HISTORY OF
CASS COUNTY
INDIANA

From its Earliest Settlement to the Present Time; with Biographical Sketches and Reference to Biographies Previously Compiled

Edited by
DR. JEHU Z. POWELL
President of the Cass County, Indiana, Historical Society

ADVISORY EDITORS:
HON. WILLIAM T. WILSON
HON. BENJAMIN F. LOUTHAIN
PROF. A. H. DOUGLASS

VOLUME II

ILLUSTRATED

THE LEWIS PUBLISHING COMPANY
CHICAGO AND NEW YORK
1913

1137038

GEN. JOHN TIPTON

History of Cass County

GEN JOHN TIPTON It is an acknowledged fact that Gen John Tipton was the most influential and distinguished pioneer citizen of Cass county, and had more to do with its early history and development than any other one man, and no history of the county would be complete without a brief sketch of him

The Tipton family is of Irish lineage Joshua Tipton, the father of this sketch, was born in Maryland but in early manhood moved to Sevier county, East Tennessee, where he married Jeannette Shields Joshua Tipton was an Indian fighter and was killed by them April 16, 1793, but it is unwritten history that his assassination was instigated by the Seviers, who held an old-time grudge against the Tiptons

It was under such conditions and surroundings that our subject was born August 14, 1786, and was only seven years of age at his father's death In the fall of 1807, he, with his mother, two sisters and a half brother, moved to Brinley's Ferry on the Ohio river, in Harrison county, Indiana territory He was the main support of the family and one of his first acts was to purchase a home for his mother, consisting of fifty acres, which he paid for by splitting rails at 50 cents a hundred These early experiences laid the foundation of his future success in life His mother died in 1827 at Seymour, Indiana

In 1809 the sheriff of Harrison county formed a company of mounted riflemen, known as "Yellow Jackets," from the color of their uniforms, and John Tipton became an active member. This company, under the command of Capt. Spier Spencer, saw active service in the Indian wars, terminating at the battle of Tippecanoe, November 7, 1811 Spencer's company was in the thickest of the fight and the commissioned officers were all killed, but there stood the brave ensign, John Tipton, at the head of the remnant of the company when General Harrison came riding up and asked

"Where is the captain of this company?"

To which John Tipton answered · "Dead, sir"

"Where are the lieutenants?"

"Both have been killed, sir"

"Where is the ensign?"

"I am here," answered Tipton

"Take command of your company," said Harrison, "and I will get relief for you in a few minutes."

General Harrison always spoke of Ensign Tipton as the coolest and bravest officer in his command. Subsequently he was promoted to the rank of brigadier-general.

At the first election held under the state constitution he was elected sheriff of Harrison county and was sent to the legislature from that county in 1819-20, and was chosen as one of the committee to select a site for the location of the state capital, and this committee, on June 7, 1820, selected the present site of Indianapolis, then in the woods, and on January 6, 1821, the legislature approved the action of the committee. In August, 1821, he was re-elected to the legislature and the following year the governor appointed him a commissioner to locate the boundary line between Illinois and Indiana. In 1823 he was appointed by President Monroe general agent of the Pottawattamie and Miami Indians on the upper Wabash and at once moved to Ft. Wayne, the seat of the agency, and he performed his duties with credit to himself and the government. In the spring of 1828, at his suggestion, the agency was moved to Logansport, where he continued to reside until his death.

In 1826 President John Quincy Adams appointed him a commissioner on the part of the United States to treat with the Indians for cession of their lands and his familiarity with the Indians greatly facilitated the opening up of valuable lands in this section of the country.

In 1831 he was elected United States senator from Indiana to fill the vacancy occasioned by the death of Hon. James Noble and in 1832-33 was re-elected for a full term of six years. While in the senate he was the chairman of the committee on Indian affairs, in those days a very important committee, for which he was eminently qualified. He recognized no party in determining his line of duty, always acting from motives of right and public duty. As a civilian and citizen he was alike successful in directing and executing, to the extent of his power, whatever purpose his conscience approved or his judgment dictated. Having made Logansport his home in the spring of 1828, he acquired title to the land upon which the town was built and, with Chauncey Carter, made the original plat of the town and later made four of its principal additions. He was awake to the true interests of the town and gave a lot for the erection of the first school and public building ever built in Cass county, the "Old Eel River Seminary" and was largely instrumental in its construction in 1828-29. He also donated the square where the present Lincoln school building stands. Under his direction the first saw and grist mills in the county were erected on Eel river, east of Sixth street, in the summer of 1828. In short, he was the instigator and moving spirit, that gave form, and imparted energy, to every enterprise calculated to improve society and stimulate progress, and the unfoldment and utilization of all the natural advantages with which Cass county has been so bountifully supplied.

In 1838 Governor Wallace directed him to raise a company of soldiers to superintend the removal of the last of the Pottawattomie Indians to their western home beyond the Mississippi, which he promptly yet kindly did, satisfactorily to all parties.

General Tipton was a member of the Masonic fraternity, having received his first degree in Pisgah Lodge No. 5, at Corydon, Indiana,

HISTORY OF CASS COUNTY 721

in 1817, and later was grand master of the state. He was instrumental in the organization of the first Masonic lodge in Logansport, which was named in his honor, "Tipton Lodge No 33," in 1828, and donated the ground for a building, the present site of the Masonic temple.

General Tipton was of medium height, rather long face but round head, low wrinkled forehead, sunken gray eyes, stern countenance large chest, stiff, sandy hair, standing erect from his forehead. He was twice married. His first wife was his cousin, Miss Jennie Shields daughter of John Shields, who became famous in the Lewis and Clark expedition. She was the mother of two children Spier S Tipton, who became a graduate of West Point, settled in Logansport, raised a company and as its captain fought and died in the Mexican war, and Matilda who died while at school in her eighteenth year. His second wife was Matilda Spencer, daughter of his old commander who fell in the battle of Tippecanoe. Three children were born to this last marriage: Harriet B, who married Thomas S Dunn of Logansport and died in the West in the later sixties leaving descendants in California, John Tipton, who married Nenah Lamb, was a captain in the regular army moved to California, where he died many years ago, George T Tipton, who was born in Corydon Indiana, in 1825, married Sarah M Purveyance in Logansport, and followed farming near the city. He died in 1873, leaving five children John, Frank M, Matilda, and Bessie B, all living in Logansport, and Fannie, who married W S Newhall and lives in Cleveland Ohio.

On February 14 1839, Mrs Tipton died and on April 4 following, the general died after a brief illness caused by exposure to inclement weather and was buried on Sunday, April 7, 1839, by the Masonic lodge, which he had organized. He was buried on Spencer square, where the Lutheran church now stands, later was removed to the old cemetery and still later to Mt Hope cemetery, where a neat marble shaft about six feet high marks the last resting place of Cass county's most illustrious pioneer.

HON DAVID D FICKLE Probably the law has been the main highway by which more men of merit have advanced to prominence and position in the United States than any other road, and it is not unusual therefore to find among the leading citizens of a community members of the legal fraternity. Among those citizens of Cass county whose connection with law and jurisprudence have led them to eminence in public life may be mentioned the Hon David D Fickle, mayor of Logansport, whose high attainments as a legist are aiding him in giving his city an excellent administration. Mr Fickle was born August 17, 1853, in Jackson township, Cass county, Indiana the seventh in order of birth of the nine children of David T and Rebeca (Engler) Fickle, natives of Ohio, of German descent.

David T Fickle, who was a farmer by occupation came to Cass county in 1844 and settled in Jackson township, at a time when that section was still in a primitive condition. He lived on the old homestead place until about 1883, at that time moving to Galveston, and there his death occurred December 22, 1894, being followed by that of his widow several years later. Beyond being thoroughly honest and upright, and believing in and acting upon the principles of the Golden Rule, the life of Mr Fickle was uneventful He was an active factor in the development of the county during its formative period, and will be remembered as one of its honored pioneers

Like so many of the farmers' sons of his day and locality, David D Fickle divided his boyhood between work on the home farm and attendance in the public schools and when he was nineteen years of age was sent to the high school at Edinburg, where he spent two years In the fall of 1875, he entered Mount Union College, in eastern Ohio, from which he was graduated three years later with the degree of Bachelor of Philosophy and succeeding this taught school until 1882, in the meantime sedulously prosecuting his legal studies On March 17, 1882, he left the law offices of McConnell, Magee & McConnell and embarked in the practice of law in Logansport, but in June, 1883, was elected county superintendent of schools to the duties of which position he devoted the following six years He resumed his law practice in 1889, but June 22, 1895, was appointed receiver for the Logansport Railway Company, and for about seven years was devoted to the work of that office, at the end of that time again taking up the practice of law In 1909, Mr Fickle became the candidate of the Democratic party for the office of mayor, to which he was subsequently elected, and to the manifold duties of which he has since given his entire attention He has given the same conscientious service to this executive office that has been characteristic of his activities in his private interests, and the citizens of Logansport have had no cause to regret of their choice Mr Fickle is a member of the B P O E , and also holds membership in the college fraternity of Delta Tau Delta

On September 28, 1887, occurred the union of Mr Fickle and Miss Carrie Larway and they have four children Florence Frances, Harold L , Helen J and Robert D The family attend the Episcopal church, all except Mr Fickle being members thereof

Hon Rufus Magee Among Cass county's native sons, few have attained to greater eminence than that secured by Hon Rufus Magee, whose versatile talents brought him prominently before the public in various fields of endeavor, and whose long and active career was given to the advancement of his state and his country no less than to his personal benefit It is all the more remarkable, in that he was practically self-educated, having entered upon his battle with life when a lad of only nine years and his subsequent struggles were marked with steady advancement and eventually crowned with well-deserved success At this time, living in quiet retirement, he is able to look back over a useful and well-spent life, content in the knowledge that his efforts have not been fruitless, and that no stain or blemish mars an honorable record of accomplishment

Rufus Magee was born October 17, 1845, in Logansport, Indiana His father, Empire A Magee, was of Scotch-Irish ancestry, and of Covenanter religion His father Daniel Magee, was a soldier in the War of Independence Empire A Magee was a millwright by trade, and came to Logansport in that capacity in 1836, here erecting the forge at what was known as Four-mile Locks, in Miami township, a structure built of what (or was) known as "kidney iron," Later he built the Aubeenaubee forge in Fulton county, on the Tippecanoe river, and then went to Lockport, in Carroll county, and operated a grist mill on selling which he moved to Monticello, where he built the mills of the Monticello Hydraulic Sompany, and died at that place about 1873

Rufus Magee resided with his parents until nine years of age, at which time he accepted a position as printer's "devil" with the *White County Jeffersonian,* and following his experience with that newspaper engaged in printing and publishing It was largely in this school that Mr Magee secured his education, although he has continued a student all of his life, and has never lost his love of literary work. For a number of years he was connected with various publications, at Indianapolis, Logansport, and other cities, and eventually, in December, 1868, purchased the Logansport *Pharos* In August, 1874, he established a daily in connection with the weekly publication, but later sold both papers For many years Mr Magee was known as one of Cass county's most prominent and influential Democrats From 1872 to 1878 he was a member of the Democratic State Central Committee of which he was secretary for two years, and in 1882 was elected state senator, receiving the re-election in 1900, and serving in all eight years In March, 1885, he was honored by the appointment to the position of United States minister to Sweden and Norway, by President Cleveland, and served as such four years and three months In 1896 he was a member of the State Central Committee, but resigned therefrom because of the silver plank in the Democratic platform On his return from abroad, Mr Magee occupied himself in the practice of law, but in 1902 retired from activities, and since that time has devoted himself to the demands of his business interests.

In 1868 Mr Magee was married to Miss Jennie Musselman, and they became the parents of two daughters

JOHN C NELSON The legists of the first several decades of the life of Logansport have passed away Of those who came to the bar during the 'sixties, most have long since laid down their briefs Some survive in retirement, enjoying the ease and dignity which lives of intellectual activity have earned, while fewer still continue to participate in the struggles which the competition of younger and more vigorous men make more severe and exacting Judge John C Nelson is one of the oldest in point of length of practice at the Logansport bar. Since the spring of 1870, now more than forty-three years, he has been in active practice, and still keeps an open office

Judge Nelson was born February 27, 1841 in Adams county, Ohio, his parents being natives of that state, while his grandparents on his father's side English, and on the maternal side Scotch, came from New Jersey and Virginia, respectively His home, from the time he was six years of age until he was twenty, was in the small hamlet of Eckmansville, where he attended the common schools and what was then known as the high school until he was sixteen years of age At that time he received a certificate qualifying him to teach in the public schools of that county his first experience as an educator being in one of the most rural parts of the county, in 1857, and his wages being $20 00 per month He followed the profession of teacher during the fall and winter months, and attended a seminary during the summer seasons until the fall of 1861, on October 18 of which year he enlisted as a private in Company A, Seventieth Regiment, Ohio Volunteer Infantry. Upon the organization of the company, he was appointed second sergeant, and when the regiment was completed he became sergeant major, in which capacity he served until December, 1861, when he was commissioned second lieutenant of Company G. The regiment, during the winter, rendezvoused at Ripley, Ohio, and in February, 1862, was ordered to the front and assigned to the Second Brigade of Sherman's Division, then being organized at Paducah, Kentucky. Upon the organization of the brigade, Colonel Buckland commanding, Mr. Nelson was detailed to act as aid upon his staff.

The division was sent up the Tennessee river on transports to Pittsburgh Landing, and was encamped about two and one-half miles from the river, the right of the regiment being near Shiloh church. During the battle of Shiloh, Judge Nelson served as aid on the colonel's staff, and on the second day of the battle was placed in command of his company, and from that time until December, 1862, did duty with it, taking part in the advance on Corinth, Grant's advance towards Vicksburg as far as Oxford, Mississippi and the subsequent return to the line of the Memphis & Charleston Railroad, the regiment then being stationed at Grand Junction. During the month of March, 1863 he was detailed and served as ordnance officer on the staff of General Denver, commanding the division until the general was relieved from the command of the division by Gen. William S. Smith, when he was relieved as ordnance officer and detailed as aide on the staff of General Smith. He continued to serve in that capacity until the summer of the same year, when he was relieved from duty at division headquarters because he declined to receive and receipt for old ordnance that was ordered to be turned over to the ordnance officer, assigning for his reason the fact that he was not the ordnance officer of the division. Upon reporting to Colonel Cockerel, who commanded the brigade, he was immediately detailed as aide on his staff, and served in that capacity until January, 1864 when he re-enlisted and was promoted to the rank of captain of Company C. While on Colonel Cockerel's staff, he was a member of the Army of Observation during the siege of Vicksburg, and after the surrender was at the siege of Jackson, Mississippi. Returning from Jackson, the division to which the brigade belonged camped on the banks of the Black river, in Mississippi, and remained there until October of that year, when it was sent, under Sherman, with the other divisions of his corps, and took part under Grant at the battle of Missionary Ridge, in November, 1863. After the regiment had re-enlisted and Sherman's army entered upon the Atlanta campaign, Judge Nelson commanded Company C, of the Seventieth Ohio Volunteer Infantry, taking part in all the battles in which the division was engaged, among which were Resaca, Dallas, New Hope Church, Kennesaw Mountain, the battle of Atlanta, July 22nd, and the battle of Ezra Church, July 27th, in the last-named of which he was severely wounded while on the skirmish line, being shot through the body. After a leave of absence of sixty days, he returned to his regiment, in October, 1864, and was shortly afterward detailed as commissary of musters of the Second Division, Fifteenth Army Corps, Gen W B Hazen commanding He was with Sherman on his memorable "March to the Sea," and with the division at the battle of Fort McAllister On the march from Savannah to Goldsboro, and at the battle of Bentonville, and then moved on to Raleigh, where the division was stationed at the time of the surrender of Gen Joseph E Johnston Judge Nelson also participated in the grand review, at Washington, D C, and afterward went West with the division, to Little Rock, Arkansas, where, August 18, 1865, he was mustered out of the service

With the establishment of peace, Judge Nelson exchanged the ponderous enginery of war for the implements of civil life, and, recognizing the need of further education attended a commercial school at Cincinnati, Ohio, until the spring of 1866. He then spent a short time as a traveling salesman for a boot and shoe house, and in July of the same year, with a friend of his, came to Logansport, and in August opened a boot and shoe store This business was conducted successfully until 1868, when he disposed of his interests to his partner, and entered upon the study of law in the offices of McConnell & Winfield and in the fall and winter of 1869-70 attended the Law school, at Albany, New York Receiving his diploma in the spring of 1870, he returned to Logansport and formed a professional partnership with Dudley H Chase, who, in 1872, was elected judge of the circuit court of Cass county In that year Mr Nelson became the partner of Dyer B McConnell, a connection which continued until Mr Nelson was elected judge of the superior court of Cass county, which office he filled during the existence of the court In 1881 he returned to the practice of law, and in the following year formed a partnership with Quincy A Myers, now judge of the supreme court of Indiana, the connection continuing for a period of twenty-five years, or practically until Judge Myers was elected to his present office

During the years 1881, 1882, 1883 and 1884 Judge Nelson served as city attorney of Logansport, was mayor of the city in 1887 and 1888, and in 1910 was again chosen to serve as city attorney, continuing as such in 1911, 1912 and 1913 Many men are honored for their ability to confer benefits,—for the wealth, or influence, or power they control Judge Nelson is reverenced for what he is A hero in war, a man of kindly spirit, and rectitude and fidelity that no temptation has been able to swerve, who has taken office only that he might serve, he has drawn about him a wide circle of admiring friends, and the veneration of all who know him

Judge Nelson was married in November, 1871, to Mary C daughter of James Cheney, whose sketch appears elsewhere Their children are Alice C, (Mrs Carl Keller) Dr James V Nelson, Allen E Nelson, of Logansport, and Helen, (Mrs R C Barnard) and Coleman C Nelson, of Cincinnati, Ohio

ORLANDO POWELL was born in Wabash county Indiana, on January 17, 1845, and is the third in a family of four children whose parents were Jacob and Martha (Troutman) Powell The father was a native of Washington county Pennsylvania, and of Welsh descent Orlando Powell was reared on the farm where he now resides, and he was educated in the district schools, such learning as he acquired there being supplemented by several terms in the Logansport (Ind) high school In the summer of 1862 he joined Company K, Ninety-ninth Indiana Infantry, with Captain George W Julian in command of his company, and he served faithfully until the close of the war His regiment participated in all the important engagements in the Atlanta campaign, including Resaca, Dallas Kenesaw Mountain, Atlanta and Jonesboro, and marched with Sherman to the sea and up through the Carolinas

Upon his return from the war he was successfully engaged in school teaching for several years later turning his attention to farming He is a man of no little enterprise and energy and he today owns a valuable farm of two hundred acres He has been prominent in the political life of his community and has held the office of township trustee for several terms He is a Republican of solid conviction, and frequently comes to the aid of the party in his district by making speeches throughout the county, having a reputation as an impromptu speaker He is a member of the G A R , and with his wife is a member of the Presbyterian church in their home community

On October 2, 1871 Mr Powell was united in marriage with Miss Sarah S McElheny, daughter of Moses and Philene (Treen) McElheny Five children have been born of their union, concerning whom the following brief mention is made Ada F born August 14, 1872, died November 17, 1889 Tacy C born July 31, 1874, Dyer J , born December 8, 1878, Martha P , born July 6, 1881 and Emma B , born March 6, 1883 The four last named are married, and Orlando Powell has five grandchildren at this writing

WARREN J BUTLER Prominent among those officials whose services have added to Cass county's reputation as one of the best-governed sections of the state, Warren J Butler, sheriff, is entitled to more than passing mention Since the time he attained to man's estate, he has been almost continuously the occupant of one public office or another and in each capacity has shown himself a conscientious, faithful official efficiently discharging the duties and holding them in the light of sacred trusts His career has been marked by constant industry and integrity since earliest youth, and his present high position has come as a result of earnest youth, and his present high position has come as a result of earnest effort and determination, directed along well-defined channels. Mr Butler was born in Fulton county, Indiana, April 19, 1863, and is a son of William T and Catherine (Phillips) Butler

Mr Butler was reared on his father's farm in Liberty township, Fulton county, and divided his boyhood between work of an agricultural nature and attendance at the common schools of his locality It was the intention of his parents that he adopt the vocation of farmer, but when he was twenty-one years of age he became deputy to his father, who at that time was sheriff of Fulton county Thus, at the very outset of his career, he received an introduction to the duties of official life, and to the responsibilities undertaken by those who enter the public arena Proving an able and trustworthy assistant, Mr Butler continued as deputy under succeeding sheriffs until 1894, at which time during the landslide of that year he found himself, with others of the Democratic faith, without office, and accordingly, during the next year,

MR. & MRS. BENJAMIN BANTA

RESIDENCE OF BENJAMIN BANTA

he acted in the capacity of attendant at the insane asylum, at Indianapolis, this being succeeded by two years in the same capacity in the asylum at Toledo, Ohio

On June 17, 1896, Mr Butler was married to Miss Minnie E McDowell, whose people were among the earliest settlers of Cass county, and soon after this event he became a conductor on the old Logansport Railway Company He continued in the service of this road, and those that succeeded it, for the following fourteen years, and was known as one of the company's most capable and trusted employes, and a great favorite with its patrons Mr Butler, however, could not resist the struggles and activities of public life, and accordingly, in 1909, again entered the field as candidate for the office of sheriff of Cass county, being returned the winner in the election that followed, and taking office in 1910 He was again elected in 1911, on the Democratic ticket, and continues to hold office, being known as an efficient and courageous officer, with an excellent record in office

Mr and Mrs Butler now reside in a comfortable home in Logansport, in which city their two children, Ben and Irene, are attending school Mr Butler has interested himself to some extent with fraternal work, and is exceedingly popular with his fellow members in the Red Men, the Eagles, the Knights of Pythias and the Masons, in the last-named of which he has attained to the Knights Templar degree

BENJAMIN BANTA The vocation of farming, as now practiced by the intelligent and practical agriculturist, is as different from the farming of several decades ago as could be imagined The day of the work-hardened, horny-handed farmer has passed In these days the agriculturist who uses scientific methods is able to retire in time to spend the remaining years of his life in the enjoyment of a well-earned competence Among those who have profited by new methods and ideas, Benjamin Banta, of Jefferson township, holds a prominent place Although now retired from active pursuits, Mr Banta is widely known, not only as one whose activities contributed materially to the agricultural importance of his section, but as a veteran of the great Civil war Mr Banta was born in Jefferson township Cass county, Indiana, June 16, 1839 and is a son of Beaufort and Elizabeth (McNairy) Banta, natives of Bourbon county, Kentucky. As a youth, Beaufort Banta removed to Ohio, where he was married, and in 1829 came to Indiana, settling in Jefferson township, Cass county, where he passed the remainder of his life in tilling the soil He and his wife had four sons, of whom three served as soldiers in the Union army during the Civil war.

Benjamin Banta was reared on the home farm, and the greater part of his education was secured in the school of experience and hard work although he made the most of his opportunities and attended the district school whenever he could be spared from home On July 22 1862, he enlisted in Company G, Seventy-third Regiment, Indiana Volunteer Infantry, being first under General Buell, and later in the Army of the Cumberland He participated in a number of engagements, including Richmond and Perryville, but February 3, 1863, received his honorable discharge on account of disability after a brave and faithful service On his return home from the war he was appointed enrolling officer in the sub-district 131 of Jefferson township As soon as he had sufficiently recuperated, Mr. Banta resumed work on the home farm in Jefferson township, where, March 12, 1867 he was married to Elvira Wilson She was born in Jefferson township, and here died September 12, 1875, having been the mother of three sons, two who died in infancy, and Everett, who married Pauline Wimer and died January 12, 1911 Mr Banta was married January 11, 1889, to Mrs Margaret Herand who was born in Boone township Cass county, Indiana, March 14, 1847, and was first married to John L Herand, by whom she had one son John A, who is single Mrs Banta was educated in the public schools of Jefferson township, and is a lady of much culture and many social graces She is a well-known member of the Presbyterian church at Pisgah, and a member of the home and foreign missionary societies She belongs to the Women's Relief Corps No 30, Logansport, Indiana, Grand Army of the Republic, of which she has been president of the Women's Relief Corps department, and has held numerous other offices, being national recruiting aid, and a delegate to the national convention in 1912, as well as holding office in the district department She also holds membership in the Daughters of Liberty, Loraine Council No 10, and in the Lady Maccabees of the World, being especially active in the work of the latter and a charter member, and is a member of the Home Making Agricultural Society

Mr Banta is a member of Logansport Post No 14, Grand Army of the Republic, and is the recipient of a pension of fifteen dollars per month In political matters a Republican, he has held numerous minor offices, but has not been a politician in the generally accepted meaning of the word Although retired from active farming, he still owns 160 acres of well-cultivated land Mr and Mrs Banta are highly esteemed in their community as people whose activities are at all times promoting good citizenship and the spread of morality and religion

GEORGE ULERICH Farming has drawn out the best efforts of some of the leading men of Cass county and developed their abilities and through their efforts in an agricultural line they have become well-to-do and prominent in their communities One of the substantial farmer-citizens of Cass county, whose intelligent knowledge of the soils and the most profitable uses to which particular lands may be devoted has made him justly regarded as one of those whose activities are advancing the agricultural importance of his community, is George Ulerich, of Clay township, who has lived in Cass county for nearly a half a century Mr Ulerich was born in Lancaster county, Pennsylvania, November 18 1853, and is a son of Henry and Caroline (Fry) Ulerich

Henry Ulerich, who was a farmer by vocation, brought his family from Lancaster county, Pennsylvania, to Cass county, Indiana, in the spring of 1866 and settled first on the old Andrew Dritt farm, where he remained for about five years, then moving to a farm near Twelve Mile, where he still resides, being eighty-seven years of age while his wife passed away some years ago

George Ulerich commenced his education in the public schools of his native county, and was thirteen years of age when he accompanied his parents to Cass county Here he completed his schooling, in the meantime assisting his father in the work of the home farm, remaining under the parental roof until he had reached the age of nineteen years At that time he started to work for George M Smith, as a farm hand, and on leaving his employ was engaged by Sam Harman, with whom he also remained a short period, succeeding which he started to work on the farm of Joseph Davidson In February, 1885, Mr Ulerich was married, and at that time began operations on his own account on a rented farm of twenty acres, belonging to John I. McDowell, but after three years removed to the farm of his former employer Mr. Davidson, where he continued two years Following this he spent five years on the farm of Barnett Brothers, and then spent one year on a farm near the schoolhouse, but eventually came to his present property, a tract of 153 acres which his wife had inherited Here he has continued to reside to the present time, working his land with his son, who lives on an adjoining property. The old log cabin built by Mrs Ulerich's father still stands on the farm, located behind the modern frame farm house which was built by Mr Ulerich, in addition to which Mr. E C Metsker has erected a new barn and made numerous other improvements on the place He has engaged in diversified farming, raising good crops, breeding cattle and finding a ready market for his dairy products An able business man, his success has been due to his strict attention to the details of his vocation and an inherent ability that has come down to him through a long line of agricultural ancestors

Mr Ulerich was married February 13, 1885, to Miss Maggie P Metsker, daughter of E. C. and Louisa C (McDowell) Metsker, who lived in Cass county for many years, and to this union there have been born two children Hugh, who is twenty-six years of age, and Harold, aged seven years. Hugh, who assists his father in the work of the farm, also received a commercial course in the commercial college He married Leta Ingmire, daughter of John Ingmire Mr Ulerich is a Democrat in his political views, but has not cared to enter the political arena, being content to devote his entire attention to the cultivation of his farm. His business integrity and honorable dealing have gained him a high reputation among the people of Clay township, among whom he numbers many sincere friends

WILLIAM A WELLS It was but comparatively a few years ago that most men ridiculed the idea of applying science to agriculture, but science has never gone backwards, it has always been progressive in nature There are still many farmers who plant, reap, feed their cattle, and let their implements stand out in the sun and rain in the careless, thriftless old way, but science is revolutionizing the farming business as it has revolutionized almost every other modern business, and the agriculturist who would attain the full measure of success must keep abreast of the trend of the times, and bring to his labors every help which modern invention and discovery will give him Among the good, practical farmers of Cass county who have realized the benefits to be derived from scientific treatment of the soil, William A Wells, of Clay township, is deserving of mention A resident of Cass county for nearly a half a century, he has attained a position of affluence through intelligent operations and in the meantime has so directed his activities as to benefit his community He was born at Kewanna, Fulton county, Indiana, February 14, 1856, and is a son of Dudley and Mary (Davis) Wells

The father of Mr Wells was a native of Connecticut and the mother was born in New York, they were married in Fulton county, Indiana, and came to Cass county in 1865. Dudley Wells was a farmer by vocation, an occupation which he followed throughout his active career, and his death occurred in Logansport, November 24, 1906, his wife having passed away September 2, 1903, in Kewanna, Indiana

William A Wells commenced his education in the public schools of Kewanna, and was nine years of age when he accompanied his parents to Cass county, here completing his studies in the district schools of Clay township while assisting his father in the work of the home farm He was thoroughly trained in all the details pertaining to the operation of a farm, and on attaining his majority started to work on his own account He is now the possessor of an excellent tract of land, which he devotes to general farming and stock raising, and on which he has made numerous improvements His buildings are substantial and in a good state of repair, his cattle are sleek and well fed, and the excellent crops produced each season leave no doubt as to his ability as an agriculturist This farm is one of the old land-marks of the township, and on it stood the first schoolhouse erected within the township limits

On September 15, 1880, Mr Wells was united in marriage with Miss Anna Freshour, daughter of George Freshour, who came to Cass county in 1835 among the earliest pioneers To Mr. and Mrs Wells was born one son—Kirk, who resides with his parents. He finished the public schools and the city high school at Logansport, and then took a full business course The son is a high Mason, having taken both the Scottish and Yorke rite of masonry. He is a member of the blue lodge, council and chapter, at Logansport, and the Shriners at Indianapolis He is a thirty-second degree Mason, and affiliates with Tipton lodge, No 33, Logan chapter No 2, Logan council No 11, St John's commandery No 24, Murat Temple, Indianapolis, Indiana Consistory of Indianapolis Mr Wells, Sr , has interested himself in fraternal work to some extent, and is a popular member of the local lodge of the Odd Fellows and the Masons Although not a politician in the generally accepted meaning of the term. he has ever been faithful to the duties of citizenship, and for the past four years has served as a member of the board of trustees of Clay township He is known as a man who lives up to his word in his business transactions, who is true in his friendships, and who, having succeeded himself, is willing to assist others to success.

GILLIS MCBEAN, SR , was born in Scotland in 1794 and died on his farm in southeast quarter, section 20, Clay township, in 1839, and lies at rest in the old cemetery. He came to America when a boy and engaged in the milling business on the Mississinewa river In 1827 he moved to Logansport before the town was laid out or even named and acted as Indian agent and kept a hotel in a double hewed log cabin, situated on the southwest corner of Third and Market streets The legislature appointed three commissioners to organize Cass county and locate its county seat, who met at the house of Gillis McBean in the summer of 1829, by direction of the legislature, and the first board of county commissioners met at Mr. McBean's house on July 25, 1829, and appointed him agent for the county

GILLIS JAMES McBANE

About 1832 he bought a farm and moved to Clay township, where he died as noted above

Mr McBean represented Cass county in the state legislature in 1833 He was married in Corydon, Indiana, to Elizabeth Kintner. From this union six children were born, to wit Margaret Catherine, Gillis James and Thomas, twins, Peter Todd and Frank, all of whom are now dead except Frank now living at Canon City, Oregon, and Gillis J., who resides at Moscow, Idaho

Gillis James McBane (originally McBean), son of Gillis McBean, Sr, was the first white child born within the original town plat of Logansport, December 30, 1829, in a double log cabin, then situated on the southwest corner of Third and Market streets, where the Kreutzberger building now stands When a child he moved with his father on what is known as the Skelton farm, on the north bank of Eel river in the southeast quarter section 20, Clay township, opposite Spencer Park When grown he worked in Coulson's, Clem's and Vigus' bakeries in Logansport Later lived with Mrs Sharts on a farm near Anoka At the breaking out of the war, 1861, he enlisted in Company G, Seventy-third Indiana Regiment Serving three years, he returned to Anoka, where he resided on a farm until 1882, when he moved to Moscow, Idaho, where he has lived ever since, engaged in carpentering and painting He made a visit to Logansport in the fall of 1912, and is still hale and hearty as shown by his picture accompanying this sketch which was taken when he was eighty-three years old. Mr BcBane was never married and says he is short on the fair sex, although his mother was a woman and the best in the world.

MRS JANE H WHITE. Among the residents of Clay township who have witnessed the wonderful changes that have taken place here during the past half a century, and have done their share in promoting the growth and development of the county, one of the best known is Mrs Jane H White, who resides with her family in a comfortable residence on Logansport Rural Route No. 4 Mrs White was born in Adams township, Cass county, Indiana, daughter of ·Joel H. and Mary (Harvey) Davis

Joel Hubbard Davis was born near Albany, New York, of Scotch-Irish descent, and some time after his marriage came to Indiana, settling in Adams township where he purchased a farm. Subsequently, when Mrs White was one year old, the family moved to Fulton county, Indiana, purchasing a farm The father died April 13, 1880, in Cass county, and the mother died November 5, 1879 Mrs White grew to womanhood in Fulton county, and was there married January 6, 1861, to John Henry White who was born of English descent in Frederick county, Virginia, son of Batley and Hannah (Hane) White In 1843 the White family located on a farm in Clay township, and John Henry White and his brother Joseph inherited their father's estate the former receiving the present home of Mrs White, where he resided for upwards of fifty-two years, dying at the age of seventy-eight years He was one of his township's well known and substantial citizens and spent his life in clearing, cultivating and improving his land In 1886 he was elected justice of the peace of Clay township, a position in which he served for some years

Mr and Mrs White became the parents of one son. Horace Mason, who was born October 20, 1861, on the present homestead He married Emma Puterbaugh, daughter of Jacob and Hannah Ida (Bauchman) Puterbaugh Mr Puterbaugh came from Dayton, Ohio, and at one time was the leading merchant of Logansport, where he still resides at the age of eighty-four years, one of the oldest living early settlers. His wife died in 1904 Horace and Emma White have had two children, namely Edith Abigail, who married Roscoe C Smith, of Indianapolis, and has one child,—Newell C Smith, aged eight years, and Fred Harvey, who married Jessie C Straw, daughter of Andrew Jackson and Anna Elsa (Walker) Straw, the former of whom is superintendent of the gardening of the Longcliff insane asylum, and they have one child who is ten months old

Mrs White, her son Horace M and wife, and their son Fred and wife, and the latter's baby, Esther, all live in the comfortable residence on the old homestead This tract, a property of 110 acres, has been greatly improved by Mr. White, who has done much clearing, draining and fencing, and it is now considered one of the valuable properties of the township Mr White is a good, practical agriculturist, who takes advantage of all the modern improvements and appliances in his work, and has risen to an enviable position among the agriculturists of Clay township Progressive in all things, in 1912 he became the candidate of the so-called Bull Moose party for the office of representative in the state legislature Mrs Jane H White is one of the best known ladies of her locality, her kindness of heart and many charities having gained her many warm friendships Although advanced in years, her faculties are unimpaired, and she recalls with unclouded memory many of the interesting incidents of early days in Cass county The members of the family are all highly esteemed in their locality, where the name has always stood for strict integrity and probity of character

LAFAYETTE M BALL A residence in Cass county that has covered nearly seventy years entitles Lafayette Ball, of Logansport Rural Route No 4, to more than passing mention as one of Clay township's old and honored pioneer citizens Coming to this township when still in infancy, he was for a long period identified with the agricultural interests of his section, and although he has now retired from the more strenuous activities of life, having reached a position when he feels he can afford to rest from his labors he still takes a keen interest in all that affects the community in which he labored for so long Mr. Ball was born in Washington county, Pennsylvania, July 24, 1843, his grandfather, Iden Ball, being a prominent member of the Society of Friends in the Quaker settlement in that county His parents came to Indiana in 1844, and first settled near Twelve Mile, one-half mile east of Bethlehem church, in which vicinity Lafayette Ball was reared to manhood During the Civil war he enlisted in the Ninety-ninth Regiment, Indiana Volunteer Infantry, which was mustered into the United States service where the Spry building now stands, on Pearl street, Logansport and with this organization served two years and ten months, leaving the service with the rank of corporal He was a brave and faithful soldier, and when his military career was ended resumed the duties of peace, which he has performed in the same able and faithful manner

On January 8, 1891, Mr Ball was married to Eleanor Johnson, daughter of Edward and Matilda (Archer) Johnson Edward Johnson was a native of Vermont and his wife of Williamsburg, Ohio, and they came to Cass county at a very early day Mr Johnson first engaging in the blacksmith business, which he gave up to devote his entire time to agricultural pursuits This latter occupation he followed throughout the remainder of his life, and passed away September 2, 1891, in which year his wife also died on August 28th Mrs Ball is a lady who is possessed of a genial, cordial and kind nature, and has ably assisted her husband in the care of their happy and pleasant home Three children were born to Mr Ball by his first marriage, namely Harry, Linda and Lillian, the latter of whom is now deceased

At the time of the marriage of Mr Ball and his present wife they settled on the old farm, formerly the property of Mr Ball's father, and originally a tract of 80 acres For some years Mr Ball continued operations there Eventually he retired from active pursuits, however, and sold a part of the land, he now owning forty-seven acres while his wife owns twenty-two and 28-100 acres, and the greater part of this is now being operated by renters, and it lies in section 8, Clay township The homestead of Mr and Mrs Ball is called "The Sunny Side Farm"

Mr and Mrs Ball are members of the Methodist Episcopal church, in which Mr Ball holds the position of steward, and both have been active in religious and charitable work He is a popular comrade of the Grand Army of the Republic. During his long residence in this section Mr Ball has seen many changes take place, and has done his share in promoting the growth and development of his community. He is honored and esteemed by those who have made his acquaintance, and has a wide circle of sincere friends The pleasant family home is situated on Logansport Rural Route No 4

RAYMOND C TAYLOR was born in Cayuga county, New York, on September 6 1834, and died in Logansport, Indiana, on the 11th day of July, 1909 He was a son of Smith Taylor, a mechanic and farmer and a grandson of Captain Noah Taylor, who won his title in fighting for American independence with the colonies during the Revolutionary war The mother of Raymond Taylor was Sylvia Barnes, and he was one of the eight children she bore her husband She was the daughter of Captain Thomas Barnes, also a soldier of the Revolutionary war period The advantages of Raymond Taylor in an educational way were limited indeed, and when he was twelve years old he began to work as a stock driver, an occupation which eventually led to his embarking in the butcher business He came to Logansport, Indiana, in January, 1864, and opened a meat market at Broadway and Sixth street, later moving his establishment to No 501 Broadway His business career in Logansport covered a period of thirty-four years, and as a result of creditable business methods he succeeded in putting aside a competency He was well and favorably known in business circles in Logansport for many years, known as a substantial man of affairs, square and true in

Vol II—2

all his business relations, and indeed, in all the relations of life, and valued by many as a good friend and neighbor

Mr Taylor was a Democrat, generally speaking, but he did not hesitate to place his support where he most approved of the candidate, regardless of party affiliation He was a Mason of the old school, which may be interpreted as meaning that he was a Mason in heart as well as in name He had conferred upon him all the degrees and orders of the York rite, and he, with his wife and daughter, were members of the Order of the Eastern Star

In 1853 Mr. Taylor married Florilla Miner, and three children were born to them, of whom a daughter, Flora M, and a son, Jay D, are now living The mother of these children died, and in 1865 Mr Taylor married Florilla A. (Doty) Taylor, a daughter of William Doty and the widow of his brother, T Doty Taylor

The life of Raymond C Taylor was practically uneventful, as great events are considered, but his career as a man in Logansport was without blemish, and he died as he had lived,—secure in the high esteem of a wide circle of acquaintances who knew him as a man and a citizen, and valued him for his many splendid traits of heart and mind

JAY D. TAYLOR, the son of the late Raymond C Taylor, of Logansport, Indiana was born at Cayuga county, New York, on July 27, 1860.

When Jay Taylor was eleven years old he decided to come west and join his father, and he accordingly went quietly about converting his worldly goods, which comprised a hog, some grain and other farm produce he had earned, into coin of the realm, and this accomplished, he started for Logansport, Indiana, without going through the formality of asking advice or permission. By husbanding his slender resources, and not being too fastidious as to his mode of travel, the boy was able to reach Logansport without undue annoyance in a financial way, and when he appeared before his father in Logansport, that gentleman forthwith took charge of the young adventurer, placing him in school where he continued until he was graduated from the high school He was then sixteen years old, and he set about learning the jeweler's trade in Logansport He was employed variously in the jewelry business with W S. Orwin, B Z Lewis, H C Eversole, and D A. Hawk. In 1889 he bought the store of Z B Lewis, located on Market street, but four months later succeeded to the business of another of the men by whom he had formerly been employed, namely,—H C. Eversole, at No 309 Fourth street. Since then he has continuously carried on his business at this place, enjoying something better than a fair degree of success In addition to the general jewelry business, he carries a complete line of optical goods, and that he may intelligently and scientifically serve his patrons, he has taken special instruction of Dr King, at Cleveland, Ohio, the Chicago Ophthalmic College of Chicago, and the South Bend College of Ophthalmics

Mr Taylor is a Democrat, a Knight Templar of the Masonic fraternity, a Knight of Pythias and a Knight of the Maccabees He was married on February 19, 1890, to Miss Loraine Ridinger, of Logansport, and one son has been born to them,—Raymond Carl Taylor, named in honor of his paternal grandfather, and who is employed by his father.

DUDLEY H. CHASE

HON DUDLEY H CHASE. The life of every public man possesses interest to his fellow citizens, particularly if his abilities have elevated him to honorable office in which he has displayed honest effort and fidelity in the performance of its responsibilities Pre-eminently is this true when judicial position is involved, and especially is interest excited when the subject is so well known and honored a man as the late Hon Dudley H Chase, whose character as a man, whose high attainments as a lawyer, whose dignity as a jurist, and whose signal services in both military and civil life, gained him a place among Cass county's citizens that will long be difficult to fill Judge Chase was born in the city in which he afterwards gained such high distinction in professional circles, Logansport, August 29, 1837, and was a son of Henry and Elizabeth (Donaldson) Chase.

Henry Chase was born at Greenfield Center, Saratoga county, New York, in 1800, a descendant of a family that came with a party of colonists from Bristol, England, and settled in the region of Massachusetts during the early history of the American Colonies In 1827 he made a visit to Delphi, Indiana, and was here admitted to the bar, but one year later moved to Adams county, Mississippi where he practiced law for four years He returned to Delphi in 1832 and from that place, one year later, came to Logansport, where he continued to carry on an extensive practice He was judge of the then Eighth Judicial District in 1839, having been appointed to that office to complete an unexpired term, but in 1844 moved to New York City, which was the scene of his legal activities for five years From the latter city he made removal to Sheboygan, Wisconsin, and there in 1854 passed away, a victim of the great cholera plague which swept the Wisconsin city during that year

At the time of the death of his mother, Judge Dudley H Chase made his home with an uncle, William Chase, in Logansport, and here his primary education was secured In 1856 he was appointed a cadet at West Point Military Academy, by the Hon Schuyler Colfax, but before entering actively upon his studies he went west, and bore a conspicuous part in the Kansas troubles of 1856, rendering valiant service as a member of Sharp's Rifle Company On his return to Logansport, he again took up his law studies. entering the office of the Hon D D Pratt, and in 1858 was graduated from the Cincinnati Law School He at once began practicing in Logansport, in partnership with his former preceptor. although later he was engaged in individual practice, and thus the outbreak of the Civil war found him As early as 1854. Mr Chase had become captain of an independent local military company, known as the "Logan Grays," and in April, 1861, this organization offered itself for service in defense of the flag, Judge Chase fully equipping the company entirely at his own expense It was accepted by the recruiting officers, and soon became Company K, Ninth Regiment Indiana Volunteer Infantry For a time Judge Chase was engaged in recruiting in Maine, taking with him fifty-two Indiana volunteers, and this was then organized into Company A, Second Battalion, Seventeenth United States Infantry, joining the Fifth Army Corps in front of Fredericksburg, immediately after the engagement at that point Subsequently Judge Chase participated in the battles of Chancellorsville and Gettysburg, and on July 2, 1863, was seriously wounded in the hip by a shell He was then employed in help quelling the draft riots in New York City, but when he had entirely recuperated from his injury, he returned to the field and took part in engagements at Rappahannock and Bristow Station, as well as the Mine Run campaign Mr Chase was forced to resign his commission on account of his wounds and February 4, 1864 left the service with an enviable record for bravery and gallantry Returning to Logansport, he resumed the practice of his chosen profession, and in that same year was elected prosecuting attorney, later being re-elected in 1866 and again in 1868 In 1872 he was sent to the bench for six years, and was re-elected in 1878, but in 1884 declined to be a candidate However, in 1896, he was elected judge of the Twenty-ninth Judicial Circuit, and as such was serving at the time of his death, July 2, 1902 As a lawyer, Judge Chase ranked among the ablest in Indiana, as a jurist his decisions were marked by such fairness and so complete a knowledge of jurisprudence that comparatively few were appealed and none were ever reversed He took a great interest in the work of the Grand Army of the Republic, his local connection being with Logansport Post No 14, and was also a member of the Indiana Commandery of the Loyal Legion He belonged to the Odd Fellows, and on a number of occasions served as eminent commander of St John's Commandery, Knights Templar, of the Masonic fraternity The loss of such a man, standing for honest government and for efficiency in all measures pertaining to the city's welfare—of a man who contributed to the city's upbuilding during his entire residence here, and who entertained and illustrated the highest ideal of good citizenship, is no ordinary loss Such men are not so plentiful that their passing away is a matter of only current interest

On October 28, 1859 Judge Chase was married (first) to Maria Durett, whose father was one of the founders of Logansport, and she died April 12, 1877, after bearing five children, namely William, Robert, who is deceased, John George and Mary On December 7, 1880, Judge Chase's second marriage occurred, when he was united with Grace M Corey, of Saratoga Springs, New York, she being a member of the Schuyler family, of Colonial fame To this marriage there were born four children Charles D, Ruth, James and Louise

Charles D Chase is the only male representative of his father's family in Logansport, and now makes his home with his mother and is engaged in the undertaking business He was born September 27 1882, was educated in the public schools, and graduated from the Myers School of Embalming, at Columbus, in May, 1903 He is a member of Oriental lodge No 272, F & A M, Bridge City lodge No 305, Knights of Pythias, Logan lodge No 40, Independent Order of Odd Fellows, and Logansport lodge No 66, Benevolent and Protective Order of Elks His political convictions are those of the Republican party, and his religious connection with the Market Street Methodist Episcopal church

EDGAR F METZGER was born in Miami county, Indiana, on December 23, 1872, a son of David L Metzger who came to Cass county in about 1885, and was a farmer in Clay township He is now a resident of Indianapolis He is a veteran of the Civil war Edgar F Metzger was reared in the counties of Cass and Miami and received his education in the public and high schools. Until he was eighteen he lived on a farm, after which he taught in the country schools of Cass county during two terms, and then began his newspaper career as a reporter on the *Logansport Reporter* He continued with the *Reporter* in various capacities until 1902, when he acquired an interest in the *Journal*, with which he continued to be associated until 1907, when he disposed of his interest and with his brother, Harry C , founded the *Logansport Tribune* In 1912 the *Journal* and the *Tribune* were consolidated and Mr Metzger is now the president of the Journal-Tribune Company

Mr Metzger has no fraternal affiliations beyond his membership in the Elks He is married

JOHN W BARNES, one of the owners and editors of the *Logansport Pharos*, was born in the city of Muncie, Indiana, July 7, 1855 His father, William Barnes, was a contractor and builder and a native of Pennsylvania He married Evaline Wachtell, a native of Maryland, at Muncie

It was in the schools of his native city that John W Barnes was primarily educated When nineteen years of age he began learning the "art preservative" on the *Muncie Democrat*, but two years later became connected with the *Liberal Republican*, a paper established for the support of Horace Greeley for the presidency During the campaign of 1876 and until 1878 he was employed on the *Democrat*, at Anderson but in the latter year came to Logansport and began work on the *Pharos* From that time until the present, a period of thirty-five years, Mr Barnes has been identified with this paper In 1881 he purchased a half-interest in the *Pharos*, and with Benjamin F Loutham, the owner of the other half, has since controlled the destiny of the oldest established Democratic newspaper in Cass county

On September 30, 1885, Mr Barnes was united in marriage with Miss Emma Grable, daughter of Jonathan and Hester Grable, residents of Cass county

HENRY JAMES MCSHEEHY Among the men who have brought fame to Logansport as a center of journalistic activity, the late Henry James McSheehy, for thirty-seven years editor and proprietor of the *Logansport Weekly Chronicle*, held a position of prestige A native of Ireland, having been born in Anniscaul, County Kerry, January 28, 1852; he was brought to the United States in boyhood by his parents and here received his education in the public schools of the city of New York, and at Lafayette, Indiana, graduating from the high school of the latter place with the highest honors in a class of sixty-eight pupils On leaving school Mr McSheehy became purser of the steamship "The City of Richmond,' running from New York to Liverpool, and in this connection became marine reporter for the *New York Herald*, which started him upon his journalistic career In those days pressboats were sent out to meet all incoming ships and Mr McSheehy's duty consisted in going aboard these vessels and secure stories and anecdotes from the passengers and crew

In 1875 Mr McSheehy was appointed by his paper to accompany Col. Robert Ingersoll on his lecture tour and while acting in this service he came to Logansport, and, noting the possibilities for a good newspaper here, immediately wired his resignation to New York and began plans for the establishment of the *Chronicle* This paper made its initial appearance April 7, 1875, and has continued to enjoy a full measure of success to the present time Since Mr. McSheehy's death, which occurred February 21, 1911, in Logansport, the *Chronicle* has been published under the same firm name by his son, Harry James McSheehy, who purchased it in May, 1911 He had the distinction of being the oldest editor and proprietor of a newspaper in Indiana in point of continuous service on one publication

Aside from his vocation, Mr. McSheehy took his keenest pleasure in fraternal work, and became very prominent therein. He was the author of the Elks' ritual, serving as chairman of the ritual committee of the Grand Lodge of Elks for two years, was for seven years exalted ruler of the Logansport Lodge of Elks and through his earnest efforts secured for the lodge the magnificent home it now occupies; was president of the building committee of the Elks and served on the building committees of both the local lodge and the Grand Lodge of Odd Fellows. In Odd Fellowship he was past grand of Logan Lodge of Odd Fellows, and when entering Grand Lodge was raised to the high office of grand patriarch He was widely known in and out of his profession, and in his death Indiana newspaperdom lost one of its most conspicuous citizens

Mr McSheehy married Miss Minnie Maurer, and they became the parents of three sons. Harry, Lloyd and Harold

CHARLES N COOK When the first settlers of Cass county came to this locality they found none of the present day developments which seem so essential a part of the landscape All the land was wild, some in prairie, other parts covered with dense timber and a portion of it under water It was a mighty task to turn the virgin sod, to fell the sturdy parent trees and to drain the pestilential swamps that were not only useless, but bred various diseases, yet these sturdy, determined old pioneers were equal to the task, and, while all did not live to see their young hopes materialized, they laid a sound foundation upon which the present remarkable structure of civilization has been built, and to them is due the initial credit One of the families to whom belongs the distinction of having commenced this great work is that bearing the name of Cook, a worthy representative of which is found in the person of Charles N Cook, veteran of the Civil war and a substantial farmer of Clay township Mr Cook belongs to an old and honored New England family, whose Puritan ancestors emigrated to America on the Mayflower He was born September 15, 1830, in Berkshire county, Williamstown, Massachusetts, and is a son of Noah and Lydia B (Bardwell) Cook.

Charles N Cook received the advantages of a common school education, and his spare time as a boy was spent in assisting his father, who was a cobbler by trade and who made many fine pairs of shoes for the college students of his town On attaining his majority, young Cook went to Marysville, California, where he entered the gardening business, but remained there only about one and one-half years, returning to his father's home in Massachusetts In 1856 Mr Cook came to Logansport, Indiana, and soon thereafter settled on a tract of land, about eleven

HISTORY OF CASS COUNTY 739

acres comprising the tract, situated west of the city limits. This land he paid fifty dollars per acre for, and upon it he began the business of gardening. He carried on that industry until August 13, 1862, when he enlisted in Company K, Ninety-ninth Regiment, Indiana Volunteer Infantry, for service in the Union army during the Civil war, and with this organization the young truck-gardener and soldier continued to participate in all of its engagements until he was honorably discharged as an invalid, on July 8, 1865, at Davis Island, N Y harbor. A brave, faithful and cheerful soldier, he won alike the respect of his comrades and the esteem of his officers, and when he had completed his career as a soldier, he returned to Williamstown, Mass and spent the summer under the treatment of a physician at the home of his parents In the fall of the same year, having recuperated his strength, he returned to Logansport, Ind , where he took a relapse of his trouble (the camp diarrhoea) and becoming so depleted in strength as to give up all hopes of recovery to health, sold his little home west of the city and at the request of a friend, went to the home of the latter in Clay township north of Logansport, where with careful nursing, on the following February was so restored to health that he married Miss Margaret Ball and commenced housekeeping on a farm in Bethlehem township and followed the occupation of a farmer as his health would permit

In the fall of 1872, Mr Cook bought a small farm of twenty acres on the north line of Clay township on which with the addition of another twenty acres adjoining he has since made his home He is now in his eighty-third year and has a well-preserved vitality for a man of his age He bought an old log cabin, hauled it to his farm with the assistance of his neighbors, fitted it up comfortably, and here he and his young wife lived

The woman who became Mr Cook's wife and faithful helpmate through life was prior to her marriage Miss Margaret Ball, who was born in Washington county, Pennsylvania, on May 5 1841, whence she came to Indiana with her parents when she was a child of three years. She was the fifth born child of her parents, David and Maria (Baker) Ball, to whom were born seven children, and of which number four are living today, Mrs Cook being the eldest The others are Lafayette, of Clay township, Joseph, of Leiter's Ford, Indiana; and William B , also of Clay township

When Mrs Cook came to Indiana in 1844, the state was in her infancy Miami and Pottawattomie Indians were there in plenty and from her childhood on Mrs Cook experienced much in the new and untaught country in which her family had settled The pioneering days of Indiana are thoroughly familiar to her, and she is well qualified to speak on pioneer conditions of Indiana that prevailed here half a century ago She lived through the period when the forest was being converted into a rough field for cultivation, saw the use of the sickle, the scythe and the cradle in the field give way to more modern methods of harvesting, saw the old-fashioned fireplace, still dear to the hearts of many of us, the andirons, the spinning wheel, the reel, the looms for weaving the jeans and linseys, all pass out of use and be supplanted by the inventions and customs of a later day None of the old time country sports are unfamiliar to her, or unforgotten. The quilting bee at which the women of the neighborhood congregated to make merry and incidentally to perform an unbelievable quantity of real work knew her cheerful presence on many happy occasions, and she was a witness at many a barn raising or log-rolling contest. In her childhood days she attended the little log cabin school in her community, and lived through the period when the old goose-quill pen was dying hard in the last days of its usefulness, when threatened by the advent of a more facile weapon. All these, and many other changes did she and her family see in the days of their early life in Indiana, and she recalls with mingled pain and pleasure the experiences of the days gone by.

Mr. and Mrs Cook are the parents of three children,—a son and two daughters. David William is a resident of Clay township. Anna Bella is the wife of William C Van Buren and makes her home in Fairfield county, Ohio, where they are engaged in the business of agriculture; they have three sons and two daughters, and Lydia Ellen, the youngest of the three, who makes her home with her parents and is devoting herself to them in their declining years. She is a young woman of admirable character, educated in the public schools of the county, and well advanced in music, a subject in which she is qualified to teach. She is a consistent member of the Bethel Methodist Episcopal church and an honored member of the Ladies' Aid Society of that church.

Mr and Mrs Cook are genuine pioneers of Cass county, and their citizenship is one of which their community may in every way be proud. They have a host of good friends in Clay township and command the esteem and regard of all who share in their acquaintance. No shadow of dishonor has fallen upon the good name of the family in all the years of their residence in the Hoosier state, and they are of the people whose identity with the state has been one of its fortuitous conditions.

HON HARRY M GARDNER. Probably in no profession or avenue of business do men become so widely known as in journalism, not always as personalities, but as influences, their printed thoughts reaching thousands where their spoken ones could be heard perhaps by only a score. Hence the responsibility of a journalist is of exceeding weight, and his influence as a molder of public opinion bears directly upon the welfare of the community in which his labors are centered. Harry M Gardner, city editor of the *Daily Reporter*, of Logansport, has spent his entire career in newspaper work, and has been connected with some of the leading public prints of the West and Middlewest. He was born at Dunkirk, New York, September 15, 1880, and is a son of William and Mary (Watson) Gardner, of Scotch and Irish ancestry, respectively. The Gardner family's advent in America occurred in Colonial days. William Gardner was a musician, a composer, and for a number of years a soloist with several of the largest musical organizations of this country. Both he and his wife are now deceased, as is also one of their two children.

Harry M Gardner received his primary educational training in the schools of Dunkirk, where he was reared, and subsequently took a course at the University of Buffalo. Shortly after this he began his newspaper career as a circulator at Dunkirk, and as a "cub" reporter on the

Evening Observer. Succeeding this he was connected with newspapers at Denver, Los Angeles, Butte, Ogden, Pocatello, Fort Worth, El Paso, and other points in the West, in a reportorial capacity, and in February, 1905 came to Logansport, Indiana, which he has since made his home, although twice before, for short periods, he had worked here. He became a reporter on the *Daily Reporter,* and successive promotions have raised him to the position of city editor of this publication.

Mr Gardner is a Democrat in his political views, and in 1913 represented Cass and Fulton counties in the state legislature. He belongs to the Benevolent and Protective Order of Elks.

ADELBERT M WALKER. Cass county, it has often been fittingly said, owes her greatest and best wealth to her farming communities and to the men who have given their lives to the cultivation of the waste places of the country, building up thriving communities and establishing happy homes in these districts that half a century ago were practically untouched by man. The present generation of Cass county farmers are carrying on to completion the worthy work begun by their fathers before them, and prominent among these may be mentioned Adelbert M Walker, one of the well established and prosperous farmers of Miami township. As such, it is wholly consistent with the spirit and purpose of this work that some mention though necessarily brief, be made of him and his work. A native son of the township and county in which he now resides, he was born here on August 19, 1872, and his parents are Eugene A and Minerva (Thomas) Walker. The father resides in Clay township and enjoys the warm regard of a goodly circle of old time friends and acquaintances. The father was a soldier in the Union army during the Civil war, giving valiant service in the cause of the North, and is a member of G A R.

Until 1898 Adelbert M Walker made his home with his parents. As a boy he attended the district schools, and ably assisted his father with the care of the home place, learning under the able instruction of his worthy parent much concerning farming activities that he has applied in his own enterprise. He married in 1893, but continued to remain at the home place with his young wife until 1898, when he acquired his present farm of one hundred and ten acres also in Miami township, and here has continued to reside. He has a fine place, well kept and carefully cultivated, and has proven himself a farmer of no slight capacity. Since he came into the possession of his present place he has built another dwelling house, more suited to the demands of his family, and as a result, two commodious dwellings now grace his farm.

Mr Walker married on September 2, 1893, Miss Mary Angle, the daughter of Benjamin Angle, of Virginia, and three children have been born to them,—Marie, Mildred and Alma. Marie received her diploma from the public schools in the class of 1912, and is taking musical instruction, Mildred is in the seventh grade; Alma is in the fifth grade.

The family are members of the Baptist church and Mrs Walker is a member of the Ladies' Aid Society of the Baptist church. They have a worthy share in the activities of that body. Mr Walker is a Republican. They have lived quietly and conservatively, and are reckoned among the responsible and reliable people of Miami township, where the family have been known to the community for three successive generations

CHARLES OGLETHORPE FENTON Among those who have made Cass county's history, it is fitting to record the name of Charles Oglethorpe Fenton He was not a pioneer of the county, he was not one of its old citizens His brief race was run in forty-nine years, twenty-seven of which were spent in Logansport Arriving here at the age of twenty-two, a stranger and without means, the advancement he made is worthy of note and emulation How did he succeed to the title of brother, friend and counsellor? Those who knew him best would tell you he was diligent, he never idled, he was prompt, he met his obligations the day they were due, not the day after. He hated gossip, for, he would say: "What an idle waste of time when there are so many good books to read!" It was his custom to carry a favorite book to his office, hoping to find some golden minutes of leisure during the stress of the day in which to read.

Charles Oglethorpe Fenton was of Irish descent, the great-grandson of Samuel and Ann (Shannon) Fenton, who sailed over the sea from Old Erin early in the eighteenth century. They settled in Newville, Cumberland county, Pennsylvania, and to them were born thirteen children, "all girls but eleven." One son, David, moved to Mantua, Portage county, Ohio His wife was Emily Dunscomb and their sons were Green and Grove The former and Louisa Frost, the daughter of Elvira Kellogg and John Frost, were the parents of eight sons and one daughter, the fourth son being C O. Fenton He was born January 31, 1863, on the "old John Frost homestead," in Mantua, where his mother had been born thirty years before When eleven years old he left the parental roof to make his own way, working for neighboring farmers evenings, Saturdays and vacations, and in the meantime attending school at Ravenna When seventeen years old he taught the district school at home, and for one summer he worked in a cheese factory, and while yet in his teens he engaged with the Central Publishing house, of Cincinnati, Ohio, to sell books, and spent eighteen monthes traveling in West Virginia, Tennessee and Texas Returning home, he again taught school, himself attending school at such short periods as he could So it is that we find him June 14, 1883, at the age of twenty, graduating from the Northwestern Ohio Normal school, at Ada, and it was to further his education he came to Logansport in April, 1885, to enter the American Normal College, then situated on College Hill, north of the city In the winter of 1885-6 he taught in Pulaski county and it was there that he met Carrie Belle Tyler, whom he married May 25, 1887. To this union one daughter was born Sagie Velle Fenton, August 17, 1888. Mrs Fenton was born in VanBuren township, Clay county, Indiana, February 10, 1866, the youngest of the four children of Roxie Velle Usher and Sage R Tyler Her father was born at Cape May, New Jersey, August 18, 1836 His father, Nathaniel Tyler, was of Scotch-Irish extraction and his mother Abigail Scull, was born in England. On the maternal side, Mrs Fenton traces her lineage back to the year 1730, when Hezekiah Usher, who kept the first book store in Boston, married Abigail Cleveland The mother of Mrs Fenton was born August 21, 1839, in Madison county, New York, the daughter of Isis

CHARLES O. FENTON

Burdick and Moses Usher When five years old she came to Indiana with her parents and grandparents, the latter being Dr. Nathaniel Usher and Lucy Palmer, of West Haddon, Connecticut. Dr and Mrs. Usher were the parents of Judge John P Usher, secretary of interior in Abraham Lincoln's cabinet. This branch of the Usher family removed to the state of Kansas

Mr Fenton also taught school at the Stone and Clymer schools in Clinton township, Cass county. At the time of his marriage he had charge of the commercial department of the American Normal College and was writing editorials and reporting for the *Logansport Times,* receiving for his newspaper work one dollar per week On May 28, 1888, he bought the *Logansport Times,* then owned by twenty Prohibition stockholders His first vote had been cast for James G Blaine, although he was born of a line of Democrats In November, 1888, he voted for Clinton B Fisk and a straight Prohibition ticket, which ticket he continued to support throughout the remainder of his life Through the medium of the *Times,* local though it was, he came to be known by the party leaders throughout the nation The sagacity, the loyalty, the persistency of this fearless editor became an inspiration He had a distinct literary style, writing prose full of fun and pathos and some verse, humorous for the most part His prose writings have been said to be something after the style of Mark Twain and some of his verses like those of Riley. His pen was his power He was a delegate to all Prohibition state and national conventions and at the last national convention he attended, at Atlantic City, in July, 1912, was assistant secretary.

In 1900 Mr. Fenton added to his newspaper work the brokerage business and as investment broker enjoyed the confidence of a large clientele and was pre-eminently successful At home his presence gave out an atmosphere of cheerfulness It was his custom evenings to spend much of the time in reading, often aloud He liked history, biography and travel and above all he loved the poets, Burns being his favorite He knew most all of his poetry and said, from the moment that he turned the knob on his office door on Fourth street to the moment he turned his door-knob at home, nine squares distant, if uninterrupted, he could and often did repeat the whole of "Tam O'Shanter" In June, 1911 he and his wife attended their daughter's graduation at Vassar College and sailed from New York to spend the summer in the British Isles, in Holland, Belgium and France It was in the land of Burns he took the greatest delight and day after day followed lovingly in the footsteps of the plowman poet. Probably his best literary productions were his travel letters written for his newspaper

Mr Fenton had often quoted. "Let me die in the harness," and so it was in the prime of a busy life that he was compelled to retire to the Battle Creek Sanitarium, Battle Creek, Michigan, for rest Even here he was reading the "Life of Washington," by his favorite American author, Washington Irving, preparing to write an article on a visit to Mount Vernon, one of a series of articles descriptive of summer vacation trip to Atlantic City, Washington, Richmond and so forth During the six weeks spent at Battle Creek he grew steadily weaker and weaker, and there, on the 31st of October, 1912, left this for a fuller life It was said of William Morris by one of his biographers that he died of being William Morris. So it was with C. O. Fenton, a man who was engaged in so many and so varied activities.

JOHN C. REA. In the annals of early settlement in Cass county, one of the names which is first to be mentioned is that of John R. Rea, whose son is now one of the prosperous farmers of Clay township. For more than eighty years this name has had a place in the history of Cass county, and has always been associated with solid worth and an industry which brings credit to the possessor and helped to create the resources and wealth of the community.

Mr. John C. Rea, the son of the old settler, was born in the village of Clymers, in Cass county, on the nineteenth of May, 1864. His grandfather's name was Daniel Rea. His parents were John R. and Elizabeth Rea. His father, who was first a resident of Connersville, this state, in 1832 came to Cass county, where he joined with the earliest settlers of this locality. A carpenter by trade, he was a very useful man in his community at Clymers, and many of the old houses of that locality were constructed by his hand and according to his plans.

His death occurred in 1884 at a venerable age, while his wife passed away in 1886 and both are buried in the Clymers cemetery.

Mr. John C. Rea received most of his education in Clinton township, and also for two years enjoyed the advantage of college training at Logansport. He has had a varied but generally progressive career, and since attaining manhood has been advancing every year to a better position in life and increased esteem of his fellow citizens. For about three years, he was engaged in teaching school in Cass county, but the greater part of his active lifetime has been devoted to farming. His present farm was formerly owned by his wife's father. The estate contains one hundred and ten acres, and Mr. Rea since locating here has made many improvements upon it, although most of the buildings were placed there by old Mr. Swigart.

On April 25, 1888, Mr. Rea married Miss Anna F. Patterson, a daughter of Simon E. and Cicely (Amos) Patterson. Mrs. John C. Rea is a native of Cass county, Indiana, and was born April 29, 1866. She was reared and educated in her native county and is a lady of pleasing and social address, ever ready to fulfill her part as wife and mother. Her cheerful and pleasant home is ever open to their many friends. She traces her lineage to the "Emerald Isle," as her early progenitors came from the "Land of the Shamrock." Mr. Rea is of Scotch ancestry. Three children have been born to Mr. and Mrs. Rea, and all are living. Harry Ralph, now a student in the Franklin College, fitting himself for the ministry, Royden K. received his diploma from the public school in the class of 1908 and has finished the high school course in Logansport, Ruth E. received her diploma in the class of 1909, and has taken one year's work in the high school at Logansport, and has also been a student in instrumental music. All three of the children are members of the Baptist church and Mrs. Rea is a member of the Methodist Episcopal church. Mr. Rea is affiliated with Burroughs Lodge, No. 495, I. O. O. F. The homestead of the Rea family is known in Clay township as "The Cedars."

ALEXANDER MILTON BUCHANAN, M D Of the pioneer families of Cass county probably none deserved mention and permanent records in the annals of this vicinity more than the Buchanan family, which became identified with Logansport in 1839, and continued prominent in this part of the state through the career of the late Dr Buchanan up to the time of the latter's death on November 29, 1905

Alexander Milton Buchanan was born at Chambersburg, Pennsylvania, on March 24, 1823, and belonged to a Scotch-Irish family, which, had been settled in Pennsylvania for many years The parents of the late Dr Buchanan were Rev James and Harriet (Berryhill) Buchanan, the former a native of Pennsylvania, and the latter a native of the capital city of that state They moved west with their family to Logansport, Indiana, in 1839, where Rev James Buchanan was pastor of the First Presbyterian church from 1840 to 1843 He had previously been minister of the Presbyterian church at Greencastle, Indiana His death occurred in Logansport in 1843, and his name is permanently identified with the early church annals of this city There were eight sons and two daughters in the family, and all of them are now deceased One of the sons, Dr Andrew Buchanan, was educted at Princeton College and Philadelphia Medical College, and for a time practiced in Cass county.

The late Alexander M Buchanan was a boy when the family came west to Cass county, and the years he spent here were during the pioneer period Among many families, education at that time was not considered a fundamental matter, but the Reverend James Buchanan was probably in advance of ordinary public opinion in that respect, and no doubt encouraged his sons to prepare for their careers with the best professional equipment that could be obtained Dr Alexander M Buchanan therefore began his studies in medicine in La Porte, Indiana, and then went east and entered the Philadelphia Medical College, the oldest and one of the best known institutions of medical learning of the time After graduating he began practice in Illinois, where he was first married Later he moved to Cass county, and spent many years of practice in both town and country He really represents the old-time doctor in this locality, and many of the older residents now living in Cass county will recall his kindly character and personality and his helpful and sympathetic attitude to all who were in distress He continued in active practice up to 1895, at which time he retired and moved into Logansport, where his death occurred in 1905 He lived at Metea this county, before returning He was a member of the Presbyterian church His first marriage occurred at Kankakee, Illinois, in 1851, when Miss Nichals became his wife He married on October 24, 1867, in Logansport, New York, Miss Minnie York, a daughter of Lewis and Delia (Babcock) York, who lived near Canandaigua, New York One daughter, Mrs Bertha L Collett, wife of W S Collett an engineer of Logansport, Indiana, was born of this union

JOHN A VINEY, of the firm of Cummings & Viney, has been a resident of Logansport for the past forty-six years, and for the four years previous, from 1861 to 1865, he was a resident of Columbus, Indiana He was born on March 11, 1856 in Greenbrier county, West Virginia, and is one of the four children born to John M. and Rachel (Lewis) Viney, two of the four yet living

John M Viney was a farmer by occupation and was originally descended from French ancestry In the subsequent history of the family they immigrated to the British Isles, and there by intermarriage became the possessors of English and Scotch-Irish blood John M Viney moved to Carroll county, Indiana, in 1860, and resided there until spring in 1866, when he came to Logansport Here ill health caused him to relinquish all active pursuits for the remainder of his days, and he died in 1871 His widow survived him six years, passing away in 1887.

John A Viney came to Logansport with his parents when a boy of ten years. He received but a very limited education in the district schools, and from the age of fifteen, when his father died, was compelled to fight the battle of life entirely on his own responsibility Until he was nineteen years old he worked in the mills on the south side of the Wabash river, and in 1875 he began learning the upholsterers trade He duly completed his apprenticeship and thereafter worked at the trade for twenty-three years, being associated with various firms in those years

In 1899, he formed his present partnership with Harvey R. Cummings, under the firm name of Cummings and Viney, and the new firm embarked in the retail furniture and upholstering business in Logansport This association has continued from then until the present time, and as both partners are practical and experienced men in their business, they have enjoyed their full share of the local trade, and are accounted among the prosperous business men of the city

Mr Viney is the president of the Logansport Credit Exchange and a director in the Logansport Commercial Club In 1881, he became a member of the Knights of Pythias, Apollo lodge No 62, in which he has served in all chairs, and is yet a member of that society He is also a member of the Knights of the Maccabees. He is a Democrat, with regard to his political affiliations

On December 24, 1877, Mr Viney married Iona E Morgan of Logansport Mr. and Mrs Viney are members of the Broadway Methodist Episcopal church, of which denomination Mr Viney has been a member for forty-four years

HOMER CLOSSON For seventeen years Homer Closson has been identified with the drug business of Logansport, as an independent man of business, previous to which he was employed in the city for nine years in the same line His venture, which he launched in 1895, has proven to be a thorough-going success, and Mr Closson is rightly regarded as one of the ablest business men of the city of Logansport today

Born near Jackson, Michigan, on September 22, 1871, Homer Closson is the son of Seymour M and Kate (Smith) Closson The father came to Logansport some thirty-five years ago, just following the death of his wife, and some years after he located in Logansport, Mr Closson married Ella McIntyre Both are living in Logansport Nine children were born to them, seven of whom are yet living

Homer Closson was a small child when his mother died, and until he was nine years of age he lived in his native county, making his home with relatives of the family and in 1880 he came to Logansport where he joined his father who had previously settled here and had married as is noted above. The boy attended the public schools of Logansport until he reached the age of fifteen, when he secured employment in the drug store of B. F Keesling. From then until the present time he has been identified with the retail drug business, either in the capacity of employe or employer. For nine years he remained with Mr Keesling, and in 1895 he began in business for himself in the place which he now occupies, his independent experience thus covering a period of seventeen years, which have been marked by a generous measure of success and general prosperity. The business has increased along conservative lines, and Mr Closson has one of the most complete and modern establishments of its kind in the city

On December 1, 1897 Mr Closson was united in marriage with Miss Alpha Hilton, of Logansport, daughter of William Hilton, an old resident of this city. Five children have been born to them Ralph W, Gertrude L, George D, Frances Jean and John H Mrs Closson is a member of the Baptist church of Logansport and of the Order of the Eastern Star

MARVIN M MINNICK Among the popular and capable officials of Cass county, none stands higher in public esteem than Marvin M Minnick, the present incumbent of the county treasurer's office, whose services have contributed materially to the public welfare A long and careful training, followed by an extended period spent in the schoolroom, as an educator, was succeeded by much experience in banking matters, thus fitting him thoroughly to discharge the duties of his office, the conscientious performance of which has thoroughly established him in the confidence of his fellow-citizens Mr Minnick bears the added distinction of being a native son of Cass county, having been born in Tipton township, near Walton, December 21, 1867, one of the six children, all living, born to Elias and Elizabeth A (Lindesmith) Minnick

Conrad Moenich (as the name was originally spelled), the grandfather of Marvin M Minnick, was a native of Hesse Cassel, Germany, whence he emigrated to the United States in young manhood, settling in Somerset county, Pennsylvania, where Elias Minnick was born in 1843 The latter was reared in his native county, educated in the public schools, and taught the blacksmith trade, but when not yet nineteen years of age enlisted, in 1861, in Company K, Ninth Regiment, Indiana Volunteer Infantry, as a private, for service during the Civil War Enlisting at Laporte Indiana, he was transferred to the Army of the East with which he fought at Cheat Mountain Grafton and Greenbrier. Subsequently his regiment joined the Army of the Cumberland, under General Rosecrans, Mr Minnick's captain being Dver B McConnell, of Logansport With this organization he fought at Corinth Iuka, Murfreesboro and Pittsburg Landing, and September 20 1863, at the battle of Chickamauga, he was captured by the enemy For seven months he was incarcerated in the awful stockade at Andersonville, and later he was transferred to Belle Isle and Florence, spending in all, about fifteen months in Confederate prisons. He was finally released on account of the close of hostilities, received his honorable discharge, and returned to the vocations of peace. Settling on a farm in Tipton township, Cass county, Mr. Minnick engaged in farming, and his subsequent life was devoted to the tilling of the soil. He was a Democrat in politics but although often solicited to allow his name to be used as a candidate for public office, steadfastly refused, preferring the peace and quietude of private life to the turmoil of the public arena. He was a popular comrade of the Grand Army of the Republic, and his religious belief was that of the Christian church, in the faith of which he died April 14, 1892. His widow still survives and makes her home at Walton, Indiana.

Marvin M. Minnick was reared to manhood on the home farm, and was given good educational advantages, attending the public schools and for three years being a student in the American Normal College. He next entered Hall's Business College, at Logansport, and after his graduation therefrom entered upon a career of teaching which covered the next seventeen years. He became widely and popularly known as an educator, but resigned from his position to enter commercial life, attaching himself to a private bank at Bunker Hill, Indiana, and later a like institution at Walton, Indiana, and for six years was cashier of these institutions. He was a resident of the latter place, in 1910, when he became the candidate of the Democratic party for the office of county treasurer, and in the active campaign that followed Mr. Minnick was returned the winner greatly aided, no doubt by his wide acquaintance and high reputation gained during his days as a teacher. Mr. Minnick gave the people of Cass county an excellent and economical administration, and in 1912 was again his party's choice for the office and elected by an increased majority. He is a Knight Templar Mason and also holds membership in the Knights of Pythias and the Independent Order of Odd Fellows. With Mrs. Minnick he attends the Methodist Episcopal church, at Walton, Indiana.

On September 15, 1896, Mr. Minnick was married to Miss Lavina H. Green, of Walton Indiana, and they have had three children, Edgar E., who is deceased, and Dallas D. and Dorothy L.

ARTHUR E. DUNN. The rapid growth of the automobile interests of the country in recent years has created an industry which has given a wide field of opportunity and enterprise to many of the young men of the present generation, who have a predilection for mechanics, and Arthur E. Dunn, of Logansport, Indiana, is one of those who have made the most of his opportunities along these lines. Since 1908 he has been in the garage business for a part of the time in partnership with one Harry Case but since 1909 he has conducted the business entirely upon his own responsibility, winning a reputation for efficiency and service in the work that has brought him a considerable prominence in the city.

Arthur E. Dunn was born on April 14, 1882, at Cissna Park, Illinois, and is one of the two sons of Edward A. and Lydia L. (Ashley) Dunn. The father was a farmer all his life. He came to Royal Center Cass county, Indiana, in 1898, and continued farming there until 1903 when he moved to Logansport, and there he died in October, 1908. His wife

passed away in April of the same year, so their two sons, Arthur E and Herbert A, were bereft of both parents in the short space of six months

The subject attended the public schools of Logansport after the removal of the family to this place, and in 1903 was graduated from the city high school The succeeding three years were spent in Lake Forest University, but he did not graduate owing to the fact that the failing health of his parents made it seem best that he return home and assist in the care of the home place After the death of his parents, in 1908, Mr Dunn entered into a partnership with Harry Case, previously mentioned, and established a garage at 320-22 Fifth stieet, in Logansport. They were successful, but the partnership was short lived, and soon Mr Dunn purchased the interest of his partner and continued the business at the original location until 1910, when he moved to No 617-623 Broadway his present location Here he maintains one of the modern and up-to-date garages of the city, the property being his own, and remodeled and arranged on its purchase to meet his own requirements and ideas of general service He carries on a general garage business, including repairing and the sale of auto accessories, and is building up a solid and substantial trade in the city

Mr Dunn is a member of the Country Club and of the Methodist Episcopal church He is married, Coad Herrington, of Pana, Illinois, becoming his bride on June 11, 1908

WILLIAM W HANEY Many lives have entered into the foundation of the state of Indiana, and none of them more worthy to be considered in a history of pioneer personalities than the late William W Haney Those who have come and enjoyed the splendid prosperity of the later era, however important their own contributions, have all owed a great debt to the pioneers who first tested the capabilities of soil and climate, who faced the hardship of existence when only the strong and the brave could remain, and who laid the foundation of a greater civilization and permanent prosperity

The career of the late Mr. Haney was not typical of the early settlers in the Wabash valley, for he was one of those remarkable men with great initiative and enterprise whose activities lie in a plane above that of the average citizen He was a leader where others followed, he founded enterprises upon which they built and enjoyed the fruits thereof, he planned and supervised the execution of undertakings which required the services of hundreds of subordinates His career is prominently associated with several of the epochal movements of early Indiana history The late Mr Haney belonged to the era of water transportation in northern Indiana, and was one of the builders of the old Wabash canal, which was the chief artery of commerce during the thirties and forties and the indistinct remains of which may be seen in Cass and adjoining counties to the present day He was also associated with the old Indiana State Bank, and his name and enterprise are linked with many of the notable events and affairs of the last century

As a succinct summary of this notable career which belongs in the annals of Cass county, nothing better has been written than the following quotation from an address by Judge D P Baldwin, delivered at the time of the death of Mr Haney—"The late Mr Haney was a remarkable man in many respects This is proved by the grand fortune he accumulated in this little city where money is scarce and riches the exception I do not hesitate to say that Mr Haney had the best financial brain of any man that, at least in my time, ever lived in Logansport At seventy-nine years, and until his last sickness his mind was as clear and quick as that of any man in mid-life Mr Haney's honesty was very remarkable. No scandal was ever connected with his great fortune. His word was sacred, he took no undue advantages, he was a remarkably friendly man, he was as kind and sociable with a tramp as with a millionaire He did not know what pride was any more than he knew what deceit and double-dealing were He was always clean-mouthed. No one ever heard him retailing scandal or speaking unkindly. Mr. Haney's great wealth brought upon him, as wealth or exceptional success always does, a great weight of envy or raillery, but he took it good humoredly No one ever knew him to get angry or excited, much less, vindictive or sullen. No one knew better of good and ill of life and humanity. Mr. Haney did not pretend to be anything else than a business man, and never sought office or promotion of any kind He did not set up to be a charitable man any more than a talented man, and yet his kindly voice, friendly ways, and unquestionable honesty gave him a happy and honored old age and made him a general favorite with all classes."

William W Haney was born in Bucks county, Pennsylvania, December 25, 1809, and his death occurred in Logansport April 20, 1889. His parents Joseph and Mary (Weaver) Haney were people of small means and for that reason, and also because of the times in which he lived, were unable to provide their son with any education except that of the primitive local schools. Though not a well educated man in the modern sense of the term, Mr. Haney had those powers of keen perception and fine memory, and so excelled in his judgment of men and his practical ability in affairs that he was never at disadvantage in his competition with the world of men His boyhood days were spent on the farm where his most useful training was probably in the acquirement of a sound physique and a practical industry. After leaving the farm he worked in a hotel, then was clerk in a store, and at the age of seventeen, without capital, began his independent career. He joined the engineering corps engaged in the construction of the Delaware division of the Pennsylvania canal, between Easton and Bristol, being on that work for a year. His next enterprise was boating coal along the river and he was also employed in a hotel at Easton With his growing ability he was next made superintendent of a division of the Pennsylvania canal, and continued in that capacity for a year, after which he returned to his former enterprise of boating coal For another two years he had supervision on a branch of the Pennsylvania canal, and then took a contract for the construction of the Delaware and Raritan canal feeder. After completing this work he acted as superintendent of the feeder

With this varied experience in constructive enterprise and general business, Mr Haney turned his attention to the west By steamboat, flatboat and pirogue he arrived in the state of Indiana, and on the fourth of July, 1835, made his advent into the frontier village of Peru The Wabash valley throughout this region was then almost an unbroken

wilderness, although there were stirrings of the great activity which the plans for the building of the Wabash canal had set in motion. Soon after reaching Peru, Mr Haney took charge of a force of men and the construction work of this canal. They opened a stone quarry below Peru for the contractor of the Peru dam, and a little later he, himself took a contract for the construction of a section of the canal at Lewisburg When this contract was finished the following year he formed a partnership with Alexander Wilson and established a merchandising business in Lewisburg, also conducting a large trade with the Indian population which had not yet been removed from Indiana Three years later he bought his partner's interest in the store, and up to the summer of 1851 was engaged in business at Lewisburg in real estate, canal script and other securities

The late Mr. Haney dated his residence in Logansport from the fifteenth of July, 1851 In this city he established a general store, but soon retired from the mercantile field His business from that time until his death was in real estate and as a private banker. During several years of this time he was president of the Logansport branch of the old Bank of the State of Indiana During the intervals of his business career he had also managed to acquire a substantial knowledge of the law, and soon after locating at Logansport was admitted to the bar, although he never practiced in the courts, confining his business in this profession to a limited office practice. The estimate delivered by one of his friends and old time associates upon his business career needs no further extension Whether as a contractor, merchant, banker or real estate man, his transactions were always marked by a high sense of honor and strictest integrity, and notwithstanding his thoroughly business character and high regard for the rigid principles of business procedure, he had the kindly nature and the genial personality which made him popular among a great body of the citizenship. At the time of his death, the late Wm W. Haney was regarded as one of the richest men in the state, as wealth was then estimated, his estate being valued at more than half a million dollars

Wm. W Haney married, December 13, 1836, Miss Louisiana Fidler, who survived him and also attained to a good old age Of two children, the daughter, Maria Emma, is now deceased and the only survivor is Mr William E Haney of Logansport, a sketch of whose career follows In the affection of his family and associates, the late Mr Haney made a secure place It is said that he was known either personally or through his kindly deeds to every man, woman and child in the city of Logansport He was a member and a liberal supporter of the Broadway Methodist church in this city Among the names of the older citizenship in Cass county none deserves higher rank or more permanent place on the rolls of honor and sincere admiration than the late William W Haney.

WILLIAM E HANEY The son of the late William W Haney is himself deservedly classed among the old settlers of Logansport, by reason of a residence in that city for more than sixty years William E. Haney's career has been one of exemplary citizenship Like many other successful men of his day, his early advantages were limited, but he had all the qualities of native ability and character which make sure success. At this time, although he has passed the age when most men feel fit for the struggles of active business, he still ably conducts the management of his extensive interests, and is a man of large and beneficent influence throughout his home city and vicinity.

William E. Haney, a son of William W. and Louisiana (Fidler) Haney was born at Lewisburg, Indiana, December 28, 1837. His education was confined to the advantages afforded by the common schools of his day, very limited when it is remembered that free public education had not yet been established throughout Indiana during the boyhood of Mr. Haney. After the removal of the family to Logansport in 1851, he had some further schooling and in better schools. In 1859 associated with his father, he started in the produce business, but after about one year moved to a farm in Eel township, where he was engaged in farming for about twelve years. Returning to Logansport at the end of that time he was for six months a boot and shoe merchant, but after the death of his partner sold out, and then for some years conducted a brokerage business on a small scale. He was also during this time becoming more and more associated with his father, in the latter's extended business enterprise. Since the death of his father his entire attention has been taken up in managing the affairs of the estate, and in handling real estate and a general brokerage business.

William E. Haney has inherited the best of his father's sterling qualities of character and business ability. He has an unassuming nature which throughout the many years of his active business career has kept him in the quieter channels of life, and he has never aspired to a place of mark in public affairs.

On April 5, 1859, Mr. Haney married Miss Christina Conrad, daughter of William Conrad, one of the pioneer settlers of Cass county. Mrs. Haney died in the spring of 1871. She was the mother of eight children, six of whom died in infancy and early childhood, while the survivors are Carrie E. and Jessie M., the latter being the widow of Miller Uhl. Mr. Haney has voted the Republican ticket throughout nearly all the years of the existence of that great party, although beyond his vote and a practical interest in home affairs and good government has never participated in politics. His fraternal association is with the Benevolent & Protective Order of Elks.

HARRY E. BURKIT. Like many others of the county officials of Cass county, Harry E. Burkit, county recorder, was born in the locality which he now represents and has passed his entire career within its borders. A product of the farm, and a member of a family that has for generations produced tillers of the soil, he has also held up the family reputation for prominence in the educational field, and for years was known as one of Washington township's most popular and efficient educators. In his official capacity he is rendering his community signal service, and his work has served to extend an already large acquaintance and to gain him many sincere friends. Mr. Burkit was born on a farm in Washington township, Cass county, Indiana near Walton, October 26, 1879, and is a son of William H. and Sarah B. (Robinson) Burkit. His grandfather, David P. Burkit, founded the family in Cass county, whence he came from Pennsylvania He is of Irish-Scotch ancestry. William H Burkit was born in Cass county, and here divided his attention between agricultural pursuits and teaching school, having passed nineteen years in the school room in Cass county His wife, also a native of the county, taught one term here and four of their six children were teaching in the county schools at the same time Mr Burkit passed away January 26, 1902, and was buried in Mount Hope cemetery, Logansport, while his widow survives, and with her children resides on the old home place

Harry E Burkit attended the district schools of Cass county, and subsequently spent two years in the Marion Normal College, and four terms in the graded and high schools at Walton Thus equipped, in 1900, he began his career as a teacher in the Long school in Washington township, and during the three succeeding terms was at the head of the district school which he had attended as a boy In all, he taught for seven winter terms, in the meantime spending his summers in the work of the farm, on which he had always resided until coming to Logansport. Mr Burkit entered Democratic politics when he was appointed deputy county recorder, and after serving four years in that office was elected, in 1911, to the office of county recorder, entering upon the duties thereof January 1, 1912 His administration has been marked by efficiency and faithful performance of duty, and the citizens of Cass county have had no reason to regret of their choice Mr Burkit has a high regard for the responsibilities of public office and is doing his utmost to give his community clean, able service He is not a politician in the generally accepted use of the term, but has at all times supported Democratic policies and candidates, and is known as one of the wheel-horses of the party in his section Mr Burkit has interested himself to some extent in the fraternal work of the Knights of Pythias, in which he has attained to the uniformed rank, and in which he has many friends He is unmarried

GEORGE W CANN Probably no better example of accomplishment in spite of handicaps and misfortunes could be found than the career of George W Cann, of Logansport, contractor in electric supplies Left an orphan at the age of five years his boyhood was one of hard and unceasing struggles, made all the more so by a serious injury, the loss of the left arm in a flouring mill, which left him to fight against still greater odds That he has risen to a high place in the business world, and has been able to overcome the obstacles placed in his path, speaks volumes for his determination, courage and ability, and his business record is replete with earnest endeavor and well-won battles Mr Cann was born July 7, 1870, at Idaville White county, Indiana, a son of George W and Mary (Hastings) Cann.

George W. Cann was but a year old when his father died. He was about five years of age at the time of his mother's death, and for one year lived with an uncle, a miller at Hoovers, in Cass county, in whose mill Mr. Cann met with an accident that cost his left arm Shortly thereafter he was placed in the Orphans Home, where he resided until thirteen years of age, succeeding which he spent three years in the home of Dr. W H Thompson, for whom he acted as office boy In the meantime he had acquired a good common school education and managed to secure a teacher's certificate. While teaching country school in the winter months, he attended two summer terms at Ladoga Normal School, and continued teaching four years At that time he came to Logansport and took a clerical position in the general offices of the Pennsylvania Railroad, where he was so employed for eight years After failing to secure the nomination for the office of city clerk, he secured a position as clerk of the city electric light department, and after two years in this connection, resigned his position and established himself in business at No 324 Broadway, where he was engaged in contracting and handling electrical supplies until April, 1911 At that time he came to his present establishment, a modern, well-equipped building at Nos 312-14 Broadway.

In 1906, Mr Cann received his nomination on the Democratic ticket for clerk of the courts of Cass county, and as such served four years He is a Cumberland Presbyterian in religion, and is a member of the Benevolent and Protective Order of Elks, the Fraternal Order of Eagles, the Improved Order of Red Men, the Independent Order of Odd Fellows, the Knights of Pythias, and several fraternal insurance bodies

On September 20, 1903, Mr Cann was married to Miss Euphemia Farnsley, of Medaryville, Indiana, and to this union there have been born three children, namely Marguerite Ellen, Mildred C and Mary Josephine The family is well known in Logansport, where its members have numerous appreciative friends

WILLIAM H REIGHTER A life of quiet effectiveness, marked by a record of many duties well done and many responsibilities faithfully fulfilled, was that of the late William Harrison Reighter, of Cass county He was one of the men who developed and made Cass county what it is He was never in the conspicuous activities of abnormal events of the world, but in the round of commonplace accomplishments and in the faithful and intelligent performance of every task that was allotted to him during his long life, he left a record which may well be envied and admired by the generations that follow him

William Harrison Reighter was born at Carlisle, Cumberland county, Pennsylvania, and his death occurred at his farm in Carroll county, April 8, 1893 His parents were George and Salome (McFeely) Reighter His father was a farmer and spent part of his life at Carlisle He owns large tracts of land in Cumberland county There were two other sons in the family, named John McF, and George Washington Reighter

The late Mr Reighter was one of the pioneer settlers of Cass county. He attained a very meagre education by private schooling and by a term or two in the common schools, and on May 14, 1839, he arrived in Cass county His first work in this county was the building of a mill in Jefferson township, and he subsequently bought eighty acres of land in Noble township Throughout his career he was one of the substantial developers of the agricultural resources of this county, and at the time of his death was owner of an estate of three hundred and twenty acres of land in Cass and Carroll counties The late Mr Reighter was in politics a Democrat He was reared in the faith of the Presbyterian church, though during his active lifetime was not a member of any church organization Neither did he have membership in any societies, but as a citizen was always public spirited, had a broad-minded view of government both national and local and was always ready to lend his aid in the promotion of any enterprise which would more effectively express the ideals of good government and a better community He was a great student both of men and books History was an absorbing study with him, and few among his contemporaries were better informed on the larger questions and topics of the past as well as the present. Personally he was of a jovial disposition and he was a delightful companion He bestowed all the riches of a noble character upon his own family circle, and they appreciated his many kindnesses and noble qualities

Mr. Reighter first married Miss Agnes Houk, and the three children of that union are all now deceased On December 7, 1854, he married Miss Cassie Graham, who was born near Pittsburgh, Pennsylvania, and subsequently moved to Ohio Her father was Israel Graham who was a native of Delaware, and who came to Cass county at an early day There are two children by the second marriage of Mr Reighter, namely Maggie, who is the wife of Samuel A Michael, and Harry T, a farmer on the old Reighter homestead in Cass county Three children have been born to Mr and Mrs Samuel A Michael, namely· W H. Lulah M, who is now Mrs. H. D Smith, and Ethyl W., who is now Mrs William R Reel The house in which Mrs Michael and family now reside was built by her father about 1855, and it has been remodeled several times, though in its associations it possesses the charms and memories of one of the oldest homesteads in this county Mrs Michael and her brother Harry have erected a beautiful monument to their father, but even in more enduring manner does his name and character exist in the minds and affections of all people who came within the radius of his acquaintance and friendship during his life

JOHN M. ETNIRE was born in Logansport, Indiana, on February 24, 1865, and is one of seven children born to Isaac and Cynthia (Baldwin) Etnire, of which number six are now living Isaac Etnire was a son of Martin, a native of Pennsylvania, who came to Cass county in pioneer times, as did also two brothers, John and Abraham

Martin Etnire settled in the heart of the woods in the cabin home which he built with his own hands, and there gave himself up to the rearing of his family and the cultivation of his wilderness farm In later life, when he was ready to retire from the activities of the farm, he moved to Deer Creek township, and there he passed the closing years of his life His son, Isaac, the father of the subject, was reared to hard work on the farm and was early inured to the hardships of pioneer life He only secured the most meagre educational advantages, the schools of the day affording but slight reward for attendance thereupon, and he lived all his days in Cass county He served in the Civil war, or, more correctly speaking, he enlisted, but after a stay of some time in Indianapolis, he and others who accompanied him, were returned to their homes, owing to some technicality which existed He was a Republican, and his religious leanings were toward the Baptist denomination

His wife is a devout member of that church. On May 5, 1912, this worthy couple celebrated their golden wedding anniversary, and they are now living retired in Logansport.

Cass county has been the home of John M. Etnire since his birth. He attended the district schools in his boyhood, and when he was twenty-one years old began farming on his own responsibility, that being the work in which he was reared in his father's home. He continued for two years, but in October, 1887, gave up the life and came to Logansport, where he launched a retail furniture enterprise. Success attended his efforts from the beginning, which was of a most humble order, and thus for twenty-five years he has continued in that field of activity. He is the oldest furniture dealer, in point of continued service in the business, to be found in Logansport, and enjoys an excellent reputation for business veracity and integrity.

Mr. Etnire is a Republican in his political faith, though not an active politician, and he is fraternally affiliated with the Knights of Pythias. With his wife, he is a member of the Presbyterian church.

On July 25, 1886, Mr. Etnire was united in marriage with Lottie Hogentogler, and two children have been born to them: Ethel M., now the wife of Arthur W. Routh, and Cecil L. Etnire.

JOSEPH TAYLOR. Among the men whose upright lives, sterling characters and high business abilities have added to Logansport's commercial and social prestige, the late Joseph Taylor is worthy of more than passing mention. Coming to this city in 1870, he here founded the firm of Joseph Taylor & Sons, which still endures and is one of the city's leading enterprises. Mr. Taylor was born in Burlington county, New Jersey, March 18, 1822, and was a son of John and Hester Taylor. When he was yet a boy his parents removed to a farm near Dayton, Ohio, and he there grew to manhood, attending the district schools, assisting in the work of the home farm, and later attending the public schools of Dayton. Prior to attaining his majority, he began clerking in a dry goods store at Dayton, but about 1845 moved to Greenville, Ohio and embarked in business upon his own responsibility. He lived at Greenville many years and became closely identified with the welfare and progress of the community. On March 25, 1850, Mr. Taylor was united in marriage with Miss Josephine C. Dawes, a daughter of Elisha Dawes, a tanner, and a man well known throughout that section of the country, and with him there, for a time, Mr. Taylor was associated in business. During the fall of 1859, he moved to a farm near Monticello, White county, Indiana, but in 1870 came to Logansport, which was his home throughout the balance of his life.

On locating in this city, Mr. Taylor founded the Joseph Taylor & Sons wholesale saddlery business, which yet endures, his sons, who continue the business, keeping the original name because of both sentimental and business reasons. Mr. Taylor was a plain, unassuming, hard-working business man, whose word was at all times as good as his bond and whose bond was always good for whatever he contracted. Upon first coming to Logansport, he established a tannery in partnership with his father-in-law, on the north side of the river, on Fifth street. Later on, this partnership was dissolved, Mr. Dawes assuming ownership of the tannery and Mr Taylor the store which they operated in connection with the other business Saddlery and hardware was a later addition to the regular line

Mr Taylor was essentially a business man, and took little interest in the struggles of the political arena outside as to how they affected his adopted community He was at all times ready to lend his hearty support and co-operation to movements which his judgment assured him would benefit Logansport or its people, and no enterprise of this nature was considered completely organized until his name was secured For almost his entire life, Mr Taylor was a member of the Presbyterian church, and his membership meant something more than a mere name, for he endeavored at all times to live and act the life of a Christian gentleman In his death, which occurred February 8, 1887, Logansport lost one of its citizens to whom the city could point with pride as representative of its best activities, and he was sincerely mourned, not only by his immediate family and a wide circle of friends, but by all who had his acquaintance and knew how hard his place would be to fill in the life of the city His widow survived him until May 2, 1892 They were the parents of nine children, and four of their sons, Zachary, Dawes, Clark and Joseph, are now conducting the business founded by their father

JOHN M JOHNSTON Under our present system of government no office carries with it greater responsibility than that of postmaster The handling of the mails of a large city entails the possession of abilities of a high order, a reputation that bears not the slightest stain or blemish, and the confidence that is only secured by the conscientious performance of every public duty John M Johnston has been postmaster of Logansport since 1906, and during this period has displayed strength, force, character and resolution qualities necessary to the best public service He has worked with his hands and trodden the familiar but difficult self-made way to success, and throughout his career has identified himself vitally with the city's interests Mr Johnston was born June 3, 1860, in Mercer county, Pennsylvania, and is the second son of Robert F and Sarah A (Donaldson) Johnston

Robert F Johnston was born in Stark county, Ohio, August 31, 1834, and was a son of John and Elizabeth (McDowell) Johnston, also natives of Stark county The family moved to Wells county, Indiana, when that section was still in its formative state, and there Robert F Johnston grew to manhood and acquired a good practical education, which was subsequently supplemented by years of close observation and wide and varied reading He was a carpenter by trade, but after coming to Logansport, in 1863, spent a number of years in the butter and egg business, and then became a traveling salesman for wholesale boot and shoe houses of Toledo and Chicago, with which he was connected for twenty-two years In this he was more successful than the average traveling man, his geniality, unfailing courtesy and good business qualifications being the principal contributing causes On January 1, 1857, he married Sarah A Donaldson a native of Mercer county, Pennsylvania, and to this union there were born four children namely Isaac S , John M , Eben E and Robert M Mr. Johnston was a member of the

Presbyterian church, was widely known in Masonry, and was one of the most stalwart of Republicans He was elected trustee of Eel township in 1895, and served as such until his death, which occurred September 26, 1898

John M Johnston was but three years of age when brought to Logansport by his parents, and this city he has always since made his home He was educated in the public schools, and for nine years following clerked in the drug store of Rodney Strain At that time in partnership with Dr M A Jordan, he entered business on his own account, purchasing the business of Mr Strain, which the partners conducted successfully for eight years and, in 1897, Mr Johnston became district agent for the Mutual Life Insurance Company, a position he was holding at the time of his appointment, June 20, 1906 to the office of postmaster, by President Roosevelt On June 10, 1910, he received his reappointment from President Taft, and still continues to act efficiently in this office His administration of the affairs of this office has been marked by a distinct advance in the service Needed reforms have been made, and innovations introduced, and the people of Logansport may congratulate themselves upon his appointment He has always been a stalwart supporter of Republican principles and for four years served as a member of the Republican county central committee.

Mr Johnston was married September 8, 1897, to Miss Emma Rosenthal, and they have had four daughters, namely · Esther, Gertrude; Margaret, who died at the age of seven years, and Frances Mr. Johnston is a member of the Masonic fraternity, being past worthy master of Tipton Lodge No 33 He also holds membership in the Logansport Commercial Club, and with other earnest and hard-working men has given of his best energies in promoting progressive anl public-spirited movements

SAMUEL E HOWE. In the death of Samuel Edward Howe, which occurred November 10, 1911, Logansport lost a business citizen whose activities had for many years had a direct influence upon its industrial importance A poor young man when he came to this city, his principal capital a generous amount of ambition and energy, he so directed his abilities that he became one of the city's leading manufacturers and his industry became an integral part of the business life of Logansport Mr Howe was born October 8, 1842, in Dixmont, in the state of Maine, and was a son of Otis Crosby Howe, who was of English descent.

After completing his education in the schools of his native state, Samuel E Howe secured a position as traveling salesman for an eastern concern, and in this capacity made his advent in Logansport A man of keen perception and farsightedness, he recognized the opportunity for establishing himself in business in this city, and accordingly started in a modest way to manufacture plow-handles In the meantime, however, he continued to discharge his duties as traveling salesman, and did so until his own business had grown to such proportions that it needed all of his time and attention As this business continued to extend over a wider and wider territory, Mr Howe embarked in other fields of endeavor, eventually becoming interested in the lumber busi-

S. E. Howe

ness, as a holder of timber lands in the South, having been induced to enter this line on account of the growing scarcity of lumber. At the time of his death his holdings were vast in a number of southern states, and since his demise his sons have handled these interests. During the war he served on the side of the Union, a member of the navy and a steward therein.

On November 3, 1870, Mr Howe was united in marriage with Miss Catherine Herrick, at Delta, Ohio, she being a daughter of James S and Martha (Sharpstein) Herrick. Seven children were born to this union, as follows. Wilson H, who married Eva Maurison, May E, who married Dr. Terflinger; Abbie C, who married Dr C W Russell, Otis C and Laura A, who are unmarried, John C, who married Jessie Grant, and Samuel E, who married Minnie Martin. Mrs Howe, who was the youngest of a very large family, lost her parents when she was still a child. She survives her husband and resides in her modern residence in Logansport, where she is surrounded by a wide circle of sincere friends. She is a faithful member of the Presbyterian church, and her late husband, while not a member, supported all religious movements generously and never refused any just request for financial assistance, for, having succeeded himself, he was at all times ready to help those who had been less fortunate than he. The factory that he first erected in company with his partner, J H Tucker, and which was the scene of his early success, is still standing. As a business man Mr Howe was very thorough in his undertakings, was frank and open, and kind to his employes. He was a man of strict integrity, and was broad-minded and liberal in his views. He contributed in a philanthropic way to all churches. His long and honorable career stands without stain or blemish to mar it, and in his death Logansport lost one whose place will be hard to fill.

FRANK AMOSS is the youngest and the only surviving member of the family of his parents, and he was born in Noble township, Cass county, Indiana, on May 22, 1877. He is the son of Jasper W and Sarah Stokes (Cox) Amoss, both now deceased. The father was born in Point Pleasant, West Virginia, in 1840, and received as a boy in his native state the advantages of the common school. He married in 1865, and they became the parents of three children. Matilda, born in 1866, and died in 1869, John, born in 1868, died in 1893, and Frank, the subject of this brief review.

While he was yet an infant, Frank Amoss moved to Logansport with his parents, and there he lived until he was about eight years of age, his mother died then, and he went back to the country to make his home with Joseph H Cox, his maternal uncle. He continued to make his home with his uncle until he had completed his high school studies at Logansport. Soon after this he made a trip to Porto Rico, and was absent in that land for about a year, investigating the opportunities which the country offered in various business lines. He then returned to Logansport, where he became deputy county treasurer under Owen A McGreevey, in which post he continued until 1907, when he received the appointment of assistant postmaster, and is still the incumbent of that position He is also connected with the undertaking firm of Chas D Chase & Co

Mr Amoss is a Republican He is a member of the Masonic fraternity, and affiliates with its various bodies as follows The Blue Lodge, Tipton No 33, A F & A M, Logan, the Chapter, No 2, R. A M., Logansport Council No 11, R & S. M, and he is the present secretary of the Benevolent and Protective Order of Elks Lodge No 66

Mr Amoss was married on January 8, 1908, to Margaret Estelle Martin of Logansport, and both he and his wife are members of the First Presbyterian church of Logansport

MURDOCK & WISE The well-known firm of Murdock & Wise opened their men's furnishing store at No 404 Broadway on October 20, 1902, with William O Murdock and Claude O Wise comprising the firm This firm has continued uninterruptedly to the present time in the same spot in which it was established ten years ago. The partners, young men of old and honored families of Logansport, began their business venture with practically no capital, but with a generous fund of inherited and acquired common sense and business wisdom They have in the ensuing years met each and every obligation as it became due and have kept their names commercially clean, their integrity being unmarred by any business shortcomings The business has been a success from the start, and much credit is due these young men for the progress which has been theirs

James H Wise was born in Canton, Stark county, Ohio, on March 18, 1846, and is a son of William and Isabel (Gregory) Wise, the former a native of Cumberland county, Pennsylvania, and the latter of Stark county, Ohio The father was a farmer and served in the war with Mexico In 1846, the family moved to Allen county, Indiana, and ten years later moved to Monmouth, Illinois where both parents died. Their son, James H Wise, was reared in Monmouth, Illinois, and there received a common school education He started out for himself in the buying and butchering of stock, and for two years he was occupied in this manner on the plains of the central west, including the states of Kansas, Nebraska, Oklahoma, Colorado, Idaho, Montana, part of the time being engaged as a cattle herder, making two trips as night herder of freight trains across the plains In 1868, he returned to Monmouth, Illinois, and resumed butchering In the following year he came to Logansport temporarily and on January 21st married Margaret Rugh, after which he returned to Monmouth and there continued his residence until 1872, when he moved permanently to Logansport, which has since been his home For forty years he has carried on, with but slight deviations, the trade of a carpenter He is a Republican and an adherent of Theodore Roosevelt He is a member of Orient Lodge No 272, A F & A M, and Logan Lodge No 40 of the Independent Order of Odd Fellows, in the latter having membership in the Canton, Encampment and Rebekah degrees He is a past brigadier general of the Patriarchs Militant Three children were born to Mr and Mrs. Wise Claude O., of the firm of Murdock & Wise, Maude, the wife of Norman E Myers, and Ira A Wise

Claude O Wise was born in Monmouth, Illinois, on June 6, 1872, the son of James and Margaret (Rugh) Wise, of whom detailed mention is made above He came to Logansport in his infancy in company with his parents, and there was reared and educated, the public schools of Logansport supplying his education In 1888, the young man began clerking in the store of Dewenter & Company, dealers in haberdashery, and for fifteen years he continued to be in their employ, during which time he became well versed in methods pertaining to the successful manipulation of such an establishment When he severed his connection with this firm it was to form a partnership with William O Murdock for the purpose of engaging in a similar business venture, and the store which they then established has continued up to the present time, and he enjoyed a pleasing degree of success and popularity in the city where both these young men have been known well and favorably all their lives Thus Mr Wise has for twenty-five years been identified with the retail men's furnishing business in Logansport and no business man in the city today is better known or has a better standing than he

The fraternal relations of Mr Wise are maintained in the Blue lodge, chapter and council of the Masonic order, the Benevolent and Protective Order of Elks, and socially he is a member of the Country Club, of which he was one of the organizers He is a member of the Logansport Commercial Club, and is a Republican in politics

On October 14, 1895, Mr Wise was united in marriage with Miss Charlotte Shroyer, the daughter of Alexander Shroyer, one of the old pioneer merchants of Logansport They have one son, J Eugene Wise. Mrs Wise is a member of the First Presbyterian church of Logansport

GEORGE W RICHARDSON A residence of something like forty-five years, during which time he has been identified with industries which have materially contributed to the importance of his community as an industrial and commercial center, entitle George W Richardson, of Logansport, to a position among the representative men of Cass county Although at the present time he has retired from the activities of life and is now living quietly in his comfortable city home, he still takes a keen and intelligent interest in all that affects his locality in any way, and is known as a citizen who may be depended upon when supporters are sought in movements of a progressive nature Mr Richardson is a native of the Old Dominion state, born in Bedford county, Virginia, December 25, 1847, a son of Washington and Jane (Payne) Richardson

Mr Richardson was reared in his native county, and there attended the district schools, although he secured only a limited education, as it was necessary that he devote the greater part of his time in his boyhood and youth to helping his father support the growing family When he was twenty years of age, in the spring of 1868, he came to Cass county, Indiana, and with the exception of one and one-half years passed in Daviess county, this state, Cass county has since been his home On first coming to this locality, Mr Richardson was successful in securing work as a farm laborer, an occupation at which he was engaged for some time, and during this period he carefully saved his wages, being industrious and thrifty and having ever in mind the idea of one day owning a home of his own Eventually, in August, 1909 Mr Richardson felt that he had earned a rest from his ceaseless labor, and with his wife moved to

Logansport, where they have since continued to reside in their comfortable, modern home. In political matters a Republican, he has taken an interest in the success of his party, was at one time known as one of the dependable men of its ranks in Miami township, and there served as supervisor for some time.

On November 10, 1870, Mr Richardson was united in marriage with Miss Eunice Montgomery, of near New Waverly, Indiana, and they became the parents of six children, as follows. Nellie J, who became the wife of William Mearns, of Cass county, William Alvah, a resident of Portland, Indiana, Charles E, who makes his home in Logansport; Gertrude, who died at the age of seventeen years, Grace, who became the wife of Elijah Booth, and Clyde, who is a resident of Keokuk, Iowa Mr and Mrs Richardson are consistent and liberal members of the Methodist Episcopal church Mr Richardson has taken some interest in fraternal work and has many friends in the local lodge of the Masonic fraternity

CHARLES E RICHARDSON Presenting as it does an excellent example of youthful industry, integrity and perseverance conducting to well-earned success, the career of Charles E Richardson, a successful Logansport business man, is worthy of emulation by those who are seeking business prestige and financial independence When Mr Richardson established himself in business in Logansport, he had little capital other than that which had been supplied him by nature, but this enabled him to found the little business which became the nucleus for his present prosperous enterprise He has been the architect of his own fortunes and a review of the steps by which he has attained his present position may not be inappropriate in a work which shows so many examples of self-made manhood Mr Richardson was born in Miami township, Cass county, Indiana, January 2, 1875, and is a son of George W and Eunice (Montgomery) Richardson A sketch of George W Richardson precedes this.

Charles E Richardson attended the district schools and remained at home until he was seventeen years of age, at which time he entered the Marion Normal school, where he spent one year He then began teaching school in Miami and Clay townships in the winter months, and during this time furthered his own studies in the Indiana State Normal school at Terre Haute Mr Richardson was so engaged at the time of the outbreak of the Spanish-American war, and April 26, 1898, he enlisted in Company M, One Hundred and Sixtieth Regiment, Indiana Volunteer Infantry, with which he went into camp There he contracted typhoid fever, and eventually received his honorable discharge, on account of disability, then returning to his home He left the service as sergeant, February 24, 1899 For about two years thereafter, Mr Richardson was employed in the capacity of fireman on the Pan Handle Railroad succeeding which he was engaged in various occupations until July 1, 1908, when he purchased a half interest in the Logansport Dye Works, at No 218 Sixth street Four months later he bought the rest of the business and in 1909 he became the owner by purchase of the building in which the enterprise is located Since 1908 he has been engaged in dyeing and cleaning after the French method, and of more recent date he has added the manufacture of soft, stiff and Panama hats to his original business His operations have proven uniformly prosperous, and he is justly rated to be one of the successful business men of his adopted city

On December 17, 1902, Mr. Richardson was married to Miss Blanche E Campbell, daughter of the Hon. B F Campbell, appropriate mention of whom will be found on another page of this work One son, Robert C, was born to this union, December 25, 1904. Mr Richardson is a Republican in his political views, and his fraternal affiliation is with the Masons, among the members of which he numbers many friends With Mrs. Richardson, he belongs to the Baptist church, in the work of which both are active, while he serves in the official capacity of member of the board of trustees

GEORGE W HOFFMANN Probably there is no more exacting vocation than that of the modern pharmacist, for, next to the physician (with whom he must co-operate), the druggist is the one upon whom we rely in sickness and accident A man of thorough training and absolute reliability, he must be also a master of several occupations beside his own, and, to make a success of his enterprise, must be capable in business, courteous in manner, and ready to serve the long hours that the vocation demands The dean of the drug trade in Logansport, George W Hoffmann received not only a thorough training in his youth, but has had the additional advantages of attendance in the school of practical experience. He has been a resident of Logansport for almost forty years, and is widely known, not only in his chosen field of endeavor, but as a man who has rendered signal services to his city in positions of public trust Mr Hoffmann was born in Cincinnati. Ohio, July 31. 1852, one of the three sons born to the marriage of George Louis and Katherine (Kalb) Hoffmann, both natives of Germany, the former of Bavaria and the latter of Hesse Darmstadt In 1848, George Louis Hoffmann left the Fatherland to escape the compulsory military service of his native land, and some time during the following year arrived in, Cincinnati, Ohio, where he secured employment at his trade of millwright Both he and his wife are now deceased

George W Hoffmann was reared in his native city, acquiring his education in the public schools and night school When he was sixteen years of age he embarked upon a career of his own, his first employment being at grinding paint Succeeding this, for three years he was employed in a drug store where he received his introduction to the business, and in February, 1873 came to Logansport, Indiana, here becoming a clerk in the drug store of G W Brown He was thus engaged but a short time when he left Mr Brown's services to become a clerk for the drug firm of Leonard, Dale & Company, which was succeeded by E H. Borgers & Company, a concern with which Mr Hoffmann continued until March, 1877 At that time he purchased a one-third interest in the firm of Leonard & Company, which then took the firm style of Leonard & Hoffmann, and this association continued until November, 1877, when Mr Hoffmann became sole proprietor In 1887, when he sold out, he became a traveling salesman for a druggists' sundries company of Detroit, but six months later entered the railway mail service, in which he also spent six months. He had for some time been interested in Democratic politics, and at this time was assistant county recorder. In 1884, he was elected to the city council of Logansport on the Democratic ticket, but after one and one-half years resigned to devote all of his attention to his private affairs. He was then in charge of the establishment of Milton Cunningham, but ill health caused his retirement after a few months. He has not been identified with political matters, having devoted himself exclusively to his pharmacy. Mr Hoffmann has spent many years in the study of pharmacy, chemistry and the most exacting science of filling prescriptions. He has conducted his business under the policy that from self preservation he must attend to his customers with quality, care and attention; he knows conditions and is familiar with the necessities of his neighborhood, supplying them intelligently, faithfully and with not only professional but personal attention. Among his associates he is known as a man of the utmost reliability and strictest integrity, and the manner in which he has ever conducted his transactions has been such as to gain him the unqualified confidence of his fellow-citizens. In his religious belief Mr Hoffmann is a Universalist. He belongs to the Knights of Pythias, the Woodmen of the World and the Knights of the Maccabees

On October 26, 1876, Mr Hoffmann was married to Miss Inez E Luther, of Logansport, and they have had four children, of whom two are living Wilhelmina, who married L H Wheeler, and George L, a research bacteriologist in the employ of the firm of Parke, Davis & Company, of Detroit

JOHN E WALLACE Although not born in Cass county, John E Wallace, the popular and efficient county auditor, has resided within its limits since his second year, and has been identified with the official life of this section since 1908. In his present capacity he has proved a painstaking, conscientious and courteous public servant, and the signal services he has rendered his community stamp him as one of Cass county's public-spirited citizens. Mr Wallace was born in Chicago, Illinois, August 7, 1877, and is a son of Mark and Mary (Farrell) Wallace

Mark Wallace was born in County Wexford, Ireland, December 5, 1848, a son of John and Ellen (Mahoney) Wallace, the former a butcher by trade. Of the five children composing the Wallace family, Mark is the only surviving son and the only one to come to the United States. As a lad of fourteen years he started his battle with life as a farm hand, and although he was able to secure ample employment at fair wages, saw ahead of him only a future filled with hard labor with little hope of accumulating a competency, and, like many other of his countrymen, turned his face toward the New World, where, as he had been assured by friends who had preceded him here, there was ample opportunity for him to prove his abilities. Accordingly he left Castle Garden in 1869 and made his way directly from New York to Logansport, Indiana, where he arrived with less than a dollar in his pocket. He soon secured employment as a section hand on a railroad, but six months later left that position to become a wiper in the round-house of the Pan Handle Railroad, and was soon promoted to the blacksmith shop, where he acted

in the capacity of helper In 1872, he was placed on an engine as a fireman, and his promotion to the position of engineer occurred in 1876, when he was given a switch engine in the Chicago yard He continued so employed until 1879, when he went out on the road, remaining in the freight service until 1893, when he was promoted to the passenger service, with a run on the north end of the Chicago division He still continues in the service of this road, being one of its oldest and most trusted employes He has been prominent in the Brotherhood of Locomotive Engineers, in which he has served as chief engineer and as first assistant chief The family has resided in Logansport continuously since 1879 In November, 1874, Mr Wallace was married, in Chicago, to Miss Mary Farrell, and they became the parents of six children, namely Annie, John E., William, Thomas, Mary and Charles

John E Wallace received his early scholastic training in the public schools, afterwards entering Hall's Business College, where he completed the prescribed course in the special branches he had elected to pursue When sixteen years of age, he started out for himself as bookkeeper for the firm of McCaffrey & Company, of Logansport, with which concern he was connected for three years, then entering the master mechanic's office of the Pennsylvania Railroad as time-keeper and clerk In 1905, he left the employ of the railroad to become bookkeeper for Dr J B Lynas & Son, and was thus employed, in 1908, at the time of his appointment to the position of deputy in the office of the county auditor of Cass county, George W Cann In 1910, he became the Democratic party's candidate for the office of auditor, and was subsequently elected for a term of four years, succeeding Mr Cann, a position which he has since filled with great ability Under Mr Wallace's administration, the affairs of the auditor's office have been in excellent condition, and he is known as one of the county's most popular and obliging officials His long and varied experience has thoroughly fitted him to discharge the duties of his position, and his work has been an important factor in advancing the best interests of the county He is interested in fraternal work, belonging to the Benevolent and Protective Order of Elks and the Knights of Columbus, and his religious connection is with the Catholic church

On May 20, 1903, Mr Wallace was united in marriage with Miss Nellie M Gallagher, and they have had three children Helen M, Harry M and John E, Jr.

JOHN J HILDEBRANDT, who died December 14, 1912, occupied a prominent place in the moral and commercial history of Logansport, a position attained through his own unaided efforts and by sheer force of character Born in Iowa, February 8, 1863, he was one in a family of six children, but one now living, born to August J. and Katherine (Gable) Hildebrandt, the former a native of Hesse Darmstadt, Germany When five years old he was brought to Logansport by his parents and he was here reared and educated in the parochial and public schools. Being of an independent and thoughtful turn of mind, he forsook the religion of his parents, joined the Presbyterian church When eighteen years of age began learning the plumber's trade at fifty cents per day This he continued for some time, his first employment being on the buildings of the county poor farm When twenty-seven years old he embarked in the business for himself, his shop being on Pearl street. He was industrious, was considered an excellent workman, and as time passed prospered An ardent disciple of Izaak Walton, he often found time to visit lake and stream and at odd moments in his shop invented fishing tackle according to ideas of his own These efforts at first became objects of ridicule for the local wiseacres, but as Mr Hildebrandt invariably returned from his jaunts with a well-filled creel, his success aroused interest Traveling men induced him to make tackle for them similar to his, and as they proved successful it was not long until the manufacture of fishing tackle of all kinds became an important adjunct to his regular business With the passing of time this enterprise grew until it became an important industry of Logansport and made the founder comparatively wealthy Such, in brief, is the history of one of the large commercial houses of Logansport Of late years Mr Hildebrandt had retired from the active cares of life, owing to failing health, and devoted much of his time to philanthropic work He was a man who loved home and humanity in general and was ever ready to extend a helping hand to those less fortunate than himself The world is better because of his having lived in it

On March 22, 1892, Mr Hildebrandt was married to Miss Katherine Markert, and they became the parents of three children Hiram H, Ruth K and Lois F He was the first president of the Associated Charities of Logansport, of which he was made an honorary president for life, was a member of the Humane Society, and the T. P. A. and on national matters was a Republican His business is still carried on by his son, Hiram II, at 408 Fourth street, shipping the goods all over the world, including Spain, Scotland and England, and is successful Mr Hildebrandt built the home at 817 High street eight years ago and where his widow now resides Mrs Hildebrandt is a member of the First Presbyterian church of Logansport.

WILLIAM H PORTER Hand in hand, in public usefulness, is the druggist associated with the physician and this mutual dependence is universally acknowledged as a condition of public safety Healing remedies are older than doctors and as far back as one may delve in ancient lore he may find mention of medicaments for some of the ills that have always afflicted the human race At times the discovery of a new drug of surprising properties, cinchona, for example, has wrought wonderful changes and has been even a factor in advancing civilization. Out of the hands of the ignorant and superstitious, the lawful administration of drugs has long since passed, and the term druggist or pharmacist now means one who, after a protracted period of study and experiment, covering a number of the sciences, has passed a thorough and satisfactory examination before a learned scientific body Into his hands there is practically placed life and death, for it is the knowledge of drugs and their effects that must guide him in handling the most careful of physicians prescriptions Thus it is no unimportant position that a druggist holds in a community, and his standing is usually of the highest Among the leading pharmacists of Cass county may be mentioned William H Porter, of Logansport, whose connection with this business here covers a period of upwards of a quarter of a century During this time he has firmly established himself in the confidence and esteem of his fellow-citizens, and has interested himself in everything that has pertained to the welfare of his community. Mr Porter was born November 12, 1865, in Carroll county, Indiana, just across the line from Cass county, and is a son of Oliver H and Rosanna (Benner) Porter all of whose four children are still living

William Porter, the grandfather of William H Porter, was a native of Fairfax county Virginia, and came to Indiana during the earliest history of the state, when it was still in its formation He settled first near Connellsville, in Fayette county, where he farmed after the primitive manner of those days, but during the latter 'thirties or early 'forties moved with his family to Cass county and settled in Clinton township There he passed away when still in the prime of life Oliver H. Porter was born in December, 1835, in Fayette county, Indiana, but practically passed all of his early life in Cass county Shortly after his marriage, he moved across the line into Carroll county, and there resided for some fifteen or twenty years, in 1879 returning to Cass county, where he continued farming until his death September 5 1898 His wife, who passed away November 13, 1888 was a daughter of Daniel Benner, who came to Logansport when this city was still a trading post and when the Indians were as numerous as were the whites

William H Porter was reared until fourteen years of age in Carroll county, and since that time has been a resident of Cass county He was trained to agricultural pursuits, and his early education was secured in the district schools but later he supplemented this with attendance in the Logansport public and high schools He received his introduction to the drug business in 1885, at which time he began clerking in the drug store of B F. Keesling with whom he continued four years, and then, in 1889 established himself in business as the proprietor of a pharmacy of his own During the twenty-four years that Mr Porter has been engaged in business in Logansport, he has gained the respect and esteem of all with whom he has had commercial transactions His establishment is well equipped, and a large stock of first-class goods is arranged in an inviting manner. Mr Porter possesses business abilities of the highest character, while his long experience has made him thoroughly conversant with every detail of his vocation Mr Porter is a thirty-second degree and Knight Templar Mason and a member of the Mystic Shrine, and has appreciated to the full the benefits of Masonry

On January 4, 1900, occurred the marriage of Mr Porter to Miss Alice Knowlton, daughter of Charles B Knowlton, one of Cass county's early settlers

CHURCHILL P FORGY. The Forgy family is one of the oldest known to American life, and members of it have from the earliest days of the British colonies been identified with life in this country, in various walks of life The first of the name to settle on American shores was John Forgy, who held an office with the British government in England He deserted his office, as the only alternative to being pressed into service in the army, and came to America, where he settled in New Jersey He was engaged in the hotel business in Trenton, when he was apprehended by the British soldiery during the Revolutionary war, and was shot by order of the government So much for the establishment of the house of Forgy in the United States

Churchill P Forgy was born in Clark county, Ohio, on January 27, 1835, and was the son of John D and Catherine (Voorhees) Forgy John D was the son of John, who in turn was the son of the first John Forgy, who lost his life in the manner mentioned above John D Forgy, father of the subject, was reared in Virginia, the mother being a native of New Jersey, where she was reared As a boy, the subject passed some time in a school at Princeton, N J, then came to Indianapolis where he worked as a printer, and afterwards came to Logansport It was at Logansport that his father had settled in 1836, where he opened up a general merchandise store and continued thus in business until 1840 afterward going to Dayton Ohio, and entering the employ of Churchill Phillips, as confidential clerk He was with them for a year or more, then moved to New Carlisle. Ohio, where he bought a farm on the outskirts of the town, and remained there until death claimed him in 1844

After some years passed in the printing business in Indianapolis, C P Forgy finally settled in New Waverly, in Cass county, engaged in the general merchandise business, and took charge of the grain elevators He continued to be thus occupied until 1902, when he retired from active business pursuits He has enjoyed a goodly share of prosperity in all his business ventures, and is well equipped to enjoy the remainder of his life free from business cares or worries

C P Forgy it may be said, was one of the four children of his parents He had one sister Maria. who is now deceased; Stern W went to the war as a captain in Gen. John A Logan's army and died from the service in the army The third son, Dickinson J., also joined the Union army in southern Illinois, serving through the war and he died in New Waverly in 1909

On December 14, 1859, Mr Forgy married Louise M Quick, the daughter of C R Quick, of New Waverly, and his wife, Lucinda (Sloan) Quick Mr Forgy is a member of the Presbyterian church, and his fraternal affiliations are with the Masonic order, in which he held the office of treasurer for a number of years He is also a member of the Odd Fellows, and has held the same important office in that society

Mr Forgy's life in New Waverly has been one of the most beneficent order, and he and his estimable wife have a host of good friends in and about the community, where they are well known for their many excellent qualities, and for the high character of their citizenship Mr Forgy's identification with the community has only been for its best good, and the place he has won and yet retains in public opinion is one that might well be envied

LOURY L QUICK, M D The state of Ohio was the home of the Quick family from the time of its locating in this country from England some generations past until it migrated to Indiana, in the spring of 1856, settling in Cass county Since that time this county has been well known to the family, and the people of this district have long been ministered to by medical men of two generations of the family. A soldier in his young manhood then a doctor, and all his life a busy and active man, Dr Quick has gained a wide acquaintance in Cass county, and his name is one that carries with it the esteem and high regard of all who know the kindly and genial Doctor in his professional capacity or in any of the relations of life

Dr Loury L Quick was born on the 20th day of December, 1846, in Clark county, Ohio, and is the son of C R and Lucinda (Sloan) Quick. The paternal grandfather of the Doctor was William Quick, and his maternal grandfather was Robert Sloan, of Dutch descent. In 1856 the Quick family came from Troy county, Ohio, making the journey during the spring which witnessed the first entry of the Wabash Railroad into Cass county They settled at first just a mile south of New Waverly, and remained there for one summer the father being occupied as superintendent of the store of a Mr Forgy of that place He was a physician and also a Methodist Episcopal preacher and engaged in practice in the vicinity of his home, where he continued until his death, and it is worthy of note in this connection that his son, the immediate subject of this review, resumed his practice where the elder gentleman laid it down.

Dr C R Quick and his good wife were the parents of five children,—two sons and three daughters Celia married J Dalzelle, Louise married C P Forgy, Raper H married Nora Lumas, and Colonel Ellsworth, who was named thus because he was born on the day that Colonel Ellsworth was shot, married Emma Grimes Dr L L Quick was the third born in that family of five

When he was but a mere youth, L L Quick enlisted for service in the Civil war and served twenty-two months in the Sixteenth Indiana Battery When he finished his military service he turned his attention to the study of medicine, determined to follow his father in the practice of that honored profession He received the first part of his medical training at what is now known as the Chicago Medical College, at Evanston, Illinois, and later spent some time at the Indiana Medical College. He then returned to New Waverly, and here he has since been engaged in the practice of medicine, and has proved himself the worthy successor of a worthy and honored father

Dr Quick has done a considerable traveling in his lifetime and is the possessor of one of the most complete collections to be found in this section of the state, both he and his wife having an unusual interest in things of the nature of historical relics

In July, 1868, Dr Quick was united in marriage with Miss Mary C Fox, the daughter of Josiah Fox, the family being one of Maryland birth and ancestry One child has been born to Dr and Mrs Quick,—Otto L, who is now forty-three years of age, and who married Carrie Black The son Otto is a train despatcher, and has held his present position for twenty-five years, being in the employ of the Santa Fe Railroad

Dr and Mrs Quick are members of the Methodist church, and he has relations with a number of fraternal and other societies among which are the Masons He is a member of Lodge No 484, A F & A M. and of the Scottish Rite body, and for thirty-four years held the office of secretary of his lodge He has also been United States Pension examining surgeon since 1882. The Doctor has always been a man who had a high regard for his duties as a citizen and New Waverly has profited much by her possession of him as a member of society, while his family has added its full quota to the social uplift of the community.

FRANK P. YEIDER. Although the gentleman whose name heads this review has lived on his present property for only a comparatively short period, he has made his name well known among the citizens of his locality through the exercise of enterprise, industry and straightforward dealings, characteristics which have always been associated with the family name. Mr. Yeider is a native of Pennsylvania, born in Lancaster county, in the Keystone State, September 17, 1851, a son of Emanuel and Nancy (Kirby) Yeider. His maternal grandfather, Nicholas Kirby, fought bravely in the War of 1812, and was one of the party of noble patriots who defended the breastworks when the British forces stormed a point on the Potomac river. Emanuel Yeider was born in Lancaster county, Pennsylvania, and was an infant of six months when his father met his death. He grew up in his native state, and in 1869 migrated to Indiana, settling first in Miami township, and later removing to a farm in Clay township, where his death occurred, January 2, 1892, after a long and honorable career. The mother died April 26, 1884.

Frank P. Yeider received his education in the schools of his native state, and was eighteen years of age when he accompanied his parents to Indiana. He continued to remain under the parental roof until his marriage, in 1876, to Miss Sabina Adams, who died November 14, 1880, leaving one son, Charles LeRoy, who was born in 1877. Mr. Yeider's second marriage occurred September 11, 1884, when he was united with Miss Mary J. Barr, and during that fall they settled on a farm near that occupied by his father. During the next February they removed to a farm in Adams township, and there continued to reside until 1890, when they went to South Bend, Indiana, Mr. Yeider having accepted a proposition offered by the Singer Sewing Machine Company. Subsequently they located in Logansport, where they continued to reside until the death of Mr. Yeider's mother-in-law, at which time they settled in Clay township, but in 1896 he disposed of his interests here and moved to the state of North Dakota, that being the place of their residence for fourteen years. The Hoosier State finally claimed them as its own, however, and in 1910 they returned to Clay township, where they have since made their home. The present Yeider homestead, a tract of eighty acres, is one of the most valuable of its size in the township. Intelligent treatment of the soil, hard and industrious labor and an inherent ability which has come to Mr. Yeider through generations of farming ancestors, have brought this land to a high state of cultivation, while he has also shown his progressive spirit by adopting modern methods and appliances. He has devoted the greater part of his time to agricultural pursuits and is not a politician in the accepted meaning of the term, but his public spirit has led him to recognize the duties of citizenship, and he has served very acceptably in the office of supervisor of Clay township. With his family he attends the Methodist church.

Charles LeRoy Yeider, son of Frank P. Yeider, married Miss Ethel Quick, and they have had three children. LeRoy James Franklin

Yeider, born March 19, 1907, Mary Sabina Ethel Yeider, born June 18, 1906, Lois Mae Yeider, born July 8, 1909

MRS SOLOMON JONES No history of Cass county would be complete that did not give an account of its women, for while our hearts are stirred by the thrilling narratives of the enterprise and deeds of the pioneers in trade, in manufactures, in the professions and in politics, ever must be borne in mind the names and the abundant works of their companions in courage and in toil The roll of these noble women of the earlier days does not contain the names of those of a later period who clamor for equal suffrage, and for equal opportunity in business and the professions, however just may be the claims and aspirations of the latter The former came to found homes, to rear children who should be fit to carry on the work which their fathers founded They were and are domestic women, not unmindful of the duties of hospitality, nor careless of the claims of social life, and it has ever been their province to bring the sweet and tender influence of their affections to soften the lot of the unfortunate and lowly

Residing on her farm in Cass township, a tract which was settled and cleared by her late husband, is one of the best-known ladies of her community, Mrs Solomon Jones, who has lived in this county all of her life She is a daughter of John E and Mercy (Rice) Howes, who came from New York state to Indiana during the early 'thirties, locating in Logansport, where they were married on the present site of the City High school Mr Howes became county treasurer of Cass county during the 'forties, and later was a member of the firm of Merriam, Rice & Howes The subject of this review grew up in Logansport, receiving her education in the public schools, and was here married to Solomon Jones, whose death occurred in 1905 Mr Jones was originally a farmer, clearing the present farm of Mrs Jones in Clay township, erecting all the fencing, and putting up all the buildings with the exception of the milk house He subsequently became collector of revenues, in the employ of the government, and on completing his term of office, entered the money loaning business. He was a citizen of integrity and industry, a hard and faithful worker all of his life, and well merited the respect and esteem in which he was universally held

Mr and Mrs Jones had one child, John, who died in infancy Later they adopted a daughter, who bore their name until her marriage to Dallas C Burke They have had two children· Helen E, who is two years old, and Desa Elizabeth, who has passed her first year. Mr Burke is employed as an operator by the Wabash Railroad, in which capacity he has worked for the past seven years, and also conducts a dairy business from the present farm of Mrs Jones, delivering milk to the various families of Logansport Mr. and Mrs Burke and Mrs Jones all live in their comfortable residence, which is situated on Logansport Rural Route No 4, and where their numerous friends are always greeted with old-fashioned hospitality

JAMES WHITWORTH The agricultural interests of Cass county are well represented by a class of hard-working, efficiently trained and thoroughly experienced men, who have made the treatment of the soil a life study and have thus been able to successfully cope with conditions and to maintain the high standard of agricultural supremacy here. Prominent in this class stands James Whitworth who for two years has resided on a well-cultivated tract of thirty acres, located in Clay township. Mr Whitworth was born in Alabama, January 5, 1865, and is a son of William and Mildred (Bowes) Whitworth, farming people of this county, the father being deceased.

Mr Whitworth received his educational training in the district schools of his native locality and like the majority of farmers' lads of his day divided his boyhood between the work of the homestead and attendance at school in the winter terms. There are a multitude of matters upon which a good farmer should be informed, and in these he was thoroughly trained by his father, while his mother reared him to habits of honesty, sobriety and integrity. He continued to remain under the parental roof until his marriage, at which time he embarked upon a career of his own and, being industrious and thrifty, carefully conserved his means and was soon able to invest in land. Since that time he has devoted his whole time and attention to the cultivation of the soil, and as a result of his activities has risen to a place of independence among the agriculturists of his section. In 1906, Mr Whitworth purchased his present tract, a farm of thirty acres located in Clay township. He has made numerous improvements, having a comfortable residence, located on Logansport Rural Free Delivery Route No 5, and appropriate buildings of modern architecture and substantial character. His property is well fenced, his live stock in a healthy condition, his implements and appliances of modern manufacture, and the entire appearance of the property bespeaks the presence of thrift and good management. Essentially a farmer, he has not cared for the struggles incident to the political arena, although he takes an interest in matters that affect his community, and has always endeavored to give his support to good men and measures.

In 1885 Mr Whitworth was united in marriage with Miss Maggie Hoover, the estimable daughter of Leason and Rachael Hoover, the former a native of Pennsylvania, while the latter was born in Ohio. Both of Mrs Whitworth's parents were married twice. They were long residents of Indiana, and were the parents of the following children Amanda, James and Elmer, who died in infancy, Benjamin, who married Minnie Rhodes, Egbert, who married Mabel Montgomery, and Maggie, who married Mr Whitworth. Two children have been born to Mr and Mrs Whitworth. Golda, born in 1886, who became the wife of Frank Griffin of Logansport, and Ruth, born in 1891 who married Glen Rader, is also a resident of Logansport, and has two children,—Harry who is two years of age, and Frank, who is six months old. The members of this family are connected with the Baptist church, and are liberal supporters of religious and charitable movements.

ELIHU S. RICE, whose death occurred April 26, 1912, was one of the "Old Guard" of Cass county pioneers. His loss was not only keenly felt among the members of his immediate family, but by his associates in business his many friends, and thousands of people all over the country who knew him only as the author of some of the most beautiful sacred music written. Born at Pavilion, Genesee county, New York,

E. S. Rice

February 2, 1827, Mr Rice was a son of Erastus and Lucretia M (Howe) Rice The father, who was a native of Massachusetts died in 1833, and six years later Elihu S, then a lad of twelve years, accompanied his widowed mother and brothers and sisters to Logansport, which city was destined to be his home during the remainder of his life   In 1843 he became a clerk for Henry Martin & Company, but in the following year the firm discontinued business, and in 1845 Mr Rice became connected with the firm of Pollard & Wilson   In 1853 Col Philip Pollard, the senior member of the firm, retired therefrom, which was then reorganized as Wilson, Merriam & Company, Mr. Rice being admitted to partnership Through various changes of this firm into Merriam, Rice & Howes, Merriam & Rice and Merriam, Rice & Company, Mr. Rice remained a partner of John C Merriam, being associated with him until Mr Merriam's death   Afterwards the firm of E S Rice & Son was formed, with his son, Frank M Rice, as junior partner and this continued until 1906, when, in order to be relieved of his many business burdens and responsibilities, Mr Rice sold the business, although it is still one of the leading establishments of Logansport, and is known as the Rice Hardware Company

In 1905 Mr Rice was elected president of the First National Bank of Logansport, a position he continuously filled up to the time of his death   For many years he was manager and principal owner of the Logansport Gas Light & Coke Company, taking charge of its affairs when it was practically a failure and demonstrating a superior business ability by making it a financial success   His long and eventful business career was characterized by fidelity and trustworthiness he was a man of charitable impulses and his many good deeds will make a long list in the general accounting of man's work during his earthly pilgrimage A good name more to be desired than riches was his   He lived uprightly, and at the ripe old age of four score and five died at peace with all the world   He was a life long member of the Baptist church at Logansport, which he enriched by substantial benefactions   While laying no claim to being a poet, he was, nevertheless, a poet in the truest sense   The world of song was enriched when he contributed to it "Shall We Meet Beyond the River?" and "Come! Let Us Sing Unto the Lord"   As a singer, his voice was frequently heard in the house of worship, and was also in great demand during presidential campaigns   During the campaign of 1856 he was a member of the famous Rocky Mountain Quartette

In 1854 Mr. Rice was united in marriage with Miss Jeannette Mabon, and she passed away in 1895, having been the mother of two children: Frank M, and Annie A, the latter the wife of George C. Taber, of Logansport   In an editorial, under date of April 26, 1912, the *Logansport Pharos* said·

"The death of Elihu S Rice removes from this community a man who was worthy of the title of exalted citizen   His was a blameless and a useful life   In every sphere of human activity, he acted a noble part   As a citizen he responded to every demand made upon him for the betterment of social conditions   As the head of a family he set an example worthy to be followed   As a business man his career was characterized by honorable dealing   As a philanthropist his good deeds were many and his favors were bestowed without ostentation He came to Logansport seventy-three years ago when yet a boy and had moved among us all these years In his intercourse with the people he was kindly, sharing their joys and with their sorrows bearing a part He walked uprightly, lived cleanly and dies respected by those who appreciate true worth in man''

Frank M Rice was born in Logansport, Indiana, February 29, 1856 Educated in the public schools and Wabash College, on completing his schooling he became a clerk in his father's employ, and continued with him until the business was sold in 1905. In 1902 Mr Rice organized the Logansport Basket Works, of which he became the first president and treasurer, and continued as such until he sold his interest in the business, in January, 1912 He has large business and realty interests, and is a director of the First National Bank of Logansport He holds membership in the Country Club, the Commercial Club and the County Historical Society, and has manifested his interest in fraternal affairs by his activities in the Masonic and Elks lodges His political proclivities are those of the Republican party, but he takes only a good citizen's part in public affairs

On November 19, 1884, Mr Rice was married to Miss Lottie F Larson, of Omaha, Nebraska, and they have had one child Ollie M, who married Wendell C Schmidt.

JOHN M CARSON Agricultural production is the basis of practically all production and the ordinary laborer, the factory, the state and the nation are absolutely dependent thereupon, the result being that agriculture is of elemental importance in the life of a person, a community and a nation Such being the case, the development of the agricultural regions must keep pace with the advancement of the times, and the farmer who would gain his full measure of success must needs take advantage of every aid that modern invention and discovery can give One of the prosperous agriculturists of Cass county who has realized and benefitted by the results to be obtained from scientific treatment of the soil, is John M Carson, of Clay township, who for ten years has been carrying on operations on his present place He was born in Jennings county, Indiana, December 5, 1855, and is a son of John H and Julia (McCammott) Carson, and grandson of William Carson and Isaac McCammott, the family being of Irish-Scotch extraction

John H Carson was born in Rutherford county, Pennsylvania, in 1818, and was one year old when brought to Indiana by his parents Here he continued to follow agricultural pursuits throughout his life, and died in March, 1877, one of his community's highly esteemed citizens During that same year, John M Carson, who had been reared and educated in Jennings county, came to Cass county, Indiana, and first located in Noble township, where he spent three years, subsequently remaining in Adams for two years, in Eel township for six years, and in Bethlehem township thirteen years, and then came to Clay township and settled on the farm on which he now resides. Here Mr Carson bought eighty-two acres of land, on which he erected a new modern residence which is one of the most attractive in this part of the county, and also made numerous other improvements which have added to the value of the farm He is an able agriculturist, and has brought to his work that thorough knowledge of the details of his vocation which only comes from years of experience His operations have been uniformly successful, and he is recognized as one of the leading agriculturists of Clay township He has never cared for public office, preferring to devote his entire attention to his farming activities, but takes an interest in all matters that affect his community, and may be relied upon to support movements for good government

Mr Carson was married to Miss Mary Criss, daughter of Lawrence W. and Barbara (Stoll) Criss, natives of Germany who were married in Logansport, Indiana and the former of whom died in March, 1877 Mr and Mrs Carson have had four children, namely. Chester Cecil, born January 15, 1886, who is now superintendent of schools at Cowan, Indiana, Dottie, born August 30, 1894, Evaline, born January 29, 1896, and John W, born May 16, 1899. The family is identified with the Bethlehem church Mr. Carson has interested himself to some extent in fraternal work, belonging to Twelve Mill lodge, No 713 Independent Order of Odd Fellows, in which he has passed through the chairs, and to the grand lodge of the state He has numerous friends in this order, and is widely and favorably known in other circles of activity in Clay township

DAVID W COOK The agriculturists of Cass county are as a class prosperous and contented, living independently upon the fertile fields, which their energy has fully developed to the present high state of cultivation Agriculture is well adapted to build up the American citizenship It not only awakens interest and gives purpose, but teaches industry and self reliance There is no other occupation that opens so wide a field for the profitable and agreeable combination of labor with cultivated thought. Of the many well-to-do citizens of Cass county who are devoting their energies to the cultivation of the soil, David W Cook of Clay township, is an excellent representative He is a native of the county of Cass, Indiana, having been born in Bethlehem township, April 7, 1867, and a son of Charles and Margaret (Ball) Cook (For the full chronological data of the parents of Mr Cook see the sketch of Charles Cook elsewhere in this work)

David W Cook was reared as a farmer's lad and received a good practical education in the public schools of his native county He remained with his parents till his marriage, and his first residence was on the McKnight Williamson farm, in Bethlehem township, thence to the Warren Gazette farm in 1896, and in 1902, he located on his present estate of sixty acres, on which his residence is located, and he has seventy-five acres adjoining the other tract His land is well cultivated and he has made substantial improvements of a modern character Mr Cook is a progressive man in his business methods, and in his political belief gives his allegiance to the Progressive party He is known by his neighbors as being a gentleman of honor and integrity, and he and his family are members of the Methodist church

It was January 21, 1891, that Mr Cook wedded Miss Bertha Deloplane, a daughter of William and Sarah (Zinn) Deloplane, and to this union five children, three sons and two daughters, have been born, and all are living except the son, William D, who died at the age of three years Everett received his diploma from the public schools of Clay township in the class of 1910, and then was a student in the Logansport Business College Frank received his diploma in the class of 1911, and he also attended the business college Both Marguerite and Sarah are in the sixth grade Mrs Cook is a native of Butler county, Ohio, and was born January 30 1872 Her parents were prominent citizens of Cass county, but both are now deceased Mrs Cook, like a true wife and mother, has ably filled her sphere in the rearing of her children and the care of her home

Mr and Mrs Cook and family are citizens of Cass county, who are esteemed for their high moral, religious and social standing and it is with pleasure that this brief review is presented for preservation in the History of Cass County, Indiana

CASSIUS M CLAY SWIGART In 1842, when adventurous settlers from the east many from Ohio, were beginning to seek homes in Cass county, Samuel Swigart and wife drove their two-horse wagon, with the family provisions and possessions, all the way from the old Ohio home to what was then practically a wilderness in this section of Indiana They were sturdy people, a commingling of German and Scotch-Irish blood producing a type that can hardly be excelled, and all their courage and resourcefulness then strength of body and spirit, were demanded by the hard pioneer experiences that they were called upon to bear in those early days The Swigart name has ever since been one that has been known and highly respected in Cass county, and a worthy representative of it may be found in C M C Swigart, who is one of Clay township's well-informed men and enterprising agriculturists Mr Swigart is a son of Samuel and Jane (McPherson) Swigart, whose other children were Frank, who married Marguerite Kline, Jessie M, who married Alice LaRose, Theodore P who married Miss Phoebe McCoy, Adam N, who married Tillie Mason, and Sarah, who became the wife of Samuel Carr Seventy years ago, when Samuel Swigart first came to Cass county, Adamsboro was a larger town than Logansport, and in that vicinity he built his first little log cabin home He continued to be engaged in agricultural pursuits during the remainder of his life, developed an excellent property on section 14, Clay township, and at the time of his death, in the early eighties was one of his township's most highly esteemed citizens He died in the faith of high morality and standard integrity His wife, who passed away in 1892, was a member of the Presbyterian church

Cassius M Clay Swigart was educated in the primitive schools of Cass county, in the Westville Academy, under Professor Laird, and two years in city schools He was also a teacher for three years in Cass county, and like the majority of farmers' lads of his day and locality, spent the summer months in the hard work of the homestead He was born February 14, 1849, and was married December 27, 1872, to Miss Rosalie E Thomas daughter of John and Elizabeth (Wilson) Thomas, and she had two sisters and one brother, namely Sarah M, who married Delbert Walker, and died in 1894, Eugene W, who married Minnie Conrad and Alice A., who never married

When Mr and Mrs Swigart married they moved to Portland, Oregon, and there he engaged in horticulture, and remained there three years In 1876 they returned to Clay township, Cass county and here Mr Swigart was engaged in the lumber business and agriculture for twenty years Then they moved to Mount Vernon, Illinois, and he was a farmer there for three years, and his farm comprised one hundred and fifty-four acres, thence to Clay township where they now reside on a splendid farm of one hundred and twenty acres equipped with good buildings, and whilst in Cass county he has pursued horticulture and agriculture, and has been reasonably successful

Mrs Swigart is a native of Miami county, Indiana, and was born September 30, 1852 Her father, John Wesley Thomas, was a native of Pennsylvania, born December 20, 1826, and died in 1908 He was a manufacturer and agriculturist and politically formerly a Republican, then a Prohibitionist He and his wife were members of the Methodist church and both are interred in the Bethel cemetery Mrs Thomas was born in Indiana, March 5, 1831, and died February 11, 1897 Mrs Swigart was reared and educated in her native county.

To the marriage of Mr and Mrs Swigart were born six children, three sons and three daughters, all living Mabel Clare, wife of Edward A Flory, a horticulturist of Miami township, was born in Portland, Oregon, and they have three sons Ernest N a resident of Clay township, and a farmer married Miss Lucy Angle a native of Virginia, and they have two sons, he is a Progressive politically and the family belong to the Baptist church Bernice M, wife of William E Packard, a resident of Miami township and an agriculturist, also assessor of the township, has seven children, three sons and four daughters, and Ruth Clare, the little granddaughter, lives with her grandparents Everett P, a resident of Clay township and an agriculturist, was engaged in railroading a number of years He wedded Miss Minnie Jones, and they have one little daughter Leona Ruth is the wife of Aaron E Packard, a resident of Clay township and an agriculturist James G. Blaine, a resident of Nightingale, Alberta, Canada, wedded Miss Hattie Kline He was engaged in railroad work for years, and is the youngest of the family.

The homestead of Mr and Mrs Swigart is known as "The Eel River Valley Fruit and Stock Farm" and Mr Swigart was the first man who successfully introduced alfalfa in Cass county, Indiana He has devoted his time to general farming and stock raising, and his operations have been uniformly successful because he has brought to his work that intelligent and conscientious devotion that never fails to be rewarded with satisfactory results His buildings are of modern design and substantial character, his land is well fenced, tiled and drained, his cattle sleek and well fed, and the entire appearance of his property shows the presence of able management Modern machinery and appliances have played no small part in assisting Mr Swigart in his march to a position of affluence for he has ever been possessed of progressive ideas, and in this connection it may be stated that he cast his fortunes in 1912 with the new Progressive political party. With his family he attends the Christian church

EUGENE A WALKER. For the full period of a half century, Mr Walker has known old Cass county, having been a resident within the boundaries of this political division of the state since 1853 He is a man of honored and respected achievements, and owns one of the handsome rural homes in Clay township

Eugene A Walker is a native of Genesee county, New York, and was born October 24, 1845. He was the oldest of four children, three sons and one daughter, in the family of Lyman G and Charlotte S (Moon) Walker Only Mr Walker and his brother Charles survive, the latter being a resident of Chicago, being married and having a family of one son, and is a Republican in politics

Lyman G Walker the father, was also a native of Genesee county, New York, where he was born March 20, 1822, and he died December 27, 1872 By trade he was a tanner and currier In 1850 he went to California, by way of the Isthmus of Panama as a seeker for gold and spent two years on the gold coast, being reasonably successful, and then returning to his old home in New York Before making this adventure he had married and had two children. Lyman G Walker traced his lineage back to Old England, and the family history in America goes to a widow Walker who came to the colonies on board the historic Mayflower, settling in the New England states, and becoming the founder of this branch of the Walkers Grandfather Obediah Walker was a soldier of the Revolutionary war and died January 30, 1832 On his monument are inscribed these words,—"A Veteran of 1776"

It was in the fall of 1853 that Lyman G. Walker, with his wife and family came to Cass county The journey was made by rail as far as Cleveland, whence they took a boat to Toledo and from there to Logansport came by the old Wabash canal After remaining until the following spring in Logansport, the father brought his family to the farm where his grandson Adelbert resided in Miami township on the banks of the Eel river Mr Walker bought other land and added to his estate until the time of his death he had a hundred and forty acres. He made practically all the improvements, since when he moved to the farm it was situated in the wilderness He was an early enough settler also to have seen many deer in this locality Lyman G Walker was originally a Whig in politics, and on the birth of the Republican party in 1856 he cast his first vote for Fremont He was a friend of the public schools and both he and his wife were members of the Baptist church, and their remains now rest in the Miami Baptist cemetery in this county. The father was also a member of the Independent Order of Odd Fellows The mother was born in Genesee county, March 29, 1825, and her death occurred April 27, 1872 She was reared in her native county, and as a mother she was devoted to the interests of her family, and set her children an example of Christian fortitude and the best virtues

Eugene A Walker was a boy of eight years when the family accomplished the migration to Cass county He was reared on a farm and to agricultural pursuits, and received his education in the public schools of Cass county The first school he attended in this county was in a log building, and the children sat upon split-puncheon slabs, supported by wooden pins driven into holes on the under side Some of the text books which he recalls as having used when a boy were the McGuffey readers and spellers. Mr. Walker was nineteen years old when he started out for himself, and his first enterprise was on a farm

He has been twice married In 1869 he married Miss Minerva C Thomas, and two children were born to this marriage, both of whom are now living Nettie, a graduate of the Cass county public schools, and a member of the Methodist church, and is the wife of Harry Kistler of Indianapolis, where he is connected with the Armour Packing Company and is very prominent in the Masonic order, having been honored with the thirty-second degree of Scottish Rites Adelbert M , who is one of the young and progressive farmers of Cass county, and his career is sketched elsewhere in this volume The mother of these children was born in Miami county, and was a member of the Methodist church Her death occurred in 1893 On November 11, 1895, Mr Walker married Miss Harriet Gallahan, who was born in Miami county and reared and educated in Cass county Her father is now deceased and her mother is a resident of Carroll county, Indiana

The first land which Mr Walker bought was eighty-four acres in Miami township He went in debt to the extent of thirty-two hundred dollars when he obtained this place in 1868, and by hard industry and thrift finally paid off in full All the improvements on the land were put there by his own work or direction, and when he took possession a log house with a board roof was about the only improvement that could properly be named as such In 1910 Mr and Mrs Walker moved to Clay township, where they now reside on a beautiful little country place of thirty-eight acres and have erected for their residence a handsome bungalow which is excellently finished and furnished, and is modern in every detail Outside of the house are a number of convenient, outbuildings for the stock, grain and machinery, and the home is situated about sixty rods from the Vandalia depot

Mr Walker is a Civil war veteran, and one of the youngest in Cass county He enlisted in February, 1865, when about nineteen years of age in Company F of the One Hundred and Fifty-first Indiana Infantry, under Captain Davidson, and his regiment was put in the Army of the Tennessee He served until receiving his honorable discharge in September, 1865 In politics he is independent, and casts his franchise in the direction in which he thinks it will accomplish the most good Mr and Mrs Walker support all elevating movements and policies for the moral and intellectual welfare of their county and township

JOHN C BARR The annals of Cass county show many records of the lives of farmers who have rounded out the duties connected with agricultural pursuits and have amassed considerable fortunes gathered from the fertile soil One who has met with well-deserved success along these lines is John C. Barr, of Noble township, who has resided in Cass county all of his life, and is well acquainted with soil and climatic conditions here Mr Barr has made farming his life work, and through intelligent management of his affairs has won his way to affluence He was born in Harrison township, Cass county, Indiana, November 2, 1870, and is a son of Thomas and Jane (Goodwin) Barr.

The parents of Mr Barr came to the United States from England in 1848, locating in Cass county In 1852, in company with his brother-in-law, Thomas Goodwin, also a resident of Cass county, he left home to seek his fortune in the gold fields of California, leaving behind him a family consisting of his wife and three children, Mary, Thomas and Jeremiah. While enroute by water, Thomas Goodwin contracted yellow fever, from which he died and his body was wrapped in a sheet and cast overboard. Mr Barr continued his journey and on reaching his destination began life by staking claims. At this he met with varying success, and after enduring the hardships incident to the rough life of the mining camp for about six years, returned to his family with sufficient means with which to purchase outright six acres of land. Through his thrift, energy and perseverance, assisted by his good-wife and his industrious family, he was able to add to this land from time to time and at the time of his death, December 14, 1893, he left an estate of sixteen hundred acres, the greater part of which was under cultivation, this being located in Harrison, Boone and Noble townships. His wife's death followed January 6, 1901.

John C Barr received the greater part of his education in the district schools, although he completed it at Royal Center. He was reared to habits of industry and honesty, and was taught the value and dignity of hard work, and thoroughly trained in the work of the farm. General farming and stock raising have always received his attention, and his success has come as a result of commendable industry and practical management of his affairs with a fixed goal ever in view.

On February 24, 1898, Mr Barr was united in marriage with Miss Daisy Fisher, the oldest daughter of Jacob and Sarah Elizabeth (Suter) Fisher, of Cass county, and six children have been born to this union, all of whom are living. Harry R, graduated in the class of 1912, and has taken violin instructions. Ray W, is in the eighth grade, also has taken guitar music; Ruth, in the fourth grade will take piano music; Nelson M., in the fifth grade, will take mandolin lessons; Grace, in the fifth grade will take piano music and Beatrice, in the third grade, is the youngest child. Mrs Barr is a native of Cass county, born May 22, 1872, and she is the third of five children, three sons and two daughters, two dead and three are living. Her mother is a resident of Jefferson township, and the father, a native of Virginia, is deceased. Mrs Barr was educated in the common schools. Their beautiful home is known as "Glendale' Farm."

Like his father, Mr Barr is a Republican in politics, and has always been a stanch advocate of public improvements. With his family, he is a regular attendant of the Baptist church, and has always been a cheerful contributor to church and charitable needs when called upon. During his long residence here, he has formed a wide acquaintance, in which he numbers many warm friends. He is known as a good and public-spirited citizen and as an excellent farmer, and has done his full share in advancing the welfare of his community.

WILLIAM L MCMILLEN. The farming interests of Noble township are well represented by a group of practical, intelligent and able men, among whom William L McMillen takes prominent place. Born July 9, 1871, in Noble township, Cass county, he is a son of Lewis and Frances Jane (McCauley) McMillen.

The McMillen family is one of the old and honored ones of Cass county, where its members have been identified with the development of the section for eighty-five years His grandparents, George and Susan (McMillen) McMillen, became residents of Cass county in 1828, entering upon life in the west in true pioneer style. The grandfather was a native of Pennsylvania and the grandmother of Highland county, Ohio Locating on a farm in Noble township, Cass county, they there reared their family of four children Lewis, Milton, William and Elizabeth J. They experienced many of the hardships and difficulties of pioneer life and to the development of a new home in the forest, but as the years passed theirs became one of the comfortable homes of the community and their labors contributed not a little to the substantial development of their section The grandfather took a prominent part in public affairs and for four years filled the office of trustee of Noble township, giving his support to the Republican party He died in 1849. at the age of forty-four years, and in the faith of the Presbyterian church

Lewis McMillen was born March 2, 1832, on the old home place in Noble township, and there he was reared to habits of sobriety, industry and honesty, and taught the value and dignity of hard work He was married October 2 1861, to Frances Jane McCauley, a native of Noble township and daughter of Elias McCauley, and they became the parents of three children. James E, Minnie and William L Mrs. McMillen died October 24, 1886, at the age of forty-four years, and many friends mourned her loss, for her sterling traits of character had endeared her to all with whom she came in contact Like his father, Mr McMillen was a Republican, and for one year served as supervisor of Noble township. He belonged to the Methodist Episcopal church, and lent his aid and influence to all movements for the public good. His business methods were honorable and straightforward, and his close application, continual perseverance and unabating energy enabled him to work his way steadily upward to a position of affluence He was a loyal citizen, faithful in his friendships, devoted to his family, and enjoyed the warm regard of all with whom he came into contact

William L McMillen received his early education in the public schools of Noble township, and his vocation has always been that of farming, he having resided on his present property since 1896 On June 2, 1895, he was married to Miss Eva May Carney of Winamac, Pulaski county, Indiana, and to this union there have been born three children, namely LeRoy who died August 23, 1896, aged six months, Naomi and Esther During the school term of 1892, Mrs McMillen was engaged in teaching the district schools of Noble township.

Mr McMillen has always given his support to Republican principles and candidates, and has several times held office, being assessor in 1900 and trustee in 1908 He is a member of the Odd Fellows lodge in Logansport, and with the members of his family attends the Methodist Episcopal church He has the reputation in his community of being a public-spirited citizen, always ready to support movements tending to advance the growth and development of his community and as one who is a liberal contributor to church and charitable enterprises

WILLIAMSON WRIGHT was born at Lancaster, Ohio, on the 18th day of May, 1814, and was a noted figure in Cass county in his day. His father, Rev John Wright, was born in Westmoreland county Pennsylvania, on February 11, 1777. He was prepared for college at Jefferson Academy Commonsburg, Pennsylvania, and was graduated from Dickinson College, Carlisle, Pennsylvania, in 1788. He studied theology under an uncle, Dr James Power, a pioneer Presbyterian minister of western Pennsylvania, and was licensed to preach in October, 1802. In 1805 he became pastor of the First Presbyterian church at Lancaster, Ohio, and he held that pastorate for thirty-one consecutive years. In 1836 he came to Logansport, Indiana, with the expectation of passing the remainder of his days here in retirement. In connection with his ministry at Lancaster, Ohio, he had worked hard in organizing other churches in a large circle, and this strenuous work had seriously impaired his health. His two sons, John and Williamson of this review had preceded him to Logansport, and here the aged father settled to enjoy his remaining days. Rev John Wright never accepted another pastorate, although he organized the First Presbyterian church of Logansport and was the first pastor of this church as well as others in Cass county, having an especial genius for that phase of his work. For fifteen years he was at the head of the Logansport Presbytery and once was moderator of the Synod of Indiana. He died on August 31, 1854. His wife was Jane Weakley, and they became the parents of three children John and Williamson, both lawyers of renown in Logansport, and Edward, who received the degree of D D, and was, as his father before him a minister of the Presbyterian church.

Williamson Wright was reared at Lancaster, Ohio, and was graduated at Miami University, Oxford, Ohio, when he was eighteen years old. He read law and when he was twenty-one was admitted to the bar. In 1835 he came to Logansport, Indiana, and he almost at once took rank with the foremost lawyers of this section. In 1840 he was elected state senator, and in 1849 was an unsuccessful candidate for Congress. It was largely through his efforts, and that of his brother, that Logansport gained its first railroad, and he was president of the company that built the road between Logansport and New Castle. He acquired ownership to considerable land in the county, but at the time of his death had disposed of all but about seventeen hundred acres.

The latter years of Mr Wright's life were devoted almost exclusively to looking after his large landed interests, but prior to that he was interested to a considerable extent in railroad matters.

Mr Wright married Eliza Sering, of Madison, Indiana, who died in 1847, leaving two children,—John and Jennie, both now deceased. In 1852 he married Kate Swift, the daughter of Rev E P Swift, D D, of Pittsburg, Pennsylvania, and they became the parents of seven children, of whom brief mention is made as follows Mary, the eldest, died when four years old. Kate married E P Tucker, Williamson Swift, Elizabeth G, who became the wife of W H Barnhart, Anne Lucy, the wife of C W Graves of Logansport, of whom extended mention is made in other pages of this work, Etta D and Elisha P S, who is dead

Williamson Wright died on the 28th day of March 1896, and his widow survived him less than a year, passing away on February 5 1897

Mr Wright was actively identified with the Presbyterian church, and his benefactions, while large, were of the most unostentatious order He was first a Whig, and then a Republican, in which political faith he continued all his life

NORMAN ELMER MYERS The whole life of Norman Elmer Myers thus far has been passed upon the farm and in the pursuit of that industry He has met with a pleasing success in his work and is accounted one of the best established men in Noble township, which has been his home all his days He was born in Noble township, Cass county, on August 18, 1872, and is the son of Henry S and Mary Ellen (Tilton) Myers

Concerning these worthy parents it may be said that the father came to Indiana from New Jersey, where he was born, locating in Noble township in the year 1858 After a residence of something like a year in this place he went west and at the outbreak of the Civil war he returned to the state and enlisted in the Fourteenth Indiana Battery He remained with his regiment through thick and thin, and was honorably discharged at the close of the war One year after the war he came to Cass county once more and settled on a farm in section 3, and in 1866 he married Mary Ellen Tilton, the daughter of Simeon and Sarah Tilton Two sons were born to these parents Frank Tilton Myers, born on March 9, 1866, in Cass county, and Norman Elmer, the subject of this review

Norman Myers was educated to a certain degree in the common schools of Noble township, and all his life with the exception of five years has been passed on the farm which he now occupies The place is located in section 9 of Noble township, and consists of one hundred and thirty acres It is a well cared for place, evidencing in every way the thrift and enterprise which mark its owner and have made him one of the prosperous men of the town

On December 5 1900, Mr Myers was united in marriage with Miss Maud Wise, the only daughter of James and Margaret (Rue) Wise. She was born in Cass county on April 18, 1874, and here has passed her life Two children have been born to Mr and Mrs Myers: Claud E, born September 7, 1901, and Mary Margaret, born on November 13, 1905

Mr Myers is a Republican in his political faith, but not more than ordinarily active in affairs of that nature, and he and his wife are members of the Presbyterian church

ANDREW BURNETTE was a native of Highland county, Ohio, born there in 1828, and was a son of Edward Burnette, who was a farmer in that county, and a descendant of French ancestry The advent of the Burnette family into America was at about the time when the American colonies gained their independence from the mother country, and they have ever since been worthy and substantial citizens of the new republic Andrew Burnette passed his boyhood on his father's farm, and such education as came his way was gained in the old-fashioned log school with its primitive and inefficient methods of instruction In 1847 he married Mary J. Horn in Ohio, and the year 1850 marked the advent of the family into Cass county, when he and his wife settled on an eighty acre farm which they had purchased, for which he paid the sum of $300. Here he built a log cabin. It was no palatial affair, indeed, it was rude and unfinished, with its stick and mud chimney, its one room, eighteen feet square, and a door and a window. But here they settled down on their new farm and set in bravely to the work of making a farm out of a piece of wild land. Andrew Burnette and his family lived on this place until 1864, when he sold it and moved to a farm in Noble township, Cass county, but some time later moved to Clay township. Here Mrs. Burnette died on February 12, 1899. The death of the wife and mother broke up the home circle, as it does too often, and Mr. Burnette thereafter made his home with his married children until he died on October 26, 1902. Mrs. Burnette was a member of the Christian church, and was one of the truly estimable women of her community, where she was held in the secure regard of all who knew her. Andrew Burnette was a Whig, later a Republican, in which political faith he labored the remainder of his life. He was a quiet, unassuming man, of kindly disposition and a most admirable character, and known in his community as a good neighbor and a genuine friend, the esteem and confidence of a wide circle of acquaintances being his. Both these worthy people are at rest in Mount Hope cemetery, in Logansport. They were the parents of three children, of whom brief mention is here made. John H., to whom a separate sketch is devoted in other pages of this work, George C., and Hannah, who is now the wife of Irvin Funston, her husband being a first cousin of General Frederick Funston, of Spanish-American war fame. George C. is married, also, and makes his home in East St. Louis.

JOHN H. BURNETTE was born in Highland county, Ohio, on February 8, 1849, and is the son of Andrew and Mary J. (Horn) Burnette, also of Highland county, Ohio, of whom extended mention is made in a separate sketch dedicated to Andrew Burnette. When John Burnette was an infant in arms his parents came to Indiana, settling first in Fulton county and later in Cass county, in both of which places they were engaged in farming. Thus has the early life, as well as the subsequent practical experience of John H. Burnette, been spent in the work of the farm. He early became acquainted with the various processes which go to make up the building up of a profitable farm from a barren wilderness, and his young life saw many of the privations and hardships incident to pioneer life. He secured such schooling as the schools of his immediate vicinity afforded, and so well did he improve his opportunities in that way that in the winter of 1869-70 and 1870-71 he taught school in his district. On April 3, 1873, Mr. Burnette married Lizzie J. Thornton, and then began farming, first in Noble township, where he remained for two years, and then in Clay township, where he was busily engaged in the pursuit of farm life from 1875 to 1908. He was always a successful farmer, and those years brought him a pleasing prosperity. In 1908 he moved to Logansport, retiring from farm life, and here he has since resided.

Mr. Burnette is a Republican and has served his city as a member of the city council for eight years, as well as filling various other local positions of trust in the city which he has made his home. He is a member of the Masonic order and of the Knights of Pythias, and with his wife is a member of the Christian church.

Mr. Burnette has been twice married. One daughter was born of his first marriage—Nellie, now living in Colorado, she married Mathew C Warren, of Fort Collins, Colorado, of the firm of Moody & Warren. The wife and mother died on February 12 1904, and on November 6, 1906, Mr Burnette contracted his second marriage, when Mrs Ida Wagner of Kewanna, Indiana, a daughter of James Murray, and the widow of Frank Wagner, a prominent Kewanna lawyer, became his wife. Mrs Burnette had four children by her first marriage, but one of whom, Don B. Wagner, is now living.

GEORGE MCMILLEN, well known and prosperous in farming circles in this township, has demonstrated in a most telling manner his fitness for the life of a farmer. He was reared on the farm but in starting out in independent life he decided to give up the humdrum existence he had so long known. Accordingly he established himself in the implement business in Logansport, but it is significant of the man that after fourteen years of honest endeavor in that business, he gave over his connection therewith and returned gladly to the farm, where he has since continued in peace and prosperity. Born on November 10, 1855, in Cass county, Indiana, George McMillen is the son of Robert and Rosanna (Harper) McMillen. The father was a millwright and passed his life in that work, death claiming him on July 7, 1890, less than a year after the passing of his faithful wife, who preceded him on the 26th of October, 1889. Both are interred in Harper cemetery in Noble township. The name McMillen is of Scotch-Irish origin.

George McMillen, their son, attended the district schools of Noble township and later finished his education in Smithson College. After his college career he turned his attention to farm work for a brief time, but in 1890 went into the implement business in Logansport, as has been already mentioned. Eight years ago the call of the farm drew him back to Noble township and he has here continued since that time, enjoying a pleasing prosperity in his chosen vocation.

On March 4, 1886, Mr McMillen was united in marriage with Miss Rose Kreis, a native daughter of Cass county, and the child of Philip and Caroline (Scheir) Kreis, who had lived for many years within the confines of the county. Three children were born to Mr and Mrs McMillen. Chester R attended the common schools, Logansport high school and then the Logansport Business College, and is now employed by the Vandalia Railroad Company. He wedded Miss Blanche Huid and they are residents of Logansport. Mabel E received a common school education and then graduated from the Logansport high school, in class of 1909, and was a successful teacher in her home township two terms. She wedded Wm J. Thornton, a resident of Logansport and an agent for automobiles. Mrs. Thornton is a member of the First Presbyterian church. Mr Thornton is a member of "The Moose." Margaret was a student in the Logansport high school. She is at home with her father.

Mrs McMillen, the mother, was a native of Cass county, reared and educated in her home county, and was during her life a devout member of the First Presbyterian church She was a lady noted for her piety, her love of home and her children Her death occurred in February, 1909 All her married life she had been an able factor to her husband in the building up of their happy home Her remains are interred in Mount Hope cemetery, where a beautiful monument stands sacred to her memory

Mr McMillen's pretty little farm of twenty-one acres lies just at the north city limits of Logansport, Indiana

Mr McMillen is a Republican, but not especially active in political matters He is a member of the Knights of Pythias, Powell Castle Hall No 62, the Foresters, and the Woodmen of the World, all in Logansport, Indiana He was brought up by his parents in the Presbyterian faith, always having attended the church of that denomination in Noble township, and he and his children are members and attendants of that church today Mr McMillen enjoys the esteem and confidence of all who share in his acquaintance, and he is known for one of the estimable and stable men of the community his life in Noble township being one that indicates in a telling manner the many splendid qualities of the man

WILLIAM R COGLEY The appeal of the soil is very strong to some men, who return to farming as a means of livelihood after years spent in other pursuits believing that in agricultural work may be attained the greatest measure of success by those who know how to till the land William R Cogley, a successful farmer and stock raiser of Clay township, was for years engaged in railroad work, but eventually yielded to the inclination that had guided a long line of agricultural forebears returned to the tilling of the soil, and has seen no reason thus far to regret of his action, for today he is numbered among the more substantial men of his locality and stands high in the esteem of his fellow-citizens Mr Cogley was born in Dauphin county, Pennsylvania on January 4, 1867, and is the son of Samuel and Mary (Enders) Cogley The family came to Cass county in 1869, and Samuel Cogley is still a resident of Noble township where he has been engaged in the business of agriculture for the past forty-four years

William R Cogley was given the educational advantages that might be secured in his day and locality, and he was early trained to farm work which he followed with more or less diligence until he had reached the age of twenty-one years At that time, he went to Logansport and in that city was graduated from Hall's Commercial College Following that addition to his education the young man went to Chicago, and for eighteen months was engaged in a large mercantile establishment He then returned to the home farm and for two years worked for his father on the home place He subsequently entered the employ of the Pan Handle Railroad, beginning as a brakeman, and by faithful attention to his duty becoming engineer with the same road He was for fourteen years employed in railroad work, and at the end of that time retired and bought a farm of eighty acres, which he is now occupying, located about two miles from the city limits, in Clay township Progressive and enterprising, he has continued to add to his improvements on this handsome property, erecting a windmill and a number of substantial and commodious buildings, and by good management and intelligent working of the soil making his land pay him yearly substantial returns for the labor he has expended upon it He has a comfortable residence, fitted with modern conveniences, and situated on Logansport Rural Route No 4

On September 20, 1893 Mr Cogley was united in marriage to Miss Minnie M Linton the daughter of George A and Mary E (Emery) Linton, both of English lineage, as is also the Cogley family Mrs Cogley is a native daughter of Cass county, born within its confines on September 15, 1872, and she is one of the eight children of her parents, of which number five are yet living

George Linton was born in Logansport and is now a resident of that city, where he has long been known as a plumber and steamfitter and where he is one of the popular and prominent men of the city He is a Mason and a member of the Knights of Pythias, and a veteran of the Civil war, through which he served with valor and distinction and received his honorable discharge when the Union no longer required his services

Mrs Cogley was reared in Logansport, and there received her education To her and her husband four children have been born, as follows George E the eldest finished with the work of the public schools of his community in 1910 receiving his diploma at the time, and is now employed as a machinist in the Vandalia shops at Logansport, Lawrence E R Weldon, and Ruth A are attending the local schools and are members of the eight, seventh and fifth grades, respectively, it being the aim of their parents to fit them for suitable positions in life by means of careful educations

Mr and Mrs Cogley are members of the Presbyterian church Mr Cogley is not affiliated with any political party, but he manifests a wholesome interest in the political affairs of his municipality, and considers it his privilege to vote for the man he regards as best fitted for the office in question, irrespective of party lines or prejudices He takes a keen and intelligent interest in all matters affecting the welfare of his community and heartily supports all movements that his better judgment tells him will make for good government and loyal citizenship Fraternally, he has membership in Tipton Lodge No 33 of Logansport, in the Masonic order

ELLIOTT E McKAIG The younger generation, whose day has come since the comforts brought by easy communication have been available, marvel at the fact that all the wealth, prosperity and conveniences have been wrought and brought about within the lifetime of men who stand among us today That men now living in Cass county fought here the wild beasts of the forest and contended with the hardships and privations of pioneer existence on these smiling farms and on the sites of cities where the roar of traffic and the heavy tramp of the iron wheels of factories have so lately drowned the voices of primeval nature, seems incredible Every year the hoary-headed band that led the van of civilization grows smaller, yet there are still many who heard the first scream of the brazen voice of the locomotive which brought to Cass county wealth and prosperity, and in this class is E. E. McKaig, an honored resident of Noble township. Mr McKaig was for many years engaged in agricultural pursuits, and when he was ready to retire took the ideal method of doing so. He retired, and yet he did not retire. He turned over the work to the broad shoulders of his stalwart son, and at the same time was in close touch with the life of the farm and ready to pass on to the younger man the benefit of the experience he had accumulated.

Elliott E. McKaig was born in Noble township, Cass county, Indiana, November 6, 1835, the fourth son in a family of nine children born to William and Elizabeth (Westfall) McKaig, the former a native of Kentucky and the latter of Maryland. His father was born of Irish descent in 1795, came to this county about 1833, and located upon a farm in Noble township, where he died in 1868. Mrs McKaig was born of German parentage in 1799, and emigrated with her parents to Ohio, where her marriage occurred to Mr McKaig, whom she accompanied to Noble township, and here she died in 1874. The children in this family were as follows: Levi Hart, deceased, and buried in Shiloh cemetery; Sarah Elizabeth, also deceased, and buried in that cemetery; Martha C., John F., who died in Kansas in 1904 and is buried there; James F., Watson C., who died in California in 1912, and was buried there; Robert N., Uriah F., deceased, who was buried in Shiloh cemetery; and Elliott E. James F. of this family died when two years of age.

Elliott E. McKaig belonged to that class from which, in the struggle in which man pitted himself against primeval forest and aboriginal inhabitant, the strongest types of manhood and womanhood were evolved. In early life he was accustomed to the hard work which develops the mind and hardens the body. His education was secured in the primitive schools, and he was trained to agricultural pursuits, which continued to be his vocation until his retirement from active life some years ago. He had ever shown a commendable public spirit, and was known as a man who always contributed liberally to movements calculated to benefit his community in any way, as well as to enterprises of a religious or charitable nature.

Mr McKaig was married July 13, 1870, to Hattie Richards, who was born December 24, 1851, in Dauphin county, Pennsylvania. She was of Dutch descent, and was the second daughter of William F. and Rebecca (Park) Richards, natives of Pennsylvania. Ten children were born to Mr and Mrs McKaig, as follows: Emma B., born September 15, 1871; Gertie, born September 21, 1872, died September 11, 1874; Willie, born April 1, 1875, who lived but eleven days; Pearl, born February 21, 1877, died September 4, 1877; infant twins, born January 1, 1878, one of whom died a few hours later, and the other when eleven days old; Mindella, born October 5, 1880; Beulah R., born November 3, 1882; Robert Neal, born September 10, 1888; and Allen Roy, born March 28, 1892. On October 31, 1893, the mother of these children was found dead in bed, having peacefully passed away in her sleep.

Robert Neal and Allen Roy McKaig attended the common schools of Noble township, and later supplemented this by attendance at the high school and commercial college in Logansport. About 1908,

Robert N McKaig left the farm and since that time has been connected with the Pennsylvania Railroad Allen R has continued to remain on the home farm, and has succeeded his father in the work of the homestead, where he is carrying on general farming and stock raising operations He is a Progressive, and inherited his sterling characteristics of honesty, industry and integrity The family has always been connected with the Methodist Episcopal church

Of the other children, Mindella was married January 3 1901, to John McCarnes, and four children have been born to this union Ethel H , Wilber E , Blanch O and Robert R , of whom Wilber E died in 1905 at the age of twenty-two months On October 28, 1903, Beulah R McKaig was united in marriage with Orla B Miller, who died in 1904 after a short illness, leaving one son, Orla E On June 1, 1908 Mrs Miller was married to William Pennock, and they have had two children Helen S and Paul Wesley

Elliott E McKaig had a long and useful career, his activities serving not only to further his own interests, but to advance those of his community as well He died February 26, 1913 and he is interred in Shiloh cemetery In the evening of life, surrounded by a wide circle of friends, and possessing the unqualified esteem of all with whom he had come in contact he furnished an excellent example of the rewards that industry brings and the contentment that comes only after a life of integrity and probity

DOCTOR JOHN B SHULTZ A life of kindly capable service to the community and to hundreds of individuals, came to a close on December 8, 1912, with the death of Doctor John B Shultz at his home in Logansport The best work of the physician does not flaunt itself before the public gaze, but is wrought in the hearts of his fellow-men The spirit of tender and knowing love for his fellowmen has ever been the trait of the true physician, and though the career of the late Dr Shultz was not conspicuous for those public honors and distinctions which mark the accomplishments of men in political and other spheres of human activity yet he left his mark upon Cass county and his long and faithful service, and the influence which he exerted over men and families deserves a more than casual tribute in this history and surely all will agree that none of the past generation was more worthy of a permanent memorial than Dr Shultz

John B Shultz was born in the adjoining county of Carroll, this state September 22, 1839 and was past seventy-three years of age when death came to him His parents were John and Elizabeth (Dunbar) Shultz, his father having been born in Pennsylvania in 1795 of German parentage, and locating in Carroll county, Indiana, in 1837 where he was one of the early settlers and where he died in 1855

Dr Shultz was educated in the public schools, and graduated from the Cincinnati Medical Eclectic Institute in 1860 The same year he located in Logansport, where he practiced in partnership with Dr James A Taylor, at 420 Fourth street, continuing to occupy that office for the long period of forty years afterwards he moved across the street to 417 Fourth street and was there when he breathed his last

Doctor Shultz, though his professional duties absorbed his energies, was still active in citizenship and an influential Republican. His party honored him by election to the position of county treasurer in 1870, re-electing him in 1872, and in 1875 he became mayor of Logansport, serving one term with honor and credit to himself and with benefit to his city. Dr. Shultz on July 29, 1883, married Miss Anna L. Cooper, of Kokomo a daughter of Dr. Wm. Cooper also of Kokomo. Her sister is the wife of Senator John W. Kern. By this marriage, Dr. Shultz had four children, of whom only one, Edwin, survives and he is now a student of Washington and Lee University, Virginia.

Dr. Shultz was tall of stature and of commanding appearance, although he always wore a smile upon his countenance. He was sociable in his nature, affable in manner, accomodating to all, pleasant and inspiring in the sick room and probably was the most popular physician that has ever lived and practiced in Cass county. Among his patients he was courteous, considerate and agreeable, never engaging in argument or discussion with them, yielding to their whims and eccentricities, and endeavoring to please the more fastidious. He disliked to hurt the feelings of any one and hated to say no or refuse a request from the most humble and would often yield to the opinions and exactions of others, although his better judgment might not approve. This engaging and agreeable personality, together with an indisputable ability in his profession was the cause of his great popularity in Cass county. During his time he had the widest acquaintance, and the most extensive practice of any physician within the bounds of this county. His presence in the sick-room was so comforting that patients have gone so far as to state that it would be a pleasure to die under his care, and with him at their side.

The late Dr. Shultz was not an erudite man nor a profound student of the libraries nor laboratories of his profession. However, he was a student of nature and the people, human nature and human ills were his study and the world his school throughout his life. He was no theorist and never argued upon technical points. He was preeminently practical, and when asked why he did this or that his answer would be, "I have tried it." A large practical experience in life was the laboratory where he had made his conclusive tests and from which he drew the experience which enabled him so successfully to serve his patients. Dr. Shultz had remarkable powers of observation and intuition and his judgment based upon these faculties were usually correct. Together with a natural ability, he possessed a large fund of energy, and throughout his life was an untiring worker. In many ways his practice represented the best of the old time country doctors. The night was never too dark, the storm too violent, the roads too muddy for him to visit a patient whether rich or poor, and the ability of the patient to pay was never a subject of his inquiry although that is not altogether true of some of the modern automobile doctors. His rule was to go wherever called and ask no questions. He adopted a rule which shows his charity in speaking of his brother practitioners, when called to succeed some other practitioner he would treat the case, but would never make comment or reflections upon the previous attendant. This was his regular rule of conduct in his fraternal relations, and he expected the same treatment from his associates.

As a practical man Dr Shultz occasionally took some very practical means in performing the exacting duties of his practice In very busy times when the old ague was prevalent during the sixties, and when nearly every case had a malarial element, it is said that he would do up packages of medicine for his patients before leaving his office, and then would make the rounds of his day's duties, examining each patient hurriedly, and throw down a package of medicine prepared in his office before starting out His liberality was extended to a fault, and often his sympathies overcame his better judgment His sociabilities, his desire to please, his difficulty in refusing a request, made him an easy mark for financial sharks, and his investments in mining stocks, realty and other speculative properties worsted him financially, and although he realized quite a fortune from his large practice, yet he died a poor man However, he was idolized by his patients, and the foregoing statements regarding his character and career are by no means overdrawn but are in fact a subdued expression of the praise and tributes accorded to his noble nature, both during and after his life He died honored by his patients, by his party and by the many members of the Broadway Methodist church, with which he had been associated for many years, and the entire community in which he had lived and practiced for nearly fifty three years, accorded him a place in its permanent esteem and memory

CYRUS TABER It is now ninety years since Cyrus Taber left his eastern home and fared forth into an unknown country in quest of fortune and adventure, for it was practically as an unknown region that Indiana existed in the year 1824 He it was who established the name of the Taber family in the middle west, or in such portion of it as is represented by the state of Indiana and men of his name have from that day to this been identified with the best interests of the state wherever they have been found within its borders Agriculture has claimed a goodly share of the activities of these men and the professions, too, have not been neglected by them while the business of merchandising has known the touch of certain of the family

Cyrus Taber was born at Tiverton, Rhode Island on January 19, 1800 In 1803 the family moved to western New York and later to Pennsylvania When he was twenty-four years old Cyrus Taber left the parental roof and, filled with the zeal and ambition of the young man who came of a goodly parentage he started west to carve out his fortune from the fastnesses of the Indiana wilderness It is possible that he did not suspect the magnitude of his task but it is characteristic of the men of his family that he did not flinch for a moment from the hardships he saw he must undergo in order to wrest any degree of prosperity from the primitive country he had invaded so cheerfully First locating at Fort Wayne, he began his battle with the wilderness, but the unhealthful conditions of the country at that time induced an attack of fever and ague from which he was a sufferer for fully a year, and the savings of $400 that he had brought with him as a working capital were utterly exhausted and he was in debt to the amount of thirty dollars before he found himself able to apply himself to any manual labor again However, upon recuperating from his illness with courage undaunted by his experience, he began the work of building log cabins and fences for the Indians and was thus associated with one Reuben Covert, it being the province of the latter to drive the oxen and haul the rails, while Mr Taber did the cutting and splitting At the end of a year he found that he had saved one hundred dollars, and with that sum he purchased his first eighty acres of land This he cleared sufficiently to place under a degree of cultivation, and applied himself to the raising of corn He saved his earnings from season to season, and as his means permitted, purchased additional land

In the light of the present day get-rich-quick methods, of which so much is seen and heard the sweat of such labor and the privations endured by Mr Taber in getting his start in the world seem almost incredible, and it requires a considerable flight of imagination on the part of the man of the world of our times to realize anything of what such toil meant Indeed, the idea is practically beyond the comprehension of the average man, despite the application of his quality of imagination

However that may be, the facts remain as stated in the case of Cyrus Taber. Because of the splendid industry and the keen business sense of the man, Mr Taber was in 1827 invited into a business partnership with Allen Hamilton, and the firm of Hamilton & Taber became a popular one in mercantile circles of Indiana Mr Taber came to Logansport in 1828 to take charge of the branch business of the firm established here, and he continued in mercantile activities here, with some slight changes until 1840, following which Mr Taber continued the business alone for three years, and in 1843 William Chase was admitted to membership in the firm In 1848 Mr Taber retired permanently from mercantile pursuits

When Cass county was organized, Mr Taber was appointed county treasurer by the county board of commissioners, that office then being an appointive one, and he served in that capacity until 1830 In 1845 he was elected to the state legislature, and in the year following was elected to the senate, serving in that body during the years 1846, 7 and 8 He was first a Whig, but in later years adopted the faith of the Democratic party

Active in all matters pertaining to the welfare of his community, Cyrus Taber was ever one of the foremost in promoting progressive movements, and it was largely through his efforts that the first railroad was induced to extend its lines into Cass county—a work whose good to the county could not well be estimated

In May, 1829, Mr Taber was married to Miss Deborah Ann Coles, of Fort Wayne, Indiana, and eight children were born to them: Stephen C, Paul, Jesse C, Allen H, William S Phoebe A, Humphrey and George Concerning Stephen C, the first born son, further mention will be found elsewhere in this work The wife and mother passed away February 15, 1847, at Logansport, and Cyrus Taber died on April 13, 1855, in Logansport, still young in years, but one who had achieved more for the good of his community and county in his lifetime than most men are permitted to accomplish in much longer earthly careers

STEPHEN COLES TABER Like his father before him, Stephen Coles Taber lived a life of the utmost usefulness and activity in his community, and occupied a leading place in Logansport for many years He was born at Fort Wayne, Indiana, on March 8, 1830, and was the eldest son of Cyrus Taber, the pioneer to whom is dedicated a separate memoir in other parts of this work, and his faithful wife, Deborah Ann Coles When a baby he was brought by his parents to Logansport, which in those early days was not more than a cross roads place There his father was engaged in the merchandise business, and Stephen Taber was reared in the young and growing town In 1849 he was graduated from Wabash College, and in 1852 he finished his studies in the law department of the State University, following which he engaged in the practice of law For many years he practiced before the Cass county bar and for a time was associated in a professional way with Senator D D Pratt The latter part of Mr Taber's life, however, was devoted largely to looking after his large property interests, the extent of which precluded the possibility of continuing with his professional labors

On September 7, 1853, Mr. Taber was married to Charlotte A Walker, who died on January 8, 1892, leaving three children George C, Charles E and Lavina Mr Taber passed away on July 15, 1908, in Logansport, after a long and busy life in this county, and his death was felt in business and social circles throughout the community

WILLIAM B SCHWALM One of the flourishing business enterprises of Logansport is that conducted by William B Schwalm, and which includes the handling of seeds, hardware, buggies, harness paints, oils and general farming implements His early years were devoted to agricultural pursuits, but eventually he ceased his farming operations and turned his attention to the mercantile field, with a large measure of success A man of progressive ideas, he has identified himself with everything that pertains to the welfare of his community or its people, striving earnestly to promote the cause of advancement and good citizenship Mr Schwalm was born October 8, 1868, in Tipton township, Cass county, Indiana, one of the eight children of Henry J and Helena (Haemel) Schwalm

Henry J Schwalm was born August 20, 1828, the only son of his parents He was reared in Hesse Cassel, Germany, and received a good practical education In 1852, with his widowed mother, he emigrated to America, arriving on a sailing vessel in May of that year After his arrival, he worked for a time by the month for an uncle, who was a farmer in Tipton township, and then began farming for himself He was frugal, honest and industrious, and at the time of his death had accumulated a fair amount of this world's goods In starting his operations, he located in Washington township on rented property, but seven years later bought a farm on section 26, Tipton township, in 1860, and there passed the rest of his life He was married May 21, 1857, to Miss Helena Haemel, who was also a native of Germany, born near Hesse Cassel, March 28, 1829, the oldest daughter of Frederich and Elizabeth (Ellerman) Haemel Eight children were born to this union, namely George H, Sarah E, Caroline M, Eckhardt A, Augustina M, Louisa L, William B and Laura E, all of whom are still living In religion,

Mr and Mrs Schwalm were Presbyterians, and their upright lives were a credit to the land of their adoption and to the community in which they resided. Mr Schwalm was a Democrat, served three terms as township assessor, and also served his county as a commissioner.

William B Schwalm was reared on the home farm and secured his education in the district schools. After attaining his majority, he continued working on the home farm for six years, and when twenty-seven years old started farming on his own account, purchasing a tract of sixty acres in Tipton township, to which he subsequently added eighty acres more. This property he later sold to his brothers, and in 1900 came to Logansport, where he embarked in the implement and seed business. His venture proved a decided success and to the original line he has since added hardware, buggies, harness and stoves.

Mr Schwalm was a Democrat up to 1912, but the policies of the old old parties not suiting him and believing in the things advocated by Colonel Roosevelt and the Progressive platform, he cast his fortunes with the young organization and was its candidate for county commissioner from the second district. Mr Schwalm is a strong advocate of temperance measures, not alone on the liquor question, but on temperate measures of all kinds. He belongs to the Presbyterian church, and is a Master Mason and a Knight of Pythias.

On June 5, 1895 Mr Schwalm was married to Louise E Ramer of Washington township, Cass county, and they have two children Merritt R and Ruth C.

CHARLES W GRAVES has been a resident of Logansport for many years and has been identified with the business activities of this city along various lines through all the years of his residence. Since 1896 he has been the owner and proprietor of what was formerly known as the Giffe Book and Music Store, and in this enterprise he has experienced a worthy success. Born in Wayne county, Indiana, October 4, 1861, Mr Graves is the son of George M and Judith M (Harwood) Graves, both of whom were natives of Massachusetts. His father first located in Cincinnati Ohio and later in Richmond Indiana, where he was in business until the outbreak of the Civil war, when he enlisted in 1861 in Company F Thirty-sixth Indiana Volunteer Infantry, rising to the rank of captain, and serving as acting adjutant on the staff of Colonel Gross. In the battle of Chickamauga he received a gun-shot wound through his right shoulder, which of itself was not necessarily fatal, but owing to his enfeebled condition, due to a recent sickness, he was unable to withstand the shock of the injury and died some days later. His body was brought to the north and laid to rest in the cemetery in Richmond. His widow was left with three small children, the only daughter, Lillie, being now Mrs John A McCullough of Logansport, Indiana. At the time of the death of the father, the eldest of the three children was about six years old, and the widow reared her little family through many hardships. She died in Logansport in November, 1904.

Charles W Graves received his education in the common and high schools of Richmond. When he was about sixteen years old he began clerking in a grocery store in his home town and later was employed as a bookkeeper. He then became a clerk in the railroad office at Rich-

mond, his older brother, George C, being chief clerk at that time, in the employ of the Columbus, Cincinnati and Indiana Central Railroad, which later became the Pittsburgh, Cincinnati, Chicago and St Louis Railway When the chief of the office moved to Logansport, in 1881, he offered Mr Graves the position of chief clerk, which he promptly accepted and accordingly came to Logansport to fill the position assuming the duties of his new office in January, 1882 Since that time Logansport has been his home Two years later Mr Graves was made chief clerk and private secretary in the office of the division superintendent, which he retained until 1894, when he resigned and bought an interest in the Logansport *Journal*, of which he became business manager He was thus associated for about two years, when he bought the Giffe Book & Music Store, and this establishment he has conducted ever since, moving to his present quarters, No 417 Broadway, in July, 1908

In 1900 or thereabouts Mr Graves was the organizer of what was known as the Logansport Co-operative Association, of which he was elected president This was brought into existence to correct the abuses that had grown up in the commercial district with regard to premium giving, trading stamps prizes, discounts, etc Thousands of dollars were lost to the general business men of the city, and many of the smaller houses were forced to the edge of bankruptcy by the unfair methods then in vogue The Logansport Co-operative Association had a precarious existence at the start, and owing to the fact of the trouble being so firmly entrenched in the general system, only the steadfast courage of those at the helm enabled them to finally stamp out the seeds of the scourge Mr Graves was also active in the organization of the Citizens' Natural Gas Company of which he was elected secretary This was in about 1891, and the company was organized to check abuses then in vogue by the concerns that at that period had charge of the distribution of the natural gas He has also been identified with the various commercial clubs and movements that have had as their object the betterment of conditions existing in Logansport and the surrounding community and has in all these various associations done most excellent and praiseworthy work in behalf of the city

Mr Graves is a Republican with progressive tendencies and is also an active worker in the temperance cause He is a member of the First Presbyterian church, of which he has been an official for years, and he is now elder and clerk of the session He is also identified with the work of the Sunday school and is a member of the board of directors of the Indiana Sunday School Association.

On October 18 1888, Mr Graves was united in marriage with Miss Anna Lucy Wright, the daughter of Williamson Wright, a pioneer of Cass county

ANDREW J. MURDOCK In ability as a financier and in general business affairs Cass county had no stronger character or one better known among all classes than the late Andrew Jackson Murdock, for many years president of the First National Bank of Logansport In the broader fields of citizenship, as well as in business, he performed a large scope of useful service which has properly identified him for all time with the history of this locality. Mr Murdock was a type and example of one who succeeds in life, though his youth was passed in comparative poverty, and with only such advantages as he could procure by his own labors and ambitions

The late Andrew J Murdock was born in Livingston county, New York, November 19, 1827 The first eight years of his life were spent in his native state, and he then accompanied the family to Michigan. Michigan, during the thirties, was almost on the frontier, and the best settled regions were but a field for hardships and privations of pioneer existence It was amid such scenes and with such limitations in advantages of education and otherwise that Andrew J Murdock was reared At the age of thirteen he was thrown upon his own resources, and from that forward depended entirely upon his own exertions for his advancement

In 1853, Mr Murdock became a resident of Logansport, so that he had identified himself with this city at an early period in its growth, and at a time when his vigorous enterprise and honorable character were important elements in the development as a city along the lines which have made it conspicuous among the larger centers in northern Indiana A year after his arrival in this city, he engaged in business on his own account, opening a store, with which his name was connected for twenty-four years He had a trade which few other merchants in the city and county could equal, and throughout his lifetime, enjoyed the confidence and good will of all with whom he came in contact. His business interests gradually extended by investments and otherwise, and in 1865 he was made a director of the Logansport National Bank, and in 1878 was elected its president Five years later this bank was consolidated with the First National Bank, of which Mr Murdock was chosen president, and this position he filled with splendid executive ability up to the time of his death, May 3, 1905 In the field of practical finance, as well as in his judgment of men, which is an element just as essential to the success of a financier as his more technical expertness in financial operations, Mr Murdock was recognized as one of the strongest representatives in Cass county Among the varied interests owned by Mr Murdock was the fine tract of land, consisting of more than three hundred acres lying between Logansport and the park on either side of the Electric railway

Though a man whose influence in business and civic affairs of Logansport, was for many years conspicuous, Mr. Murdock was a citizen who was never in the public eye, as the general sense of that term is understood, and modesty was his chief characteristic He was always a Republican in good standing, and supported the party candidates and principles, though never seeking office for himself His contributions and support were accorded to nearly every important enterprise of public nature in Logansport for thirty or forty years yet his name appeared less frequently than that of many whose active support was less. On August 4, 1862, Mr Murdock was married, and his home and family always represented the chief sphere of his leisure activities He wedded Maggie C. Chadwick, of Newark, New Jersey, daughter of Thomas and Margaret (Pickles) Chadwick Their three children are May, wife of

Samuel Patterson; Flora, wife of Samuel Emmet Mulholland, Gertrude, wife of Edward H Donovan. Mr Murdock attended the First Presbyterian church, being a prominent contributor thereto, and he built the Murdock Hotel The Murdock home was one of the social centers of Logansport, and the family have always been among the most representative of this city

MOSES B LAIRY In the roster of those who have gained prominence at the Cass county bench and bar, are to be found many eminent names, none of which, however, have stood out in greater relief than that of the Hon. Moses Barnett Lairy, Judge of the Appellate Court, who has gained an enviable distinction through the medium of his great experience, his great good sense, his stainless integrity, his perfect impartiality, his wide discernment and his abundant learning A worthy representative of a family that for years has been identified with the commercial, agricultural, professional and public interests of the county, he early entered upon a legal career, and so ably has he directed his activities that today he is recognized as one of his State's leading jurists Judge Lairy was born in Harrison township, Cass county, Indiana, August 13, 1859

Daniel Lairy, the paternal grandfather of Judge Lairy, was born in Ohio and as a young man became a pioneer to Tippecanoe county, Indiana, settling within its borders when that section was almost an unbroken wilderness and there spending the rest of his life Thomas Lairy, son of Daniel, and father of Judge Lairy, was born in Butler county, Ohio, January 20, 1807 As early as 1837 he entered land from the government in Harrison township, Cass county, but did not move to this property until many years later He had accompanied his parents to Tippecanoe county in his boyhood, and was reared to manhood among pioneer scenes, receiving his early training in the hard work of plowing, planting and cultivating the fields Subsequently, he moved to LaFayette, where for a number of years he was engaged in carpentering Mr Lairy was married (first) to Belinda Miller, who died without issue, and his second union was to Mrs Eliza (Barnett) Thornburgh, daughter of Moses Barnett, a pioneer of the county While a resident of LaFayette Mr. Lairy belonged to the militia, and served in a company during the Black Hawk war He was a member of the Christian church, in the faith of which he died January 11, 1877, his widow surviving him a long time and passing away May 14, 1892. They had two children · Moses B and John S

Moses Barnett Lairy was reared on the Cass county farm which his father had entered from the government, and attended the district schools of Harrison township until he was seventeen years of age, at that time being compelled to give up his studies to operate the home farm, his father having died. Later he spent one term in the Northern Indiana Normal School and then began teaching school in the winter terms, his summers being spent on the home farm His first experience as an educator was at Fletchers Lake schoolhouse, just across the line in Fulton county, and in all taught for about nine years carefully saving his earnings that he might further his own studies in the

Northern Indiana Normal School During the last years of his school teaching experience, he took up the study of law under the direction of Judge Dudley H Case, and in 1888 entered the law department of the University of Michigan, where he was graduated with the class of 1889 Succeeding this, in September of the same year, he began practice in Logansport, alone, but four years later became associated with DeWitt C Justice For fourteen years he also maintained a professional partnership with M F Mahoney A Democrat in politics and an active worker in his party's interests, as his abilities became recognized his name began to be mentioned for judicial honors, and in 1894 he was made his party's candidate for the judgeship of the Cass county circuit court Political conditions at that time, however, caused his defeat with the others on the ticket On April 1, 1905, he was appointed by Gov Matthews to fill the unexpired term of Judge D B McConnell, resigned and on completing his term of twenty months was succeeded by Judge D H Case His election to the Appellate bench occurred in 1910, since which time he has continued to faithfully and capably discharge the duties of his high office maintaining the dignity and best traditions thereof and being known as a fair and impartial judge Fraternally, he is connected with the Masons and the Benevolent and Protective Order of Elks

On April 14, 1892, Judge Lairy was married to Miss Mazetta Rogers, daughter of Thomas B Rogers, of Logansport she having been for some years a teacher in the public schools of the city They attend the First Presbyterian church

HON JOHN S LAIRY Occupying a position of high credit and distinction among the leaders of the legal profession in Cass county, Hon John S Lairy, judge of the twenty-ninth judicial district, has, during a long and useful career, exemplified the best type of American citizenship As a lawyer, he early took a foremost position among the practitioners of the Logansport bar, his gifts as a speaker and his capacity for close, logical reasoning making him a peculiarly forceful and effective advocate As a judge he has made a record that holds out a stimulus and example to all men who are called upon to bear the high responsibilities of a place upon the bench The sound judgment, the well-balanced judicial mind, the intellectual honesty and freedom from bias which are required in a judge—these attributes have been all his and have enabled him not only to give opinions which are widely quoted, but to maintain the best traditions of the judicial office Judge Lairy was born in Harrison township Cass county, Indiana, September 7, 1864, and is a son of Thomas and Eliza (Barnett) (Thornburgh) Lairy

Judge Lairy belongs to an old and honored family which originated in Ireland, and the American progenitor of which came to this country in 1727, soldiers of the name fighting in the Colonial army during the War of the Revolution Daniel Lairy, the paternal grandfather of Judge Lairy, was born in Ohio, and some time after his marriage made removal to what was then the wilderness of Tippecanoe county Indiana, the rest of his life being spent in clearing and cultivating a farm Thomas Lairy, son of Daniel, and father of Judge Lairy, was born

January 20 1807, in Butler county, Ohio, and as a lad was taken to Tippecanoe county, Indiana, where he was reared amid pioneer scenes Later, he moved to LaFayette, where he was engaged in carpentering, and while residing in that locality, pre-empted land from the Government in Harrison township, Cass county, for $1 25 an acre, although he did not settle thereon until during the fifties The rest of his life was spent in farming, and his death occurred January 11, 1877, in the faith of the Christian church, of which he was a life-long member While a resident of LaFayette, he was a member of the state militia, and served with a company during the Blackhawk war Mr Lairy married (first) Belinda Miller, who died without issue, and his second union was with Mrs Eliza (Barnett) Thornburg, daughter of Moses Barnett, a pioneer of Cass county Mrs Lairy passed away May 14, 1892 having been the mother of two sons Moses Barnett, judge of the appellate court, and John S

John S Lairy was reared on the home farm and secured his early education in the common schools and the American Normal School, at Logansport He then spent several years in teaching school, in the meantime devoting himself to the study of law, and in 1895 and 1896 attended the law school of the University of Michigan, at Ann Arbor, where he was graduated in 1896 with the degree of Bachelor of Laws In August of that year he entered upon the practice of his profession in Logansport, which city has been his home to the present time Shortly after beginning practice, Judge Lairy served two years as deputy state's attorney, his services in the discharge of the duties of this office bringing him favorably before the public In 1900 he became the Democratic candidate for the office of judge of the twenty-ninth judicial district, and was subsequently elected, taking office in 1902 He was reelected in 1906 and in 1912 again became the candidate of his party for reelection Judge Lairy has shown himself a worthy member of the Indiana bench, the soundness and equity of his decisions having never been questioned A hard student and a man of high scholarship with a well-poised mind, and ever ready with his legal knowledge, his opinions have been widely quoted and he has not only attained a position of prominence in the field of jurisprudence, but his business and personal excellencies have made him a leader of worth and sagacity He has interested himself in fraternal work to some extent, being a member of the Elks, the Knights of Pythias and the Loyal Order of Moose, in all of which he has numerous warm friends

On July 17, 1912, Judge Lairy was united in marriage with Miss Ica Campbell, whose home was in Logansport

BENJAMIN F KEESLING is of Indiana nativity, his birth occurring at Mechanicsburg, in Henry county, on February 18, 1850 Mechanicsburg might well have been named Keesling, for here in 1828 came Peter Keesling with George, John, Jacob and Daniel, all brothers, and each of these brothers married in the course of time, and each reared a large family So numerous did they become in that vicinity that practically every person one met either bore the name of Keesling, or was related to the family by marriage Originally the family came to America from Germany and for generations lived in Virginia With the spirit of the pioneers, members of the family moved to Ohio, and from there moved to Indiana and settled at what is now Mechanicsburg

John Keesling, the grandfather of Benjamin F., built his log cabin in the woods from growing timber and there passed some time in grubbing, clearing, planting and harvesting, the regular routine of the pioneer farmer He subsequently built a farm house One of his sons, Peter Keesling, the father of Benjamin F, was married to Margaret Loy, who become the mother of ten children. Peter Keesling, like most of the others of his name, was thrifty and industrious and possessed of the necessary courage to fight the battle of life to a successful issue, even under the adverse conditions of those primitive days

Benjamin F Keesling was born in Henry county, February 18, 1850. Growing up on the farm he learned all that could be taught him of farm life, and hard, continuous work was the portion of his youthful days After attending the neighboring schools he went to the graded schools at New Castle When about twenty years of age he began clerking in a general store at the latter named place, but in April, 1874, came to Logansport and associated himself with Dr John Needham in the drug trade A few years later he bought the interest of Dr Needham in the business and continued in it alone until 1900, when the property was destroyed by fire The ensuing four years he was in Boston and Pittsburg, then returned to Logansport and in December, 1907, bought the Metzger Brothers' interest in the Logansport *Daily Journal* With his son, Arthur R, the Logansport Daily and Weekly *Journal* flourished until October, 1912 when it was consolidated with the *Tribune*, and is now the *Journal-Tribune*. Under the new arrangement, Mr. Keesling became a stockholder and is the present secretary-treasurer of the corporation

Mr Keesling is a Republican, and in 1892 was elected treasurer of Cass county, being the only successful nominee on his ticket On February 18, 1875, Mr Keesling married Anna B McCune, of Middletown, Indiana, and one son, Arthur R, was born to them Mrs Keesling is a member of the Methodist church

JACOB SELLERS For sixty years a resident of Cass county, during fifty-five of which he has made his home in Logansport, Jacob Sellers is entitled to a position among the representative men of his city not only for the length of time which he has spent within its borders, but also as a citizen who has continuously had the best interests of his community at heart Mr Sellers has devoted the greater part of his time to the cultivation of the soil and to attention to his duties in the railroad shops, but he has never been so engrossed in his own affairs that he has not found time to lend his interest and support to those movements which he believes will benefit his adopted city or its people Mr. Sellers was born August 15, 1834, in Wittenburg, Germany, in what is widely known as the Black Forest His father, Michael Sellers, was a baker by trade and died in the old country, his widow, who bore the maiden name of Katherine Cook, married (second) Gottlieb Frick, and the family emigrated to the United States in 1847, and located at Buffalo, New York, where they lived five years In the spring of 1853 the family came to Cass county, Indiana, and located four miles east of Logansport, where Mr. Frick found employment working for Thomas Green, who operated a large forge there, and succeeding this went to what is known as the "Indian Reserve" in Washington township They moved to Logansport three years later, and here both Mr and Mrs. Frick passed away

Jacob Sellers was thirteen years of age when he accompanied his parents to the United States, and his education was confined to a few terms in the common schools The greater part of his life has been passed in farming and working in the railroad shops, and his success has been due to well-applied energy, ambition and perseverance, in connection with integrity of the strictest order While so doing he has gained and maintained the entire confidence of his fellow-citizens, who have recognized in him a man of general worth and probity of character Mr Sellers was married June 20, 1867, to Miss Fredericka Adler, daughter of Christopher Adler, who was a native of Austria and came to the United States in 1853 Mr Adler died on his farm near Winamac, Indiana To Mr and Mrs Sellers six children have been born, as follows Carrie C, who became the wife of Edward Hanke, Edward D, a sketch of whose life will be found in another part of this work, Charles J, Mamie, who married Manuel Connor and is now deceased, Frank F, and Emma L, who became the wife of Clarence Ammons, and is a resident of Logansport

Early in 1865, Mr Sellers enlisted for service in the Union army during the Civil war, becoming a member of Company C, One Hundred Fifty-fifth Regiment, Indiana Volunteer Infantry Owing to the war being practically over, he was detailed to do guard duty until peace was declared, when he received his honorable discharge and returned to the duties of private citizenship.

EDWARD D SELLERS. Among the prosperous establishments of Logansport, one which started in a modest manner and has enjoyed a rapid and continuous growth is the clothing and furnishing business of Helvie & Sellers, composed of Samuel S Helvie and Edward D Sellers The junior member of this partnership has been engaged in this line of endeavor ever since boyhood, and has brought to his work a boundless enthusiasm, coupled with wide experience, natural business ability and inherent integrity which has gained him the confidence of his patrons and fellow-citizens Edward D Sellers is a native of Logansport, and was born July 4, 1871, a son of Jacob and Fredericka (Adler) Sellers

Jacob Sellers was born August 15, 1834, in the Black Forest, Wittenberg, Germany, and is a son of Michael and Katherine (Cook) Sellers, the former of whom, a baker by trade, died in Germany, while the latter married (second) Gottlieb Frick, and emigrated to the United States in 1847 First locating at Buffalo, New York, the family spent five years in that city, and in the spring of 1853 came to Cass county, Indiana, and settled four miles east of Logansport, where Mr Frick found employment with Thomas Green, the proprietor of a forge. Later, they went to what is known as the "Indian Reserve," in Washington township, but three years later moved to Logansport, and there both Mr. and Mrs Frick passed away Jacob Sellers was thirteen years of age when he accompanied his parents to this country, and his education was secured in the common schools, in which he passed a few terms. He has passed the greater part of his life in agricultural pursuits and in working in the railroad shops and has been uniformly successful in his ventures. On June 20, 1867, he was married to Miss Fredericka Adler, daughter of Christopher Adler, who was a native of Austria and came to the United States in 1853, dying on a farm near Winamac, Indiana. Six children have been born to Mr. and Mrs Sellers Carrie C., who married Edward Hanke, Edward D., Charles J., Mamie, who married Manuel Connor and is now deceased, Frank F., and Emma L., who became the wife of Clarence Ammons, and lives in Logansport. The father of these children fought valiantly in the Union army during the Civil war.

Edward D. Sellers received his education in the public schools of Logansport, and at the age of sixteen years commenced upon his business career as a clerk in the clothing store of Harry Frank, with whom he remained for five years. Succeeding this for two years he clerked for Joseph Grace, and in 1896, in partnership with Samuel S. Helvie, he embarked in the clothing and furnishings business under the firm style of Helvie & Sellers, an association that has continued to the present time. The firm has enjoyed a healthy growth and now has a large trade, embracing some of the best business in Logansport. Mr Sellers is a young man of the highest business integrity, with a reputation for straightforward and honorable dealings. He has been industrious and enterprising, and has never failed to take advantage of modern ideas and methods. In politics he was formerly a Republican but since 1912 has been allied with the new Progressive party. His fraternal connection is with the Masons.

On June 6, 1900, Mr Sellers was married to Miss Mattie Gibbons, formerly a resident of Sheldon, Illinois.

WILLIAM B. ENYART. A citizen who has left his impress on the business interests of Logansport, and whose activities entitle him to rank with the solid substantial men of the city, is William B. Enyart, for thirty-five years the proprietor of a bottling establishment here. He belongs to that class of business men who have found time from their personal operations to give to the public needs, and at various times has been elected to positions of trust and responsibility, in which he has proven himself able and conscientious. Now, at an age when most men are willing to turn over their interests to men of the younger generation, he still conducts the management of his enterprise with unabated activity and energy, giving to its smallest details the close attention that has been the secret of its success. Mr Envart has spent his entire career within the confines of Cass county with the exception of the time when he was serving as a soldier in the Union ranks during the Civil war. He was born in Clay township September 19, 1845, and is a son of Israel and Temperance (Foy) Enyart.

Benjamin and Sarah (Miller) Enyart, the grandparents of William B. Enyart, came to Cass county in 1834, settling in Clay township, where for many years they kept a tavern known to all the old settlers as "Four-Mile House." The grandfather, who died in December, 1845, was detailed as a teamster during the War of 1812. In religious belief he was an old-fashioned Methodist. Israel Enyart was born in January, 1821, and was reared to hard work, clearing grubbing and doing general farm labor, and the limited education he acquired was secured in the little log schoolhouse, having but few chances during his entire life to receive schooling. He lived with his people until he reached manhood, and then went to farming on Mill Creek, near Kewanee. Two years later he bought a tract of land on section 21 Clay township, where the balance of his career was spent. During his later life he joined the church, and died a Christian. His chief characteristics were honesty and liberality, and whatever he possessed was always ready for his neighbors' use. Mr. Enyart married Temperance Foy whose people came to Cass county from Virginia in 1835 and to this union there were born six children. William B., Mary Elizabeth, who is deceased, Hiram Wilson, also deceased, Sarah A., who is now Mrs. Alexander Davidson, and Lavina and Asbury Newton, who are both deceased. Mr. Enyart died January 12, 1892, and his widow followed him to the grave in August, 1896.

William B. Enyart was reared on the old home farm, and secured his education in the common schools. When just past eighteen years of age, November 2, 1863, he enlisted in Company H, Seventy-third Regiment, Indiana Volunteer Infantry, with which organization he participated in numerous engagements, including Athens, Decatur, Alabama, although the latter part of his military career was spent in doing garrison duty. He received his honorable discharge, after a brave and faithful service, December 11, 1865, and returned to the pursuits of peace, learning the plasterer's trade, at which he worked for fourteen years. In 1884 he turned his attention to the bottling business, and this he has carried on to the present time, having built up an excellent trade through the exercise of native integrity, high ability and honorable dealing. For some years he was in partnership with a Mr Chambers, under the firm style of Enyart & Chambers, but is now associated with his son. Known as a thoroughly reliable business man whose operations have been of a strictly legitimate nature, he has gained the confidence and respect of all who have done business with him. He has invested in realty to some extent and is at this time the owner of some paying property in Cass county as well as city real estate in Logansport. Mr. Enyart is a Republican in his political views, and in 1902 was a member of the common council from the Fourth ward. In 1904 he was again elected to that office, serving in all four years and in 1906 was the successful nominee of his party for the office of county sheriff. Two years later, however, he was defeated for re-election with the other members of his ticket. He is a popular comrade of the Grand Army of the Republic, and his fraternal connections are with the Benevolent and Protective Order of Elks, the Fraternal Order of Eagles and the Loyal Order of Moose.

On March 10, 1873, Mr. Enyart was married to Miss Louisa Tippett, a native of Cass county, Indiana who died some years later leaving four children. Charles M., who is associated in business with his father, Nora S., who married Frank Etnire, Carrie B., and Frank L.

Mr. Enyart was married (second) February 11, 1886, to Kate May, a native of Pulaski county, Indiana

JOHN S KLINE is a pioneer of pioneers in the state of Indiana, where for sixty-nine years he has made his home, and this residence is the more notable when it is known that he is living today in the identical spot where his family settled when they migrated from Ohio in 1844, bringing him as a boy of seven years Few men in any part of the country can boast a continued residence of almost seventy years in one spot, or indeed in one single community His life has been a busy and active one, and he has taken an industrious part in the industry of the township, which has long been and still is that of farming

The natal day of John Samuel Kline was August 27, 1837, and his birth occurred at Eaton, Ohio, where the family had long lived He was the son of William Kline, who served as a soldier throughout the War of 1812, and who after settling in Miami township, devoted his remaining days to the business of farming He died at the age of sixty-two and his widow, who in her maiden days was Isabel Snodgrass, died at Logansport, when she was ninety-three years old They were the parents of six children, concerning whom brief mention is made as follows Jacob M, who married Miss Marietti Baldwin, William T, married Miss Letitia Sizor, Mary became the wife of Peter Heffley, Margaret married Frank Swigart, Henry married Miss Ella Leas, and John S, who is the immediate subject of this brief sketch

In 1844 the Kline family migrated from their native state, making the trip into Indiana overland, the wagon route being most popular in those early days, and eleven days were consumed in the journey, which would not be made in a few hours The father secured land in Miami township, and they settled down to country life, occupying a little log house that already graced their home farm Here John S Kline was reared and educated With the passing years he took a wife, Mary Etmre, the daughter of Abraham Etmre She was a native of Canton, Ohio, and she died on September 20, 1864 The present Kline residence was begun by William Kline, the father prior to his death, which occurred in 1855, and was completed by John S Mr Kline, early in his career, bought eighty acres of land, to which he has added from time to time until today he has a farm comprising one hundred and thirty and a half acres

Two children were born to John S and Mary Kline, Joseph Slaton and Charles The latter died in 1904, but the other son, who is known as Slate Kline, still shares the home place with his father He is now fifty-one years of age, and is his father's business partner Slate Kline has been twice married His first wife, who was Cora Scott, died in 1902, and he later married Anna Williams They have one child, Victor S Kline, now three months old. To the marriage of Slate Kline with Cora Scott were born three children, named as follows Hattie, now the wife of Blaine Swigart, and living near Strathmore, Canada, on a farm, Mary, who is engaged in teaching school, and Charles who has finished high school and intends to take up farming The other son of John S Kline, Charles Kline, who died in 1904, left one son, Kenneth, who is now of age and resides with his mother at Los Angeles, California

Family Group of —
Mr & Mrs Rob M Elliott

The Kline family are members of the Baptist church and their politics are those of the Republican party, whose stanch adherents they are in all things. They are among the best known and most estimable people in the township, and enjoy a high standing in the community.

ROBERT M ELLIOTT. While the soil of Cass county is very fertile, water plentiful and easily obtained and weather conditions nearly ideal, good crops cannot be raised unless the land is properly worked and scientifically conditioned, and the high standard set by the agriculturists of the county is therefore of great credit to them. Many of the leading farmers of this county have lived here all of their lives, thus becoming thoroughly familiar with the character of the soil and climate, and in this way being able to direct their operations along lines that will insure success, and in this class stands Robert M Elliott, of Clay township, the owner of 110 acres of well cultivated land. Mr Elliott was born June 18, 1864 in Cass county, and is a son of Alfred and Emily (Williamson) Elliott. His father, a native of Montgomery county, Indiana, came to Cass county in 1849, and here erected a frame house, the first one of this character to be built in the county. His subsequent life was devoted to tilling the soil, and he was uniformly successful in his operations, at the time of his death in 1900, being considered one of the substantial men of his community. His widow still survives him, at the age of seventy-three years, and makes her home on the old farm. They were the parents of six sons and two daughters.

Robert M Elliott acquired his education in the district schools of his native locality and was reared to the work of the home farm, his boyhood being divided between agricultural work in the summer months and attending school in the winter terms. Thus he acquired a good education and a sturdy body, well fitting him for the duties he was to be called upon to discharge in later life. He continued to remain under the parental roof until 1894, in which year he was married to Miss Eleanor G McDowell, a daughter of John McDowell, who brought his family to Cass county from Ohio.

Mrs Robert Elliott is a native of Cass county, Indiana, born October 7, 1869, and a daughter of John and Amanda (Dritt) McDowell. There were three daughters in the family—Mrs Elliott eldest. Adria, wife of James Cassel, a resident of Logansport and proprietor of The Star Laundry, has three children; Elizabeth, wife of Wiley Sharp, also of Logansport, has four children. John McDowell was of Scottish lineage but was born in Stark county, Ohio. He served as a soldier in the Rebellion and was a stanch Republican politically. Mrs McDowell was of German lineage and was born near Lancaster, Pennsylvania. She died September 14, 1912. Both he and wife were members of the Presbyterian church. He died April 27, 1889.

At the time of his marriage, Mr Elliott began farming on a tract of sixty-five acres, located in Clay township which was the property of Mrs Elliott's parents and subsequently purchased this, and some time later he added to this an additional tract of forty-five acres, and on this latter property erected all the buildings. He also owns a fine tract of land in Sanilac county, Michigan, has bank stock in Logansport, and other good securities. In addition to general farming, he has been engaged in dairying to some extent, and his operations have succeeded because of his untiring industry, his thorough knowledge of his business, and the intelligent manner in which he has directed all of his actions. He is a thorough believer in the efficacy of scientific methods and uses modern machinery and appliances in his work. Among his associates Mr Elliott is known as a man of the highest business integrity, whose success has been gained through no chicanery or questionable methods. He has for some years been a member of the Benevolent and Protective Order of Elks, in which he has numerous friends. In politics, he has always given his support to Democratic policies and candidates, and from 1901 to 1904 served very acceptably as a member of the board of county commissioners of Cass county.

Mr and Mrs Elliott have one daughter Esther E, who is living with her parents. She graduated from the public schools in the class of 1910 and attended two and one-half years in the city schools of Logansport and has also taken musical instruction. The members of the family are affiliated with the Presbyterian church.

Mrs Elliott was educated in the public schools of Cass county. She has nobly filled her sphere as wife and mother and her pretty home is her haven. The beautiful estate of Mr and Mrs Elliott lies on the highest point of ground in northern Cass county and is known as "The Summit Lodge."

JOHN McDOWELL a highly respected citizen of Clay township, died at his home on Saturday, April 27, 1889. He had suffered for years with lung trouble, but only during the past two years was he compelled to quit work. He contracted a deep cold while serving a second term on the petit jury which hurried his end. The deceased was a man of good character, upright in all his dealings, and well liked by all who knew him. The funeral services were conducted by Rev Dr Putman and the remains were interred at Mt Hope cemetery.

Mr McDowell was born in Stark county, January 24, 1840, and was therefore forty-nine years of age. His father moved to this county while John was yet a boy. He has three brothers living Silas McDowell, of Noble township, Butch McDowell, of Silver Lake, and Isaac McDowell, of Illinois. He has also three sisters, but one of whom is living, Mrs C E Metzger, who resides in Clay township.

Mr McDowell was married to Miss Amanda Dritt in March, 1868. To this union three daughters have been born, who with their mother survive to mourn their loss.

ROBERT GUTHRIE was born on April 2, 1850, in Cass county, Indiana, and received his education in the common schools of the county and in the Logansport Seminary. He is the son of William and Margaret (Japp) Guthrie.

William Guthrie was the son of John and Elizabeth Guthrie and was born in the city of Perth, Perthshire, Scotland, in the year 1795. The son of wealthy parents he was graduated from the University of Edinburgh, and soon after, on the demise of his father, finding that the law of primogeniture and entail was against him and stung by a sense of outraged justice, he turned his back on the home of his youth and emigrated to the United States. He settled in Switzerland county, Indiana, in about the year 1825, and here he engaged in general farming.

He married Margaret Japp, the daughter of Thomas and Agnes Japp, who was born in the year 1812 on the river Doon, in Scotland. Orphaned in infancy, she emigrated to America with foster parents in the year 1819, and with them settled in Switzerland county. Here she became acquainted with William Guthrie. Their acquaintance ripened into friendship and culminated in their marriage in 1828. To their union thirteen children were born.

Mr. Guthrie continued his farming operations in Switzerland county until 1848, when with his wife and nine children, he moved to Cass county, settling in the wilderness along the shores of Rock creek seven miles south of the then village of Logansport, and here began that Herculean task that required stout hearts and willing hands,—the building of a new home in the wilderness. The children who then graced the family home were John, William, Agnes, Thomas, Jane, Alexander, Ann, Joseph and James, having previously lost their son Isaac by death and here, surrounded by primeval forests and confronted with all the hardships and privations incident to pioneer life, the family was blessed with three more children,—Elizabeth, another who died in infancy unnamed, and Robert, the subject of this sketch.

Here in this new home William Guthrie spent the remainder of his life,—a life largely given over to the clearing away and subduing of the forests, and devoted to the best interests, the upbuilding and the onward march of civilization. To him and such as him we owe our gratitude. He died on September 9, 1855. In 1857 his widow married again, Richard Downham becoming her husband, and they continued to reside upon the farm until 1864, when she accompanied her husband to the west but returned again in 1873, widowed for the second time in her life. She spent her declining years in Cass county, dying on July 2, 1880.

Robert Guthrie upon leaving school accepted a position as salesman in his brother's clothing house in Logansport but in the following year took up the study and practice of law, being admitted to the bar in June 1876. Soon, however he gave way to the allurement of the wilds and embarked in the lumber business in which he continued with varying success until September 20, 1883, when he was married to Miss Laura A. Funston. Five children were born to this union: May Anna, John Roy, Alta Lola, Edna Elizabeth, and Jane Nora. Mrs. Guthrie was born on January 28, 1860, in Clark county, Ohio, and was the only daughter of William and Rebecca (Black) Funston. She moved to Cass county with her parents on March 9, 1865, and the family settled on a farm in Noble township. She was educated in the common schools of Cass county.

Subsequent to his marriage, Mr. Guthrie gave up the lumber business and settled on a farm in Harrison township, which place he continued to operate until April 1896, when he located in Logansport and engaged in the real estate and insurance business, afterward accepting a position with the Pennsylvania Railroad Company, in which capacity he served until November 17, 1903, when he moved with his family to a farm in Noble township. Here he is still employed in the peaceful occupation of farming, truck gardening and horticulture.

In 1908 the ex-students and teachers of East Sandridge organized a pioneer school reunion association, the first of its kind in Cass county, and Mr. Guthrie was elected president of that organization. His address delivered at the reunion the following year is here presented in full

Fellow students. When I look into your faces and survey these surroundings. I am forcibly reminded of those beautiful lines which read like this ' How dear to my heart are the scenes of my childhood, when fond recollections present them to view.'' We are brought back here today, not only in remembrance, but we are brought face to face, as it were, with the scenes of our childhood. Brought back once more to Sandridge, back to this old familiar school-house playing ground. A place made sacred by memories of the past. For here it was you spent so many of your childhood days. 'Twas here you skipped and played in childish glee, and here again you toiled o'er lessons hard, then played your games of ball, of tag, and blindman's buff. 'Twas here you planned the spelling bee, the bob sled ride, or the social party at a patron's house. And now to think you're here again! to look each other in the face and grasp each other by the hand. No wonder recollections of the past come crowding to our mind. And now what of Sandridge? Sandridge holds a warm place in the hearts of many. Sandridge throughout all the years that she has existed as a place of learning has maintained a reputation for being one of the very best common schools in all this broad land. And the reason for this may be found in the fact that in the very beginning she was surrounded by a loyal, peace loving, honest and honorable constituency. And the children of those sturdy pioneers who came here to receive instructions in the fundamental principles of an education emulating the examples set by their fathers, though none have risen to preeminence among men, yet, upon the whole, they have made honored and respected citizens. Men and women who have gone into the world and have fought and are still fighting the great battles of life, and discharging the duties of citizenship in a way that has been a credit to themselves, a credit to the school and a credit to the great commonwealth of Indiana

And now, fellow students at East Sandridge, I am glad to be with you here today for I see among you those who have passed the zenith of their lives, who years ago, as boys and girls while the flush of youth was yet upon their cheeks and the fire of ambition shone in their eyes, roamed these woods and fields, who coasted down, and played upon this ridge of sand. You are here today, fellow students, to engage in reminiscence and recreation, to once more commingle your voices in commemoration of those happy days gone by, God bless you all

An original poem by Mr Guthrie, entitled "Early Recollections" is here presented as written.

    Somewhat back from Rockcreek's swampy, muddy banks,
    Midst prickly ash and wild hawthorn,
    With its clapboard roof and latch string door,
    Stood the old log cabin where I was born
    Its broad and ample fireplace
    Was built from sticks and mud and clay
    And round its cheerful glowing hearth

We worked and played and sang each day
How well do I remember
Those awful swamps and sloughs,
For when we'd walk around a while
Water came in our shoes
And when we'd take a ramble
At the surrounding woods to peep
Some ancient frog behind a log
Would say "Knee deep, knee deep."
Then when the August sun shone forth
And the leaves began to dry
The way we'd have the ague chills
Was enough to make one cry.
My father settled in those swamps,
From across the deep blue sea
But how he lived and reared us kids
Seems passing strange to me
But he was wise and very learned
From delving into lore
I've often thought he had some coin
Brought from Scotland's shore
However that may be he loved that land
Which then was but a jest,
But now it don't require a sage
To tell that it's the best
But many changes have taken place
Since the day that I was born,
Where once was naught but woods and swamps
Grow fields of ripening corn

WILLIAM H STOUGHTON Probably there is no class of people who so quickly grasp anything new and progressive like the modern farmer. Although residing away from the hustle and the bustle of the city, a considerable distance from the manufacturing centers, it is really surprising to note how familiar the agriculturist is with improvements that relate to his vocation It is in this way, and in this way only, that the farmer of today is able to attain to a full measure of success, for this success comes only as a result of full and prosperous crops, which, in turn, come only from treatment of the land by modern methods Among the progressive farmers of Cass county, who have recognized the value of using up-to-date measures in their work, William H. Stoughton, of Noble township holds a prominent position He is a native of Cass county, and was born February 22, 1858, a son of Ira and Nancy (Mathews) Stoughton

Ira Stoughton was born in New York, and was married October 17, 1852, to Nancy Mathews, a native of Indiana They settled down on a farm in Cass county, and their children were all born here, as follows: Horace, September 24, 1853, Mary E, January 8, 1856, William H; and Elsie J, June 18, 1873. Horace was married first to Martha E. Helvey, deceased, who was the mother of four children, Arthur G, Lutie, who died at the age of six years, Leora, who married in November, 1900 Edward Smith, a farmer of Roann, Indiana, who has one child.—Arthur M., and a child who died in infancy. Mr. Stoughton married for his second wife Ollie Miller, of Ohio, and they have had one child, who died at an early age. Mary E. Stoughton was married April 7, 1880, to Allen G. Benton, of Cass county. Elsie J. Stoughton was married May 15, 1902, to Harry A. Jamison, who is connected with the Vandalia line of the Pennsylvania system.

William H. Stoughton was educated in the common schools of Noble township and his entire career has been devoted to farming and stock raising. On March 9, 1880 he was married to Miss Hattie E. Michael, of Cass county, daughter of Charles and Lucy A. (Bowyer) Michael, who were long residents of Cass county. Mrs. Stoughton was educated in the schools of this county. In the fall of 1880, Mr. and Mrs. Stoughton went West, and for about five years were residents of Southern Illinois. While there, October 30, 1884, a son, Ira Ray, was born to them. They subsequently lived for about nine years in Southwestern Kansas, and then moved on to Texas. They were living in the Lone Star State in 1900 when the terrible flood caused such damage to the city of Galveston and it appears as though only a dispensation of Providence saved their lives. At the time the storm began Mrs. Stoughton was at home with her son, and as the hurricane increased she became alarmed and with great difficulty managed to make her way to the home of a neighbor. They had not yet reached their refuge when a terrific blast struck the little home which they had just left, completely demolishing it, with all the other buildings on the place casting its timbers some thirty rods distant and driving great beams so deep in the ground that later they could not be extracted by the utmost exertions of a strong man. There is no doubt but that Mrs. Stoughton and her son would have been killed had they remained in their own home. In the meantime Mr. Stoughton who had started home when the storm began to threaten to become serious, was overtaken by the terrific hurricane some seven miles from home, and there was compelled to remain himself suffering greatly as well as being in an agony of anxiety as to the welfare of his loved ones whom he was powerless to help.

When the little family was again readjusted, Mr. Stoughton gathered his scattered belongings together and returned to Cass county, and here his son continued the studies started in Texas, completing them in the commercial college at Logansport. He is now engaged in assisting his father in the work of the home farm which has been brought to a high state of cultivation, and has been improved with good buildings and modern appliances. In political matters, Mr. Stoughton is a stalwart Prohibitionist although his only interest in public matters is that taken by every good citizen and voter. With his family he attends the Presbyterian church.

WILLIAM RILEY. Classed among the prominent and enterprising farmers of Washington township is found William Riley, another of the men whose success in life has been gained through the medium of their own efforts. From boyhood when he was left an orphan Mr. Riley's life has been one of incessant industry, and in the face of discouragement and misfortune, he has slowly but surely worked his way up the ladder of success, and his efforts have been rewarded by the accumulation of a fine farm of eighty-five acres lying on the Riley road, about seven miles from Logansport. Mr. Riley was born June 15, 1851, in the city of Cleveland, Ohio, and is a son of Andrew and Catherine (Hoover) Riley. His father, a marble cutter by trade, came to Indiana when a young man and took up land in Cass county, but subsequently entered the railroad contracting business, and in that line was engaged at the time of his death. At that time William Riley was but seven years of age, and during the next three years he lived with an elder brother. The latter, however, enlisted in the Union army at the outbreak of the Civil war, and the youth was left alone in the world. After drifting around for some time, seeking a home he was taken in charge by his uncle, on whose farm he was reared and who gave him the advantages of a country school education. Mr. Riley continued to reside with his uncle until he was twenty-seven years of age, in the meantime carefully saving his earnings, with the end ever in view of one day being a property owner himself. His ambition was realized, in 1878, when he became the owner of his present property, a tract of eighty-five acres of fine land, which he has brought to a high state of cultivation. From time to time, as his finances permitted and circumstances demanded Mr. Riley added to the buildings and improvements on his land, thus adding to the value of a property that in itself was of much worth. He has devoted himself to general farming, and has also been successful in the raising of livestock. This land was all cleared by Mr. Riley from its virgin state, and its present condition reflects great credit upon his industry, enterprise and good management. The multitudinous duties of his work have precluded the idea of his entering the political field as a seeker for personal preferment, but he has observed the duties of good citizenship, and has given of his time and means in supporting movements for the public welfare.

On October 8, 1882, Mr. Riley was united in marriage with Miss Charlotte Gotschall, and to this union there have been born three children, as follows: Maude, who married Fred Stackhouse, a Cass county farmer, and has one child,—Ray Harvey, who is single and lives on the home farm, which he is assisting his father to cultivate; and Katie, who also lives with her parents. The family belongs to the United Brethren church in which all of its members have numerous friends. The life of Mr. Riley is worthy of emulation by aspiring youths and teaches the lesson that integrity and industry are bound to bring success.

H. HARVEY GOTSHALL. Among the agriculturists of the second generation who are carrying on the work that their fathers commenced in the development of Cass county, Harvey Gotshall is entitled to prominent mention. He was born on the old Gotshall homestead in Washington township, December 16, 1866, and is a son of Henry and Maria J. (Rodrick) Gotshall.

Peter Gotshall, the grandfather of Harvey Gotshall, was a native of Pennsylvania, and in 1837, with a large party of emigrants seeking homes in what was then the far West, with twenty-eight teams altogether, came by way of Pittsburgh, Pennsylvania, and Richmond, Indiana, with the intention of settling in Illinois. On the way, however, Mr.

Gotshall stopped for a visit in Indiana, and was so attracted by the community that he rented a piece of land eight miles south of Terre Haute, on which he remained until 1845, in that year coming to Cass county, and settling in Noble township Here he spent the remainder of his life in agricultural pursuits, dying in 1857, when fifty-seven years of age He married Ann Woodling, who survived him until seventy-nine years of age, and they had a family of seven children. John, who resided in Kansas City, Missouri, Henry the father of Harvey, Elizabeth, deceased, Frank, Jacob and Eliza, who were residents of Noble township, and Alva, deceased

Henry Gotshall was born April 25, 1827, in Pennsylvania, and was ten years of age when his parents emigrated to Indiana His early education was secured in the primitive subscription schools, and it was not until he was twenty-one years of age that he secured advantages in the first free school taught in the state The entire subsequent period of his active life was devoted to farming, and his success was commensurate with the hard, intelligent and persistent labor which he expended upon his work He was a Whig and later a Republican in politics, although only a voter, and with his family attended the German Baptist church Mr Gotshall was married to Mary J Rodrick a native of Maryland, who came as a child to Washington township and they became the parents of the following children Sarah, who died leaving five children, Alice, who died at the age of seven years, Charlotte who married Wil-William Riley and has three children Hamlin Franklin, deceased, who lived on a portion of his father's land, Amanda, who married Charles Wilson, of Tipton township, and had two children; and Harvey

Harvey Gotshall received his education in the country schools of Washington township, which he attended during the winter terms, his summers being devoted to the work of the home place He has always devoted himself to agricultural pursuits, and at this time is the owner of 64 acres of good land in Washington township, where he raises large crops and breeds valuable live stock Like his father, he is known as a good, practical agriculturist, and one who takes advantage of new methods and modern farming machinery, and his property shows the presence of good management

In March 1907, Mr Gotshall was married to Miss Hattie Amen, daughter of David and Mary (Hunter) Amen, and they have one child in the family, Everett Mr Gotshall has never sought public office, preferring to devote his entire time to the cultivation of his land He is a public-spirited citizen, however, and lends his support to all progressive movements in the way of education, religion and good citizenship

WILLIS R TOUSLEY Fifty years in the service and still at the key, such is the record of W R Tousley, of Anoka, one of the oldest operators of the Pittsburgh, Chicago & St Louis Railroad Railroading in all of its various branches attracts young men, there is something about the glamour of the vocation that draws youths from every walk of life It is also true that commensurate rewards and steady employment are given those who are willing to work hard, to place their company's interests before their own, to at all times sacrifice self for the service for those who are not willing to do so, and who have not the necessary ability, the great railroad systems have little use. The railroad man is a soldier no less than he who fights under his country's flag, his first duty is to obey orders absolutely. It will thus be seen that a man who has remained in the service for one of the large transportation companies for a period covering a half a century of time, must necessarily be possessed of the qualities of intelligence, integrity, faithfulness to duty and keen perception, and all of these Mr Tousley possesses in no small degree. Although he has reached an age when most men are willing to retire from active labor, and is the owner of a comfortable home which the years of constant industry have secured for him, like others before him he feels himself bound by the ties of loyalty to his company, and is loath to leave its service.

Mr. Tousley was born February 19, 1848, at Clinton, Michigan, and is a son of Isaac and Julia (Murdock) Tousley. His father came from the East, in young manhood, settling first in Michigan, and later in 1851 coming to Logansport, where he followed merchandising and painting as a contractor up to the time of his death. He and his wife were the parents of five children, as follows: Edwin, W R , Henry, Charles who is deceased, and Fannie.

W R Tousley was little more than two years old when he was brought to Logansport by his parents, and here he received his first instruction in the old public school at Tenth and Market streets. Subsequently, he attended the old Stone Seminary and the high school, but when his father died he was compelled to seek employment, and accordingly became a messenger boy in the service of the Pittsburgh, Chicago and St Louis Railroad, with which he has been connected in one capacity or another to the present time. He was advanced to the position of agent after some time, his evident endeavor to properly perform his duties attracting the attention of his employers, and while thus engaged he learned telegraphy, eventually becoming an operator. It was in that capacity that Mr Tousley came to this junction, one of the important points on the line, where he still continues to faithfully perform his duties, one of his company's most trusted employes.

Mr Tousley was married twice, first to Miss Alice Jack and one child was born, Charles E. Mrs Tousley died and Mr Tousley wedded the sister to his first wife, Miss Sarah Jack, and four children graced this union, namely: M G , C A , Lillian, and C T. Mr Tousley is a member of the Masonic lodge of Walton, Indiana, and the I O O F. at Anoka, Indiana, and in both orders he enjoys the true friendship and brotherhood of the orders. His political inclinations are in sympathy with the Democratic party, although he has never cared nor sought for public office. He has been thrifty and industrious, and is now the owner of a pleasant home in Anoka, as well as a farm of one hundred and twenty acres in Washington township, the latter of which is being operated by renters. Mr Tousley is respected and esteemed by all who have his acquaintance, as a man who has lived an upright and honorable life, and as a citizen who has ever held the best interests of his community at heart.

JAMES HORNEY No longer does the traveler through Cass county view neglected farms and poor, unremunerative stock, the agriculturists of this section today being men of experience and ability However, it is not every farm that shows the same sleek and shining cattle, well nurtured and thoroughbred in appearance, that may be found on the handsome, highly-cultivated farm belonging to James Horney, in Noble township Mr. Horney is a native of Cass county and has passed his entire life here, being thoroughly familiar with soil and climatic conditions, and thus able to manage his operations satisfactorily He was born February 10, 1849, and is a son of James and Matilda (Page) Horney

James Horney, Sr, was born in North Carolina, October 18 1804, and his wife, a native of Virginia, was born March 6, 1816. He came to Cass county in 1829, and in 1836 James Horney, Sr, was sheriff of the county, being later elected associate judge with Judges Biddle and Wright For a number of years he held the office of township trustee, and during the drafting period of the Civil war was chosen by a number of drafted citizens to take a voluntary contribution of $2,700 to Indianapolis to buy up substitutes to take their places This he succeeded in doing and returning home within twenty-four hours. He died February 6, 1882, on his farm, after a life given in large part to the benefit of his fellowmen, and one which left a distinct impress upon his community. His widow survived him some years, and passed away April 9, 1898

James Horney, Jr.. was educated in the district schools of Noble township, to which community he had been brought with two older children when a mere child He was reared to farming pursuits, which he has followed all of his life, and in connection with which he was for some years an extensive buyer of timber for James Van Buskirk, a dealer of Logansport Like his father, Mr Horney bears an enviable reputation in business circles, and is known as an able farmer and good citizen On November 4, 1875, Mr Horney was married to Miss Nancy J Wilson, daughter of John and Keziah (Maple) Wilson, and one of eleven children About 1836 the parents of Mrs Horney came to Cass county with their two oldest children, locating in Lewisburg By trade Mr Wilson was a blacksmith and at Lewis he established himself in business, a great deal of his trade being with the Indians in sharpening arrowpoints, etc , and he also did a large business shoeing horses for the boatmen on the canal that ran through Logansport. An incident worthy of note, in that it shows his ability and good workmanship, relates of his shoeing a team of oxen for a company of young men en route to California, these shoes not being removed until the party reached its destination some six months later During the Civil war, he purchased a farm in Miami township, and there he resided for some forty years, dying about the year 1901.

Two children have been born to Mr and Mrs Horney, namely Harry D , born August 23, 1878, and George A , born July 4, 1884

Mrs Horney was born in Lewisburg, Indiana August 5, 1850, and there reared and educated in the common schools She is a devout member of the Baptist church Both of the sons of Mr and Mrs Horney are living, the eldest is Harry D , born August 23, 1878 He received his diploma from the common schools and pursued a full commercial course at Logansport He has been an accountant, working for one firm in Philadelphia, Pennsylvania, for fifteen years He is now an agriculturist and a resident of Braidentown, Florida He wedded Miss Harriett F Jordan, and she is a member of the Baptist church He is a Republican George A, born July 4, 1884, also received his diploma one of the highest grades in the county at that time, then he was a student in the Logansport high school and subsequently took a commercial course, at the Logansport Commercial College. He married Miss Hazel H De Laroter (whose progenitors were French) and they have one little son, Richard Albert, aged two years. George is a carpenter by trade. He was a member of the Indiana National Guards, and his wife has embroidered a handsome piece of embroidery—exhibiting all the officers' and guards' names in beautiful needlework. Mrs Horney received her diploma from the public schools and was one of eighty-one who passed the examinations, and one of the number was a great-granddaughter of the old Indian Chief Godfrey In politics Mr Horney was a Republican until recent years, but now believes in voting rather for the man than the party. He has never been an office seeker himself, having been content to confine his activities to the cultivation of his land

Mr and Mrs James Horney of this sketch have one hundred and twelve acres of good land in Noble township They passed the winter of 1912 in Florida Their comfortable home lies on the Pleasant Grove Pike, two miles north of the city, and is known as "Forest Home," the abode of hospitality

HARRY FULTZ One of the most successful farming men to be found in this section of Cass county may be designated in the person of Harry Fultz, who has a fine farm of eighty acres in Noble township, where he is regarded among the most prosperous and influential of the citizens of his community.

Harry Fultz was born in Logansport, on July 26, 1871, and is the son of Andrew J and Julia Ann (Boyer) Fultz The father was an Ohioan, born in Stark county, where his people had long lived, and the mother came from Pennsylvania in 1868, settling in Edward township. Her people were of German descent. Andrew J and Julia Fultz became the parents of three sons, two of whom died young,—Charles when six years of age and Lawrence in infancy. Harry being the only surviving child of his parents

When he was a child, the parents of Harry Fultz moved to Peoria, Illinois, and from there located in Iowa They later moved back to Indiana, settling in Noble township and here Mr Fultz lives today on the farm they occupied there in his boyhood Concerning the father of Mr Fultz, it may be said that he was born in Stark county, Ohio, on August 31, 1844 His mother died in 1854, when he was but ten years old, and when he was sixteen having been accustomed to making his own way for some years, he engaged in railroad work,—a business he followed with great success until 1898 He was an engineer on the road for twenty-eight years and he has the distinction of having run the first coal burning engine from Logansport to Chicago over the Chicago

& Great Eastern Railroad After leaving off railroad work, Mr Fultz settled on a farm in the vicinity of Logansport, and there lived until the time of his death

It was the occupation of the father in his capacity as a railroad engineer that necessitated the several changes of residence that Harry Fultz experienced as a boy These changes, however, it is safe to say did him no harm, and he has for some years been devoting himself to the farm work with an intensity and fervor that have won him success and well-being in a financial way, and the regard and esteem of all who regard with favor the energetic application of a man's best qualities in the work he sets himself to do

On February 7, 1895, Mr Fultz married Miss Lena Quade, the daughter of Frank L Quade and his wife, Louise (Schwab) Quade, and they have three children Burton, born June 15, 1896, LeRoy, born July 11 1904, and Alice, born February 27, 1905

The family are members of the Presbyterian church, and Mr Fultz maintains an independent attitude in his political activities

CHARLES B E YOUNG One of the business men of Logansport, whose activities have covered a period of twenty-two years, and whose energy, sagacity and industry have enabled him to build up a large and important enterprise, is Charles B E Young, proprietor of a harness store, where are also sold carriages, automobiles and their accessories Mr Young has been a resident of Cass county since his second year, was reared and educated here, and here received his business training His actions at all times have entitled him to the respect and esteem of his fellow-men and as a public-spirited citizen he has rendered signal service to his community in assisting to a successful conclusion many movements for the public welfare Mr. Young was born in Franklin county, Indiana, February 14, 1863, and is a son of Alexander and Susan (Teague) Young

Alexander Young and wife, with their three children, Carrie Alta R (since deceased) and Charles B E, came to Cass county in 1865, locating on a farm nine miles east of Logansport, on Pipe creek After their arrival here another son, Albert, was born Alexander Young was a farmer all of his life, and attained a reasonable amount of success, but passed away when still in middle life, February 12, 1872 His widow still survives him, as do also three of their children During the Civil war, Mr Young was a member of the Indiana Home Guards that repelled the attack of the raiding Confederate general, Morgan

Charles B E Young grew up on the family farm on Pipe Creek, his boyhood being passed in assisting his father, and during the winter terms he acquired his education in the country district and public schools of Logansport Just prior to attaining his majority, he became a drug clerk in Logansport, continuing in that business for seven years For one year succeeding this he traveled for a wholesale cigar and tea house of Indianapolis, but in 1891 decided to enter business on his own account, and accordingly, on August 1st of that year, purchased the harness shop of Charles McNitt He has continued to be the proprietor of this establishment to the present time, and of recent years has added carriages and automobiles and their accessories to his stock His business has enjoyed a steady and healthy growth, yielding commensurate returns for the labors of Mr. Young who is an energetic, though well-balanced, business man. In national affairs, Mr Young gives his political support to the Republican party, but in local matters reserves the right to vote for the man he deems best fitted for the office, irrespective of party lines He is a Royal Arch Mason and a member of the Independent Order of Odd Fellows, takes much interest in fraternal work, and is popular with his fellow lodge members

On June 8, 1893, Mr Young was united in marriage with Miss Sarah F. Place, and they have become the parents of three children: Helen, Clark and Frances Mrs Young is a member of the Methodist Episcopal church, where she has a wide circle of sincere friends

JOHN T FLANEGIN Thirty-three years ago, John T Flanegin came to Logansport and opened a modest stove and tinware store, taking a position among the early merchants of Market street, where he has since continued his operations During the period to the present time he has enlarged his establishment and his stock, which now includes general shelf hardware, and today he is known as one of the substantial veteran business men of the city Mr Flanegin was born on Raccoon creek, in Washington county, Pennsylvania, July 11, 1847. He is one of two children, both living, born to John and Mary (Johnston) Flanegin, who were natives of Pennsylvania and descended from Irish parentage In the old country, the name was Flanekin, but for some unknown reason the name here has been spelled in its present style

John T Flanegin was reared in southeastern Ohio, whence his parents removed when he was a boy, and there received his education in the public schools When fifteen years of age he became a clerk in a general store at Zanesvile, Ohio, and subsequently held a like position in a store at Pittsburgh, Pennsylvania For some years following, he was engaged in working out at various occupations, such as herding cattle, clerking, driving drays and various other vocations, but upon the sickness and subsequent death of his father he returned to the Ohio town, where he resided until 1880 That year saw his advent in Logansport, and marked the beginning of his successful career as a merchant. Having had some experience in the tinware business, he opened a shop, and also installed a line of stoves, and to this, with the passing of years, he added general shelf hardware. Coming here in moderate circumstances, through industry, energy and an intelligent comprehension of the needs of his locality, he has built up a business that has gained him a position of prestige among his fellow merchants He is known as strictly reliable in all his dealings, having an enviable reputation for integrity, and among his associates is recognized as a shrewd and capable business man, possessed of foresight and acumen An American first, last and all the time, he endeavors to lend his influence to the cause of good government and general progress, and those movements which promise the advancement of his community's interests are sure to find in him a loyal supporter In his political proclivities he is a Democrat, although he has never sought personal preferment in the public arena Mr Flanegin has taken some interest in fraternal matters, being a member of the Masons, the Knights of Pythias and the

Benevolent and Protective Order of Elks, in all of which he is popular with his fellow members

On January 6, 1875, Mr Flanegin was married to Miss Alice A. Moore, of Bloomington, Illinois, and to this union there have been born three children: Blanch, who became the wife of C L. Baker, Thomas J, and Lorin A Mrs Flanegin died February 3, 1910, in the faith of the Presbyterian church, of which her husband is a member.

GEORGE A LINTON is one of the oldest native-born citizens of Logansport, his birth having occurred in this city August 9, 1848, on North street, in the second house east of the present site of the Masonic Temple Samuel B Linton, his father was born at Chillicothe, Ohio, and was a carpenter and contractor, coming to Logansport in that capacity in 1825, when there were but three houses in the place He did not remain long at that time, but moved on to LaFayette, where he continued to reside for two years, but in 1827 settled permanently in Logansport, where he made his home during the balance of his life He here worked at his trade, but with the passing of time the structures erected by him have been rebuilt In addition to a number of residences and business establishments, he built two canal boats to ply on the Erie canal and these he operated from shortly after the completion of the canal until the year 1840 Joseph Dale was associated with him in the building of one of these boats Attracted by the glowing reports from the gold fields of California, Mr Linton started overland for that locality in the spring of 1852 and was there three years, building flumes and flatboats on Feather river and at Sacramento He returned to the east in 1855, but again returned to California in 1859, to recuperate his failing health, going by boat around Cape Horn, a trip that lasted six months Seeing the futility of his mission he remained there but a short time returning to Logansport and dying in July, 1860 He was married twice, first to a Miss Blaine, a cousin of the Hon James G Blaine, and she bore him seven children, none of whom are now living His second wife was Eliza Dale, daughter of Christopher Dale, who bore him two children Thomas, who died in infancy, and George A Mr Linton was a man rather small in stature, weighing about 150 pounds His frequent association with the Indians enabled him to speak the Pottawatomie and Miami tongues Resolute and firm he never embarked on any undertaking without carrying it into execution In his later life he joined the Methodist Episcopal church and died in that faith He was a Whig in politics and later became a Republican, and served Logansport as town marshal in 1857 and 1858

George A Linton has always claimed Logansport as his home, although he has not lived here continuously He received his education in the public and paid schools of this city. On February 4, 1862, when not yet fourteen years of age he enlisted in the field service in the Union army and was assigned to duty in Knetucky, under General Nelson, for whom he was mounted orderly. In February, 1863, he was sent back to procure horses and while there his guardian, Capt Alexander Hardy, who had been made such while young Linton was at the front, secured him and permitted him to enlist in the Twenty-fourth

Indiana Light Artillery He participated in the pursuit of General Morgan, who had made raids into Indiana and Ohio, and from here went into Eastern Tennessee, under General Burnside. They were penned in at Knoxville until relieved after the battle of Missionary Ridge, and from Knoxville (including all the attendant campaigns preceding and following the battle) went to Charleston, Tennessee, in the spring of 1864 There the command was merged with the Second Brigade Twenty-third Army Corps, under General Schofield, and entered the Atlanta campaign, having seen the first engagement at Snake Creek Gap, Dalton, and the continuous fighting until July 21 It was at the battle of Kenesaw Mountain that Capt Alexander Hardy, commanding the company of which Mr. Linton was a member, fired the gun loaded with a spherical shell that killed General Pope After the fall of Atlanta, Mr. Linton was a member of the command that pursued General Hood north and participated in the battles of Franklin and Nashville. Here they went into camp at Fort Negley, and this, with the exception of some guerilla fighting, completed Mr Linton's military career. He was wounded at Leonore's Station, through the left wrist and arm, and was discharged August 3, 1865, at Indianapolis, by order of the War Department

Returning to Logansport, he was engaged in the occupations of peace until February, 1867, when he enlisted in the general field service of the Regular Army and was stationed at Vicksburg, Mississippi, there passing safely through the cholera epidemic. He was then assigned to the Eleventh United States Infantry of the Fifth Military District, which comprised Mississippi, Louisiana and Texas, and was under the command of Gen Joe Reynolds, at San Antonio, Texas, being detailed to the Mounted Police whose duty it was to quell the disturbances of the frontier desperadoes, the Indians and the off-scourings of both armies, and in general to see that law and order were maintained He was finally discharged March 4, 1870 He returned at that time to Logansport and for a time was engaged in railroad work, but in 1879 embarked in the pump and well business, in which he continued until 1895 Since that time he has been associated with Adam Graf in the plumbing and heating business A thoroughly reliable and capable business man, Mr Linton has the confidence and esteem of his associates, and his judgment is always consulted on questions of importance He is a Republican in politics, but has not entered actively in the struggles of the public arena, for his whole attention has been given to his business enterprises He takes a keen and intelligent interest in the welfare of his city and its people, however, and always supports measures that make for good government and good citizenship He is a valued member of the local lodge of Masons and has risen to the Knight Templar degree

On June 11 1870, Mr Linton was married to Miss Mary E Emery, and they have had eight children, as follows· Horace B , Minnie, who married William R Cogley, Gertrude, who married M McMeans, Mary E, who became the wife of L E Slick, Elizabeth, Alice and Carrie, who are deceased, and Charles A Mrs Linton died July 14, 1912, in the faith of the Methodist Episcopal church, of which Mr Linton is a consistent member and liberal supporter.

JOHN ALBER, for many years identified with the crockery business in Logansport, and one of the widely known and prominent business men of the city, was born in Logansport, Indiana, on September 11, 1852. He is the son of Jacob Alber, who was a native of Lichtenstein, Austria, and his wife, Sophia Dierkson, a native of Bremen, Germany.

Jacob Alber learned the trade of a housepainter and decorator in his native land and in Italy, and in 1848, or thereabouts, he emigrated to the United States. He first located at Wabash, Indiana, but in 1849 came down the canal to Logansport, where he began working at his trade. He also became connected with the trade of a stone mason, and worked for a time as a bricklayer, as well as at various other employments of a kindred nature. In 1850 he met and married Sophia Dierkson. She came to Baltimore with a family of the name of Albers, and from there to Indiana with the family of James G. Cox, who settled in Bethlehem township, in Cass county, Indiana. There they were married, and during the remainder of his life Jacob Alber worked at his trade in and about Logansport. He was ever a hard-working and industrious man and in later life was reckoned fairly well-to-do. He was twice married. By his first wife he became the father of two children,— John and Philip, the latter of whom died at the age of two years.

The father, who was born January 7, 1821, died July 24, 1891, and the mother, born on May 15, 1813, died April 4, 1883.

John Alber is the only surviving child of his father. He was educated in the public schools of Logansport, and at Notre Dame University, from which he was graduated in 1868. His first employment upon leaving college was a clerk in the store of Mitchell, Walker & Rauch, boot and shoe dealers of Logansport, and he remained with them for a year. He then accepted a position with Morris & Snider, as a clerk in their crockery establishment, then as traveling salesman. In 1880 he severed his connection with that firm and began traveling for Hollweg & Reese, wholesale crockery dealers of Indianapolis, and for twenty-nine years Mr. Alber remained with them with the exception of a two-year-period when, in partnership with W. H. Snider, he was engaged in the wholesale and retail crockery business in Logansport. When that association was suspended Mr. Alber resumed his old place with the Indianapolis house, continuing with them until 1909. In that year he again embarked in the wholesale and retail crockery business in Logansport, and again his business partner was W. H. Snider. On January 17, 1911, Mr. Alber bought his partner's interest in the business and has since conducted it alone, with a pleasing degree of success.

Mr. Alber is a Republican in his politics. He is a Mason of the Scottish Rite branch, and a member of the Knights Templar and Murat Temple of the Ancient Arabic Order of the Nobles of the Mystic Shrine.

On April 14, 1879, Mr. Alber married Miss Betty B. Dawes, daughter of Elisha Dawes, and they have one daughter,—Aline Sophia, now the wife of Joseph T. Graffis, whose home is at Indianapolis. Mrs. Alber is a member of the Episcopal church.

HENRY TUCKER, for forty-seven years a resident of Logansport, is of New England nativity, his birth occurring in the village of Norway, Maine, on March 27, 1843. His paternal grandfather located at that place in the year 1802 and established himself in the harness and saddlery business, and upon his death he was succeeded by his son, Benjamin, and a son of the latter succeeded him, at the close of the Civil war, in which he served in the Army of the Potomac. Upon his death a nephew took over the business, and he continues in it to the present time, thus making four generations of the Tucker family in a direct line to have conducted the harness and saddlery business in Norway, Maine.

Benjamin Tucker was the father of Henry Tucker. He was born at Norway, Maine, there married Sarah Millett, the mother of Henry, and passed his life in the place of his birth, employed in the business which descended to him on the death of his father.

Henry Tucker attended the district schools and the academy in his boyhood, and learned the harness and saddle-making trade under his father. While he was yet a boy, on November 9, 1861, he enlisted in Company G, Fourteenth Maine Volunteer Infantry, receiving the appointment of corporal of his company. In 1862 he was promoted to sergeant and with his regiment became a part of the command of Gen B F. Butler, on the expedition to Ship Island, Mississippi, and thence to New Orleans, arriving at the latter place the day Mumford was hanged by order of General Butler for pulling down the American flag from the city hall. By reason of ill health, Mr Tucker received an honorable discharge from the service on July 5, 1862, and for some time thereafter was unable to actively engage in any arduous undertaking On May 1 1864, his strength renewed by his continued relaxation from duty, he reenlisted and became first sergeant of Company H, Maine State Guards, stationed at Fort McClary, Portsmouth Harbor. He received his final discharge on July 4, 1864

Mr Tucker then determined that his education was not sufficiently complete, and he accordingly took a course of study in the Business College of Bryant & Stratton at Portland, Maine, after which he set out for the west in search of a favorable locality in which to engage in business. For a year he made his home at Elgin, Illinois, but in April, 1866, he came to Logansport, Indiana, and in the following August he bought the J W Fuller harness shop. Here for a period of nearly forty years Mr. Tucker was engaged in the business at that stand, and in the course of his business transactions during that time gained an acquaintance with almost every man in Cass county. For the past few years, however, Mr Tucker has been occupied with the undertaking business, in which he has experienced a goodly measure of success.

In the quiet, unobtrusive way which characterizes Mr. Tucker, he has lived so as to leave an indelible impress for good upon every enterprise with which he has been identified. He is a Mason, having joined the order in Maine many years ago, but is now a member of Orient Lodge No. 272 A F. & A M of Logansport, of which he has served as worshipful master. He is also a member of Logan Chapter No 2, of Logansport, the Council No 11 of Logansport and St. John Commandery, No 24, serving as eminent commander in 1881-82, and the oldest in point of membership of the Scottish Rite in the county. He is also a member of Logansport Post No. 14 Grand Army of the Republic

Mr Tucker has been twice married. In 1871 he married Emma Stalnaker, who died about one year later. In 1876 he married Julia Merriam, daughter of J A. Merriam, one of the leading business men of Logansport, and they are the parents of two daughters,—Minnie and Florence both of whom are married Minnie is the wife of N. W Blemming, now living in Fort Scott, Kansas, and Florence is married to J. Burt Winter, of the firm of Elias Winter & Son, who was born and has always lived in Logansport

ISAAC HIMMELBERGER was one of the noted men of Cass county and was always a credit to the community wherein he made his home He was born August 13, 1840, in Berks county, Pennsylvania, and was one of seven children born to Charles Himmelberger and his wife, Lavinia (Hain) Himmelberger.

Reared at Lancaster as a boy, Isaac Himmelberger received not more than a common school education. When he was eighteen years old he moved with his parents to Meyerstown, Pennsylvania, and there he was later associated with his father in the milling business, and still later with an uncle, Levi Hain, in the grain business. From Meyerstown he came to Indiana in 1865, and with Levi Hain, Henry Sherk and John Myers, engaged in the lumber business about two miles north of the town of Walton, in Tipton county. Here they established a sawmill in the swamp, acquired a tract of three hundred and eighty acres, and at once began to convert the towering timber into lumber When the work here had been completed and the supply of raw material been exhausted, Mr Himmelberger and Perry Kessling leased a tract of land near Onward, there erected a mill, and began the work of sawing as they had done near Walton Mr Himmelberger then came to Logansport and in partnership with a Mr Dewey, built a mill and established a general lumber business, buying timber throughout the entire country surrounding them It was during this time, in 1878, that he became the candidate of the Republican party for the office of sheriff of the county, and notwithstanding the fact that the nominal Democratic majority in the county was something like six hundred, Mr Himmeberger was elected He served a two year term in the office of Sheriff, and it was during this period that he bought out his partner's interests in the business. Soon after his retirement from office he went to Buffington, Missouri, and there started a sawmill, moving the equipment from Logansport to the Missouri town, to augment the equipment of the mill already in operation there A few years later he formed a partnership with John Burris in the stave business at Dexter, Missouri, in connection with his other business, and this partnership existed but a comparatively short time, but Mr. Himmelberger still continued the lumber business at Buffington, Missouri, and later at Morehouse, Missouri, a place of which he was really the founder and builder His son, John, was associated with him at these two latter places At Morehouse he built one of the largest hardwood lumber plants ever known in the southwest, if not, indeed, in the entire country. They acquired approximately 100,000 acres of land and at times employed more than two hundred mill hands. Mr Himmelberger, while yet in the prime of life and while the future yet held glowing promise of attainment, was suddenly stricken with an illness which culminated in his death on July 16, 1900

His was a life that held many lessons He began his independent

career without other means than his own courage and willing hands His courage never faltered in all the years of his activity, and repeatedly he was called upon to overcome obstacles that would have overwhelmed many with dismay, and would have been the sure defeat of many another Through all the years he steadily pressed forward, achieving a success far beyond that which the average man meets At no time was the honesty and fairness of his dealings ever questioned With him "whatever was worth doing at all was worth doing well" and that old axiom he held up for the constant admonition of all who were associated with him in his work He died as he had lived,—an honored and respected citizen, and his untimely death was deeply mourned by all who came within the circle of his acquaintance

In 1860 Mr Himmelberger was married to Catherine Haak, and seven children were born to them, four of whom lived to reach years of maturity, as follows John, who is now engaged in conducting the business in Missouri which was founded by his father, Jane, the wife of Samuel Fisher, Lillia, the wife of H. J Crismond, and Nettie, who married W. O Murdock, and is now deceased Mrs Himmelberger, who still lives and is the grandmother of twelve children, is the daughter of Henry and Sarah (Bassler) Haak, who were natives of the state of Pennsylvania, and like the Himmelbergers people of German ancestry.

JOHN W GUARD was born in Dixon, Illinois, on March 1, 1863, and is one of the five children of John L and Anna Mary (Gable) Guard, all of the five being alive today

John L Guard, the father of the subject, was a minister of the English Lutheran church, an occupation which he followed all through his busy and active life He was a native of Virginia, descended from German-Hessian ancestry, and his wife's people originally came from Bavaria Rev John L Guard died in Carroll county, Indiana, on October 18, 1895, and his wife died in Peoria county Illinois, in March, 1868

Carroll county, Indiana, was the home of John W. Guard until he was fifteen Camden was the town where he was reared, and he lived on a farm between the ages of fifteen and twenty-one He received his preliminary education in the common schools of his community further advantages not being afforded him In 1885 he came to Logansport, Indiana, and there engaged in the draying business, which appeared to him to offer a chance of success He handled the draying contracts for Elliott, Stroyer & Company, wholesale grocers, they being among his largest patrons, and after he gave up draying he was for three years engaged in ranching in southwestern Kansas, after which he returned to Logansport, in 1890, and for sixteen years thereafter was employed as a clerk in the retail grocery store of Lewis Ray He then bought an interest in the Rice Hardware Company, and has since been engaged in that business, at present being the treasurer of the corporation

Mr Guard is a Republican, and his fraternal relations are with the Masons, in which he is a member of Tipton Lodge No 33, A F & A M He is a member of St Luke's English Lutheran church, as is also his wife, who was Miss Anna Hildebrandt, and to whom he was married on November 23, 1903

MOSES R. FRAZEE. With the exception of a four years' period which he spent in Minneapolis, Minnesota, Moses R. Frazee has been a resident of Logansport for the past fifty-two years. He was born on August 26, 1834, in Miami county, Ohio, a son of David and Mary (Price) Frazee. The father of David Frazee came to America from the Isle of Jersey, and the mother was a native of Wales. David Frazee was a farmer and Moses R. made his home upon the farm home until he was about fifteen years old. He helped with the work of the home place as a boy and attended the old fashioned school common to his time, finishing his schooling with two years in the schools of Piqua. After this latter experience he clerked in a general store for something like two years, in the employ of I. B. Whipple. He then went to Marion and managed a store which Mr. Whipple owned there, and some fifteen months later, in 1857, he came to Logansport. Here Mr. Frazee embarked in a general dry goods business on his own responsibility. His stock in the early days consisted of boots, shoes, general dry goods, produce and clothing. He sold his store in 1866 and went to Minneapolis, where with his brother-in-law, William Murphy, he built a flouring mill and for four years was engaged in the milling business. This was one of the old stone buhr mills and had a capacity of three hundred barrels daily. During this time the firm of Frazee & Murphy had sold a two-thirds interest in the business, and finally disposed of the remaining one-third to Charles Pillsbury, and under his management and eventual control the mill was changed over to the patent roller process, and made millions for its owners. Mr. Frazee returned to Logansport in 1870 and once more embarked in the dry goods business, in which he has been continuously engaged since that time, and he is the oldest merchant now doing business in this city.

On August 21, 1864, Mr. Frazee was united in marriage with Miss Mary Higgins, a daughter of Capt. A. M. Higgins, who was one of the early and well known men of the county. Three children were born to Mr. and Mrs. Frazee, as follows: Helen, who died in infancy, Jessie, who lived to be five years old, and Stuart R., who died on November 20, 1912. The wife and mother died on November 5, 1902.

Mr. Frazee is a Republican and cast his first presidential vote for John C. Fremont. He is one of the best known men in Logansport, esteemed by a large circle of friends and acquaintances who have known him for many years as one of the substantial citizens of Logansport.

WILLARD ELLIOTT. Among the old and honored families of Cass county whose members have been identified with the growth and development of their section's commercial, industrial and agricultural importance, that of Elliott is among the best known. Its members have for years resided in Harrison township where the history of the family has been commensurate with that of the community, and have contributed in no small degree to its public service. A worthy representative of the name is found in Willard Elliott, of Logansport, assistant clerk at the City Light Company, and a man who has represented his city and county in various positions of trust and responsibility. Mr. Elliott was born December 26, 1868, in Harrison township, and is a son of Alfred and Emily (Williamson) Elliott.

Joseph Elliott, the grandfather of Willard Elliott, was a farmer by occupation, and owned a tract of land in Harrison township which had been secured from the government by one Skinner, who erected log buildings thereon. When Mr. Elliott secured this tract of eighty acres, the wolves were still plentiful in the community, and pioneer conditions of all kinds had to be met and overcome, but he was of a sturdy and persevering character and managed to make a good home for his family, replacing the log buildings with more modern structures of frame and making various other improvements. Alfred Elliott followed in his father's footsteps as a farmer, and was also engaged for some years as a carpenter contractor. He died in 1902, at the age of sixty-five years.

Willard Elliott secured his education in the public schools of Harrison township, and grew up on his father's farm, it being his father's intention that he adopt the vocation of agriculturist. As a young man, however, Mr. Elliott entered the field of politics, becoming deputy auditor of Cass county, a position which he held for several years. Subsequently he became receiver for the Baldwin banks, and after three years in that position became connected with the City Light Company, where he now acts in the capacity of assistant chief clerk. Here he has displayed his ability in numerous ways, his services having been of a high order.

On April 29, 1894, Mr. Elliott was united in marriage with Miss Mary Burton, who was born in Cass county, daughter of Levi Burton, a complete review of whose career will be found in the sketch of J. J Burton in another part of this work. One child has been born to this union. May Burton, born March 18, 1896. Mr Elliott has interested himself to some extent in fraternal work, being a valued member of the local lodges of the Knights of Pythias and the Benevolent and Protective Order of Elks. They attend the Christian church, where they have numerous friends. Mr Elliott is known as a man who has taken a leading part in every movement that has had for its object the betterment of the community, and his long and honorable career has been marked by constant fidelity to duty and the strictest integrity and probity of character.

JEHU T ELLIOTT has long occupied a place of prominence in the commercial and civic life of Logansport, where he has been engaged in business since the year 1871. Many and varied are the changes which have marked the growth and development of this city, but every succeeding change in the business of Mr Elliott has served but to mark its greater advance and its higher status in the business interests of the city.

Born in Cambridge City, Indiana, on March 24, 1844, Mr Elliott is the son of William and Eliza (Branson) Elliott. His early school privileges were but meager, owing to the facilities for education which that period provided, and he was but twelve years old when he set about making his own way in the world. From then until the present time he has been self-supporting, and it is small wonder that success and prosperity should attend the efforts of a man who as a lad of twelve had the courage and hardihood to shoulder the responsibility of his own future. His first independent work was as a salesman for his brother Dewitt C

Elliott, with whom he remained until he reached his majority, and in 1865 he engaged in the dry goods business as a partner with Henry and A R Shroyer, under the firm name of Shroyer, Elliott & Company, but some little time later they disposed of their business, and Mr. Elliott purchased the grocery store which his brother owned in Newcastle, Indiana There he continued to operate until 1870, when he went to Chicago and secured a position as a bookkeeper in a packing house After a year he gave up his work and came to Logansport, where he became identified with the wholesale grocery concern of Elliott, Pogue & Shroyer which firm was later changed to Elliott, Shroyer & Company. In 1889 the brother of the subject died, he being a member of the firm, and in the next year Mr Shroyer withdrew, leaving the firm Elliott & Company In 1896 Mr Elliott sold his interest to William M and S J. Elliott His next business move was to engage in the wholesale grocery business again, the firm name being J T Elliott & Son Some little time later Elliott & Company and J T Elliott & Son consolidated under the firm name of J T Elliott Company, and in 1907 was reorganized under the firm name of the Elliott Grocery Company (Incorporated), J T Elliot being president of the company That firm still exists and is one of the most prosperous and well known institutions in the business directory of the city, bearing a reputation that is unassailable, and occupying a leading place in the community Since the reorganization in 1907 Mr Elliott has been president and manager The firm conducts a wholesale grocery business and furnishes employment to twenty-five people, including road salesmen Mr Elliott has been in his present quarters since 1874, and has been identified with the wholesale grocery business for forty-one years, a record of which he may well be proud

Mr Elliott is a Republican, and has ever taken an active and interested part in the political and civic life of his city He was for eighteen years a member of the Logansport school board, and much credit is due him for the work he did as a member of that board and a number of beautiful schoolhouses were built during his term of office as evidence of his achievement He has long been a member of the Wholesale Grocer's Association of Indiana and of the Traveling Men's Protective Association He is a Mason of high degree, and has been since 1866 He was a member of the board of directors for the Masonic Association for the construction of the Masonic Temple of Logansport, which gave to the city a magnificent building in the Temple Mr Elliott was president of that board, and much of his enterprise, energy, loyalty to the order, and general public spirit is manifested in the splendid structure which resulted from the efforts of the society, under his direction He has been for years also a member of the Knights of Pythias and of the Modern Woodmen, as well as of the Benevolent and Protective Order of Elks in later years He was a director of the latter named order when their magnificent Temple was built in Logansport A number of the Methodist Episcopal church at Broadway, this city, Mr Elliott has been its treasurer for thirty-five years, a splendid record for service, surely.

On May 16, 1865, was celebrated the marriage of Mr Elliott and Miss Caroline Shroyer, of Newcastle, Indiana Three children were born to them Harry S , Esther E , the wife of Harry Uhl, and Arethusa, the wife of Edward B Bliss Mr and Mrs Elliott have occupied the same residence in Logansport for the past thirty-eight years, and have a host of friends in the city

JOHN R MILLMAN Among the enterprising and progressive young farmers and stock raisers of Cass county may be mentioned John R. Millman, who is engaged in cultivating his father's farm of one hundred and sixty acres, located on the Millman road, about four and one-half miles southeast of Logansport Mr Millman comes of a long line of agriculturists, and has spent his entire life in the work of cultivating the soil Although still a young man he has demonstrated his ability, and his enthusiasm and progressive spirit has resulted in the cultivation of an excellent property. John R Millman was born November 7, 1880, at Remington, Jasper county, Indiana, and is a son of Orville M and Lizzie (Benson) Millman

Orville M Millman was born in Putnam county, where he was reared and educated, and when still in young manhood, in 1872, migrated to Jasper county There he was engaged in agricultural pursuits until 1895, in which year he brought his family to Cass county and settled first north of and then in Tipton township He is still engaged in active pursuits and is the owner of a fine farm of fifty-eight acres Mr. Millman married Miss Lizzie Benson, of Jasper county, Indiana, and they became the parents of four children, namely. John R , Hattie, who lives with her parents in Tipton township, Lawson A , and William F , also at home

John R Millman secured his early education in the common schools of Jasper county, and finished it in the country schools of Cass county, whence he accompanied his parents when fifteen years of age He has always lived at home, and his training in agricultural matters has been most thorough. At the age of eighteen years he began farming on his own account, and being the oldest of his parents' children was put in charge of the home farm upon attaining his majority He has shown skill, good judgment and thorough knowledge of all the details of modern farming, believes in the use of modern machinery and methods, and is considered an excellent judge of stock. Like his father, he has always supported the principles and candidates of the Republican party, but has not cared to identify himself with public life, having been too busy in his farming operations He has found time, however, to lend his support to those movements which he has been led to believe will benefit his community or its people, and has also been identified with fraternal work to some extent as a member of the Masonic order, Tipton, Lodge Logan. in which he has many warm friends, as he has, indeed, in the various walks of life

On December 18 1907, Mr Millman was united in marriage with Miss Edna Martin, who was born in Cass county, a member of an old and honored family of this section, and a daughter of William P. and Eliza (Berry) Martin, farming people. Mr. and Mrs Millman have one little daughter, Margaret R , born November 8, 1912 Mr and Mrs Millman are consistent members of the English Lutheran church Their comfortable home, situated on the Millman road, is often the scene of pleasant social gatherings, as both the young people are popular in social circles of the community

JEROME McCLAIN. Among the citizens of Cass county who devoted their lives to the development of the agricultural interests of this section, one who will be remembered by the older generation was the late Jerome McClain, who for many years cultivated a fine tract of land on the McClain road, about six miles south of Logansport. Coming to this vicinity in young manhood, when the country was still in its formative shape, he materially aided in bringing about the present prosperous conditions, and will be remembered as a man of the highest integrity and probity of character. Mr. McClain was born January 5, 1824, in Dayton, Ohio, in a house on McClain street, named in honor of the family, and as a youth learned the trade of carpenter, and also worked at harness making and blacksmithing. He was still a young man when he migrated to Cass county, and here, in the city of Logansport, was married. After the birth of his oldest child, Frank McClain, he returned to Ohio in November, 1848, and for ten years worked at his trade in Dayton, but in November, 1858, again came to Cass county, this time taking up land and clearing a space for a log cabin. During the remainder of his life, Mr. McClain was engaged in tilling the soil, and became one of the best known and most highly esteemed of his community's citizens. He cleared the greater part of a valuable eighty-acre farm, which is still in the possession of the family, and on which he erected good buildings, made other improvements and continued to carry on general farming and stock raising. In his death, which occurred September 2, 1911, Cass county lost a good, practical agriculturist, and a citizen who always had the best interests of his community at heart.

Jerome McClain was married in Logansport to Miss Cazahne Holly, a member of an old Cass county family, and they became the parents of eight children, as follows: Benjamin F., now a resident of Kokomo, Indiana, who is married and has nine children; Pulaski, who is still operating the old homestead; Sarah E.; Granville M., who also resides at Kokomo, and has four children; Dowell, who is deceased; Mary E.; Margaret C., also Doc and Noah, deceased.

Pulaski McClain, son of Jerome McClain, was born in Dayton, August 8, 1853 and his sister, Mary E., who lives with him and manages the household affairs, was born on the old home place on McClain road. His early education was secured in the Galveston schools, and later he attended the district schools, his summer months always being spent in the work of the home place. His sister secured her education in the West school in Washington township. On completing his education, Mr. McClain commenced working at odd occupations, and being possessed of much more than the average mechanical ability, has had little trouble in finding plenty of employment, in addition to managing the home farm of eighty acres. He is known as one of the enterprising men of his community, and both he and his sister have many warm friends in the vicinity of their home. They are attendants of the Christian church in Washington township. The McClains are of Scottish lineage, and the original spelling of the name was McLean.

JOHN M. LAROSE. In the earlier history of this country, there are many accounts of the trials and brave sacrifices of those who are numbered among the pioneers of certain districts. The tide of civilization

A Family Group of

HISTORY OF CASS COUNTY

was then ever moving westward, and as soon as a section was fairly well developed, there would always be some venturesome souls eager to press still further towards the frontier, making new boundary lines for the outposts of civilization Without these the United States would not he from ocean to ocean, but would still be clustered along the Atlantic seaboard, without these courageous pioneers, who braved the savage Indian and wild beast, the great commonwealth of Indiana would still be a waste of prairie and timber land, and where is now heard the cheerful bustle of urban existence, the prairie chicken and wild turkey would wing their low flight Among the families that are largely responsible for the Cass county of today, that bearing the name of LaRose is well known, and a worthy representative of this name is found in the person of John M LaRose, of Clay township, the owner of a part of the old LaRose homestead He was born on the property which he now occupies, April 25, 1854, and is a son of John S and Lucretia (Chestnut) LaRose, natives of Ohio

The ancestry of the LaRose family can be traced back to John Lewis LaRose, the great-great-grandfather of John M. LaRose, who was a native of Germany and came to America in 1740, locating in Lehigh county, Pennsylvania, where the Rev. John Jacob LaRose, the great-grandfather of John M, was born and reared. He was a tailor by trade, but when the War of the Revolution was inaugurated he put aside all business and personal consideration to aid in the cause of independence. The son of this Revolutionary soldier, Philip J LaRose, was born in Guilford county, North Carolina, and was there married to Mary Shearer, also a native of that county In 1826 they left their southern home and came to Wayne county, Indiana, and in 1834 made removal to Cass county, locating on an eighty-acre tract of land in Clay township To that property Mr LaRose kept adding from time to time as his financial resources increased until his landed possessions aggregated over 700 acres His was a busy and useful life, and his success was well merited He died March 28, 1871, at the advanced age of ninety-one years, and the community thereby lost one of its honored pioneer settlers He and his wife had a family of eight children, among whom was John S LaRose The latter, following in the footsteps of his father, made agricultural pursuits his life work, and became one of the successful and greatly esteemed citizens of Clay township. He married Miss Lucretia Chestnut, and they had two living children John Marion and Annie V

John Marion LaRose attended the district schools of the vicinity of his home, and supplemented this by three years of attendance in the city schools of Logansport On completing his studies he at once settled down to agricultural pursuits, which he has followed with uniform success throughout his career He now has 210 acres of land, all in a high state of cultivation, on which he has made numerous modern improvements which have greatly enhanced the value of the property The family residence, which succeeded the little log house in which Mr LaRose was born, is located on an elevation on the farm, and can be seen for miles in every direction. Mr LaRose is known as a good practical agriculturist, and as one whose abilities are such as to allow him to gain a full measure of success from his labors His standing as a citizen is equally high, and among his business associates he is known as a man who lives up to all of his obligations The homestead house is known as "The High View Stock Farm," and he raises the "Mule Foot" swine which is registered

On March 5, 1876, Mr LaRose was united in marriage with Miss Nancy Miranda Brown, who was born in Cass county, daughter of Isaac and Elizabeth J (Custer) Brown, for years a prosperous farmer of this locality. To this union there has come one child. John Brown, born in 1895 Mr and Mrs LaRose are members of the Methodist Episcopal church, while his political affiliation is with the Democratic party.

GEORGE W. BURKHART. A resident of Cass county since 1866, George W Burkhart, veteran of the Civil war, former manufacturer of lumber, retired farmer and public-spirited citizen, has had a long and honorable career, and has been closely identified with the growth and development of this section His life furnishes an example of the success that is to be gained through upright living, strict integrity and constant devotion to the principles of honorable dealing and public-spirited citizenship, and among the people of his community he is held in the highest esteem. Mr Burkhart was born September 17, 1846, in Center county, Pennsylvania, and is a son of John G and Susan (Felmey) Burkhart His father a native of the Fatherland, came to the United States when about sixteen years of age, and subsequently followed the trades of miller and baker, in addition to carrying on agricultural pursuits. He successively lived in Pennsylvania, Ohio (where he worked at his trades in Bucyrus and Sandusky), Fulton county, Indiana, and finally Cass county, where his death occurred in his sixty-sixth year, some time during the Civil war A thrifty and industrious German, he accumulated a competency and some years before his death was able to retire. Mr Burkhart married Susan C Felmey, a native of Pennsylvania, who passed away at the age of fifty-five years, and they became the parents of three children: John W, who now lives in Kent, Wisconsin, George W, and Cecelia, who married Thomas Detmore, and had three children —Oliver, Lucinda and Nora

George W Burkhart was five years of age when taken to Ohio by his parents. and there he was reared to hard work, being given only three months schooling in all his life If his education was slight, his opportunities for culture of a genuine sort were more so, but one cannot be in Mr Burkhart's presence long before realizing that he is a man of wide knowledge and general information, close observation and much reading having given him an education that has made up for what the earlier years lacked He was thrown upon his own resources at the age of thirteen years, at which time he began to work at odd jobs, chopping wood and working as a farm hand in fact accepting whatever honorable employment presented itself In 1861 the family came to Fulton county, Indiana, where young Burkhart worked on a farm for about one year, and in 1862 he began his military career as a private in Company A, Twenty-sixth Regiment, Indiana Volunteer Infantry, Col John G Clark commanding, with which organization he served faithfully for three years He was in the Thirteenth and Sixteenth Army Corps, and later connected with the Department of the Gulf, and throughout a long and arduous service maintained the reputation of a cheerful, brave and faithful soldier, winning alike the respect of his comrades and superior officers Among his battles were Vicksburg, Nashville, Yazoo Pass, Prairie Grove, Sterling Plantation, Mobile Bay and Spanish Fort, and numerous minor engagements and skirmishes For about a year he also participated in the Missouri troubles, during the time when the notorious Quantrell and his gang of desperadoes were terrorizing that state

On the completion of his military service, Mr Burkhart returned to the vocations of peace, and for a number of years he followed lumbering and engaged in the manufacturing and sale of building material, but eventually turned his attention to agricultural pursuits, and still owns forty acres of land south of Logansport and a well-cultivated property of one hundred and seventy and three-fourths acres on the Kokomo Road His ventures have been characterized by honest dealing, and although he is now retired from active pursuits he still holds the confidence of a wide business acquaintance. For a number of years Mr. Burkhart was actively engaged in Democratic politics, especially as a "stump" speaker, but in 1912 cast his fortunes with the young Progressive party, whose candidate he became for joint representative In the years of 1898 and 1899 he was representative of Cass county, Indiana, in the state legislature In a number of township offices he demonstrated his ability as a public executive, and his services are still in demand as an orator at various gatherings, celebrations and social events Probably no other man in his part of the county is better posted upon the history of the country, especially as to its presidents and eminent statesmen

On April 11 1872 Mr Burkhart was united in marriage with Miss Rosetta H Seybold, daughter of John G and Ursula (Munger) Seybold and six children have been born to this union John Irvin, who married Pearl Kay, Harry F, of Fulton county, who married Susan Weisner and has two children —Zoe and Luretta, Joseph A, who married Anna Leffert, and has two children,—George and Harry, Frank, who married Ethel Kochel, and has two children,—Rosetta and Bernice, Clarence, residing in Logansport, and Geneva, who is single and resides with her parents

HARRY C. JONES On the Kokomo road about four miles from Logansport, is situated the finely cultivated eighty-acre farm of Harry C Jones, a tract which has been in the family since 1857, and on which Mr Jones was born He is one of his section's enterprising and energetic agriculturists, belonging to that class of farmers who are quick to adopt advanced methods and progressive ideas, and among his neighbors and associates is recognized as a man who at all times is ready to aid movements tending to better his community Mr Jones was born on his present property, August 10, 1855, and is a son of Josiah and Emily (Updegraff) Jones His father, a native of New York, spent his early years in the Empire State where he was engaged in farming, and was about forty years old when he migrated to Indiana Here he settled in Cass county on the present farm of Harry C Jones, then a wild tract on which there had been no improvements made He spent his subsequent years in clearing and cultivating this land, and died with a comfortable competency and the esteem and respect of those with whom he had come into contact Josiah and Emily Jones had two children Harry C , and Jennie, now Mrs John M Burkit

Like all country boys of his day and locality, Harry C. Jones divided his early years between attendance at school in the winter terms and working on the farm in the summer months He was reared to habits of industry and sobriety, taught to realize the value of hard work, and thoroughly trained in all the details of farm labor In the meantime his mind was being trained in the district schools and the old stone seminary in Logansport, after leaving which he continued to work on the home place. At the time of his father's death, Mr Jones inherited one-half of the homestead, and after a few years, when he decided to make a home of his own he puchased his sister's interest in the property, and since that time has been its proprietor At that time Mr Jones was married to Miss Sarah J Vernon, March 25, 1875 and they have had a family of nine children, as follows William H , who married Anna Ramer, and has one child,—Blanch J , Arthur C , who married Pearl Nichols, and has one child,—Howard N.; Josiah P , who married Flora Barnes, and has one child,—Harry E. , Frank V , who married Elsie Bopp and they have one daughter, Dorothy; Charles E , who married Ida Mosby, and has one child,—Ralph V., Thomas E , who married Mae Condon, and Quincy A , who wedded Miss Mildred Dussard, Paul Revere and Carl B , all of whom reside at home and assist their father in the work of the farm This eighty-acre tract is one of the finest of its size in Washington township Years of intelligent, practical and painstaking cultivation have resulted in the development of an excellent property, which produces large crops annually Mr Jones is a Republican in his political views, but is not a politician in the generally accepted use of the term, although in 1912 he allowed his name to be used as a nominee for the office of commissioner His fraternal connection is with Lodge No. 417, Independent Order of Odd Fellows, in which the family is well represented, six of Mr Jones' sons also belonging to this order. He also holds membership in St Paul's Evangelical Lutheran church, which he attends constantly and supports liberally The homestead of Mr and Mrs Jones is called "The Cedars" and is the abode of hospitality

CHARLES QUINCY PALMER Industry, perseverance, intelligence and good judgment are the price of success in agricultural work in these modern days of farming, when the hard, unremitting toil of former days has given way to scientific use of modern machinery and a knowledge of the proper treatment of the soil Cass county boasts of many skilled farmers who treat their vocation more as a profession than as a mere occupation and take a justifiable pride in their accomplishments. In this class may be mentioned Charles Quincy Palmer, of Washington township, the well-tilled tract of two hundred acres owned by his father and himself being located not far from Logansport and who is also carrying on operations on his father's tract, the latter being retired from active life Mr Palmer was born in Washington township, Cass county, Indiana, May 28, 1874, and is a son of John and Mary (Best) Palmer.

His father was born in Irwin, Ohio, from whence he came to Indiana during young manhood, and here carried on agricultural pursuits with well deserved success until his retirement several years ago There were three children in the elder Palmer's family, namely Charles Quincy; George H, who makes his home in Logansport, and Dr A L, a well known physician of Logansport, who is acting in the official capacity of coroner of that city.

Charles Quincy Palmer was given the advantages of a good education, attending both the district schools of Washington township and the graded schools of Logansport, and after leaving the latter resumed work on the home farm Subsequently, he learned the trade of horseshoer, which he followed for six years in connection with his agricultural operations, but eventually gave up this vocation and now devotes his entire attention to tilling the soil The two hundred-acre tract has been put in a high state of cultivation, the buildings thereon are modern and in a good state of repair, and altogether the property gives eloquent testimony to Mr Palmer's skill as a farmer. He has realized and taken advantage of the use of modern methods in his operations, and may take pride in the fact that he has one of the valuable properties of his community Among his neighbors he is known as a man of the strictest integrity in all matters of a business nature, and one who, having succeeded himself, is at all times ready to assist others to a like success Essentially a farmer, he has taken little interest in politics, but movements which have for their object the betterment of his community may always depend upon his support and co-operation. In fraternal matters, Mr Palmer is popular with the members of the local lodge of the Fraternal Order of Eagles, in which he has passed through all the chairs

On March 21, 1900, Mr Palmer was united in marriage with Miss Martina Miller, daughter of John and Elizabeth (Simmons) Miller. They have no children. Mr and Mrs Palmer attend the English Lutheran church, in the work of which Mrs Palmer has been very active, and both are popular in the social circles of Logansport, their home being but three miles south of that city.

NEWMAN H SETTLES Since earliest history the vocation of tilling the soil has been numbered among the most honored vocations A liberal profession, embracing a knowledge of the physiology of the earth and the products that grow out of it, it requires also a philosophy of economics that understands the necessities of demand and supply by which these products are kept moving over the face of the earth Among the good, practical agriculturists of Cass county, who thoroughly understand their vocation, and are securing a full measure of success through the application of intelligent treatment of the soil, none stand higher than Newman H. Settles, who for thirty-five years or more has been cultivating land in Noble township. Mr Settles is a native of Ohio, born March 10, 1846, a son of John and Julia Settles, natives of Virginia and New York, respectively. Mr. Settles' parents were married in Ohio, and from that state came to Adams county, Indiana, in 1859, and thence to Cass county, first locating in Harrison township, on a farm of eight acres. There the father erected a shop and followed the cooper trade until 1872 when he moved with his wife to Kansas and in that state died in 1904, Mrs Settles having passed away in 1882.

Newman H Settles was a lad of thirteen years when the family came to Cass county, Indiana, and here his education was completed in the common schools On the completion of his studies he entered business with his father, from whom he had learned the trade of cooper, and after his father had moved to the West he continued to operate the business until 1877 At that time he took up his residence in Noble township where he rented a larger farm, and here, through tireless industry, constant thrift and persevering determination, aided by a keen intellect and a comprehensive knowledge of land values, he has been able to accumulate a handsome property of eighty acres in section 12. In 1903, in which year Mr Settles bought this farm, it was in poor condition, due to mismanagement on the part of the former owner, but during the ten years that it has been in Mr. Settles' possession, he has developed it into one of the valuable tracts of his township Modern buildings have been erected, innovations have been introduced, and scientific treatment of the soil has tended to increase the productive ability of the property.

On October 28, 1864, Mr Settles was married to Miss Anna Crawford, who was born in Ohio, September 15, 1852, daughter of Robert and Margaret Crawford, who came to Cass county in 1854 and settled on a farm in Boone township. Six children were born to this union Julia, Willard, Margaret, Jennie, John and Franklin Julia died in 1872, at the age of eleven months, Willard was married (first) in 1896 to Miss Ida Smith, of Cass county, and had two children Eva and Paul. His first wife died in 1902, and in 1906 he was a second time married the ceremony taking place in Detroit, Michigan In 1904 Jennie Settles was married to William Wright, of Logansport, and they have two children · Dorothy, born in 1905, and Margaret, born in 1908 Margaret Settles was married in 1910 to Charles Lew, an engineer on the Pennsylvania Railroad On December 25, 1909 John Settles married Miss Florence Grable, of Cass county, and on September 17, 1912, Franklin Settles married Miss Anna Holland, also of Cass county

Newman H. Settles has never cared for public office, although a supporter of good government, and an active participant in progressive movements With his wife and children, he attends the Methodist Episcopal church ·

HENRY RHOADES It has been given to some to help develop the country, to shape their surroundings according to their needs, and to bring forth the present high degree of civilization Cass county Indiana, became the home of many a sturdy pioneer, who did not ask for anything more than raw land to work upon Bravely, uncomplainingly, these forerunners of civilization went to work, and many of them still survive to see the fruits of their years of labor Among these is Henry Rhoades, himself a pioneer and a member of an old and influential family of the Hoosier state, who is now the owner of eighty acres of fine farming land about five miles from Logansport Mr Rhoades, who has the added distinction of being a veteran of the Civil war and an honor to those who wore the blue, was born October 17, 1846, in

Pulaski county, Indiana, and is a son of Mike and Mary (Niss) Rhoades. His father, who was born in Pittsburg, Pennsylvania, came from that city to Pulaski county, Indiana, in 1848, and there spent the rest of his life in cultivating a farm He was the father of eight children, namely. William, deceased, Daniel, Henry, Sarah, deceased, Hattie, Kate and Angelina, and Silas, deceased.

Henry Rhoades was reared to agricultural pursuits, and received his education in the district schools, starting to work out on neighboring farms when he was only twelve years of age. He was so engaged when the Civil war broke out, and with other youths of his locality, went to Winamac, Pulaski county, and there enlisted in the Union army, becoming a member of the Eighty-seventh Indiana Volunteer Infantry His regiment was assigned to the Army of the Cumberland, and he subsequently participated in a number of hard-fought engagements and took part in the famous "March to the Sea," under Gen W. T Sherman After completing a brave and honorable service, Mr. Rhoades returned to Pulaski county and to agricultural pursuits, remaining in that section until he was about twenty-five years of age, when he came to Cass county. Being possessed of but little capital, commencing at the lowest round of the ladder of life he worked on shares until he was able to purchase his present land, which he has developed into one of the best tracts of its size in Washington township General farming and stock-raising have held his attention, and he is known as an able agriculturist, who is thoroughly conversant with modern ideas and methods, and whose activities have served to contribute to the farming importance of his township

On December 23, 1869, Mr Rhoades wedded Miss Florence C. Fink, daughter of Jacob and Mary (Skillen) Fink Her parents came to Cass county from Pennsylvania in an early day In the Fink family there were three children Florence, Sarah and Eli, and all of the children are living

Six children have been born to Mr and Mrs Henry Rhoades Daniel W, who married Miss Myrtle Lucy and they have four children Orvilla, Henry, Lester L and Wayne, Mary, wife of Burton Nethercutt, the parents of six children Orville. May Henry, Russell Mosie, Bessie and Paul, Elizabeth, wife of Herman Leffert and they have five children Herbert, Irene, Arthur, Mary and Wayne, Lottie, wife of Oliver Marshall, who have four children. Florence, Hazel, Harold and Opal, Walter who married Flossie Reese and has no children, and Harvey, who wedded Edna Rush and has one child, Helena

In his political views, Mr Rhoades is a Democrat, but he has never sought public office, preferring to give his entire attention to his farming operations With his wife and family, they attend the Lutheran church, of which he has always been a liberal supporter Mr. Rhoades belongs to that class of men who appreciate their success the more because it has been self-gained, and because it has come through honest effort and by no questionable means, aided by his estimable wife His standing as a citizen is high, and during his long residence in Cass county he has gained and maintained many sincere friendships His good wife shares equally well the friendship and good wishes of their many friends

Mrs Rhoades has a sunshiny smile and a royal welcome for all who may enter the portals of their pretty home

NELSON WARNER CADY, M D In a career of thirty-five years as physician and surgeon of Cass county, Dr Cady has come to rank among the foremost men of his profession in this county, has done much good service both as a doctor and as a citizen for the welfare of his home city, and is well known for his ability and high character in his profession over the state

Nelson Warner Cady was born October 3, 1850, at Indianapolis, and belongs to an old family of Indiana, and its members have been distinguished for worthy and honorable position in practical affairs and social life The parents of Dr Cady were Charles Warner Cady and Abigail Aikman Kiersted. The father was born at Keene, New Hampshire, in 1810, located in Indianapolis about 1840 as the first general fire insurance agent in the state, and died in that city in 1855 The mother was born at Fort Washington, (now Cincinnati, Ohio), in 1824, and died at her home in Indianapolis in 1900 She was a type of Indiana's noble women during the last century She was deeply interested in the work for the soldiers during the Civil war and made and presented a regimental banner to Lew Wallace's regiment of zouaves The father, during his early manhood, learned and followed the trade of saddler, but subsequently took up fire insurance and after some years in the business had the distinction of establishing the first fire insurance office in the state of Indianapolis Besides Dr Cady, the other children of the family are mentioned as follows: Eudora Dunn Cady, who married Woodford Tousey, and who died at Indianapolis in 1913 in her seventieth year, Albermarle Cady, who died in infancy, Anna Kiersted Cady, born in 1845, and died in 1901, first married W O Stone and second Dr Hammond of Indianapolis, Ella Wilder Cady, who married John Lawrie, a merchant; Jeremiah Kiersted Cady, born in 1855, and married Paget Daniels, is now an architect in Chicago.

Dr Cady after leaving the Indianapolis high school, entered Cornell university at Ithaca, New York, where he was graduated Ph B in 1874 His medical education was acquired in the Bellevue Hospital Medical College of New York, and he was graduated M D in 1877 Many years ago Dr. Cady acquired the art of stenography, and was among the first young men in Indianapolis to use this art as a reporter on the *Indianapolis Journal,* and he has practiced more or less through all his career, being now a contributor to newspapers and medical journals

Dr. Cady located in Logansport, Indiana, in June, 1877, and has practiced medicine in this city for more than thirty-five years With a genius for mechanics, as well as for the subtler arts of his profession, Dr Cady has used his skill in inventing a number of fracture splints of a new design, and now used extensively by the profession For several years he held a position on the Logansport board of health, and has been as public-spirited in his citizenship as in his profession.

Dr Cady for many years supported the Republican party, but his politics now is of the Progressive brand He is a member of the Cass County and Indiana State Medical Society, and of the American Medi-

"SUNNY LAWN HOMESTEAD," RESIDENCE OF MR. AND MRS. HORACE M. FUNK

cal Association His fraternal affiliations are with Orient Lodge No 272 A F and A. M., Logan Chapter No 2 R. A M and Logansport Council No 11 R and S M.

Dr. Cady was married August 22, 1883 to Miss Jennie M Miller, of Waverly, New York, a daughter of Samuel W. and Adaline Parmenter Miller, her father being a butcher by trade Dr Cady and wife have the following children. Margaret Abigail Cady, born August 20, 1864, died February 5, 1886, Eudora Helena Cady, born March 2, 1888, living at home with her father, and Wallis Albermarle Cady, born February 14, 1888, and now a newspaper reporter at Toledo, Ohio. The family worship with the Episcopal church

HORACE MILTON FUNK Among the progressive and enterprising agriculturists of Cass county, one who has gained success through the medium of his own efforts, and now holds an enviable position among his fellow-citizens, is Horace M Funk, the owner of one hundred and twenty acres of well-cultivated land in Clay township. Mr. Funk has been an agriculturist all of his life, and has lived at various places in Indiana, and wherever his activities have been located he has gained the friendship and good will of all with whom he has come in contact He is a native of Pennsylvania, and was born September 19, 1859, a son of Joseph G and Mary (Ward) Funk, and a grandson of George Funk

The parents of Mr Funk came to Cass county in 1867, Mrs Funk, his grandmother, being the owner of the first farm on which they settled and this property Mr Funk and his father worked on shares For some time the family lived in a frame residence in Clay township The farm of Mr Funk's parents is now one of the valuable properties of the township Joseph G. Funk is still operating this land, but the mother passed to her final rest on April 4, 1894

Horace N Funk received his education in the district schools of Clay township, and his boyhood and youth were spent in assisting his father and in learning the multitude of details with which a good farmer must be conversant On attaining his majority he began operations on his own account, but he continued under the parental roof until 1889, when he went to Miami township, and there carried on operations for one year Returning to Clay township in 1890 he continued farming there until the following year, when he went to Peru, Indiana, and continued to live there until removing to Adams township in the fall of 1892 He spent about four and one-half years in that vicinity, and then purchased another property, but before he had settled thereon grasped an opportunity to sell it at a satisfactory advance, and then came to his present farm, a tract of one hundred and twenty acres in Clay township Here he has made a number of valuable improvements, having a handsome residence situated on Logansport Rural Free Delivery Route No 5, with appropriate barns and outbuildings His land is in a high state of cultivation, and yields bumper crops in return for the intelligent labors which Mr Funk expends upon it Through honorable dealing and strict integrity in all his transactions, he has gained a reputation for honesty and straightforwardness, and no citizen of his locality stands higher in public esteem He is a

Republican in his political views, and, although not a politician in the generally accepted meaning of the term, has recognized the duties of citizenship, and has served his township both as trustee and supervisor. With his family, he attends the Christian church, and has ever been a liberal supporter of those movements which go to make for morality, education and good citizenship.

Mr Funk was married to Miss Mattie G. Scott, February 6, 1889, daughter of Benjamin D and Belinda (Carr) Scott, and they have had three children, namely Ruth A, who became the wife of William English, and lives in Clay township, Ward S, eighteen years old, and Eveleen E, ten years of age Ruth and Ward both received their diplomas from the public schools and the daughter Ruth was a student one year in the high school and Ward has finished the full curriculum of the high school Eveleen is in the sixth grade Mrs Funk was a daughter of Benjamin D and Belinda (Carr) Scott Benjamin Scott was a native of Cass county, born in 1831, and he died in 1895, aged about 64 years He was a carpenter and joiner, also an agriculturist and a Republican in his political sentiment. His wife was a member of the Christian church Mrs Funk was educated in the common schools and the American Normal, formerly of Logansport, and she was a successful teacher in Clay and Miami townships

Mr Funk is an honored member of the Knights of Pythias, also of the Maccabees The comfortable home of Mr and Mrs Funk is known as "The Sunny Lawn Homestead," and their home is ever open to their many friends

JAMES ALVIN HIGGINS is well known among the farming men of Cass county as one of the most successful breeders of hogs in the vicinity of Logansport He has devoted his entire life to the farm and its diversified interests, winning prosperity and success in all his undertakings, and his position is one of no little prominence in the city and county which has represented his home and the center of his activities all his life Born on the 6th day of December, 1848, in Logansport, James Alvin Higgins is the son of Alvin McCaslin and Eliza Jane (Reyburn) Higgins

Alvin M Higgins was a man of eastern birth and ancestry, and he came to Indiana in 1834 from Portland, Maine En route to Fort Dearborn (Chicago) in company with his brother, both were stricken with a dangerous illness at Peru The brothers were taken into the home of Col William M Reyburn and there were cared for by those kindly and gentle people The brother died, but Alvin Higgins was nursed into convalescence by the daughter of his good samaritan host, and upon his ultimate recovery he married the lady who had saved his life Alvin and Eliza Higgins, upon the happy culmination of their romantic acquaintance and courtship, established a home in Logansport, and here Mr Higgins took up the trade in which he had been trained in his boyhood—that of a tin and copper smith He opened a small shop, which was later supplemented by a line of stoves and hardware, and to him was accorded the distinction of having been the first man to introduce the heating stove into Cass county Mr Higgins, it may also be said, was the first man in Cass county to own a thoroughbred Durham bull, and it was about the year 1855 that he made the purchase. He was one of the first to recognize the importance of introducing blooded stock into the country, and with a Mr Buchanan, made the purchase. The transaction was one fraught with considerable difficulty, as they were obliged to go to Kentucky to make the purchase —a big undertaking in those early days.

Mr and Mrs Higgins were the parents of eight children, of whom the following brief facts are here incorporated William R, who was educated for the ministry He began preaching in 1865 and was called out of Cass county. He died in Terre Haute, Indiana, on July 4, 1895 Emma B died on the 8th of January, 1846, Sarah C died February 12, 1890, Mary C died on the 4th of November, 1902, Eliza Jane died on May 4, 1894, James A, of this review, Ella F. died on June 19, 1907, Elizabeth A. died on January 8, 1902 With but a single exception, the deceased members of this family lived past middle age, Emma B having died when she was about five years old. The wife and mother died on August 8, 1859, and Mr Higgins died on March 5, 1885 Mr. Higgins was a captain of a military company, organized in Logansport and he saw active service on various occasions when Indiana troops were called into action, in the troubles incident to those early days He was a man of much public spirit and a citizen who never shirked his duties and responsibilities in the way of public service. He served two terms as city councilman and one term as probate judge He was county treasurer during two terms of office and was a member of the school board during practically all of his life in Cass county In all of these offices he served faithfully and well, winning the respect and esteem of his fellow citizens and establishing a reputation for solid worth and integrity that will live while the same endures He was a member of Logansport Lodge, A F. and A M, and was a charter member of the first Odd Fellows lodge in Logansport, and had a similar experience with regard to a lodge known as the Sons of Temperance In about the year 1858, Mr. Higgins disposed of his tinsmith and hardware business and engaged in the lumber industry, making black walnut the principal item to which he devoted his operations He died on March 5, 1885, after an illness of a year or more, and his death deprived Logansport and Cass county of one of the most worthy men they had ever known

James Alvin Higgins was educated in the schools of Logansport, finishing his education with the high school He saw himself as one of the successful farmers of the future in Cass county and early in life set about the realization of his young ambition Thus all of his business life has been devoted to farms and farming, and success has most generously rewarded his efforts In later years Mr Higgins turned his attention to hog raising, and that enterprise has taken the best part of his time since then

On the 22nd of January, 1873, Mr Higgins was united in marriage with Miss Emma Thornton, the eldest daughter of Harvey and Catherine (Murray) Thornton Mrs Higgins was born in Cass county and was given her early education in the schools of Noble township, later attending school in Cincinnati, for a year, and completing her studies at the Presbyterian Academy in Logansport—that institution standing in the relation to Logansport as the high school of today

Three children came to Mr and Mrs Higgins, as follows Warren T, born on August 5, 1874 Reyburn A, born on February 27, 1877; and Mary E., whose natal day is September 23 1881 All three are living The second son, Reyburn, married Lillian Stewart Jones on July 8, 1909 and he is engaged in educational work as a teacher in the schools of Louisville, Kentucky Mary is also a teacher, and is carrying on her work in the schools of North Vernon, Indiana.

The family are members of the Presbyterian church, in which Mr Higgins was carefully reared by his staunch Presbyterian parents, and all are worthy members of society, filling admirably the places they have made for themselves in their various communities

WILLIAM H DRITT Cass county, it will not be denied, owes much of its present day prosperity and growth to the pioneer farmer who came in and opened up the waste places of the county more than a half century ago and set on foot a cycle of solid improvement that has gone on from then until now and is still in progress In 1848 the father of William Dritt settled on the identical spot now occupied by the latter, and devoted the remainder of his life to the business of converting the rugged wilderness into a series of blossoming meadows How well he succeeded in his work, self-imposed, though it was, is no secret to any who are familiar with the history of Noble township, and the worthy work of that sturdy pioneer has been worthily carried on by his son, who is the subject of this review

Born February 24, 1865, William Dritt is the son of Daniel and Sarah (Schilling) Dritt. They had seven children, but only two are living Daniel Dritt was born in Pennsylvania, of German parentage and ancestry, on January 29, 1826, and was the son of Andrew and Elizabeth (Fishel) Dritt He died on July 9, 1881, and the wife and mother died June 18, 1898

William Dritt was reared on the home farm, and upon his father's death fell heir to the old home place, where he has since carried on the work of the farm. He was married on February 16, 1888, to Miss Ella Cornell

Mrs Dritt is a native of Miami county, Indiana, born February 28, 1869, and the eldest of two daughters born to Jeremiah and Maria (Moose) Cornell Mrs Dritt and her sister Clara, wife of Albert Chandler, a decorator, live at Peru, Indiana Mr. Cornell was a native of Indiana, and was an agriculturist He was educated only in the common schools was a soldier in the Civil war and received his honorable discharge Both he and his wife were members of the Presbyterian church Mrs Cornell was also a native of Indiana, and her parents were natives of New York. Mrs Dritt was educated in the common schools She is a lady of excellent judgment and has well performed her part in the building up the home and in the rearing of her children. She is a member of the Presbyterian church, also an honored member of the Progressive Club in Logansport, a club devoted to literature, art and music.

The following children were born to Mr and Mrs Dritt· Ethel

S received her diploma from the public schools in 1904 and graduated from the Logansport high school in 1909, and she has taken musical instructions She wedded Elmer Young, resident of Logansport, and a salesman Florence P received her diploma from the public schools in 1906, and then attended the Lincoln Seminary of Logansport, and has also taken music She married J Jay McCormick, a resident of Logansport, and he is engaged in the elevator business. Harry J. received his diploma from the public schools in 1908, and was a member of the graduating class in Logansport high school in 1913 He is associated with his father on the farm Madge graduated from the public schools in 1908, and the Logansport high school at the early age of seventeen in the class of 1912 She is a vocalist of more than ordinary merit. It is noticed in this sketch that Mr and Mrs Dritt have given their children the best of advantages in acquiring good educations, fitting them for the higher walks of life The homestead of the Dritts is known as "Glen Dale Farm," and their many friends will always find a cordial welcome there The farm comprises one hundred and sixty acres, and many of its present day improvements in the way of buildings, etc , may be credited to the present occupant of the place

Mr Dritt is one of the leaders of thought and opinion in his community, and attends the Presbyterian church, his life has been one entirely consistent with his profession of faith He is a Republican, and has pronounced political views, though he is not more active in the field of politics than good citizenship demands of him He and his family maintain a high place in the esteem and regard of their many friends in and about Noble township, where they are known for their many excellent traits of heart and mind, and where they are regarded as the best of neighbors.

WILLIAM PURCELL POWELL, deceased, was born on February 25, 1828, in Ohio, the son of Benjamin and Sarah (Carroll) Powell He came with his parents from Jefferson county, Ohio the place of his birth, to Indiana, in 1835, and they located in Cass county, settling on a wild tract of land in Harrison township, of which they hoped to make a farm for themselves Here they built a cabin home and set about clearing up the wilderness and improving the place as best they might They were pioneers in the truest sense, and the first election ever held in his community was held in the old Powell home

Here was William Purcell Powell reared, and here in early life he married Harriet Smith, who died without issue. His second wife was Mrs Delilah Isabell Gressinger, a daughter of James and Mary Ann (Carrier) Spacey, and the widow of Adam Gressinger Mr. Powell was one of the old fashioned men who held as one of the tenets of his faith that honesty was one of the cardinal virtues—a belief still in good repute to some extent, but not held so commonly perhaps as in those early times He was extremely temperate in his habits, and this, no doubt, led to his retaining his mental faculties unimpaired to the end of his days He was a Democrat in politics, always keenly alive to the progress of the times, but never sought public office He was a Universalist in his religious belief and during his later years derived much simple and wholesome pleasure from the study of the Scriptures He was a man of much courage and unlimited faith in the future, an example of which is given in the fact that he began his married life with a cash capital of fifty cents His first home was no sooner completed than it was destroyed by fire, but it was characteristic of the man that adversity of that order was insufficient to keep him down He at once rebuilt his home, and with the passing of time, he prospered, not by waiting on fortune, but by the hardest kind of work, economy and the application of excellent business judgment in his every-day affairs A noteworthy trait in him was his sturdy honesty and his high general character He was a kindly man in his disposition, temperate in all things, charitable and generous in his benefactions for the public good He died as he lived, an honored and respected citizen, death coming to him on October 5, 1876

J E Hertsell still retains and operates the fine old place that his grandfather came into possession of when he first came to Cass county, Indiana, more than half a century ago, although he no longer makes his home on the place, having a fine home of his own acquired in Clay township where he carries on the business of farming on an extensive scale, and along the most approved modern methods

Born in Miami township, Cass county, on October 21, 1885, J E Hertsell is the son of Jesse and Jennie (Bird) Hertsell The father was the son of another, Jesse Hertsell, and the mother was the daughter of one Eli Bird, people of English descent The family located in Miami township when Jesse Hertsell was a youth, and he passed his life on the farm his father purchased, and upon his death, which occurred in February, 1912, the old home came into the possession of the son

J E Hertsell received such education as the schools of Miami township afforded, and early in life began to devote himself to the work of the farm He has been successful in his operations along these lines and has acquired a fine place of his own in recent years, located in Clay township, and there he makes his home In 1909 Mr Hertsell married Ruth Mannen, the daughter of Henry Mannen, and two children have been born to them Reta, who died when six months old in 1910, and Helen Esther, who is now fifteen months old

M Hertsell and his wife are members of the Baptist church, and take an active share in the works of that body, while Mr Hertsell has membership in the Knights of Pythias They occupy a secure place in the esteem of their many acquaintances in Clay township, as well as in Miami township and enjoy the friendship of many who know them for their many excellent qualities of character.

Jesse Martin For many years the citizen whose name heads this short review was one of the leading agriculturists of Washington township, and his entire career was one of industry, integrity and honorable dealing Although not a native of Cass county, he came to this section at an early date, and his activities were such as to gain him the respect and esteem of his fellow-citizens, not alone in business matters, but in the political arena and in the work of the church Mr Martin was born May 4, 1834, in Somerset county, Pennsylvania, a son of Peter and

Rebecca (Long) Martin He died February 11, 1909, and his wife died September 8, 1908

Peter Martin, on first coming to Cass county, purchased land on section 27, Washington township, but in 1848 removed to section 22, where the rest of his life was spent. He and his wife were the parents of eight children, all born in Pennsylvania and reared in Cass county, as follows Francis, Simon, Jesse, Herman, Caroline, Catherine, Manassas and Matilda All are now deceased

Jesse Martin commenced his education in the public schools of his native state, where he resided until he was fourteen years of age, and after coming to Indiana, completed his schooling in a private institution of Logansport For several years thereafter, he devoted his attention to teaching school during the winter months, while he farmed in summers, but eventually gave up the educator's profession in order to give his entire time to farming and stock raising, in which he became very successful He took a keen interest in the affairs of his community, was well and favorably known among the leading business men of his township, and for upwards of half a century was identified with the work of the Presbyterian church, in which he acted as elder. He had a family of eight children, of whom seven are living Emeline, deceased, who was the wife of John Wendling, Edwin F, who married Edna Crane, and had five children, Stanley, deceased, Esther, Joseph, Rachel and Jesse, Roland, who married Lina Schwalm, and had six children—Earl, Ethel, Eunice, Helen, Ruby and Lois, Albert, who married Julietta McCreary; Irvin, who married Emma Foreman; John P, Manassas, who married Laura Schwalm, and has one son—Roy, and Frank, single, who lives on the old homestead of 120 acres

John P Martin, son of Jesse Martin, was born on the old homestead farm, October 18, 1868, and received his education in the public schools of Cass county, in the meantime assisting his father in the work of the home farm from the time that he was old enough to grasp the plow handles At the age of twenty years, he began farming on his own account, purchasing eighty acres of land from his father, on which he has made numerous improvements, including modern substantial buildings He has always been a leader in Republican politics, and for a time lived in Indianapolis while serving as a member of the clerical force of the state senate. Like his father, he has been a member of the Presbyterian church During his long career in Cass county he has ever possessed the respect and confidence of his fellow citizens, and in a work of this kind deserves honorable mention

WILLIAM H SHARP The career of William H Sharp, one of the foremost of Washington township's representative agriculturists illustrates strikingly the opportunities that are open to young men of foresight, good judgment and business ability, for solely through the medium of his own efforts and good business talents he has steadily advanced until he is now one of the most substantial of his community's citizens Since early manhood he has engaged in buying cultivating and selling farming land, and his operations have carried him all over Cass county where he is known as a man of the highest integrity At this time he is operating a tract of sixty acres, located on the Kokomo road, about five miles from Logansport Mr Sharp was born August 3, 1860, in Pickaway county, Ohio, and is a son of Samuel M and Isabel (Bailey) Sharp.

Samuel M Sharp was born in Columbus, Ohio, November 11, 1837. The family is of Scotch-Irish extraction, and was founded in the United States by Abraham Sharp, the great-grandfather of William H Sharp, a native of Erin and a carpenter and millwright by trade. On first coming to America, Abraham Sharp settled in Maryland, and while working at his trade there made a tool chest, which many years later was in the possession of J S P Marshall, a resident of Missouri, who was also in possession of many interesting facts regarding this old and honored family Mr Sharp became one of the pioneers of Franklin county, Ohio, and at a point three and one-half miles southeast of Columbus cleared a tract of land and made a comfortable frontier home In that county he married a Miss Howard, who lived to the remarkable old age of one hundred and two years, eleven months and seven days, passing away in Illinois where Mr. Sharp had entered a quarter section of land, on the present site of the city of Peoria The children of this union were William, the grandfather of William H ; Elizabeth, who was married in Ohio to John Reader, George, who married Susan Cramer, Nancy Rachel, who married Andrew Shanklin; and Nathaniel, who married Mary Gregg

William Sharp was born May 12, 1806, and was married to Miss Mary Teegardin, who was born July 17, 1812, in Pickaway county, Ohio, a daughter of John and Mary (Brobst) Teegardin, and she died March 21, 1880 The first two persons of the name of Teegardin to come to this country were George Teegardin, the father of John, Barbara, Anna (Graul), Aaron and Mary, the grandmother of William H Sharp, and William, the father of Peter Abraham and others George and William Teegardin came to Ohio in 1811, settling on land near Ashville which their father, Aaron, from Westmoreland county, Pennsylvania, had entered, the latter, two years later, located there with his sons. His children were George, William, Jacob, Daniel, a daughter who married Mr Lauffer, Solomon, and Ann, who first married a man named Kanouse and afterwards a man named Fippen George married a Miss Brobst, daughter of Jacob Brobst. The Teegardins have been generally members of the Lutheran church. John Teegardin became a pioneer farmer in Pickaway county, Ohio and during the War of 1812 fought valiantly in the ranks of the American army.

William Sharp, after his marriage, settled on a farm in his native county, and was successfully engaged in agricultural pursuits there until his death, which occurred in the prime of his life, at the age of thirty-seven years, June 30, 1845 He was a member of the Methodist Episcopal church, and was a man whose many excellent traits of character won the confidence and respect of all with whom he was in any way associated His children were Nancy, Peter, Samuel, Samuel M., Aaron T and Margaret

Samuel M. Sharp, father of William H Sharp, was given but meagre educational advantages in his youth, as his father died when he was eight years of age, and he was compelled to early begin his battle with life. He was reared by his mother and guardian, the latter his uncle,

Aaron Teegardin, a farmer of Pickaway county, in whose household he remained until he was twenty years of age. He was married in Pickaway county to Miss Isabel Bailey, who was born in Madison township, that county, daughter of Reason W and Annie (Hoymen) Bailey, and granddaughter of William and Phoebe (Wells) Bailey. Her father a native of Maryland, and a carpenter by trade (although he spent the greater part of his life in agricultural pursuits) moved from Maryland to Ohio and subsequently to Indiana locating in Clay township, Miami county, where he died in 1873, at the age of seventy-two years. He was an industrious man, honest and upright in every way, and was a worthy member of the Lutheran church. His children were as follows Eliza A, Mary, Mahala Isabel, Jama Solomon L, Joseph L, Louis B, Phoebe and Ellis.

After his marriage Samuel M Sharp settled on a farm in Pickaway county and made that place his home until 1873, when he moved to Miami county, Indiana, arriving there on the 4th of March. He began life without any capital whatever, but by industry and good judgment, and with the assistance of his loyal and loving wife, he accumulated a competency. On locating in Miami county, he purchased 100 acres of land, to the value of which he added greatly by honest, well-directed toil. Both Mr. Sharp and his wife were actively identified with the Church of the United Brethren in Christ, aided materially in the erection of the first house of worship in their neighborhood and were always prominent in church work, Mr Sharp being class leader in the local church of his vicinity. His political inclinations made him a Democrat, and fraternally he was connected with the Masons. The following children were born to Mr and Mrs Sharp Mary M, William H, Eliza M, Jennie D Annie M, Maggie M, George L, Myrtle A, Leon C, Edmund G, Ruby N, and two who died in infancy.

William H Sharp was about twelve years of age when he accompanied the family from Ohio to Miami county, Indiana, and during his entire school period he assisted his father in the work of the farm. In young manhood his first real business venture was the clearing of a heavily timbered tract of 100 acres of land, the timber from which he sold, thus making for himself a considerable capital with which to start operations. At the age of twenty-one years he went to Wabash county and worked on a farm for three years, at the end of which time he first came to Cass county, here spending the next five years. He next purchased a team and began farming on shares of sixty acres, but after a short time returned to Miami county. There he was engaged in cultivating a rented farm for a short period, but eventually came back to Cass county and bought ninety acres of land, which he farmed for eight years, finally selling that to purchase his present property. Mr Sharp has been uniformly successful in all of his business ventures because of the exercise of shrewdness and excellent business acumen. He is an able judge of land values is known as an efficient farmer, and among all who have had business dealings with him is held in the highest respect.

On March 3, 1892, Mr Sharp was married to Miss Carrie W Buchanan daughter of James and Mary (Buchanan) Buchanan. They have no children Fraternally, Mr Sharp is connected with the Masons, Tipton Lodge No 33, and he and Mrs Sharp are attendants of the Lutheran church He has Democratic proclivities, and, while not a politician in the generally accepted meaning of the term, has served efficiently as a member of the election board The pretty homestead of Mr and Mrs Sharp is known as 'The Cedars''

JOHN L WARNER Cass county is largely agricultural but its thriving towns, its numerous industrial enterprises, its schools and its churches prove that a vigorous life underlies every activity, although here as in every section of the world, dependence is necessarily placed on the products of the land and the labor of those who develop it No matter how men may toil or how much they may achieve in any direction, they must be fed and it is the farmer, in the background who turns the wheels, who fights the battles, and who provides for the survival typified in ' the passing of the torch '' Happily there are in Cass county contented owners of land who intelligently and willingly carry on the peaceful pursuits of agriculture and, although they do not seek such a term of approbation, are, nevertheless, benefactors of mankind They are often men of wide information on many subjects, usually are men qualified for offices of public service, for the proper cultivation of the soil and a realization of its utmost yield require knowledge on many subjects Among the representative citizens of Cass county who have devoted their energies to the tilling of the soil, none are held in higher esteem than John L Warner of Clay township, a man who has impressed himself upon the community not only as an agriculturist but as a public-spirited citizen whose services in official office have aided materially in his locality's effort towards good government

Mr Warner was born January 22, 1867, in Clay township, Cass county, Indiana, and is a son of Fielding G. and Florence (Maurice) Warner, and a grandson of David Warner His father was of French and Welsh descent and was born at Dayton, Ohio, November 4, 1837, and died December 27 1907 in Clay township, while his mother, who was born in France and came to this country when she was nine years of age, still survives and makes her home with Mr Warner's brother, Samuel, who lives on the farm adjoining that of John L Warner Mr Warner's parents had six children, as follows David, who died when aged one year, Alice, who married Will Smith and died when thirty-four years of age, Emma, who was eight years old at the time of her death Florence who died at the age of six years, John L ; and Samuel, who married Blanche Powell, and has one child Florence, who was born December 3, 1907

John L Warner attended the district schools of Clay township and is a graduate of Hall's Business College in Logansport, Indiana He was reared to agricultural pursuits, in which he has been engaged all of his life His present farm, a tract of one hundred and seventy-two acres, is one of the finest in this part of the county, and during the twenty years he has resided here he has brought his land to a high state of cultivation New and modern structures have been erected by Mr Warner, and his entire property testifies eloquently to his able management and

"SOMMERLOWE," RESIDENCE OF MR. AND MRS. JOHN L. WARNER

good judgment. Progressive in all matters, in 1912 he allied himself with the so-called Bull Moose party, and at the present time is efficiently serving as a member of the county council. He has also served as trustee of Clay township and has always brought to his official services the same conscientious devotion to duty that has made him so successful in his business affairs. His brother, Samuel Warner, is the present assessor of Bethlehem township. With his family, Mr Warner attends the Christian church.

On December 20, 1888, Mr Warner was married to Miss Minnie Alma Shilling. One child was born to this union Florence Ruth, who died at the age of five months.

Mrs Warner is a native of Clay township, Cass county, and was born May 12, 1865, a daughter of Samuel and Elizabeth (Maurer) Shilling, and her parents were natives of Ohio, of German lineage, and both are deceased.

Mrs Warner was educated in the common schools and the city schools of Logansport. She is a member of the Bethel Methodist Episcopal church and a member of the Ladies' Aid Society in the Spring Creek Christian church.

Mr Warner is a member and deacon in the Spring Creek Christian church. They are people who enjoy life in their beautiful country seat, known as "Summit Lodge," and they have a five-passenger Hupmobile touring car. They are citizens who stand high in the social world of Cass county.

ADELBERT L HOOVER. The name of Hoover has long been prominently associated with the agricultural history of Cass county, where for years members of the family have contributed materially to the growth and development of what is now one of the most prosperous sections of Indiana. They have also enrolled among those who have promoted movements for the advancement of education, morality and good citizenship fairly earning the right to be classed with their community's representative men. Adelbert L Hoover, a well-known member of this old and honored family, is maintaining the high standard set by his forebears, and is one of the agriculturists of Washington township who take a pride in developing their land through the use of modern methods and appliances. He was born August 22, 1871, in Richland county, Wisconsin, and is a son of Thomas and Laura (Yates) Hoover, the former of whom brought the family to Cass county more than a quarter of a century ago and is still living on his farm. There were four children in the family Mrs Mary Berryman, William, Jacob and Adelbert L.

The early education of Adelbert L Hoover was secured in the public schools of Wisconsin, and his tuition was completed in the institutions of Cass county whence he had come when he was about fifteen years of age. During his early youth, in his struggles to secure a property of his own, he met with the usual difficulties that bar the path of a youth who without capital or influential friends is seeking a competence and independent position, but each experience added to his fund of knowledge and prepared him to better face the next obstacle. Industry and perseverance finally triumphed, and at this time he is the owner of a handsome property of 100 acres, which produces large crops, and on which he has made many valuable improvements. He devotes his whole time to general farming and stock raising, in both of which lines he has met with uniform success and among his neighbors and associates he is known as a good, practical farmer and an excellent judge of live stock.

On May 2, 1901, Mr Hoover was united in marriage in Cass county with Miss Margaret Alma Martin, daughter of Herman and Margaret (Blozier) Martin of this county. They have had no children. Mrs Hoover is a member of the Union Presbyterian church of Washington township and has taken an active part in work of a religious and charitable nature. Fraternally, Mr Hoover is popular with the members of the local lodge of the Independent Order of Odd Fellows, No 314 of Wallen, while his political connection is with the Democratic party, in the activities of which he has taken a leading part in his section, although he has never cared for nor sought public office. Mr Hoover's life has been a busy and a useful one, his business methods have ever been unmarred by stain or blemish and at all times he has been true to the obligations and duties that have rested upon him. As a man who has the best interests of his community at heart he enjoys widespread esteem, and his acquaintance is large and his friendships numerous. Mr and Mrs Hoover's homestead is known as "Cottage House" and is one of the pretty properties of the county.

JAMES VERNON. Cass county is the home of some excellent citizens who have employed themselves in tilling the soil. Many of these have spent their entire lives on the property which they are now cultivating, and in this class stands James Vernon, of Washington township, who owns forty acres and farms about eighty acres on the township road. A member of a family which has been connected with agricultural affairs for a number of generations, his whole training has been along this line, and as a result he has made a success of his operations, and is justly considered one of his community's most skilled agriculturists. Mr Vernon was born in the old home, which still stands on his present farm, August 12, 1850 and is a son of Pickering and Elizabeth (Burkit) Vernon. His father a native of Greenville. Darke county, Ohio, came to Indiana in young manhood, and purchased land from the government in Cass county for $1.50 per acre, here spending the remainder of his life as a farmer, and dying advanced in years with the respect and esteem of the people of his community. He married Elizabeth Burkit a member of an old and honored Cass county family, and they became the parents of nine children, as follows: William, who is deceased. Ensley, John, James, Jane, Thomas and Margaret, who are deceased, Mary, and Daniel, who is deceased. Both Mr and Mrs Vernon were deeply religious people and reared their children to honest, God-fearing lives.

James Vernon was given only ordinary educational advantages during his youth but close observation and much reading and discussion of timely subjects have made him an exceedingly well-informed man. With his father and brothers he spent his youthful days in clearing, grubbing and general farm labor and when he reached the age of twenty-four years embarked upon a career of his own. For some years he rented land from his father, working faithfully and industriously, and carefully saving his earnings until such time as he was able to invest in property his first small purchase forming the nucleus for his present farm. Mr. Vernon is one of the most progressive of farmers, and is always ready to adopt new methods and to experiment with new inventions. As a result, his land is in a high state of cultivation, and is considered one of the most valuable farms of its size in this part of the township. Although general farming has occupied the greater part of his attention, he has also devoted himself to some extent in raising stock, his success in this line having been commensurate with the labor he has expended upon it. Mr. Vernon has never cared to enter public life, his ambitions being satisfied in his farm and his home, but he is known as a public-spirited citizen, and any measure which commends itself to his judgment as one which promises to be of benefit to the community can depend upon his hearty support. He holds membership in the Christian church which he attends consistently and supports liberally.

Mr. Vernon was married September 25, 1873, to Miss Mahala F. West, daughter of Paynter and Catherine (Myers) West, and to this union there were born two children, namely: Rose, deceased, who was the wife of Alva Knapp, a Cass county farmer, and had one child, Ellis, who is also deceased; and Blanch, who married Emmett Small and had two children—John and Zelma Olive. On September 7, 1909, Mr. Vernon was married to Mrs. Katie (Eberley) Honicker, and three children have been born to them—Frank, Walter and Carrie. The pretty homestead of Mr. and Mrs. James Vernon is known as "Park Lawn."

ROLLIN T. MARTIN. It is a noticeable fact that the agriculturists of any section who have the best farms are those who take the most pride in the prosperity of their community and the most active part in the upbuilding and development of the section in which they reside. This holds true in Cass county as elsewhere, and one of these representative farmer-citizens is Rollin T. Martin, who has always been in the leading ranks of any movement likely to prove of benefit to his locality. Mr. Martin has spent his entire career in this part of the state, and is thoroughly acquainted with soil and climatic conditions, as well as with the most minute detail of the vocation of farming. He was born May 9, 1862, on the old Martin homestead in Washington township, Cass county, Indiana, and is a son of Jesse and Christina (Mummey) Martin. Jesse Martin was engaged in agricultural pursuits in Cass county, and a full sketch of his career will be found in another part of this work.

Rollin T. Martin was reared in his native township, securing his education in the district schools, which he attended only when the weather was such that farm work could not be done. He continued to assist his father until he reached the age of twenty-two years, at which time he began farming on his own account. Later he bought his present property from his father, and this tract of eighty acres situated on the Walton road has continued to be his home until the present time. Mr. Martin is an able agriculturist and an excellent judge of live stock

He has made numerous valuable improvements on his land which is equipped with a comfortable home, a commodious barn, and outbuildings for the shelter of his stock grain and implements, all substantial in character and of an attractive architectural design. Modern methods and improved machinery are used exclusively, and the excellent crops that are raised justify the procedure.

On May 14, 1885, Mr. Martin was united in marriage with Miss Caroline M. Schwalm, of Cass county, a member of an old and honored family of this section, and to this union there have been born six children, namely: Earl G, who was educated in the schools of Logansport, and now resides at home assisting his father in the management of the farm; Ethel L, who also resides with her parents; Eunice P and Helen M, who are teachers in the public schools of Cass county; Ruby G, who is attending the Walton high school; and Lois E, a graded school pupil. The family is connected with the Presbyterian church of which Jesse Martin was a charter member, while Rollin T is now acting in the capacity of deacon. Mr. Martin bears the reputation of being a man who has always attended strictly to his own business, and has not been desirous of entering public affairs. However, he takes an interest in all that affects his community, and his hearty co-operation and support are given to those measures which he feels will be of benefit to his community. The Martin farm is noted for its Short-horn cattle, which bring top-notch prices in the markets. The homestead of Mr. and Mrs. Martin is known as "Maple Lawn Farm," and is the abode of hospitality.

MANASSEH M. MARTIN. One of the old and honored families of Cass county is that of Martin, whose members have been identified with the agricultural interests of this section for many years, and whose activities have served in material manner to promote the growth and development of the community and its interests. Styles and methods of farming have changed during the past half a century, but the family contributes to the new school of practical, scientific farming just as it did to the old style. A worthy representative of the name is found in Manasseh M. Martin of Washington township, who is cultivating an excellent tract of sixty acres, located on the Walton road, about nine miles southeast of Logansport. Mr. Martin has been a life-long resident of this section and years of experience have given him a practical knowledge of conditions in this vicinity, where he is known as an industrious agriculturist and exemplary citizen. He was born on the old Martin homestead, located in Washington township, Cass county, Indiana, January 11, 1871, and is a son of Jesse and Christina (Mummcy) Martin. Jesse Martin was for many years one of the leading farmers of his part of the county. A complete review of his life and labors will be found on another page of this work.

Manasseh M. Martin secured his education in the same manner as most farmers' sons of his day, being a student in the district schools when he could be spared from the work of the home farm, principally during the winter months. He was thus fitted mentally while securing a strong constitution and a knowledge of the principles of his chosen vocation, for even in his youth he had decided to follow in the footsteps of his forefathers and to continue a tiller of the soil. He remained on the old homestead, assisting his father until he reached his majority, at which time he left the parental roof and started to make his own way in the world. Not long thereafter he located on his present property, which then had but few improvements and was far from being fully productive. With youthful energy he settled down to develop his land determined that he would one day be the owner of one of the best farms of its size in the township. That he has succeeded in his efforts, is shown by the general appearance of the property, every detail of which gives evidence of a wise and capable management. General farming has been given the greater part of his attention, although he has also devoted some time to the raising of stock, and is known as a good judge of cattle and horses. Like other successful men of his locality, he has realized that one of the surest ways to advance one's private interests is to advance the interest of the community, and has acted acordingly, lending his hearty support to every movement that is calculated to advance public progress. He has been identified with Republican politics for some time, and was chairman of the precinct committee although his identification with public life has been rather as a director than as an active participant in search of honors. With his family, he attends the Presbyterian church.

Mr. Martin was married May 14, 1895, to Laura E. Schwalm, the estimable daughter of Henry and Helena (Haemel) Schwalm, a sketch of whose careers will be found in another part of this work under the caption of George Schwalm. Mr. and Mrs. Martin have had one son, Roy E., who graduated from the public schools in the class of 1911, and who is a practical agriculturist, being associated with his parents. Mrs. Martin is a native of Cass county, born September 16, 1871, and educated in the common schools. She has been treasurer of the Missionary Society for ten years and is in the office yet. She has been one of the efficient Sunday school teachers for twenty-two years—of girls—and some of these girls are now married. Mrs. Martin and her class put in two stained or art glass windows in the Presbyterian church in Washington township. She has been one of the most active ladies in the county in all work pertaining to the advancement of her home community. She has been an able factor in the establishment of her beautiful home known as "Shady Nook." She is a member of the Home Makers' Club of Cass county, which was organized February, 1913.

WILLARD E. SHANTEAU, proprietor of the Twin Beeches Farm, a tract in Washington township that has been developed from its virgin state to its present excellence by its owner, was born March 28, 1870, in a house at the corner of Twelfth and Broadway, Logansport, Indiana, and is a son of Sylvester and Lydia (Rogers) Shanteau.

Sylvester Shanteau was born near the city of Toledo, in Lucas county, Ohio, where as a lad he drove horses on the canal. Subsequently, he worked his way to Logansport, Indiana, where he learned the trade of blacksmith, an occupation which he followed during the remainder of his life in Cass county in connection with farming. He became one of his community's best known citizens and at the time of his death was in comfortable circumstances, and had a wide circle of warm friends. Mr. Shanteau married Miss Lydia Rogers and they became the parents of seven children, namely: Willard E., Marcus Frank, who resides in Logansport, Charles, of Cincinnati, Ohio, and three who died young.

Willard E. Shanteau was still a lad when brought to Washington township by his father, and here he secured his education in the public schools during such time as he could be spared from the work of the farm. He was an ambitious, industrious lad, making the most of his opportunities and thoroughly training himself in every detail of farm work, and by the time he was twenty years of age was able to make his first payment on his present farm, a tract of forty acres of land. This property was in rather poor condition, but Mr. Shanteau's intelligent treatment of the soil, his untiring perseverance and his patient industry have worked wonders, and the land is now considered one of the valuable tracts of the township. General farming and stock raising have received his attention, and his ventures have proved successful because of his close application to his work. He has not entered public life and cares but little for politics except as a voter, but has interested himself to some extent in fraternal work, and is a popular member of the local lodge of the Modern Woodmen of America at Walton.

Mr. Shanteau was married November 25, 1890, to Miss Fannie L. Jenness, daughter of Perry and Margaret (Walters) Jenness, residents of Logansport, and to this union there have been born three children, two sons and one daughter. Owen, now eighteen years of age and who resides with his parents, assists in the cultivation of the home farm and spends the winter terms in teaching school in Washington township. The members of the family are affiliated with the Christian church, in which all have many warm friends.

JOHN J. HUMMEL. Some of Cass county's best agriculturists are men who originally engaged in other pursuits, but who, coming of families whose members had for generations been tillers of the soil, eventually found the call of the land too strong and returned to the occupation of their forefathers, finding therein the medium in which they have worked their way to success and independence. In this category is found John J. Hummel, who is carrying on operations on a well-cultivated tract of 188 acres, situated on the Hummel road, about six and one-half miles from Logansport. Mr. Hummel is one of his section's good, practical farmers, and his large crops testify to his ability to cultivate his property under the most modern methods. He was born on the old Hummel place, in Washington township, Cass county, Indiana, September 3, 1871, and is a son of George A. and Elizabeth (Deitz) Hummel. His father, a native of Hummelstown, Dauphin county, Pennsylvania, came to Madison county, Indiana, in 1862 as a young man, but after a short stay there made removal to Cass county, and here he was engaged in farming up to the time of his death, in August 1908. He and his wife were the parents of five children, namely: Anna, who is deceased; John J., of this review; William G., living on the old home place; Mrs. Minnie E. Cripe, and Mayme M., who also lives on the Hummel homestead.

"PLEASANT VIEW STOCK FARM," RESIDENCE OF MR. AND MRS. REUBEN G. BALL.

John J Hummel secured his education in the district schools in the vicinity of his father's farm, in the meantime being trained to the occupation of agriculturist. He also devoted himself to learning the carpenter's trade, became a skilled mechanic, and for some years was so engaged, erecting many houses, barns and other structures in this section. In 1892, Mr Hummel returned to farming, purchasing his present property, then a poorly cultivated tract which boasted of but minor improvements and was considered of only nominal value. Twenty years of intelligent treatment has worked wonders with this soil, and Mr Hummel may now lay claim to being the owner of one of the handsome properties of his county. He is always quick to take advantage of new innovations, realizing that modern methods bring better results than the hit-or-miss operations of former years, and the appearance of his farm testifies mutely, but eloquently, to the presence of good management. His stock are sleek and well fed, and Mr Hummel bears the reputation among his neighbors as being an excellent judge of cattle.

In March, 1897, Mr Hummel was united in marriage with Miss Nora B Shanks, daughter of Henry and Mary (Blue) Shanks, and to this union there have been born two children. Forest J, who is now in his third year of high school, a member of class 1914, and Ide Lorea, who is attending the Young America school in the seventh grade. Mr Hummel has interested himself to some extent in fraternal work, and is a popular member of the Odd Fellows Lodge No 477, and Moose lodge. His religious belief is that of the Lutheran church and Mrs Hummel's of the Baptist.

REUBEN GEORGE BALL Among the pioneer families of Cass county whose long connection with the agricultural interests have made their names well known in this section of the state, none have attained greater prestige, perhaps, than that of Ball. Coming to the then wilderness of Indiana at an early day representatives of this name bore their full share in the early development of the locality, and their descendants have ably carried on the work which they started. Located in Clay township on Rural Free Delivery Route No 5 is the handsome property belonging to William B Ball a tract that is now being intelligently operated by Mr Ball's son Reuben G Ball a young man of industry and enterprise who has inherited the sterling traits of character which have gained the bearers of the name the esteem and respect of their fellow-citizens in years past. Reuben G Ball was born August 28, 1886, on the old Ball homestead, which he now operates and is a son of William B and Jennie (Coons) Ball. The family was founded in Cass county by his grandfather, David Ball, who was born in Philadelphia, Pennsylvania, October 2, 1811, and came to Indiana in young manhood. Here William B Ball was born in a little log house, the original pioneer home of the family, and grew to manhood in the woods, being trained to agricultural pursuits. He still survives and is one of his township's leading citizens. William B Ball was married (first) to Jennie Coons the daughter of George Coons, also an early settler, and she died on November 11, 1892. In 1905, Mr Ball married (second) Mrs Etta (Grauel) Metzger, the widow of Dave Metzger.

Reuben G Ball received his education in the district schools of Clay township and was reared to the work of the farm As a young man he also learned the trade of carpenter, which he followed for five years, and spent another year in the west, working in Montana On his return, he resumed farming, and on the day following his marriage located on the present property, which he has since been conducting for his father This tract consists of 100 acres, and is in a high state of cultivation, the land being fertile with an abundant water supply, and supplied with all modern appliances and improvements A fine set of buildings enhance the value of this farm, the residence, built in 1898, and the barn, erected in 1900, having been put up by Mr Ball and his father Mr Ball is a man of progressive ideas, and has demonstrated that he is fully capable of obtaining a full measure of success from his operations

On March 6, 1912 Mr Ball was married to Miss Agnes B Wilson, who was born in Benton county, Indiana, daughter of Robert and Jane (Henderson) Wilson natives of Scotland Mr and Mrs Ball are the parents of one little daughter Catharine Irene, born January 16, 1913 Mr and Mrs Ball are members of the Baptist church, and have been active in its work In his political views Mr Ball is a Republican, but so far he has found no time to devote other than a good citizen's interest in matters of a public nature However, his support and cooperation are given to movements calculated to be of a beneficial nature to his community or its people He is a member of the Eel River Lodge, I O O F, corner of Fifth and North streets, Logansport A young man of pleasing personality, he has a wide acquaintance in Clay township, and is highly regarded by a wide circle of personal friends The homestead of Mr and Mrs Reuben Ball is known in Clay township as "The Pleasant View Stock Farm"

HARRY N LITTLE Some of the most enterprising agriculturists of Cass county belong to the younger generation who bring to their work the enthusiasm and ambition of youth, while they profit by the experiences of those who have preceded them A large proportion of the farmers of this class come of old agricultural families, whose members have for generations been tillers of the soil, and thus they contribute to their labors a natural inclination that is helpful in solving the many problems that arise to try the abilities of the agriculturist Harry Little, an energetic and successful young farmer and stock raiser, may be said to belong to this class For about five years he has been operating his father's property, a tract of 172 acres of well-cultivated land, located about two miles northwest of Onward, and the satisfactory results he is securing from his labor stamps him as one of his section's able young farmers Mr Little was born on the old Little homestead, in Miami county, Indiana March 17, 1886, and is a son of Lewis and Alice (Sullivan) Little His father one of the leading farmers of Miami county, has been engaged in tilling the soil all his life and is still engaged in extensive farming and stock raising operations there He and his wife have had five children namely Susan, who became the wife of John Williams, Minnie who married Arthur Mays, Laura, who is the wife of Homer Reed, Charles and Harry.

Harry Little was reared on his father's homestead place in Miami county, and there commenced his schooling which was finished after he came to Cass county. He was thoroughly trained in the multitude of duties with which the modern agriculturist must be familiar to obtain a full measure of success, and continued to work in association with his father until he reached the age of twenty-two years. At that time, having demonstrated his ability he was placed by his father in the management of the farm on which he is now carrying on operations, and which, in the short space of five years, he has made one of the finest in his part of Tipton township. The greater part of his attention has been given to general farming, although stock raising has also come in for a share of his activities, and in all departments of farm work he has shown himself possessed of ability, good judgment and farsightedness. Numerous improvements on this land have been made under his supervision, and substantial buildings have been erected, the latest being a modern home, equipped with all comforts and conveniences substantial in character, and of architectural beauty.

On August 26, 1908, Mr. Little was united in marriage with Miss Olive E. Mays, the daughter of Edward and Florence (Mackey) Mays, of Cass county, and to this union there has been born two sons, Gordon M. and Nelson L. With his wife, Mr. Little attends the Christian church, in the work of which they have been active, and in which they have numerous friends. He has not taken other than a good citizen's interest in matters of a political nature.

CHARLES B. WILSON. Belonging to a family which has resided in Cass county for more than eighty years and has taken an important part in the advancement and development of the agricultural interests of the county, Charles B. Wilson of Tipton township, holds prestige as a worthy representative of his section's best farming citizenship. He is now the owner of 176 acres of excellent land, in addition to cultivating which he is serving capably as a member of the township board of trustees. Mr. Wilson was born in a log cabin located just across the road from his present farm, on the Marion road, about seven miles from Logansport, and is a son of Andrew and Eleanor D. (Tucker) Wilson.

Andrew Wilson was born in Virginia, April 7, 1812, and when six months old was taken by his parents to Greenbrier county, in that state, where he was reared to manhood. About the year 1829 he left the Old Dominion, journeyed overland by team, and settled near New Waverly, and in 1839 came to Tipton township and took up a government claim. Here he purchased two hundred and ten acres of land at a dollar and a quarter per acre, built a little log cabin, and at once began the difficult task of developing a farm from the heavily timbered land. As the years passed he continued to add to the improvements of his property and when he died, December 22, 1892, he was one of the substantial men of his community. He was a member of the United Brethren church, and in his political affiliations was a Republican. On November 10, 1842, he was married to Miss Eleanor D. Tucker, who was born in Clark county, Ohio, daughter of James and Charlotte (Dunn) Tucker. To this union there were born the following children: William H., born December 4, 1843, and now deceased; Harry G., born in 1845, a resident of Chicago, Marcellus T, born in 1847, a resident of Tipton township, Alice, born December 26, 1818, who married A J Sharts, Carrie, born May 4, 1851, a resident of Los Angeles, California, Linnie J, born August 8, 1853, who married Andrew Shirley, Mary Louise, born June 22, 1855 deceased, James A, born October 5, 1857, who died in infancy, Jennie, born February 24, 1859, who married J M Stucky, and is now deceased, Charles B, Martha E, born November 1, 1863, who married Thos East, and Laura, born October 12, 1868 who married Grant Hughell, resident of Madison county

Charles B Wilson divided his boyhood days between work on the home farm and attendance at the old Wilson school, and he subsequently was a student in Logansport for one year. On reaching his majority he engaged in farming on his own account, and as the years passed gradually bought more and more of the old homestead, finally purchasing the interests of the other heirs to his father's estate. He now has a well-cultivated property of 176 acres, and is justly regarded as one of his township's most substantial citizens. He uses the most approved modern methods in his work, takes a pride in being able to advance his interests by the use of the latest invented machinery, and a consequence has attained a full measure of success. He is known as a man of public spirit, who has the welfare of his community at heart, and his neighbors and associates cheerfully testify to his integrity in matters of a business nature

Mr Wilson was married to Miss Amanda Catherine Gottschall January 1 1884. Mrs Wilson was born in Cass county, Indiana, August 25, 1863 the fifth in a family of six children, two sons and four daughters, born to Henry and Maria Jane (Roderick) Gottschall. Both of her parents are deceased. Mrs Wilson was reared and educated in her native county and is a lady of pleasing address, sociable, and has a kind word for all. The eldest of Mr and Mrs Wilson's children is Chester H, who received his diploma from the public schools, class of 1912, and put in one year at high school work at Onward Ind. Byron A received his diploma from the public schools at the age of thirteen and spent one year in high school. Clara Louise is in the seventh grade and has also taken music. Mr and Mrs Wilson are giving their children good practical educations. Mr Wilson is a trustee of Tipton township and was elected to that office in 1908 for four years but his term is extended and will end in 1914. Mr and Mrs Wilson are consistent members of the United Brethren church and he is affiliated fraternally with the Independent Order of Odd Fellows, of Anoka, Indiana. Their homestead is known as Maple Grove Stock Farm

ADELBERT C BOWYER One of the best known families of Cass county and of the most highly esteemed ones is represented worthily by Adelbert C Bowyer a well known farmer in the vicinity of New Waverly in this county. A sketch of the family is presented elsewhere in this work in the biography of John Bowyer the paternal grandfather of the subject, and for details of the father of Adelbert Bowyer the reader is referred to the life of John M Bowyer mentioned above. It suffices to say at this juncture that Adelbert C Bowyer is the son of Allen W and Elizabeth (William) Bowyer and the grandson of Lewis M Bowyer, pioneers of this section of the state and esteemed throughout their long and useful lives as only honest and worthy men are honored

Adelbert C Bowyer was born in Miami township in this county, on February 7, 1866 As a boy he attended the school at Walton and the Cross Roads, after which he turned his attention to the farm and its care early learning much of the practical side of farming as a result of his association with his father in the home work At the age of twenty the young man had rented a tract of farm land from his paternal grandfather, who assisted him greatly by the advice and instructions he was so well qualified to offer The lessons he had early learned in industry and general good management soon enabled him to purchase land in the vicinity of Walton, where he lived for some years, eventually buying his present farm near Lewisburg The place is a well managed one of one hundred and fifty acres lying on Pipe creek, and is well known for one of the most thrifty and productive places in the community Prosperity and contentment are attributes of the Bowyer home that are readily discernible to the most casual observer and the family is one that enjoys the friendship and high regard of all who share in their acquaintance

Mr Bowyer in young manhood married Miss Mary C Fidler, February 27, 1887 and to them have been born two children, Clifford A, their first born married Luella Flannigan, and Wayne W, is the younger child

Fraternally Mr Bowyer is affiliated with the Improved Order of Red Men, Kokomo, Howard county, and he and his family are members of the New Light Christian church He gives all due attention to the duties of citizenship, and has a share in all the works of civic improvement carried on in his town and county The homestead of Mr and Mrs Bowyer is known as "Pine Lodge"

OSCAR WILSON Among the members of that class of self-made men of whom Cass county has reason to be proud, men who, unaided have fought the battles of life without capital or influential friends and have worked their way to the top through the sheer force of their own ability and industry, Oscar Wilson, now a farmer of Tipton township, takes prominent place He has been a resident of this part of Indiana all of his life, and has accumulated a handsome property of 200 acres, located on the banks of the Wabash river, near Lewisburg Mr Wilson was born April 7 1856, near Peru, in Peru township, Miami county, Indiana, and is a son of Absalom and Magdalena (Fisher) Wilson The parents of Mr Wilson both came from Clarksburg, West Virginia, not long after their marriage, settling in Miami county, where they passed the remainder of their lives in the cultivation of the soil They were the parents of nine children, namely Oscar, Thomas J, George F Omer, Absalom, Olive, Margaret A Ella and Noah

Oscar Wilson received his educational training in an old log school house in the vicinity of his native home, which he attended during the short winter terms the whole period of his boyhood being devoted during the spring, summer and fall months to work on his father's farm For some years after attaining his majority he rented land from his father but subsequently acquired enough means to purchase a property on Big Indian creek in Pulaski county, where he managed to bring 160 acres of land under a high state of cultivation, although when he first located thereon it had been in its virgin condition, without improvement of any kind. There he continued to reside until 1895, in which year he came to his present location, here purchasing 100 acres, to which he has added from time to time, now having 200 acres of some of the best land to be found in this part of Cass county. He has carried on general farming and stock raising, and has made improvements of a substantial and valuable nature, the general appearance of his land testifying to his ability as an agriculturist and business man. Among his neighbors and associates, Mr Wilson bears a high reputation for integrity and probity of character, and he is generally esteemed by all who know him. Mr and Mrs Wilson reside in their modern, eight-room residence, recently erected by Mr Wilson, and equipped with all modern conveniences and comforts. Here they entertain their numerous friends with old-fashioned hospitality.

On February 22, 1881, Mr Wilson was married to Miss Julia C Scovel, daughter of Harmon and Cornelia (Huested) Scovel. Her father, a native of Germany, emigrated to the United States when nineteen years of age, locating first in New York, and later at Fort Wayne, Indiana, and finally settled on a farm in Allen county. Mr and Mrs Wilson have had five children. Elma M and Zelma C, twins, the former of whom is deceased, while the latter resides with her parents, Carrie, who is deceased, Nola L, residing at home, and Harmon, who is a student at Defiance, Ohio. Mr Wilson is a member of the Independent Order of Odd Fellows, No 52 of Peru, Indiana, among the members of which he numbers many sincere friends. His religious affiliation is with the Christian church, of which for years he has been a consistent member and liberal supporter. He has been a lifelong adherent of Democratic policies and candidates. His career has been a long and honorable one, and now he may look back over a life that has been not alone of benefit to himself but to his fellowmen, content in the knowledge that no stain or blemish mars an honorable record.

GEORGE P SHARTS. Among the old and honored residents of Cass county who are devoting their activities to the cultivation of the soil, George P Sharts, of Tipton township, holds prominent place. Mr. Sharts has been a resident of Tipton township since 1849, and has borne no small part in the development of this section from a practical wilderness, into one of the most productive sections of Indiana, and bears a high reputation among the people of his vicinity, who know him as an industrious agriculturist and a citizen who has always had the best interests of his community at heart. His present sixty-acre farm is located on the Galveston road about ten miles from Logansport. Mr Sharts was born November 9, 1839 near Germantown, in Montgomery county, Ohio, and is a son of George and Frances (Bear) Sharts. His parents were born in the vicinity of Hagerstown, Maryland, from whence they moved to Frederick county, that state, and later removed to Montgomery county, Ohio, where they resided for some years. In 1849 they came to Cass county, Indiana, settling first on the farm now occupied by N B Richinson, and lived in a little log house for some years, until this shelter was replaced by a dwelling of more modern character and architecture. A large portion of this land was covered with a heavy growth of timber, which was cleared by Mr Sharts and his sons, and there he spent the remainder of his life, his death occurring in 1853 when he was fifty-three years of age, and that of his wife in 1875, when she was seventy-two years old. They became wealthy and substantial people of their section, although the elder Sharts did not live to see his labors bear their full share of fruit. George P and Frances (Bear) Sharts became the parents of the following children. Mary M, Rose Ann and Elizabeth, who are all deceased, Mrs Catherine Hahn, Mrs Jane P Phillips, Abraham and John, who are both deceased, George P, William O who is deceased, Abijah J, who is engaged in farming in Tipton township, and Caroline Lucas, who is deceased

George P Sharts was only sixteen years of age when his father died, and, being the eldest of the sons he was called upon to bear the brunt of the farm work as soon as he was old enough to do so. His educational advantages were somewhat limited, but he made the most of his opportunities, and being an intelligent and observing youth soon acquired a good schooling. On leaving the parental roof, he started working out among the agriculturists of his locality, thriftily saving his earnings with the end in view of becoming the owner of land of his own, and this ambition has been accomplished for his present land is now one of the best properties of its size in this part of the township. He is engaged in general farming and stock raising, and the success that has rewarded his efforts may be taken as an indication of his ability in his chosen line of endeavor. Mr Sharts is a member of the local lodge of the Masonic fraternity at New Waverly No 484, and his religious connection is with the Christian church, which he attends consistently and supports liberally

On February 13, 1861, Mr Sharts was united in marriage with Miss Maria Surface, who was born July 21, 1843, daughter of the Rev Adam Surface. She was born in Preble county Ohio, and joined the United Brethren church when she was fifteen years of age, continuing to be a faithful member thereof until her death, December 19, 1885. Mr and Mrs Sharts had two children · George A. born August 20, 1876, who lived only six months, and Elnora M, who married Fremont Haynes, is a resident of Tipton township. The home of Mr Sharts is known as "The Sunset View Farm."

JOHN A RUSH. To the uninitiated in farm lore, no especial credit attaches to the accomplishment of the man who begins his farming activities as a renter, dependent upon the extent of his crop for the means to reserve to himself the privilege of harvesting another crop in the following year, but to one who has seen something of the trials of the renting farmer, or better yet, has experienced in some measure the hardships that follow thick and fast through some seasons, the success that a renter finally evolves stands out, brave and staunch. John A Rush is one of these men who command the admiration and esteem of every honest man who has witnessed something of his rise in agriculture in the past forty years. He is known today for one of the ablest and most successful farmers and stock raisers in the county, and his place is situated in the fine farming neighborhood south of the Wabash river, near the mouth of Hart creek in Tipton township. A native of the county, here reared, he has been identified practically all his life with the industry of agriculture and its associated business of stock raising, and from his slender start as a renter, he has accumulated a very substantial and productive property while in his capacity as a citizen and a member of the social community, is one of the most highly esteemed men in Tipton township.

Mr. Rush was born on the old Lendall Smith farm, near Onward, in Tipton township, on March 11, 1857. His parents were John and Elizabeth (Colvin) Rush and the father was a native of the state of Pennsylvania, whence he came to Indiana as a boy with his parents, and it may be mentioned here, that they were the first of the name of Rush to locate in Cass county, which has ever since known the business and social influence of the family. The ten children of John and Elizabeth Rush were named as follows, and nearly all of them are living today in places of usefulness in various parts of this county. Silas, the eldest, is now deceased; Mary, William, John A., of this review, Frank, Milton, Ira, Willard, Charles and May.

As a boy John A. Rush attended the common schools of Miami county, and there he received a practical schooling that well equipped him for the career he has since followed. While a school boy he was being trained thoroughly in the duties of the farm, building up a sound physical constitution that has stood him in excellent stead all through his rugged life in the farming industry. At the age of twenty-three he began independent farming as a renter, and from his good management and the profits of his labor, was in later years able to purchase his present estate. In early life he wedded Emma J. Grimes, the daughter of John and Nancy (Gard) Grimes and to them have been born three children as follows: Minnie B., the eldest, is the wife of Harry Griffith, they have three children—Dorsey, Esther and Thelma, Edna May, the second child of the Rush home, is the wife of Harry Rhodes, and their one child is named Helen, Walter E., the third and youngest child, is yet a school boy and gives promise of a life of usefulness in maturity.

Mr. Rush and his family are active members of the Christian church, and are prominent in the social affairs of the community. During his residence in Tipton township, Mr. Rush has taken an active and wholesome interest in civic affairs, and any improvements calculated to better conditions in his community never fail of his generous support.

JOHN T. DECKER. Too much cannot be said in praise of the worthy influence emanating from the life of a man who devotes his entire life to the development of a given section of the country, and who continues in that work despite the discouragements and misfortunes that may attend his efforts. It may be said that the man who devotes his life to the wresting of prosperity from the soil is benefited as much thereby as is his community, and some truth is found in that counter-claim, but the fact remains that it is thuswise that prosperity comes to any community, and so it must continue to be attained. Among the well established farming men of Cass county who have given years of toil to the

upbuilding of his particular part of the town may be mentioned John T Decker, who is a native son of the county, born within its confines on April 10, 1862, and thus has better than half a century of identification with the county to his credit His parents, Moses and Sarah (McHenry) Decker, came from Ohio in their younger days, here settling and passing their remaining days The Decker family is one of New Jersey ancestry and associations, and is of German and Irish blood Moses and Sarah (McHenry) Decker were the son and daughter of John Decker and John McHenry and they were married in Cass county where they settled down on a farm and here reared their family The father built with his own hands the log cabin in which his children were born, and there he lived in quiet and contentment until death claimed him in 1897

John T Decker, the Miami township farmer whose name heads this review, lived on the old home place until December, 1911 when he moved to his present fine place of two hundred acres He was married November 15 1881 to Miss Esther A Scott Mrs Decker is a native of Fulton county and was born December 10, 1861, and educated in the common schools Both her parents are deceased She is a lady who has the universal respect of all who know her, as she is a woman of pleasing and agreeable personality, and has always aided her husband in counsel and advice Her pretty and comfortable home is her paradise To Mr and Mrs Decker one son was born, Claude, who was taken by death when he was a promising young man of twenty-four years He was provided with many noble attributes of character and loved by all Since deprived of the aid and companionship of his one son, Mr Decker has continued to care for his farm without the help of any, and he has one of the most attractive and productive places in the township He is regarded as one of the prosperous and competent farming men of the vicinity, and his standing among his fellow-men is one of the highest order, and of which he is in every way worthy With his good wife he attends the Christian church, and he is a Republican in his political faith He has served his township on occasions as supervisor, giving praiseworthy service on those occasions, and he is known for one of the capable and consistent citizens of the township

JOHN M BOWYER A resident of Cass county for more than seventy years, and of Tipton township for a period exceeding forty-five years John M Bowyer is entitled to mention as one of the old and honored citizens of his section, and as such is deserving of mention in a work of this nature Mr Bowyer has devoted his whole life to the cultivation of the soil in Cass county, and has witnessed and participated in the wonderful changes that have transformed what was once a wilderness of timber and brush into one of the most productive agricultural sections of Indiana He is now the owner of ninety acres of fine farming land on the Anoka river about ten miles southeast of Logansport Mr Bowyer was born April 24, 1841, in Miami township, Cass county, and is a son of Lewis and Malinda (Wilson) Bowyer His father, a native of Germany, came to the United States in young manhood, and first settled in Pennsylvania, from which state he came to Indiana at an early day, locating in Cass county, where the remainder of his life was passed in farming and stock raising He and his wife became the parents of fourteen children, of whom only two survive at this time John M and Sylvester

John M Bowyer began to receive instruction in agricultural work when he was still a small boy, and long before he had passed his early 'teens was able to do his full share in the work of the home place In the meantime he was securing his literary training in the district school of his neighborhood, which he attended during the short winter terms He grew to manhood in Miami township, and with his father laid out a part of Lewisburg from the home property, there continuing to reside until reaching majority At that time he began to carry on operations on his own account and was so engaged at the time of his marriage, November 30, 1865, to Miss Mary S DeLawter She was a daughter of Ezra and Sophia (Heck) DeLawter, who were born in Frederick county, Maryland, the former in 1818 and the latter in 1817, and who went to Ohio as young people with their parents, being married in the Buckeye state Mr and Mrs DeLawter had four children, namely: Mary S, who married Mr Bowyer, Sarah E., who married a Mr Esquire Fenton, Jacob W., who makes his home near the Bowyer place, and Rebecca, who married Mr. M. T Wilson Dr DeLawter became an early settler of Cass county, and here spent the remainder of his life in agricultural pursuits Mr and Mrs Bowyer have had eleven children, as follows Charles Lewis, who married Maggie Layton, and has eleven children; Ella E , who is deceased, Horace, who married Minnie Helver, who died leaving three children: Milfred, Maria and Ocal; Edward, Effie Mae, who is deceased, Alvin, who married Rosa Timmons, and has six children Elmer E , who is deceased, Carrie, who married Clyde Smith and has one child. Josephine, Marshall, deceased, who married Mattie Robinson and has one child Susan, Iona, who married Seward Sullivan and has three children Helen, Cleo and Carl, and Owen, who married Ruth Wilson Mrs Bowyer is a member of the Methodist church

Shortly after his marriage, in 1866, Mr Bowyer came with his wife to Tipton township, which has since been his home His ninety-acre farm is in a high state of cultivation, gives eloquent evidence of the presence of good management and untiring industry, and is considered one of the valuable tracts of the township Mr Bowyer has been a lifelong Republican, but has not entered public life having been content to devote his activities to his farm. He is one of his township's highly esteemed citizens and has gathered about him a wide circle of sincere friends

AARON FLORY The farming industry has received long and careful attention from men of the name of Flory in Cass county, and horticulture has come in for its full share of the attention of Aaron Flory, the immediate subject of this review, and his father, David Flory The winter banana-apple was produced by these gentleman after years of experimenting and discouragements and the science of horticulture is directly indebted to them for this addition to the fruit bearing trees of the country

Aaron Flory was born on the 5th of September, 1866, on the old homestead farm in Miami township that his father has settled some years prior to his birth In the log cabin built by the father on the place all but three of the children of David and Sarah (Heffley) Flory were born David Flory was the son of Henry Flory, a native of Dart county, Ohio, and it was in about 1843 that the father of the subject came from that place to Cass county He was twice married His first wife, whose maiden name was Richardson, died in about 1844, leaving him two children, William and Henry He later married Sarah Heffley, and she bore him ten children They may be mentioned as follows: Frank, who married Grace Adams, James who married Lizzie Adams, a sister of Grace, Samuel, who died in infancy, Mary, who became the wife of Dr. J C White, Isabelle, died at the age of twenty-one, Florence, died when she was twenty-two years old, David, who married Marguerite Kelley, Charles, who married Ottie McCauley, Edward, who married Mabel Swigart, and Aaron, the subject of this brief record

David Flory was a cooper by trade, and he devoted his winters to that work, while he gave himself to his farming and horticultural research work in the summer seasons He was a devoted student of horticulture, and with his son succeeded in producing the famous winter banana-apple, as mentioned in a previous paragraph. During his later years he discontinued his work as a cooper, and confined his attention to the farm thereafter

Aaron Flory has by skilfull work and careful attention to business come to be the owner of a nice place in Miami township of eighty acres and ninety acres in Clay township both places being in a fine state of improvement, and in appearance indicating something of the care and labor that their owner has expended upon them Mr Flory is recognized among the substantial farming men of the community, where he enjoys the friendship and esteem of the best people He is a member of the Christian church with his family, and is a Democrat His fraternal relations are with the Knights of Pythias

On August 19, 1892, Mr Flory was married and he and his wife became the parents of three children Evan L, born May 28, 1892, Wilmer B, born December 23, 1895, and Marselles N, born May 18, 1902

SCHUYLER FLORY Another of the younger generation of Cass county farming men who have ably demonstrated their fitness to carry on the worthy work inaugurated by their fathers in the taming of the wilderness sections and the settling of the waste places is Schuyler Flory, who has passed all the years of his life on the farm he now occupies He was born there on April 20, 1886, and his parents, who reside in Logansport, Indiana and operate the farm in partnership with their son, Schuyler Flory of this review, are David M. and Marguerite (Kelly) Flory The father is a son of another David M Flory, and the mother is a daughter of Nelson Kelly

Schuyler Flory was educated in the district schools of his native community, and received an excellent training in farm lore at the hands of his father, who has long been known for one of the most practical and successful farmers and horticulturists in the township of Miami The farm, which comprises seventy-four acres, is operated on shares by father and son, and the arrangement has continued to prove itself a most satisfactory one. The principal business of the place is the cultivation of small fruits, in which they have experienced a pleasing success and gained considerable prominence as producers of that variety of fruit.

The Flory farm, as it stands today, represents many hours and weeks of unremitting toil on the part of the father and son and to the former must be given the credit for having erected every building that stands on the farm today. The place is well kept, wisely cultivated and is a source of pleasure and profit to its owners to whom it is endeared through long years of constant association. The family are members of the United Brethren church, and Mr. Flory and his son are adherents to the faith of the Democratic party, though not active beyond the demands of good citizenship.

JOHN S. CROCKETT. It is difficult for those of the present generation to realize the numerous difficulties and hardships with which the pioneers of Cass county were forced to contend. First were those of getting here from homes far distant. Many of these early residents endured weeks of wearisome travel, literally passing through fire and flood to reach their destination. Then, after a habitation was secured it often was a very meager protection against the elements and wild beasts. Subsequently came the clearing and subduing of the virgin soil, and the cost of the first plowing was often three times the cost of the land if purchased from the government. Other difficulties were appearing, but through them all these sturdy, courageous, self-reliant men battled bravely and steadfastly, valiant soldiers in the strife of peace. Without them, this section would still be the haunt of the wild beast, the prosperous, luxuriant farming land would not know the plow. Among the citizens who have assisted materially in the growth and development of Cass county, none stands in higher regard than John S. Crockett, of Washington township. This venerable citizen is the owner of a fine tract of land one mile east of the Kokomo road, about seven miles south of Logansport, of which he has himself cleared every acre of the eighty. Mr. Crockett was born April 19, 1837, in Carroll county, Indiana, six miles from his present home, and is a son of William and Mary Ann (Stanley) Crockett, natives of Ohio and Kentucky respectively. William Crockett moved to Carroll county in young manhood, and he and his wife were the first couple to be married in Washington township, that county, the ceremony being performed in 1835. John S. was the oldest of their ten children, also the oldest living descendant of either the Crockett or Stanley families.

John S. Crockett is a self-made man in all that the term implies. His education was secured in the little time that could be spared from his duties on the home farm for like other farmers sons of his day and locality, and especially the older sons, he was expected to be his father's assistant, and to share with him the hard work pertaining to the subduing of a practical wilderness. Mr. Crockett came to his present farm in 1848 embarking upon his career with but little capital, his early home being a little log cabin. By degrees he managed to clear and cultivate his land gradually adding improvements as his means would permit. He has continued to reside on this property, and although he has reached an age when most men are content to transfer their duties to younger shoulders he is still actively engaged in the management of his affairs, unimpaired in faculties or energies. Mr Crockett is not a politician, but the confidence in which he is held by his fellow-citizens has resulted in his election to a number of township offices in which he has shown himself capable and conscientious. He is regarded as one of the pillars of the Universalist church.

Mr Crockett was married in 1859 to Miss Mary J Circle, of Ohio, who is now deceased, and they had a family of eight children, namely: Frank H, Clara C, Leroy M, Ella J, Mattie, Rebecca, Charles and Mary Elizabeth, the last-named deceased. The family further consists of twenty-six grandchildren and five great-grandchildren.

THOMAS L EAST. About seven miles from Logansport, on the Anoka road, is situated the farm of Thomas L East, a tract of seventy-seven and one-half acres of well-cultivated land that represents the result of a life of industry and well-applied energy. Mr East embarked upon his career with but a meager capital of cash, nor was he possessed of influential friends who could start him on the road to independence and position, but his possessions as expressed in ambition, determination and perseverance were large, and today he finds himself one of the successful farmers and stock raisers of his township, with a full appreciation of his success because it has been self gained. He is a native of Kentucky, born September 15, 1857, in Garrard county, a son of James and Elizabeth (Land) East. His father was born in the same county, where the grandfather also named James East, founded the family at an early day. The father grew to manhood in the Blue Grass state, and there engaged in agricultural pursuits, in which he continued to be engaged throughout his life, meeting with a fair measure of success. He and his wife were the parents of ten children, of whom five grew to maturity: Thomas L, Calvin, Owen, Daniel and Sallie, all born and reared in Garrard county.

On completing his education in the district schools, which he attended during the winter terms while working on the home farm in the summer months, Thomas L East came to Indiana to live with an uncle, Owen Land, who was the owner of an extensive farm in Brown county. There he grew to manhood, and on leaving his uncle's home came to Cass county and began working as a farm hand. He was industrious and ambitious, and carefully saved his earnings, having determined to become the owner of a farm of his own, and eventually he was able to make his first payment on his present farm in Tipton township, this section having been his home ever since. He is now the owner of seventy-seven and one-half acres, all in a high state of cultivation, on which many fine improvements are to be found. The buildings are of substantial character, including a modern residence, good barns and appropriate outbuildings, and the entire appearance of the property bespeaks the thrift and good management of its owner. Essentially an agriculturist, Mr East has not entered the political arena, nor has he identified himself with organizations of a social or fraternal nature but has applied himself assiduously to the work which he chose in his youth as the medium through which to attain success. He has succeeded in a monetary way, and has also gained the esteem of his fellow-citizens and the warm regard of a wide circle of friends.

On April 6, 1880, Mr East was married to Miss Martha Wilson, who was born in Cass county, a daughter of Andrew and Eleanor D (Tucker) Wilson. Her father, a native of Virginia, came to Tipton township in 1839 and took up government land, on which he spent the remainder of his life, passing away December 22, 1892, one of the substantial men of his community. His wife was a native of Clark county, Ohio, and they had children as follows: William H, Harry G, Marcellus T, Alice, Carrie, Linnie J., Mary L, James A, Jennie, Charles B, Martha and Laura. Mr and Mrs East have had two children: Calvin and Edith, both residing at home with their parents. Edith graduated in the public schools and then from the commercial course in Marion, Indiana. She is a member of the North Baptist church. Calvin was educated in the common schools and at home. The homestead of Mr and Mrs East is called "Cedar Lawn."

CLARENCE A ARCHEY At an early period of our American history, representatives of the Archey family located in the Old Dominion. Energy, honesty and industry have been some of the marked characteristics of the family, and the elemental strength of character in Clarence Archey, of Tipton township, shows that these qualities are predominant in his nature. Mr Archey is one of Cass county's examples of self-made manhood, for he has been self-supporting since his twelfth year, and at this time is known as one of his township's enterprising and progressive young farmers, and one who is rapidly forging his way to the front. Mr Archey was born in Shelby county, Indiana, August 12, 1874, and is a son of Thomas and Belle (Lacy) Archey. His grandparents, Peter and Abbey Archey, were F F V's in the Old Dominion, from which state they migrated to Shelby county at an early day, and there spent the remainder of their lives in the peaceful occupation of farming. Thomas Archey was born in Breckenridge county, Virginia, and was a small lad when he accompanied his parents in their migration to the Hoosier state. He was reared in Shelby county, became a farmer on reaching his majority, and passed the entire period of his active career in tilling the soil. For some years he has been living a retired life, and now makes his home in Lafayette Indiana, his wife having passed away many years ago.

Clarence Archey was the only child born to his parents and lost his mother when he was but ten months old. When about two years of age he was taken to Tippecanoe county, and there spent his boyhood in farm work, attending school during the short periods when he could be spared from the work of the farm. His opportunities for an education were not great, but he was an ambitious and intelligent youth and made the most of his chances thus securing a somewhat better schooling than many who were given greater benefits. He was only twelve years of age when he embarked upon a career of his own, but had been thoroughly trained in all the subjects with which a good farmer and stock raiser must be conversant, and his subsequent use has been steady and continuous. At the present time he is renting the old Louthian farm, where he carries on general farming and stock raising, in addition to

Yours Truly

Chas. E. McCoy

which he devotes some time to working on shares His private interests have always demanded his entire time and attention, and through careful management, sound judgment and unflagging industry he has been able to overcome many obstacles and discouragements and to gain a place for himself in the esteem and respect of his fellow-citizens

On August 27, 1902, Mr Archey was united in marriage with Miss Edna Layman the estimable daughter of Benjamin Layman, and to this union there have been born four children Robert L, who is attending school, Madeline M, residing at home; and Mildred and Thomas, who are deceased Mr Archey holds membership in the local lodge of the Independent Order of Odd Fellows at Anoka, Indiana, in which he has many warm friends With his wife, he attends the Seven Mile United Brethren church where he acts in the capacity of superintendent of the Sunday school

REV CHARLES E McCOY The ministry of the Christian church has held the chief interest and activity of Charles E McCoy for the past fifteen years, but he has of late found time to give some little attention to the business of farming, and at the present time he is busily occupied in the work of building on his farm He has been pastor of a number of churches, among them pulpits at Independence, Kokomo and Winamac, and lastly he was located at New Waverly, where in addition to his duties as pastor he had charge of the postoffice His life has been a busy one from his earliest time, and he has proven his worth as a live citizen in whatever community he has lived since he reached man's estate

Born on April 7 1874, in Monroe township, Howard county, this state, Charles E McCoy is the son of Sampson and Jane (Vernon) McCoy Sampson McCoy was born in the state of Ohio, and his father was a native of the state of Maine, coming from that state to Ohio, and his son drifting into Indiana in young manhood The McCoy family is one of pure Irish ancestry, the first American ancestors having come to these shores from Ireland at an early date Sampson and Jane (Vernon) McCoy became the parents of thirteen sons and daughters, the most of whom lived to assume places of responsibility in their various communities.

Up to the age of twenty-one years, Charles McCoy lived on the home farm, and from then until he had reached the quarter century mark he was employed variously in the community At that age he married, and he established his first independent home in Winamac, Indiana, where he took charge of the church of the Christian denomination, and discharged the duties of a pastor with all satisfaction He then moved to Howard county, where he was occupied in the ministry for a few years, when he moved to Kokomo, Indiana, and once more resuming the pastorate of the Winamac church From there he moved to Miami township, in Cass county, and took charge of the Christian church at New Waverly, at which point he has also been occupied as postmaster In later years he has done some farming, as well as his ministry

Rev McCoy's primary educational training was begun in the public schools Then he entered the New London, Indiana, high school and spent two and a half years there, after which he entered the Frankfort,

Indiana, high school, and there finished the third year of the high school work Next he took the full normal course of instructions, and then entered the theological department of the DePauw University in 1894, and completed part of the course there Then he entered and completed the full four-year course in the Northwestern Indiana Christian Conference, and has been chairman of the educational executive board and is the present incumbent Rev McCoy is a man who is well qualified for the profession or calling of the ministry, since he is a logical and cultured gentleman of pleasing personality, and has been an able factor in the affairs of his home township He is ever ready to lend his aid to all measures for the advancement and elevation of the moral, spiritual and intellectual development of his county and state

Rev Mr McCoy is a member of the Masonic order at New Waverly, Indiana, and has been a trustee of Miami township for the past four years

On July 23, 1899, Rev Mr McCoy was united in marriage with Miss Blanche Griffith, the daughter of Tatman and Irene (Adams) Griffith, the father of Dutch ancestry, born in Jennings county, and the mother was born in Cass county, Indiana Four children have been born to Mr and Mrs McCoy Ursela Irene born April 22 1901 Leland D, born February 13, 1902, Paul G, born February 27, 1904 and Chelsa E, born February 5 1907 Politically Rev McCoy was a Republican, but now gives his allegiance to the Progressive party

FRANZ S MARTIN The pioneers of this great middle west were those who blazed the way to civilization, and made the wilderness to bloom and blossom like the rose Mr Martin, the subject of this sketch, was the founder of a family of most worthy descendants who have aided very materially in building up the great commonwealth of Cass county, Indiana He was a direct descendant of the German, as his grandfather, Peter Martin emigrated to America in 1780, and settled in Pennsylvania, near Philadelphia

Mr Franz S Martin was born October 22 1830 and died April 30, 1907 in Somerset county, Pennsylvania He was educated in the primitive schools of that state and was more than an ordinary mathematician He was mostly self educated and was a teacher He with his parents in 1849 came to Cass county and the trip from the Keystone state overland was made in one of the old fashioned wagons crossing swollen streams and over mountains and finally reached Cass county The family settled on section 27 in Washington township, and the first habitation they lived in was a log cabin with a puncheon floor and afterwards the largest frame house in the township

Mr Martin wedded Miss Caroline Sine November 29, 1853 and eleven children, three sons and eight daughters were born and all are living but one Charles H married and is a resident of Logansport, he was an agriculturist and is a Democrat politically Mary H, widow of Rev Amos Jones is a resident of Zion City, Illinois, Rev Jones was a Presbyterian Herman E is represented elsewhere in this work Rebecca is the wife of Dr M J LaRose a resident of Zion City, Illinois and a health officer Harriet is a resident of Zion City Illinois George W is a resident of Memphis, Tennessee, employed in the lumber interests, he married Miss Anna Gregg Ellen V is a resident of Zion City, Illinois she was educated in Logansport Indiana, and at Hanover College in Indiana, and was a successful teacher for fifteen or eighteen years in Cass county, Indiana Lucy D is the wife of Rev Mahlon Krauss, a resident of Richmond, Indiana and he is a member of the Methodist church Carrie V is the wife of Cyrus B Carleton, a resident of Rochester, Indiana, and a dealer in grain Elsie J is the wife of Dr F M Kistler, a resident of Royal Center, Indiana, and a practicing physician

Mrs Martin was born in Maryland January 8 1834 and died May 8 1910 She was but a child when her parents left Maryland for Pennsylvania, and there they resided for years and from Pennsylvania the Sine family came to Cass county overland by wagon She was educated in the common schools and was a devout Christian of the Presbyterian faith She was a mother and friend to the poor and needy and the hungry never went from her door in need

When Mr Martin was about twenty-two years of age he went to Iowa and purchased one hundred and sixty acres of land but sold it and came to Cass county and here he remained during his life and was a successful man and accumulated five hundred and twenty-five acres, all in Washington township so it is readily seen that he had been a man who had been careful and had taught his children the lessons of economy and integrity Politically he was a Jacksonian Democrat and he adhered to those principles till late in life and then advocated the Prohibition principles Officially he was assessor of Washington township eight years He was a man who was appealed to by the citizens to take an active part in the affairs of the community and in the adjusting of estates He was ofttimes selected as delegate to the county and state conventions at various times In 1876 he attended the Centennial at Philadelphia and the scenes of his childhood Religiously he was an ardent supporter of the Presbyterian doctrines and was one of the charter members of the Union Presbyterian church of Washington township, which is now in 1913, one of the most prosperous religious societies in Cass county. He was one of the trustees of the official board and was elder of the church a number of years and was one of the leading factors in the Sunday school, being superintendent

It was in March, 1887, when Mr and Mrs Martin vacated the old homestead on the farm and located at 1408 North street Logansport but he had several properties in the city Both Mr and Mrs Franz S Martin were citizens of Cass county who as shining lights to the younger generation show that honesty of character as well as true integrity present to a finished earthly existence They were well known for their deeds of benevolence and good will, and no needy one would have left their hospitable door empty handed Both are interred in Mt Hope cemetery, where beautiful stones stand sacred to their memory

WILLIAM KEISER Practical scientific farming has taken the place of the old hit-or-miss style and as a result land that at one time could be purchased for almost nothing is today worth hundreds of dollars an acre Much of this has been brought about by the use of improved machinery and the application of scientific methods as well as by general progress and the increase in population One of the practical farmers of Tipton township, whose activities have been of such a nature as to firmly establish him in a position among the representative men of his community, is William Keiser, the owner of ninety-two acres of land located on the Keiser road Mr Keiser has been an eye-witness to and an active participant in the wonderful change that has transformed this part of Cass county from a practical wilderness into a veritable flower garden Mr Keiser was born on the old Hilderbrandt farm in Tipton township, Cass county, August 15, 1856, and is a son of Eckhart and Anna Catharina (Dorn) Keiser, natives of Germany Eckhart Keiser was an industrious hard-working citizen, but in his native land lacked the opportunities to achieve success Accordingly, when about forty years of age, he gathered his little family together and brought them to the United States, settling in Cass county, Indiana He had only a small capital, and was entirely lacking in influential friends, and consequently his progress was slow Faithful labor and commendable perseverance, however, paved the way to success and at the time of his death he was the owner of a snug little farm, on which he raised good crops He and his wife were the parents of four children, namely Martha, who is deceased, Henrietta, Minnie the widow of Harvey Schuman, now living in Walton, and William.

William Keiser's boyhood was spent in his little log cabin home, on his father's farm, and in the district schools The greater part of his education was secured in the school of hard work, as he was his father's only son and it was necessary that he give all of his time possible to the work of the fields Thus he was reared to habits of industry, frugality and thrift, and given a thorough training in all the details of farm work At the age of twenty-one years Mr Keiser commenced farming on shares, and a short time thereafter he had accumulated enough capital to warrant his embarking in business on his own account He therefore purchased a small tract of land, to which he has since added from time to time, and now has ninety-two acres, all in a state of cultivation He is known among his neighbors as a man of integrity, who can be depended upon to support movements that make for progress and development An excellent farmer, he is also a good judge of livestock, as his herd of sleek well-fed animals proves He has made a number of modern improvements to his place, and the most approved methods find in him a willing disciple

On November 11, 1885, Mr Keiser was united in marriage with Miss Lucinda Smith, daughter of Alexander and Mary (Burkit) Smith of an old family of Cass county and three children have been born to this union, namely Roswell Melroy, Charles G , and William L Roswell M received his diploma in 1905 at the public schools and from the Walton high school in 1909, and he spent four summers in the Valparaiso University, and he also taught two years in the common schools and two years in the former high school He is a Democrat and is a member of the Presbyterian church Charles C received his diploma from the common schools in 1907, and graduated in Walton high school in 1911 He is a student at Winona Indiana, and a member of the Presbyterian church William Leslie received his diploma from the common schools in 1908, and graduated in Walton high school in 1912 He is a member of the Presbyterian church With their family, Mr and Mrs Keiser consistently attend the Presbyterian church Mr Keiser is a Democrat and is a member of the I O O F, No 314, and the M W. of A. No 7244, in Walton, Indiana

HARVEY O. BIRD. The younger farming men of Cass county have wrought worthily and well in carrying forward the splendid work of development that was put in motion by their fathers and grandsires in years gone by, and it will hardly be denied that the greater part of the real prosperity of the county and the wealth of the communities have resulted from the application and energy of these sturdy farmers and honest and admirable citizens Among the more prosperous and comfortably situated agriculturists of Cass county, of whom there are indeed many, H O Bird of Walton is one who is deserving of especial mention in this historical and biographical work dealing with the county of Cass in Indiana He was born in Deer Creek township, this county, on February 27, 1887, and is the son of J. W and Essie (Rhinehart) Bird, of whom the former is now deceased J W Bird was born in Ohio, where he devoted himself to farming and was very prominent in the community that represented his home for years before he identified himself with the fortunes of Cass county He was the father of seven living children, named as follows Francis A , Harriet, who married a Mr Walter Barnes, Benjamin F., Harvey O , of this review, Charles R ; Eva J , and Ruby

Harvey O Bird in boyhood attended the Crockett school in his community, and during his vacation seasons applied himself diligently to the work of the home farm, as was required of him. He was nineteen years of age when on February 22, 1906, he married Ercie Banks, the daughter of Harry and Lorinda (Rush) Banks, and one son, Clark Bird, has been born to them

Mr and Mrs Bird are members of the Christian church and have an active part in the work of the church in its various departments Politically Mr Bird is identified with the Republican party, and takes the interest of a good citizen in all affairs of a political and civic nature in his community, where he has a prominent place of which he is well deserving

LOUIS KAUFMAN. Located on the township line between Washington and Tipton townships is situated the ninety-acre farm belonging to Louis Kaufman, a veteran agriculturist of Cass county, whose residence here covers a period of almost a half a century His energies have always been devoted to his farming interests, and he is known as an honorable, upright business man, whose sterling worth has gained him high regard. Mr Kaufman was born at Dayton, Montgomery county, Ohio, April 27, 1858, and is a son of Henry and Anna (Wiegand) Kaufman His father, a native of Germany, left the Fatherland in young manhood, and settled in Montgomery county, Ohio, where he carried on agricultural pursuits, as he did also in Darke county, where he subsequently moved About the year 1865 he came to Washington township, Cass county, Indiana, here continuing to follow farming until his death He was a successful business man of his day and locality, took a keen and intelligent interest in the needs of his township, and succeeded in winning the respect and esteem of those about him. He and his wife were the parents of five children: George, Elizabeth, Martha, Louis and Catharine.

Louis Kaufman secured his education in the public schools of Montgomery and Darke counties, Ohio, mostly in Cass county, Indiana, and during the summer months worked on his father's farm, assisting him materially in his work and gaining a thorough knowledge of the multitudinous subjects on which a good farmer should be informed. He was about six years of age when he accompanied his parents to Washington township and continued to remain under the parental roof until his marriage, when he embarked upon a career of his own. He had been a thrifty and industrious youth, and had carefully saved his earnings, so that he was able to make a payment on a farm in Washington township of seventy-five acres. This he sold and purchased his present farm, which is situated about nine miles southeast of Logansport, on the Washington-Tipton township line. Here he settled down to clear and cultivate the soil, each year seeing further advancement made, until he now has the full ninety acres, except eight acres of timber, under the plow. He carries on general farming and also devotes some attention to stock raising, and his success has been such as to make him one of the substantial men of his community. He has erected commodious buildings, with modern conveniences, for in this matter as well as in others he believes in the use of up-to-date methods and ideas. His machinery is of the latest and most highly improved manufacture and his entire property is a model of neatness and order.

October 10, 1896, Mr. Kaufman was united in marriage to Miss Anna Lebert, who is deceased. He was married to Miss Augustina Schwalm, September 7, 1898, and to this union there have been born two children, Wilbur and Helena, and both are in the eighth grade in the public school, and both are taking music. With his family, he is connected with the Presbyterian church, where he has been liberal in his support of religious and charitable movements. He is independent in politics, casting his vote for the man best fitted for the party. He has also stanchly supported measures which he has felt will advance his community, taking a keen interest in those things which vitally affect it. Thus he has become a potential force in his locality, where he is looked to for counsel, advice and leadership. The pretty homestead of Mr. and Mrs. Kaufman is known as "Hill View Farm."

OSCAR B. FERGUSON. Upwards of half a century ago the father of Oscar B. Ferguson settled in Cass county, and at a time when the most primitive conditions existed throughout this region, set himself to the herculean task of hewing a farm and a home out of the pristine wilderness that prevailed. Only those who have seen something of the hardships of such an undertaking are capable of making any adequate estimate of the courage, energy and perseverance that these sturdy people brought to bear in the taming of the wilderness and in the eventual evolving of a home from the conditions then existing. When Oscar Ferguson came into possession of the place it had passed beyond the stage of storm and stress peculiar to the early years, but he has done his full duty in carrying it forward to its present state of cultivation and giving it the appearance of fruitfulness and prosperity that it now wears. The place comprises one hundred and thirty acres on the boundary line pike and its owner is properly regarded as one of the prosperous and successful men of the community.

Born in Adams township, in Cass county, Indiana, December 13, 1865, Mr. Ferguson is the son of James P. and Mariah V. (Dillman) Ferguson. They were farming people of Adams township, where they passed their lives for the most part, and became the parents of six children, as follows: Oscar B., of this review, Luman N., now deceased, Henry D., Sylvia M.; Cora D. and Maud E. The father, James P. Ferguson, was the son of Richard and Phoebe Ferguson. The thickly timbered district in which he settled in his young manhood has, as intimated above, since that time given place to fertile hills and valleys and during the years when the transformation was being slowly wrought he reared the goodly family just mentioned.

Oscar B. Ferguson as a boy attended the Thomas school near his home, and later, through the wisdom of his father, who recognized the studious qualities which his son evidenced, he was permitted to attend Logansport Seminary and the Central Normal at Danville, Indiana, so that he secured educational advantages in advance of what the average youth of his day received. He married Miss Arna R. Bowyer, the daughter of Charles G. and Isabelle (Craighead) Bowyer, but no children have been born to them. In the goodness of their hearts, however, they took a little girl, Mary M. Enyart, to rear and educate, and it can be truthfully asserted that little Mary will have a home of sweet influence and religious training, as well as high moral teaching. Mrs. Ferguson's father, Charles Granles Granville Bowyer, was a descendant of the well known Bowyer family of Virginia, and he was born in 1837 and died on the 18th day of February, 1912. She was one of the seven children of her parents, the others being: Mary D., Mavilla B., and Vesta J., all deceased. May B., Willard N., and Ellis. The surviving children are all filling places of usefulness in the various spheres to which they have been called.

Mr. Ferguson is prominent in his membership in the Masonic fraternity at Walton Lodge No. 423, and in the Knights of Pythias, Powell Lodge No. 62, Logansport, Indiana. He is also a member of the Order of the Eastern Star as is his wife, and both are popular and prominent in social circles of their community, where they are held in the highest esteem and regard by all who share in their acquaintance. Mr. Ferguson has always taken a wholesale interest in civic activities in the community, and in politics has voted with the Republican party, but has never been an office seeker at any time in his life, content with the duties of citizenship, but averse to the responsibilities of official life. The beautiful estate of Mr. and Mrs. Ferguson is known as "Locust Lawn," and it is the abode of hospitality and good cheer. They are citizens who take great interest in church work and are members of the Disciples of Christ church at Walton, Indiana. They take great interest in the Sunday school also.

OLIVER J. PIERSON. Cass county's history has been developed by the men who first settled here, and more pages are constantly being added by those whose lives are now being enacted. The agricultural sections of this county are extensive, in fact it may be called a farming county, so that a large number of its residents are engaged in tilling the soil and raising stock, with benefit to themselves and profit to their communities. An excellent example of the progressive, up-to-date Cass county farmer is found in the person of Oliver J. Pierson, of Washington township, the owner of forty-two and one-half acres of land, which he has brought to a high state of cultivation. Although not a native of Cass county, Mr. Pierson can lay claim to being an "old settler," as he was but one year old when brought to this section. Here he has continued to be identified with agricultural matters to the present time, in the meanwhile establishing himself firmly in the confidence and esteem of his fellow-citizens by upright living and honorable dealing. Mr. Pierson was born September 25, 1867, in White county, Indiana, and is a son of Matthew H. and Mary A. (Jenness) Pierson.

Matthew H. Pierson was born in Preble county, Ohio, from whence he migrated in young manhood to White county, Indiana, in which locality he was married and had one child. He subsequently came to Cass county, in 1868, and here was engaged in agricultural pursuits during the remainder of his active career, fairly winning the regard of his neighbors and accumulating a competency. He and his wife became the parents of six children: Oliver J.; Mrs. Carrie Small, Mrs. Gertrude Ramer, Emma, the wife of Adelbert Flanigan, who had one child,— Estella D., who is living with Mr. Pierson; Mae, who married Benjamin F. Crockett, and has two children,—Gilbert P. and Herbert P., and Mrs. Maud Toney.

Oliver J. Pierson was reared to agricultural pursuits, and secured his education in the common schools. His entire life has been spent in farming, and at the age of twenty-four years he became the possessor, through purchase, of his present land. He has brought his property to a high state of cultivation through the use of modern methods, and in addition to producing large crops devotes some attention to the raising of valuable livestock. He has made a study of soil conditions, rotation of crops, and kindred subjects necessary to scientific treatment of his land, and as a result is known as one of his township's foremost agriculturists. In addition to his Cass county property he is the owner of valuable holdings in the state of Texas.

On August 30, 1892, Mr. Pierson was married to Miss Effie E. Martin, daughter of John T. and Caroline (Martin) Martin, and to this union there has been born one son, Donald M. Mr. Pierson's fraternal connection is with the local lodge of the Modern Woodmen of America, Camp 7244, at Walton, Indiana, in which he was venerable counsel and in which he numbers many friends. With his family, he attends the Presbyterian church.

SAMUEL W. ULLERY, who was long connected with the business interests of Logansport, where he was known for one of the most reliable and enterprising merchants of the city, was born at Covington, Ohio, on January 17, 1843, and was a son of Jacob and Elizabeth (Fager) Ullery, both of German descent.

Jacob Ullery was born in Maryland and there reared, moving to

Ohio in young manhood and there passing the remainder of his days He was a farmer and it was in the many details of farm life that Samuel W Ullery passed his younger days He attended the district schools, securing in his somewhat intermittent period of study, a limited education, but that handicap was insufficient to deter him from his purpose, which was to succeed in some established business His business career he began as a hardware merchant in his native town, but in 1848 moved to Greenville, Ohio, where he conducted a similar business until 1866 Three years later he came to Logansport, Indiana, and under the firm name of S. W. Ullery & Company, with William M Wilson as his partner, he embarked in the hardware business again. In 1886, Mr Wilson withdrew from the firm, upon which G L Ullery, a son of the head of the firm, became a partner under the firm title of S W Ullery & Son, a name that endures to the present time, although both father and son are now deceased

Samuel Ullery was a prosperous man, although his prosperity was never of a spasmodic order He made constant, steady progress in the business world, his achievements being ever wrought through the application of his powers of keen discernment and practical business sense, together with the abundant energy which characterized his life In the early years of its life, the business was conducted in a retail way, but gradually developed into a wholesale establishment, though still continuing its retail trade

Mr Ullery was one of the organizers and a director of the State National Bank of Logansport, and also for a time was vice-president of the bank Upon the reorganization of the National Bank of Logansport, he became one of its stockholders

In all his many business relations and dealings, Mr Ullery s reputation as an honorable, straightforward business man was never questioned As a private citizen he commanded the respect and confidence of his fellow men He was a Republican in politics, although never an aspirant for public office

In 1849 he married Sarah Kessler, and for thirty-six years there continued a most ideal marriage relation, broken by the death of Mrs Ullery They were the parents of two children G Lincoln, who died June 20 1901 and Juniata, the only survivor of the family, and the wife of George P Bliss, the present manager of the firm of S W Ullery & Son, of whom extended mention is made in other pages of this work. Mr Ullery died on June 1, 1899

GEORGE P BLISS Since 1897 George P Bliss has been connected in an important capacity with the hardware business of S W Ullery & Son, and in recent years became manager of the company, which position he now holds Born at Bluffton, Wells county, Indiana, on May 5, 1852 he is the son of Jeoffry Bliss, who was engaged in the business of making fanning mills during the early part of his business life, and later was identified with mercantile pursuits, at Bluffton, where he passed away

George P Bliss remained at home until he was about fifteen years old, and attended the public schools of his native community He also assisted his father in the making and painting of the fanning mills, and later secured work as a clerk in a local store For some time he worked in the private bank of John Studebaker & Company, and still later, he was for a number of years employed as a bookkeeper In the following years he was variously engaged in a number of places, fourteen years being passed in a flouring mill at Toledo, and something like five years in Cleveland When the Clover Leaf Railroad was yet a narrow gauged track to St Louis, Mr Bliss was engaged as paymaster of the road for about four years, after which he served for a matter of two years as cashier of a bank at Markle, Indiana

In 1897, Mr Bliss came to Logansport in the capacity of clerk and bookkeeper in the wholesale and retail hardware concern of S W Ullery & Son, and ever since has been identified with the firm Upon the death of the junior Mr Ullery, Mr Bliss became manager of the establishment and he is yet serving in that important position

On November 18, 1896 Mr Bliss was united in marriage with Juanita Ullery, and they have one son, Harold P Bliss Mr Bliss is a member of the Country Club and the Logansport Commercial Club, and is a director of the latter organization He is a Republican, and with his wife attends the First Presbyterian church of Logansport, of which she is a member

HERMAN E MARTIN Among the enterprising agriculturists of Cass county who have been progressive in inaugurating improvements on their properties, and have shown their ability and progressiveness by taking advantage of modern inventions to increase their capability and decrease the cost of production, Herman E Martin, of Washington township, holds a place in the foremost ranks Coming of an agricultural family, which for years have contributed its members to the tilling of the soil, he has made a place for himself among the substantial men of his community, and his finely cultivated tract of one hundred and fifty-eight acres, located on the Ramer and Martin road, about nine miles from Logansport eloquently testifies to his ability as a farmer

Mr Martin was born on the farm which he now occupies March 14, 1859, and is a son of Franz and Caroline (Sine) Martin Like most of the farmers sons of his community, Mr Martin secured his education in the district schools during the winter months, his summers being devoted to helping his father in the cultivation of the homestead a part of which he assisted in clearing On attaining his majority, he worked on the farm at home, and also worked at the carpenter's trade, which he had picked up in his youth and thus earned the means to invest in a tract of eighty acres in Tipton township On this land he labored industriously and with a fair amount of success for a period of eleven years, carefuly saving his earnings At the end of that time he disposed of his Tipton township land, and bought his father's old homestead, which he has continued to operate to the present time Mr Martin is a self-made man in the truest and best sense of the word Giving his closest attention to the smallest details of his work, at all times being willing to experiment with new innovations, and constantly seeking methods which would advance his interests he has been able to add materially to his property, and to make it one of the most valuable of its size in this part of the county General farming has received the

"PINE LAWN," RESIDENCE OF MR. AND MRS. HERMAN E. MARTIN

greater part of his attention, and he has also spent some time in raising stock, and his crops have been large and prosperous, while his cattle bring top-notch prices in the markets While he has at all times seized every opportunity to advance his interests, he has always done so in an honorable manner, never taking an unfair advantage of others, and for this reason has won the respect and confidence of his fellow-citizens

Mr Martin was elected trustee of Washington township in 1900, and served four years in that important office At the present time he is chairman of the county council The members of the Cass county council at the present time are Messrs Herman E Martin, John Warner, Alva Crook, Dr. Z U Loop, Daniel Woodhouse, William Farrell and Allen Snyder. Mr Martin is also a member of the board of trustees of the Presbyterian church.

Mr. Martin was married December 25, 1882, to Miss Melissa Stough, a daughter of Samuel and Maria (Garman) Stough of Cass county To the marriage of Mr and Mrs Martin, the following children were born Edith Myrle, who married Rev. Alexander E. Cameron, and resides in Morning Sun, Iowa, where he is pastor of the Presbyterian church Mr Cameron was educated in the University of Chicago while his wife was graduated from the public schools at the age of fourteen, and spent one year in the Logansport high school and later was a student at the Marion Normal College. For two terms she was a successful teacher in her own county before her marriage She and her husband are the parents of three children Colin E, Frances M., and Paul P. Ralph Emerson second of the family, received his diploma from the public schools and was a student in the Marion Normal He died February 19, 1907 A member of the Presbyterian church, he was a young man of model habits and character, and was greatly beloved by all Chester Monfort, third. finished the public schools, and is now a practical farmer associated with his father He is a member of the Presbyterian church, and cast his first ballot for William J Bryan Hazel Eunice, the fourth, married Evan G Marquardt, of Toledo, Ohio, where he is a hardware merchant They have a little daughter named Carolyn Mrs Marquardt after attending the public schools spent two years in the Oberlin Musical Conservatory as a student of both instrumental and vocal, and is an accomplished young woman, highly capable of presiding over her home and has active membership in the Presbyterian church. Inez Helen, who attended the public schools and graduated from the Logansport high school, was a student in the Eastern College of Music at Manassas, Virginia, and is now engaged in teaching music, and is likewise a member of the Presbyterain faith Armeda Marie is a graduate of the public schools, and is proficient in music, being also a member of the same church as her parents Homer Carlton, after leaving the public schools spent two years in the Logansport high school and is now taking a course from the Scranton School of Correspondence, Raymond Stough is a student of the eighth grade, and Doris Esther, the youngest of the family, is in the sixth grade of the public schools Mr and Mrs. Martin have made it their ambition to give their children the best of educational advantages, and have thus fitted them for the higher places of usefulness in the world

Mrs. Martin was born in Cass county, September 21, 1859, the third in a family of six children, three sons and three daughters, and five of the Stough family are living in 1913 The father, born in Pennsylvania, sprang from good old German stock, and when a young man came west to the state of Indiana, where he was married By vocation he was a brick and stone mason, and had the distinction of erecting the first Lutheran church in Walton, Indiana In this connection it should be stated that Mr Martin's father erected the first Presbyterian church in Washington township Mr Stough was a Democrat in politics and was the first superintendent of the Lutheran Sunday school in Walton, and was known throughout that community as one of the best vocalists and a great lover of music Mrs Stough, the mother of Mrs. Martin, was born in Pennsylvania, and died at the age of seventy-four, while her husband passed away when seventy-seven years old Mrs. Martin was educated in the common schools and with a fine endowment of character, a pleasing personality, she has ably filled her part of wife and mother to this happy Cass county home She is a devout member of the Presbyterian church Mr and Mrs Martin's hospitable home, which is always open to welcome many friends, is known as 'Pine Lawn "

JOHN H PERSINGER The real history of the Civil war is written deepest on the hearts of those who participated in that mighty conflict. The sacrifices of the volunteers did not cease when peace was declared, for none of them came out of the war as they had entered it Those who were fortunate enough to escape bullet, shell and imprisonment, were for years troubled by the seeds of disease, while shattered nerves will be the mementos of others as long as life lasts The brave, gallant, dashing and laughing youths who left their homes to fight for the flag of their country returned to those homes, when they did return, saddened, sorrowed men, old in experience if not in years The country owes a debt of gratitude to the "boys in blue" which it can never repay, and for this reason the veterans of the Grand Army of the Republic still inspire respect and veneration even after the passage of more than a half century of years Cass county sent its full quota of brave, hard-fighting men to the front when secession reared its gory head, and among these none had a more honorable record than John H Persinger, whose service covered more than four years Mr Persinger is now a resident of Tipton township, where he is engaged in agricultural pursuits, and throughout his life has performed the duties of peace in the same able, cheerful and faithful manner that characterized his actions when serving in the ranks under the "Stars and Stripes "

John H Persinger was born October 2, 1835, in Warren county, Ohio, and is a son of Eli and Sophia (Blinn) Persinger His father, a native of Virginia, removed to Ohio in young manhood, and about the year 1850 brought his family to Indiana, the remainder of his life being passed in agricultural pursuits in Cass county, where both he and his wife passed away. They were the parents of the following children Christopher, who is deceased, John H , Mary Ann and Julia Ann, who are now deceased, Harrison and Amanda. John H. Persinger received his education in the district schools of his native state, where he was reared to agricultural pursuits, and taught the dignity and value of hard labor He was still engaged in assisting his father when the War of the Rebellion broke out in all of its fury, and with youthful patriotism he at once offered his services to the Union army They were accepted and he was enrolled upon the list of privates of the Forty-sixth Regiment, Indiana Volunteer Infantry, Captain Thomas This hard-fighting regiment was detailed to the Army of the West, and participated in some of the bloodiest engagements of the war, at all times acquitting itself with the utmost gallantry Mr Persinger continued to take part in all the movements of this regiment for four years, and after a service marked by bravery in action and duty well performed, he received his honorable discharge and returned to his home from Louisville, Kentucky He at once resumed farming, and at the time of his marriage came to Tipton township, where he has since made his home, now being the owner of some valuable property He carries on general farming and stock raising, has wisely invested his means, and is considered one of his locality's substantial men He receives a pension from a grateful government Mr Persinger is popular with the comrades of the local Grand Army post, and has numerous friends in business and social life

In 1868, Mr Persinger was united in marriage with Miss Mary Miller, who was born in Cincinnati, Ohio, and they have had three children Mitchell, Ira and Mrs Bessie Berk Mr Persinger is a member of the Independent Order of Odd Fellows

WILLIAM SMITH Located in "Hilltop," Washington township, about six miles south of Logansport, is the eighty-acre farm of William Smith, a tract that compares favorably with any of its size in this part of Cass county From his boyhood Mr Smith has been engaged in agricultural pursuits, and the position he has gained among the successful farmers and stock breeders of his locality has come through conscientious labor and intelligent management of his affairs Born January 31 1844, near Hamilton, Butler county, Ohio, Mr Smith is the son of Samuel and Elizabeth (Schafer) Smith

Samuel Smith was born in Pennsylvania, and was a young man when he left his native state and journeyed to Ohio He did not remain in the Buckeye state for long, however, but pushed on to Indiana, and here settled at once in Tipton township Cass county, having made the journey by way of wagon He became successful in his operations, was a large land owner, and in his death Tipton township lost one of its best citizens He married Elizabeth Schafer, and they became the parents of eleven children, as follows· William, David, John Elizabeth, Sarah, Samuel, George, Mary, Daniel, Alta and Caroline

William Smith was a lad of nine years when he accompanied his parents to Tipton township, and completed his education in the log schoolhouse of his locality, in the meantime assisting his father in the work of the home farm. He was married first to Miss Sarah Long, a sister of Simon Long, a sketch of whom appears elsewhere in this work, and she died after becoming the mother of four children Marvin, who married first Anna Showtax, and they had three children,—Marie, Gladys and Irene; he married a second time and had four children,—Adah, Leffie Evelyn and Charles William B married Ruby Easton, and had two children,—Fern and Hazel Walter married Ellen McMillen, and had two children,—Sarah and Josephine. William Smith was married October 8, 1902, to Mrs. Mary H. (Beeler) Atherton, the widow of August Atherton, by whom she had eight children: Ida, Albert, Gertrude, Daniel, Walter, Cora, Willie, deceased, and Elmer. Mrs. Smith is the daughter of Daniel B. and Margaret (Schater) Beeler. Mr. Beeler was born in Pennsylvania, and removed to Darke county, Ohio, in young manhood, becoming one of the successful farmers and stockmen of that locality, where the rest of his life was spent. He was the father of six children: William, Joseph, Lizzie, Mary, George, and Samuel.

After his marriage, Mr. Smith settled on his present farm in Washington township, which he has brought to a high state of cultivation. He is thoroughly conversant with crop and climatic conditions, understands crop rotation and other scientific methods of gaining the best results from his land and is a believer in the use of modern farming machinery. He supports movements tending towards progress and is always found among those who are advancing their community by promoting its interests. He has always been a man of temperate habits, and indicates his inclinations by supporting the candidates and principles of the Prohibition party. His religious faith is that of the Christian Science church, and he is a man who has good reason to be a devotee to the Christian Science and its great miraculous healing of body and mind. The Scientists are to erect one of the most beautiful and costly church edifices in the city on the corner of Ninth and North streets, Logansport.

CHARLES O. ROUSH. In every community there may be found among its citizenship men who direct their lives in harmony with the old rule known as that of the "Three P's—Push, Pluck and Perseverance." Given to any town one or more men of that stamp, a fair degree of prosperity must inevitably characterize that place, for they invariably stand for prosperity and advancement whatever may be the nature of the community wherein they are found. C. O. Roush is undeniably one of these plucky and persevering men. His farm, one of the fine places of the township of Tipton, is in section seventeen, and its eighty acres is intersected at one corner by the Pennsylvania Railroad. Its owner, one of the young and successful agricultural men of Cass county, began his career in that uncertain and ofttimes unsatisfactory status of the renter, has risen above many unpropitious conditions, and is today one of the most capable and prosperous farming men in the county, as has already been said.

C. O. Roush was born on June 23, 1882, and is a son of Christopher and Martha (Long) Roush. The father, who was born in Wabash county, was for many years a farmer in Benton, and after a successful career, is now living retired from active business. His four children were: Charles, Mary, Tammie and Burdette.

Charles O. Roush attended the Green school in Jasper county this being one of the largest schools in the county. His schooling was interspersed with vacation periods of active work on the home farm, and throughout his boyhood days he was carefully instructed in the duties and responsibilities of farm life, so that when he had finished his school work, he was well equipped to take his place as an intelligent and practical farmer. The lessons learned under the able tutelage of his father have stood him in excellent stead in the years of his independent farming career, and have gone far toward establishing his present success For seven years after he began his work on his own responsibility Mr Roush was a renter, and from his savings in that length of time he was able to purchase the George Enyart farm, which is his present home The improvements in evidence on this farm today are all of first-class order, the dwellings and outbuildings, fences and well-kept fields, all offering indisputable testimony to the thrift, energy and good management of this young husbandman

Mr Roush was married on November 26, 1902, to Miss Cynthia Julian, a daughter of Elias and Harriet (Dresbach) Julian. The father of Mrs Roush was a farmer, originally from Sheldon, Illinois, and he was the father of eight children, as follows Milton, Milo, Guy, Lucien, Cynthia, Amanda, Nancy and Ruth To Mr and Mrs Roush have been born two daughters, Lillian and Harriet, both of whom are attending school in the home community The family are members of the Methodist Episcopal church

CHARLES E. JAMES Agricultural methods have changed very materially during the past decade or two, and now that even the chief executive of the nation is taking a deep interest in progression among the farmers, there is every reason to suppose that still further advance will be made along all lines Interurban service, telephones, automobiles, and the consequent bettering of the roads on account of the latter, have brought the farmers much closer together, and as well have placed them in close touch with the centers of activity, and the man who today devotes himself to the cultivation of the soil is more independent than any other worker in the world Among the progressive and enterprising farmers and stock raisers of Cass county, one who has recognized the value of modern methods and innovations and has profited accordingly is Charles E. James, whose well-cultivated tract of land is located in Noble township Mr James is a native of this township and was born October 13, 1881, a son of John and Nancy J (James) James, who came to Cass county, locating on the farm on section 2, where Mrs James is still making her home John James was an agriculturist throughout his life, was a loyal and public-spirited citizen, and in his death, which occurred in 1906, his community lost one of its best and most highly esteemed men

The early education of Charles E James was secured in the district schools of Noble township, and in boyhood he was accustomed to the hard work which develops the mind and hardens the body Spending his time in assisting his father on the home farm, he was thoroughly trained in all the details of agricultural work, and this he chose as his life vocation, nor has he had any desire to follow any other line of endeavor He has been uniformly successful in his operations because of hard, industrious labor, intelligently directed along well-defined lines, and the soil of his land has responded gratefully for the work expended upon it, yielding him large and profitable crops. Mr James has realized the value of modern machinery and scientific methods, and is an advocate of progress along all lines, not only in his own work, but in movements making for the public welfare Such movements have always had his hearty support and co-operation He has never had any desire for public office, being essentially a farmer, and has never, therefore, entered the public arena, although a stanch advocate of good government

On August 7, 1901, Mr James was united in marriage with Miss Nora Lontz, who was born March 1, 1882, in Carroll county, Indiana, daughter of William A and Sarah Lontz The latter died in December, 1885 Mr Lontz served one term as county assessor of Cass county his term ending in 1902, and shortly thereafter he left for the West, where he has since made his home Mr and Mrs James have had one child Clarence E, who was born April 14, 1903 Both Mr. and Mrs James are widely and favorably known in Noble township and are recognized as representatives of Cass county's best people

JAMES M DENISTON Among the citizens of Cass county who are adding to the commercial importance of their section by their activities in the business field, James M Deniston, of Onward, holds a foremost place A product of the farm, reared to agricultural pursuits, he belongs to that class of men whose versatile talents allow them to meet with success in more than one line of endeavor, and has proven himself as able a business man as he was a farmer He is now the proprietor of a general store at Onward, where he handles a large trade in merchandise and farming implements, his customers being drawn from a wide contiguous territory Mr Deniston was born December 25, 1862, in Miami county, Indiana, and is a son of Thomas B and Elizabeth (Wilkinson) Deniston His father, a miller by trade, came to Miami county, Indiana, from Ohio, and here spent the rest of his life in agricultural pursuits He and his wife had six children Eva, Clara who is deceased, James M, Belle, deceased Charles and William. The mother of these children died in 1873

James M Deniston attended the district schools of Miami, but the greater part of his education was secured in the schools of hard work and experience An energetic, industrious youth, he spent his early years in faithful labor, carefully saving his earnings with the idea ever in view of becoming the owner of a property of his own His perseverance and industry were rewarded by the accumulation of a farm of one hundred and twenty acres, located in Pulaski county, Indiana, on which he carried on operations for a number of years, but in 1892 he decided to enter upon a commercial career, and accordingly traded ninety acres of land for his present store. Here, by good judgment, honorable dealing, and attention to minor details as well as large ones, he has succeeded in building up a large trade, carrying a full line of articles demanded by the people of his community and an up-to-date stock of farming implements He is known as a man of the strictest integrity and possesses the full confidence of all who have had dealings with him In addition to attending to the affairs of his store, he also carries on agricultural operations in Cass county.

Mr Deniston was married in 1882 to Miss Rebecca Leffel, and to this union there were born four children, namely William, a resident of Logansport and bookkeeper in the First National Bank He graduated from the public schools, and then took the teacher's course

Charles A Brandt
And Wife.

"BELVEDERE," RESIDENCE OF MR. AND MRS. ALBERT O. BRANDT

of the Marion Normal, of Marion, Indiana, and taught two terms. He also graduated from the Logansport business college. He wedded Miss Anna Leffel, and they are members of the Christian church, and he is a Mason. Herman C., graduated from the public schools and is an agriculturist in Pulaski county, Indiana. He wedded Miss Alice Kelsey, and they have two children, Herbert and Mildred. He is a member of the United Brethren church and a Mason, and his wife is a member of the Progressive Brethren. Minnie is the wife of T. J. Sullivan, a resident of Adams township, and they have one son Lloyd. He is an agriculturist and a Mason. Mabel, the youngest, is at home and in the sixth grade of the public schools. Mrs. Deniston is a native of Cass county, Indiana, and was reared and educated in her home county. She and her husband are consistent members of the United Brethren church, located at Twelve Mile, Adams township, Cass county. Mr. Deniston has interested himself to some extent in fraternal work, and is affiliated with the local lodge of the Masonic order at Twelve Mile. All matters pertaining to the betterment of his community or its people find in him a hearty supporter, while among his associates he is known as a man who, having succeeded himself, is always ready to help others to succeed.

ALBERT O. BRANDT. Noble township is the home of some excellent citizens who have employed themselves in tilling the soil. Many of them have spent their entire lives on the farm and have known no other occupation, and in this class stands Albert O. Brandt, who for the past thirty years has been engaged in cultivating his present tract of land. Mr. Brandt was born in Noble township, June 21, 1859, and is a son of Charles A. and Rosanna (Adair) Brandt. He has a full genealogical tree, and traces his lineage back to 1760, as his progenitors came from Germany.

Charles A. Brandt was born in Fairfield county, Ohio, December 14, 1828, and is a pioneer of Noble township. He is the oldest son born to John and Hannah (Coulson) Brandt. His father immigrated to Indiana in 1837, from Fairfield county Ohio with his wife and three children, having been persuaded to come by David B. Coulson and Jacob Bimesdorfer, brothers-in-law, who were at that time residing here. Charles A. Brandt was but nine years of age at the time of the immigration, and when he was seventeen years old he was apprenticed to E. B. Williams of Logansport, with whom he remained one year, learning the trade of wagon maker. He continued working at his trade in Logansport and LaFayette until 1850, when he started for Oregon, but on account of illness he did not proceed farther than St. Louis, Missouri, being compelled to return home from that point. Again in the following spring, he started on another trip, with Oregon again as his destination. Leaving Logansport March 18, 1851 by ox-team in company with two other young men he journeyed to St. Joseph, Missouri where he joined a company then en route for his point of destination. On September 27th of the same year the party reached Oregon City, and shortly thereafter Mr. Brandt journeyed to California and there engaged in mining. Some months later he returned to Oregon and engaged in the packing business, in conveying provisions from there to the mines in California by pack mules. In this line he was quite successful, and continued in the business until June, 1854, when he decided to return to Indiana, although the return journey was filled with difficulties as regarded methods of travel Leaving San Francisco, June 1, 1854 on the steamship Yankee Blade, he traveled to Panama, went thence by foot to Cruces on the Chagres river, and then by railroad to Aspinwall, a distance of twenty miles, for which he had to pay $12 50 in gold He then again boarded a steamship, and landed at New York City, June 22d He left New York on the following day, going by rail to Buffalo, where he laid over one day, and then continued by rail as far as South Bend, Indiana, arriving in Logansport June 27th on a stage-coach He has resided in Cass county since that date In 1855, he located on a farm in section 20, Noble township, and in 1864 he purchased and removed to a farm on section 21, in the same township, where he resided until 1889 At that time he made removal to his present farm in the same township In 1857, with his father and brother, he built a grist-mill on what is known as Cottonwood creek, and was here engaged in milling until 1860. In the spring of 1860, Mr. Brandt made a trip to Pike's Peak, Colorado, but returned in the fall of the same year, and in the fall of 1866 went to Kansas, and returned one year later, these trips being more of a prospective nature than with any idea of permanently locating there

On March 30, 1855, Mr Brandt was united in marriage with Miss Rosanna Adair, who was born August 5, 1834, in Noble township, the daughter of Benjamin and Anna (McMillen) Adair of Ohio and Pennsylvania respectively Two children were born to this union James M, born October 28, 1857, and died the following day, and Albert O On March 30, 1905, the golden wedding anniversary of this honored couple was celebrated, an added interest at the time being the wedding of their granddaughter, Nellie R, the daughter of Albert O Brandt. After a long and useful life, Mrs Brandt passed away June 5, 1909 Mr Brandt's political faith is that of the Republican party, with which he has been connected since its formation, prior to that time having been a Whig With his family, he attends the Shiloh Christian church Mr Brandt takes a deep interest in biographical and genealogical matters, having in his possession much information in regard to Cass county and its early history and being a pleasing and entertaining conversationalist He has ever been honest and straightforward in his dealings, and his reputation is that of an excellent neighbor, a true friend, a capable business man, and a loyal citizen

Albert O Brandt received his education in the district schools and the county normal school, and has always been engaged in farming He has lived on his present property since November 8, 1883, and is now engaged in farming his own land and working with his father, and like him is known as a man of good habits, loyal to his township's interests, and a capable man of business On September 12, 1880, he was joined in marriage with Miss Annie B Grable, daughter of Joram and Lucy Anna (Carson) Grable, of Adams township, Cass county Mrs Brandt is a native of Cass county, Indiana, born August 31, 1858, and is the fifth in a family of six children one son and five daughters, but there are only two children of the Grable family living, Mrs Brandt and her sister, Samantha, wife of Isaac Watts, residents of Pulaski county, Indiana

Mrs Brandt was educated in the common schools and also received a normal training for the profession of teacher She taught five years in Cass county She is a member of the Shiloh Christian church and of the L A S Her father was a native of Pennsylvania, and was a well educated gentleman, and followed the profession of teacher both in Pennsylvania and Indiana, but most of his life was spent as an agriculturist. He was a Republican, and both he and his wife were members of the Presbyterian church

To the union of Mr and Mrs Brandt there have been born two children. Olive A, born July 10, 1881, who died September 1, 1881, and Nellie R, born September 21, 1886, who was married March 30, 1905, to Oliver O Leach, an agriculturist, who resides near her parents On this last-named occasion, the house was decorated in white and gold, and three guests were present who had attended the wedding of Mrs Leach's grandparents, fifty years before. Mrs Leach received a good education, receiving her diploma from the public schools in 1899, and in 1900 entered the Logansport high school, and spent two years there as a student She is a musician of merit, and taught music in her home township Both she and her husband are members of the Shiloh Christian church

Mr Brandt has always been a faithful member of the Shiloh Christian church, which he attends regularly, and is an official worker in the township and county Sunday school association, in connection with his church In politics he has always been a staunch Republican, but has never cared for public office, preferring to devote all of his time and attention to his farming operations His fraternal connection is with Royal Center Lodge No 585, Free and Accepted Masons, in which he has many warm friends, as he has, indeed, in all circles of his community The homestead of Mr and Mrs Brandt is known as "Blakemore."

MARION E REED Among the public-spirited men of Cass county who are filling official positions with marked ability and conscientious devotion to duty, none stands higher in general esteem than Marion E Reed, postmaster at Onward, a capacity in which he has acted for more than six years In choosing the men who handle the United States mail, the government is careful in securing only those individuals who have proven their worth in business, their loyalty as citizens and their general fitness for public office as displayed in their past careers Mr Reed has not only met all of these qualifications, but by his courteous and obliging manner has won the friendship of all who have had occasion to come in contact with him in his official capacity He is a native of Cass county, and was born on the Reed homestead, about one and one-half miles east of Onward, November 4, 1869 a son of George M and Martha J (Smith) Reed Mr Reed's mother's people were natives of Pennsylvania, from whence they migrated to Ohio and later to Cass county, Indiana, where they were engaged in tilling the soil. George M. Reed was born in Cumberland county, Pennsylvania, a son of John and Jane (Brandt) Reed and was brought by his parents to Cass county as a lad, the family settling on government land, which George M assisted in clearing from its native state. He is remembered as one of the very early settlers of Cass county and as an able agriculturist and sterling citizen. He and his wife were the parents of seven children, namely Marvin, who is deceased, and Marion E, Virgie, Estella, Edward, Homer and Otho.

Marion E Reed first attended what was known as the Cross Roads school and later the Kinsey school, and finished his education in Onward. He was reared to the occupation of farming and remained under the parental roof until he was twenty-five years of age, at which time he embarked in agricultural pursuits on his own account, being engaged therein for about ten years. He then turned his attention to mercantile pursuits, in which he was engaged until recently, and in which he met with the same success that had rewarded his agricultural efforts. He has recently sold his business, and now resides quietly on his valuable town property, devoting his attention to looking after his realty interests. Mr Reed has been a lifelong supporter of Republican policies and candidates and on January 8, 1907, received the appointment of postmaster of Onward from President Roosevelt, a position which he has held to the present time.

On March 27, 1895, Mr Reed was married to Miss Lovina Wessinger, who was born in Miami county, Indiana, a daughter of Isaac and Margaret (Blubaker) Wessinger, and they have had two children Roscoe E, who is dead, and Janice, who is attending school in Onward in the third grade. Mr Reed holds membership in the Ancient Order of Gleaners lodge, located in Walton. With his family, he attends the Christian church, in the work of which he has always been active. The family name has always stood for reliability and good citizenship, and Mr Reed is ably maintaining the high standard set by his forebears.

LEWIS B WALTERS The town of Onward, Indiana, is situated in the center of a great grain belt, and one of the chief industries of the locality is the handling of the products of the agriculturists of the section. A prosperous and growing enterprise of Onward is the grain elevator of N E Walker & Company, the superintendent of which, Lewis B Walters, has risen to his present business through well-applied energy and inherent business ability. Mr Walters has been identified with the grain business for nine years and for four years of this time has been a resident of Onward, where he is known as a citizen who takes an interest in all matters pertaining to the welfare of his community. He is a native of the Hoosier state, having been born in Clinton county, near Frankfort, March 24, 1876, a son of Samuel and Amanda (Finney) Walters.

Samuel Walters was born in Pennsylvania and came to Indiana with his parents when still a babe, the family settling in Clinton county, where Mr Walters was reared and educated. He became engaged in agricultural pursuits, and was working on a farm when the Civil war broke out, when he enlisted in the Eighty-ninth Regiment, Indiana Volunteer Infantry, for three years. In his first large battle, at Mumfordsville, Kentucky, he was captured by the Confederates, but was exchanged and sent home on a three months' furlough to recuperate from a serious illness contracted in a southern prison On rejoining his regiment, he served under General Smith, in the Army of the Potomac, so continuing until receiving his honorable discharge at the close of his service He was a faithful and gallant soldier, and when his military term had expired returned to the occupations of peace, and throughout the remainder of his active career devoted himself to the tilling of the soil

Lewis Walters received his education in the district schools of his neighborhood and the public schools of Clinton, after which he became engaged in farming In 1904 he entered the grain business and was on the road for one year In 1909 he came to Onward and became associated with the firm of N E Walker & Company where he has since remained Faithful devotion to his duties and earnest application in behalf of his company's interests gained him rapid promotion, and at this time he holds the position of general superintendent of the Onward elevator He is widely known in the grain trade, and has won an enviable reputation as a shrewd capable man of business

On September 6, 1899, Mr Walters was married to Miss Effie Newlin, daughter of Alfred G and Ella (Mote) Newlin, and they have the following children Lawrence A , in the seventh grade of the public schools, Samuel A , in the fifth grade, and Bernice and Gertrude Mrs Walters was born in Iroquois county, Illinois, March 7, 1880, the fourth in a family of ten children—six sons and four daughters—and three are living at present Her mother is living in Clinton county, Indiana. Mr Walters is a member of the Independent Order of Odd Fellows, No 455, at Onward, in which he has numerous friends He has been a lifelong adherent of Republican principles and has served his township as a member of the election board With his wife and children, he attends the Christian church at Onward

JOHN H MINNICK Among the successful agriculturists of Cass county who have devoted their lives to the tilling of the soil, and who now have large, well-cultivated properties to show for their years of labor, John H Minnick holds a prominent place He has spent his entire career within the borders of the county, and his life, from earliest boyhood, has been one of industry and energy Today he is the owner of a handsome tract of ninety-one acres, located on the Thomas road which, through intelligent handling, he has made one of the valuable tracts of his locality Mr Minnick was born in Tipton township, Cass county, Indiana, July 5 1855, and is a son of Henry and Mary (Bechdol) Minnick His father, a native of Somerset county, Pennsylvania was brought by his parents to Cass county in boyhood, and here he took up agricultural pursuits, in which he was successfully engaged during the remainder of his life Henry and Mary Minnick became the parents of eight children of whom six survive at this time Daniel, William, Charles, Joshua, Charlotte, who became the wife of Mr. Fred Gibson, of Tipton township, and John H

The early education of John H Minnick was secured in the old Flynn school in Tipton township, which he attended during the short winter terms, his summers being devoted to the hard and unremitting work of the home farm. An industrious and energetic youth, he was ambitious to thoroughly learn every detail of farm work, in which he was trained by his father while by his mother he was taught to be honest and upright in his dealings. Thus growing to manhood, he continued to work with his parents, and to remain on the homestead until his marriage, when he established a home of his own and embarked upon a career, following the training of his youth and engaging in agricultural pursuits. Selecting his present property on the Thomas road, he settled down to improve and cultivate it, and to make it one of the valuable tracts of the township, and in this he has been successful, as a visit to his well-tilled fields will demonstrate. His buildings are substantial and of a modern style of architecture, and the general air of prosperity that pervades the whole place shows that Mr Minnick made no mistake in his choice of a vocation.

October 3, 1873, Mr Minnick was united in marriage with Miss Lillis Doud, and to this union there were born four children, namely Merlon, who is deceased; Jennie, who married Wm Ramer, Clarence, who is deceased, and Alvin, who resides at home and assists his father. The last named, Alvin, finished the public schools and then took a business course at the Miami Business College. The following paragraph is taken from one of the Walton papers.

"Lillis Minnick was born near Chili, Miami county, Indiana, April 10, 1853, and died at her home near Walton, Cass county, Indiana, June 10, 1907, aged fifty-four years and two months. She was the daughter of Lorenzo and Lydia Dond. On October 30, 1873, she was united in marriage to John H Minnick. To this union were born four children, three sons and one daughter. A husband one son one daughter three sisters, two brothers, two grandchildren and a host of friends are left to mourn her departure, two sons, three brothers, two sisters, father and mother having gone on before. She was converted and united with the M E church at Chili at the age of fifteen, but later united with the Christian church near her home, of which church she remained a faithful member until called to go to her Heavenly Father. She expressed a desire to live, yet she was willing to go. There has departed from our midst a devoted wife a faithful, sacrificing mother, a sincere friend, beloved by all. The funeral services were held in the Christian church northwest of Walton, June 13 1907, at 10 a m conducted by Rev. W M Amos in the presence of many sympathizing friends, and interment was made in the Walton cemetery 'We cannot say and we will not say that she is dead, she is just away. With a loving smile and a wave of the hand she has wandered into an unknown land and left us dreaming, how very fair it needs must be, since she lingers there. And you, O you who will often yearn for the old-time step and the glad return, think of her just the same, we say, she is not dead, but just away.' " FRIENDS

On April 27, 1909, Mr Minnick was married to Mrs Edna (Patton) Swafford daughter of Joseph and Elizabeth (Berry) Patton Mis Minnick is a native of Cass county born January 4, 1874 and she is the younger of two children, both living. She was educated in the common schools and at the Walton high school. She wedded Archibald Swafford and six children were born and only two are living Gettis O., who graduated in the common schools and is a resident of Tipton, engaged with the Pennsylvania system, and Harry B, in the fourth grade. Mr and Mrs Minnick are members of the Presbyterian church, in the congregation of which they have many friends. He has taken a prominent part in township affairs, not particularly as an incumbent of public office, but as a man who is ever ready to give his time and means to promoting movements for the public welfare. He is held in high esteem by his fellow-townsmen, and may be justly named one of the representative men of his township. Mr and Mrs Minnick's beautiful estate is known as ' Pleasant View Lawn '

WILLIAM P BURKIT One of the representative farmers of Washington township, who has been an eye-witness of the marvelous growth and development of Cass county during the past four decades, and who has contributed materially to that development, is William P Burkit, township trustee and a man who has always been devoted to the best interests of his community. During a long and honorable career, he has given his attention to the cultivation of the soil, and at this time is the owner of a well-cultivated tract of 380 acres of some of the best land in Washington township, situated about nine miles southeast of Logansport. Mr Burkit was born February 21, 1866 in an old log cabin in Washington township, Cass county, which had been built by his father, Alvin Burkit. The latter was a native of Jefferson township, Cass county, where he received his education and was reared to manhood, beginning his operations as a farmer when still a youth. A self-made man in the truest sense of the word, he was honored and respected by his neighbors as an energetic, industrious farmer and reared a family that was a credit to the community. At about the age of eight years Alvin Burkit came to Washington township, and during the remainder of his lifetime cleared the greater part of the farm that is now the home of William P Burkit. He married Miss Sarah Small, also of Washington township, and they had a family of six children, of whom but two now survive · William P. and Charles A , the latter now residing in the city of Logansport. The mother, now aged seventy-two years, is a resident of the city of Logansport, Indiana.

William P Burkit passed his boyhood much as other farmers' sons of his day and locality. His early education was secured in the district schools, which he attended during the short winter terms, the summers being spent in assisting his father in clearing the home farm. He had reached his twenty-sixth year before he embarked in farming on his own account, at that time renting a small property from his father. An industrious, sober and thrifty youth, he was soon able to purchase a small tract of land, and to this he has added from time to time, until he now has one of the finest farms in his part of the county, 380 acres in area, all in a high state of cultivation. In addition to his home property, he owns two other valuable farms, and is justly considered one of his township's most substantial citizens. The homestead farm presents a strikingly different appearance than it did during Mr Burkit's boyhood. The little log cabin that was his birthplace has been replaced by a modern residence, erected by Mr Burkit, and numerous other changes and improvements have been made, the entire property giving evidence of the presence of able management. A Democrat in politics, in 1908 Mr Burkit became his party's candidate for township trustee of Washington township, and in the election that followed he was returned to the office by a handsome majority. He has since continued to discharge its duties, laboring faithfully in behalf of the best interests of his community and its people.

On June 17, 1891, Mr Burkit was united in marriage with Miss Matilda Zollman, who died August 29, 1895, daughter of Charles and Martha (Bell) Zollman. One child was born to this union—Virginia A —who is now the wife of Chester Buschbaum. Mrs Burkit was a devoted member of the Presbyterian church, was actively interested in church and charitable affairs, and was widely known and greatly beloved.

GEORGE H SCHWALM. To its enterprising and progressive agricultural class, Cass county owes its marvelous development during the past several decades, a development that has transformed what was once almost a valueless waste to a center of agricultural, commercial and educational activity. A great many of the pioneers of this section have passed to their final reward, but their sons and grandsons are continuing their work and just as sturdy, self-reliant and industrious a class of men may be found here today as those who braved the dangers of an unknown region during the county's formative period. A family that has contributed of its members to work of this development is that bearing the name of Schwalm, a worthy representative of which is found in George Schwalm, whose postoffice address is Logansport Rural Route No 3, and who is cultivating his own property of 100 acres and the homestead, which consists of eighty acres, in section 26. Mr Schwalm was born March 2, 1858, in Washington township, Cass county, Indiana, and is a son of Henry and Helena (Haemel) Schwalm.

Henry Schwalm was born in Germany, August 20 1828, and was educated in the Fatherland, from whence he came to the United States in 1852 and began working for his uncle, Henry Schwalm. Subsequently, he took a lease to clear forty-five acres of land in Washington township, and from that time continued to carry on agricultural operations on his own account, becoming the owner of the old Schwalm homestead. On May 21, 1857, he was married to Miss Helena Haemel, daughter of Frederick and Elizabeth (Ellerman) Haemel, and they became the parents of eight children, as follows. George, Sarah E, who married Mr D P Hurd, Mrs Caroline M Martin, Eckert A, Mrs Augustina M Kaufman, Louisa L, who is single and resides with Mr and Mrs Kaufman, William B, a resident of Logansport, and Mrs Laura E. Martin. All the members of this family, except Mrs Hurd, are members of the Presbyterian church and take an active part in church work.

George Schwalm received his education in the Flynn public school in Tipton township, and as the eldest son of his parents spent his boyhood and early youth in assisting his father in the work of the home place. When he was twenty years of age, he began teaching school, carefully saving his earnings and investing them in farming land, and when he had accumulated a small capital he gave up the vocation of educator and returned to farm work. He has since been engaged in tilling the soil and in raising stock and has met with uniform success in all of his ventures

On September 21, 1882, Mr Schwalm was united in marriage with Miss Laura E Martin, daughter of Simon and Eliza (Shuman) Martin, and she died leaving four children Grace, Edna M., Florence I and Edith R., all living at home Mr Schwalm was married to Miss Orpha C Bechdol, and they have two children Mary H. and Elma C Mrs Schwalm is the ninth in a family of twelve children, three sons and nine daughters, born to Elias and Mary J. (Stough) Bechdol, and there are seven living Both parents are deceased and both were members of the Lutheran church The Schwalm family is connected with the Presbyterian church Mr Schwalm has not cared for the activities attendant upon public life but, willingly lends his support to progressive movements, and on a number of occasions has shown that he has the welfare of his section thoroughly at heart The pretty estate of Mr and Mrs. Schwalm is known as "Eutopia"

WILLIAM H. SNYDER. Many of Cass county's leading agriculturists are carrying on operations on the farms on which they were born, and which were taken up by their fathers from the government and developed from their virgin state Having spent their entire lives on these properties, their owners are thoroughly conversant with climatic conditions and the needs of the soil, and are thus able to secure a full measure of success from their labors. In this class stands William H Snyder, of Tipton township, an agriculturist of long standing, and a citizen who has at all times held the respect and esteem of his fellow-townsmen. In his early years Mr Snyder was engaged in other lines of endeavor, but eventually returned to the old homestead, content that his abilities fitted him best for the occupation of his forefathers Mr Snyder was born on the old Snyder homestead in Tipton township, located about one mile west of Onward, at the junction of the Thomas and Snyder road, July 1, 1857, a son of Levi and Madeline (Rothenberger) Snyder His father, a native of Pennsylvania, left that state as a young man and came to Clinton county, Indiana, from whence he enlisted in the United States army for service during the Mexican war After the close of that struggle, he came to Cass county, and here took up land, cleared a farm and spent the remainder of his life in farming, his death occurring in 1900, at an advanced age He and his wife were the parents of three children William H , Mary E and Mrs Martha J Shank

William H Snyder was given excellent educational advantages, attending the district schools near his home in Tipton township, and completing his studies under Professor Neff, at the normal school During this entire period, he had spent his spare time in assisting his father on the home farm, being thoroughly trained in the vocation of farming When he was twenty-one years of age he left the parental roof and engaged in school teaching for a period, but subsequently served an apprenticeship to the carpenter trade, which he also followed for some time Eventually, however, he again turned his attention to the tilling of the soil, and in 1900 bought the interests of the other heirs to his father's land, of which he is now the sole owner. He has eighty acres of land, all in a high state of cultivation, and his able management of the property is evidenced by its general air of prosperity and the large crops raised thereon He believes in the use of modern machinery and methods, has made a thorough study of crop rotation and other measures which have so advanced agriculture during the past several decades, and his property compares favorably with any of its size in the township Mr Snyder is essentially a farmer and has not cared for public life, taking only a good citizen's interest in matters of a political nature His fraternal connection is with the Knights of the Maccabees, and in religious matters he affiliates with the German Reformed church, while his wife belongs to the United Brethren faith and daughter to the Methodist

Mr Snyder was married to Miss Rachael M Surface May 1, 1884, and they have had three children Leotine B, deceased, who married W H Haas and died without issue, Edgar F, who resides at home, and William R. Mrs Snyder was born June 17, 1865, and was educated in common schools Both of her parents are deceased Edgar received his diploma from the common schools and was a student in the Marion Normal College He was superintendent of the high school one year, and is again superintendent for 1913-14 He is a member of the B P O E and deputy county treasurer of Cass county William R received a public school diploma and graduated from the county high school in Onward and was a teacher in Cass county but is now messenger at Logansport State Bank He is a member of the Red Men

JOHN W KENDALL is another of the progressive farming men who have added not a little to the development and prosperity of Cass county and Noble township as a result of his up-to-date and modern methods of operation He was born on August 26, 1855, in Carroll county, Indiana, and came to Cass county in 1883 He is the son of Thomas and Maria (Graves) Kendall, the father having been a Civil war veteran He enlisted in an Iowa regiment and saw much of the hardships of actual war It was during his service that he contracted an affection of the lungs that resulted in his death in 1908 The mother is still living in Cass county

When John W. Kendall came to Cass county, a young man of twenty-three or thereabout, he settled on what was then known, and is yet called the Tabor farm, in Washington township There he began the business of general farming, an occupation in which he has ever been successful and prosperous In 1894 he branched out in the diary business, and in 1905 he came to Noble township here settling on the farm he now occupies on what is called College Hill Here he has enjoyed a pleasing degree of success in his general farming and dairying The farm, which comprises eighty acres, has under Mr Kendall's care reached a splendid state of improvement and cultivation, and is known to be one of the best kept places in the township, while the place boasts one of the most complete and perfect silos in the state of Indiana, the same being built on a twenty-four inch foundation, four bricks deep, and is thirty feet high,— one of the most valuable adjuncts in connection with the operation of his dairy farm

On January 2, 1881, Mr Kendall married Miss Henrietta Wright,

and to them were born seven children, named as follows Pearl, Gertrude, John Ellis, Harry N, Jesse, Hattie and Ethel Harry N died in 1897 at the age of four years, and Ethel was taken by death in the same year, at the tender age of two years In August, 1912 the eldest daughter Pearl, married Charles Emmery, a manufacturer of mineral waters and pop in Logansport Gertrude married George Case, in 1906, and they conduct "The Island View Hotel" in Logansport, Indiana

Mr Kendall has always been an adherent of the Republican party, though not particularly active in the ranks, and his fraternal relations are represented by his membership in the Redmen and the Tribe of Ben Hur The family attends the Universalist church A man of much public spirit and enterprise, Mr Kendall has always been a strong cooperator in every movement of a public nature that has for its ultimate object the betterment of the community and may always be depended upon to give generously of his means and his support in any worthy cause promulgated for the good of his fellows

HON DYER B MCCONNELL, for many years one of the prominent legists of Cass county, was born in Highland county, Illinois, on February 15, 1835 He is one of the ten children born to Dr James B and Sarah Dean (Stewart) McConnell, five of that number now living James B McConnell was a physician and came to Cass county in 1848 locating in Royal Centre, where he practically passed the remainder of his professional life He died at the home of his father, Samuel C McConnell, a farmer of Harrison township Samuel C McConnell came from Ohio to Cass county in 1839 and followed farming in Harrison township He was a native of South Carolina and of Scotch-Irish ancestry, but his southern nativity did not prevent him from being a strong abolitionist and a member of the first anti-slavery organization in the county The McConnell family came to America in Colonial days, religious prosecution in their own country causing their emigration

Dyer B McConnell received his scholastic training of earlier years at Russelville, Brown county, Ohio He came to Cass county in 1852 and finished his education with a four months' term in a private school, conducted by Messrs Glenn and Rogers, graduates of Miami University in Logansport He was reared in the expectation that he would embrace the medical profession, but for seven years he taught school in Indiana and Illinois and subsequently engaged in the manufacture of lumber in Harrison township On August 27, 1861, Mr McConnell enlisted in Company K, Ninth Indiana Volunteer Infantry as a private He went first to West Virginia and served three months on scouting duty on Cheat Mountain In January 1862 he camped with his command at Felterman and at this time, January 29, 1862, was elected second lieutenant of his company On April 12th following he was made first lieutenant upon the death of Lieutenant Joseph S Turner Close upon this promotion followed his election to the post of captain on August 21, 1862 He continued in the service until October 29, 1864, when he resigned owing to ill health but he was not mustered out until November 9, 1864 His military service from April, 1862 was joining the command of Don Carlos Buel at Nashville, Tennessee They moved in the direction of Pittsburg Landing in March and reached there on the evening of the first day of the fight At that time he was acting quartermaster of his regiment By special request he was relieved of his duties as quartermaster that he might participate in the second day's fight, and he was in command of Company K after the wounding of First Lieutenant Turner, who commanded the company, the captain acting as major of the regiment During this engagement the Ninth Regiment lost more men in killed and wounded than any other regiment in that action The Century Company, in their pictorial history of the war, paid a high tribute to the efficiency and bravery of the Ninth on the second day of that fight Succeeding this engagement, he was in the Corinth campaign, then was on the campaign through Mississippi to Florence, Alabama, thence north into Tennessee Mr. McConnell's history from this on was the history of the Ninth Regiment. He participated in the battles of Greenbriar and Buffalo Mountain, the second day of the battle of Shiloh, all the engagements of Corinth, Perryville, Kentucky, Stone river (two days' fight) Chickamauga, Lookout Mountain, Mission Ridge, Resaca, Peach Tree Creek, Kenesaw Mountain, Buzzard's Roost, Dallas, New Hope Church, Jonesboro, Lovejoy Station, and the reduction of Atlanta Mr McConnell was then sent in pursuit of Hood to Dalton, Summerville and Galeville, and at this latter point separated from General Sherman's command After various other engagements and campaigns, he went to Pulaski, Tennessee, where he resigned from the service

Returning to Logansport, Mr. McConnell took up the study of law and was admitted to the bar in 1865 Soon thereafter he was appointed by Governor Morton prosecuting attorney for the common pleas court He continued in active practice until elected judge of the Twenty-ninth Judicial Circuit in November, 1888. He served the unexpired term caused by the resignation of Judge Maurice Winfield, and in 1890 commenced serving his own term of six years He resigned in 1895, then continued in practice until 1904, when he became referee in bankruptcy, his private practice being reduced considerably by his service in that office

On February 4, 1864, Judge McConnell was married to Hattie Gibson, who died on December 19, 1910 They were the parents of eight children, the following being those who yet live Edgar Boyd, May, Elizabeth, Helen, the wife of George Ross, and Grace Judge McConnell is a progressive Republican in his politics and is a member of the Grand Army of the Republic

Since 1910 Judge McConnell has been practically retired from active business pursuits

STEWART T McCONNELL, for over half a century a lawyer in the active practice of his profession at Logansport, and the present senior member of the firm of McConnell, Jenkines, Jenkines & Stewart, is a son of Dr James B McConnell, who came to Cass county, Indiana, in 1848, and lived for many years at Royal Centre Appropriate record is made of the life of Dr McConnell in connection with the biography of Judge Dyer B McConnell immediately preceding this

Stewart T McConnell was born in Highland county, Ohio, in the village of Greenfield October 16, 1836, and his boyhood days were passed in attending the neighboring school and assisting an uncle, with whom he lived, in farming Before attaining his majority he attended a scientific and classical school for four years, paying his way with the proceeds derived from his own labor He came to Cass county in 1859, and taught school for a number of terms Influenced by the advice of Judge Horace P Biddle, he decided to become a lawyer and while teaching school he became a student of Hon D D Pratt and Judge D P Baldwin In December, 1861, he was admitted to the bar and very shortly thereafter engaged in the practice of his profession For a period of more than fifty years Mr. McConnell has occupied a conspicuous place in the legal history of Cass county, and in most of the important litigation covering this period, his name is to be found as counsel As counsellor or trial lawyer he has few equals in the state, which is famous for great lawyers While aggressive, he is invariably courteous and thus commands the respect of his fellow members of the bar His knowledge of the law is profound and a legal position once assumed immediately commands the instant attention of court and jury.

Contrary to the usual custom of lawyers, Mr. McConnell has never sought political honors, although at one time he was the nominee of both political parties for the office of common pleas prosecutor and served as such one term He has always manifested a deep and practical interest in education, temperance and religion, and to all matters pertaining to the public weal his support is enthusiastically given

On April 3, 1860, he married Miss Louisa Gibson, and to them were born four children Mrs McConnell died in the spring of 1884, and in November of the following year he married Eloise Landis Stuart.

Few men in Cass county stand higher in public confidence and esteem than does Stewart T McConnell.

DR ARTHUR N BAKER Among the professional men of Logansport who have gained success in their chosen fields of endeavor, Dr Arthur N. Baker has firmly established himself in a position of prestige in the practice of optometry He has been a resident of. the city practically all of his life, and is a native of the Hoosier state, having been born at Culver, Marshall county, February 19, 1869, a son of Dr Ira J and Eliza A (Duddleston) Baker, of Wyandotte county, Ohio Dr Ira J. Baker was a physician and came to Logansport about 1877, this city still being his home and that of his wife During the Civil war he served in the Union army as a member of the signal corps

Arthur N Baker attended the public and high schools of Logansport, succeeding which for several years he was a teacher in the Cass and Fulton county schools He then became a student in the Chicago Opthalmic College and Hospital, where he was graduated June 1, 1895, and subsequently took a post-graduate course at the Northern Illinois College of Opthalmology and Otology where he was granted a diploma in May, 1899 In June, 1895, Dr Baker established himself in the optical business in Logansport, and here he has continued to the present time, from a small and modest beginning having built a substantial business along optical lines exclusively Here he has his own instruments for grinding lenses and for the prosecution of the various other operations of his chosen vocation, and by his skill has gained a position in the confidence of the people and a reputation in optical circles Upon the passage of the law in 1907 creating a state board of five members, appointed by the governor, of Registration and Examination in Optometry, Dr Baker was chosen one of its members, and he has since continued to be a member of that board He is a Democrat in politics, and his fraternal connections are with the Masons the Knights of Pythias and the Benevolent and Protective Order of Elks

In April, 1894, Dr Baker was married to Miss Lillie Condon, and they have been the parents of one daughter, namely Helen Maurine

HARRY FIDLER In the annals of Cass county are found numerous instances of youths who have risen to affluence and prestige in social and business life, but it is doubtful if any cases can be discovered that parallel the career of Harry Fidler, of Logansport, whose phenomenal advancement has brought him within the comparatively short period of two decades, from selling newspapers and blacking shoes to the management of one of the city's leading business establishments Mr Fidler is still a young man, but his accomplishments have been great, and a sketch of his remarkable career should prove of a beneficial and encouraging nature to those who have become discouraged because of the apparently insurmountable obstacles placed in their path

Harry Fidler was born in Logansport, Indiana, September 25, 1881, and is one of the two surviving children of a family of six born to August W and Lydia J (Powell) Fidler His opportunities for securing an education in his youth were extremely limited, and when he was only ten years of age he went out upon the streets of Logansport, selling daily papers, and carrying his little boot-blacking kit The bright, cheery and ambitious youth soon applied for and secured the position of errand boy for the jewelry establishment of Charles Church, and on leaving that occupation was employed as an assistant in the office of Dr J H Shultz This proved the turning point of Mr Fidler's career, for Dr Shultz so impressed upon him the importance of securing an education that he began to attend the public schools whenever he could be spared from his duties and also undertook a course of private instruction Later, having tasted of knowledge, he thirsted for more, and attended the Logansport Business College where he made an excellent record in his studies For a short time succeeding this he was employed in the drug store of W H Porter and in May, 1900, he became office assistant for Seth M Velsey, where his services were so satisfactory that within the short space of three months he was given entire charge of one branch of the business, and in 1903 was given full management of the office At the time of the deaths of his father and Mr Velsey, which took place about the same time, the settlement of both estates fell upon the shoulders of the youth and both were settled to the entire satisfaction of all concerned By express stipulation in the will of Mr Velsey, Mr Fidler was given absolute charge of the settlement of the Velsey estate, one of the largest in Cass county, and within twenty-two months this had been accomplished Since that time Mr Fidler has succeeded to the business founded by Mr Velsey, and has given his attention to its management to the present time

Mr Fidler was instrumental in raising funds for the erection of the Protestant and Catholic mausoleums at Mount Hope cemetery. He is a thirty-second degree Scottish Rite and Knight Templar York Rite Mason, a member of the Mystic Shrine, a Knight of Pythias and a member of the Benevolent and Protective Order of Elks For ten years he has been an officer of rank in Logan Company No 26, Uniformed Rank, Knights of Pythias, of which, for the past eight years he has been captain He has been an unswerving Republican all of his life Although his duties in a business way have been such as to preclude the idea of his entering actively in the struggles of the political arena he takes a keen and intelligent interest in all matters that affect his community or its citizens and has stanchly supported measures making for education, morality and good government He has the utmost confidence of all with whom he has come into contact in a business or social way, and his friends in Logansport are legion

On November 8, 1911, Mr Fidler was united in marriage with Miss Fay Lucy, of Logansport.

JOHN G KEIP Since his seventeenth year, John G Keip, of Logansport, one of this city's leading business citizens, has been the architect of his own fortunes, and his long and interesting career is a striking example of the fact that true success is the result obtained by steadfast integrity, constant industry and unremitting perseverance Mr Keip came to Logansport, September 1, 1894, and within his recollection the city has grown and developed from a rude, undeveloped community into a municipality noted as a center of education, culture and commercial activity, its public improvements have been fostered and forwarded, and many of its handsomest business structures have been erected As resident manager of one of Logansport's principal enterprises, the Columbia Brewing Company, Mr Keip holds a position of unquestioned prestige in business life and his public spirit has led him to identify himself with all movements calculated to benefit the city and its people.

John G Keip was born in the city of Toledo, Ohio, November 8, 1857, a son of Joseph and Katherine (Rees) Keip, natives of Germany, both of whom are now deceased His father was a painter and decorator at Toledo, where his death occurred in 1871 Receiving his early education in the public schools of Toledo, Mr Keip supplemented this by attendance at Canisius College, Buffalo, New York, where he was graduated in 1875, and for a number of years succeeding worked in various clerical capacities In 1880 he made removal to Chicago, where he became a clerk in a wholesale clothing establishment then becoming the traveling representative of a Chicago wholesale house in Kansas, a position which he held for four years At this time he became interested in politics, and for a time was employed in the water and police departments in Chicago, following which he accepted a position in the Department of Internal Revenue It was while acting in the capacity of revenue officer that he received his initiation into the distilling and brewing business, the details of which he thoroughly mastered In 1900 the Columbia Brewing Company went into the hands of a receiver, and Mr Keip was appointed to close up its affairs When the estate had been settled, he accepted the position of manager of the new concein, and since that time he has acquired a proprietary interest in the business, has continued steadily with it, and is its present resident manager As the directing head of this large enterprise, Mr. Keip has displayed marked ability, and his reputation among his associates is that of a well-balanced man of business, capable of handling large issues and thoroughly the master of every detail of the company's operations His business interests have been so large and important that in late years he has given but little attention to political matters, but at all times has displayed a keen and intelligent interest in movements concerning his city's welfare He has been identified with fraternal work to some extent and at this time is a member of the Elks, the Moose, the Eagles and the Travelers Protective Association

While still a resident of Chicago, November 19, 1884, Mr Keip was united in marriage with Miss Etta Provost, and they became the parents of three children, all of whom are deceased Mr and Mrs Keip also adopted three children, one of whom died, one returned to its parents, and one, Bertha Henrietta, is now living with Mr Keip Mrs Keip passed away March 15, 1912, as the result of injuries sustained in an automobile accident some two years previously Mr Keip was married to Annie M Clark, of Michigan City, Indiana, on November 5, 1912

WILLIAM T WILSON Among those who are members of the Cass county bar may be found many native sons of this section, men belonging to old and honored families, members of which have been prominently connected with commercial, professional and public life for many years It is in this class that William T Wilson holds prestige, for he has not only gained a high reputation in his chosen profession, as well as along business lines, but is a son of one of Logansport's early merchants, the late Thomas H Wilson

Thomas H Wilson was born May 31, 1818, near the village of Denton, Caroline county, Maryland a son of John and Sarah (Hopkins) Wilson, both of English descent. The sixth of a family of ten children, he passed his early years on a farm, and at the age of eleven years, at the time of the death of his father, he went to live with an uncle, Thomas Hopkins, who was his guardian, and in whose store and mill he worked for some time In 1834 he became a clerk in a store at Camden, Delaware, and in 1837, when this firm was dissolved, came with one of his employers, Daniel Atwell, to Logansport, Indiana Here, in 1840, he became one of the principals in the mercantile establishment of Pollard & Wilson, which concern, in 1843, built a grain warehouse on the Wabash & Erie Canal. Mr. Wilson, through his extensive mercantile, commission and forwarding interests, became widely and favorably known throughout this part of the state About 1853, owing to changes the firm became Wilson, Merriam & Company, although the firm of Pollard & Wilson continued to do business until the death of the senior partner in 1856 Failing health, caused by close attention to his duties as executor of the estate of Mr Pollard, led to Mr Wilson's resignation from the firm, but he continued in the produce trade until 1875 In May, 1865, he became president of the Logansport National Bank, and served as such until his death December 27, 1877 He was originally a Whig in his political views but when the organization of the Republican party was

brought about, he cast his fortunes with the new movement He was reared, religiously, in the faith of the Friends, or Quakers, but all religious denominations benefitted by his liberality, and no charitable movement with a worthy cause ever appealed to him in vain In his death the poor, needy and afflicted lost a true friend, who had never forgotten them Mr Wilson was thrice married, his first union occurring in 1842, when he married America Weirick She died three years later, and in 1849, Mr Wilson married Mary A I Dexter, who passed away in 1854 His third marriage took place in 1856 when he was united with Elizabeth E Hopkins, who survived him until 1898. Mr Wilson had four sons William T , Ellwood G , Thomas H. and John Charles.

William T Wilson was born in Logansport, Indiana, in 1854, and his early education was secured in the public schools Subsequently, he entered Princeton University, New Jersey, from which institution he was graduated in 1874, and in the following year commenced reading law in the office of the Hon D D Pratt, of Logansport, being admitted to the bar during the same year He immediately entered upon the practice of his profession, and has gained an enviable reputation among his associates and in the confidence of the people of his community His practice has been of a general character, and he is known as a thoroughly learned and sound lawyer, a logical and convincing reasoner and a persuasive and successful advocate. He is a Republican in politics although of the kind that seeks the establishment of the right principles of government rather than the acquisition of the honors of office or the spoils of partisanship Since 1877, the year in which his father died, he has been officially connected with the First National Bank of Logansport, of which he has been a director for a quarter of a century, and various other positions of prominence have been capably filled by him With Mrs Wilson, he attends the Presbyterian church

In 1880 Mr Wilson was united in marriage with Miss Martha L McCarty, daughter of Joseph P. McCarty of Logansport. Their four children are Thomas H , associated with his father in the practice of law, Elizabeth, wife of Mr Frank H Worthington, of the Vandalia Railroad, residing at Terre Haute, Joseph and Dorothy Dexter, living at home

SIMON LONG. It has been stated, and truthfully, that agriculture offers blessings in the greatest plenty, but does not allow us to take them in idleness True there are those who are content to travel along the rut of mediocrity, taking from their land a bare living but the full measure of success in farming only comes to those who are willing to work hard and faithfully, to observe changed conditions and practices, and to constantly remember that the only true success in life is that gained through the practice of honorable dealing In this connection it is not inappropriate to briefly sketch the career of Simon Long, a selfmade man of Cass county, whose long and honorable career has been crowned with well-deserved success secured through the medium of his own efforts Mr Long was born September 10, 1845, in Cass county, Indiana, and is a son of William and Elizabeth Long His father, a native of Pennsylvania, came to Indiana in young manhood, and here spent the remainder of his life in agricultural pursuits He and his wife were the parents of nine children, namely: Eliza, who is deceased; Mrs Catherine Beal, Sarah, Angelina, William, Aaron and Samuel, all of whom are deceased, Simon; and Joseph, also deceased

Simon Long received rather limited educational advantages in his youth, the death of his father making it necessary that he early start out in life for himself, but in his later years he has accumulated a wide fund of information, and is known as a man of good educational attainments. When he was still a small lad he went to live at the home of an elder brother and at fifteen years of age began to gain experience in the world by working out on neighboring farms His salary was small and his hours long, but the youth was industrious and persevering, and carefully saved his earnings, and thus, by the time he had reached the age of thirty years, he was able to purchase the farm on which he now resides This land was almost entirely uncultivated and what improvements had been made upon it were of a primitive nature, but the industry and integrity with which Mr. Long took up his work soon changed conditions, and as the years have passed the land has become productive and the buildings modern and substantial He now has eighty acres in a high state of cultivation, it being located near the Marion road, five miles from Logansport Mr Long is justly considered one of the able agriculturists of this part of the county, and as a citizen he is known to be progressive and public-spirited During his long residence here he has formed a wide acquaintance, in which he numbers many sincere friends

On March 28, 1871, Mr Long was united in marriage with Miss Mary Anna Leedy, daughter of Daniel and Jane (Nelson) Leedy, one of the old and prominent families of Cass county, and she died in 1909, and was laid to rest in Mount Hope cemetery Eight children were born to this union, namely: Charles who married Myrtle Shuey, and has two children, Benton and Norma, Jasper, who married Dot Stover, and has four children, Mae. Glenn, Homer and Donald, Wilda. who married August Snyder, and has three children, Dorothy, Wayne and Verda; Angeline. who married Homer Cragen, Joseph, who married (first) Freda Snyder, and (second) Mrs Emma Cohan Henshaw, Ruby, who married Carl Wilson and Jennie and Albina, who are deceased With his family, Mr Long is a member of the English Lutheran church, which he attends consistently and supports liberally

MICHAEL L FANSLER Probably no family has contributed more materially to the professional prestige of Logansport than that of Fansler, members of which have attained eminence in law and medicine and have rendered signal services in public office Among the worthy representatives of the name may be mentioned the late M D Fansler, and Michael L Fansler, father and son, whose records have been associated intimately with the history of Cass county

M. D Fansler was born June 25, 1857, in Wyandotte county, Ohio, his parents being Dr. David N and Mary D (Caldwell) Fansler The family is of a mixed ancestry, being Irish-Scotch on the mother's side and German-French paternally Dr David Fansler was an early physician of Logansport, but in his later years removed to Marion, Indiana, where his death occurred M D Fansler received his early education in a minor capacity in a printing office, and was practically self-educated, yet he became one of the leading figures at the Cass county bar Coming to Logansport in 1879, he became prosecuting attorney in 1884 and held that office until 1888, following which he returned to private practice, in which he was engaged up to the time of his death, May 2 1896 Mr Fansler was admittedly one of the finest orators that ever practiced before the Cass county bar Of fine taste and great erudition, his reading covered a wide range, both in the line of his profession and in the broader field of polite literature He loved books and was a discriminating critic and possessed the happy faculty of being able to store up the useful and essential things in his mind, which was a perfect treasure house of knowledge In his death Cass county lost not only one of its most able legists, but a citizen who in every walk of life was honored—esteemed not for what he had but for what he was On May 4, 1881 Mr Fansler was united in marriage with Miss Johanna (Nannie) Mulcahy, whose father, a native of Ireland, came to Indiana in 1870 and until his death was an employe of the Pennsylvania Railroad Four children were born to Mr and Mrs Fansler, of whom three are still living

Michael E Fansler was born in Logansport, Indiana, July 4, 1883, and has never known any other home than this city He received his preliminary educational training in the public schools, and in 1901 entered Notre Dame University, from which noted institution he was graduated in 1905, receiving the degree of LL B He at once entered upon the practice of his profession at Logansport, where he now has a large and representative clientele In 1906, Mr Fansler formed a professional partnership with George C Custer, with whom he continued four years, Mr Custer being prosecuting attorney during this time and Mr Fansler assisting him in the prosecution of criminal cases. In 1910 Mr Fansler succeeded Mr Custer in that office, and this was followed by his re-election in 1912 During these two terms, Mr. Fansler has demonstrated his ability as a lawyer and his entire fitness for public office He holds the duties of his office in high regard, and has brought to his work the enthusiasm and conscientious attention to detail that made him so successful in his private practice He has inherited much of his father's oratorical ability, has a wide and comprehensive knowledge of law and jurisprudence, and during his career has been connected with many notable criminal trials In his political views he is a Democrat and he has at all times been a stanch adherent of the principles and candidates of his party Mr Fansler's religious views are those of the Catholic church

On June 30, 1909, Mr Fansler was married to Katherine Hall, formerly of Peru, Indiana

ABRAHAM L JONES To the realty dealers of this section, Cass county owes much for its growth and development during the past several decades Those who are expert in land values, who have the peculiar ability necessary to encourage settlement from outside communities, and whose activities serve to promote the erection of structures which add to the commercial and industrial prestige of their community, form the medium through which Cass county, and notably the city of Logansport, have gained their present high place as centers of all lines of business activity. Among this class of citizens stands Abraham L. Jones, of Logansport, who in comparatively a short space of time has risen from a humble farmer's youth, working for a meagre stipend, to the position where his operations involve several hundreds of thousands of dollars annually. Mr. Jones is a native son of Indiana, born in Madison county, August 24, 1864. When six years of age he came to Cass county with his parents, Richard T. and Drusilla (Nighbarger) Jones, who located on a farm in Clay township. During the next four years Richard T. Jones was engaged in operating a rented farm, but then moved across the line into Fulton county, there purchased land and continued to be engaged in agricultural pursuits during the remainder of his life. He died in 1900, and on the same day that he was laid to rest his widow passed away. They were the parents of eleven children, of whom four sons and five daughters survive, and of these three reside in Cass county.

Abraham L. Jones resided with his parents until his eighteenth year, in the meantime attending the district schools and assisting his father in the work of the home farm. The spring before his eighteenth birthday, he secured employment on a neighboring farm, and until twenty-five years of age was thus engaged, then turning his attention to railroading, as a fireman in the employ of the Pennsylvania Railroad. Fourteen months later he began braking on a freight train on the Vandalia road in the service of which he continued for nearly one year, and then started to work at the carpenter's trade, which he had picked up in his youth. During this time, Mr. Jones had saved his earnings industriously and thriftily, and when an opportunity presented itself he invested in several Logansport building lots, on which he erected houses. This was his introduction into the real estate business, and as time passed he continued to follow the same system, building up an excellent business from a humble nucleus. Financial depression came on, however, property values declined, and Mr. Jones retired from the real estate field for a time to engage in the grocery and meat market business, a venture which occupied his attention for a year or more. He then again returned to the real estate field, conditions having become more settled, and he now does a business that averages approximately $200,000 annually. Men there may be who have risen as rapidly in the business world as Mr. Jones, but none has done so more steadily or surely through legitimate means and the medium of their own efforts. While he has always been ready to grasp any opportunity that presents itself, he has also respected the rights of others, and has not taken a questionable advantage of his associates or business competitors. In political matters he is a Republican, but his inclinations have led him to support the more progressive branch of the party. His religious faith is that of the Christian Science church.

On June 29, 1890, Mr. Jones was married to Miss Ida J. Kinnaman, daughter of Nathan K. Kinnaman and they have two daughters, Fay and Margery.

GEORGE B. FORGY, investment banker and broker of Logansport, Indiana was born at New Carlisle, Ohio, on September 13, 1851, and is the son of John A and Polly (Brown) Forgy. He has been a resident of Cass county since he was a child of three years, and his identification with Logansport dates back to the year 1879, in which year he established himself in his present business His success has been one worthy of the name, consistent with the energy and enterprise which he has invested in his operations, and he is well known and esteemed most highly in all circles in Logansport, whether of a business or a social nature

The father of Mr Forgy, John A Forgy, was also born near New Carlisle Ohio, and there he was reared and in young manhood married Mary Brown, who died leaving three children He then married his second wife, who was a sister of his deceased wife, and she bore him one son, George B, of this brief review She, too, was called by death, and in later years he married Catherine Forgy, the widow of a cousin, and she accompanied him to Cass county, Indiana, in 1853, and settled on a farm in Miami township Mr Forgy subsequently laid out the town of New Waverly, and he was identified with various activities during his life He farmed, but did not confine his attention to that work He was for a time engaged in the merchandise business at Waverly operated a saw mill for a season and sold lumber, being generally known for one of the most inveterate traders, withal one of the most successful, that lived in Cass county in his time He was a prominent member of the Presbyterian church, and a fine, manly character, regarded as one of the most congenial and approachable men in the county He manifested the most unbounded faith in his fellow man, and was always found ready and willing to aid with counsel and more substantial aid in the form of finances, any worthy cause that was brought to his attention This trait redounded to his great financial disadvantage in his later years and he died a comparatively poor man, as far as this world's goods is regarded, but rich in the love and gratitude of the many who had occasion to know his generous kindly heart and his open-handed benefactions

George B Forgy, the only child of his second marriage, came with his parents to Cass county when he was a small child He was reared at New Waverly, the town which his father virtually made, and received in that place a common school education When he was about eighteen years old he started out for himself, and his first work was that of a fruit tree salesman for John Wampler, an old Dunkard nurseryman of the vicinity of Dayton, Ohio His next venture was as a clerk in a dry goods store at Peru, Indiana, and soon after was placed in charge of the collections in four states for the Howe Sewing Machine Company, the headquarters of which large concern was then located in Peru He was associated thus for something like five years, when, in company with E W. Shirk, he organized the Tipton County Bank, the two being equal owners in the firm They continued at Tipton for three years, and in 1879 Mr Forgy came to Logansport and established himself in his present business, that of an investment banker and broker He has continued successfully up to the present time and is rightly regarded as one of the solid and substantial financial men of the city and county Mr Forgy is a Mason and his political affiliations are with the Republican party, but he is not especially active in the interests of the party, being more attentive to his own affairs than any others. In 1876 Mr. Forgy was united in marriage with Miss Alice O. Crowell, of Peru, and one son has been born to them—Ben C., who is now engaged in operating a farm in Boone township, Cass county. Both Mr. and Mrs. Forgy attend the Presbyterian church, but neither of them are members of that or any religious organization.

SILAS McDOWELL was one of the well known farmers of Cass county, and as such is deserving of more than passing mention. He was born in the state of Ohio, Starke county, on September 8, 1840, a son of John A. McDowell, who came to America in the later '50's and farmed on the Michigan road in Clay township until his death. Silas McDowell was favored with but little education in his youth, and his whole life was one of hard and unremitting toil. He was yet in his teens when he came to Cass county with his parents, and being the eldest of seven children, all of whom grew to maturity, much of the burden of the work of the old farm fell upon his young shoulders. He made his home with his parents until he married, after which for about two years he rented and operated land belonging to his father. When he was sufficiently prosperous to warrant the venture he purchased eighty acres of unimproved land in Noble township, on which he caused to be erected a small five-room house. In this he settled with his little family and began the strenuous work of cleaning up his potential farm. As his means increased from year to year, he finally added an additional eighty acres in Noble township and then seventy-five acres in Clay township, which gradually brought him generous returns. Beyond the fact of his hard work and clean, wholesome life his life was as that of the average man, and his career uneventful. His industry and his splendid practical business sense made it possible for him to accumulate a considerable property, a fact which enabled him to extend material aid to each of his children when they started out in life for themselves.

A Republican in politics, he was in no sense a politician or a seeker for official preferment at any time, his life being all too busy in the care and maintenance of his family and his property. It is doubtful if he possessed a stronger characteristic than that of his rugged honesty and his intense distaste of anything that savored of trickery. He was a generous man and contributed liberally of his means to the support of all worthy objects that came to his notice, and was a valued member of the Cumberland Presbyterian church, to which he gave generously all his life.

Mr. McDowell married Catherine Dritt and eight children were born to them, as follows: Andrew, who was accidentally killed at the age of twenty-three, Horace B., who married Martha Wadkins and lives at Akron, Indiana, Willard N., married Lucy Sweeney and now lives in Logansport, Jennie E., the wife of Theodore Sharp, of near Saginaw, Michigan, Minnie E., who married Warren J. Butler, present sheriff of Cass county, Harry D., appropriate mention of whom follows this sketch, Charles E., who married Cecil Powers and resides in Logansport, and Sarah, who died in infancy. Mr. McDowell died on March 26, 1896, and his widow survived him until September 4, 1906.

HARRY D. MCDOWELL was born on his father's farm in Noble township, on the 14th of December, 1870, and there was reared. He is the son of Silas McDowell and Catherine Dritt his wife, and is one of the eight children of these parents. Further mention is unnecessary with regard to the family, as a full sketch is dedicated to the father just preceding this.

The district schools of his native township supplied the early education of Harry D. McDowell after which he took a thorough course at Hall's Business College. Between the years of 1895 and 1908 the young man farmed on his own responsibility, occupying a part of his father's generous estate, but in 1908 having purchased the James Reed hardware and implement store in Logansport in association with his brother, Charles E., he gave up his farming, and moved to the city, where he has since made his home. Charles E. McDowell had moved to Logansport some time prior to this and established himself in the meat market business, Harry D. being his partner in the venture, which proved a successful one. The two brothers have continued in partnership up to the present time, and are now the owners of a considerable valuable land, a meat market and a hardware and implement business, and are reckoned among the capable and prosperous business men of Logansport.

Harry D. McDowell was married on April 29, 1896, to Miss Sarah J. Dalzell and to their union seven children have been born, named as follows: Frederick, Blanche, Doris, Gladys, Harry, George and John. Mr. McDowell is a Republican in his political adherence, and his wife is a member of the Presbyterian church.

CARLTON A. PRICE, well known in Logansport and surrounding district in the monument business, was born in White county, Indiana, on January 26, 1873 and is the son of William H. and Mahala (Shull) Price, and a grandson of Aaron and Mary (Hancock) Price. The family is one of Scotch-Irish ancestry, which made its early advent into this country in Colonial days.

Aaron Price and his wife came to what is now Logansport in 1827. At that time but one log cabin marked the site of the future city, and the surrounding country was in a state of wildness such as to make true courage one's most valuable asset in attempting to establish a home in the region. Mr. Price located on a tract of land near Lockport in Carroll county, later moving to the vicinity of Idaville, where he lived retired until his death in 1882. He was a great hunter and enjoyed to the utmost the pursuit of the wild game that inhabited the country in his early days in Indiana. He worked on the old canal at times, but the best years of his life were spent in farming, in which he experienced much of success and prosperity. Seven children came to their home, and of that number William H. Price was the fourth born.

William H. Price was reared on his father's farm and has always followed the business in which he was there trained. In 1894 he moved to near Camden, in Carroll county, and three years later moved to North Dakota, where he now resides. He and his wife became the parents of ten children, seven of whom are yet living.

Carlton A. Price is the third born child and the second oldest living child of his parents He passed his youthful days on the old home place and as a boy attended the neighboring district school, in common with the other youths of his community He was just past his majority when he set out for himself and began an independent farming career, but in 1902 he gave up that plan and came to Logansport, where he set about learning the trade of a granite cutter He liked the work, became a skillful workman, and in five years from the time he identified himself with the business as an apprentice, he bought the marble shop of Henry L Foust, and has since been successfully engaged in the monument business in Logansport His business relations and activities are not confined alone to this city, but reach out to other cities and towns in the county and adjoining states in which he is coming to be well known in his line of enterprise

Mr Price is a Democrat, independent in his views, and holds membership in the Woodmen of the World On November 12, 1902, he was united in marriage with Eva McManus of Washington township, and they are the parents of two children,—Forrest and Kathleen

WILLIAM S RICHARDSON was born in Logansport, Cass county, Indiana, on April 25, 1838 When he was one year old his parents moved to what is now a part of the city of Logansport, and here he lived continuously from that time, covering a period of seventy-five years In those years he lived an active and helpful life in the community, and conducted a business in carpentering from early manhood until recent years, when he retired from the cares of active industrial life

The early opportunities of Mr Richardson for the securing of an adequate education were extremely limited, and such learning as he possesses was acquired in the practical school of experience. He learned the carpenter trade under the instruction of his father, who was also engaged in that trade during his life-time, and on December 1, 1861, was sworn into the United States service as a member of Company B, of the Forty-sixth Indiana Volunteer Infantry He was made quartermaster sergeant early in his military service and upon the resignation of the quartermaster was promoted to the rank of first lieutenant With his regiment he participated in all the engagements and movements of his command, the detailed history of which is to be found in the article devoted to the Forty-sixth Regiment in other pages of this work, and he was discharged from the service on September 11, 1865

After the close of the war, Mr Richardson returned to Logansport and there resumed the work of his trade, and in that work he continued steadily until in more recent years, when he gradually withdrew from business life and was afterwards practically retired from the building industry and the cares of business life

On August 17, 1865, when he was home from the war on a furlough, the young lieutenant was united in marriage with Susan Flory, the daughter of Emmanuel Flory, an old settler of the county She was born in Montgomery county, Pennsylvania, in March, 1840 They became the parents of one child, who died in infancy

Mr Richardson was made a Master Mason on December 11, 1865, and was also a member of the G A R He was a member of the Broadway Methodist Episcopal church, as is also his wife, and for thirty-five years he sung in the Methodist choir, as well as being a member of the G. A. R quartet for some years The death of this honored old citizen occurred on the 12th of February, 1913

FRANKLIN HENRY WIPPERMAN was born on December 15, 1861, at Angels Camp, Calaveras county, California, and is the son of Henry and Matilda (Ossenbeck) Wipperman, both German people Henry Wipperman was born in Germany on February 23, 1832, and came to America when but a few months old in company with his parents They settled in Indiana in September, 1837, making Clinton township their home, and there Henry Wipperman received the meager training afforded by the log-cabin schools of that primitive period In 1852 he went to California, prior to which time he had learned the carpenter's trade, and he remained in California until 1866, when he returned to Cass county and there remained until his death, which took place on February 7, 1904 He was a man who enjoyed the confidence and esteem of his fellow citizens at all times, and at one time in the eighties he held the office of county commissioner He married Matilda Ossenbeck on February 14, 1861 She was born in Cass county, the daughter of German born parents, her birth occurring on September 21, 1837, on the farm which remained her home during her young life While yet in her teens she went to California in the expectation of bettering her health, and there she completed her education in Stockton, where she met and married her husband She returned to Indiana with her husband in 1866, and in July of the following year death claimed her.

Franklin Henry Wipperman was the eldest of the two children born to these parents, his brother dying at the age of two months, shortly following the death of their young mother The common schools of his native community afforded Franklin Wipperman his early education, and in 1885 he was graduated from the Logansport high school. He passed his early days on the home farm in Washington township, in Cass county, and continued there until he was about twenty-nine years of age, or until December 1, 1890 when he removed to the city of Logansport and engaged in the abstract business, buying a part interest in the old John F. Dodd's office and later becoming full owner In 1902 Mr Wipperman was induced to become secretary and treasurer, in the new Logansport Loan & Trust Company, just organized at that time, and he has remained in that office up to the present writing

Mr Wipperman has devoted himself assiduously to business and has given no attention to public affairs of an official nature and has never been an office holder He was reared a Democrat, but broke away from the party in the famous money campaign of 1896, since which time he has voted for Republican candidates for president until 1912, when he was drawn into the Progressive party In local affairs, his support is given to the individual whom he regards as being best fitted to the office, it being his firm opinion that party prejudices have no place in local governments

On June 18, 1890, Mr. Wipperman was united in marriage with Clara M Bazin, daughter of Josiah and Matilda Bazin, of Logansport, Indiana Mr Bazin was an old time and faithful employe of the Pennsylvania Railroad until he was pensioned by that road, and came to Logansport from Griggsville, Illinois in 1872. Two children have been born to Mr and Mrs Wipperman. Frederic Bazin, born January 6, 1892, and Walter Kendall, born January 21, 1898. The elder son is a graduate of Cornell University and Walter Kendall has recently completed the local high school course, both being yet pursuing their education in the higher branches.

Mr Wipperman is a member of the Apollo Lodge, Knights of Pythias, since 1886, and of the Uniform Rank of the same order since 1888. He was a member of Ebenezer Lutheran church in Clinton township since he was fifteen years old until the year 1888, when he transferred his membership to St Luke's Lutheran church in Logansport and he has held various official positions in the church and synod of this denomination in the years that he has been associated with it as a member.

JOSEPH ENSMINGER CRAIN was born in Montgomery county, Indiana, January 2, 1844, and is one of the five sons and three daughters born to James Harvey and Elizabeth (Ensminger) Crain, of which family three sons and two daughters are living today.

James H Crain was born at Lebanon, Ohio, on August 27, 1809, and when ten years of age moved with the family to Montgomery county Indiana, and was there reared on the home farm. He received a common school education, after which he learned the carpenter's trade, thereafter following that business for something like fifteen years after he became of age. His father, Elihu Crain, was a brick mason by trade and he it was who built the first brick building in the city of Cincinnati. James H Crain with his wife and two children came to Cass county, Indiana, in 1845, and located on a farm in Washington township, three miles south of Logansport. He followed farming during the remainder of his life and died on February 22, 1897. Although a man of but limited schooling, he was exceptionally well informed. He realized the importance of an education and lost no opportunity to supply his early lack in that respect. By a course of self-imposed study and systematic reading, he acquired an excellent practical education and was known as one of the best informed men of his day in Cass county. In his religious views Mr Crain was a Baptist, and was one of the charter members of the Second Baptist church in Logansport. His wife was born at Harrisburg, Pennsylvania, February 28, 1822, and died on September 9, 1902. She was reared a Presbyterian and later in life embraced the Baptist faith.

Joseph E Crain has never considered any place but Cass county as his home. He was brought up on the old home farm in Washington township, educated in the district schools and under the tutelage of his father, who looked to the education of his children in the common school branches and industrial pursuits. His real start in life was probably at the time when he enlisted in the Civil war. Three times did he endeavor to enter the service before he was finally accepted, being once rejected for being under age, and once owing to rheumatic troubles from which he suffered. On January 28, 1865, he was enrolled as a member of Company F, One Hundred and Fifty-first Indiana Volunteer Infantry, and was discharged on September 19, 1865 His military activity consisted largely of doing guard and picket duty at Nashville and Tullahoma, Tennessee He had the rank of corporal at the time of being mustered out of the service For two years after the close of the war Mr Crain was occupied in farming, and in the fall of 1867 he moved to Logansport, where for seventeen years he was employed in carpentering Since then he has devoted himself exclusively to architecture, the last ten years of his life as a carpenter being devoted to the especial study of that subject He is regarded as one of the most capable architects in Logansport today, and among the buildings which he has erected and designed are the Masonic Temple, the Market Street Methodist Episcopal church, the Elliott building, the Crawford building, the McCaffrey building, the Windfall M. E church, the Frankfort Protestant Methodist church, the Kimmel M E church, and scores of other churches, private residences and commercial buildings in and about Logansport Two residence buildings designed by Mr Crain are especially deserving of mention. these are the Himmelburger residence and the residence of J W Rogers

Mr Crain is a Progressive Republican in his politics, and he has taken an active part in the political life of the country and his city In 1894 he was elected county commissioner, serving one term of three years, and in 1904 he was elected a member of the county council, serving three years in that body He is a man who has ever performed his full share in the good works that have been carried on in his community, both in a civic way and in his private capacity. He has long been a member of the Market Street Methodist Episcopal church,—forty-three years having passed since he first became thus identified, and for thirty-five years he has been a member of the board of trustees of that church He is a member of the Masonic fraternity, and is Past Worshipful Master of Tipton Lodge, No 33, Ancient Free & Accepted Masons He is also a member of, and past commander of Logansport Post, No 14, G A R , and he is a member of the famous Logansport Grand Army Quartet, organized in 1878 In further reference to his musical prowess, it may be mentioned here that for thirty-two consecutive years Mr Crain was the leader of his church choir

On October 19, 1865, Mr Crain was united in marriage with Miss Sarah Elnor Updegraff, of Washington township, Cass county, and seven children were born to them. of whom brief mention is here made as follows Edna M , who married Edwin F. Martin, is a resident of this county, Schuyler Colfax married Hattie Weymer, who is now deceased, and he is engaged in contracting in Portland, Oregon, Barton Keep married Elizabeth Pherson, and is now engaged in the Round Oak stove business, and lives at Dowagiac, Michigan, Rodney James, who married Eva Cline, is a railroad engineer, and makes his home in Logansport, Harriet Ann is the wife of George Shank of Grand Rapids, Michigan; Charlotte Belle is in Portland, Oregon, and is engaged in keeping house for her brother, Schuyler Colfax, Horace Ensminger, who married Elsie Landerholm, is engaged in commercial pursuits in Portland, Oregon

GEORGE A. CUSTER. Among the men whose high attainments have brought prestige to the Cass county bar, none are more deserving of mention in a work of this kind than George A. Custer, of Logansport, whose well-disciplined intellect, admirable self-control, great ability and many years of industrious application to all branches of professional practice have rendered him a bright ornament to a bar which boasts of many men of great intellect and wide range of knowledge in the field of jurisprudence. Having taken a prominent part in a number of noted trials during the past fifteen years, both in private practice and as a city official, he has been always cautious, always honorable, always fair, and the influence of his example has had much to do with giving the Cass county bar its enviable reputation of being one of the most honorable in the state. Mr. Custer has the added distinction of being a native of Cass county, as his birth occurred in Clay township, August 11, 1873, one of the two living children of a family of three born to George D. and Katherine (Morehart) Custer. His father, a native of Fairfield, Ohio, came to Cass county, Indiana, about 1870, and began farming in Clay township. Here he was married and continued to reside until the opening of the Rosebud Reservation, in Gregory county, South Dakota, when he journeyed to that section and purchased a relinquishment of a claim. Subsequently, he was followed by his daughter, who also bought a relinquishment, and they are now residing in Tripp county. Mr. Custer has always been prominent in Democratic politics wherever he has resided, but has not aspired to public office. His wife passed away in 1879. Her father, Adam Morehart, with his wife and family, came to Cass county from Pennsylvania by ox-team at a very early period in the history of the county, and here spent the rest of his life in agricultural pursuits in Clay township.

George A. Custer lived on the home farm until eight years of age, at which time he removed with his father to Marion, Indiana. There he continued a public school education that was begun in Clay township, and this was concluded in Logansport. Subsequently, after reading law for one year in the office of Judge John C. Nelson, of this city, he became a student in the State University at Bloomington, and was graduated therefrom June 16, 1897. He at once came to Logansport and began practice with Charles E. Yarlott, under the firm style of Custer & Yarlott, and was later associated with W. C. Dunn, of Chicago, Illinois, under the firm style of Custer & Dunn, succeeding which he was in individual practice for a short time. In 1906 he was the Democratic nominee for the office of prosecuting attorney and in the election that followed was easily elected, leading his ticket with a majority of 536 votes. In 1908 he again became his party's candidate, and this time was elected by the still further increased majority of 970 votes the largest majority ever given a candidate in Cass county. During this latter term, Mr. Custer was appointed by Governor Marshall to prosecute in the case of "State of Indiana ex rel George A. Custer, prosecuting attorney, within and for the Twenty-ninth Judicial Circuit of the State of Indiana, vs the Chesapeake & Ohio Railway Company of Indiana, et al." This was a case where it was charged the defendants were making an attempt to unload about $40,000,000 watered stock upon the public, attracted widespread attention, was considered to be of great importance as setting precedents, and ended in a victory for the state as represented by Mr Custer At the time of his first election, Mr. Custer had formed a partnership with Michael L Fansler, who became his deputy, and this continued four years, but since the expiration of Mr Custer's second term of office, he has been engaged in individual practice As a lawyer, conducting cases from the original consultation, through their preparations in his office and conflicts at the bar, to the final engrossment after the last decree of the last tribunal, Mr Custer is systematic, patient, vigorous and powerful He is an associate most valuable, an antagonist most worthy On February 10, 1911, while in Washington, D C, on business, he took the examination and was admitted to practice before the Department of the Interior, of which the patent office is a branch His registered number is 9934, and he is the only lawyer in Cass county to be so registered Mr. Custer has also contributed special articles on legal subjects, which have been widely quoted, to legal journals all over the country, including such a well-known authority as Hawkins' Legal Counsellor and Form Book Fraternally, he is connected with the Masons and the Benevolent and Protective Order of Elks

On November 12, 1903, Mr Custer was married to Miss Julia McReynolds, of Kokomo, Indiana

BENJAMIN F LONG To properly interpret the law in all its complexities and unerringly apply its provisions to establish human rights and defeat injustice, demands such a comprehensive knowledge not only of books but of life itself that he who reaches a high plane in this profession must command more than negative consideration in the minds of his fellow men It is told in both history and romance that a kind of law is upheld among savages, but when explained it resolves itself into the old axiom that "might makes right," and in modern, civilized life it becomes the task of the exponent of the law to overcome this only too prevalent idea Hence, on a solid educational foundation, must be built up a thorough knowledge of what law means to the present day man and how it can be applied to circumvent evil, protect the helpless and bring happiness and safety to the deserving Among the legal practitioners of the Cass county bar whose activities have brought them prominently before the public, none stands in higher esteem than Benjamin F Long, of the firm of Long, Yarlott & Souder, of Logansport A native of Cass county, he has spent his entire life within its limits, and belongs to a family that has been well known here for more than three-quarters of a century Mr Long was born in Washington township, Cass county, Indiana, January 31, 1872, a son of William and Joanna (Penny) Long His grandfather, William Long, Sr , was a native of Somerset county, Pennsylvania, from whence he moved to Indiana with his family in 1843 and located on the old home place in Washington township, where he spent the rest of his life in agricultural pursuits He was widely known as Major Long, that title having been acquired while he was a member of the Pennsylvania State Militia William Long was the eldest child of Major Long and, like his father spent his life in farming He died October 5 1893, in the faith of the

English Lutheran church, while his widow followed him to the grave December 12, 1902

Benjamin F Long was reared on the home farm, and during his boyhood attended the district schools In 1891 he graduated from the Logansport high school and during the succeeding two winters taught the district school which he had attended as a lad, in the meantime assisting his father in the work of the farm during the summer months In 1893 he entered the state university at Bloomington, but after two years was compelled to leave the university on account of lack of funds, as he had been paying his own way through college With a commendable spirit of determination, he returned to Logansport and secured a position as teacher of history in the high school, there continuing from 1895 to 1899, and in the latter year reentered the state university, where he completed the prescribed course in literature and received the degrees of Bachelor of Arts and Bachelor of Laws Returning again to Logansport, he entered upon the practice of his profession, and shortly thereafter was selected associate professor in the law department of the state university, a position which he continued to hold for one year He then resigned his chair and came again to Logansport, where he has since continued in a lucrative practice From 1903 to 1906, Mr Long served as deputy prosecutor, being a partner of the prosecuting attorney, George W Walters, under the firm style of Walters & Long, from January 1, 1903, to January 1, 1908 Since the latter date he has been a member of the firm of Long, Yarlott & Souder, and has been very successful in obtaining a representative clientele. He is recognized as one of the learned, thorough and reliable attorneys, and among his confreres is respected as a legist who respects and recognizes the unwritten ethics of the profession In politics he is a Republican, but has taken no very active part in public matters With his wife he attends the English Lutheran church

Mr Long was married September 10, 1902, to Miss Lucy Nichols, of Marshalltown, Iowa, and they have one son· Benjamin.

CHARLES H STUART Among the families of Cass county which can claim residence here of three-quarters of a century or more, that bearing the name of Stuart holds prominent place In its ranks have been found eminent professional men, soldiers, merchants and financiers, leaders in public and civic life and prominent figures in social activities One of the representatives of this name who is well known to the legal profession of Cass county, is Charles H Stuart, United States commissioner at Logansport, and an attorney of deserved reputation

Hon William Z Stuart, the Cass county progenitor of the branch of the family to which Charles H Stuart belongs, was an early attorney of Cass county, whither he came early in 1836 He was admitted to practice at Logansport, February 20, 1837, and soon attained rank among the legists of the state, many of whose names subsequently became widely renowned Of necessity, his practice covered all branches in the early days, but during his later years he gained reputation as a railroad lawyer and for a long period was chief attorney for the Wabash Railway Company Beginning in 1843, he served one year as state's attorney, and from 1853 to 1857 he was judge of the state supreme court He married (first) Minerva Potter, who died, leaving three children Venitia, Selden P and Francis H Later, Judge Stuart contracted a second marriage

Selden P. Stuart, son of Hon William Z Stuart, and father of Charles H. Stuart, was born September 16, 1842, at Logansport, Indiana, and at the outbreak of the great Civil war was a student in the preparatory school. On December 26, 1862, he enlisted in Company K, Ninety-ninth Indiana Volunteer Infantry, subsequently being promoted to first sergeant, and to second lieutenant of his company, May 1, 1865, and received his honorable discharge June 5, 1865 For the most part he was actively connected with all the movements of his company until the close of the war, the one exception being when he was detailed as acting aide-de-camp to General Oliver, brigade commander He married Eloise Landes, and they became the parents of two children, one who died in infancy and Charles H Mr Stuart died in November, 1881, while his widow still survives him and is now the wife of Stewart T McConnell, an attorney of Logansport

Charles H. Stuart was born in Logansport, Indiana, May 7, 1878 and here prosecuted his preliminary studies in public and private schools Subsequently he became a student in the Culver Military Academy, Culver, Indiana, and then entered Lawrenceville Academy, New Jersey, after graduation from which, in September, 1896, he started upon his collegiate course in Princeton University. He was graduated therefrom in 1900, with the degree of Bachelor of Arts, and returned to Logansport, where he was admitted to the bar in September of the same year. Shortly thereafter, however, he went to Chicago, Illinois, where he acted in the capacity of clerk in the First National Bank for two years, being connected with the legal department During this time he also attended the legal department of Lake Forest University, and in 1902 he returned to Logansport and entered upon the active practice of his profession Mr Stuart has succeeded in building up an excellent professional business of a representative character, and is recognized by his confreres as a legist who respects the unwritten ethics of the profession Well versed in the principles of law and jurisprudence, he has been a constant and assiduous student, and the success that has come to him in his chosen field of endeavor has been an appreciation of his high abilities. During the past eight years, Mr Stuart has served as United States commissioner at Logansport In 1912 he cast his fortunes with the new Progressive party, and at that time became its candidate for the office of judge of the circuit court of Cass county As a citizen he stands high in the esteem of his fellows, being known as a man of progressive spirit and one who is at all times ready to contribute of his time or means to any worthy cause promising the welfare of Logansport or its people He has been interested in historical work, and at this time is secretary of the Cass County Historical Society.

On June 17, 1903, Mr Stuart was married to Miss Marie Watson Rogers, of Cass county.

DAVID C. ARTHUR was admitted to the bar in 1899 and he has been engaged in practice continuously since that time, his activities being conducted in Logansport, both as an independent practitioner and as a partner in the firm of Fickle & Arthur. Mr Arthur was born in Darke county, Ohio, on February 25, 1862, and is one of the family of ten children born to his parents, Abner and Mary (Bowman) Arthur, of which number eight are yet living.

Abner Arthur was a farmer by occupation, and in 1867 he removed to Randolph county, Indiana, where he and his good wife yet live. David C Arthur was reared in Randolph county, and received his elementary education in the district schools of the home community. For a time he attended the National Normal University at Lebanon, Ohio, also attending the state university at Bloomington, Indiana, for two terms. This schooling was secured through the strictest economy and the most strenuous effort, for the young man found it necessary to earn his own way. He worked on the farm, taught school, made brick and tile, did janitor work, in fact, did anything he might find at which he found it possible to turn an honest penny in his efforts to secure an education. After he left Bloomington, he engaged in teaching, and it was while thus engaged that he came to Logansport in 1894 as principal of the high school. He was thus employed for five years in this city, and while here he took up the study of the law in the offices of Kistler & Kistler. In 1899 he was admitted to the bar and at once began the practice of his profession in Logansport. He continued in independent practice for a time, then entered into a partnership with John M Ashby, which association endured for two years. Since 1909 he has been the partner of Hon D D Fickle, doing business under the firm name of Fickle & Arthur.

Mr Arthur is a Democrat in his politics. In 1910 he was elected a member of the city school board, of which he is secretary, and his early educational work has especially qualified him for the duties of that position. Mr Arthur has been identified with many of the secret, benevolent and fraternal organizations of the city, and is popular and prominent in whatever circles he is found. He is a member of the Presbyterian church, in which he has for many years been an elder, and his wife also holds membership in that church.

On Christmas day, in 1894 Mr Arthur was united in marriage with Miss Ellen Jameson, of Lebanon Ohio, and they are the parents of two children, Mary and Robert.

SYLVESTER S CRAGUN Of the many valuable farms found in Cass county, one of the most valuable is that known as Hill Top farm which is devoted to stock raising and is located on the Hill Top road. Here its owner, Sylvester S Cragun, is breeding a superior line of Percheron horses and other valuable stock, and his activities have made him well known among the successful men of his community. Mr Cragun belongs to an old and honorable family and was born in Clinton township, Cass county, May 20 1852, a son of Zachariah and Elizabeth N (Shideler) Cragun The family was founded in America by Patrick Cragun, who came from Dublin, Ireland, prior to the Revolutionary war, and took part in the struggles of the American colonists that resulted in the winning of independence. Patrick Cragun was the father of several children, among them Joshua Cragun, the grandfather of Sylvester S.

Zachariah Cragun was born in 1824, in Clinton county, Indiana, on

"INGLESIDE" RESIDENCE OF MR. AND MRS. SYLVESTER S. CRAGUN

his father's farm, and was nineteen years of age when he came to Cass county. He had been reared to agricultural pursuits, working on the farm during all of his school period and until he was married, was employed as a farm hand. Subsequently he became the owner of a tract of his own, and the remainder of his life was passed in tilling the soil. His wife was born near Eaton, Preble county, Ohio, and was a small girl when she came to Cass county with her parents, who became prominent farming people of Clinton township.

Sylvester S. Cragun was born in a little log cabin on the old Cragun homestead, as were his two sisters, Dora, who became the wife of Andrew Y. Shanklin, and Ellen who is now deceased. He was educated in the common schools of his day, and was an able assistant to his father in the clearing of the home place, on which he remained until reaching his twenty-fourth year. At that time he left the parental roof and embarked upon enterprises of his own, eventually accumulating enough capital to purchase his present tract, Hill Top farm, a property of eighty acres, which he has brought to a high state of cultivation. He feeds his farm products to his stock, and has been unquestionably successful in his breeding operations. He is recognized as an excellent judge of livestock, and his advice is often sought by the stockmen of his community. In business affairs he has ever proved reliable and trustworthy, and his reputation is that of a man of integrity in business matters and public-spirit in affairs affecting his township. With the birth of the so-called Bull Moose party, in 1912, he was one of the first men in the United States to be nominated as a candidate on that ticket, making a very creditable campaign for the office of commissioner of Cass county. He is a member of the Anoka Lodge, Independent Order of Odd Fellows, No. 630, and Logansport Lodge, Free and Accepted Masons, Tipton Lodge at Logansport.

On March 29, 1877, Mr. Cragun was married to Miss Candace S. Marshall, daughter of John and Margaret (Kendall) Marshall, the former of whom was born in Kentucky in 1804 and came to Carroll county, Indiana, in 1834. Mr. and Mrs. Marshall had eleven children, of whom five are still living: George K., Susana, Sarah, Candace S., and James J. Mr. and Mrs. Cragun have had four children: Harry M. and Ruth, who are both deceased, Homer J., who finished the public schools and spent two years in high school, married Angeline Long, and is engaged in farming; and Miss Margaret, a graduate of the Cass county schools, class of 1909, also spent two years in the Logansport high school and then attended commercial college.

Mrs. Cragun was born in Carroll county, Indiana, October 23, 1856, the youngest in her father's family. She received a good common school education and in her life's work she has ably performed her part as wife and mother in the building up of their beautiful home and rearing her children. She is an honored member of the Jewel Rebecca Lodge of the city of Logansport. Mr. and Mrs. Cragun and children are eligible to become members of the Sons and Daughters of the Revolution. Their homestead, "Ingleside," is a beautiful estate located five miles from the city of Logansport, Indiana.

JAMES D. McNITT A name that has become widely known in business and financial circles of Logansport during the past decade is that of James D McNitt, president of the Logansport Loan and Trust Company, and a citizen who has shown himself possessed of all the essential qualities of a useful and successful business man Quick to perceive, ready to act, he meets minor business questions with great ease, while careful to act rightly, larger matters are the subject of full consideration His operations in the feeding, buying and shipping of stock have been extensive, and in every line of business activity he is known as one whose commercial ideals are of the strictest nature Mr. McNitt has been a resident of Indiana since he was six months of age, coming here from Juniata county, Pennsylvania, where he was born July 3, 1845 His parents, James G and Jane (Nagney) McNitt, were also born in this country, but were of Scotch ancestry James G. McNitt, his father, came to Cass county, Indiana, by wagon in 1845, the trip consuming six weeks, and located on Crooked creek, in Jefferson township, where he was engaged in farming until his death in 1847 His widow survived him nine years, her death being brought about by fighting a prairie fire Thus the six children were left to shift for themselves, and all are now deceased with the exception of James D

James D McNitt was the youngest of his parents children, and his boyhood was divided between attendance at the district school and work on the farm Later he took a course of one term in the Old Seminary, at Logansport, and thus equipped, taught district school. After three terms, however, he decided his abilities could be directed to better advantage in a different field of endeavor, and accordingly he turned his attention to farming and stock raising About the year 1873, Mr McNitt ceased active agricultural pursuits and came to Logansport, where he embarked in the wholesale and retail grocery business with a partner, under the firm style of Uhl & McNitt, a connection that continued profitably for eleven years, the buying of wool being an important factor in the conduct of the business. However, the constant confinement and excessive labor connected with his duties, told heavily upon Mr McNitt's strength, his health began to fail, and he was finally compelled to sell his mercantile interests He again took up stock buying, feeding and shipping, and to this he has given the greater part of his attention ever since, with marked success In 1902, Mr McNitt assisted in the founding of the Logansport Loan and Trust Company, and on the completion of the organization, he was elected its president, a position in which he has served to the present time Honorable and honest in his affairs, courteous and easily approached, considerate and broad in his judgment of general business conditions and tendencies, and a most certain and intuitive judge of the character of men, Mr McNitt deserves and receives the full esteem and regard of his associates, and is justly judged one of the community's foremost men of business

In December, 1872, Mr McNitt was married to Miss Mary Ellen Uhl, daughter of Joseph Uhl, and seven children were born to this union· Caroline N, Mary Ethel, deceased, S Miriam, Robert J, Willard C, Helen U and Esther U Mr and Mrs McNitt have given their children excellent educational advantages, sending them to the best colleges and universities in the country and fitting them for whatever positions in life they may be called upon to fill He was president of the city schools of Logansport nine years The family are consistent members of the Broadway Presbyterian church, Logansport Mr McNitt is a Democrat in politics, but has never aspired to public office, preferring to give his entire time and attention to his business affairs He is always ready, however, to support movements for the welfare of Logansport or its people, and to co-operate in advancing education, morality and good citizenship

GEORGE WASHINGTON BISHOP. A career of more than half a century of time, during which he has risen from obscurity and a humble position in life, to an acknowledged position among the foremost business citizens of his community, proves the right of George Washington Bishop to the title of representative man of Walton In this long period he has been identified with various interests, commercial, industrial, agricultural and financial, in all of which he has left the impress of his remarkable business capacity, his great quickness of perception and his wonderfully systematic mind Although now retired from business activities, having reached an age when he feels himself entitled to a rest from the worries and struggles of former years, he still exerts a distinct influence in the life of the city, with whose history his own has been almost commensurate Mr Bishop was born September 18, 1836, at Tiffin, Ohio, and is a son of David and Eliza (Douden) Bishop His father, a native of Pennsylvania, went to Kentucky in young manhood, and later made his home for some time at Cincinnati, with Gov. R. M Bishop's father who is a second cousin of George W Bishop, succeeding which he moved to Tiffin, Ohio, and there passed away at a ripe old age He and his wife were the parents of twelve children, all of whom reached years of maturity Mrs Ellen Huffman, John T, Mrs Mary Lightner-Darling, Mrs Julia Betts, Eliza, W H, Alvina Booker, Mrs Lovina Flynn, Catherine Shafer and Ida Baumgardner. all of whom are deceased, George Washington and Laura Penrose

George W Bishop remained under the parental roof until he was fourteen years of age, working with his father, who was a carpenter, and learning the trades of carpenter and bricklayer In 1852 he first came to Walton, Indiana, walking about two hundred miles to Lewisburg, as the railroads had not reached this point and the canal was frozen over. He then returned to Tiffin, but in October, 1854, again came to Walton and for a time worked at his trades Soon, however, he recognized the opportunity for entering the mercantile field, and, returning to Tiffin, Ohio, invested his modest capital in a little stock of general merchandise, which he brought back to Walton The business thus started became one of the large enterprises of the town, Mr Bishop's intelligent management, tireless industry and sound business sense serving to constantly widen its scope and extend the range of its operations For twenty years he was also engaged in the manufacture of excelsior, and then turned the store over to his sons His next venture was the buying of the Bank of Walton, which he sold four years later and retired from active life Mr Bishop is the owner of three handsome farms, one being the Bishop home place, on the Walton and Bunker Hill road, a tract of sixty-five acres north of Walton a part of which is in the city limits, another is the old Harrison McVeedy farm on the township line road a tract of 160 acres about two and one-half miles northwest of Walton, and the third tract, of 117 acres is located in Jackson township, about two miles southeast of Walton.

Mr. Bishop was married April 25, 1860, to Miss Sarah Corbley, and they became the parents of five children Ida and Alonzo, who are deceased, Myrtle, the wife of Aaron McKee who has two children—Harold and Keith, Claude a sketch of whom appears elsewhere in this volume, and George Walter. Mr. Bishop was married again, April 2, 1891, to Mrs Vora (Watson) Sumption widow of David Ward Sumption a full review of whose career will be found on another page of this work, and to this union there has been born one son. Richard Edgar, a graduate of Walton High school who spent two years in Wabash University and is now at Purdue University. Mr. and Mrs Bishop attend the Lutheran church, and have interested themselves in its work He is a member of the Independent Order of Odd Fellows and she was a Rebekah. The high rewards that are attainable in fortune, character and influence through a life of industry and probity guided and regulated by a sense of Christian obligation, are illustrated in Mr Bishop's career. With no extraordinary endowment of faculty, unaided by inheritance or friendly support he was content to enter into the life which a rising community offered in a humble station and to follow up the opportunities that opened before him with steadiness and industry, gaining, step by step the rare fruits of well directed enterprise. Today he finds himself in the possession of a handsome competency and the friendship of his fellow men and the head of a family which reflects credit upon the wise and guiding hand that has trained its harmonious members to lives of usefulness and honor.

DAVID WARD SUMPTION Although a resident of Walton for only a comparatively short period, the late David Ward Sumption will be remembered by many of the older citizens here because of his connection with the manufacturing interests of the city, as well as one of the pioneer "Knights of the Key" whose occupation called them to various parts of the state. Mr Sumption was born in 1857, at St Joe, Indiana, and was a son of Robert and Barilla (Ward) Sumption, the former of whom was for a number of years an inn-keeper and hardware merchant at Ridgeville, Randolph county, Indiana. There were four children in the family Mrs Josephine Tyrrel, who now resides at Santiago, California, Albert who is traveling auditor for the Union Pacific railroad, with headquarters at Carney Nebraska, David Ward, and William who is deceased.

David Ward Sumption was educated in the common schools of Jay county, Indiana, and learned the trade of telegrapher at Union City, subsequently becoming railroad agent at Ridgeville. Later he spent a short time at Elwood after which he returned to Ridgeville, where for a few years he was engaged in the hardware business, but again took up his vocation as a telegraph operator and as such came to Walton in 1873 here continuing as agent for five years He then turned his attention to the manufacturing business which he followed until his removal to Madison, Nebraska and his death occurred in Madison county, Nebraska, April 15, 1881. After his death, his widow took up his work, but gave up that occupation to engage in school teaching, an occupation which she followed until her second marriage to George W. Bishop, of Walton.

Mr. Sumption was married to Miss Vora Watson October 27, 1870, and they became the parents of three children, as follows: Gertrude, a graduate of the State Normal school, at Terre Haute, and for some time a school teacher, married Sanford Bell, and had three children — Portia, Geneva and Josephine, and the family home is now located at Denver, Colorado. Homer, now residing in San Diego, California, who married Amelia Walters, of Sheridan, Wyoming, and has one child,— Vora; and Josephine, director of music in the Denver (Colo.) College, and organist in Trinity Methodist Episcopal church, who married F. M. White, of Noblesville, Indiana. Mr. Sumption was a member of the Universalist church, and was a man of integrity and probity of character. He was always interested in fraternal work, and was popular with the members of the Independent Order of Odd Fellows and the Knights of Honor. Those who knew him will remember him as a man who was always ready to assist others, who never knowingly made an enemy, and who never lost a friend except through death.

JOSEPH T. McNARY has been actively identified with the growth and development of Cass county for more than a quarter of a century. Born in Harrison county, Ohio, September 26, 1850, he is a son of James and Harriett (Thompson) McNary, both of whom were natives of Washington county, Pennsylvania. His scholastic training was obtained in the schools of Bloomfield, Ohio and Union College, from which latter institution he received his diploma in 1864. He first came to Cass county, Indiana, in 1865, but the ensuing two years he passed in Tipton county, teaching school and studying law, upon which he had settled for his professional career.

In 1868 Mr. McNary continued his legal studies under O. P. Blake of Peru, Indiana, and in connection with legal pursuits, was engaged in handling real estate at Peru until 1870. Since the latter date he has resided in Logansport. It would seem that real estate dealings are especially to his liking, for he has never ceased to be more or less engaged in transactions along that line, and for the past ten years practically his entire attention has been devoted to the real estate and loan business. For a number of years John R. McNary, his brother, was associated with him.

Actively identified with the Republican party since early manhood, Mr. McNary was first elected to the city council of Logansport in 1881, and by continued reelection, served some sixteen years in that office, during which time some of the most important laws on the city government were enacted. It was also during this time, and largely through the instrumentality of Mr. McNary that the first traction line of the city was built and since that time, he has been closely identified with the construction of all the other lines. The purchase of Spencer Park by the Street Railway was another important measure in which Mr. McNary bore a conspicuous and worthy part. The deal was engineered entirely by Mr McNary, and the gift to the city by the Street Railway Company of eighteen acres was through his influence. It was dedicated and named McNary Park and afterwards called Spencer Park. He was closely identified also with the locating of Riverside Park. He assisted in the reorganization of the State National Bank after its failure and for many years has been a part of almost all important public events in Logansport. The Northern Indiana Hospital for the Insane became a Logansport institution largely by reason of his personal efforts, and many another movement has felt his influence in a direction that would be of the greatest possible benefit to his home city.

Mr. McNary has achieved success in life wholly through his own efforts. He came to Logansport with scarcely a dollar to his name, but success in his case came only after years of tireless energy and industry. Of late years he has devoted a considerable time to travel, and there is not a state, territory or important or interesting city in the Union that he has not visited. He has made one trip abroad, and is planning to continue his travels as opportunity affords.

Mr. McNary was united in marriage on October 7, 1875, to Miss Belle Thompson, of Wabash county, Indiana, and their beautiful home in Logansport is a most ideally happy one.

OTTO FIKE. The citizens of Walton, Indiana, need no introduction to Otto Fike, the popular general blacksmith who has built up a thriving business through excellent workmanship, general reliability and courteous treatment of customers. His career from boyhood has been one of steady industry and persistent endeavor, and is worthy of emulation by the aspiring youths of today, teaching an example of upright living and well-directed effort. Mr. Fike is worthy in every way of the respect in which he is held, and among his many acquaintances he can count many friends.

Otto Fike is a native son of Indiana, having been born in Miami county, August 26, 1883, and is a son of David and Lavina (Dickson) Fike. His father was born near Mexico, Indiana, from whence he went to Bunker Hill, Indiana, and there carried on his business of blacksmith and general mechanic. He and his wife were the parents of two children: Edward, who is an automobile trimmer; and Otto. The early education of Otto Fike was secured in the district schools of Miami county, but later, when his parents moved to Logansport, he went to the public schools, there finishing his training. He was a resident of Logansport for eighteen years, and there, in Joseph Erny's shop he began to learn the trade of blacksmith. When he had thoroughly mastered all the details of this vocation, he came to Walton, where he has since continued to carry on a profitable business. Mr. Fike is alert and shrewd in business dealings, but his career has been free from transactions otherwise than those of a legitimate character. He is an excellent mechanic, and his trade is attracted from a wide contiguous territory. Public life has held out no inducements to him. He has been too busy making a place for himself among the business men of Walton to think of political preferment. His home and his business have always been of the greatest value to him. However, he has not been unmindful of the duties of citizenship, as is demonstrated on every occasion when movements for the welfare of the community are promoted, for in him they find an intelligent, energetic and reliable supporter

In March 7, 1906, was solemnized the marriage of Mr Fike with Mrs Sarah (Brooher) Laird, who had two children by a former marriage. Juanita and Violet Mr and Mrs. Fike have had one son David Edward   The family belongs to the Lutheran church, and is liberal in its support of religion and charity   Both Mr and Mrs Fike have a wide acquaintance and their friends are legion.

EDWARD F SMALL   A complete account of the little business and agricultural community at Walton and vicinity could not be comprised, with reference to the affairs and activities of the last half century, without mention of the firm known as Small Brothers, comprising W. L, Ed F, and Otho A. Small, three brothers who for many years have been influential factors in the business enterprise of this part of Cass county

Mr Edward F Small, the second of these enterprising brothers, was born on the old Small homestead in Washington township, Cass county, on the twenty-third of March, 1867, his parents, Andrew Jackson and Mary (Ijams) Small   One in a family of seven children Edward F Small obtained his education in the common schools, and a principal part of his early training consisted in the work and experiences of the home farm   It was after attaining to manhood and some independent venturing of his own that he founded the association with his two brothers for engaging in the grain business. The firm of Small Brothers, starting from this point in business affairs, enlarged the scope of their operations, and through their individual application to business, they extended and built up a business which is one of the largest and most successful of the kind in Cass county   It has had a substantial and steady growth, always being expanded on the solid basis of capital and prospect of assured returns

Mr Edward F Small was married November 18, 1903 to Miss Flora E Flanagan a daughter of Charles and Jennie (Waite) Flanagan   Mr and Mrs Small are the parents of two children, named Inez and Herbert   Fraternally he is affiliated with the Independent Order of Odd Fellows, No 314 at Walton, and also the Masons Lodge, No 423 and he and his family are members of the Christian church

WASHINGTON L SMALL   Among the really useful men of a community are found those in whom their fellow citizens can rely in affairs of public importance, to whom they can come for assistance in seasons of financial distress, men who have won this confidence by the wisdom of their own investments and by the honorable lives they have led on every field of effort and as neighbors and friends   Very often, in prosperous towns, these men are retired farmers, frequently they are bankers   Such a man is W L Small, president of the Cass County State Bank, of Walton, an energetic business man, well qualified to conduct the affairs of of a financial institution, whose material success has been alike beneficial to himself and to the place in which he has labored   Mr Small was born on a farm in Washington township, about nine miles from

Logansport, Indiana, September 20, 1847, and is a son of Andrew Jackson and Mary (Ijams) Small. The eldest of his parents' seven children, his education was secured in common schools, which he attended when he could spare the time from the duties of the home farm. He was thrifty and industrious as a youth, carefully saving his earnings with the idea ever in view of embarking upon a career of his own, and eventually, with his two brothers Ed F. and Otho A. Small, entered the grain business. Instead of hiring their work done by others, the three brothers performed their own labor, each striving earnestly for the success of their enterprise. This method soon began to show results, and as time went on and their capital permitted they added to their holdings and equipment and were successful in building up one of the important industries of this section. During this time W. L. Small had continued to be engaged in farming, and at this writing is the owner of an excellent tract of 170 acres with modern buildings and valuable improvements. In 1911, Mr. Small became a stockholder in the Cass County State Bank, and soon thereafter he was elected to the presidency of this institution. That his choice displayed good judgment on the part of the directors is shown by the fact that since he has been shaping the policies of the institution the business has developed an increase of fifty per cent. His personality had much to do with instilling confidence in the depositors, while among his associates he is recognized as a shrewd, careful and farsighted citizen, and a man of the strictest integrity and probity of character.

Mr. Small was married to Mary E. Spohn, January 6, 1881, and to this union there has been born four children, namely: Frank, who is single and engaged in managing his father's farm; Emmet, who married Blanch Vernon, daughter of James Vernon, and has two children,—Zelma and John; Claude; and Nora, who married Peter Erny. The family is connected with the Christian church. Mr. Small is not a politician, nor has he sought political preferment, but he is at all times ready and anxious to do his full duty as a citizen and no movement of importance is considered complete until his name is enlisted in the ranks. Like other successful business men here, he takes a pride in the accomplishments of his city, in that he has assisted in making these accomplishments possible.

OTHO A. SMALL. The average Cass county farmer, of an industrious and energetic nature, is generally loath to retire from the work in which he has spent the best years of his life and acquired a competence but when he does turn over his interests to other hands and moves to the near-by town or village, he becomes one of his new community's good citizens, investing his capital in its industries and adding his support to its progressive movements, thus being a welcome addition to the section's population. Among the retired farmers now living in Walton, is Otho A. Small, who is probably better known as "Bert" Small, and who for years was engaged in carrying on agricultural operations in this vicinity. Mr. Small has resided in Cass county all of his life having been born on the old Small homestead place in Washington township, June 5, 1869, and is a son of Andrew Jackson and Mary (Ijams) Small.

Mr. Small comes of an agricultural family, and in his youth he was

MR. AND MRS. J. CHARLES THOMAS AND FAMILY

trained to agricultural work and to habits of industry, sobriety and honorable living As a youth he secured such advantages as were to be obtained in the district schools of his community, and he continued to assist his father in conducting the home place until he was nineteen years of age At the age of nineteen years he and his brother, Edward F Small, rented small pieces of land, on which they managed to get a start in life, after they had refused to be disheartened by a number of hard knocks Working industriously on their own property and in the meantime assisting their father in cultivating his land, the boys secured a little capital, and eventually realized their ambition of entering the grain business, in connection with which they bought and sold stock Later the three brothers Edward F, Otho A and W L, built an elevator at Walton, and this was developed into one of the leading business enterprises of the place "Bert" Small is known as a business man who has ever borne a high reputation because of honorable transactions He always devoted himself strictly to legitimate lines, and the business which he assisted in developing will stand as a monument to his ability He is now living in quiet retirement, in the enjoyment of the fruits of his early labors It is not to be supposed, however, that he has dropped entirely out of the life of the community, for he still interests himself in its movements, and, as spectator, takes a keen and intelligent interest in the battles of the political arena He belongs to the Odd Fellows, in which he has a number of warm friends, and is a deacon and trustee of the Christian church

On February 3, 1897, Mr Small was united in marriage to Miss Carrie Jane Pierson daughter of Matthew and Mary Jeanette Pierson, and they have had one son. Orel R, fourteen years of age, a bright, intelligent lad, who is attending the Walton public schools and will enter the Walton high school In 1908 Mr and Mrs Small erected their pretty modern residence in Walton, Indiana

J CHARLES THOMAS "When agriculture flourishes," observes Xenophon, the Greek historian and philosopher, "all other pursuits are in full vigor, but when the ground is forced to lie barren, other occupations are almost stopped " This statement is as true in these modern times as when it was written many centuries ago To the farm each country must look for its sustenance, and it is therefore of such vital importance that those in whose charge must be placed the agricultural interests of any community must be men of ability in their vocation, able to produce their full share of the necessities without which other industries are sorely handicapped Among the agriculturists who have raised the agricultural importance of Cass county to such a high standard as that it now enjoys is found J Charles Thomas, of Clay township, who was born May 23, 1857, a son of William and Porter and Margaret (Stafford) Thomas

William Porter Thomas was the son of Giles Wheeler Thomas, who was born near Baltimore, Maryland, on October 31, 1794, five years prior to the death of General Washington He learned the trade of a tanner in Blacksburg, Virginia, under the instruction of Harmon Sifford, and migrated to what was then known as Champaign county, Ohio, now called Clark county, and there he wedded Agnes Black, a daughter of William Black She was born on April 28, 1798, and died on October 4, 1851 In later years Giles Thomas married a second time, Mrs Julia (Stafford) Funston, connected by marriage with the famous Funston family of which Gen Frederick Funston, of the United States Regular Army and of Philippine war fame, is a member, becoming his wife She was born on September 10, 1804, and died in September, 1881 Giles Thomas died on January 6, 1870 His son, William Porter Thomas, the father of J Charles Thomas of this brief review married Miss Margaret Stafford, a daughter of Ralph (native of Ireland) and Catherine (Saylor) Stafford, and to them were born a goodly family of ten children, seven growing to manhood and womanhood, and six are living at this time They are named as follows· Giles Stafford and George Wheeler, twins, of whom Giles S , who is a resident of Geneva, Nebraska, was married to Sadie Wheeler and is a retired agriculturist and was a soldier in the Civil war

George W , who lives in Peru, Indiana, married Grizzie Black, and is a retired farmer. He was also a soldier in the Civil war The brothers were members of Company K, Ninety-ninth Regiment, Indiana Volunteers Martha Virginia married Uriah W. Oblinger and both died in Nebraska Uriah W Oblinger was a soldier in the Civil war, a member of Fifty-seventh Regiment, Indiana Volunteers Ellen Annette is the wife of D S Bailey of Minneapolis, Minn , a contractor and builder Samuel Greene, a farmer of Middletown, Indiana, married Sarah Pawabaker William Rowen, a farmer of Tipton township, married Lorretta Miller and J Charles Thomas of this review

J Charles Thomas received his education in the district schools of Tipton township, and there was reared to agricultural pursuits, remaining on the home farm and assisting his father with the home duties until his marriage, when he left the parental roof and engaged in farming on his own responsibility He is now the owner of a fine tract of sixty-eight acres of well cultivated land, on which he has brought about numerous improvements, including the erection of a number of substantial buildings He has devoted his life to the business of general farming and the success he has attained has been the result of his own industry, perseverance and faithful labor Mr Thomas was for many years a supporter of the principles and doctrines of Republicanism, but of recent years has transferred his allegiance to the Prohibition party He has interested himself in fraternal work, and is a member of the Woodmen of the World, and of Tipton lodge, Ancient Free and Accepted Masons Mr Thomas and his family are members of the Methodist church

On January 17, 1886, Mr Thomas married Miss Jeannette Beal, daughter of John D and Catherine (Long) Beal, the latter a daughter of William Long Mr Beal came to the United States from France about the year 1830, at that time the family name being rendered D'Beel, since then the present form coming into popular usage His wife came from Pennsylvania in 1840 and their marriage occurred in Cass county, Indiana, in 1859 They settled in Washington township, where Mr Beal was engaged in the business of farming until his retirement from active farm life, since when they have been living at No 25 Market street, in Logansport, Indiana, where their golden wedding anniversary was celebrated in 1909 Mr and Mrs John D Beal had eight children, as follows Joseph A, who married Mollie Thornton, John Henry, who married Libbie Herr, Jeannette, Mrs Thomas, William V, who married Effie Carney, James Adrian, who married Julia Grover, and three others, who are deceased

Mr and Mrs J Charles Thomas are the parents of four daughters, namely Mabel Annette, the wife of Everett Hubler, to whom one daughter has been born—Vere Catherine by name Mrs Hubler was graduated from the public schools of her native community and was a student in the Marion normal, after which she was engaged as a teacher in Cass county Her husband is one of the more successful farming men of Allen county, Indiana Ethel Ursula was educated in the public schools and she has since specialized in instrumental music, in which she is quite successful Eulalia Marie is also proficient in musical ability, and Margaret Catherine, the youngest of the four, is yet a student in the public schools, and will graduate with the class of 1914

Mr and Mrs. Thomas have given to their daughters the advantage of the best education available, and their school instruction has been amply supplemented by the most admirable home and church training —a phase of education which is all too often neglected in American homes, but which is the basis of all genuine training and the foundation of the happiest homes With the exception of the eldest, the daughters are at home with their parents

Mr Thomas and his estimable wife who has long been his able counselor in all the affairs of life, are citizens who are held in high regard by all who know them Their cozy homestead known as "Rose Lawn," is one where genuine hospitality abounds

Both parents come of families that gave worthy service to the flags of their respective countries, and it is of such blood that the best citizenship must inevitably spring The paternal grandfather of Mrs Thomas, John D D'Beal, was a native of France and a soldier under Napoleon Bonaparte, with whom he was serving at the time of the famous retreat from Moscow, while the maternal grandfather of Mr Thomas was a soldier in the Revolutionary war, through which connection members of the family today are eligible to membership in the society of the Sons and Daughters of the American Revolution, a distinction dear to the hearts of all patriotic Americans today, and one which is a true patent of American nobility

HENRY FRANKLIN SMALL There has been no period in recorded history when the caring for the dead has not been a feature of even savage life, and the ceremonies have been of a character that has been marked by the measure of civilization Study habits and customs of every nation and it will be found that a reverence has been paid to the dead, oftentimes such as was not given to the living, and even the most brutal savage tribes in the deepest wilderness, even those who still make human sacrifices as a part of religious rites, can point to their stone crypts, their burning temples, their funeral barks or their tree-top burials There never has been, however, a time when the proper, dignified sanitary conduct of funeral obsequies and disposal of the remains of those whose life work has ended has been so complete as at present. Funeral directors and undertakers of the present day in America are no longer mere mechanics but, on the other hand are carefully trained in this profession and often are graduates of more than one college. Methods of body preservation which formerly were considered lost arts are well known now and have been vastly improved upon. Henry Franklin Small, whose tact dignity and kindly sympathy have made him a comforting figure in the homes where death has visited, is the proprietor of a modern undertaking and embalming establishment at Walton Indiana. He was born July 16, 1848, in Washington township, Cass county Indiana near the present home of W L Small, and is a son of Daniel and Nency (Overleese) Small.

The grandfather of Mr Small was a native of Germany, and in young manhood emigrated to the United States, settling in Maryland, where he spent the remainder of his life. Daniel Small was born in Maryland, and there passed his boyhood and youth, but when still a young man migrated to Indiana and for a short time resided near Crooked Creek. Subsequently, he came to Cass county and took up government land, making the first settlement in Washington township. There he and his wife spent the remaining years of their lives devoting themselves to the tilling of the soil. They were the parents of nine children, as follows: Harriet, Susanna, Andrew Jackson and Margaret, who are all deceased. John Elizabeth and Alexander, who are both deceased; Mrs Sarah Burget, a widow living in Logansport, and Henry Franklin.

Henry Franklin Small was reared on the old homestead, where he worked during the greater part of his school period. At the age of twenty-five years he left the parental roof and came to Walton where he took up the trade of carpenter, and gradually drifted into contracting. During the next twenty years he followed this line of endeavor, and many of the structures erected by him still stand, their excellent state of preservation testifying to good workmanship and honest material. At the end of that period, Mr Small took up the undertaking trade, and first attended the Indianapolis School of Undertaking, from which he received his diploma, succeeding which he took the Barnes course in Chicago and received his certificate. He immediately returned to Walton, and here he has continued in this business to the present time, now being the proprietor of a well equipped establishment, furnished with every device for the proper handling of the dead and with every comfort for the bereaved. His reputation is that of a man of unquestioned integrity and probity of character, and well merits the high respect and esteem in which he is universally held.

Mr Small was married (first) to Miss Elizabeth Younglove, and after her death married her sister Hattie Younglove they being daughters of Charles and Elizabeth (Hoyt) Younglove. Mr Small has interested himself in fraternal work, and is a member of the Masons, the Odd Fellows, the Order of the Eastern Star and the Tribe of Ben Hur.

HENRY A CROCKETT. Although he has reached an age when most men begin to think of laying aside the cares and duties of active business strife, Henry A Crockett, of Washington township still continues in the management of his affairs, and each day attends to his various duties, thus satisfying an energetic nature that from his boyhood has caused his life to be one of constant industry. A member of an agricultural family, which has for generations contributed its full quota of men to the farming vocation, he has followed in the footsteps of his forefathers and has devoted his entire career to the tilling of the soil. Mr Henry Crockett has passed almost his whole life within the borders of Cass county, has here achieved a success, and today ranks with the foremost of his community's valued citizens. He was born September 13, 1849, in Deer Creek township, Cass county, Indiana, and is a son of Asher and Susannah (Plank) Crockett. His father, a farmer, was born near Greenville, Ohio, from whence he came to Cass county, Indiana, in young manhood, and here spent the remainder of his life. There were six children in the elder Crockett's family, namely Henry, Jane, Elizabeth, Sarah, James and Alice the latter deceased.

Henry A Crockett was reared in Cass county, where he secured his early education in the district schools, but when still a lad the family moved to Miami county, and there he completed his studies. He eventually returned to Cass county, and settled on his present farm, an excellent tract of eighty acres which is located on the Crockett and Richeson road. Mr Crockett has continued to devote his attention to the tilling of the soil, and his property is one of the valuable ones of the township. As the years have passed and his leisure and capital would permit, Mr Crockett has made numerous improvements in the shape of substantial buildings and draining and tiling. His ventures have proved uniformly successful, and through the use of good judgment, natural ability and constant industry, he has accumulated a competence, gained a position of importance among his fellows and reared his family in comfort. Mr Crockett is essentially a farmer but has not ignored the duties of citizenship, and at this time is acting capably in the capacity of justice of the peace.

On January 15, 1876, in Cass county, Mr Crockett was united in marriage with Miss Catherine Knight, of Cass county, Indiana, and to this union there have been born eight children. Carrie who lives with her parents; Benjamin Franklin (Frank), who is engaged in farming in Tipton township, married Mae Pierson and has two children,—Gilbert and Herbert; Harvey, who married Ethel Hymon, and is the father of one child,—Opal; Laura and David, who are residing at home; Mae, who married Daniel Brunner, and has three children,—Wilmer, Florence and Velma; Chester who married Hannah Pippinger, has one little son, Clifford Keith; and June, who lives with her parents. The members of this family attend the Christian church, where they all have numerous friends. Judge Crockett belongs to the class through whom communities prosper, for with others he has been an agitator for the advancement of progress. During his long and honorable career, he has formed a wide acquaintance, and no citizen stands in higher esteem in his community. The beautiful estate of Mr and Mrs Crockett is known as "Highland Crest."

CHRISTIAN F WENDLING. That the farmer is the backbone of the nation is a trite saying, but nevertheless a true one, and no circumstances or conditions might arise that would ever lessen the importance of the agricultural industry to the country at large or decrease the prominence of the active and successful farmer in the scale of values prevailing today throughout the broad land. Many successful and ambitious farmers are to be found in Cass county, and the late Christian F Wendling occupied a high place in the agricultural class in the county. Following in the steps of his worthy father, Mr Wendling came to be one of the most prosperous farmers in Walton or, indeed, in the county, and as such is properly accorded a place in an historical and biographical work of this nature.

Born in Butler county, Ohio, October 8, 1858, Christian F Wendling was the son of Michael and Mary (Schmitt) Wendling, Mr Wendling was a native born German and Mrs Mary Smith Wendling was a native of France Michael Wendling was credited with being one of the most skillful farmers in Cass county, and it is therefore but fitting that more than a merely cursory mention be made of him in this sketch dedicated to his son He was born in Alsace, then a part of France, but now within the border of Germany and was the son of John and Margaret (Schini) Wendling He was fifteen years of age when he came to America, in company with his parents, who immigrated hither in 1845 Up to that time he had received excellent educational advantages, being versed both in French and German in his native schools The family first located on a farm in Butler county, Ohio, and there the parents of Michael Wendling passed their remaining days, the father being seventy-two years of age when he died He was twice married, his first wife having died in Germany, and his second wife having been the mother of Michael, who was one of the three children of the second marriage, the others being Christian and Catherine

In 1863 Michael Wendling came to Indiana, and in this state located in section 34, Washington township, Cass county, which place thereafter represented his home and the scene of his farming activities until the day of his death He was a successful farmer, carrying on his affairs prudently and scientifically, and while the tract of land he first selected in Cass county was not the most promising then to be found within its borders, he proved that all land is good land if properly treated, and his place came to be one of the richest and most productive in the county.

On January 10, 1854, Michael Wendling married Miss Mary M Schmitt, a daughter of George and Barbara (Mochel) Schmitt, both natives of France. where Mrs Wendling was born on the 3d of July, 1830. She same to America in 1848, alone, and settled in Pittsburg Pennsylvania Seven children were born to Mr and Mrs Wendling, as follows· John H., born in 1855 and married to Emmeline Martin they living in Cass county and are well and favorably known here George W. is a civil engineer, Christian F is the subject of this sketch William D , a Cass county farmer, is now deceased; Charles C , Jacob S., deceased and Eli E Mr. Wendling was a stanch Democrat, and was all his life a member of the Lutheran church. He died on the 14th of November, 1904

Christian F. Wendling was born on the 8th day of October, 1858 He received his education in the common schools of Cass county, where he was reared from the age of five years, the family removal from Butler county to Cass county taking place at that time. He was well disciplined in farm work in his youth, and was identified with the home place until the age of thirty-two, when, in 1887, he married and established a home of his own. His wife was Miss Laura B. Walker, the daughter of T. H. and Maggie (Bennett) Walker, and their marriage took place on the 14th of April 1887. Four children were born to them. George C., Jesse E., Grace B. and Alonzo E. George C. received his diploma from the Walton high school, class of 1910, graduating with honors, and is now in his third year at Purdue University, studying civil engineering. Jesse E. completed the eighth grade. He married Miss Laura Preiser, and they have one daughter, Margaret Wilodene, born March 4, 1913. Grace B. received her diploma in 1906. Alonzo E. received his diploma with the class of 1911, and entered the Walton high school.

Mrs. Wendling is a native of Cass county, born May 31, 1872, and was educated in the Walton public school. Her parents are both living in Kokomo, Indiana, and her father was formerly engaged in merchandising. In earlier years he was a teacher, and he was educated in Ohio.

Mr. Wendling became the owner of a fertile and productive farm of eighty acres, situated about a half mile from the town of Walton, where his family united with him in making a comfortable and happy home. He demonstrated beyond all question his skill as a farmer, and the early training he received at the hands of his father was to him a boon in his independent career, although he was never content to continue in the industry without progressing in the scientific knowledge pertaining thereto. He took a hearty interest in the civic and political affairs of the community and was one of the best known men in his district, wherein he was long and favorably before the people. Fraternally he was a member of the Masonic order, lodge No. 423 at Walton; of the Maccabees, Tent No. 103, and of Ben Hur Lodge, Tribe No. 233, and was a charter member and a deacon of the Lutheran church of Walton, his family also sharing in his religious faith. Mr. Wendling occupied a place of respect and esteem in the town and county, and his death, on the 9th of February, 1913, was mourned by a large circle of friends. He was laid to rest in the Odd Fellows cemetery.

CASSIUS M. IDE, successful and prosperous in the business of diversified farming, in which he has been occupied in Cass county for a number of years, was born on April 13, 1856, in Howard county, Indiana, and came to Cass county in 1872. He is the son of Reuben P. and Sarah (Gifford) Ide and he was a small child when his father died in Howard county, Indiana. The mother married a second time, and he was one of the three children of her first marriage. When they came to Cass county in 1872 the family comprised the mother and her three children. Bedford B. Ide, the brother of the subject, still lives in Cass county, and for a long period has held a responsible position with the Pan Handle Railroad. The sister married Alexander Copland and is a resident of Logansport.

Cassius M. Ide received the rudiments of an education in the public schools of Howard county, his schooling continuing up to the age of twelve years, after which he took upon himself the business of finding a living. His first independent venture was in the draying line in Logansport, and he continued to be connected with the work there for five years. For three years thereafter he was interested in an active way in the livery business in the same city, and by that time he felt he was ready to settle down to farm life. With his wife he came to the farm inherited by Mrs Ide, consisting of one hundred and twenty acres in section 16, Noble township, where he has since continued to be occupied with a general or diversified farming business. He has experienced an agreeable amount of success in his work, and is accounted one of the prosperous and progressive farmers of the township.

On October 31, 1883, Mr Ide was married to Miss Jane Braithwaite, who was born in Cass county, June 2, 1860, the daughter of James and Peggy (Eglin) Braithwaite, who came to these parts from Yorkshire, England, their native land, in 1844 and 1848, respectively. They were married in Cass county, June 28, 1851, and in the following year, 1852, moved to Kosciusko county, Indiana, where they continued to reside for four years. Then they returned to Noble township, Cass county, and purchased a farm of eighty acres, which location was their home until the death of Mr Braithwaite, July 10, 1882, when he had reached the age of seventy-one years. A few years after locating in Noble township he purchased two other farms in the same township, one of 160 acres and one of 80 acres. Mrs Braithwaite is living and is a resident of the city of Logansport. She was eighty-two years of age January 12, 1913. Mr. and Mrs Ide became the parents of four children. Nolo Fay, born October 10, 1884, graduated from the public schools and spent three and a half years in the Logansport high school. She wedded Carl Hardy, an agriculturist, and they have a little daughter, Peggy Fern, born July 4, 1903. James Reuben, born August 27, 1886, received his diploma from the public schools and spent two years in high school, after which he pursued a commercial course in Logansport. He was census enumerator of Noble township in 1910, and is at present serving his fifth term as financial secretary of the Cass County Detective Association. He is now with his parents on the farm. His fraternal relations include membership in the Odd Fellows order at Logansport, of which he was financial secretary two years and is now its permanent secretary. He affiliates with the Republican party and is a member of the Christian church. Mary Juanita, born November 7, 1888, graduated from the common schools and in the Logansport high school, class of 1908, and wedded John Webber, February 10, 1909. He is an agriculturist. Both Mr and Mrs Webber are members of the Cumberland Presbyterian church, and they are residents of Harrison township. Jane Braithwaite, their daughter, was born March 31, 1913. Clay Braithwaite, born September 27, 1897, the youngest of the children of Mr. and Mrs Ide, graduated from the common schools and is now a student in the Logansport high school. He is a member of the Christian church.

Mr Ide is a Republican and has always lent his support to the furtherance of that party, and his fraternal relations are represented by his membership in the Independent Order of Odd Fellows Eel River Lodge, No 417, and the Knights of Pythias, both of Logansport. He was one of the promotors in the erection of the Odd Fellows Temple in Logansport, a building which is a credit to the city He is a stockholder therein, and for twelve years has been one of the building's trustees It is also a fact worthy of mention that in the engraving of the old seminary on Thirteenth street, which was replaced in 1874 to be seen in the prospectus which preceded this publication, Cassius M Ide may be seen at the base of the belfry of the seminary, with arm outstretched and viewing the scene below He and his family have always attended the Christian church Their homestead in Noble township is named after the old Braithwaite homestead in Yorkshire, England, ' Greenat ''

FREDERICK M MARKERT, remembered by many of the oldest settlers as one of the early coopers in Logansport, was a native of Wurtemburg, Germany, his birth occurring on March 31, 1822 He was reared in his native country, received but a limited education and after serving seven years in the German army he enlisted again and served an additional period He learned fruit gardening after his military service was concluded, his principal attention being given to the culture of the grape. It was about 1846 when he emigrated to the United States, and after landing at Castle Garden, New York he went to Cleveland, Ohio, and there worked at the cooper's trade for two years In 1848 he came to Logansport, Indiana, via Lake Erie, to Toledo, and from there by the Erie canal Until 1850 he worked in the old Cecil flouring mill cooperage shop, located on the south bank of Eel river at the intersection of Sixth street. In 1851, in association with Gotlieb Schaefer and Charles Luy, he embarked in the brewing business on the north side of Columbia street, between Sixth and Mary streets, but three years later disposed of his interests in that enterprise and once more engaged in the cooperage business, his location being on Pleasant Hill For many years he continued in this business, retiring in 1886 He died on April 3, 1901

In 1854 Mr Markert married Fredericka Rombold, who was also a native of Wurtemburg, Germany, and eight children were in time born to them, concerning whom brief mention is made as follows Fred C died on May 17, 1911, Charles F, is a resident of Logansport, George H , who married Dora Schaeter, lives in East St Louis, Illinois, William, died when twelve years of age, Katherine, is the wife of John J Hildebrandt, of Logansport, Christine, married Dr J Z Powell, of Logansport, Andrew, died in infancy, and John D , who married Agnes Morgan, now lives at East St Louis, Illinois

Mr Markert was a member of no religious organization, but to a certain extent held to the belief of the Swedenborgians, in his political faith he was a Democrat Mrs Markert died on October 5, 1897, a member of the Evangelical church

CHARLES F MARKERT is a son of Frederick M and Fredericka (Rombold) Markert, natives of Wurtemburg, Germany of whom detailed mention is made in an article dedicated to the father in other pages of this work Charles F was born on the place where he now resides, Pleasant Hill, in Logansport, Indiana, his birth occurring on

October 11, 1858, and this city has always been his home. A common school education was granted to him, after which he started out for himself, being eighteen years old at that time. He learned the cooper's trade with his father, and later learned the trade of a marble polisher with C B Sanderson, but he did not adhere to either of those occupations for any length of time. In 1881 he turned his attention to gardening, and he has since continued in that work without interruption, and his efforts have resulted in a most favorable manner He was the first gardener in Cass county to undertake hot house gardening, and in that work he enjoyed a pleasing success and prosperity

His marriage with Miss Catherine Newman, a daughter of John Newman, a well known farmer of Harrison township, was solemnized on November 12, 1891, and four children have been born to them— George L, Esther F H, Ellen L and Mary A Mr Markert is a Democrat and he and his wife are members of the Evangelical Association

NATHANIEL TILTON, a well known general agriculturist of Noble township, has been an important factor in farming circles of Cass county, and his popularity is well deserved as in him are embraced the characteristics of an unbending integrity, unabated energy and an industry that never flags. He has been interested in all that affects his community, and has especially identified himself with movements making for the advancement of religion, education and morality. Mr Tilton was born October 25, 1854, on a farm in section 1, Noble township, Cass county, Indiana, and is a son of John Tilton

John Tilton came to Indiana from Ohio with his wife and eight children, locating on the farm now occupied by Nathaniel Tilton, where he spent the remainder of his life in agricultural pursuits, and was also associated with other earnest and hard-working citizens in advancing his community's interests After coming to Cass county he and his wife had two other children Maria Ann, who was married in 1877 to George Fergus, and still resides in Cass county, and Nathaniel

Nathaniel Tilton received his education in the district schools of Clay township, and was reared to the vocation of farmer, which he has followed all of his life He is progressive in his methods and ideas, and each year finds his property further improved with good buildings and other features His land is in a high state of cultivation, his crops are always large and bring top notch prices in the markets, and the appearance of his farm testifies eloquently to the presence of able management He has always been a strong advocate of public improvements, ever being among the first to declare himself in favor of what he thinks will benefit his community or its people Although not a politician in the generally accepted meaning of the word, he served for two terms as supervisor of district No 1, Noble township

On April 12, 1877 Mr Tilton was married (first) to Miss Henrietta Roberts, a native of Fulton county, Indiana, and to this union there was born one son, William I, November 30, 1881 While this child was still in its infancy, its mother died very suddenly, in February, 1882 During the following year, Mr Tilton married (second) Miss Eva A Ulerick, who was born in Pennsylvania, October 30, 1857, and whose parents, Henry and Caroline (Fry) Ulerick, came to Cass county.

"UPPER VALLEY FARM," RESIDENCE OF MR. AND MRS. NATHANIEL TILTON

Indiana, from the Keystone state in 1864 Mrs Tilton came with her parents to Cass county, where she was a little maiden of eight years and here she was reared and educated Her father was a native of Pennsylvania, but of German lineage, as his mother came from Germany He was a butcher by occupation and was a self-made man, and is now a resident of Cass county He is a Democrat politically and is a member of the United Brethren church and his wife was a member of the German Baptist Mrs Ulerick died November 20, 1889

Mr and Mrs Tilton have had two children, namely Henry A, born March 14, 1884, and Chauncey E, born January 2, 1889 Henry A graduated from the common schools, and then took a full commercial course at the Logansport Business College, and he paid his way partially by raising melons The first year he cleared $150 by this industry At the present time he is connected with the R T Crane Iron and Steel Company of Chicago, and is located at Lima, Ohio, where he has charge of the business in that locality He is one of the stable young men that Cass county, Indiana, claims, and is strictly a self-made man He married Miss Bessie Vernon and they have one little son, Vernon, aged five years Henry Tilton and wife are members of the Christian church and were converted under the preaching of Rev "Billy Sunday. He is a Republican and a member of the K of P

Chauncey E is one of the successful young farmers of Noble township and he and wife have a model little home near his parents' home He is a young man of good practical education, and is associated with his father on the estate. He wedded Miss Myra Yund, and one little son, Leslie Kenneth graces this marriage Chauncey is a Republican and he and wife are members of the Presbyterian church

Mr and Mrs Tilton may be proud of the honorable lives of their children, who are a credit to their aged parents

Mrs Tilton is a lady of most genial manners, sociable and cordial, and a model housekeeper, and she and her worthy husband are citizens who are held high in the respect and esteem of the people of Noble county

Their pretty homestead is known as "The Upper Valley Farm."

Both the Tilton and Ulerick families have been close attendants of the Presbyterian church, and their members are widely known in religious circles. Mr Tilton succeeded his father as elder in the church, a position he has held since the elder man's death. During his long residence in Noble township, Mr. Tilton has formed a wide acquaintance, in which he numbers many warm friends, while everywhere he is known as a man of the highest business integrity and moral probity

ELMER DALLAS SNYDER, M D Having risen to influence and obtained recognition through solid merit, founded upon good natured abilities, ripened by liberal scholastic training and matured by thorough scientific study and long, continuous and assiduous practice, Dr Elmer Dallas Snyder, of Onward, Indiana, is known as one of the leading medical practitioners of Cass county. He belongs to that class of professional men who value their success the more because it has been gained through their own individual effort, rather than through outside influence and assistance, and during the fifteen years that Onward has been his field of endeavor has impressed himself favorably upon his fellow-townsmen by the interest he has manifested in the welfare of his community. Dr. Snyder was born on his father's farm, located one mile west of Onward, in Cass county, December 1, 1865, and is a son of David and Maria (Waite) Snyder.

The Snyder family originated in Germany, from whence the great-grandfather of Dr. Snyder emigrated to the United States, settling in Berks county, Pennsylvania. From that section the grandparents of Dr. Snyder, Henry and Mary (Martz) Snyder, came to Cass county, Indiana, with their eleven children, who were named as follows: Simon, Levi, Elizabeth, Henry, William, Sarah, John, David, Kate, Mary and Leah, of whom David and Mary are still living. Henry and Mary (Martz) Snyder both passed away in Cass county, where they had been engaged in agricultural pursuits. David Snyder was born in Carroll county, Indiana, and accompanied the family to Cass county more than a half a century ago. Like his father, he was a farmer, and was so engaged until his retirement when he and his wife moved to the state of Washington, their present home. They had five children: Dr. Elmer D., Mrs. Dora Smith, Alonzo D., Mrs. Cora Mays and Mrs. Nora Bell.

Dr. Elmer Dallas Snyder was reared to agricultural pursuits and spent his boyhood in assisting his father in the work of the home farm, but it became his early intention to enter upon a professional career. The necessary funds for an education along medical lines were lacking, but he did not allow this to stand in his way, for he had inherited much of his father's ability to make his own way in the world. His early schooling was secured in his native locality, and subsequently he attended the schools of Logansport, following which he took up the vocation of educator, thus earning the means with which to gain his cherished medical training, which was secured in the Louisville Medical College. Following his graduation from that institution in 1893, he began practice at Kewanna, Fulton county, later moved to Burr Oak, Marshall county, and finally settled in Onward, his home locality, where he is now firmly established in a representative practice.

Dr. Snyder was married first to Miss Ettie M. Apt (no issue), and on March 15, 1907, he married Mary Catherine Eckert daughter of John and Leah (Eckhart) Eckert, members of a prominent family of Carroll county. Dr. and Mrs. Snyder are members of the Methodist Episcopal church, and in addition to the various medical organizations he belongs to the Knights of the Maccabees. Although not a politician, having preferred to give his entire attention to his professional work, Dr. Snyder has not been insensible to the duties of citizenship, and for a period served capably and faithfully in the capacity of county coroner.

SAMUEL S. HELVIE. Among the better known and more prosperous business men of Logansport, Samuel S. Helvie holds a leading place, and in his capacity as such is eminently deserving of some mention, however brief it may be, in a historical and biographical work of the nature of which this publication partakes. Mr. Helvie has experienced a gradual rise in life in a financial and business way, and from a farm home in Tipton township, has come into his present important place in the business life of Logansport

Born in Tipton township, Cass county, Indiana, on November 30, 1852, Samuel S Helvie is one of a family of thirteen children born to Samuel M and Anna (Ulery) Helvie, eight of that goodly number being alive today The father was a Virginian by birth and when a boy moved with his parents to Miami county, Ohio, where he later married Anna Ulery, the daughter of a well known Kentucky family He received in his boyhood but little education out of books, and was early inured to the hard work of the farm, on which he lived until his marriage In April, 1849, with his wife and ten children, he came to Cass county, Indiana, the journey being made from Virginia to this county in a wagon, drawn by horses, the popular method of travel in those early days. They settled in Tipton township on a slightly improved farm, owned by W W Haney, and here Mr Helvie continued to be engaged in farming activities until his death, April 14, 1878 The widow survived him until September 26, 1896 Both these worthy people were members of the United Brethren church Mr Helvie was a lifelong Republican, but was never an aspirant for political office or favor His life was a quiet and uneventful one, and he lived among his acquaintances in Tipton township, esteemed and respected in the highest manner He was honest as the day, to employ a term often used in speaking of him by those who knew him best, and was a good friend and neighbor, ever ready to lend a helping hand to those less fortunate than himself He was a man particularly fond of hunting, and was known to be one of the best marksmen in Cass county

Samuel S Helvie was the youngest of the children of his parents, and he was born after the family removal to Tipton township There he was reared and educated, and being the family Benjamin, remained at home until he was seventeen, contrary to the custom of other members of the family When he was seventeen he set about learning telegraphy at Anoka, and after he had mastered the key, he was stationed at Anoka Junction as night operator, a place he continued to hold for almost seventeen years In 1886 he began operating the flouring mill at the falls of Pipe creek, his father-in-law, John Costenborder, having been the original builder of the mill He continued to be the active operator of the plant until the fall of 1890, when he gave up his personal connection with it and employed a miller to handle the place for him, upon which basis it was then operated for the ensuing three years

From early manhood Mr Helvie had taken active interest in politics as a Democrat, and in 1890 he was the nominee of his party for the office of county auditor, to which office he was elected by a majority of two hundred and seventy-two He served a term of four years, when, in accordance with the prevailing rule, he retired from office, after a period of service marked by the greatest efficiency and general satisfaction to all concerned Upon the expiration of his term of office, Mr Helvie accepted a position as clerk in a clothing store in Logansport in the employ of Joseph G. Grace Two years later, on November 26, 1896, Mr Helvie, in association with Edward D Sellers, succeeded to the business under the firm name of Helvie & Sellers, and they have since that time become firmly established in the commercial world of Logansport Their business is a prosperous one, and both partners hold enviable positions in the community.

On October 30, 1874, Mr Helvie was united in marriage with Elvira Costenborder, and to them nine children have been born: Lewis E, Walter M, Gertrude M, Ora E, Harry A, Etta, Bertha, Marie and Ocle Mr Helvie is a Mason of the Knights Templar degree, and Mrs Helvie is a member of the Christian church of Logansport, where the family attend

DANIEL W. CLARY The Clary family in Cass county dates back to the period before the removal of the Indians from this part of the state, and the different members have witnessed all the transformations in conditions from the time of the first settlement down to the twentieth century era Daniel W Clary has long been a prominent farmer and citizen of Harrison township, which is his native home, and has acquired a position of influence in this township

Daniel W Clary was born in Harrison township, August 14, 1864. His parents were Isaac N and Rebecca (Remley) Clary The paternal grandfather was John Clary, and the maternal grandfather was Daniel Remley The father of Daniel W Clary came to Cass county at a very early date When his father first started out for himself he bought a place of about 310 acres, on which he put up a rail pen and slept on a rail bed for some time In this rough abode he lived though with some improvements in conditions, until his marriage, at which time he erected a log cabin home, and thereafter lived in increasing comforts until his death His marriage occurred in 1843 He was a resident of the county at the time the Indians were removed to their western homes, and he took some part in assisting in this removal He spent many years of an active and prosperous life in the county, and in 1893 moved from the farm which he had first settled to the place now occupied by his son In 1863 he had bought the present homestead there, and occupied it for the following year All the substantial buildings were erected by the father, though Mr Daniel W Clary has himself, during his proprietorship, instituted a great many improvements and has continued to keep the farm apace with modern progress in agricultural conditions

Daniel W Clary was married on the twenty-third of November, 1887, to Miss Martha E Conn, a daughter of David and Sarah (Herbert) Conn David Conn was a soldier in the Seventy-ninth Indiana during the last two years of the Civil war, and his death occurred on April 17, 1886 Mr and Mrs Clary are the parents of three children, their names being· Berlin A, born October 17, 1888, received a common school education, David Earl, born January 3, 1902, in the sixth grade, and Lillie Ellen, born August 28, 1907. All the children live at home The family are members of the Zion M E church, and Mrs Clary is a member of the Ladies' Aid Society in the church Mr Clary is a Democrat in politics and one of the influential citizens of this community

GEORGE H LYNAS The life work of the late Dr J B. Lynas, of Logansport, Indiana, whose death occurred January 28, 1901, was the founding and developing of a business that has become one of the principal industries of the city and is of national reputation Entering upon the manufacture of proprietary medicines in a small way, only as an accommodation for his numerous patients, in the alleviation of whose ills he had spent many years, he found that instead of retiring from active life, as he had planned, he was but entering upon a still more strenuous career, and one which was to make his name known all over the country The business, thus started in a humble way, has grown and developed, until its agencies are found from coast to coast, and its products, which first included only certain medicines of the doctor's own compiling, now cover a wide range of household necessities

Dr J. B Lynas was born in Dearborn county, Indiana, February 14, 1835. In 1862 Dr Lynas was married to Miss Sarah E Reed, who was born in Wisconsin and who died in Logansport, January 18, 1911. George H. Lynas, son of Dr. Lynas, and the present directing head of the great enterprise that bears his name, was born in Logansport, January 10, 1874, educated in the public schools, and at the age of eighteen years entered his father's business, with which he has been connected to the present time His administration of its policies has served to advance the business in no small way, at the same time following his father's strict rule of honorable and upright dealings with the thousands of agents working for him He was married October 31, 1905, to Miss Ethel Hanawalt, of Logansport Dr J B Lynas received his preliminary education in the public schools of Henry county, whence he had been taken by his father when five years of age, and after spending some time in the study of medicine received his diploma from the Eclectic Medical School, Indianapolis, in 1874 At that time he entered upon the practice of his profession in Logansport, and during the years that followed built up a wide and representative clientele throughout Cass county. It was the desire of Dr Lynas, however, to retire from active practice, but at the same time to meet the wishes of his patients, and accordingly he started to manufacture remedies at his home, these being compiled from old and well-proven remedies which he had used in his practice and which he had found successful in the relief and cure of many diseases At the start he little foresaw the extent that this business was destined to grow to, but it was not long before the merit of his goods caused the demand to exceed the supply that could be manufactured in the limits of the doctor's home, and, accordingly, in 1884, he established a laboratory at No 409 Fourth street During this time the business began to extend outside of the limits of Cass county, and when it began to reach out into other states the firm purchased and moved to No 210 Sixth street Dr. Lynas was the dominating factor of this great organization until his death, and his wise administration of its affairs made him one of Logansport's best known business citizens, but even after his demise the business continued to grow, and in 1904 was incorporated under the name of Dr J B. Lynas & Son, with a capital stock of $100,000 In 1906 it was found necessary to again seek larger quarters, and accordingly they purchased and located in the present factory and laboratory, at Nos 517 and 519 Market street Here Dr. J. B Lynas & Son have a well equipped building, fitted with the latest improvements and appurtenances, the utmost care being taken to preserve sanitary conditions The products now include, in addition to the well known J B L medicines, all kinds of spices, teas, sachet powders, fruit colors, toilet articles, toilet soap, extracts, perfumes, stock preparations and miscellaneous articles. The J B L trademark is a guarantee of absolute purity and excellence and the agents of the company located in all parts of the United States are instructed at all times to replace any article that is not satisfactory, thus, without flaring newspaper advertisements the confidence of all users of these J B L products are gained. It is this policy of giving customers the benefit of honorable and upright dealing that has had all to do with the phenomenal success of the enterprise. The first officers of the incorporated company were George H Lynas, president, and Sarah E Lynas, vice-president and treasurer. At this time George H Lynas retains the presidency, while Dr J F Noland is treasurer, and R C Overmeyer is secretary. April 1, 1913, there was between fourteen and fifteen hundred people working for J B Lynas & Son. They are located in nearly every state in the union. At the above date they were employing additional workers at the rate of about sixty per month. To take care of this fast increasing business, many traveling representatives, as well as a large office force, are required.

ROBERT F FRUSHOUR. One of the citizens of Cass county who began their career in primitive and often times log cabin homes to labor with courage and industry to develop a wilderness of forest into a broad landscape of farms and have subsequently reaped the rewards of such diligence in ample material prosperity, is Mr Robert Frushour of Harrison township, whose postoffice address is Logansport. This family is one of the oldest in Cass county, and two generations have assisted in the progress of this county.

Robert F Frushour was born in Bethlehem township Cass county October 16, 1856. His parents were George V and Charlotte (Rowan) Frushour. Both grandfather and father came to that county at a very early date from Virginia, where they bought a great deal of land, most of it from the government, and set to work with characteristic industry to develop homes out of the forest. The only roads in the country at that time were the rough trails blazed through the woods, and the pioneer scenes and difficulties, which are described on other pages of this history, were, almost without exception, experienced by the Frushour family during its career here. The brothers and sisters of Mr Robert F Frushour were as follows. Harmon T, whose first wife was Harriet Orwin and his second wife was Anna Turner, both himself, as also his wives now being deceased. George, Jr, who married Lucy Thompson. William V who married Etta Gundrum, Anna, who became the wife of Arthur Wells, and Ida, who was the wife of Ira Maudlin.

On February 18, 1880 Mr Frushour married Miss Mary E Brown. Her parents were Isaac and Elizabeth (Custer) Brown. One of her grandfathers was also named Simpson. Various members of her family became early residents of Cass county, having located here during the decade of the early forties. The brothers and sisters of Mrs Frushour were as follows. George who married Effie Schilling. Albert who died at the age of forty-two. Samuel, who married Anna Newberry, Jay, who died at the age of thirty-one years, unmarried, Nancy, who married John M LaRose The father of Mrs Frushour died in 1872, and her mother passed away in 1884

Mr Frushour and wife were the parents of the following children Della, born August 18, 1881, is now the wife of John Spencer, Olive, born May 27, 1883, married Lora Early, and Lottie, born July 24, 1888, married Harley Moore Industry and thrifty management have been characteristic of Mr Frushour's career throughout his many years of activity as a farmer He has been the owner of three different farms in this immediate section of the county, and has improved them all with excellent buildings, and other facilities for high-class agriculture At the present time, he is just completing the building and general improvement of his third farm Much of the land has been cleared by his own labor, or under his immediate supervision, and he is a farmer who has never relaxed his attention to business, and keeps all his interests to the highest point of efficiency He still works untiringly, and his prosperity is well deserved and earned He and his family are members of the Presbyterian church His pretty home is known as "Forest Glenn," located about five miles from the city of Logansport

BENJAMIN F YANTIS Seventy-seven years ago the family of Benjamin F Yantis made their way by ox team and by boat from their home in Spencer county, Kentucky, to Cass county, Indiana, and from then until the present writing, Cass county has been the home of this representative family, and has known the activities and influence of its members. The subject, Benjamin F Yantis, was born in Spencer county, Kentucky, on February 2, 1831, and was thus a young lad when the migration of the family changed his home to Cass county. He is the son of Aaron and Martha (Cockran) Yantis The father, Aaron Yantis, came from Germany with his brother George in the year 1760 and settled in Kentucky The mother of the subject was of Scotch parentage With the arrival of the family in Logansport from their Kentucky home, they settled there, remaining for two years, and then taking up their residence on a farm at the place where the street car line now ends, within fifty yards of the city limits It was in the spring of 1841 that they removed to the George H Harland farm in Bethlehem township for six years and then to the present farm or the one that is now owned and occupied by Benjamin F Yantis

Benjamin F Yantis was one of the eight children of his parents One brother, John, secured some prominence in engineering as the result of much work on the Wabash & Erie canal in Indiana The Yantis residence was destroyed by fire in 1906 and since that time Mr Yantis has replaced the old brick residence with a new and handsome brick house, one of the finest to be found in the township The place boasts many improvements, all of which have been installed by the owner and proprietor.

Mr. Yantis has taken his place in the activities of the township in a public way, and one time served as township treasurer He was drainage commissioner of the county for six years and served as trustee of the township for nine years, giving the most efficient service on all those positions, and proving his merit and calibre as a citizen

On September 13, 1855, Benjamin F Yantis married Mary J. Hill, the daughter of Joseph and Esther (Jenkins) Hill Eight children were born to Joseph and Esther (Jenkins) Hill, concerning whom brief mention is made as follows William married Sarah Horn, Stephen J married Hannah Conrad, Elizabeth A married Isaac W Wilson, Mary J. married B F. Yantis, Martha A married Jackson L. Thompson, Orlando married Savina Garber, Hannah died at the age of seven years, and Israel J. married Martha Gordon

Mrs Yantis is a native of Washington county, Pennsylvania, born May 21, 1831, and she was reared in her native state Her father was a farmer and lawyer in Pennsylvania and Indiana He was a Republican, and he and his wife were members of the Methodist Episcopal church, although she was reared as a Quaker Both of Mrs. Yantis' parents are dead The mother died in Fulton county, Indiana, June 21, 1873, and the father died in Bethlehem township, May 12, 1876 Father Hill was a splendid scholar, a fine penman and could write the German text To the marriage of Mr and Mrs Yantis were born eight children, four sons and four daughters, five are living, as follows· Mary E , wife of Charles J Moss resident of Chicago and engaged in mercantile business, they have three children, two sons and one daughter They are members of the Episcopal church Elvira A is the wife of Sumner E Buck, a farmer in Bethlehem township They have four children, one son and three daughters, and are members of the Methodist Episcopal church. Ruth A resides at home with her parents She was educated in the common schools and then took the Logansport teachers' course and musical instruction in Chicago, both vocal and instrumental She is a member of the Presbyterian church Joseph A is a farmer in Bethlehem township. He married Miss Frances Calvert They are members of the Baptist church and he is a deacon therein and a Republican in politics. Lyman A is a farmer in Bethlehem township He wedded Miss Maude Evans, and they have two sons and two daughters The name Yantis is of German extraction and was formerly "Yandes " Two brothers came from Germany during the time of the Revolutionary war and were soldiers in the war

Mr Yantis, though now in the eighty-third year of his life, is active and strong, and is enjoying these later years of quietude and plenty in the home he has so long cherished and cared for He is a prominent man in his community, and has all his life enjoyed the esteem of all who have shared in his acquaintance The estate of Mr. and Mrs Yantis is known as "Highland Place "

NOAH L BESS has had a successful agricultural career, covering a number of years, and as one of the skilled farmers and stockmen of Washington township is deserving of personal mention in connection with biographical sketches of other representative men of this locality Mr Bess is a native of Missouri, having been born in Bollinger county, April 24, 1868, and is a son of John and Malinda (Shell) Bess, the latter of whom lives with her children John Bess made removal to Illinois about 1875, settling in McLean county, where he became a leading farmer and land owner, and where the rest of his life was spent He

"ENGLEWOOD" RESIDENCE OF MR. AND MRS. NOAH L. BESS

and his wife were the parents of seven children, of whom three are now living Noah L , Jefferson Monroe and Siebert I

Noah L Bess was about seven years of age when he was taken by his father to McLean county, Illinois, and in that locality he secured his education in the public schools Reared to agricultural pursuits, he has followed the vocation of farming throughout his active years, and about 1900 came to Cass county and settled on his present farm in Washington township, a tract consisting of 124 acres of well-cultivated land Here he has made numerous improvements, erecting handsome buildings, thoroughly ditching, draining and tiling the land, and keeping his implements in the finest condition That he is an able manager is testified by the general prosperous appearance of the farm, and he has demonstrated his ability as a stock grower by breeding some of the best stock to be found in his section He is essentially a farmer, and has not cared for public life, his private affairs having left him no time to take an active part in politics aside from casting an intelligent ballot in the support of the principles which he believes will best secure the welfare of the nation He is regarded as one of the busiest most energetic and enterprising men of Washington township, and his methods in his business dealings have firmly established him in the respect and confidence with all who have come into contact with him His fraternal connection is with the Modern Woodmen of America of Forest, Illinois, and he is popular among the members of the local lodge of that order

Mr Bess was married in Bollinger county, Missouri, to Miss Ellen Perkins. October 9, 1888, a member of an old and honored family of that county, and to this union there has been born one son, Grover I, who was born in McLean county twenty-three years ago He was educated in that locality and has been reared to an agricultural career, now being his father's aid in the management of the home farm In November, 1910, Grover I Bess was united in marriage with Miss Lena J Furst, who also belongs to an old Illinois family, and they have one daughter, Jessie May All of the members of this family belong to the Union Presbyterian church. Mr. Bess has a No 17 Buick, five-passenger touring car and he and family can take many hours of pleasure and recreation Their beautiful homestead is known as "Englewood"

JOHN A FRUSHOUR The leading hardware establishment in the village of Lucerne, in Harrison township, is that conducted by John A Frushour. Mr Frushour took charge of this business some years ago, and by his ability as a merchant has succeeded in more than doubling his trade, and now has an enterprise which is probably second to none of its class in northern Cass county

John A Frushour was born in Harrison township on the tenth of January, 1861 The family have been residents in this county for more than seventy years, and have always been industrious citizens, and highly respected for their personal character The name Frushour, however, is of Belgian lineage Mr Frushour's grandfather was named Mathias, while his father was the late John W Frushour The maiden name of the mother was Cecelia Bierd The late John W Frushour, the father, was twice married. The nine children by his first wife were as follows Michael W , Samuel J , James E , John A , Francis X , Eleanor E , George M , Edward W , and Sarah J. His second wife bore the maiden name of Amanda M Boyle. and she was the mother of four children, namely Mary R , Joseph E , Rose and Margaret The father of the Lucerne merchant, came to Cass county about 1840, his original home having been in Morgan county, Virginia He was accompanied by his father, and their first settlement was in Noble township, on what is known as the old Tipit farm He resided at different places in Noble township, and finally moved into Harrison township, which was his home until his death, at an advanced age in 1911 His first wife passed away in 1871.

John A Frushour married October 22, 1892, Miss Mary A. Hoynes, a daughter of James and Margaret (Glenn) Hoynes Seven children were born of their marriage, six of whom are living and one deceased, namely John Leo, born January 15, 1894, and died February 14, 1911, James A , Ruth, Austin G , Margaret E , Edward H , Mary C

Mr Frushour was reared in his native vicinity where he attained such schooling as afforded him a practical preparation for life, and remained at home working on the farm and other occupations, until the time he was thirty-one years of age During his youth he had acquired the trade of a carpenter, and when he began life on his own account, it was as a carpenter contractor, a business which he followed for about twenty years, with considerable success It was on retiring from that occupation that he entered the hardware business at Lucerne, where he has since been a prosperous merchant He bought out the present establishment, and as already noted, has more than doubled the business in the years in which he has been engaged in same His family attend the Catholic church, St Elizabeth's, in Harrison township

LUYE J CLARY Both industry and enterprise are required in the development of a first class farm from land which is in practically its native state Mr Clary, of Harrison township, has been characterized by these two qualities, and though still a young man he has succeeded beyond the ordinary and is considered one of the most substantial men of his vicinity

Mr Clary was born in Harrison township, September 22, 1877 His grandfather and his father were both named Isaac His mother's maiden name was Susan Julian, a daughter of Samuel Julian Mr. Clary had three brothers and three sisters, whose names are as follows. William, Arthur, who married Blanche Morrison, Harvey, who married Mollie Tucker; Ida, who married Ervin Hull, Nellie, who married Roy Wolford, and Fern, who married George Bell

On the eighteenth of February, 1906, Mr Clary was united in marriage with Miss Daisy Wolford, a granddaughter of Abraham and daughter of Phillip Wolford Her father was one of the old settlers of Cass county and the name Wolford is well known in this vicinity. The brothers and the one sister of Mrs Clary are as follows · Mary, who was the wife of Bert Herd, George, who married Cora Clary, Owen, married Hazel Deck; and Rowell, at home in Harrison township Mr and Mrs Clary are the parents of one daughter, Esther, who was born November 17, 1906 After their marriage, Mr and Mrs Clary lived for some time in Fulton county, where they were farmers for four years and in that time did a great deal to establish a firm foundation for their subsequent prosperity. Mr. Clary had forty acres in that vicinity and during his residence there rebuilt the house, put in a cellar and also constructed a silo and many other minor improvements about the estate. From there he and his wife moved to the present farm in Harrison township, Cass county, where he owns eighty acres in the homestead, besides fifty-one and one-half acres situated about half a mile from here. The land, when he took hold of it, had no improvements, and he has built a good house and put the entire place in condition for profitable agriculture. Mr. and Mrs. Clary are members of the Christian church, and in politics he is independent. The pretty homestead of Mr. and Mrs. Clary is known as "The Sunny Side Farm."

RICHARD WINN. Among the foreign born citizens of Cass county who have contributed their full quota to the best development and advancement of this district, the name of Richard Winn stands well to the forefront, and it is wholly consistent with the spirit and letter of a work of this order that more or less extended mention be made of his life and deeds on the pages of this historical and biographical record. Richard Winn has for many years figured prominently in the agricultural activities of Harrison township, this county, and of late years has concerned himself to a large extent with mercantile lines, although his interest has not been of an active nature. He has served in numerous public offices of prominence and has been prominent in church work for many years. He is now practically retired from all business activities, and his winters are spent in the warmth and sunshine of Florida.

Born in Yorkshire, England on August 3, 1836, Richard Winn is the son of Richard and Alice (Batty) Winn, and the grandson of William Winn, a farmer in England. Richard and Alice Winn were the parents of a goodly family of eight children, named in the order of their birth as follows: William, Richard Edmund, Thomas, Agnes, Isabelle M., Thomas B. and Leonard W.

In Harrison township Richard Winn, Sr., with his family, settled down in the resumption of farm life, further devoting himself to the business of cattle raising, in which he achieved a worthy success, his operations being more than usually extensive. He found that his entire time was absorbed by his own affairs, and thus never saw the day when he felt free to dip into political or municipal affairs. He was sixty-nine years old when he died in August, 1875, honored and esteemed by all who knew him.

Richard Winn, Jr., was twenty-four years old when he married and settled down on the home farm, on which he lived and prospered for many successful years. His farm, comprising five hundred acres, was one of the finest in the county, and yielded abundantly to his skilful manipulation. He later interested himself in the grain business at Lucerne, securing a half interest in a grain elevator at that place, and continued to be thus-identified for many years, also becoming connected with certain other mercantile enterprises, all of which brought him bountiful returns, although his interest was always that of the silent partner, he never having connected himself actively with their operation.

Success always attended his efforts, and his identification with a business venture ever seemed sufficient to insure its practical success

On August 23, 1860, Mr Winn married Miss Isabelle Herd, the daughter of John and Agnes (Stainton) Herd, who, like the Winns, were also natives of England, Yorkshire being their ancestral home Mrs Winn was a daughter of John and Agnes (Stainton) Herd, and there were nine children in their family, five sons and four daughters, and there are five living Mis Richard Winn, Thomas, a retired resident of Gas City, Indiana, and married. William, a retired resident of city of Logansport, George, an agriculturist of Harrison township, and Elizabeth, widow of Peter Castle, a resident of Logansport, Indiana

The children of Richard and Isabelle (Herd) Winn are named as follows. Agnes, the eldest, married Edward Morrison, and they have two children, Blanch and Mary John was accidentally killed some three years ago, he had married Mary J. Hall, who with their four children yet survive him, they being named, Maurice, Paul, Chester and Harold, last deceased, Mary Ellen, the third born child of her parents, married James Stevens and they have four children, Myrle, Ethel, James Monroe, and Florence, Alice died at the age of five years Thomas died when three years old, Charles Emmett married Edith Myers, and they have five children, Earl, Dott, Mildred, Victor, and Irene, Harry married Violet McCoy, and they had two children Wiley and Ruth, deceased, James married Catherine Wyand, and their only child died in infancy Florence wife of W A Brown, has eight children, Ralph, George, Carl, Mabel, Elmer, Russell Harold and Horace Edna, the youngest born of the family, is married to Ervan S Grove.

Mr. Winn has been more or less prominent in municipal affairs during his career, and has held a number of important offices in the service of his town and county He served two terms as county commissioner, was trustee of his township for a number of terms and has held other similar offices He has long been active in the Zion church and is at present, and has been for some years, one of its trustees It is some years since Mr Winn has been active in business having retired to enjoy the fruits of his labors extending through several decades of useful and valuable citizenship He has long enjoyed the high esteem and regard of his fellow townspeople, and is known for one of the most valuable men of the community, and an example of a high order of citizenship which the present and coming generations can not do better than to emulate

WILLARD WINN The president of the Bank at Lucerne, also the owner of a Harrison township farm of two hundred and twenty acres, is one of the native sons of this township, and represents a family, which has been identified with the development of this part of Cass county for more than sixty-five years The Winn family came here when most of the country was in the wilderness, before any railroads were built, and by their own labors they contributed in no small degree to the substantial development and improvement of this part of Indiana

Willard Winn was born in Harrison township on March 2, 1866 His father, William Winn, was for many years a well known citizen of the township, and passed away in 1908. The mother, whose maiden name was Susan Michael, was a daughter of Peter Michael, whose original home was in Virginia, from which state the Michael family came to Indiana. Richard Winn, the grandfather of Willard was a native of England, and in 1847 came to America and settled his family on a farm in Harrison township Cass county. The place had already undergone considerable improvement, since it had a three room brick house, which at the time was considered one of the most substantial residences in this section, but nearly all of the land was covered with dense timber, and it was many years before the arduous labor of the members of the family succeeded in getting all of the land ready for cultivation. It was in that old brick homestead and on that farm that William Winn, the father, was reared, and after attaining his majority he started out for himself, and during his long lifetime won a commendable degree of prosperity.

Willard Winn had three brothers, whose names were Albert, Edmond and Gilbert. In November, 1886, Mr Willard Winn married Miss Peggy Burton, a daughter of Levi and Ann (Eglin) Burton. Mr and Mrs. Winn are well known in social circles of Harrison township, and possess a very attractive and beautiful homestead. The two hundred and twenty acres of land, comprising the farm are among the best in the township. Mr Winn began his career by attending the district schools, and with the advantages of only such an education and largely upon his own resources, he has acquired a position where his influence counts for much in this part of Cass county. He is a breeder of fine registered stock, such as The Short Horn Cattle, Shropshire Sheep and blooded Barred Plymouth Rock chickens, and he is also a producer of "The Winn's Improved Reid's Yellow Dent Seed Corn." The estate of Mr and Mrs Winn is known as "The Indian Creek Stock Farm," located about ten miles from city.

JACOB W CLARY. Beginning life in a log cabin in Harrison township and reared amid conditions which might truly be called of pioneer character, Mr Jacob Clary has now for more than forty years been one of the prospering farmers of this county, and has acquired many evidences of his thrift and business ability, as also the thorough esteem and respect of his fellow citizens.

Jacob W Clary, who was a son of Isaac N and Rebecca (Remley) Clary concerning whom further details appear in other biographies in this work, was born in Harrison township, Cass county, December 14, 1848. At the time of his birth, the family habitation was a log house and he was old enough to witness some of the first trains which ran over the first railroad in this county, and has been a witness of nearly every other subsequent development of importance in this part of the state.

Mr Clary was married on the fourteenth of November, 1869, to Miss Eliza Rush, a daughter of David and Lavina (Julian) Rush. Mrs Clary, after more than thirty years of happy married life, passed away on March 29 1901. She was born December 14, 1853, and was forty-seven years of age at the time of her death. Her remains now rest in Harrison township. The ten children of Mr and Mrs Clary were named as follows: Lonzo, who married Nellie Wilson; William, who died at the age of two years; John, who married Anna Conn; Minnie, who married

Bert Helkert, Rene, who married James Lamostros, Charles, who married Cora Thomas, Bertha, who married John Cummins, Cora, who married George Wolford, Hanford, who married Jessie Day, and LeRoy who is unmarried and resides at home Mr Clary moved to his farm in Harrison township, near Lucerne, in 1872 It was then unimproved with buildings, and everything in this nature has been the result of his own labors and management He is now the owner of two hundred acres, some of the best land in the northern part of Cass county, and his business-like methods of cultivation have resulted in a substantial prosperity for himself and family The first house on his farm was a small two-room structure, situated in the woods, and it was in that little cabin that he and his wife resided for six years, and some of the children already mentioned were born in this place His father had given him eighty acres at the beginning of his career and it was from this nucleus that he built up his present estate, consisting of almost three times as much in quantity and many times more in value than what he started with Mr. Clary also owns several houses in the town of Lucerne He is a member of the Presbyatrian church, and fraternally is affiliated with the Independent Order of Odd Fellows in Lucerne. In politics he is now a Democrat. Mr Clary married February 20, 1913, Mrs Mabel Mummert, and they reside in the village of Lucerne, Indiana

JOSHUA TUCKER For a period of about forty years, Mr Joshua Tucker has been one of the progressive farmers of Harrison township He has spent practically all of his life in this vicinity, which is the location of the original settlement of this family in this county more than eighty years ago No name is better known in that part of Cass county than Tucker, and few have with such credit to themselves and value to the community carried on their burden and life work during all these years of residence

Joshua Tucker was born on a farm just a mile north of his present homestead in Harrison township, on the thirty-first of March, 1850 His father's name was Abraham and that of his grandfather Michner. The maiden name of his mother was Margaret Witters, who was a daughter of David Witters The grandfather came from Lafayette to Cass county about 1832, and was one of the first settlers who secured his land from the government He cleared up a large tract, and his descendants still possess a considerable part of the land which he obtained direct from the government The grandfather is buried in Noble township, and the father rests in Zion cemetery at Harrison township.

On September 28, 1873, Joshua Tucker married Miss Barbara Bailey, a daughter of Henry and Catherine (Mogle) Bailey The children in the family of Mr and Mrs Tucker are as follows Harry A born July 7, 1874, William W born September 24, 1876 Charles M born December 28 1879, Walter J born July 12, 1883, Arthur T born November 20, 1888, Elmer R born May 17, 1893, and Russell L born April 25, 1896

Soon after their marriage, in 1873, Mr Tucker and his wife moved to their present farm, where he is the owner of ninety-two and a half acres. This place, when he first took possession nearly forty years ago, was very little improved, and had poor buildings, and was not yet developed to a point of highly profitable cultivation Since then Mr Tucker has not

only developed the land and the possibilities of the soil as a means of producing wealth, but has also made many improvements which increase the comforts of the place as a home, and now enjoys one of the best rural homes in the northern part of Cass county. During his youth in this county, Mr. Tucker had to walk a mile to school, and the term lasted for only about four and a half months out of the year. He thus came to know many of the deficiencies and difficulties of life in the early years of this county, and is in a position to realize and to appreciate the modern advantages. He and his wife are members of the Methodist church, and in politics he is a Progressive. He is also affiliated with the Knights of the Maccabees.

CAPTAIN DANIEL H. MULL, one of the most highly respected citizens of Logansport, died at his home in this city on January 12, 1903. After earning his rank and title by gallant service in the Civil war he was for nearly forty years identified with the commercial life of Logansport and his loss was not only a personal one, but also left a gap to be filled in the business world. Of a genial and generous disposition, he made friends wherever he was, and his undoubted ability and capacity for hard work made him a valuable man in the world of business and in the civic community. His father, Daniel Mull, was a German and his mother, Miss Anna Sites, of Irish descent, both of North Carolina, soon after their marriage they settled in Indiana. The late Captain Mull was born December 27, 1821, at Spencer, Owen county, Indiana, being in his eighty-third year when death came to him. His trade was cabinet-maker, and carpenter, and it is interesting to note that he helped to build the original Methodist church on Eighth and Broadway in Logansport. In the family were two other sons and three sisters, and John Mull of Spencer, Indiana, was the last to pass away of that generation of the family.

Daniel Hart Mull obtained a common school education in Owen county, and was a young man when he came to Cass county, being unaccompanied by any other members of the family but had a sister (Mrs. Richard Hensley) living here, with whom he made his home until his marriage. He enlisted at the outbreak of the Civil war, and rose to the rank of captain of Company H in the Seventy-Third Indiana Infantry.

He was taken prisoner May 3, 1863, and twenty-three months of his military experience were passed in Libby Prison. On the close of the war he engaged in the retail shoe business, and for many years was a leading member of the firm of D. H. Mull & Company, and also of the firm of J. B. Winters & Company. The late Captain Mull was a stanch Republican in politics, but never occupied official position. His fraternal affiliations were with Tipton Lodge of the Masonic order, and with the Grand Army of the Republic.

On May 28, 1846, Captain Mull married Sarah Simpson Jones, daughter of Thomas Jones, who at one time served as sheriff of Cass county. Mrs Mull died on July 30, 1904. Of their five daughters, two survive namely Mrs Anna R Clark of Indianapolis and Miss Fannie Mull of this city. The attractive homestead at 801 North street in Logansport was built by Captain Mull more than sixty years ago and is a landmark in the residence district and the center of many kindly memories and associations for the family Captain Mull and family in early years worshiped at the Methodist church, and his body now rests in Mt Hope Cemetery

DR JOHN J BURTON A career of honorable and useful activity, largely devoted to the service of his fellow-men, has been that of Dr John J Burton, in Harrison township Dr Burton is now one of the oldest physicians in point of years of practice in his section of Cass county, and he is one of the best examples of that ideal type of the country doctor

Dr John J. Burton was born in Harrison township on the twenty-third of March. 1850 The family have been residents in this section since pioneer days, and as farmers and public spirited citizens have always done their part in the community The doctor's parents were John and Susan (Sagaser) Burton, the latter a daughter of Henry Sagaser Dr. Burton's father was born in 1816, and died in 1868, while his mother was born in 1815, and died in 1876 The father was a native of Yorkshire, England, and was about two years of age when his family crossed the ocean, and settled in northern Indiana. The doctor's mother was a native of Kentucky, and the five daughters and three sons who comprised the family of which the doctor is a member were named as follows: Sarah Jane, who married John Morphet, Amanda, who married Peter Montgomery, Elizabeth and Emma, who died in infancy, Elizabeth, who married Richard Brown, Leonard R, whose first wife was Emma Baker, and whose second wife was Lena Batty John J, the doctor, whose marriage is mentioned in the following paragraph, and William L, whose first wife was Priscilla Murry, and who married second Jane Conn

Dr John J Burton, when a boy, attended the district schools near the farm on which he was raised Subsequently he studied in the high school at Logansport, and when his ambition has been set upon the study of medicine, and the privileges afforded him for preparation, he entered a medical college at Cincinnati, where he continued his studies until graduation, with his medical degree May 9, 1876 On returning from college, he began his practice in the vicinity of his old home, and has built up his patronage in the vicinity of people who have known him all his life, and who thoroughly esteem him for his ability and integrity of character There is now only one physician practicing in this county, who was here at the time he began his practice Dr Burton has never held any office, though he is a Democrat in politics, and his family are members of the Christian church He was married June 21, 1877, to Miss Mary B Lumbirt, a daughter of Hiram and Maria (Anderson) Lumbirt The doctor and wife have no children.

REV JOSEPH TODD For many years a minister in the service of the Presbyterian church, but since 1904 engaged in the merchandise business in a general way, Rev Joseph Todd has seen life from the viewpoint of the clergyman and the business man, and in these widely separated fields of activity has met with experiences that have rounded out his mentality and his entire nature in a most inclusive manner As postmaster for nine years in Lucerne, appointed by President Roosevelt, he has seen something of service in the civil service department, and his fraternal relations in the popular organizations of the country have given him an acquaintance with men that he would never acquire, either in his churchly or business relations with fellows

Joseph Todd was born in Home county, Ohio, on June 23, 1861, and is the son of William and Mary (Moorehead) Todd. The father was the son of another William Todd, and the mother was the daughter of James Moorehead. The father of the subject was a farmer in Home county, who died in 1889, but the mother yet lives. As a boy, Joseph Todd had the advantages of the schools of the community wherein he made his home, which schooling was later supplemented by four years' study in college in Wooster University in Ohio. He succeeded in preparing himself for the ministry, and served in his ministerial capacity in his native state, also in White county, Indiana. He preached three years in the Presbyterian church in Lucerne, that service completing fourteen years of work in his ministerial capacity. In 1904 he returned to Lucerne, and since has here been engaged in the general merchandise business, in which he has realized a substantial success. He has served as postmaster of the place for nine years, but beyond that has held no other office of a public nature.

Fraternally Mr. Todd is a member of the Masonic and Odd Fellow societies and has considerable prominence in both orders.

On September 29, 1893, Mr. Todd married Miss Cora Baker, the daughter of William P. Baker and his wife, who was Lydia Needham in her maiden days. Six children were born to them: Orville W. was born on December 31, 1896; Mildred A., born June 13, 1898; Louis I., born July 22, 1900; Forrest E. and Edna Fay, twins, were born on October 27, 1907, and Thelma M. The family has made its home in Cass county since April 1, 1892, moving hence from White county, this state, and prior to that time had resided in the state of Ohio, where Mr. Todd and his wife were born. Both Mr. and Mrs. Todd were the children of fathers who fought for the preservation of the Union, the senior Todd having served throughout the war in the One Hundred and Sixty-sixth Ohio Infantry, while Mr. Baker served in the Eighty-seventh Indiana.

No family in Lucerne enjoys a wider circle of friends than does the Todd house, and they are accounted among the more substantial people of the community.

CLAYTON C. CAMPBELL, M. D. Perhaps it is true that each individual is born with one natural gift, but not every one seeks to discover it, or, finding it, has the opportunity to nurture or develop it. History and biography prove, however, that many of the most brilliant professional men of our land have felt this natural bent from youth—in the direction of law, medicine, the church or literature, and, with enthusiasm, controlled by circumstances, have sought advancement along this line. Not so many, perhaps, have reached the cherished goal in their most receptive years, some, indeed not until middle life, but here and there are found those who, at the open door of manhood, find also the door open to their chosen field of effort. Respectful attention, in this connection, is called to Dr. Clayton C. Campbell, of Walton, Indiana, whose persistent devotion to the self-imposed duties of his profession have gained him a position among the medical practitioners of his section that might be envied by many men a number of years his senior Dr. Campbell was born August 14, 1879, in Preble county, Ohio, and is a son of Rome and Jennie (Disher) Campbell. There were four children in the family: Clayton C , Mrs Isa Lairy, Mrs Ethel McNeely, and Leonard, who is a civil engineer of Cambridge, Ohio.

Clayton C Campbell received his early education in the common schools of Eldorado, Ohio, and was still a lad when his father died, at which time the little family moved to Indianapolis, the courageous mother making it possible to keep her children about her by establishing herself in business as a milliner In that city young Campbell accepted odd jobs at whatever honorable employment presented itself, carefully saving his money in the meanwhile, as he already had intentions of entering, if possible, upon a professional career Finally he was able to enter the drug business, and after seven years spent therein had enough capital to pay for his first year's tuition in the College of Physicians and Surgeons, Indianapolis, following which he took special courses on diseases of the eye with Dr G S Row, of Indianapolis He entered medical college in 1900 and graduated therefrom in 1904. He was president of the college Young Men's Christian Association, and was interested in all branches of its work and when he entered the Deaconess Hospital was the first man of his college to become connected with that hospital Thus thoroughly prepared, Dr. Campbell entered upon the practice of his profession in Indianapolis, but one year later went to Harrodsburg, Monroe county, and after two years in that town came to Walton, which has since been his field of endeavor. He is now in the enjoyment of a large and representative practice, and his success in a number of complicated cases has served to establish him firmly in the confidence of the people of his community

In 1904 Dr Campbell was married to Miss Mary I. Garvin, of Cambridge Ohio, and to this union there were born three children Clayton C , Jr ; Elizabeth, who died when three years of age; and Flora A. Dr. Campbell is prominent fraternally. He is a past master of the Masonic Lodge No 723, Walton, and a member of the Knights of Pythias, the I O O F, the Modern Woodmen of America and the Red Men He is also a member of the County District and State Medical Societies. The family has always been prominent in the work of the Lutheran church, in which Dr Campbell is serving as deacon. He has been actively interested in everything pertaining to the upbuilding of Walton.

AMBROSE ELLIOTT A family which has been represented in Harrison township and Cass county for the greater period of its history is that of Elliott, represented by Mr Ambrose Elliott of Harrison township, where he is one of the most prosperous and progressive farmers.

Ambrose Elliott was born in Montgomery county, Indiana, February 9, 1840 His parents were Joseph and Martha (Lincoln) Elliott Both of them came to Cass county at an early date The father, who was of English descent, was for many years a substantial citizen and gave his family the best advantages procurable at the time, and under the conditions of life as it was then lived in this section of Indiana Mr. Ambrose Elliott was married, after growing into manhood in this county, to Miss Agnes Winn, a daughter of Richard and Alice (Battie) Winn. After their marriage Mr and Mrs Elliott located upon a farm in Harrison township which contained one hundred and eighty-five acres, and which had been bought by his father About forty acres of this land was cleared and a large part of the labor, during his early years as a farmer, was spent in clearing off the land and increasing the quality of cultivable soil Mr and Mrs Elliott became the parents of five children whose names are as follows: Harvey, born December 6, 1867, married Susie Lovett, and they were the parents of two children, Floyd and Earl, Ida, the second child, born March 16, 1871, became the wife of Isaac Wilson and was the mother of four children, Ethel, Edna, and Roy still living, while Harvey died at the age of two years; Wilbert, born December 4, 1874, married Myrtle McCaughy, and they were the parents of two children, Lottie and Margaret, Elmer, born September 10, 1877, married, for his first wife, Viva Mahaffy, and for his second wife, Grace Burkell, Albert, the youngest of the family, was born March 30, 1880, and married Effie Brown, by whom he has two children, Forrest and Maud For several years now, Mr Elliott has lived retired, his earlier career having been prosperous to a high degree and giving him a competence with which he can enjoy his remaining years in leisure. In politics he is a Democrat, and has membership in the Methodist church.

BENJAMIN FRANKLIN STUART Though now a resident of Carroll county, Mr Stuart had all his early associations with Cass county, and his family were identified with this county from 1856. He has had an active career, and is held in the highest esteem in old Cass

Benjamin Franklin Stuart was born in Floyd county, Indiana, July 26, 1852, and is of Scotch descent on his father's side, and English on his mother's Robert F Stuart, his father, was born near Natchez, Mississippi, in 1818 When thirteen years old he came to Floyd county, Indiana. He married Susan Atkins, who was born in Floyd county in 1830. Neither of the parents had many advantages in the way of schooling but were practical and substantial people, and did well for their family. They came to Cass county in 1856, locating two and a half miles west of Royal Center, in Boone township While the father lived on a farm, he spent most of the time working at the cooper's trade He was the first man to operate a cooper shop in Royal Center and shipped the first load of barrels from that place to Chicago. In politics he was a Whig, an Abolitionist and Republican He voted and supported the Republican ticket from 1856 till the time of his death He never held any office and exercised his influence on civic affairs as a private citizen. He was a member of the Presbyterian church, and his death occurred on his farm in 1875. Benjamin F Stuart had five brothers and two half-sisters and one half-brother, namely· Carolina, born in 1845, Maria, born in 1847, Stephen G., in 1849, Thomas J, in 1854, Robert A, in 1858, John M, born in 1860 and died in 1875; Warren E, born in 1863; Charles H, born in 1867, and died in the same year

Benjamin Franklin Stuart, as a boy, attended school at the Burr Oak schoolhouse in Boone township, and the Herman school in Jefferson township Later he was in the graded school at Burnettsville, and the State Normal school For forty years Mr Stuart has been interested in and connected with the public school system, as student, teacher, and as patron He was four years old when the family came to Cass county, and many years of his life were spent in Boone and Jefferson townships, but at the present time he has his home on a farm in Carroll county For eight terms he taught country school, and is still remembered by many of his old pupils Later he took up farming as a regular occupation and has done quite a business as a dealer in live stock and as an auctioneer His only noteworthy connection with public affairs to be mentioned was as trustee for the Seceder Cemetery Association, and outside of this has been content to exert his influence outside the medium of any public office He is a Republican, and has been an admirer of the careers and personalities of Blaine, Harrison and Taft

On June 2, 1880, Mr Stuart married Miss Mary I Love at Idaville, the minister performing the ceremony having been Rev Gilbert Small Mrs Stuart's parents were William and Deborah Love, who were substantial farming people, and for fifty-eight years lived on one farm, located two and a half miles south of Burnettsville The children of Mr and Mrs Stuart are mentioned as follows. Lucretia born in August, 1881, and died February, 1893, William, born May, 1883, died July, 1883, Robert F , born June, 1884 now a student at Purdue University, Pearl A , born June 18, 1887, a graduate in music and formerly a teacher of that art, and now the wife of Larry Guthrie, a farmer in Carroll county, Mary Love, born October, 1891 a former student of the State Normal school, and now engaged in teaching, John M , born August 18, 1894, now in the fourth year in the Burnettsville high school, Mason W born September, 1896, and in the third year in the Burnettsville high school

Mr. Stuart and family are members of the Presbyterian faith What Mr Stuart regards as the best remembered and most eventful day in his life, contains incidents which are of interest beyond their individual associations with his own career He looks back to a day in the early history of Logansport, in the month of October, 1860, a day of great festivity, when Cassius M. Clay was the principal orator of the occasion Young Stuart was then eight years old just at the time when impressions are deepest and the memory will persist throughout life. He then saw for the first time the flag of the country, and heard the fife and drum and the "wide-awakes" marching to the music He also heard the roar of cannons for the first time Then it was that he looked upon the dashing waters of the Wabash and the Eel rivers and viewed the long covered bridges which existed at that time He saw a grist mill—the forest mill, and marveled at the canal and its boats, and the old aqueduct and escaping waters All those things were wonderful to the boy of eight years and all of them are pictures of a past-time in Logansport and recall some of the institutions which were once an intimate part of life and activity in this county.

CLAUDE C BISHOP. A representative of one of the old families of Cass county which since early days has been prominently connected with the commercial development and substantial progress of this section of the state, Claude C Bishop is now worthily sustaining the high reputation of the family by his honorable connection with the mer-

THE PLUMMER FAMILY REUNION—1912. SPENCER PARK, LOGANSPORT, INDIANA

cantile interests of Logansport. He was born at Walton, Cass county, June 13, 1869, a son of George W and Sarah (Corbly) Bishop His father, a native of Tiffin, Ohio, is a carpenter by trade, but for the greater part of his active career has been engaged in mercantile pursuits, and at this time is residing at Walton, Indiana, where he is widely and favorably known among business men

Claude C. Bishop was reared at Walton, and primarily educated in the public schools of that place Subsequently this was supplemented by attendance at the National Normal School, at Lebanon, Ohio, at the age of nineteen years and in 1890 he was graduated from the scientific course of that institution From this date for three years he and his brother, George W Bishop, Jr, conducted a store at Walton, which had been founded by their father, but in 1893 he decided to take up the study of law, and accordingly entered the legal department of the University of Michigan, at Ann Arbor He was graduated therefrom in 1895, and immediately thereafter came to Logansport and established himself in practice, but in 1897 returned to Walton and again took up merchandising. In 1906 he again came to Logansport and with his brother bought the elevator formerly belonging to the Johnson Elevator Company This the brothers conducted until May, 1911, when George W. Bishop, Jr, retired from the firm, and Mr C C Bishop has since been the sole proprietor In addition to running this elevator in a successful manner, Mr. Bishop has dealt in coal, flour, feed and tiling By his honorable and upright business methods, he has gained and maintained an enviable reputation, and among his business associates he is regarded as a shrewd, far-sighted man, whose judgment may be relied upon in matters of importance In politics a Republican, he has been active in the support of his party's principles and candidates, and in 1912 was the candidate for the office of representative to the State Legislature Fraternally, Mr. Bishop is connected with the Masonic order and the Benevolent and Protective Order of Elks. His career has proven that true success in life may be attained through the medium of personal effort and consecutive industry, and that the road to success is open to all young men who have the courage to tread its pathway, keeping ever in mind the rights of others

On April 7, 1892, Mr. Bishop was married in Walton, Indiana, to Miss Lulu Minnick, of that city, daughter of Justus Minnick Three children have been born to this union, namely Ralph H, John H and Helen M Both Mr and Mrs Bishop have many friends in Logansport, and are well known in social circles

MOSES L PLUMMER Practically all his life a resident of Cass county, Moses L Plummer gave the active years of his career to the farming industry in this section of the state, and it may be said in all sincerity and truth that few men in Cass county held a higher place in public confidence and esteem than did Mr Plummer when he died His life was characterized by the highest integrity and usefulness, and it is to such men as he that the splendid reputation which the county bears for stability, progressiveness and prosperity, is in a great measure due

When the late Moses L Plummer was a lad of eight years his parents came to Cass county and settled in its fertile farming district Here he was reared, and here he lived continuously until death called him January 1, 1871

Born on August 2, 1825, in Fayette county, Indiana, he was the son of John and Nancy (Ladd) Plummer. The father was born on the 6th day of September, 1772, in North Carolina. In 1800 he located in Virginia, moving thence to Georgia, where he was married in June, 1810. In the following year he came to Ohio, and in 1814 moved into Fayette county, Indiana, remaining there busy in the farming industry until the year 1833, when he came to Cass county. Here he purchased a goodly farm, secured his patent rights from the government, the place being situated in section 16, in Clay township, and known down to the present day as the old Plummer homestead in Cass county. He died at his home there on July 4, 1855, when he had reached the fine old age of eighty-three years, and his widow followed him on July 7, 1859. They were the parents of eight children, as follows: Noble, Mary A., Thomas, Elihu, Elizabeth, John, Nancy and Moses, the latter named being the subject of this review.

As has already been mentioned, Moses Plummer was a boy of eight when he first saw Cass county. He was educated in the common schools and gave the usual amount of his time to the work of the farm home that the average country youth contributed to such employment. When he discontinued school the young man remained at home and gave diligent and faithful service at the family homestead, and when he married on December 22, 1884, he left home and rented a place, it being his intention to establish an independent home. He was very successful in his farming enterprise, and though he rented for the first few years, he eventually secured a place of his own and gained a position of prominence and undeniable influence in the county as a farmer of means and intelligence.

Mr. Plummer married Miss Catherine Yohea, December 22, 1854, the daughter of Henry and Lydia (Ault) Yohea, who came from Washington county, Pennsylvania, many years ago and located in Ohio. They later moved to Fulton county, where Mrs. Plummer was reared. Six children were born to Mr. and Mrs. Plummer. The eldest Elihu, married Caroline Sullivan and they have two children—Charles W. and George A. Plummer. Emma is married to William O. Thomas, and they have three children living and one dead—Alvan M., Bessie and Owen and Otho M., deceased. Mary married George J. Nichols, who is now deceased, and they have one living son—Kedar J.; John L. lives at home on the old homestead, and Etta, the next to youngest of the family, shares the old home with him, John having been born on the old Plummer place. The family received their schooling in the schools at Onward and are living lives of usefulness in the communities where they are established in homes of their own, all bearing the same high reputation that characterized the life of their deceased father in the many years that he passed in Cass county as an active participant in the industrial affairs of the district.

Mrs. Plummer and her children have two old parchment deeds, one executed June 25, 1841, and signed by President John Tyler, the other dated April 1, 1848 and signed by President James K. Polk. This makes the third deed of the kind found in Cass county, and are valu-

Philip Voorhees

able heirlooms in the Plummer family. The son John has his great-grandfather's will, dated October 26, 1805, and in the deed he willed three negroes, valued as follows one at $2,500, one $2,000 and one at $1,800 This deed was executed in Florida

The Plummer family each year has a family reunion and herewith is presented a protrait of the reunion of the family at Spencer Park, Logansport, Cass county, Indiana, in 1912. The pretty homestead is known as "Wood Lawn" in Tipton township

PHILIP VOORHEES first came to Logansport, Indiana, in 1889, here identifying himself with the lumber industry of the place Since that time he has made continued progress in his business, and has added a planing mill, in addition to which he has engaged in the handling of hardware, cement and lime His success has been of a solid growth, each year marked by a significant advance in his fortunes, and he is today one of the leading business men of the city Born in Coshocton county, Ohio, on April 16, 1857, Philip Voorhees is the son of Stephen and Eliza Ann (Heishman) Voorhees

Stephen Voorhees moved from Coshocton, Ohio, with his family to Carroll county, Indiana, locating southwest of Delphi, and there engaged in farming He was a cooper by trade, and in the winter he occupied himself in that manner, giving up his summers to active farming The first winter that Mr. Voorhees was in that community he worked in the woods, hauling his cordwood to Delphi, where he disposed of it The following summer he rented a field and planted ten acres of it to corn In the autumn, while he was engaged in making barrels, before he thought the corn ready for the harvest, the owner of the field appeared on the scene, harvested the ten acres of corn, husked it and made off, thus beating Mr. Voorhees out of his season's work This experience, however, was not sufficient to daunt the courage of the man, and he located a farm, which he operated in summers and applied himself to coopering in the winter seasons He passed the remainder of his life in Carroll county and carried on his daily work until the infirmities attendant upon advancing age made it impossible to longer keep up his activities Although he was a renter for a number of years, good management and economy made it possible in time for him to secure a farm of his own, and when he died he left a competency to his widow He died in 1903 aged seventy-three, and she survived him until 1909, and was eighty-two years of age at the time of her passing She was a member of the Methodist Episcopal church and was a devout and much loved woman These parents had a family of fifteen children The first born and the last two died in infancy, six sons and six daughters yet surviving

When Philip Voorhees was two years old he came with his parents from Ohio to Carroll county, Indiana He was the youngest of the family at that time As a boy at home he shared in the work of the farm, early learned something of the cooper's trade, and when he was nine years old made a creditable barrel, much to the pride of his father He attended the district schools and remained in the home until he reached man's estate When he was seventeen years old he began working at the carpenter's trade and he continued in that work until 1889, when he engaged in the saw mill and lumber business at Flora, Carroll county, Indiana. In 1897 he came to Logansport and straightway identified himself with the lumber business. He operated saw and planing mills for some time, and was afterwards at Flora, and eventually worked into the handling of hardware, cement, lime and builders' supplies. He is also interested in a cream separator factory at Lebanon, Indiana, known as the "Dairy Queen Separator Company," and he is the president of the company, which was organized in 1911. He is the owner of several hundred acres in Dakota, in Jefferson county, Indiana, and in Lafayette county, Arkansas. He is now engaged in those various lines of enterprise, and is enjoying a pleasing success in the business world of Logansport. One son, Arthur V, has a one-fourth interest in the business with Mr Voorhees.

On March 27, 1885, Mr Voorhees was united in marriage with Miss Flora Baer, of Carroll county, Indiana, and Arthur W, previously mentioned, is their only living child, one other having died in infancy.

Mr and Mrs Voorhees are members of the Christian church, and Mr Voorhees supports the platform of the Prohibitionist party. He is a member of the Order of Ben Hur.

BENJAMIN F LOUTHAIN More than thirty-five years ago Benjamin F Louthain first attached himself to the *Logansport Pharos*, and since 1877 he has been the chief editorial writer on its staff. That he has borne an emphatic part in the moulding of sentiment in Cass county along lines of public interest and civic development is undeniably true, and it is a truth patent to all that the influence of such a man as he has ever proven himself to be could only be for the best good of the community in which his opinions and utterances hold sway.

A native son of Cass county, Benjamin F Louthain was born on the farm of his father, a short distance from the then village of Logansport, in the year 1847. His parents, William Preston and Elizabeth (McGrew) Louthain, were pioneers of the Wabash valley, and their son was reared in pronounced primitive fashion, as might be expected in consideration of the period and station of the family. It is significant of the boy that he was always a student, and his tastes in that line were early demonstrated by his buying a United States history with the first money he ever earned. Diligent effort made it possible for him to enter the high school at Logansport when he was seventeen, and it was but a short time from then that he began work as a teacher. He was soon made principal of the school in Walton, Indiana, in which position he was especially successful. It was in about 1875 that he began to take a lively interest in the activities of the Democratic party, and in that year he was appointed deputy sheriff of Cass county, in which position he acquitted himself in a most creditable manner. He was particularly active in the campaigns of his party in the year of 1882, 1884, 1892, 1894 and 1896, in those years serving as chairman of the Democratic county central committee, and has since held the same position in the party. In 1890 he served as a member of the Democratic state central committee, and his public services also include membership on the board of trustees of the State normal school at Terre Haute.

The *Logansport Pharos* has long been recognized as the able exponent of the principles of the Democratic party, and it has in Mr Louthain one of its stanchest advocates

Mr Louthain has always given a deal of thought to the public school system of education, and has been the friend of advanced methods and more efficient service throughout He has given valuable service to the city as a member of the school board, and for four years was postmaster of the city

On May 4, 1881, Mr. Louthain was united in marriage with Mrs Matilda M Emshe, of Logansport

GEORGE W WALTERS Displaying energy and resource, and measuring up to the standards and requirements of his profession, George W. Walters, of Logansport, has attained to an enviable place at the Cass county bar, and is well deserving of mention among those who have added to his adopted city's professional prestige Losing his mother when he was an infant, his life from earliest boyhood has been passed practically among strangers but his commendable perseverance has won him recognition as an attorney, and his admirable personal qualities of character have drawn about him a wide circle of appreciative friends Mr Walters was born in Boone township, Cass county, Indiana, July 19, 1862, and is the one survivor of the two children born to Jacob and Emily (Washburn) Walters His father, in early life a farmer, and later justice of the peace in Boone township is now deceased, while his mother, as before stated, died when he was an infant

George W Walters was reared in the village of Royal Centre, where he secured his education during the winter terms, while his summers were spent in working at whatever honorable employment presented itself Ambitious and industrious, he seized every opportunity that came within his reach to gain an education, and when only sixteen years of age had qualified to teach school, in which vocation he continued for eight years, at intervals For four years he was superintendent of the Royal Centre schools, but in 1883 gave up teaching to enter the National Normal University, of Lebanon, Ohio, being graduated from the scientific course thereof in 1884 Four years later, Mr. Walters came to Logansport and took up the study of law in the offices of McConnell & McConnell, and in the following year became an employe of the United States government at Washington, D C, as a special agent of the labor department In 1893 he returned to Logansport and entered upon the active practice of his profession, which he has continued to follow to the present time In 1903 and again in 1905 he was elected prosecuting attorney of the twenty-ninth judicial district, serving, in all, four years, and during this time displayed high abilities as a public executive Mr Walters has accomplished the task of the translation of the aspiring boy to the full-fledged lawyer with an acknowledged position at the bar His early years were a period of struggle, of privation, of incessant labor with head and hands, but never with lessening of purpose, rather with eye firmly fixed on the goal, each obstruction in the way an incentive to increased endeavor and greater energy Such a career should carry its own lesson and prove inspiring to the youth of today who consider themselves handicapped by lack of funds and influential friends Formerly a Republican, Mr Walters in 1912 transferred his allegiance to the new progressive movement that resulted in the birth of the so-called "Bull Moose" party. His fraternal connections are with the Masons, the Benevolent and Protective Order of Elks and the Knights of Pythias

In 1886 Mr. Walters was united in marriage with Miss Lillian Barron, and they have two daughters Edna and Mildred They attend the Broadway Methodist Episcopal church, in which they have many sincere friends

DR. ADELBERT LEE PALMER in the nine years of his identification with the medical profession in Logansport has come to be one of the best known and most successful practitioners in the city or county His advance has been constant and his rise in the public favor has seen a healthy growth since he established himself in practice in Logansport after he received his M D degree from Rush Medical College at Chicago, and once more has it been demonstrated that a man need not cut himself off from his native community in order to experience success in his chosen field of activity, the old aphorism to the contrary notwithstanding

Born in Washington township, Cass county, Indiana, on September 27, 1878, Dr Palmer is a son of John and Mary (Best) Palmer John Palmer is a native Ohioan, born near Ironton, that state, of Scotch-Irish ancestry He was a farmer, and first came to Cass county in 1852 in company with his parents, settling on a farm in Clinton township, but after a short time the family moved to Logansport, thence to Washington township, where he has since resided, thirty-five years representing the time he has spent on the place he made his own in that locality In 1870 he married Mary Best, whose people were Pennsylvanians, and they became the parents of three sons, Charles Quincy, George Harrison and Adelbert Lee The mother died on July 20, 1910 Mr Palmer has served in varied local positions of trust in this community, and is known as a strong Democrat in his political faith, while he is a member of the Masonic fraternity

Dr A L Palmer was reared on the home farm located three miles south of Logansport, on the Kokomo pike, and thus his acquaintance with the city has dated from his earliest boyhood He attended the district schools in boyhood, later the schools in Logansport, and in September, 1897, he entered the State University of Michigan for the purpose of taking preliminary instructions in the study of medicine. He remained there until June, 1898, then matriculated at Rush Medical College in Chicago, and in 1903 was duly graduated from that institution with the degree of M D The newly fledged doctor straightway turned to his home community and there established himself in medical practice, and so well has he succeeded that he has never considered a removal to other fields being well content to exercise his skill in the city which has known him all his life, and which has not been slow in recognizing his talent.

In 1905-6 Dr Palmer was secretary of the city board of health, and in the latter part of 1909 and in 1910 was county coroner of Cass county, being appointed to fill an unexpired term In both these offices he discharged the duties intrusted to him admirably and to the entire satisfaction of all concerned In 1910 he was elected to succeed himself in the office of coroner, his re-election following in 1912. Dr Palmer is a Democrat in politics, and his fraternal relations are centered in the Masonic order, in which he has membership in the Knights Templar and the Ancient Arabic Order of the Nobles of the Mystic Shrine He is also a member of the Cass county and Indiana state medical societies and the American Medical Association

On June 28, 1906, Dr Palmer married Miss Daisy Grace, daughter of William Grace, of Logansport

JOHN P HETHERINGTON, M D, has been established in practice in Logansport since 1890, and has found a sure place in the esteem of the community at large in the passing years, as well as winning a high position in the ranks of the medical profession in this section of the state. Born in Cicero, Indiana, on February 15, 1869, Dr Hetherington is the son of Dr. Augustus and Catherine (Teter) Hetherington

The Hetheringtons spring from one of the old Scottish clans known to history in Scotland from the Middle Ages The American ancestors of the doctor came to America in the late half of the seventeenth century, settling in New York The father, Augustus S Hetherington, was a native of the state of Ohio, and he died in Hamilton county, this state, when his son, John P, was scarcely more than an infant. The widowed mother later wedded Dr. D. L. Overholder, of Logansport. Dr. Hetherington died in 1872 when he was but forty-two years of age

Until he was five years old, Cicero represented the home of John P Hetherington, after which he went to Logansport, where he remained until he was about fifteen He was a student in the schools of the city during those years In 1887 he began reading medicine under the advice and instruction of Dr McIntyre at Unadilla, Nebraska, and in the following year matriculated in the Eclectic Medical Institute in Cincinnati, from which he was graduated in 1890, with the highest honors in his class Almost immediately the young doctor established himself in practice in Logansport, in association with Dr J B. Shultz, with whom he continued for the long period of twenty-one years. Since then he has conducted an independent private practice

Dr Hetherington is local surgeon for the railroads and the interurban roads at Logansport, and he has the distinction of being one of the first doctors in this community to introduce the X-ray into his professional work, and probably the first to own a heavy X-ray machine. While engaged in general practice, he has given especial attention to surgery and has won a considerable local prominence in that branch of his work He is a member of the American Medical Association, the county and state medical societies, and also a member of the Wabash & Pennsylvania Railroad Surgical Association In a fraternal way he is affiliated with the Masonic order, being a Knight Templar of St John's Commandery, and a member of the Knights of Pythias He is a member of the Broadway Methodist Episcopal church. In the line of public service Dr. Hetherington has done good work as county coroner of Cass county, as well as serving on the city council at one time

Dr Hetherington has been twice married His first wife was Mary Lux who was a past grand matron of the Eastern Star of Indiana She died in April, 1910 The doctor later married Mrs Bertha Miller, of Muncie, Indiana

MICHAEL F MAHONEY Undoubtedly while some men achieve success along certain lines and in certain professions, there are those who are born to them their natural leanings and marked talents pointing unmistakably to the career in which they subsequently achieve distinction With some the call of the church cannot be disobeyed, to others the science of healing appeals, the business mart or the political arena engages many, while there are still others who early see in their visions of the future their achieving in the law and the summit of their ambition. To respond to this call, to bend every energy in this direction, to broaden and deepen every possible highway of knowledge and to finally enter upon this chosen career and find its rewards worth while—that has been the happy experience of Michael F Mahoney, one of the leading attorneys of the Logansport bar Mr Mahoney was born at Delphi, Indiana, December 18, 1863, one of the eight children, six now living, of Michael and Katherine (Ryan) Mahoney His parents were natives of County Limerick and County Cork, Ireland, respectively, and each came with their parents to the United States, locating at Delphi, Indiana, where they were married For twenty-seven years Mr Mahoney, Sr, was in the employ of A T Bowen, the old-time banker of that place In 1867 the family moved to Washington township, Carroll county, and there Michael Mahoney was reared

Until he was eighteen years of age Mr Mahoney divided his time between work on the home farm and attendance in the country schools In 1884 and 1885 he attended the State University at Bloomington, and in 1886 and 1887 Georgetown College, Washington, D C He then came to Logansport, and in April, 1887, entered the law office of Michael D Fansler, then prosecuting attorney He practiced in the justice and city courts until he was admitted to the bar by examination, and immediately thereafter became Mr Fansler's assistant In 1888 he became assistant to John W McGreevy, prosecuting attorney, and served as such four years In 1892 he became his preceptor's partner, the firm being known as Fansler & Mahoney, which continued uninterruptedly until Mr Fansler's death in May, 1895 In November of that year Moses B Lairy, present appellate judge retired from the circuit bench, and with him under the firm style of Lairy & Mahoney, Mr Mahoney continued in practice until January 1, 1911 By a singular coincidence Judge M B Lairy was elected appellate judge, defeating Judge J M. Rabb, who had served on the appellate bench for four years, and Judge Rabb, on June 1, 1911, became Mr Mahoney's partner under the firm name of Rabb & Mahoney, which has since continued During the session of the legislature of 1889, Mr Mahoney was committee clerk in the house of representatives in 1894 he was county attorney, and also held that office in 1896, 1897, 1898 and 1899; in 1908 and 1909 he was a member of the Logansport school board In political matters he is a Democrat and in 1888 was secretary of the Democratic county central committee Ever since being admitted to the bar, by reason of his legal associations, Mr. Mahoney has been connected with nearly all of the noted criminal cases in the judicial circuit He is a Roman Catholic in religion, and belongs to the Sigma Chi college fraternity

On June 20, 1894, Mr Mahoney was married to Katherine Farrell, and they have two children, Madeline and Raymond

DAVID PAYSON HURD Although he has been the owner of his present farm on the Walton and Bunker Hill road for only seven years, D. P. Hurd is one of the old residents of this part of Cass county, whence he came as a lad of seven years. His subsequent career covers a period spent in the grain business and in extensive agricultural operations, and at this time he is the owner of an eighty-acre tract two miles west of Walton. In all of his operations, Mr. Hurd has been uniformly successful, and he has not only been fortunate in a material way, but has succeeded also in firmly establishing himself in the good graces of all with whom he has had transactions. Mr. Hurd is a native of the Prairie state, born April 12, 1861, at Lawn Ridge, Marshall county, Illinois. His father, a native of Nashua, New Hampshire, migrated to Illinois in young manhood, and was there married and settled down to agricultural pursuits. In 1868 he came to Walton, Indiana, and embarked in the sawmill business, in which he continued throughout the remainder of his life. He also did an excellent business in handling grain, and was known as one of Walton's substantial business citizens. He and his wife were the parents of six children. Walter, deceased, D P, Matilda, Willard, Lyra and Frank.

D P Hurd was a boy of seven years when he accompanied his parents to Walton, and there he received his education in the public schools. In the meantime, he had assisted in the work of his father's mill, gaining experience that had proved very valuable to him in subsequent years. He was ambitious and industrious, and when he had thoroughly mastered all the details of the grain business, he embarked therein on his own account and soon built up a thriving trade. Eventually, however, Mr. Hurd decided to enter agricultural pursuits, and accordingly, in 1906, he purchased his present handsome property, a tract of eighty acres which he has brought into a high state of cultivation. He is progressive himself, and believes in progressive measures, which he has applied to his work with a large measure of success. Experience has shown him that modern ideas and methods obtain far better results than the old hit and miss style, and he uses the latest improved machinery in his work. His buildings are large and substantial and the entire place speaks of the presence of able and thrifty management.

On April 13, 1882, Mr. Hurd was married to Miss Mary C Bowyer, who died not long thereafter. On November 26, 1885, Mr Hurd was married (second) to Miss Sarah E Schwalm, and they became the parents of the following children Lyra M, Jessie H, Henry N, George M, David O and Mabel. Lyra M. received her diploma in public schools and spent two years in the high school at Logansport. She died at the age of twenty-three. She was a member of the Lutheran church and was a teacher in the Sunday school a member of the Ladies' Aid and Literary club. She is interred in the Walton cemetery, where a beautiful stone marks her grave. Jessie H received her diploma in the public schools and she graduated from the Walton high school in 1908. She spent one term in Valparaiso University and one term in Earlham College. She is a member of the Lutheran church. Henry N received his diploma from the public schools and graduated from the Walton high school in the class of 1912. He is at home and an agriculturist. George M received his diploma from the public schools and also graduated from the Walton high school, class of 1913 He is at present at Winona College David O. finished the public schools and received his diploma Mabel died August 14, 1909 Mr and Mrs Hurd's children have all received the benefits of good education, fitting them for the higher walks of life Mrs Hurd is a native of Cass county, born April 9, 1859, and was educated in the common schools She is a model housekeeper and her home is her paradise She is secretary of the Ladies' Aid Society With his family, Mr Hurd attends the Evangelical Lutheran church He has found no time to enter politics as a seeker after personal preferment, but in him good government and good citizenship have always found a stanch friend and supporter, as do movements tending to advance the cause of education, morality and general progress

I. N. CRAWFORD. A resident of Logansport since 1869, I N Crawford has had a career crowded with varied experiences, marked by ventures of extent and importance, characterized at all times by the strictest integrity and adherence to honorable business methods, and stamped with the approval of all with whom he has come into contact A pioneer of Indiana in various lines of business activity, he has identified himself with diversified enterprise, in all of which he has met with uniform success, and today he is justly regarded as one of the foremost of his city's commercial geniuses Mr. Crawford was born February 17, 1843, at Pittsburgh, Pennsylvania, a member of the family of five sons and one daughter, all living born to James and Ann Jane (Creighton) Crawford, farming people of the vicinity of Pittsburgh

I N Crawford was reared to agricultural pursuits and educated in the public schools of his native locality in a log schoolhouse with puncheons floor and with the cracks filled with mud These same cracks afforded the scholars much pleasure in kicking out the mud to get fresh air Mr Crawford believed that further west better opportunities were furnished for ambitious and energetic young men, and accordingly when twenty-five years of age he left home. For some time he traveled through the middle West, visiting St Paul, Chicago and other points, but eventually decided to cast his fortunes with the growing town of Logansport, and in 1869 embarked in a lumber business at Fifth and North streets Three years later he disposed of his interests to his brother, and started buying and shipping lumber, being the first here to ship poplar to Boston In 1873 he bought an interest in a hardware store and was associated with T J Immel for two years, but in 1875 bought Mr Immel's interest and ever since that date has been the sole owner of this establishment, one of the oldest in the state Not long thereafter Mr Crawford secured a half interest in a stone quarry at Alton, Illinois, and for three years divided his time between Alton and Logansport, but eventually traded his interest in the quarry for a steamboat, with which he carried salt, cotton and provisions to the Cherokee, Choctaw and Creek Indians, having previously effected a contract with these tribes for that purpose About the year 1886 he embarked in sawmilling on the St John's river in Florida, becoming the pioneer in shipping cypress shingles to the East, furnished lumber for the Ponce de Leon, Csnomica and Aleazar hotels, and for five years shipped on the high seas, his product going to the Bermudas and eastern port cities of the United States The mill burned about 1891, and after a few years spent in retirement, recuperating from his strenuous labors, Mr Crawford started a sawmilling business at Dixon, Kentucky There he continued for some five or six years, and while located at that point secured the contract for the building of the Bourbon county (Ky) courthouse, a deal that concerned some $250,000, and which he successfully completed After a few years Mr Crawford turned his attention to farming at West Baden in Orange county, Indiana, but in September, 1912, disposed of this land. During all of this time Mr Crawford had continued to conduct the hardware store in Logansport. For about fifteen years he has been a stockholder and director in the City National Bank, of which he is vice president, and at this time acting president Mr Crawford is a man of sound judgment, and not only can plan brilliant business enterprises, but has the business ability to carry them into successful operation His career has been governed by the strictest regard to the ethics of commercial life and his reputation is unassailable. In addition to the activities before mentioned Mr Crawford is the possessor of an excellent military record, being a veteran of the war between the states. He enlisted in 1862 for nine months' service in Company H, One Hundred and Twenty-third Regiment, Pennsylvania Volunteer Infantry, with which organization he participated in numerous engagements, including Second Bull Run, South Mountain, Antietam, Fredericksburg and Chancellorsville. He was never absent or sick a day, and received his honorable discharge at Harrisburg in 1863 by reason of the expiration of his term of service He is a valued comrade of the Grand Army of the Republic In political matters he is a Republican, but has not cared for public life

In 1869 Mr Crawford was married to Miss Isabel J. Ross, of Allegheny, Pennsylvania They are members of Broadway Presbyterian church

Although past seventy years of age Mr Crawford claims that he can throw more dirt off of his feet on the store floor than many of the young American boys of the present generation

JOSEPH S CRAIG, who died in Logansport on March 28, 1910, was a man of more than usual force of character He was born in Greenville, Darke county, Ohio, on January 19, 1830, and was a son of James and Matilda (Quinn) Craig. By the time he was eight years of age both his parents had been claimed by death and he was reared to early manhood by an uncle, J C Quinn When he was sixteen years old he began life's battle upon his own responsibility, and in June, 1849, went to Huntington, Indiana, where he married Emily Johnson. He moved to LaGro, Wabash county, where his three children were born, and where Mrs Craig died in 1862 In the following year, 1863, he moved to Wabash. where he served as deputy sheriff for the county until his enlistment in Company G, Seventeenth Indiana Volunteer Infantry He subsequently helped to recruit the One Hundred and Thirtieth Indiana Volunteer Infantry and mounted to the rank of captain After being honorably discharged at the close of the war he was engaged in merchant tailoring at Wabash until 1872, when he came to Logansport, and this city ever afterwards was his home Here he conducted a merchant tailoring establishment successfully and profitably He was a man whose sterling character commended him to his fellow men at all times, and held the esteem and confidence of all who knew him. He joined the Odd Fellows in 1856 and was a charter member of the Knights of Pythias lodge of Logansport, and a Methodist in religion. In 1866 he remarried, his second wife being Minerva Pickering

WILLIAM D CRAIG is the only living child of his parents, Joseph S and Emily (Johnson) Craig He was born at LaGro, Indiana, September 4, 1856, and was reared at Wabash where he acquired his early education in the public schools He came to Logansport in 1872, and having worked for his father in the merchant tailoring business, he became a partner in the business, under the firm name of J S. Craig & Son

In 1889 Mr Craig disposed of his interest in the business and embarked in the manufacture of overalls under the name of the Thomas Manufacturing Company, and in a short time he became the sole owner of the business He continued in the manufacturing of overalls until 1907, since which time he has devoted his entire time to the manufacture and jobbing of juvenile suits It is probable that not more than a few people in Logansport realize that the business conducted by Mr Craig in this line is one of the largest manufacturing establishments of the city He is also running a branch factory in Tipton, Indiana, started in May, 1913 He employs as many as one hundred people, mostly girls, and does an annual business of one hundred thousand dollars, his product being marketed in almost every state in the Union

Mr. Craig is a Republican, and is a member of the Benevolent and Protective Order of Elks, the T P A., and the Country Club. He is also a member of the Deutsch Verein.

In April, 1888, Mr Craig married Miss Frances M Place, and they have one child, Virginia D Craig

JOHN E BARNES During a period covering more than a half century, John E Barnes, of Logansport, has been engaged in contracting and building in Cass county, where his activities have left a distinct impress upon the community and contributed materially to its progress and development A self-made man in the broadest meaning of the title, his advancement has been steady and continuous, and today he holds an enviable position among the business men of this flourishing Indiana city. Mr Barnes came to Cass county in November 1854, with his parents, the family locating in Logansport His father, Thomas Barnes, was a native of England, where he married Ann Bearne, and they became the parents of twelve children, all with the exception of one being born in Great Britain, and six of whom still survive Thomas Barnes was a stonemason by trade, and followed that vocation and contracting throughout his career For one year after coming to this country he resided in Brooklyn, New York, and his death occurred in Logansport about the year 1864

John E Barnes was born in England, September 8, 1841, and was thirteen years of age when his people came to Logansport He received only a limited schooling in his youth, and the ample education which he now possesses was obtained in the school of experience. Even before he had attained his majority, he began his career as a contractor, and this occupation, in a large extent, he has followed throughout life. He was for eleven years in partnership with John Medland, under the firm style of Medland & Barnes, which firm, among other structures, erected the Cass county courthouse, the First Presbyterian church, and a number of business blocks and school buildings. Since closing his partnership with Mr Medland, Mr. Barnes has had his sons associated with him, and they have erected the Logansport public library, the Logansport high school and a number of the buildings of the Culver Military Academy, and also rebuilt the Presbyterian church. Mr. Barnes' buildings are monuments to his skill and reliable workmanship, and he has always been known as a man of the highest integrity, who has at all times lived strictly up to the letter of his contracts. A Republican in his political proclivities, he has served efficiently as a member of the city council, and as a member of the board of trustees of the waterworks.

In 1864 Mr. Barnes was married to Miss Elizabeth J Bates, and they have been the parents of eight children, of whom the following six still survive Clara A, who married George W. Funk, Charles H, W W. Curry, James I, and Benjamin F and George W, twins. The family is connected with the Universalist church. Fraternally, Mr Barnes is connected with the Masons and Odd Fellows, is president of the Odd Fellows' Hall Association, and holds the position of secretary of the Odd Fellows' Hall trustees. He is also president of the Home for the Friendless, a position to which he was elected to fill the vacancy occasioned by the death of former President Rice. Since the winter of 1854 Mr Barnes has not only been an eye-witness to the development of Cass county, but has done his part in bringing about the changes which have contributed to its present prosperous condition. As one of its leading and public-spirited citizens he is held in the highest esteem, and his many friends testify readily to his personal character and great popularity.

JAMES I BARNES No record of the successful business men of Cass county would be complete did it not contain a sketch of the career of James I Barnes, whose work in the construction of many of Logansport's most substantial buildings has been of a character to leave its impress on the city for many years to come. A native of this city, educated in its public schools and reared in the business in which he has gained such high reputation, he early displayed a certain progressiveness, a marked intuitiveness and a prophetic shrewdness that promised a subsequent distinction in his chosen field of endeavor, a promise that has been amply fulfilled. James I Barnes was born January 5 1872 in Logansport, Indiana, and is a son of John E Barnes. On completing his public school education, he at once associated himself in business with his father, whose partner he was until the elder man's retirement. That his work has been of an extensive and substantial character is evidenced by the list of large enterprises with which he has been connected among his contracts being the following The Haney residence, the Western Motor Works building, Rauth packing house, English Lutheran church, Strecker bakery building, Maiben laundry building, Elks temple, Odd Fellows building, Aldine flats, all in Logansport, Royal Center high school building, James Taylor building and electric light plant at Royal Center, Ind the Goodman and Harlecker buildings at Monticello, Ind high school and bank building at Attica, mess hall for the military academy at Culver; a church building at Centralia, Illinois, township high school building at Kinmundy, Illinois, high school buildings at Pennville, Shelbyville and New Salem Indiana, ward school building at Alliance, Ohio, high school buildings at Milford and Sidney, Ohio, Carnegie Library at Gary, Indiana, and high school at Pawnee, Illinois All of this work has been accomplished during the past five years, in addition to which Mr Barnes has laid stone and gravel roads in Cass county Indiana, to the extent of twenty-five miles

In August, 1899, Mr Barnes was married to Miss Emily C Englebrecht, of Logansport, Indiana, and they have had six daughters. Dorothy Lucile, Emily Aldine, Doris Eleanor, Marjorie May Clara Louise and Elizabeth Jane The last-named, who was the second in order of birth, is deceased Mrs Barnes is a member of the German Lutheran church, and is well known in religious work and social circles Mr Barnes belongs to the Masons, the Knights of Pythias and the Elks He is a Republican in his political views but has taken only a good citizen's interest in public matters, and, to use his own language, has never aspired, and never will, to public preferment Essentially a business man, he has devoted his entire attention to his large interests, his ambitions being satisfied by the prestige he has gained among the men to whom Logansport is indebted for its commercial importance

JOHN HERMANN, M D, who died August 8, 1889, was one of the strongest characters in the medical history of Cass county, a man of unusual force of character, one whose career and achievement in his field of endeavor if fully chronicled would alone fill the pages of a reasonably large volume of intensely interesting material He was born in the Kingdom of Wurtemburg Germany, August 27, 1834 His father occupied a prominent place in the political history of the Fatherland, having served as commissioner of public domain, an office that entailed the keeping of the king's forest As a boy, Dr Hermann attended the primary educational institutions, subsequently being graduated from the Polytechnic school at Stuttgart He then entered the University of Tubingen, from which he received his medical diploma, succeeding which he received the appointment of physician in the Orthopedic hospital at Coustatt, where he remained two years With many of his countrymen he became embroiled in the revolutionary movement for free suffrage and home rule, which, proving a failure, he was obliged to flee his native land, and in 1864 came to America and for a time practiced his profession at Buffalo, New York While there, he met and married Miss Angeline deVillers, the daughter of a French army surgeon Unfortunately, he here lost the greater part of his means through unsuccessful investments, and largely because of this he determined to start anew in another locality

Locating in Chicago, Illinois, Dr Hermann succeeded in getting fairly started and had a home prepared, but while he was going to meet his family, who had remained behind in Buffalo while he was establishing a residence for them, his property was destroyed by fire, and he was once more practically without means Nothing daunted, with his family he

"WALNUT DELL STOCK FARM," RESIDENCE OF MR. AND MRS. WILLIAM H. RAMER

started for the East in 1867, but owing to the illness of his daughter he stopped off at Logansport, Indiana While at the hotel, where he was compelled to remain a few days, it was learned that he was a physician, and he was importuned by the German residents to remain His success in several complicated cases won him early recognition, and he soon had more calls than he could attend to alone Thus encouraged to remain, for nineteen years he was associated in successful practice here with Dr. William H Bell. Dr Hermann was a superior diagnostician and a physician of unusual ability Large in stature, jovial in nature, he radiated cheer in the sick room or wherever he went His wide experience in this country and abroad, his extensive acquaintance with notable men, his education and profound knowledge along special lines, all made him an ideal companion and one whom it was a pleasure to know. Dr Hermann was a notable example of the professional success and social prestige to be gained by foreign-born citizens, and his career may prove encouraging to those who are struggling to overcome obstacles in their endeavor to reach a position of independence Dr Hermann and his wife had four children, Arthur J , Jennie, the wife of Dr. Francis M. Bozer, Francis J., and William

Dr Francis Joseph Hermann, the second son of Dr John Hermann, was born in Logansport, Indiana, July 4, 1875, completed his literary education at Canisius College, from which he was graduated in 1893, and received his early medical training under the preceptorship of his father In 1894 and 1895 he attended Rush Medical College, Chicago, and the succeeding two years was a student at Bellevue Hospital Medical College, New York, which granted him a diploma in 1897 In this same year he began practicing in the office he now occupies, and here he has since continued As a physician and a citizen, Dr Hermann is an able successor to his distinguished father, and well merits the universal esteem in which he is held On June 26, 1907, he was united in marriage with Miss Honora I McHale, of Logansport

WILLIAM H RAMER Among the citizens of Cass county who are rendering their community signal services in public office may be mentioned William H Ramer, of Washington township, who in the capacity of assessor has given the voters of his community no reason to regret their choice. Essentially an agriculturist, reared in the atmosphere and to the work of the farm, he has proven himself an efficient, painstaking and courteous public official, and has added to the friendships that long years of honorable dealing had previously gained for him. Mr Ramer has spent his entire life on the farm on which he now lives, a well-cultivated tract of 120 acres, located on the Ramer road, about nine miles southeast from Logansport Here he was born February 4, 1870, in the old home, a son of Justus and Georgina (Ritter) Ramer

Henry Ramer, the paternal grandfather of William H , was a native of Germany, and in his youth came to the United States, locating first in Pennsylvania, where he carried on farming until 1841 In that year he made removal with his family to Cass county, Indiana where his subsequent years were spent, and where he died honored and respected by all Justus Ramer, his son, was born in Pennsylvania, and was a lad when he accompanied his father to Cass county Like him, he devoted his attention to the tilling of the soil, meeting with success in his ventures and gaining the respect of his fellow-citizens He married Georgina Ritter, and they became the parents of six children, namely William H, Mrs Louisa Schwalm, George, a resident of Chicago, Illinois, Mis Emma Jenness, and John and Myrle, of Washington township

The education of William H Ramer was secured in the district schools of Washington township, which he attended during the winter months, and, being the eldest of his parents' children, when his father died the management of the home place and the care of the family devolved upon him, although at that time he was but eighteen years of age Thoroughly trained in farm work, industrious persevering and ambitious, he was able to take up the work of the home place where his father had left it and his subsequent success has resulted from constant and industrious labor, well directed He has a tract of 120 acres, on which he raises excellent crops, and here he has made numerous improvements of a modern character His buildings are substantial, his stock sleek and well-fed, and his farming implements of the most modern manufacture, and the entire appearance of the property gives eloquent evidence that he is a practical and scientific agriculturist

On June 3, 1896, Mr Ramer was married to Miss Jennie Minnick, a daughter of John H and Lillis (Doud) Minnick, of Washington township, and two children have been born to this union Blanche M, who is a high school student, and Edgar M, who is in the seventh grade school Mr Ramer has taken a keen and intelligent interest in political affairs, and in 1908 was elected assessor of Washington township, a position which he continues to fill to the entire satisfaction of all concerned He is a member of the I O O F, Walton lodge, No 314 and he is a past grand With Mis Ramer, he attends the Presbyterian church, in the work of which all the members of the family are very active The beautiful estate of Mr and Mrs Ramer is known as "Walnut Dell Stock Farm"

JASPER NEWTON NEFF, M D. Belonging to a family that has made Cass county its home for upwards of three-quarters of a century, and members of which have, during this time, been identified with the various occupations, professions and industries to which this section of Indiana owes its importance, Dr Jasper Newton Neff, of Logansport, prominent physician and extensive land owner, holds a position of prestige in the business and professional life of his locality He has been a resident of Logansport since the fall of 1895, and while his large landed interests and the duties of his vocation have demanded the greater share of his attention, he has not been unmindful of the duties of citizenship, his public-spirit having been manifested on various occasions when the welfare of the city or its people has been at stake Dr. Neff was born on his father's farm in Deer Creek township, Cass county, Indiana, January 2, 1852, and is a son of Jacob and Henrietta (Berry) Neff, natives of Ohio His father was a son of Joseph and Polly (Sink) Neff, who came to Cass county from the Buckeye State in 1838, and during the rest of their lives lived in Deer Creek township. They became the parents of six children, namely: Jacob, Allen, Josiah, Frank, Alexander and Mary, all of whom are deceased Jacob Neff was still a lad when he accompanied his parents to Deer Creek township, and there he grew up and was married to Henrietta Henderson Berry, daughter of Henderson

Berry. Following their marriage they located on a farm in Deer Creek township, there spending the rest of their useful lives in the tilling of the soil They became the parents of four sons, all of whom were well educated and fitted for whatever positions they were called upon to fill, and all have reached honorable places in life, Joseph H. being a leading member of the bar of Logansport, Indiana, Dr. Jasper N, the well-known Logansport physician; Francis M, being a musician of distinguished ability, residing here in Logansport, and Dr Jacob L, having reached a recognized position among the medical practitioners of Logansport, Indiana

Until he was seventeen years of age Jasper N Neff worked as a farm hand in Cass county, during which time he attended the neighborhood school Subsequently he spent one year in the Lebanon (Ohio) Normal school, and was eighteen years of age when he passed the required examination necessary to secure a teacher's certificate. At that time he was placed in charge of a school in Deer Creek township, and during the next three years he divided his time between teaching this school and attending the normal While here he decided to enter the profession of medicine, and accordingly gave special attention to the study of anatomy, physiology and chemistry, and in 1876 graduated with honors at the College of Physicians and Surgeons, Indianapolis, where he received his degree of Doctor of Medicine At this institution the late Dr Robert N Todd, president of the college, acted as his preceptor, and in addition to his kind encouragement and assistance, gave him his personal attention during a severe spell of sickness, for which Dr Neff will ever hold his memory in grateful remembrance. After his graduation Dr Neff established himself in practice in Walton, Indiana, where he continued in the enjoyment of a large and representative clientele during the next twenty years During this time he had been a heavy investor in farming property, and through intelligent transactions and shrewd foresight his holdings had become so large and required so much attention, that it was his intention to retire from active practice, and with this end in view came to Logansport He has not been permitted, however, to leave the ranks of active practitioners, although he now confines himself to office practice and consultation He is widely known in professional and business activities of Logansport, and with his family enjoys the friendship of a wide circle of congenial friends, his home being a center of social refinement

In 1891, Dr Neff was married to Miss Lavina Flynn, who died in 1894, and in the following year he was married to Mrs Flora Bennett, daughter of Thomas Elwood Trueblood, for many years one of Howard county s most prominent and highly respected citizens

Dr John H Barnfield was born in Jersey Shore, Lycoming county, Pennsylvania, July 2, 1864, and is the son of William Nelson Barnfield, a Pennsylvania lumberman Dr Barnfield was reared in his native town, and after completing the course prescribed by the village schools became a student at Millersville state normal school He then took up the study of medicine under Dr J F McClure, of Watertown, Pennsylvania, and in 1883 entered Jefferson Medical College, from which he was duly graduated in 1886.

Dr Barnfield began the practice of his profession in Irvona, Pennsylvania, and while there was surgeon for the Witmer Land and Coal Company He remained in that place for three years, then became medical examiner in the relief department of the Pennsylvania Railway Company, serving in that capacity for four and a half years In June, 1894 he came to Logansport, and established himself in the general practice of medicine, and this city has represented the scene of his professional activities since that time In 1905 Dr Barnfield took a post-graduate course in the Chicago Polyclinic, thus further fortifying himself in the knowledge of his profession

Dr Barnfield is a Democrat in his politics He is a member of the Logansport Commercial Club, in which he is chairman of the executive committee He is a member of the Cass county and state medical societies, and of the American Medical Association

Dr Barnfield was married in 1894 to Miss Mae S Schlater, of Richmond, Indiana

IRA BLACKBURN A native citizen of Cass county, whose worth and character are material factors in the recent progress of this community, is Ira Blackburn, whose rural home is situated in Harrison township, an old place which has been in the family for many years Three generations of the Blackburn family have been identified with Cass county, and they have always been known as thrifty citizens, and worthy members of the community. In ancestry they are of English and French descent

Ira Blackburn was born in Harrison township, Cass county, January 26, 1874 His grandfather was James Blackburn, and his father was David Blackburn The latter, who is now a retired resident of Harrison township, married Susan Batty, a daughter of Thomas Batty David Blackburn, the father, was also born in Cass county, and his father, the grandfather of Ira, put up the first building that stood on the farm now occupied by the grandson This was in the pioneer days, when practically all the country was new, and the Blackburn family found their land in its virgin state, and have made practically all the improvements that have appeared thereon during the succeeding years

Ira Blackburn was reared in his native locality, attending the country schools and on attaining manhood became a partner with his father in the management of the home farm He and his father now conduct the homestead together, and make a very profitable business out of its cultivation Mr Ira Blackburn is owner of forty acres of his own situated opposite the old homestead On June 1, 1898, he married Miss Mattie A Herd, a daughter of John and Emma (Burton) Herd The three children born to their union are Blanche born May 22, 1901, June, born June 24, 1904. and Mae, born June 2, 1911.

JESSE W NEFF One of the representative farming men of Bethlehem township who is worthy of mention in this biographical and historical work by reason of his accomplishments as a tiller of the soil and one of the world's workers, is Jesse W Neff, a resident of this township since July, 1889 He was born on May 15, 1852, in Darke county, Ohio, and is the son of Alfred J and Nancy (Wilson) Neff His paternal and maternal grandparents were Wilson Neff and James Wilson, and his father's people were of German ancestry

Alfred J and Nancy (Wilson) Neff became the parents of seven children, four of whom are now deceased John V. died in infancy; Frank P died in 1871, Laura died in 1879, Ira W died in 1879 also. James L, Emma and Jesse W yet survive

Jesse W. Neff came to Cass county on July 15, 1889, from Miami county, where he had previously been located He settled on a small farm and devoted his time to the improvement of that place and to the acquiring of more land Today he and his wife have a fine place of one hundred and forty acres in an excellent state of cultivation, with comfortable buildings of every description, all new and modern, and the work of their own hands.

On June 27, 1888, Mr Neff was united in marriage with Miss Keren Harter, the daughter of John and Mary E (Kreider) Harter. She was born in Miami county, Indiana, December 16, 1860, and there reared Four children have been born to Mr and Mrs Neff, as follows: Ruth, who died at the age of three years, Leon H, born June 27, 1892, Paul V, born October 22, 1894, Jessie, born November 23, 1896, and Wayne B, born November 17, 1902

The family are members of the Presbyterian church, and Mr Neff is prominent in the local lodge of the Independent Order of Odd Fellows, which he joined at the age of twenty-one years, and has been faithful and true, and in which he has held many offices He is a Democrat and a leading citizen of his community In 1910 Mr Neff's father died, but his widowed mother still lives on the old home place in Miami county, where they located a number of years ago

LEMUEL POWELL, a pioneer farmer of Bethlehem township, was born in Jefferson county, Ohio, on October 24, 1834 He came to Cass county with his parents, Josiah and Margaret (Mugg) Powell, when he was two years old, and has resided continuously in the county since that early date. At that time Bethlehem township was a wilderness, with a cabin in a small clearing here and there, and with no schools or churches in the community Mr Powell has borne a worthy part in the development of the township and making of it what it is today, and is by reason of that fact deserving of an honorable mention in the pages of this history

Mr Powell was educated in the old log school house of his boyhood days, and acquired a fair education for his time He is a quiet, unassuming man of the strictest honesty and probity, and no man in the county bears a better reputation for uprightness of character and genuine moral worth than does Mr Powell Although he is small in stature, he makes up for this in the excess of mental and physical energy he has ever displayed, and which have redounded to the good of the community which has represented his home so many years With his wife he owns two hundred and fifty acres of fine land, all lying in Bethlehem township.

Mr Powell was married on February 7, 1864, to Sarah A. Roberts, who died on November 15, 1866, leaving one son, Choral G, born May 13, 1865 This son is now married, his marriage to Laura W. Douglass occurring on December 7, 1892, and they have a family of seven children

On December 5, 1872 Lemuel Powell married a second time, when Mary Martha Gray became his wife Three children were born to this latter union, as follows John V, born on September 5, 1874; Warren, born April 17, 1876, died July 10, 1892, being drowned accidentally, and Edna, born October 12, 1880 John V and Edna are still under the parental roof, and there care for their aged parents and the entire family are highly esteemed in Bethlehem township—the elder ones as worthy citizens who have helped to reclaim the district from a state of wilderness which existed when the white man made his first appearance in these parts in the early thirties, and the younger ones as worthy successors of their parents, who may be expected to do well their part in the further development of their native country Mrs Powell is a native of Jefferson township, Cass county, where she was born July 9, 1839 She is the youngest of six children and the only daughter born to James and Catharine (Duncan) Gray, and is the only survivor of the family She was educated in the common schools of the neighborhood and several terms walked two miles to attend the log cabin school, so well known at that time in that section of the county Mrs. Powell was a member of the Presbyterian church.

Mr Powell is a Republican politically and cast his first presidential vote for John Fremont, the first Republican candidate, and has voted for each Republican candidate since Mr. and Mrs Powell have two of the old parchment deeds executed March 30, 1837, that bear the signature of President Van Buren.

LEVI B HORN. The business of farming has occupied the best years of the life of Levi B Horn thus far, and he is known for one of the successful and well-to-do agricultural men of the township of Bethlehem, where many of the leading citizens of Cass county may be found devoting their energies to the tilling of the soil and enjoying to the fullest their free communion with Dame Nature in the pursuit of their calling. Levi B Horn, unlike many of his neighbors is not a native resident of the county, nor of the state He was born in Washington county, Pennsylvania, on September 12, 1851, and is the son of Thaddeus and Lina (Burson) Horn, his paternal grandfather being George Horn The Horns are of German ancestry, while the Bursons are of Scotch descent

Mr Thaddeus Horn did not receive any but the most meager common or district school education, but the business of life has kept his wits sharp and his mind has been one ever open to impressions and to expansion, so that his lack of schooling has been in a large measure overcome In 1852 Mr. Thaddeus Horn came to Bethlehem township and purchased the old John White farm from Joseph Sellers and for a few years he lived on the place and gave diligent attention to its cultivation. He later sold the farm to a Methodist minister of the name of Terrill, and he himself became identified, in a way, with sawmill work, where he continued for a year He then turned back to farming, and bought the Noah Martin farm, another well-known place in Bethlehem township, and the Henry Barnett place He later added to this by repeated purchases until today Levi Horn, his son, has a fine place of one hundred and sixty acres When Thaddeus Horn came into possession of the farm it was covered with a heavy growth of timber, the most of which has given place to clean

"FOREST GLEN HOME," RESIDENCE OF MR. AND MRS. ABIAH J. SHARTS

and smooth fields that are under the careful cultivation of their owner Levi Horn saw to most of the building work that has been carried on at the place, and has a number of commodious buildings of all descriptions On the whole, his enterprise has yielded a satisfactory income, and he has a home of which any man in the community might well be proud In addition to his farming interests he is also a stockholder in the First National Bank.

On April 2, 1874, Mr. Horn married Fannie, the daughter of Aaron and Jane (Cuthberson) Tilton Nine children have been born to them, of which number three are now deceased Those who live are named as follows Mary A, the wife of William Lemmon, Bertha E, the wife of R J Johnson, Franklin Y, married to Amy Dreutzer, Ada wedded Kirk Wells, Flora and Burson The deceased children were named Amy, Carrie and Fannie

The family are members of the Presbyterian church, in which Mr Horn has been an elder for forty years His position in the community is wholly consistent with his place in the church, and he is known as one of the most estimable and honorable men in the township Fraternally he is a member of the Masonic order, belonging to Orient Lodge No. 272 The daughters, Bertha, Ada and Flora, are members of the Eastern Star The present beautiful homestead of Mr and Mrs Horn is known as "The Aberdeen Stock Farm," as Mr Horn is a breeder of the registered Aberdeen cattle, which are known by cattle breeders throughout the United States

ABIAH J. SHARTS In naming the representative farmers of Cass county, any work would be incomplete that did not give a sketch of the career of Abiah J Sharts, of Tipton township, located on a farm of one hundred and sixty acres on the Anoka road, about one-half mile east of Anoka Mr Sharts was born October 24, 1845 in Montgomery county Ohio and is a son of George P and Frances (Bear) Sharts His parents were natives of Maryland, born in the vicinity of Hagerstown, from whence they moved to Frederick county, Maryland, and later to Montgomery county, Ohio In 1849 they came to Tipton township, Cass county, Indiana, settling first on the farm now occupied by N B Richinson, and lived in a little log house until this primitive dwelling was replaced by one more modern in character A great deal of the land was covered with a heavy growth of timber, which was cleared by Mr Sharts and his sons, and here he continued to reside during the remainder of his life, his death occurring in 1853, when he was fifty-two years of age, while his wife passed away in 1875, being seventy-two years old. From a small beginning they became wealthy citizens of their community, while their standing among their neighbors was that of honest, God-fearing people who always endeavored to live up to the dictates of their conscience They were the parents of the following children Mary M and Rose Ann, who are deceased, Elizabeth, also deceased, Mrs Catherine Hahn, Mrs Jane P Phillips, who died January 7, 1913, Abraham and John, who are both deceased; George P, an agriculturist of Tipton township, William O, who is deceased, A J and Carolina Lucas, deceased

Abiah J Sharts received his education in the old Wilson district school, a log building which was standing until within recent years, although it had not been used for a long period He was only eight years of age when his father died, and this necessarily cut his schooling off before it was completed, as his services were needed to help in the work of the homestead He was so engaged when the Civil war broke over the country, and when not yet eighteen years old, in June, 1863, enlisted for service in the Union army, as a private of Company F, One Hundred and Sixteenth Regiment, Indiana Volunteer Infantry Capt Sangford C Thomas, Army of the Cumberland He was mustered in at Indianapolis, and from there went with his command to Lafayette, Indiana, and later to Detroit, Michigan, where he was in camp until sent to Cleveland, Ohio Later he was transferred to Camp Nelson, Kentucky, subsequently participating in the battle of Knoxville During the greater part of his services he was under General Burnside, doing guard duty at Cumberland Gap, Greenville and Tazewell, Tennessee He served until March, 1864 when he was mustered out of the service at Lafayette, Indiana, and returned to the pursuits of peace On returning home, he once more took charge of the farm, which he operated until 1879, and then removed to his present property, a tract of one hundred and sixty acres, which he has brought to a high state of cultivation and improved with substantial buildings and other modern improvements He is known as an excellent agriculturist with a thorough knowledge of all the details of his vocation, and as a business man whose word is as good as his bond He belongs to the Independent Order of Odd Fellows at Anoka, Indiana, was a member of the Grand Army of the Republic, and has many friends in both With his family, he attends the United Brethren church where for years he has been a liberal supporter of its movements

On October 10, 1867, Mr Sharts was married to Miss Ellen Alice Wilson, and to this union there have been born six children Harry who is deceased, Benjamin F, graduated from the common schools and is at present cashier of the City State Bank of Logansport, Indiana He taught two terms of school in Tipton and one in Washington township He belongs to the Masons, and both he and his wife are members of the Presbyterian church He married Pearl McManus and has two children, Victor and Robert Elmer E, graduated from the common schools and spent one term in Logansport Business College. He married for his first wife Mamie Richinson, and had one child, Truman, he married a second time and by this marriage has two children Thomas and Alice Blanche M, graduated from the public schools and from the business college and is a finished stenographer She is the wife of George D DeYoe, and they are residents of Chicago Walter, deceased Charles, a resident of Tipton township and one of the young progressive farmers, was born on the farm on which his father originally came on many years ago, and has here resided all of his life He is now the manager of his father's property, and is known as one of Tipton township's good, practical young agriculturists He resides in a modern residence erected by his father He graduated from the public schools and spent one year in high school He wedded Miss Edith Mason, and they have two little children Paul and Margaret Mr and Mrs Sharts may well be proud of their children, as they all hold high places in the esteem of the people who know them

Mrs Sharts is a native of Cass county, Indiana, born December 26, 1848, and she is the fourth in a family of twelve children, five sons and seven daughters, born to Andrew and Eleanor (Tucker) Wilson, and there are five of the children of the Wilson family still living, and all are residents of Indiana, except Mrs Carrie Stukey, of Los Angeles, California, and Harry G Wilson, a resident of Chicago Mrs Sharts was reared and educated in her native county She has worthily filled her place as wife and mother in the building up of their beautiful home in Tipton township which is known as "Forest Glen Home" and it is the abode of hospitality Mr and Mrs Sharts have a fine Great Western five-passenger touring car, and they enjoy life

JOHN W REDD Continued hard work and persistent effort have won for John W Redd a degree of prosperity he might never otherwise have attained and he has to thank his own sturdy energy for his present success, rather than any outside agency He was born on April 7, 1835, at Battle Ground, Indiana, and is the son of William and Martha (Shigley) Redd, the people of the latter being of German descent The father was a son of Joseph Redd, a native Pennsylvanian, and was born in Washington county, that state He was yet very young when he left his native state and moved to the Pan Handle in Virginia, where he engaged in the operating of a distillery, going thence to Wayne county, Ohio, and from there to Tippecanoe, Indiana Bethlehem township in Cass county, saw him next, and it was in the year 1838 that he arrived here and settled down on a farm

Thus it was that William Redd came to be reared in Bethlehem township, and here he has passed practically all his life He was reared amid the quiet country scenes peculiar to the time, attended the country schools at intervals, and was well taught in the business of farming In due time he chose a wife, who in her maiden days was Mary Ann McCarthy, the daughter of Berryman McCarthy, who in his young manhood was shot and killed while on his way to the house of a friend, being mistaken for a deer by a careless hunter, John Rush by name The mother of Mrs Redd in her maiden days was Phoebe Marsh, and she and her family were residents of Fulton county Four children have been born to Mr and Mrs Redd, as follows William B, the eldest, married Lou Burrows, Phoebe E married Charles White, Ida F, married R E Merritt, and Joseph A, married Dollie Livingston

Mr Redd has lived on his present farm since 1862, and with the passing years many goodly improvements have found place upon the premises, so that he farm is one of the finest in Bethlehem township today He has not always been a landed proprietor, as one might say, and the first forty-five acres of land he acquired caused him much hardship and many hours of honest toil But to toil he has never been a stranger, and work is no hardship to one of his energetic and wholesome nature, so that with the years that have gone, he has been able to add bit by bit to his place until it is now represented by two hundred and eighteen acres of well cultivated lands The first thirteen years of his residence here was marked by his occupancy of the log cabin home that stood upon the place when it came into his possession, and which has later given place to the present commodious dwelling

Mr Redd is a Methodist and politically he is of the Progressive party He has taken a lively interest in the political activities of his community, and is known for a man of excellent qualities of citizenship

ANDERSON B STANTON came to Cass county, Indiana, from Indianapolis, in 1874, thus having lived here for thirty-nine years He was born in Shelby county, Indiana, on December 13, 1843, and was the son of Eli and Eunice (Barnard) Stanton Eli Stanton followed farming through the greater part of his life He was a pioneer of Shelby county, having located there when the district was practically all dense woods He was a Quaker, reared in that rugged and simple faith by his parents, and his life exemplified in every way the training he had received in the faith His faithful wife died in March, 1850, and he later married Elizabeth Gardner, a cousin of his first wife She, like his earlier helpmate, was a Quaker Three children were born of this second marriage In 1864 he sold his place and returned to Union county, Indiana, where he had lived previous to his Shelby county experience, and there he passed the remainder of his life, death claiming him in 1895

Anderson B Stanton, the immediate subject of this somewhat brief review, was reared in a Quaker home and under the strict influences which characterize a home in which that sturdy old religion predominates Plenty of hard work was provided for him in the work of the farm, and three months schooling in each year constituted his educational privileges When he had attained his majority, he still continued on the home place with his father When he was twenty-three years old he found himself in debt to the amount of forty dollars, and he left home and hired out as a farm hand, in order to secure the money to pay his obligations He soon found work more remunerative and also more suited to him, and for a number of years was employed by the Singer Manufacturing Company as general agent in Indiana and Illinois In the latter part of 1874 he opened a music store in Logansport, and since that time he has continued to make his home in this city He continued in the music store until the year 1877, when he sold the place, and has since been engaged in farming and in handling stock He owns a fine farm of four hundred and three acres in Washington township, which he oversees, and is known as one of the most successful men in an agricultural way in the county—a fact no doubt due in large measure to his thorough early training in farming in his boyhood home

Mr Stanton is a Republican in politics and a member of the Christian church since he was twenty-eight years old He was married on November 25, 1875, to Priscilla A Justice, and they are the parents of three children, as follows Nellie the wife of George Kistler James J, a practicing physician of Logansport, of whom more extended mention is made elsewhere in this work, and Elizabeth Cady Stanton

DR. JAMES J. STANTON was born in Logansport, Indiana, on July 9, 1880, a son of Anderson B. and Priscilla A. (Justice) Stanton, and the grandson of Eli and Eunice (Barnard) Stanton, concerning these ancestors appropriate mention being made in the sketch devoted to Anderson B. Stanton, in other pages of this work so that further details with regard to the parentage of Dr. Stanton are superfluous at this juncture.

Dr. Stanton was reared on his father's farm, to a large extent, and he was an attendant of the schools of Logansport during the winter seasons. In 1899 and 1900 he was a student at Hiram College, in Hiram, Ohio, and in September, 1901, entered Jefferson Medical College, at Philadelphia, Pennsylvania, from which he was duly graduated on June 2, 1905. For one year following his graduation he was occupied as house physician at McKeesport (Pa.) hospital, and on September 1, 1906 the young doctor opened an office in Logansport. He has since continued here in active practice. He conducts a general practice, with special attention to surgery, and in the years that he has been identified with the professional life of Logansport, he has acquired a pleasing reputation for efficiency and progressiveness which makes his future success a well assured fact.

Dr. Stanton is a member of the county and state medical societies, and fraternally is affiliated with the Masonic order and the Benevolent and Protective Order of Elks. He also retains membership in the Nu Sigma Nu, his college fraternity.

The doctor was united in marriage with Miss Jean Murray, of Logansport, on June 22, 1910.

JOB SMITH. It requires very few words to tell of hopeful pioneers settling in a forest and with energy attacking the subjugation of the land and developing cultivated and productive farms thereby, but this outline is but a superficial covering for some of the most trying experiences through which men and women have bravely and triumphantly passed and which deserve to be remembered. The first log cabin of the Smith family in Indiana, was built in 1836, in Bethlehem township, Cass county, after a space had been cleared, by William R. Smith, on his timbered tract of 240 acres, to which he and his wife had come after weeks of tedious travel from an eastern state. In all probability it was but poor protection at first against the elements and possibly the Indians and wild creatures of the forest, but its comforts were increased as time went on, family life developed and expanded, and within its walls were born and reared the three children of the family. The Smiths were pioneers in every sense of the word, the ancestry belonging to Scotland, and as typical of that land their sturdy independence and moral qualities made them leaders and organizers of the stable institutions and promoters of good government in the section which they had selected as their home. Among the worthy representatives of this family is found Job Smith, of Bethlehem township, who for many years was engaged in farming here, and who still resides in this township. Mr. Smith was born October 28, 1841, in a log cabin on the farm which he now owns, and is a son of William R. and Amanda F. (Simpson) Smith, and a grandson of Job Smith and James Simpson. His parents were natives of New Jersey, and were married in Ohio, in which state they lived for about twelve years, and then, in 1836, made their entrance into Indiana. They continued to be residents of Cass county until their deaths and were numbered among their township's substantial and highly respected people. They had four children, namely: Job, James, who married Amanda Campbell, Rachael, who married Joseph Champ, and Hannah who died at the age of five years.

Job Smith received only meager educational advantages in his youth, the district school being two miles from his home and the school term lasting only three months in the winter, but he was an intelligent and ambitious youth, made the most of his opportunities, and managed to gain a good education. On completing his studies, he was engaged in teaching for two years, and then turned his attention to farming, which occupied his attention throughout the balance of his active career. He is now the owner of 133 acres of well-cultivated land, on which he erected all of the present substantial buildings, and this is known as one of the valuable properties of his township. For the past eight years he has lived a retired life, having been afflicted with blindness. He has been a life-long member of Spring Creek Christian church, of which he was deacon for many years. Mr. Smith is highly regarded in his locality, being known as a kind neighbor, an honorable business man, and one who has always been true to his friendships.

On January 16, 1868, Mr. Smith was married in Miami county, Indiana, to Miss Emmeline Code, daughter of Powell and Lydia (Carlisle) Code, the former of whom died in 1878 and the latter in February, 1904. Mrs. Smith's parents came to Indiana from New York state and settled in Miami county at a very early date, first erecting a log cabin and later replacing it with a more modern structure. They were the parents of six children as follows: Christopher, who married Sallie Murden; John, who married Caroline Charles; Ira, who remained single and died at the age of thirty-nine years; Angeline, who married James Hallock; Josephine who married Henry Lewis; and Emmeline. Mr. and Mrs. Smith have had the following children: Omar T., born February 8, 1869, who married Daisy Lawrence; Nora E., born February 8, 1872; Ego born January 14, 1875; Milo J. born February 19, 1877; Laurie, born March 17, 1880, who married Edith White; and Elmer born August 31, 1884, who died in July, 1908, and Bernice B November 7, 1886.

GEORGE W. CONRAD. Many of the leading agriculturists of Cass county are residing on the farms on which they were born and which in their youth, they helped to clear from the virgin growth of timber. Life-long experience has given them a thorough knowledge of soil and climatic conditions, and this has aided them materially in gaining the position of prestige that they now hold. In this class stands George W. Conrad, of Bethlehem township, experienced farmer and well-informed citizen, whose entire career has been spent within the limits of Cass county, where he has gained and maintained the esteem of his fellow-citizens through strict integrity and honorable dealings. Mr. Conrad was born on his present property, a part of the old Conrad homestead February 8, 1867, and is a son of Stephen G. and Margaret (Cowel)

Conrad His grandfather, David H. Conrad, was born in Pennsylvania, of German descent, and came to Indiana in 1840, locating in Cass county, where he continued to be engaged in agricultural pursuits up the time of his death. Stephen G. Conrad was born in Washington county, Pennsylvania, and was a young man when he accompanied his parents to Indiana, here assisting his father in the work of the home farm until the outbreak of the Civil war, when he enlisted for service in the Union army as a member of Company F, Indiana Volunteer Cavalry. On his return from the war, he resumed his agricultural operations in which he was employed during the remainder of his active career.

George W. Conrad received a district school education, and was reared to the occupation of agriculturist, which has been his vocation throughout life. In his boyhood and youth he worked so faithfully for his father, that on attaining his majority he was given eighty-five acres of land, and to this he has continued to add from time to time, as his finances have permitted, until now he is the owner of 210 acres. The present buildings were all erected by Mr. Conrad and his father, but have been greatly improved during the son's residence here, and the land, heavily wooded at one time, is now all under the plow and yields abundant crops. Mr. Conrad has kept abreast of the times, and takes advantage of all the improvements and inventions which have been brought about by invention and discovery. He has not entered politics except as a voter for Democratic principles and policies but has never failed to support movements for good government, and those measures which affect his township or its people have always had his intelligent attention. With his family, he attends the Methodist church, where for some years he has held an official position.

On September 6, 1890, Mr. Conrad was married to Miss Dora M. Bray, of Fulton county, Indiana, and they have had six children as follows: Russell L., Harry N., Thelma B., Ethel G., Edith M. and Ida Pearl. The members of the family are highly esteemed in the community where the name has stood for integrity and probity for nearly three-quarters of a century. The pretty homestead of Mr. and Mrs. Conrad is known as "Walnut Glenn Homestead."

IRA B. MAUDLIN is one of the well established and prosperous farming men of Bethlehem township, where he has made his home for many years—practically since his infancy, for the old home of his parents is located in this township, where they located in 1864. Farming life has always been his portion, and in it he has demonstrated a measure of ability and capability sufficient to win him a place among the more prominent men of his community.

Born in Kewanee Fulton county, this state, Ira B. Maudlin is the son of Benjamin and Abigail (Woolf) Maudlin who were the son and daughter of Edwin Maudlin and Jonas Woolf. They came to Bethlehem township in 1864 and here the father ended his days, death claiming him in 1898. The mother yet lives, and is a member of the household of her son, Ira B. of this review and has reached the age of eighty-two years. The old homestead of the Maudlin family is located one mile south of Fletcher's lake in this township, where the father first acquired the ownership of one hundred and twenty acres of land and built a log house for the shelter of his young family The land was covered with a dense growth of timber, which the passing years saw give place to rolling fields that enriched their owner in a comfortable degree The old log house still stands there, as a monument to the industry of its builder Four children were born to these parents—two sons and two daughters Amos, the eldest son, was twice married, first to Irene Beattie, and later to a Mrs Rosa Landis Marguerite married George Hollenback, and Hannah died about 1880

Up to the age of twenty-seven years Ira B Maudlin remained at home, and performed his share of the work of the home place As a boy he received certain advantages of schooling somewhat limited it is true, but as good as the average country youth of his day received, and he has made good use of such learning as he did acquire in those early days He was born on January 29 1863 just prior to the time when his parents moved to their Bethlehem township farm, so that his earliest recollections begin with that old place May 29, 1889, Mr Maudlin was married, and he settled then on his first independently operated farm This was a place of seventy-five acres, and adjoined his father's place It boasted a small frame house, which he improved from time to time and built on as occasion made necessary and is today a fine old farm house He added to his land holdings until he had a total acreage of one hundred and fifteen acres, and there he remained until 1911, when he removed to his present fine place of one hundred and five acres The farm is under an excellent state of cultivation has fine new buildings, and is in every way suited to the convenience and wishes of the family. May 29 1889, Mr Maudlin married Miss Ida Frushour the daughter of George and Charlotte (Rowan) Frushour, and they have one son, George B, who was born on November 19, 1890 He received his diploma from the public schools in 1906 and then entered the Media High School of Bethlehem township for two years In 1908 he entered the literary and commercial department of the Marion Normal at Marion, Indiana, for one term and then was a student in the Logansport High School He is a practical agriculturist and assists his father on the place Mrs Maudlin is a native of Cass county, born May 23, 1862 and reared and educated in her native county Mr Maudlin erected a lovely home in 1911, which is heated by furnace, has acetylene light and is finished in hardwood The homestead is known as "Oak Lawn "

Mr Maudlin has long been a prominent man in his township and has been identified with much of its public life He was a trustee of his township from 1904 to 1908 and gave excellent service in that office. He and wife are members of the Methodist Episcopal church at Fletcher's Lake, and he has long been a trustee and a steward of the church

DAVID N JAMESON has been a resident of Cass county since 1853 in which year he migrated from his native state, Ohio, and settled in Clay township He was a boy of twelve at that time, and since then he has been identified with the history of this part of the county, in a more or less prominent and significant manner Though he began his independent career without other assets than his native ability and determination, he is today well established in a worldly way, and is one of the comfortably situated farming men of Bethlehem township

Born in Ashland county, Ohio, on March 27, 1841, David N Jameson is the son of John and Minerva (Nickols) Jameson The father, John Jameson, was the son of Albertus Jameson, and the family was long identified with the history of Ohio in the years of her earliest growth and development The mother of the subject was born in Ashland county, Ohio, and she died when her son, David, was a small boy The father died in March, 1857 He came to Cass county in 1853, bringing his family with him, and settling in Clay township, and there he spent the remainder of his life

John Jameson was married three times and by his marriage to Miss Minerva Nickols there were three children born, but David N, the subject, is the only child living of the three different marriages, and he was the oldest of the three born

When David N Jameson was fifteen years old he went to live with an older brother, and he remained there for five years, or until the outbreak of the Rebellion With the first intimation of war, he enlisted in the army and served until 1863 when he was honorably discharged Three months of his time he was with the Ninth Indiana, the remainder of his period of service being spent in the Twenty-ninth Indiana Regiment Following his return from the war April 16, 1863, Mr Jameson married Mary E Metsker, the daughter of David and Margaret (Edgar) Metsker, who with his wife died in the year 1849 After the marriage of Mr Jameson, he settled in Cass county on his present farm, and here he has since resided carrying on an active agricultural business in the community, and his seventy-five acres of fine land is regarded as among the best in the county The place, as it stands today, represents years of the most arduous toil with much of disappointment, as well as much of prosperity and happiness as the reward of his efforts He built primitive log cabin buildings on the place where he first took possession, and with the passing of time the farm took on a prosperous and well-kept appearance that spoke well for the industry and effort of its owner

Two children were born to Mr and Mrs Jameson The eldest Samuel Edgar, died in 1892, when he was thirty years of age The other, John W, married Gertrude Fergus, and they have seven children, named as follows· Edith, Charles, Glenn, George, John L, Frank and Louise All this fine little family are living, and their grandparents find much pleasure in the contemplation of their growth and development Mrs Jameson is a native of Cass county, born September 21 1842, and she was the eldest of four children, one son and three daughters born to David and Margaret (Edgar) Metsker, but is the only survivor of that family She was educated in the common schools Mr Jameson has been a teacher in the Sunday school for twenty years also superintendent

The family are members of the Presbyterian church, and Mr Jameson is a member of the Grand Army of the Republic The pretty homestead of Mr and Mrs Jameson is known as "The Sunny Crest Grange"

JAMES CHENEY Among the notable men whose careers were in large part spent in Cass county, and the county-claims for the honor and distinction of its citizenship, the late James Cheney was one of the most successful as a banker and business man He came to Cass county before the war and was for many years identified with financial affairs of such importance that he had more than local prominence, and was a well known figure in the banking circles of New York city His death occurred at Fort Wayne, Indiana December 13 1903, and his remains now rest in the Logansport cemetery

James Cheney was born in Sutton, Vermont December 15, 1817, and was of English and New England stock His parents were Roswell and Abigail (Willard) Cheney His mother was a relative of Frances E Willard The father was a contractor in Vermont and after finishing his common school education, James Cheney went into the same business and assisted his father for a number of years He left New England when a young man and in 1840 located in Toledo Ohio, and in 1856 came to Cass county

The late James Cheney organized at Logansport one of the branches of the old Indiana State Bank and served as cashier of the local institution From that time until his death he was closely identified with the larger interests of financial and business affairs In 1859 he engaged with Mr Uhl in the milling business and subsequently was in the real estate business He removed from Cass county in 1871 to New York city, where he was known as a banker and in the stock and bond business He held a seat for a number of years on the New York Stock Exchange and was connected with the National City Bank and with the Farmer's Loan and Trust Company A fact of his business career which is specially noteworthy is that he was one of the organizers and builders of the first Atlantic cables during the decade of the fifties

The late Mr Cheney was affiliated with the Masonic order, and his church was the Presbyterian On May 1, 1842, he married Miss Nancy B Evans of Defiance county, Ohio where she was the first white child born Her father was Pierce Evans The children of the late James Cheney and wife, three daughters and one son, are mentioned as follows Mrs Alice Knight of Fort Wayne, Mrs Helen Kimberly, of Wisconsin Mrs Mary C Nelson in Logansport, and Willard Roswell Cheney of California

HENRY S MURDOCK, of Cass county, has had a more varied career than usually falls to the lot of the average man If the story of his life was properly written, it alone would make an interesting volume of reading Mr Murdock was born December 10, 1835, at Clinton, Michigan, and is the only survivor of a family of six children born to Tilson and Fannie (Blossom) Murdock, who were natives of Vermont, and of Scotch ancestry The father was a farmer, but for the most part, worked at carpentering He moved to Clinton, Michigan, at a time when the country was in a most primitive condition, and there passed the remainder of his days

The boyhood of Henry S Murdock was passed in a manner not unusual in those days, and in the course of his early years acquired the rudiments of an education in the district schools of his native community When old enough to begin to work, he secured a place clerk-

ing in a general store at Clinton, and was there employed for several years. His mother and married sisters having removed to Logansport in the intervening years, Mr. Murdock in 1853 came to this city, the canal furnishing his mode of travel from Toledo. Here he began clerking in the store of Thomas Stevenson his brother-in-law a general stock of goods being on hand at this place, including linsey-woolsey, delaine, calico, ginghams and all the required dry goods staples common to the times, as well as complete lines in other branches. About the year 1856 he began clerking for his brother Andrew J. Murdock who had embarked in a merchandise business at the corner of Fourth street and Broadway, but in 1860, in partnership with Joseph McGaughey, he began in the general dry goods business for himself. When he left for the war a brother-in-law, Jacob H. Hicks, took his place in the firm, with the understanding that on Murdock's return he was to pay simple interest on invoice. This arrangement was scrupulously carried out. In August, 1862 he enlisted in the Seventy-third Regiment Indiana Infantry and the rendezvous was at South Bend. He was made orderly sergeant. They left there August 1862, and went to Kentucky. For a time his command was stationed in Kentucky and Tennessee, but the first real engagement in which he participated was the battle of Stone river. Following this he became a part of Colonel Straight's command, which steamed down the Cumberland river to the Ohio river, thence to Paducah where the brigade was provisioned, and from there to Eastport, Mississippi, via the Tennessee river. Here the command disembarked and were deployed as cavalry to resist the rebel general, Forrest, who was threatening to break through. The history of the capture, imprisonment and escape of Colonel Straight has been told in history and story. Mr. Murdock was captured May 3 1863, he was incarcerated first in Libby prison, where he was relieved of all his valuables and where he remained for one year. He was then confined in another prison across the river for a short time, after which he was taken to Macon, Georgia and from there to Charleston South Carolina. At this place he was in three different prisons, and at one time was exposed to the fire of Federal gunboats at Morris Island three miles distant. From Charleston he was taken to an open camp at Columbia, and while here succeeded in making good his escape in December, 1864. By traveling at night and "laying up" in the daytime, getting food from negroes and directions from the few loyal men he encountered he succeeded in getting two hundred miles near the Union lines, but was finally recaptured near Pickens North Carolina courthouse taken back to Columbia Camp—then taken to Wilmington, North Carolina where he was exchanged in March 1865. After a brief visit home, he rejoined his command in Northern Alabama but the war by this time was virtually at end, and until his final discharge in July, 1865, with the rank of First Lieutenant, he was employed at guard duty.

Following the close of the war Mr. Murdock resumed merchandising in Logansport, with his brother, Andrew J., as a partner, thus continuing for nineteen years. Andrew J. Murdock then became president of the First National Bank, and Henry S. Murdock continued in the merchandise business until 1900, since when his time and attention have been occupied in looking after his private property interests.

Such, in brief, is the career of Henry S Murdock Much could be said of intense interest to embellish these plain statements, but lack of space prevents

In 1868 Mr Murdock was married to Miss Emma Woods, who died in 1870, leaving one son, Harry W Murdock, of Lockport, New York In 1874 at Des Moines, Iowa, Mr Murdock married Theodosia Owens, who died in 1900, leaving four sons William O, Karl F, Charles E and J Fred

Mr Murdock is a Republican and although one of the party's staunch followers he has never sought office. He is also a member of the Grand Army of the Republic

JAMES McTAGGERT was born in County Tyrone Ireland, August 15, 1824, and was one in a family of five sons and three daughters born to John and Rose (McGovern) McTaggert The father, John McTaggert, was a teacher, land agent and collector, and his children received rather better than average educational advantages James McTaggert passed his youthful days at home and while a young man he spent a year in Scotland, working at whatever honest employment he might turn his hand to, and returning to his home in Ireland in 1847 The unhappy conditions existing then in Ireland caused him to turn to America as a place where he might prosper better than in his native land, and the winter of 1847 found him aboard a sailing vessel bound for New York, and after a journey of seven weeks he landed in America It chanced that aboard the vessel were some of his Irish acquaintances who were bound for Logansport, Indiana, and they induced him to accompany them to that point, a decision he was not slow in arriving at, as he had set sail with no objective point in mind, other than that he intended to come to America They made the trip from New York by Hudson river to Albany, thence by canal to Buffalo, by lake to Toledo, and from that place down the Erie canal to Logansport The spring of 1848 found the little party from Ireland arriving at Logansport, and during a part of the summer ensuing Mr McTaggert was occupied at farm work, receiving a stipend of fifty cents per day He found employment for a time in helping to build the old seminary, after which he became a canal boat captain He was industrious and ambitious, and he frugally saved every possible penny from his earnings until he was able to buy a horse and cart With this capital he began doing contract work, the excavating of cellars and basements being his line of work From that he branched out into street contracting, and from time to time added new ventures to his enterprise Mr McTaggert built the macadam work on Fourth street between Market and Broadway, and this was the first macadamized street in Logansport Among other contract jobs which he handled, was the building of a section of the Pennsylvania Railroad In 1856 Mr McTaggert gave up contracting and turned his attention to the grocery business, locating at the corner of Fourth street and Broadway He owned the property where his store was located and here he continued in a thriving grocery business until 1871, when he sold the store, and in 1872 engaged in the retail clothing business on Market street In 1882 he retired from active business pursuits, and he died on April 28, 1886

It is a significant fact that, despite his early hardships and the slenderness of his resources when he set sail for America, Mr McTaggert was able to build up a business in various lines, that permitted him to be accounted a fairly wealthy man when he died. Every success he met with in his business career came as the direct result of his well placed efforts and the sturdy determination with which he went about every business project he took in hand. He was always a hard working man, and he had the advantage of knowing the value of a dollar to the last penny. His means, as they were accumulated with the passing years, were carefully and wisely invested, and he died in comfortable, if not indeed, affluent circumstances. After he had become established in business here, Mr McTaggert saved money with which to bring his parents and others of the family from Ireland, and in February, 1851, he married Sarah Donahoe, a daughter of James and Rose Donahoe, of County Tyrone, Ireland. They became the parents of eight children, three of which number died in infancy. The remaining five were Catharine A, the wife of James McGourty, Sarah C, now Mrs John McGreery, Rose, John Joseph, who died when twenty-eight years of age, Mary J, the wife of Richard McGreevy. The mother died on June 20, 1908. She, like her husband, was a devout member of the Roman Catholic church all her life.

Mr McTaggert was a Democrat in his political convictions, and served in the city council with credit to himself and to the good of the city in 1868 he was the nominee of his party for the office of county treasurer, but was defeated by Dr Schultz by the narrow margin of 86 votes. Though not an office holder to any extent, he was a citizen of sterling worth always interested in the good of the community, and bearing his full share of the civic burdens.

FINIS E FOUTS For the past eighteen years, Finis E Fouts has been engaged in farming and stock raising operations on his present farm, a well cultivated tract located on the Kokomo road in Deer Creek township. During this period he has established a reputation for integrity and honorable dealing, and is now accounted a worthy representative of one of the honored pioneer families of Cass county that have been identified with the progress and development of this section of the State since an early epoch in Indiana's history. Mr Fouts was born on his father's farm in Cass county, November 21, 1866, and is a son of Solomon and Margaret (Bridge) Fouts. His father, who, with Mr Neff, shared the distinction of being the first two white children born in Montgomery county, Indiana, came to Cass county in 1834, and here spent the remainder of his life, accumulating a handsome competency and attaining a high position in the esteem and regard of his fellow-citizens.

Finis E Fouts was given the advantages of a good education, first attending the old Runaway school in Deer Creek township, later going to the district schools in Carroll county, and finally, in 1894, entering Purdue University, where he took a course in agriculture and mechanical engineering. In the meantime, he had spent his vacations in working upon the home farm, thus getting practical experience in the vocation which he intended to make his life work, and eventually, well equipped, embarked upon a career of his own. Mr Fouts came to his present property in 1895, and here he has met with unqualified success. His land, brought to a high state of cultivation, yields him a golden tribute in return for the labor and care he bestows upon it. All of the machinery and buildings on the place are of the most modern construction, and indicate the owner to be a most progressive and enterprising farmer, and such is the reputation he bears throughout the community. In addition to general farming, he also carries on stock raising, and his business is so carefully and systematically managed that he has won a high degree of prosperity, and at the same time has gained and retained the respect and confidence of those with whom he has had business transactions. He takes a pardonable degree of pride in what he has accomplished, in that it has been won through his own unaided efforts.

On October 29, 1891, Mr. Fouts was married first to Miss Nellie M. Pottenger, daughter of Thomas and Hannah (Sater) Pottenger, and to this union there were born five children, namely: Glenn P., Elda, Marvin, Rufus and Laura. His second marriage took place July 6, 1911, when he was married to Mrs. Louanna (Kitchell) Shanks, daughter of Daniel Kitchell and widow of the late Frank H. Shanks, and this union has been blessed by the birth of one daughter Margaret. By her first marriage, Mrs. Fouts had three children Carol E., Ellen C. and Frank J. Mr. and Mrs. Fouts are members of the Presbyterian church, and have been liberal in their support of religious and charitable movements.

GEORGE DAVIS was among the earliest pioneers of Cass county. His parents were Virginians and were of Welsh ancestry. He married Katherine Miller and settled at Richmond, Indiana, at a time when the Indians were more numerous than the whites. He was a carpenter by trade, although he followed farming for the most part throughout his life. In the late fall of 1834 together with his family, he came to Cass county, a pair of cows hitched to his wagon being the means of transportation, the cows doing double duty in that they provided food for the children, as well as taking the place of horses or oxen. Upon their arrival at Eel river, they were compelled to have the cows shod in order that they might cross upon the ice. They located on one hundred and sixty acres of land on section 19, in Jefferson township, half of which was pre-empted from the government, and here they began clearing, grubbing and farming. Mr. Davis also worked at his trade, and many of the log cabins and old fashioned log barns were designed and built by him.

Mr. Davis was a soldier of the war of 1812, and served in all of General Harrison's campaigns. His father, Joseph Davis, assisted the Colonies in their struggle for independence and he was a participant in some of the great battles of the Revolutionary war. To George Davis and his wife six sons and three daughters were born, three of the sons serving in the war with Mexico. George Davis was in many ways a unique character. He abhorred the liquor traffic and many times had difficulty in getting his crops harvested because of his unwillingness to provide whiskey for the farm "hands." He was a member of the Methodist Episcopal church at Burnettsville, which he helped to organize, and of which he was an official for years. He died in 1840.

Richard Pedrick Davis was the youngest of the sons of George Davis. He was born at Richmond, Indiana, in 1828, came with his parents to Cass county when he was six years old and as a boy assisted with the work of the home farm. His chief characteristic was his untiring energy. He once worked for two weeks to get enough money to buy an axe. His opportunities for education was extremely limited, but being a keen observer and possessed of an unusual fund of good, practical sense, he was able in later years to supply in a measure the training which his early years lacked. Along in the early history of the Burnettsville Normal School he attended that institution for three years, after which he taught school for several terms. His remuneration at one school was $25 for a three months' term, and he was compelled to chop his own wood, act as janitor, and "board around" as well. He was one of the best men that ever lived in Cass county, and for forty years was an elder in the Christian church. He served four years as justice of the peace, was deeply religious, and an outspoken advocate of the cause of temperance, and was an ardent Democrat.

In partnership with his brother, David, Richard P. Davis operated the first threshing machine ever brought to Cass county.

To his marriage with Jane Hildebrand, which occurred in 1850, nine children were born, six of that number growing to maturity and being named as follows: Sarah Ellen, Lucy Ann, George B., Mary Jane, and Fred and Frank, twins. Mr. Davis died in April, 1906, and his widow survived him until May, 1911.

The eldest son of Richard P. Davis is George B., born July 14, 1857. He completed his schooling in Burnettsville Academy, and since 1875 he has been a teacher in the public schools. For the past ten years he has been principal of the Franklin school, in Logansport. He married Minnie Cullen in 1881, and Fannie, John C., Mary E. and Dr. Charles S. are their children. Mr. Davis is present chairman of the Democratic County Central Committee.

Frank Davis, present commissioner of Cass county, was born on March 6, 1864, and is the twin brother of Fred Davis, the youngest children of Richard P. Davis. At the age of nineteen years he and Fred started farming on shares, continuing to be thus occupied for six years, after which Frank Davis bought out his brother's interest and continued alone. In 1892 he bought sixty acres of land, later adding forty-eight acres thereto, and in addition, he and Fred, by purchase, now hold the old homestead place in partnership. In 1908 he was elected county commissioner on the Democratic ticket, re-elected in 1910, and in February, 1911, moved to Logansport, where he now resides. On January 9, 1889 he married Emma Byers, and they have two children Jessie M. and Jefferson Grover Cleveland. The latter married Mamie Strosser, and they have one daughter, Maxine. They live on the old place, thus making the fifth generation to have resided on this homestead.

Mr. Davis is a Democrat, and Odd Fellow, and an exceptionally able county official.

GEORGE I. WOLF. This prominent farmer and highly respected citizen of Deer Creek township may be counted among the pioneers of Cass county, since he has faithfully done his share in the development of his section of the state, both materially and intellectually. Such men constitute the mainstay of a commonwealth, and it becomes the duty of the biographer to encourage the formation of a character that builds up the best interests of the state. Mr. Wolf is a self-made man, having gained his present position through individual industry, and the salient features of his career go to show that he has ever displayed an enterprising, energetic nature, even from boyhood. Born in Preble county, Ohio, in 1834, he is a son of Jacob and Barbara (Hiser) Wolf. His father, a native of Frederick county, Maryland, migrated to Preble county, Ohio, in young manhood, and after some years there, came to Carroll county, Indiana, in 1836. There he spent the remainder of his life in agricultural pursuits, dying advanced in years, with the full respect and esteem of his fellowmen and having accumulated a comfortable competency.

George I. Wolf spent his boyhood days in Carroll county, where he secured his education in the district schools, in the meantime gaining a thorough knowledge of farming by assisting his father in the work of the homestead place. He early learned the dignity and value of labor, being taught to be industrious and honest, and his success in after life was due in large part to the benefits accruing from this early training. He continued to remain under the parental roof until he had reached his majority, at which time he started upon a career of his own, first on rented property and later on a farm for which he went into debt. He subsequently cleared off his indebtedness, sold his land and came to Cass county, where he purchased the farm on which he is now carrying on operations, a tract of eighty-three acres, located in Deer Creek township, not far from Young America. His modern home is located on Galveston Rural Free Delivery Route No. 13, and he also has commodious barns and appropriate outbuildings, of handsome architecture and substantial character. His land has all been brought to a high state of cultivation and yields abundant harvests, while his ventures in stock raising have met with an equal measure of success.

In 1859 Mr. Wolf was married to Miss Margaret Tolen, who also survives, and they celebrated their Golden Wedding anniversary in 1909, at which were present their children and grandchildren, as well as many of their friends, who recalled pioneer days in Cass county and wished the aged couple many more years of happy life. Mr. and Mrs. Wolf have been the parents of seven children: Mary, who became the wife of W. L. Burrows, Sarah, who married Wm. Henry, Eva, who became the wife of Abraham Smith, Ladosky, wife of Mr. Michael, Anna, wife of David McClusky, Carrie, at home, and Charles. Charles, who is married, resides on the old homestead and is his father's manager, having gradually taken over the elder man's duties. He is maintaining the family reputation for integrity and industry, and is known as one of his section's good practical farmers. The family is connected with the German Baptist church.

Dr. C. L. Thomas. Thirty years of devotion to his profession is the record of C. L. Thomas, M. D., a veteran physician of Washington township—thirty years of his life given to the calling which he chose as his life work in young manhood, a third of a century of time spent in the alleviation of the ills of mankind. Such is indeed a faithful service, a record of which no man might be ashamed. Always giving of his best energies, always faithful to his trust, never sparing himself in the accomplishment of his tasks, his life has surely been a useful one,

and he may now look back over the years that have passed with a sense of duty well done and take a pardonable pride in a work that has served to assist humanity, as well as to add to the professional prestige of his adopted community. Dr. Thomas was born October 25, 1846, in Carroll county, Indiana, and is a son of Samuel and Catherine (Johnson) Thomas. His father, a native of Virginia, accompanied his parents to Indiana in boyhood, and the remainder of his life was given to farming and the millwright business, dying in advanced age, with the entire respect and esteem of the people of his community. He and his wife were the parents of eight children.

Dr. C. L. Thomas prosecuted his preliminary studies in the country schools near Asbury church, and was reared to the occupation of farming. The young man, however, had decided upon a professional career, and accordingly took the examination and certified as a teacher in the public schools. At this time, however, the Civil war came on, and young Thomas, fired with patriotism, joined a regiment of Indiana volunteers, and fought bravely in defense of the country's flag. On the completion of his military career, he resumed teaching in the district schools and was so engaged until he entered upon his medical studies. He spent some time in preparation at Battle Ground, Tippecanoe county, Indiana, and in 1879 received his degree of Doctor of Medicine at Indianapolis, subsequently spending some time in practice at Burlington, Carroll county, and eventually coming to Logansport. Here he has continued to the present time, in the enjoyment of a large and representative practice, which is not confined to his immediate community, but is drawn from all over this part of the county. A deep thinker and consistent student, he has ever devoted himself to research and study, and has taken a special course in Bellevue Hospital, New York City. His sympathetic nature and kind and gentle personality have assisted him greatly in his work, and have made the aged physician one of the most beloved of his profession in Cass county. He has taken a keen interest in the work of the various medical organizations, and at this time is president of the Cass County Medical Society, in addition to acting as a member of the pension board. The Doctor specializes on medical and surgical diseases and treatment of the eye and his practice is not confined to Cass county but to all the adjoining country.

Dr. Thomas was married in 1876, to Miss Mary E. Cheney, of Clinton county, Indiana, and they have had one son: Willard, who married Miss Jessie Wilson, and has two children. Marie and Charles. The family is highly esteemed in this vicinity and its members number many warm friends in Logansport, near which city their home is situated.

FRED G. DROMPP is a native son of Logansport Indiana born in the city on December 28, 1869, and is the son of Gottlieb F. and Sophia (Arnold) Drompp, both natives of Wittenberg, Germany.

Gottlieb Drompp was reared and educated in his native land and there he married. He came to America in young manhood, and after a year spent in Chicago, came to Logansport, the time of his arrival here being in the '50's. Here he learned the cooper's trade, a business which claimed his attention through the remainder of his life. He was a member of the German Lutheran church and reared his family in that faith. He died on December 29, 1891, his widow surviving him until February 22, 1894. They were the parents of twelve children, six of whom are yet living.

Fred G. Drompp has always made his home in Logansport. He was educated in the German Lutheran parochial school, and when he was fourteen he became a bundle boy in the old Keller-Troutman & Company dry goods store. He remained with this firm until it ceased to exist, working his way up from bundle boy to a clerkship. He was later employed in the store of George W. Seybold & Brother until July 12, 1900, when he, associated with Henry Kammerer and Ferdinand Graas, under the firm name of the Stewart Dry Goods Company, embarked in the dry goods business in Logansport. Their beginning was a humble one, and they occupied a room at No. 315 Fourth street. The firm was duly incorporated, with a capital stock of $15,000, Mr. Drompp being president, Mr. Graas, secretary, and Mr. Kammerer, treasurer. This firm has ever since continued without change in its personnel, and the business has prospered with the passing years. In 1903 an additional room was requisitioned for the growing demands of their patronage, and the firm employs about twenty-four people, aside from the members of the firm. They carry a complete stock of dry goods, ladies ready-to-wear goods, carpets, rugs, curtains and linoleums—and is one of the leading houses in its line in the city. Mr. Drompp is also a director of the City National Bank.

Mr. Drompp is a Democrat, but not an active politican. He is a member of the German Lutheran church and is treasurer and trustee of that body.

On June 18, 1895, Mr. Drompp was married to Miss Lena E. Grahs of Union City, Indiana, and they have two children. Esther A., attending high school, and Frederick G., who attends the German Lutheran parochial school.

LeRoy F. Bird. Many of the leading agriculturists of Cass county are carrying on operations on farms upon which they were born and where they have spent their entire lives, and this may be given as one of the reasons for their success. Having passed their entire careers here, they are thoroughly conversant with climatic conditions and the needs of the soil, and as a result they can bring to their work an intelligent knowledge of what methods will bring the best results. In this class stands LeRoy F. Bird, the owner of 170 acres of fine land situated in Deer Creek township, section 5, an enterprising agriculturist and public-spirited citizen. Mr. Bird belongs to that class of men who have not been content with what has been accomplished by their fathers, but have continued to improve their properties and to contribute to the general prosperity of the community. He was born on his present farm, December 13, 1857, and is a son of Benjamin F. and Harriet (Small) Bird. His father, a native of Decatur county, Indiana, engaged in agricultural pursuits early in life, and continued to be so engaged throughout a long and useful career. He was known as a practical farmer and shrewd business man, and won the respect and esteem of his fellow-townsmen by his integrity and honorable dealing. Benjamin F and Harriet Bird were the parents of three children, namely William, deceased, formerly a farmer of Cass county, who married Estella Rhinehart, and had seven children, Adelbert, Hattie, Benjamin, Otis, Eva Charles and Ruby, A F, who makes his home in Walton and LeRoy F.

LeRoy F Bird secured his early educational training in the old Deacon district school in this township, after leaving which he attended the Walton public schools for some time In the meanwhile he spent the summer seasons on the homestead, assisting his father in his work, and learning to cultivate the soil and raise stock. Ambitious and enterprising, he applied himself assiduously to his tasks, gaining a thorough knowledge of his chosen vocation and carefully saving his earnings He has never left the old homestead, and still carries on operations there, having met with a full measure of success. His crops are large and find a ready market, and he is known as a good judge of cattle, his herds being sleek and well fed

Mr Bird has never married He is a popular member of the local lodges of the Independent Order of Odd Fellows and the Knights of Pythias, and was reared in the faith of the Universalist church, of which his parents were life-long members Public life has never attracted him, and the only interest he has taken in political matters is that of any good citizen who has the welfare of his community at heart. His many friends testify to his general worth as a neighbor and a man

WILLIAM R DEACON Although now living retired from active pursuits, the greater part of his time being devoted to looking after his farm William R Deacon still takes a keen and intelligent interest in matters pertaining to the welfare of Cass county, where he has resided for nearly half a century A veteran of the Civil war, when he had completed his service to his country, he returned to his Indiana home, and here for a long period was connected with the painting and decorating business A brief sketch of his career will show that he has ever lived an industrious and energetic life Mr Deacon was born April 4, 1841, in Liberty, Union county, Indiana, and is a son of W C and Sarah (Dawson) Deacon His father, a native of Lexington, Virginia, was about thirty years of age when he walked to Liberty, Indiana, and there he followed the trade of painter, which he had learned in his native state, continuing in Liberty from 1832 to 1864 in which year he came to Deer Creek township, Cass county He continued to spend the remainder of his life in this section and died with a comfortable competence and with the esteem and respect of those who knew him He and his wife became the parents of six children; namely: William B, George, Mary E, Martin, and Lucy A, who are deceased, Alice J and Annie

William R Deacon was educated in the schools of Liberty, Indiana, and as a youth was engaged in assisting his father, thus learning the trade of painter and decorator He was so engaged at the outbreak of the Civil war, when he went to Richmond, Indiana, and enlisted in the First Battalion, Fifteenth United States Infantry, under General Buell On the completion of a brave and gallant service, he came to Cass county and joined his parents, and here for a time was employed in a sawmill in Deer Creek township. Succeeding this he began to work at the trade of decorator, and was so engaged during the remainder of his period of activity. An excellent workman, thoroughly reliable in his transactions, he soon secured a large business, and built up a reputation for responsibility and honesty.

On May 11, 1865, Mr. Deacon was united in marriage with Miss Sarah J. Zeek, the estimable daughter of Isaac and Catherine (Robinson) Zeek, and to this union there have been born five children: Albertus and Lucy, who are both deceased; Minnie, at home; Edna, who is the wife of John Jackson; and George Franklin, who married Minnie Sprinkle, and has one child, Geraldine. With his family, Mr. Deacon attends the Methodist church. His daughter, Miss Minnie Deacon, belongs to the Rebekahs. Mr. Deacon has formed a wide acquaintance during his long residence in Cass county, and in it he numbers many warm friends, drawn about him by his many excellencies of mind and heart.

LORA WILSON. An example of well directed industry conducing to success is found in the career of Lora Wilson, of Deer Creek township, an enterprising and progressive agriculturist who has won financial independence and a position of prestige through the medium of his own efforts. Some twenty years ago he began his farming operations as a renter of land, and his progress has been steady and continuous until today he is the owner of a well-cultivated tract of eighty acres, and is classed among his township's successful farmers and stock raisers. Mr. Wilson was born on the old Wilson farm in Deer Creek township, Cass county, Indiana, March 28, 1874, and is a son of George Washington and Catherine (Beamer) Wilson.

George Washington Wilson was born on a farm in Union county, Indiana, near the village of Liberty on May 11, 1843, and when he was twelve years of age accompanied his father to Cass county, Indiana. His educational advantages were meager, as his services were needed in cultivating and improving the home farm of one hundred and sixty acres of wild land, on which, when the family first settled thereon, not one furrow had ever been turned.

Upon the death of his father in 1871, Mr. Wilson took charge of the homestead, which he continued to operate during the period of his activity, and in addition, accumulated a tract of seventy-eight acres on section 20, in Deer Creek township. He placed both tracts under a high state of cultivation, made most of the improvements on them, and continued to carry on general farming and stock raising for many years, attaining financial success and the confidence of all with whom he had transactions. He was a Republican in politics, and his religious affiliations were with the Christian church. On January 29, 1873, George W. Wilson was married to Miss Catherine Beamer, and to them were born six children, as follows: Harry, now a farmer of Deer Creek township, Lora, of this review, Stella, Carl, William A. and Almi I., the last two named now being deceased. George Washington Wilson was a Republican and a lifelong member of the Christian church He was born on May 11, 1843, and died on March 30, 1911, and his wife was born September 1, 1845, in Virginia and is living

Lora Wilson was early trained to the duties of farming, spending the summer months in assisting his father on the home place while the winter seasons were passed in attendance at the district schools of his native township He received the equal of a grade school education of the present day, after which he had some training in the Normal schools of various nearby cities, and his education was terminated by a year in the agricultural department of Purdue University. When he was eighteen years old he began teaching school, and for the ensuing five years he gave himself to that work, spending the summers either in school, in the pursuit of further knowledge, or helping with the work of the home farm, which he so well knew how to carry on. Mr. Wilson was twenty-one years old when he began to farm independently, renting the farm of his father as a beginning and operating the place on shares for something like ten years At the end of that time he had so prospered that he was able to purchase an eighty acre tract for himself, and his attention since then has been devoted to the cultivating and improving of this place It may well be assumed that Mr Wilson has made many improvements along modern lines in the conduct of his farm, and the erection of commodious and substantial buildings is not the least feature along the line of such improvement His stock in its appearance indicates his thorough knowledge as a breeder, and modern machinery of all kinds betrays the progressive spirit of the man in his farming capacity

Mr Wilson has maintained the family reputation for honesty and integrity in business affairs, and his pleasant personality has gained him a wide circle of sincere friends He is a Republican, and is a member of the Masonic fraternity, but has no other associations that would detract from his attention to his farm and his home

On March 22, 1905, Mr Wilson was united in marriage with Miss Grace Idel Billiard, of Carroll county, Indiana She is the daughter of Lewis and Susan Amanda (Debolt) Billiard Lewis Billiard was a farmer of Carroll county, and served as a soldier during the Civil war Mrs Wilson received her education in the grade and high schools of her native community, and takes her place among the most estimable and highly regarded women of the township, where she has a host of good friends Three interesting children have been born to Mr and Mrs Wilson, Florence, George and Lucille, all of whom were born on the farm near Young America, where the family home is maintained The eldest was born on September 9, 1906, the second on November 19, 1909, and the third born claims July 7, 1912, as her natal day

JOHN W COST was born at Fairfield, Green county, Ohio, July 24, 1844, his parents being Henry Joseph and Anna (Steele) Cost. He was of a family of four children, three sons and one daughter, all of whom are deceased except John W Mr. Cost was six years of age when the family made removal to Dayton, Ohio, and there the mother passed away February 8, 1858, following which they removed to Logansport, Indiana In his early boyhood, Mr Cost attended school at the old seminary, and when he was sixteen years of age began an apprenticeship with George W Brown, in the drug trade. He was so engaged in 1863, when he enlisted in the One Hundred and Sixteenth Regiment, Indiana Volunteer Infantry in the six months' service, and March 1, 1864 his time expired and he was mustered out of the service. During the following week he re-enlisted in the Seventy-third Regiment, Indiana Volunteer Infantry remaining therewith until February 1, 1866, and during these enlistments participated in a number of important engagements, among them being. Stone River, Murfreesboro, Tennessee, Decatur and Athens, Alabama, and Franklin and Nashville, Tennessee. In addition there were a number of minor engagements and skirmishes, in all of which he took an active part. At the close of his services he returned to school in the old seminary for one year, and then resumed his training in the drug business, this time with Henry Bringhurst. During the following five years he engaged in the drug business with Rodney Strain, and at the end of this time embarked in business on his own account, in the old Magee Block, in what is now known as the George Hoffman store location, on Fourth street. Succeeding this, Mr Cost moved to the Thomas Bringhurst room on Broadway, now occupied by Hall Smith's jewelry establishment, and in 1883 he came to Young America where for thirty years he has been considered one of the town's leading business men.

On October 11, 1876 Mr Cost was united in marriage with Miss Amanda Stapleton, the eldest daughter of J J Stapleton, and to this union there have been born two children Joseph Albert and Clara Alice. Joseph Albert Cost is now timekeeper for the Kokomo factory of the Pittsburgh Plate Glass Company, Alice Cost became the wife of W. E Kirkpatrick, of Young America. Mrs Amanda Jane (Stapleton) Cost was born in Bethlehem township, Cass county, Indiana, March 4, 1855, and has been a resident of this county all of her life.

The foregoing is a brief review of the salient points in the career of one of Young America's ablest and most highly esteemed business men, a veteran in the drug trade, and a citizen who has ever been devoted to the best interests of his adopted community. During the thirty years that he has been the proprietor of an establishment here, he has ever held a reputation for the strictest integrity and business honor, and each year has seen the extension of his wide circle of friends. He is a popular member of the Masonic fraternity, and with his family, attends the Christian church.

JOHN W SPRINKLE. Among the progressive and enterprising agriculturists of Cass county, one who has gained financial independence and business prestige through the medium of his own efforts is John W Sprinkle, of Deer Creek township. Embarking upon a career of his own when he was a young man, without financial assistance or influential friends, he so well directed his efforts that today he is the owner of a handsome property of 160 acres of land, on the Walton road, in addition to having other valuable interests. Mr Sprinkle was born on what is known as the old Sprinkle home place, near Sprinkle Chapel, in Cass county, Indiana, February 13, 1862, and is a son of John and Margaret (Roach) Sprinkle. His father, a native of Rockbridge county, Virginia was a machinist by trade, but after coming to

Cass county, in young manhood, followed farming and stock raising, and also operated a sawmill and threshing machine. He and his wife were the parents of eight children, as follows: Ellen, who became the wife of a Mr Orr, Wilson, William, who is deceased, Elizabeth, deceased, who was the wife of a Mr McDonald; Hannah, who married a Mr. Britton, John W, George; and LeRoy.

John W. Sprinkle began his education in the old Logan school and subsequently became a student in the Babb school, where he completed his training. On finishing his studies, he took up the trade of machinist, under the preceptorship of his father, and subsequently worked in the sawmill and with the threshing machine, traveling all over this and surrounding counties, but when the land became partly cleared, he turned his attention to farming. On reaching his majority, he embarked upon a career of his own, and through industry, energy and perseverance has gained an enviable position among the agriculturists of his section of the county. Starting in a modest manner, as the years passed and his finances would permit, he added to his land, to his stock and to his improvements, and now has a tract of 160 acres that is well cultivated and fitted with modern buildings. He believes in the use of modern machinery and scientific methods, and the success which has rewarded his efforts marks him as one of the substantial men of his community. He is also the owner of 320 acres of government land in South Dakota, located near Redfield. A man of the highest integrity, his business dealings have always been of a strictly legitimate nature, and his methods have gained him an enviable reputation and a wide circle of friends.

Mr. Sprinkle has been twice married, his first wife, Eva Crawford, dying without issue. His second marriage was to Miss Lillie Ruth, of Cass county, a member of a prominent farming family, and to this union there have been born five children as follows: Clifford, who married Pearl Plank, and has three children, Pauline, Luella and Ellsworth; Addie, the wife of James Kay, who has one daughter, Frances; and Gracie, Edith and Gladys, all of whom reside with their parents. The family is connected with the Methodist Episcopal church, in the support of which they have always been liberal. Mr Sprinkle holds membership in the local lodge of the Independent Order of Odd Fellows.

SAMUEL HURSH. A substantial representative of the agricultural interests of Deer Creek township is found in the person of Samuel Hursh, the owner of 160 acres of excellent farming land, located about one and one-half miles east of the village of Young America. Although a resident of Cass county only since 1903, he has become widely and favorably known among the citizens of his locality, and his ability and integrity have been recognized by his election to official position, in which he has served efficiently and conscientiously. Mr Hursh is a native of the Hoosier State, and was born March 26, 1863, in Carroll county, a son of Martin V and Sarah E (Quinn) Hursh. His father, a native of Butler county, Ohio came with his parents to Indiana in boyhood, settling in Carroll county in 1842. There he continued to be engaged in agricultural pursuits during the remainder of his life, accumulating a comfortable competency and being highly esteemed as a neighbor and citizen. He and his wife are both deceased and are buried in the cemetery at Flora, Indiana They were the parents of six children, namely Samuel, Ada, Minnie, Mollie, Fannie and Ambrose. Martin V Hursh was a member of the Independent Order of Odd Fellows

Samuel Hursh attended the Carroll county schools, and was reared to the vocation of farming, an occupation in which his ancestors had been engaged for generations At the age of twenty-one years, he left the parental roof and embarked upon a career of his own in Howard county, Indiana, where he continued operations until 1903, which year saw his advent in Cass county Settling in Deer Creek township, Mr Hursh began to cultivate and improve his 160-acre farm, and his substantial buildings in good repair and his well-tilled fields give eloquent evidence of his thrift and enterprise This property, known as the old Harness farm, is being devoted to general farming and stock raising, in both of which lines Mr Hursh has attained a full measure of success Through the careful direction of his business interests and by indefatigable industry, he has acquired a handsome property and at the same time has so conformed to the ethics of business life that he has the unqualified confidence of all with whom he has had trade transactions

In August, 1894, Mr Hursh was united in marriage with Miss Alice Harness, the estimable daughter of Jackson and Louise (Fisher) Harness, and to this union there have been born three children Obie, who is engaged in farming in Deer Creek township, married Miss Laura Snider and has two children, Robert and John, Ica, residing with her parents, a graduate of the local schools, and Oca, also living at home, who is still a pupil in the schools of the township Mr Hursh is a popular member of the Independent Order of Odd Fellows, as was his father, and takes a great deal of interest in its work His political belief is that of the Democratic party, and at the present time he is serving as a member of the board of trustees of Deer Creek township, where he is laboring faithfully in behalf of the best interests of his community and its people With his family, he attends the Christian church

JOHN L MAURICE came to Logansport, Indiana, in 1862, and with the exception of about four years has ever since made this city his home He is a native of Departemant des Voge, Canton de St Die, France, his birth occurred on June 13, 1841, and in 1852, when he was eleven years old, he came with his parents, Nicholas and Margarte (Maikuere) Maurice, to America

Nicholas Maurice located on a small tract of land near Dayton, Ohio, after coming to this country and engaged in the business of agriculture, in which he continued until his death

All the education John L Maurice ever received was in the schools of his native county and a winter in the schools of Dayton When he was twelve years of age he started out on his own responsibility and his first employment was as a farm laborer, and for his services he received four dollars a month and his keep He continued working as a farm laborer with gradually increasing wages, until he grew older, and in 1861 he went to Indianapolis Indiana, where for a year he was employed as a clerk in an ice cream parlor The next year he

came to Logansport and for a year thereafter he worked in the blacksmith shop of John Jackson. On July 9, 1863, he enlisted in the Mississippi Marine Brigade and at first was a member of Company D Cavalry, which later became Company K Infantry. The duty of the command to which Mr. Maurice belonged was to patrol the Mississippi river and disperse bands of guerrillas. His military career was one of continual activity, and while he participated in no general engagement, he was continually exposed to attacks from the rebels. His command took part in the Red River expedition under General Banks, and he was finally honorably discharged from the service with the rank of corporal, his discharge taking effect on January 21, 1865. His original company comprised one hundred and four men, and of this number only sixteen were left at the close of the war. Succeeding the return of peace to the land Mr. Maurice returned to Logansport, soon thereafter going to Dayton, Ohio gardening about two years, and at the butcher business one year. He then returned to Logansport again and established a meat market at the corner of North and Sixth streets. For a period of thirty-eight years he conducted a market at this corner, and he still owns the corner where the shop stood, although he retired from active business in 1910. He was at that time the oldest living butcher in Logansport. It is a fact that when he first began his meat market he had to borrow the money to buy a horse, and when he first opened his doors his capital was so limited that he could only buy one beef at a time. He has prospered in the most unmistakable manner, and bore the reputation of being an excellent butcher, a careful buyer, a good salesman, always courteous and square in all his dealings with his patrons, and enjoyed during his entire career the patronage of many who first frequented his little shop with its modest supplies. Mr. Maurice is a man of excellent habits of life, temperate and saving, and these qualities have made possible the accumulation of his present property.

Mr. Maurice has been twice married. He has two sons by his first marriage—David W. and Charles L. In 1893 he was married to Mrs. Indiana Connolly, the daughter of James S. Wilson, an old pioneer of Logansport, and the widow of Robert J. Connolly. Mrs. Maurice has one son by her first marriage—Wilson J. Connolly. She is a member of the Second Presbyterian church.

Mr. Maurice is a Republican and is a member of the Benevolent and Protective Order of Elks.

JAMES S. WILSON. An old and distinguished citizen of Logansport in Cass county was James S. Wilson, who came to Logansport on a canal boat, became identified with the local milling industry, and for many years was one of the leading manufacturers of the city. James S. Wilson was born at Elizabethtown, in Allegheny county, Pennsylvania, October 9, 1823, was of staunch American stock, and a son of Andrew and Elizabeth (Shooley) Wilson natives respectively of Pennsylvania and England. Until he was twelve years old he received an education in the common schools of his native town, and his first practical experience was as a clerk in a drug store. This he followed for three years, and it led him to take up the study of medicine, but he soon abandoned his intention of becoming a physician and instead went West and found a position as steward on a packet boat plying along the Wabash and Erie Canal in the freight trade between Logansport and Toledo In this way he visited Logansport and practically became a permanent resident in 1845 For several years he was connected with the canal transportation, and in 1850 left that and accepted a clerkship with William Beach & Co in the Forest Mills, an illustration of which old mills will be found on other pages of this history Seven years later, having a thorough experience in all departments of the mill, he formed a partnership with Cecil & Co, and subsequently became proprietor of the Logansport mills He was a prosperous miller and local manufacturer until 1890, at which time he sold out the water power and mills to the city of Logansport, which converted it to the use of municipal power and lighting purposes

On May 21, 1844, Mr Wilson married Delilah Creding, of Akron, Ohio To their marriage were born two children. Indiana, first married Robert Connolly and after his death became the wife of John L Maurice and now lives in Logansport, Virginia became the wife of G W Stevens, who is president of the C & O Railway with residence at Richmond Virginia James S Wilson was a Republican in politics, and was affiliated with the Independent Order of Odd Fellows and the Elks of Richmond, Virginia

JAMES G JOHNSON After spending many years in mercantile lines in Young America, J G Johnson is now living retired from active pursuits, the greater part of his time and attention being given to looking after his realty interests. A worthy representative of an old and honored family, he has been a resident of Indiana since infancy and his entire career has been one of industry and energy conducing to well-merited success J G Johnson was born September 27. 1838, near Cincinnati, in Hamilton county, Ohio, and is a son of William and Sarah (Godfrey) Johnson His father, born and reared in Hamilton county, received excellent educational advantages, became a physician, and after some years of practice came to Spencer county, Indiana, in 1838, and here lived for several years, then came to Young America, Cass county, where he practiced medicine Thence he moved to Durham, Missouri, where he died He became a well-known member of the Indiana medical profession, accumulated a comfortable competency, and when he died left a wide circle of friends to mourn him He and his wife were the parents of five children, namely: William, Martha, Robert, Eliza Ann and J G, all dead but the last named

J G Johnson was educated in the common schools of Spencer county, and his boyhood was spent much the same as that of any other country physician's son He was eighteen years of age at the time he first came to Cass county, at that time locating in Deer Creek township, where for some time he worked as a farm hand Subsequently he became apprenticed to the trade of mason and after thoroughly mastering its details followed that occupation for some time eventually, however, turning his attention to mercantile pursuits Mr Johnson became one of the pioneers in his chosen line in Young America and for years was a leading business man of this town Always trustworthy and reliable, he built up a business that covered the entire contiguous territory, and, while he was shrewd and farsighted in his business operations, his transactions were ever of a legitimate nature, and not only did he establish himself in the confidence of his business associates through the force of his integrity, but also gained the friendship and esteem of his customers by a pleasant, genial and obliging personality He continued to enjoy a steady and well-balanced trade until several years ago, when feeling that he had earned a rest from his years of labor, he retired He still retains an active and intelligent interest, however in all that affects his community, giving the support of his influence his time and his means to promoting its welfare Although nearing his seventy-fifth year, his faculties are unimpaired his memory is excellent, and he recalls in a pleasing conversational manner many incidents and experiences of early days in Young America Everywhere he has the respect and esteem of his fellow citizens Mr Johnson holds prestige in the Masonic fraternity as the first man in Young America to receive his Masonic emblem With his family, he attends the Christian church On July 19, 1862, Mr Johnson was married to Miss Margaret P. Burrows, and they had three children William H , Sarah J and John All these children died before the mother Mr Johnson is a Prohibitionist, but is not an office seeker

A A SEGRAVES One of the native sons of Indiana who has conferred honor and dignity upon the state of his birth is A A Segraves, general farmer and stock raiser of Deer Creek township, who owns and operates a handsome tract of 180 acres on the Kokomo road Reared to agricultural pursuits, he has made this his life vocation, and his success has come as a result of persistent industry, unfailing energy and integrity in business matters that have won him the confidence of his associates Mr Segraves was born January 2, 1859, in Carroll county, Indiana, and is a son of William and Mary (Plank) Segraves

Elam and Martha (Moore) Segraves the paternal grandparents of A A Segraves, were natives of the Old Dominion, from which state they migrated to Ohio as pioneers, settling near Eaton. There their son, William, was born and reared, taking up the occupations of farmer and carpenter and subsequently coming to Carroll county During the Civil war, William Segraves enlisted in the Seventy-second Regiment, Mounted Indiana Volunteer Infantry, and he starved to death with others at Andersonville prison He and his wife were the parents of three children, namely A A , James H , who died unmarried, March 2, 1885, and Martha, who became the wife of William Johnson and has three children

A A Segraves was a boy when brought to Deer Creek township and here he secured his educational training in the district schools, finishing his course in the Swamp school In the meantime he had spent the summer months in working upon the home farm, thoroughly assimilating all the details of agricultural work, and continued to remain under the parental roof until he was twenty-four years of age, at which time he embarked upon a career of his own He began his operations by renting land from John Hendrickson but subsequently became his stepfather's partner, and since then his rise has been steady and continuous His present farm of 180 acres, on the Kokomo road. has been brought to a high state of cultivation and improved with good buildings, and is known as one of the valuable tracts of the township Mr Segraves has other business interests and in numerous ways contributes materially to the importance of his community as a center of business activity

On May 8, 1884, Mr Segraves was married to Miss Clara Crockett, a daughter of John Crockett, a sketch of whose life appears in another part of this work Five children have been born to them William E an enterprising young agriculturist who is managing his father's interests married Lola Bowman and has two children, Irena and Geneva, also Mary, deceased, Earl, of Saskatchewan, Canada, manager of his father's half-section of rich farming land, who married Mabel Noakes and has three children, Anal, Harold and a baby daughter, and Mary Mabel, Ruth and Lenna, all at home with their parents Mr Segraves is a member of the Knights of Pythias, and with his sons holds membership in the Independent Order of Odd Fellows, Mrs Segraves being a member of the Rebekahs The family's religious affiliation is with the Universalist church Mr Segraves has proved himself in all the relations of life an earnest, honest, upright man, and a citizen of whom any community might be justly proud

ALLEN SNYDER Cass is essentially an agricultural county It has its factories its mills and its business houses, and the professions are, of course well represented, but the chief industries here have been those of farming and stock raising, and along these lines the leading citizens have attained their positions of prestige Among the men who have devoted their lives to the tilling of the soil, and through their operations have added to the general prosperity and welfare of the community, Allen Snyder takes prominent place He is the owner of two farms, of one hundred and sixty and forty acres, respectively, and has also been active in public affairs, being at present a member of the common council of Logansport He has been a resident of this section all of his life, having been born in the old house now standing on his present farm in September, 1863, a son of William and Catherine (Senseman) Snyder William Snyder was born in Lancaster, Pennsylvania, and came to Cass county, Indiana, as a young man, taking up land in the vicinity of Galveston where he spent the remainder of his life in agricultural pursuits He and his wife were the parents of fourteen children as follows Samuel, John, who is deceased, William, Charles, Allen, of this review; Justina, who is deceased, Elizabeth, Mary, Jennie, Martha, Minnie, Frank Sarah and Henrietta

Allen Snyder first attended the Runaway school and later the Peppermint and Washington schools in Washington township, and during his entire school period worked on the home farm, assisting his father and brothers in clearing, cultivating plowing and harvesting, and in the thousand and one tasks that occupy the busy farmer's attention William Snyder had a large farm and there was plenty for each of the sons to do, but their educations were not neglected, nor was their moral training forgotten, the good mother rearing them to habits of industry, honesty and thrift On attaining his majority, Allen Snyder embarked upon a career of his own on a part of his father's farm, and as the years passed he added to his holdings and continued to put up new buildings and make other improvements until his farms are considered some of the most valuable in the township Although he does not engage as actively in the farm labor as in former years, Mr Snyder still superintends the operations, and is known as a practical farmer and excellent judge of cattle, of which he has large herds.

On March 5, 1887, Mr. Snyder was united in marriage with Miss Anna Eckerle, daughter of Leopold and Nancy (Mallory) Eckerle, who came to Cass county from Ohio, and here took up land at an early date There were eight children in the Eckerle family: Frank, Charles, Anna, who married Mr Snyder, Alice and Martha, who are deceased, William, Rose and Mary Mr Eckerle, a retired mechanic, still survives and makes his home at Flora, Indiana Mr and Mrs Snyder have had five children Eddie L, who has charge of the home place, where he resides, married Myrtle Bone, Howard, who married Mary Lambert, Rollie, Marvin and Vera Mr Snyder has taken a keen interest in public matters, and was recently elected a member of the common council of Galveston, where he has rendered efficient and conscientious service He is a member of the Knights of Pythias of Young America and of the Democratic party He has a widespread reputation for integrity and honorable dealing, and his friends are only limited to the number of his acquaintances

ANDREW J GRAY, M D, physician and surgeon at Young America, Indiana, is one of the eminent professional men of this part of Cass county, and his activities as doctor, civic official and public-spirited citizen have marked him as a representative of the best type of progressive American citizenship, and gained him the esteem and confidence of his fellow townsmen and the sincere regard of a wide circle of personal friends Since locating in Young America, in 1890, Dr Gray has identified himself with various movements for the public welfare, his connection with which has caused his election to positions of honor and trust, and in his discharge of the duties of which he has displayed the same faithfulness and conscientiousness that have marked his professional career Dr Gray was born October 1, 1854, in Jackson township, Cass county, Indiana, and is a son of John and Harriet (Culver) Gray.

John Gray was born in Juniata county, Pennsylvania, and was reared to agricultural pursuits On leaving the Keystone state, he went to Butler county, Ohio, but remained there only a short time, subsequently coming to Carroll county, Indiana, where his father had taken up land. Mr Gray spent the remainder of his life here in agricultural pursuits, and died with a comfortable competence and with the full esteem and respect of his numerous friends He and his wife were the parents of four children, namely. Jacob, James, Joseph and Andrew J, of whom James is deceased

Andrew J Gray received his early education in the common schools of Jackson township, and during the summer months assisted his father in the work of the farm Following this he took a finishing course at Walton and then prepared for a collegiate course by attendance in the preparatory school at Valparaiso Succeeding this he entered the Indiana Medical University, at Indianapolis, where he was graduated with the degree of Doctor of Medicine in 1897, and immediately entered upon the practice of his profession at North Grove, Miami county Indiana where he continued for ten years. In 1890, Dr Gray came to Young America, where he has since become the possessor of a large and representative professional business. He has been a close student and is the possessor of a valuable medical library the perusal of which occupies whatever time he can spare from his professional duties. He has a well-appointed office, equipped with the most highly improved equipment of the profession and everything that will in any way add to the comfort and convenience of his patients. He belongs to the Cass County and Indiana State Medical Societies and the American Medical Association, in the work of which he takes great interest, and his fraternal connections include membership in the Independent Order of Odd Fellows and the Knights of Pythias

On November 10, 1891, Dr Gray was married to Mrs Kate P Hamilton, the widow of Joseph Hamilton, of Kokomo, Indiana, and they have one child Joseph P who is engaged in teaching school in Cass county. For four years Dr Gray served efficiently in the office of trustee of schools, and during his administration the present Young America high school was erected. At the present time he is a member of the board of Cass county commissioners, and is giving his best services in behalf of the community in which he has resided for so many years

CLAUDE BECK It is almost entirely upon the standing of its business men and leading citizens, upon their reliability, integrity, enterprise and public spirit, that the standing of any community rests. That locality is indeed fortunate when it can boast of a number of self-made men for while they have been advancing their own interests they have at the same time been forwarding the growth and prosperity of their community and, having succeeded themselves are almost invariably ready to assist others to success thus materially contributing to the public welfare. Among the citizens who have been the architects of their own fortunes and who have builded wisely and well, none stands higher in general esteem than Claude Beck, of Deer Creek township Losing his father before his birth, his life from earliest boyhood has been one of incessant activity and today he is the owner of a finely cultivated tract of more than two hundred acres of land. Mr Beck was born August 18, 1872, near the village of Liberty, Union county, Indiana, and is a son of Alvin and Cynthia T (Showalter) Beck. His father, also a native of Union county, was a farmer by occupation, and died when still in the prime of life, leaving his wife with five small children, George E, Edwin A, Bruce and Garry who are now deceased, and Claude

The educational advantages of Claude Beck were somewhat limited, owing to the fact that it was early necessary for him to become self-supporting, but he attended the schools of Young America, made the most of his opportunities, and, being ambitious and industrious, managed to acquire a much better education than many who had much better chances. When still an infant he was brought by his mother to Cass county and here when still a lad he began his career as an agriculturist. When yet in his teens he started operations on a tract of rented land

FRANK V. GUTHRIE

in Deer Creek township, and as the years passed invested his earnings in property until at the present time he has, as before stated, two hundred acres. Here he has made numerous improvements, his buildings being large and substantial and of modern architecture, and his machinery being of the latest manufacture and in the best of repair. The greater part of his attention has been given to general farming, but he has also experimented in stock raising with a full measure of success. In business affairs Mr Beck is a man of keen discrimination and sound judgment, of energy and perseverance, and the prosperity which has attended his efforts is the merited reward of his own faithful labor

In May, 1892, Mr. Beck was married to Miss Mary A. Roach, and they have had a family of eight children Maude, who is deceased; Ethel E., who became the wife of Carl S Zook and resides on her father's farm Ruby S, Tonawanda, Virgil, Alvin, Bruce and Victor The children have all been given good chances for an education, and fitted for the positions in life which they may be called upon to fill Mr Beck is a popular member of the local lodges of the Independent Order of Odd Fellows and the Knights of Pythias

FRANK V GUTHRIE It not infrequently occurs that the men in a family will display an inclination to follow the same business or vocation and this is especially true in the professional occupations Where the son has inherited the father's predilection and ability, it is but natural that his bent should be along the same line, and Cass county furnishes a number of instances of one profession being passed down from one to the succeeding generation An example of this kind is found in Frank V Guthrie the capable county attorney of Cass county, whose career before the bar is but a continuation of the success gained by his father in the practice of law It is probable, however, that Mr Guthrie's high position can be accredited as much to his hard, faithful work, as to any qualities of a hereditary character, for his has been an active and industrious career, filled with earnest, painstaking endeavor directed along well-defined lines He is a native of Cass county having been born in Washington township, August 19, 1865 and is one of six children, five sons of whom are now living born to Alexander and Mary (Brosier) Guthrie

Alexander Guthrie was born in Switzerland county, Indiana and was ten years of age when he accompanied his father, William Guthrie to Cass county Here he was reared on his father's farm, early in life became a school teacher, and eventually took up the study of law, a profession which he followed for about thirteen years from 1870 His death occurred in 1906, and he is survived by his widow

Frank V Guthrie attended the public and high schools of Logansport, graduating from the latter in 1886 and following this began the study of his chosen profession under the preceptorship of his father Subsequently he entered the office of DeWitt C Justice, although prior to this time he had been elected justice of the peace, an office in which he served four years In 1892 Mr Guthrie took the examination and was admitted to the bar, and since that year has continued in constant practice in Logansport He was associated with his former preceptor in a professional partnership until Mr Justice's death, and since that time has practiced alone. He was not long in securing recognition as a lawyer of high attainments, and soon acquired a large and representative practice. His activities in Democratic politics won him the chairmanship of the Democratic Central Committee of Cass county in 1906, and as such he served until January, 1912. In the meantime, on January 1, 1909, he was the successful nominee of his party for the office of county attorney, a position in which he has served with the greatest ability to the present time. Mr Guthrie has been connected with much of the important litigation of recent years in Cass county, and has acquitted himself in an able manner in all the cases with which he has been connected. Among his associates at the bar he is recognized as a valuable associate and as an antagonist to be feared. His religious connection is with Eel River English Lutheran church, while fraternally he belongs to the Odd Fellows Lodge No 417, and Lodge No 66 of the Benevolent and Protective Order of Elks.

On June 25, 1890, Mr Guthrie was married to Miss Catherine Miller, of Logansport, who was born and reared here, and to this union there have been born two sons namely Earl F and Asa E.

BART SWAFFORD The life history of the gentleman whose name heads this brief review has been commensurate with that of Cass county, where he has made his home since 1866. It is difficult for the enterprising and energetic farmer, after spending long years of earnest toil in cultivating a property, to retire from active pursuits and turn his property over to younger hands, but when he eventually arrives at the conclusion that he has reached an age when he is entitled to rest from his labors, he generally removes to a nearby city or village, and there becomes a welcome addition to its population as a man whose long experience makes him valuable in forwarding his community's interests. This remark is in no sense inappropriate to Mr Swafford, who is now living a life of retirement in Lincoln, whence he removed when he turned over the management of his 160-acre farm to his sons.

Bart Swafford was born in Preble county, Ohio, on the 22d day of May, 1845, a son of Archibald Swafford. His parents were farming people of Preble county, where they spent their lives, both now being deceased. They were the parents of eight children, namely: William, Bart, John, Emmett, Reese, James, Mary and Ella. Bart Swafford received his education in the district schools of his day and locality, and was reared to agricultural pursuits on his father's farm. He was thrifty and industrious in his youth, carefully saving his earnings with the view of becoming a property owner himself, and in 1866 was able to realize his ambition when he came to Deer Creek township and purchased his present land. Each year he added to his property and made improvements thereon, until it became one of the valuable tracts of the township. He erected a modern home, substantial barns and good outbuildings, and was successful in the raising of good stock and abundant crops. At the time of his retirement he moved to Lincoln, where he has since resided, and has taken a keen interest in the growth and development of his adopted place. He has not entered public life, having no desire for public office, but has done a good citizen's part in promoting the welfare of his community and its people, and has never been backward in supporting those movements which he has believed would work out for the ultimate good of all concerned

Mr Swafford was married to Miss Melinda Toney, and they reared a family of seven children, namely. Reese, John, Archibald, Beverly, Emmett, Dennis, who is now deceased, and Mrs Roxie Maryland

Beverly and Emmett Swafford, sons of Bart Swafford, are the owners of a sixty-acre farm just across the road from the homestead, and also rent the latter place from their father Both were educated under the veteran Cass county teacher, John Babb, working on the farm during their school period and continuing to be tillers of the soil after attaining their majority They have been successful in farming and stock raising operations, and have maintained the family reputation for industry and integrity

WILLIAM O BURROWS One who has considered the pursuits of private life as abundantly worthy of his best efforts, and who has concentrated his interests, energies and attention upon his home county, labored persistently for its advancement and growth, and at the same time has promoted his private interests so that he holds a place of prestige among his fellow citizens, is William O Burrows, of Deer Creek township, the owner of 145 acres of excellent farming land

The subject always closest to Mr Burrows' heart has been agriculture, and he has not only gained an enviable position in his chosen calling but has marked his career by a memorable showing forth of the utmost fidelity to principle and to the highest standard of human conduct He was born on the old Burrows homestead, owned by his brother, John E Burrows, in Deer Creek township, Cass county, December 21, 1855, and is a son of Joseph and Mary (Custenborder) Burrows. His father, a native of Greene county, Ohio, came to this township as a young man, and during the remainder of his life was engaged in the cultivation of the soil, becoming one of his community's substantial and influential citizens He and his wife became the parents of six children, namely Sarah, who became the wife of Peter Pierson, Priscilla, who married David Studebaker Mary C, Amanda, widow of Chauncey C Mummert, William O and John E

William O Burrows commenced his education in the old Thomas school and passed all of his school days in the country His boyhood was spent much the same as other farmers' youths of his day and locality, there always being plenty of work on the homestead to keep his hands busy and his mind occupied In the meantime he was securing experience of a practical nature that was of great value to him during the years that followed He was always industrious and ambitious, and on attaining his majority embarked upon a career of his own, first renting land and later going into debt for his present property He was able after some years of labor to clear his land from its incumbrance, and from that time his rise has been steady and continued He is engaged in general farming and stock raising, in both of which lines he has met with a full measure of success, and his land is constantly increasing in value As a farmer Mr Burrows is inclined toward modern methods and ideas In his every-day citizenship he displays the same enterprise and practices the same creed He has enriched his community and added to its importance by developing a choice property, and for this reason, if for no other, deserves a place among Deer Creek township's representative men

On December 31 1879, Mr Burrows was married to Miss Eliza J Blue, daughter of Uriah and Mary (Cohen) Blue, and they have had the following children Grace, Delbert, who married Grace Seward and has four sons—Harold Robert Arthur and Richard, Elmer, who died at the age of fifteen years, and Margaret, who is attending school. Uriah Blue was born in Carroll county, Indiana and there spent many years on a farm, but eventually came to Cass county He and his wife were the parents of four children Eliza J , who married Mr Burrows, Ella M , Mary Ann and Oretta Mr and Mrs Burrows are prominent members of the German Baptist church

JOHN R BABB There is no vocation in which man can engage that is more highly honored than that of the teacher Placed under his care are the plastic minds of youth, eager for knowledge easily impressed, and the responsibility resting on the shoulders of the educator is a heavy one Each year the standard of education has been placed higher, and he who would keep abreast of his calling must constantly study, even as those under him study For forty years John Babb has been engaged in teaching in the public schools of Cass county, and during this time he has made a name for himself in his profession, has been also a successful agriculturist, and as a citizen has gained the respect and good will of all with whom he has come in contact He is now the owner of a farm of forty acres, on which he still resides, located on Lincoln rural free delivery route No 15, in Deer Creek township, although he has retired from active agricultural pursuits Mr Babb is a native of Ohio, born near Greenville, in Darke county, August 31 1850, a son of William H and Mary C (Anderson) Babb His father brought the family to Cass county when John Babb was still a lad, settling on a farm in Deer Creek township, where he continued to be engaged in tilling the soil during the remainder of his life He met with a reasonable amount of success and was known as one of his section's industrious men and practical farmers and as a citizen who ever had the welfare of his community at heart He and his wife were the parents of ten children, of whom five grew to maturity, namely John, James N , David B , Reese M and Ulysses S , who is deceased

John Babb commenced his educational training in the old Salem school, originally a log church, following which he attended the public schools of Valparaiso and a preparatory school at Lebanon, Ohio Thus equipped he secured his teacher's license and at once entered upon his pedagogic work, in which he has since become known all over Cass county In the meantime he has followed farming to some extent, devoting himself to his calling in the winter months, and spending his summers in cultivating his fields, although he retired from the latter occupation some years since Mr Babb is known as an ideal educator, who has the much-desired quality of being able to impart to his students his own extensive knowledge Many of his pupils have gone out into the world and made names for themselves in various lines of endeavor, and have frequently given credit to their preceptor for his wise and valuable teachings that started them off well prepared for the serious business of life

Mr Babb was married in 1877 to Miss Indiana Toney, who died, leaving two children Claude D., who married Florence Kelly, and has three children—Omer, Elwin and Wilma, and Clyde, who married Laura Daggert, and has two children—Hilda and Robert.

Mr Babb belongs to the Methodist Episcopal church and has been liberal in his support of religious and charitable movements He has not entered public life, having had no desire for personal preferment, but has not been unmindful of the duties of citizenship, and has done all in his power to further the interests of his community and to aid in securing good government His long connection with educational matters has made him widely known, and everywhere he is esteemed as a man whose long life has done much to better his locality and those about him

JAMES ALEXANDER NELSON An excellent illustration of the rewards to be gained through a life of industry, energy and probity, is to be found in the career of James Alexander Nelson, of Deer Creek township. now the owner of 403 acres of valuable land, whose success has been attributable to individual worth A resident of Cass county since boyhood, he has been closely identified with the growth and development of this section, and has done his full share in bringing about the wonderful changes that have marked Cass county's history during the past several decades James Alexander Nelson was born September 25, 1851, in Union county, Indiana, and is a son of John and Nancy (Allen) Nelson. His father, also a native of that county, spent his life in tilling the soil, and became one of his community's prominent and substantial citizens. There were four sons in the family John, William, Jacob, who is now deceased, and James A

The early education of James A Nelson was secured in the schools of Lybrook Union county, and he was still a lad when he was brought to Cass county, here completing his studies in the common schools He was reared to agricultural pursuits, and remained with his mother until he was twenty-one years of age, at which time he embarked on a career of his own, taking up a tract of land in Deer Creek township As the years have passed and his finances have permitted, he has added to his land from time to time, and now has about 403 acres, over 200 acres of which have been cleared by himself

He carries on general farming and stock raising, using the most approved methods, and has taken advantage of modern machinery in cultivating his land Progressive along all lines, he has recognized that the successful farmer best helps himself who helps the community, and accordingly has done all in his power to advance the interests of Deer Creek township His reputation in business circles has ever been that of a man of integrity and honorable principles and he justly merits the high esteem in which he is universally held

Mr Nelson was married to Miss Ella Barnhart, and they have been the parents of six children, namely Roy, who married Esther Peters, and has one daughter—Geneva I, Bertha, who married a Mr Babb, and has two children—James and Esther, Edna single and residing at home with her parents, and Everett and Emmett, who are attending school. The oldest child, May, died at the age of sixteen years. With his wife and children Mr. Nelson attends the New Light church. He is a Democrat politically.

MARTIN VAN BUREN BURROWS. Among the residents of Deer Creek township who are successfully carrying on the work of breeding and dealing in live stock and developing the fields according to modern methods of farming, is numbered Martin Van Buren Burrows whose home is on Galveston rural free delivery route No. 13. Here he has a farm of seventy-one acres on which he has carried on operations for many years, during which he has gained a widespread reputation for integrity, probity and good citizenship. He was born November 15, 1837, in Greene county, Ohio, and is a son of Benjamin and Mary (Stottler) Burrows. His father, a native of Maryland, migrated west to Ohio in young manhood, settling in Greene county, where he was engaged in farming until he brought the family to Cass county in 1865. In addition to carrying on farming he followed the trade of blacksmith for a long period, and accumulated a large tract of land. He became widely known in his part of the county and was accounted one of Deer Creek township's best citizens. He and his wife were the parents of three children, namely: Martin Van Buren, William Jackson and Mrs. Mary Founda, both of whom are now deceased.

After completing his education in the common schools of Greene county, Ohio, Martin V. Burrows started upon his career as an agriculturist. His early training was secured in his native county, for, being his father's youngest son, he was put to work in the fields almost as soon as he was large enough to grasp the plow-handles. Reared carefully, by Christian parents he was taught the value of industry and honesty, being trained under the teachings that success in life was only to be obtained through the medium of constant application and tireless perseverance.

Mr. Burrows was about twenty-eight years of age when he accompanied his parents to Cass county, Indiana, and here his first farm consisted of rented land. It was not long, however, until he purchased a property of his own, although it was some time before he had it entirely clear of indebtedness. Laboring faithfully and intelligently along well-defined lines, as the years passed he was able to make improvements on his land, to add thereto from time to time, and as his means would permit to erect substantial buildings to take the place of those originally built. His labors have borne fruit, and today he finds himself in possession of a handsome property which compares favorably with any of its size in the township. He always has been known for his integrity in matters of business, is accounted a good neighbor, and his numerous friends testify to his general popularity.

On June 16, 1859, Mr. Burrows was united in marriage with Miss Mary Campbell, daughter of John and Elizabeth (Braun) Campbell. The Campbells were from Indiana, while the Braun family migrated to this state from Pennsylvania. Six children were born to Mr. and Mrs. Burrows as follows: Anna, who passed away at the age of fifteen years;

Warren L, who married a Miss Wolf, and has two children—Otis W and Etta M, Frank, the wife of Jacob Cripe, who has four children—Lee and Mae, twins, Fern and Geneva, Albert, who married (first) Ella Vernon, by whom he had one child—Blanch, and married (second) Elsie Hart, and has two children—Grace and Ross, Mary, the wife of Ira Smith, who has two children—Edna and Earl, and Walter who married Mattie Bruner Mr and Mrs Burrows belong to the Dunkard church

OTHA A DAVIS Residing in a pleasant home on his 120-acre farm, located on Walton route 16, about ten miles south of Logansport, Otha A Davis is numbered among his community's successful agriculturists. A man of strong individuality and indubitable probity, he has gained position through the exercise of industry and perseverance, and has at the same time promoted the general welfare while enhancing individual prosperity Today he ranks among the most progressive and enterprising agriculturists of Deer Creek township and has gained a position of distinctive prominence by reason of his superior ability, close application and sound judgment He has also maintained a lively interest in the industrial and popular activities of the community and has contributed materially to the general progress and upbuilding

Otha A Davis was born August 3, 1869, in Washington township, Cass county Indiana, on the old Anthauer farm, and is a son of N M and Mary (Deacon) Davis His father came from near Eaton, Preble county, Ohio, to Cass county, and here continued to be engaged in agricultural pursuits during the remainder of his life, accumulating a comfortable competency in worldly goods and gaining and retaining the respect and esteem of his business associates and neighbors

He and his wife had a family of four children, as follows Elmer E, a farmer of Deer Creek township, Otha A, of this review Elizabeth, who is deceased, and John W, who is engaged in business in Chicago, Illinois

The educational training of Otha A Davis was secured in Deer Creek township, where he attended Deacon School District No 2 during the winter months while in the summers he assisted his father in plowing, cultivating, planting and harvesting and in the multitudinous duties that form a part of the life of the busy Indiana farmer When he was nineteen years of age, he began farming on his own account, first renting small tracts of land, later increasing his tracts, and eventually buying from his earnings a property of his own This he brought to a high state of cultivation and disposed of at a profit, and at that time bought his present farm, a tract of 120 acres, which he is devoting to general farming and stock raising, in both of which lines he has met with success The general appearance of his farm at once stamps the owner as a man of intelligence and good management as well as one of untiring energy, the buildings being substantially built and of modern architecture, the fields being well laid out and neatly fenced, and the cattle healthy, sleek and well fed He takes an interest in political matters, especially those of a local nature, but merely as an onlooker, having never had any aspirations for public office He has been interested to some extent in fraternal work, being a valued member of the Free and Accepted Masons the Independent Order of Odd Fellows and the Knights of Pythias, being senior warden in the last named and popular in all, while Mrs Davis belongs to the Daughters of Rebekah

On December 26, 1888 Mr Davis was united in marriage with Miss Luella Jane Crockett, daughter of John Crockett, a review of whose career will be found on another page of this work Seven children have been born to Mr and Mrs Davis, namely One who died in infancy, Emmett, a Logansport business man, who married Esther Hyman, Homer E., who assists his father in the work of the home farm, and Janet, Lowell, Wilmer and Joseph all residing with their parents The family attends the Universalist church, and its members have ever been liberal in their support of religious and charitable movements

THOMAS McELHENY A native son of Logansport, widely known and highly regarded by all classes, Thomas McElheny, clerk of the court of Cass county, has spent his entire career in this city, and has won recognition in business and public life through the medium of his own efforts and abilities Since the time when he completed his schooling, as a small lad, he has made his own way in the world, directing his ambitious activities along well-defined paths and characterizing his operations with a high regard for the rights of others and an earnest desire to assist his city and its people that has won him friends everywhere Thomas McElheny, or "Tom" as he is more familiarly known, was born in Logansport, Indiana, October 20. 1878, a son of Robert and Ida (Mason) McElheny

The McElheny family was founded in the United States by the great-grandfather of our subject, who came to this country from Ireland The grandfather, Thomas R McElheny, was born in Dayton Ohio, from whence he came to Cass county, Indiana, in pioneer days, locating in Logansport, Indiana, where with his son Robert he was engaged in the grocery business for many years Contrary to what might be expected from their nationality the members of this family were Protestants Robert McElheny was a member of Company B, Forty-sixth Regiment, Indiana Volunteer Infantry, serving one year during the Civil war, after the close of which he returned to the pursuits of peace, spending the rest of his life in merchandising, and passing away February 29. 1898 His widow survives, living in Logansport, and has been the mother of nine children, Thomas, the fourth in order of birth, being one of three survivors

Tom McElheny was reared to manhood and has always resided in Logansport His education was secured in the common schools, and when still a small lad he began to make his own way in the world, accepting whatever honorable occupations presented themselves Being of a thrifty and industrious nature, he carefully saved his earnings, and when twenty-four years of age established himself in a general insurance business Four years later he added a real estate department to his enterprise and in both lines he has met with well-deserved success The companies represented by Mr McElheny & Company organized in 1902, are as follows. Home Insurance Company Insurance Company of North America, North British and Mercantile,

Fireman's Fund, Fire Association, Franklin, Royal, Standard Fire Globe Indemnity, Ocean Accident Guaranty Corporation, New York Plate Glass Hartford Steam Boiler, International Live Stock, Standard Accident, National Surety Company, National Life of Vermont

While he has supported the Republican party as a rule in national affairs, he has been broad-minded enough to criticise what he deems wrong in his party's policies and probably could be better termed an independent Republican In 1910 he entered the public arena as a candidate for the office of clerk of the Cass county court, was elected by a handsome majority, and has continued to capably fill that office to the present time Mr. McElheny has been prominent fraternally as a member of the Masons, in which he holds membership in the Blue Lodge, Chapter and Council He is also a Scottish Rite Mason and a Shriner a member of Murat Temple, Indianapolis He holds membership also with the Knights of Pythias and Benevolent Protective Order of Elks With his family he attends the Methodist Episcopal church

On June 7, 1904, Mr McElheny was married to Miss Mabel Pitman of LaFayette, Indiana, and they have three sons Tom, Jr, Joseph and Richard

EDGAR D ROBINSON From the Old Dominion state have come many of Cass county's best agriculturists, men reared to the soil who have brought with them many of the sterling, sturdy traits of their forefathers In this class stands Edgar D Robinson, of Deer Creek township who migrated to Indiana in young manhood with no capital save a laudable ambition, an energetic spirit and a persistent nature, which, however constituted a sufficient foundation upon which to erect a structure of success Today, Mr Robinson is the owner of eighty acres of excellent land, and has a recognized place among the substantial men of his community He was born in Virginia on the 3d of May 1865, and is a son of Alexander and Caroline (Cather) Robinson, natives of that state, where they spent their entire lives in farming and both have now passed away and are buried in their beloved Virginia

Edgar D Robinson received his educational training in the schools of his native vicinity, and from earliest boyhood was trained by his father in the duties of the farm He continued to assist his father until he was twenty-two years old at which time he left the parental roof and came to Cass county, which has since been the scene of his labors On his advent here, he first located at Walton, where he secured employment working on the farm of the Wendlings, situated near that place He was thrifty, industrious and enterprising, carefully saving his earnings and was eventually able to secure his present property, a farm of eighty acres This land had but few improvements when Mr Robinson became its owner, but since that time it has been converted into one of the most valuable tracts of its size in the township As time has passed and his resources have permitted, he has added to his buildings and equipment, making necessary improvements in a modern way and keeping his implements and buildings in the best of repair Although the greater part of his attention has been given to general farming, he has also met with some success as a stock raiser, his sleek, well-fed herds of cattle giving evidence of his ability in this line In business matters he has always displayed the strictest integrity thus winning and retaining the confidence and respect of those with whom he has had transactions

Mr Robinson was united in marriage with Miss Ursula DeHaven, and to this union there has been born one child Clarence Mrs Robinson is a consistent member of Salem Methodist Episcopal church, and they are liberal in their support of church and charity He has shown some interest in fraternal matters, being a member of the Masonic order, but aside from this has given his entire attention to his farm and his home, which have satisfied his ambitions He has not cared for public life and is no politician, taking merely a good citizen's interest in matters that affect his community It is such men that form the bone and sinew of any section, and to them must be given the credit for the great advance enjoyed by Cass county along agricultural lines

JOHN HYNES The pioneers of Cass county have done their work, and the result of their efforts is shown today in the magnificently developed farms, the flourishing towns and cities the splendidly kept roads and the perfectly equipped schools All this was not brought about in a day, but is the result of years of unceasing endeavor, coupled with constant faith in the locality and appreciation of its possibilities One of the representative farmers of this locality, who belongs to an old and honored family, and who has himself been identified with the agricultural history of his part of the county, is John Hynes, the owner of 318 acres of well cultivated land in section 11, Clinton township Mr Hynes was born on the farm which he now occupies, August 18, 1849 and is a son of John and Nancy (Coble) Hynes

John Hynes, the elder was born in Westmoreland county Pennsylvania, in December, 1811, and in 1828 came to Cass county and entered land Returning to Montgomery county, Ohio, he was married to Nancy Coble, who was born near Dayton, Ohio, in December, 1811, and in 1832 they returned to Cass county, where they spent the remainder of their lives in agricultural pursuits, Mr Hynes dying in 1890 and his wife in 1881 They were the parents of fourteen children, of whom four are living at this date Nancy J who is the widow of Hugh Fitzer, Margaret who is the widow of W K Canada Ella, the wife of William H Tyner, and John, of this review

John Hynes was reared on the homestead place, and attended the district schools during the winter terms until he was twenty-one years of age, in the meantime spending his summer months on the farm He was first married to Miss Ella Parks, who died without issue, as did also his second wife, who bore the maiden name of Alice Hilderbrand His third wife was Ella Loesh On November 19, 1885, Mr Hynes was married (fourth) to Jennie Gasaway, who was born in Clinton township and educated in the district schools here and they became the parents of two children Alda, who resides at home, was given an excellent education in music and is now a teacher, and Rachel, also single and at home, a graduate of the district and high schools and Purdue University, in which institution she took the short course

Mr and Mrs Hynes and their children are members of the Christian church at Pleasant Hill, where Mr Hynes is acting as an elder He is a member of Burrows Lodge No 495 I O O F, and of the Grand Lodge, and is past grand therein, and of Logansport Lodge of the Tribe of Ben Hur He is a Democrat in his political views, served as assessor of Cass county for four years, and at this time is superintendent of the Hynes & Porter gravel road

Mr Hynes has devoted his entire life to agricultural pursuits, and at this time is the owner of 318 acres of good land Farming, as conducted today is an enterprise requiring close calculation and scientific management, a technical trade full of demands for exact information and the deft touch, and to win the full measure of success the modern farmer must be a man of sobriety, industry and energetic nature A glance at Mr Hynes' well-regulated property will assure the visitor that he is possessed of all of these faculties, while his sleek cattle, well-fed hogs and standard bred horses testify to his ability as a stockman Personally he is a man of pleasing address, and his many admirable qualities of mind and heart have won him hosts of friends and admirers He has invested his means judiciously and intelligently and is a stockholder in the Farmers and Merchants Bank at Logansport.

HON WILLARD C FITZER The unusual and versatile talents that go to make for success in diversified fields of endeavor are seldom possessed in full degree by any one individual but in the case of the Hon Willard C Fitzer, of Clinton township, it would seem that nature had been prodigal in her gifts The brilliant professional man seldom proves the successful agriculturist, or *vice versa*, and while it is not unusual for either to become the influential legislator, it is not so frequent that one man combines all the qualities of the three Mr Fitzer is an excellent example of an exception to this rule, as he has proven his ability and has made a distinct success of his farming operations, and in the legislative halls is a recognized power. He is a native son of Cass county, having been born in Clinton township, a son of Hugh and Nancy J (Haynes) Fitzer

Hugh Fitzer was born in the state of Ohio, and as a young man in 1831, migrated to Indiana, settling on the farm in Clinton township on which his son Willard C now resides He became a large owner of land, one of his community's public-spirited citizens, and his death, which occurred in 1906, was sincerely mourned by a wide circle of friends Although a modest and unassuming man, who never allowed his name to be used in connection with public office, he took a keen and intelligent interest in politics, and always worked energetically in the interests of the Democratic party With his wife, he attended the Methodist Episcopal church, and everywhere was known as an honest, industrious and law-abiding citizen Mr Fitzer was married in Clinton township to Nancy J Haynes, a native of Indiana, and they became the parents of two children Hon Willard C and Harry J

Willard C Fitzer was reared on his father's farm, and in boyhood entered the district schools of Clinton township, which he continued to attend until he was seventeen years of age At that time he took up his studies in the preparatory department of Purdue University, and one year later entered upon a regular course of four years in that institution, being graduated therefrom with the degree of Bachelor of Sciences, in 1890. At that time he became a student in the law department of the University of Michigan, where he received the degree of LL. B. in 1893, and almost immediately thereafter opened a law office in Logansport, which was the scene of his professional endeavors during the next ten years. During this time he acted in the capacity of prosecuting attorney of the twenty-ninth judicial circuit of Cass county, to which office he was elected on the Democratic ticket, having inherited his father's political proclivities. Subsequently he was sent as a representative to the sixty-seventh general assembly, from Cass county, his services in which were given their appreciation when he received the re-election in the sixty-eighth general assembly, of which he is now a member.

Mr. Fitzer returned to the Clinton township farm in 1904, and since that time has given the greater part of his attention to the raising of pure-bred Angus cattle and high grade sheep and hogs. A capable, practical farmer and stockman, taking advantage of modern ideas and methods, his success has been due to intelligent effort, directed along well-defined lines and at all times characterized by the highest degree of integrity. The home farm, a tract of 620 acres, has been brought to a high state of cultivation, and its entire appearance denotes the presence of able management, thrift and industry. Although his farming operations and the duties of his public office leave Mr. Fitzer little time for outside affairs, he has not been insensible to the social amenities, and is popular with the members of Tipton Lodge No. 33 A. F. & A. M., Bridge City Lodge No. 305, Knights of Pythias, and B. P. O. E. Lodge No. 66.

JEROME JUSTICE. Many of the leading agriculturists of Cass county have spent their entire lives within its limits, a number having been born on the land which they are now cultivating. In this class is Jerome Justice, a farmer of section 11, Clinton township, who was born on the farm he is now cultivating, January 4, 1856, a son of James M. and Mary (Shortridge) Justice.

The Justice family is one of the old and honored ones of the county, and can be traced back to the year 1610, when Mr. Justice's forefathers were driven out of Ireland taking refuge in Holland, from which country the progenitor of the family in this country came in 1743. Six brothers of the name were living in the American colonies at the outbreak of the Revolutionary war, all enlisted in the colonial army, and three died while wearing the uniform, one of the others the great-grandfather of Jerome Justice, being with General Washington during the memorable winter at Valley Forge, and afterward living to the remarkable age of one hundred and four years. The grandfather of Jerome Justice, John Justice, was a Pennsylvania school teacher, and married Rosa Hood a native of Ireland, their children being: Joseph, who was a paymaster in the Army of the Cumberland during the War of the Rebellion; John who was an auctioneer and peddler in Cass county prior to the advent of railroads here; Frank, a clerk and trader; William, who passed his life in Winchester, Kentucky; Clarissa, who became the wife of Benjamin Porter; Rosie, who married William Porter, a pioneer of Cass county of 1832; and James M.

James M. Justice, the father of Jerome Justice, was born in Lancaster county, Pennsylvania, in 1809, and upon coming west in early manhood located in Fayette county, where he was married (first) to Malinda Porter, daughter of William Porter. Soon thereafter they made removal to Cass county, and October 8, 1837, became residents of Clinton township, their home being located three miles west of what is Clymer station. Mr. Justice entered a quarter section of land from the government, developed a fine farm, and made his home thereon for fifty-six years. He was a very successful farmer, managing his interests with that ability, foresight and energy that seldom fail to bring the desired financial returns. In addition to his agricultural pursuits he also practiced veterinary surgery. In his political views he was a stalwart Republican and on that ticket was several times elected to the office of township trustee. He belonged to the Christian church, was a man of exemplary habits, and his many excellencies of character won him the regard of all with whom he came in contact. In his death which occurred July 17, 1894, his community lost one of its best citizens. Mr. Justice's first wife died, leaving seven children, as follows: Elizabeth, the wife of Warren Millard, of Carroll county, Indiana; Rosanna, deceased, who was the wife of Isaac N. Myers; William; Joseph, who is deceased; James, who belonged to the One Hundred and Eighteenth Regiment, Illinois Volunteer Infantry, during the Civil war, rising to the rank of brigade quartermaster; Clara, the wife of A. C. Chapman of Sacramento, California, and Caroline, who became the wife of Robert Houston. Mr. Justice was married (second) to Mary Shortridge, who was born in Fayette county, Indiana, and they became the parents of seven children, of whom five are living: Jerome; Lorinda, the wife of William Shaffer, of Carroll county, Indiana; Frank, a contractor living in Logansport; Parker, a veterinary surgeon of Winnipeg, Canada, and Millory, a retired farmer of Burroughs, Carroll county, Indiana.

Jerome Justice was reared to agricultural pursuits on the home farm, and as a youth was given excellent educational advantages, attending the district schools, the seminary at Logansport, the Ladoga Normal School and the Danville Normal School, and eventually was given a teacher's certificate, of which, however, he never made use. On completing his education he made a trip to California, where he remained for two years, at the end of that time returning to Cass county, where he took up farming on the homestead. He now owns 118 acres, of which eighty were originally included in the property settled and cleared by his father, and the entire tract is now in an excellent state of cultivation, producing large crops and giving ample evidence of Mr. Justice's ability as an agriculturist. In addition to farming he carries on stock raising and his ventures have proved successful, because he has applied himself to his work, has given his personal attention to each detail thereof, and has used intelligent, practical and modern methods, equipment and machinery.

In 1889 Mr. Justice was married to Miss Belle Martin, who was born and reared in Carroll county, Indiana, and there educated in the district schools and she died March 29, 1890, having been the mother of one child, Martin E., a graduate of the Winona schools, of Indiana College and the University of Illinois, who is now engaged in farming in Carroll county. Mr. Justice was married November 16, 1892, to Miss Jennie Myers, who was born in Miami county, Indiana, and there reared and educated. One daughter, Ethel B., was born to this union, December 31, 1895. She was educated in the common schools of Clinton township, and has also been given a musical education in Logansport, being a young lady of no small talent.

In political matters Mr. Justice is a Republican, although in the campaign of 1912 he was disposed to incline towards the young Progressive party. During his long residence here he has gained a wide acquaintance among which he numbers many friends. He has been reliable and straightforward in all his dealings, and his neighbors and numerous acquaintances are invariably unstinted in their commendation of his methods.

CHARLES B. CHAMBERS. Undoubtedly travel and experience are helpful in the successful pursuit of any calling, for in this way the mind is broadened, new ideas are introduced and strange methods are given a trial, thus adding to the traveler's stock of information and widening his scope. Few of the citizens of Clinton township have enjoyed better advantages along this line than has Charles B. Chambers, who is engaged in farming and stock raising on section 10, and whose career is of interest because it has been marked by constant endeavor along well-defined lines, showing the success that may be gained by a poor boy whose only capital in early life is pluck and energy. Mr. Chambers was born on a farm in Clinton township, Cass county, Indiana, March 1, 1859, and is a son of Thomas and Christiana Chambers, the former a native of Kentucky and the latter of Germany. His parents came to Cass county as young people, were here married, and spent the rest of their lives in farming. They were the parents of four children, namely: Richard, Charles B., Samuel L. and V. P.

Charles B. Chambers was reared on his father's farm in Clinton township, and was attending the district schools at the time of his father's death. Although he was but fourteen years of age he was compelled to give up his studies and start to work to assist in the support of the family, his first employment being at wood chopping. Later he started to work on neighboring farms, and continued to be so engaged until his marriage, in 1879, when he became engaged in operations on his own account. Thrifty, industrious and energetic, as the years passed he added to his land from time to time, in the meantime carrying on general farming and stock raising. In this connection he has traveled throughout the southwest, observing the methods of breeding stock in various sections of the country and taking advantage of any innovations with which he was formerly not familiar. He has a fine home on his farm of 171 acres.

In 1879 Mr. Chambers was married to Miss Emma Neff, also a native of Clinton township, a daughter of Washington Neff, an agriculturist of this part of the county, and they had three children: Charles B., Jr., who was educated in the common, high and commercial schools; Bessie, the wife of Ira Cree of Logansport and a graduate of the common and high schools and a private school of Logansport; and Russell who is taking a post-graduate course in the Logansport high school. The wife and mother died May 16, 1913.

Mr. Chambers has interested himself in fraternal work to some extent, being a member of Eel River Lodge No. 417, I. O. O. F., at Logansport. In his political affiliations he was a Republican until 1912 in which year he cast his vote with the new Progressive party. He has shown a deep interest in the cause of education, and all that tends towards the advancement of the moral, physical or material welfare of his community. He has done much to bring about desirable results and, as such men are all too few in any community, is esteemed and respected accordingly by all who know him.

ASA J. SHIDELER. Among the enterprising and progressive agriculturists of Cass county who have spent their entire lives on the farms which they now occupy, Asa J. Shideler, of Clinton township, holds a prominent place. Born and reared in Clinton township, from earliest youth he has been trained to a knowledge of soil and climatic conditions here, and the result has been the development of a property which produces abundant crops and gratefully repays its owner for the toil he has expended upon it. Mr. Shideler was born on his present farm, the old Shideler homestead, March 10, 1867, and is a son of Abraham and Elizabeth (Mummey) Shideler.

George Shideler, the grandfather of Asa J. Shideler, was born in Washington county, Pennsylvania in 1793, went to Lancester county in young manhood, and later to Preble county, Ohio and as early as 1832 came to Cass county, settling among the pioneers of Clinton township on a farm which he had purchased while on a visit some four years before. His subsequent years were spent in clearing, cultivating and developing this land, and throughout the remainder of his life gave his entire attention to agricultural pursuits, his only outside connection being that which he maintained with the Dunkard church, of which he was a faithful member. His death occurred at the home of his son, Abraham, in 1875, and his wife followed him to the grave in 1881. Mrs. Shideler had been Miss Elizabeth Neff, a native of Washington county, Pennsylvania and a daughter of Jacob Neff, a farmer of the Keystone state. She and her husband had the following children: Lavina, who was the wife of Martin Miller, Mary, who was the wife of Thomas Dillard, Catherine, who married Jacob Neff, Naomi, who married Adam Yost, Jonathan, Jacob, Elizabeth, the widow of Zachariah Cragun, of Clinton township, and Abraham and Isaac, twins, the latter a retired clothing merchant of Logansport. Of these children, Elizabeth and Isaac are the only survivors.

Abraham Shideler, son of George and father of Asa J. Shideler, was born on the Shideler homestead in Clinton township July 22 1835, and there spent his entire life, his death occurring in May 1910. His parents trained him to habits of honesty, industry and thrift, and he was early taught to respect the dignity and value of hard work. While assisting his father in the work of the homestead, he attended the district log schoolhouse of his vicinity during the winter terms, this training being supplemented in his after life by close observation, much reading and years of practical experience. He made farming his life work and his unquestioned success was ample evidence of his intelligent and well directed efforts. Politically a Republican, he was widely known in public life from a period shortly after he attained his majority, when he was elected township assessor, a position to which he was re-elected in later years. In November, 1894 he was called to the office of county commissioner, in which he served until December, 1897, and during the last year was chairman of the board, the Market street bridge in Logansport being but one of the many improvements brought about through the energy and influence of Mr Shideler and his fellow-commissioners. He was fraternally connected with the Masons, in which he had reached the degree of master, and his religious faith was that of the Christian church.

On April 14, 1859, Mr Shideler was married to Miss Elizabeth Mummey, daughter of John and Barbara (Libenguth) Mummey, the former a representative of a Pennsylvania family of German origin, and to this union there were born three children. Amelia, the wife of Herman Homburg, living at No 209 Burlington avenue, Logansport, Elmer G, who died at the age of twenty-four years, five months, and Asa J.

Asa J Shideler was reared on the home farm, and secured his education in the district schools, which he attended until he was about eighteen years of age. At that time he began to give his entire attention to farming, which has been his occupation to the present, and now resides on the old Shideler homestead of 160 acres, in addition to which he has a property of 132 acres in Clinton township. A man of congenial and affable manners, he has gained the esteem of his neighbors and business associates, and in his wide acquaintance numbers numerous warm friends. As an agriculturist he is recognized as a man who is thoroughly conversant with all the details of his business, and as a citizen he has demonstrated his public spirit whenever movements for the betterment of his community have been in need of his support. He is a popular member of Tipton Lodge No 33, A F & A M, and his family is prominently connected socially. Mr Shideler has taken an active interest in politics, and at one time served on the Clinton township Republican Central Committee, but in 1912 cast his fortunes with the new Progressive party, the principles of which he ardently supports.

On November 25, 1896, Mr Shideler was united in marriage with Miss Florence Tyner, who was born, reared and educated in Clinton township, daughter of William and Ella (Hynes) Tyner. Two sons have been born to this union. William Abraham, born December 1, 1897, a student in the district schools and Elmer G, born April 25, 1899, also a district school pupil.

MATTHEW MORONEY Celtic blood flows in the veins of Matthew Moroney in generous measure. Indeed, his paternal and maternal ancestry were of Irish birth and breeding, and his parents were born and reared in County Clare, in Ireland, whence they came to America's shores in 1850. It may be said concerning these worthy people that they came to America in their early wedded life, the year being 1850, and from New Orleans where they landed their journey to Indiana, where they eventually settled, covered a period of about five years. They first stopped at Memphis Tennessee, going from there to Cincinnati, where

Matthew Moroney and Wife.

the father was employed variously. At Hagerstown, Indiana, he stopped with his little family for some time, then came on to Cass county, Indiana, where, in 1853, he settled on a farm some three and a half miles from Lucerne, the place being now owned and occupied by John Hall. Four years he spent there, then moved to the farm that is owned today by his son, the subject of this review.

The father was Matthew, son of Matthew Moroney, and the mother was Marguerite Manix, both of fine old County Clare families, where they were born and bred. When they settled on the farm which is now the home of the subject he was yet unborn. The place was more a wilderness than a farm, and the building that might be termed a dwelling was a one room log cabin. The head of the little family straightway secured the aid of a carpenter to make a suitable addition to the home, and while the work of building was being carried on Matthew Moroney was born, on November 8, 1860. The carpenter who was employed upon the new home, built a cradle for the new comer, which, though crude and rough as it doubtless was, held him as close and warm as any much more elegant shelter could possibly have done. The father later built the barn, which still stands on the old place, although it has in recent years been moved from its original location. At that early time, little if any clearing had been done on the place, hardly worthy as yet to be called a farm, but Mr Moroney gave himself unreservedly to the task of cleaning up the land and making a productive farm from it. He succeeded most admirably, and when he died in 1876 left a fine place to his son, Matthew of this review. He was fifty-six years of age at that time, and his widow survived him for twenty years, passing away in 1896 when she was seventy-seven years old. She, it may be said, had been twice married. Her first marriage, also contracted in Ireland, culminated in widowhood, when she was left with three children, named as follows: Nancy Burke, who later married Patrick Kearney, Mary, the wife of David Campbell, and John Burke, who is unmarried. By her second marriage she had three children,—Matthew, Marguerite and Katherine. Marguerite married William Murphy, and is now deceased; Katherine married John Carroll, and is also dead.

Upon the death of the father, Matthew Moroney continued on with the home farm, and finally came into its ownership. He has made worthy progress in the farming industry and has carried to completion the work that his father began many years ago, winning the right to be regarded as one of the substantial and progressive farming men of the community.

On November 9, 1881, Mr Moroney married Mary Backus, the daughter of Richard and Rose (Fitzsimmons) Backus. For one quarter of a century Mr and Mrs Moroney traveled life's journey—but in the year 1906, she passed away. Mrs Moroney was an affectionate and loving wife and mother, and a friend to all. She was a lady who commanded the universal respect and friendship of all with whom she came in contact. She had faithfully reared her children in religious teachings, and her daily life was a lesson to her children. She was ever ready to counsel and advise her husband in life's battle, and when she passed "to that bourne from whence no traveler returns," the golden circlet in the home was severed. She was a devotee to the Catholic faith and was ever loyal to her church, which was the Saint Elizabeth Roman Catholic church in Harrison township, where her husband and children are also members. She passed away loved and respected by all who knew her, leaving her husband and nine children, named as follows: Alice, born August 25, 1882, Katharine, born January 21, 1884, William, born October 3, 1886, Matthew M, born March 29 1889, Rose, born on September 19, 1890, Charles, born December 28 1892, Nellie, born August 21 1898, Mary, born February 25, 1901, and Richard, born September 18, 1902.

Mr. Moroney has taken his place among his townsmen as one of the wide-awake men of the community, and has been called to serve as trustee of Harrison township for one term, as well as in the higher office of county treasurer of Cass county, in which official position he acted with all efficiency for two terms, the quality of his service being one that fully justified the people in returning him to the office and which marked him as a capable and praiseworthy citizen and public official. He is a Democrat, stanch and firm in his political convictions, and his religious affiliations are with Saint Elizabeth's Roman Catholic church, of Harrison township.

Mr. Moroney is also a member of the B P O E lodge, No 66, and the Knights of Columbus, No 561, located at Logansport Indiana. The pretty homestead of Mr Moroney is known as "Forest Lodge."

FREDERICK W SEYBOLD It is due to the efforts of the energetic, progressive and intelligent farmers that agricultural conditions in Cass county are now in such a healthy condition. Intelligent working of the soil, recognition of the value of crop rotation, and the use of modern machinery have improved conditions wonderfully during the past several decades and one of those who have assisted in the advancement of the county, and especially in Clinton township while at the same time he has furthered his own interests, is Frederick W Seybold the owner of a valuable tract of 240 acres located in Clinton township. Mr. Seybold has carried on general farming and stock raising, and his ventures have proved uniformly successful because of the intelligence and energy he has brought to his work. He was born in Cass county, Indiana, near Logansport June 15, 1876, and is a son of Frederick and Mary A (Wolfe) Seybold, the former now a resident of Logansport, while the latter is deceased.

Frederick Seybold was born near Dayton, Ohio January 26 1832, and is a son of John G and Jacobema (Fulmer) Seybold both natives of Germany. They were the parents of twelve children, as follows John G Frederick Henry, Jacob William P Mary A, Elizabeth Catherine Jacobema, Margaret, Christ and David. The grandfather of Frederick W Seybold remained in the Fatherland until his fourteenth year at which time, in order to escape being forced into the army of Napoleon, he ran away from home and made his way to England. He had not yet reached his majority in 1814 when he managed to secure passage to Montreal, Canada, which city was the home of a wealthy uncle, engaged in the wholesale clothing business for whom he was an errand boy for two years, receiving for his services his board and clothing. The year 1816 saw his advent in the United States, where, at New York City, he learned the baker's trade, an occupation which he followed in the metropolis and other cities for several years, his next migration being to North Carolina where he spent the year 1820 In 1821 he returned to New York and married Jacobenia Fulmer, and in the following year came west in a one-horse wagon and settled on a farm near Springsboro, Warren county, Ohio In addition to farming, Mr Seybold also worked on the Ohio canal and accepted whatever honorable employment presented itself, and by the year 1832 was able to purchase sixty acres of land in Montgomery county, near Dayton, Ohio to which he later added forty acres more, and there passed the remaining years of his life, passing away in 1865 His widow survived him some years and was ninety-two at the time of her death, which occurred in Ohio

Frederick Seybold, the son of the progenitor, and father of Frederick W Seybold, was born and reared on his father's farm in Montgomery county, Ohio, and in his youth attended school in a log schoolhouse near his home When twenty-eight years of age, in 1859, he made his way to Indiana and purchased 108 acres of land, near the corporate limits of Logansport, in Cass county, and to this he added from time to time until he was the owner of more than five hundred acres of some of the best land in the county His success in life has been due to his own efforts, as he started out in life with little capital save his own energy, ambition and ability, and won his way to the front solely through his own industry and intelligent management On January 13, 1859 he was married to Miss Mary A Wolfe, who was born in Montgomery county, Ohio, daughter of Jacob Wolfe, and to this union there were born seven children, of whom three survive Lydia, the wife of Alva Myers, of Logansport Indiana, Alfred, who married Eva Guthrie and lives in Logansport, and Frederick W Frederick Seybold is now retired and lives in his comfortable home in Logansport He has always been a stalwart Democrat, and takes an intelligent interest in public matters, having been elected to a number of township offices during his active years

Frederick W Seybold was reared on his father's farm, which was situated near the corporate limits of Logansport, and attended the public schools of that city, also spending two years in the high school On completing his education, he at once entered upon his career as a general farmer and stockman, and has given the greater part of his attention to the latter branch, buying, shipping and feeding cattle, hogs and colts, and finding a ready market for his stock in the various large points From time to time he has added to his land, now having 240 acres of excellent property, and as the years have passed has added to his buildings and equipment His present residence, erected at a cost of $9,000 contains fourteen rooms, with seven rooms in the basement and is fitted with every modern comfort and convenience Like his father, he is an adherent of Democratic principles, and takes a keen interest in public matters albeit more as a spectator than as an office seeker His fraternal connection is with Lodge No 323 of the Fraternal Order of Eagles, of which he is a member of the board of trustees

On December 14, 1898, Mr Seybold was married to Miss Maude Gotchall who was born in Noble township, Cass county, Indiana July 13, 1876, and to this union there have been born two children· Hazel, born September 4, 1899, and Madge, born February 20, 1900, both students in the district schools

CLARENCE BRUCE REED Agricultural conditions in Cass county have changed to such an extent during the past several decades that the enterprising farmer has been compelled to a large degree to alter his methods of treating the soil if he is ambitious to keep up with the march of progress and attain a full measure of success, otherwise he falls into the rut of mediocrity and must be content to follow, not to lead, in the ranks of his vocation New scientific discoveries have been made powerful machinery has been invented, new innovations have been introduced, all calling for close and constant attention on the part of the man of progress, and Cass county can boast of its full quota of men who have been quick to recognize the advantages of the new school of farming. Among them may be mentioned Clarence B Reed, of section 5, Clinton township, whose 120-acre tract bears mute but eloquent evidence of the presence of able and intelligent management Mr Reed has spent his entire life in his present locality, having been born in Clinton township, June 8, 1858, a son of William and Catherine (Schuey) Reed

William Reed was a native of Erin, and was brought to this country by his parents when a lad of ten years, the family settling in Indiana in the southern part of the state There he was reared, and in young manhood came to Cass county, where he was married to Catherine Schuey, who was born in Pennsylvania and was brought to Indiana in girlhood After their union, Mr and Mrs Reed settled on the farm now occupied by Clarence Bruce Reed, here spending the remainder of their lives The father passed away in 1884 and the mother in 1887, and they were the parents of a family of eight children, four being alive today, as follows Clarence Bruce, Robert R Thomas L, and Emma G, the last named being the widow of Fred J Neville

Clarence B Reed was reared on the farm that he now owns and received his education in the district schools, which he attended until he was twenty-one years of age He received a careful training in every detail of farm work, and on attaining his majority began farming and stock raising on his own account, in which he has since engaged, gaining unqualified success Mr Reed is now the owner of 120 acres of the old homestead, on which he has made numerous improvements, including modern buildings, tiling, draining ditching, etc He takes a pride in being able to increase the productive power of his property and to decrease the cost of production thus placing himself among the men to whose efforts the cause of progress owes so much In political matters he is a Republican, but he has only interested himself in politics as a voter, never having had a desire for the struggles of the public arena In fraternal circles he is a member of the Elks of Logansport, and a popular member of Lodge No 323, Fraternal Order of Eagles, of which he has served as a member of the board of trustees and his wife is well known among the Ladies of the Maccabees, Lodge No 86, of Logansport She is also a property owner, having 110 acres of well-developed land in section 15 Clinton township.

On January 1, 1890, Mr Reed was married in Clinton township to Miss Rosabelle Rhorer, also a native of this township, born December 11 1862 daughter of Jacob and Jane (Justice) Rhorer, farming people of Cass county Mr and Mrs Reed have been the parents of one child, Gail who died in infancy

WILLIAM J GRANT A striking example of the success to be attained through the medium of well-applied industry, intelligent effort and a life of integrity and probity, is found in the career of William J Grant, of Clinton township, who has retired from active pursuits after many years spent in tilling the soil Left an orphan at a tender age, his boyhood was filled with hard work of the most unceasing character, and the succeeding years were ones in which many obstacles were met and overcome, but he ever kept his face toward his cherished goal, with the result that today he is in possession of a handsome competency and holds an undisputed position among the citizens of his locality Mr Grant was born in Canada, April 6, 1851, and is a son of George and Hannah Grant

Mr Grant was ten years of age when he came to the United States with a party of immigrants who located in White county, Indiana, and there he was reared to manhood His educational advantages were decidedly limited, but he was a keen and intelligent youth and made the most of his opportunities, which supplemented by years of observation and study have given a wide fund of general information He began working on a farm in White county at the age of fourteen years, and on November 11, 1874 was married to Miss Sarah Davis who was born in White county March 18, 1859, a daughter of Noah and Mary (Steele) Davis, the former a native of Connersville, Fayette county, Indiana and the latter of White county Mr Davis located in White county when a lad, when that section was covered with a dense woods, and there spent the rest of his life in farming On August 1, 1879, Mr and Mrs. Grant came to Cass county, locating first for about one year in Logansport where he was engaged in working by the day Succeeding this he also worked at day laboring in Clinton township for some time, but subsequently started operations on his own account on a rented farm, on which he continued to reside until 1897, and at that time purchased what is now known at Maple Ridge Farm, his present property, a tract of seventy-six acres Here he made numerous improvements, his buildings including a beautiful country home, in which he and his wife are now living retired enjoying the fruits of their early labors Mr and Mrs Grant have had three children, namely Ira J, who married Jennie Beal of Remington, Indiana, where they now reside, Asa E, a farmer of Tipton township, who married Bessie Thomas, and Alice M, deceased, who was the wife of Ira Bonta

The members of the Grant family are affiliated with the Church of God, and Mr Grant's fraternal connection is with Eel River Lodge No 417, Independent Order of Odd Fellows. He has Democratic inclinations in political matters, and while he has never been an office seeker, has served in the capacity of township supervisor. Mr Grant deservedly bears the honored title of self-made man Everywhere and at all times he remembers that he has worked hard and faithfully, but the struggles of earlier years are forgotten in the peace and contentment that a life of industry brings, and now, in his latter years he may look over an honorable career, unblemished by the stain of questionable dealing

HARRY E AMOSS The owner of a well-cultivated farm of fifty-six acres, Harry E Amoss is now serving as trustee of Clinton township, and is one of the leading and influential citizens of Cass county Mr Amoss has always been a farmer having been reared to those pursuits and adopted them as a vocation when he embarked upon a business career of his own, and the success which has rewarded his efforts is but the result of the understanding of his own capabilities and the selection of a business to which he was especially suited Mr Amoss was born on a farm in Clinton township Cass county Indiana, November 8, 1862 and is a son of William and Mary A (Rea) Amoss

The grandparents of Mr Amoss John and Matilda (Cohen) Amoss, were early settlers of Clinton township and the Cohens were large landholders in this vicinity William Amoss was born in Virginia (now West Virginia), and came to Cass county, Indiana, as a single man Here he was married to Mary A. Rea, whose people were from Virginia, and whose members had contributed to the soldiers from their state that fought in the War of the Rebellion Mr Amoss was a farmer by occupation, and continued to be so engaged until his death, which occurred August 16, 1912 He and his wife were the parents of six children, of whom four still survive, namely Addie, single, who lives on a part of the old homestead place, Walter, who is a miner and resides in Wyoming, Arthur who lives on the old home farm, and Harry E

Harry E Amoss was educated in the public schools of Clinton township and at the age of seventeen years began to give his whole attention to farming He continued under the parental roof assisting his father and brothers, until his marriage November 12, 1890, to Miss Lizzie Sherman, who was born in Clinton township, Cass county, February 29, 1864 and educated in the public schools here One child has come to this union Rea, born October 20, 1891 who is a graduate of the township schools and of the Logansport high school, and is now assisting his father to cultivate the home farm Mr Amoss is accounted one of the practical and progressive agriculturists of the community He uses the latest improved machinery in the development of his farm, studies the best methods for producing the various cereals adapted to this climate, practices rotation of crops and above all brings to his work that unflagging industry which spells for the greatest degree of success His life has been one of well-directed effort, and with his success has come that content that is known only by those whose consciences are clear of any questionable methods, and who have been the architects of their own fortunes

Fraternally, Mr Amoss is connected with the Independent Order of Red Men, and I O O F in which he has held high office His political belief is that of the Republican party, and on that ticket was elected to the office of trustee of Clinton township, a position which he still fills with credit to himself and to the entire satisfaction of his fellow-citizens He has given to his official duties the same faithful services that have characterized his private affairs, and has aided all movements for the public good, being a member of the building committee of the high school at Clymers Faithful in his friendships, he enjoys the warm regard of all with whom he has been brought into contact

WILLARD BRIGGS Two miles west of Clymer, in Clinton township, Cass county, is situated the well-cultivated eighty-acre farm belonging to Willard Briggs, former trustee of Clinton township, and a citizen who has spent his entire career within the limits of the county Mr Briggs has devoted all of his active years to the cultivation of the soil, and it would be difficult to find one who is better versed in agricultural conditions in this part of the county, while his standing as a public-spirited citizen is equally high Mr Briggs was born in Clinton township, Cass county, Indiana, March 19, 1867, and is a son of Duncan L. and Sarah J (Gerton) Briggs

Duncan L Briggs was born in the State of New York, and was an infant of two years when taken by his parents to Ohio There he embarked upon his own career at the age of sixteen years as a boatman on the Erie Canal and Lake Erie, following this kind of employment until he had reached his thirty-third year When he was thirty-four years of age, Mr. Briggs was married, and at that time turned his attention to agricultural pursuits, in which he was engaged in Cass county during the remainder of his life, his death occurring January 20 1912, and that of his wife December 25, 1910 They were the parents of two children Willard, and Elizabeth, the latter of whom, now deceased, was the wife of John Patterson

Like other farmers' sons of his day and locality, Willard Briggs gave part of his boyhood to the work of the home farm During the winter terms he added to his fund of literary knowledge, but the summers were all devoted to following the plow or other farm labor, and he thus built up his constitution and became thoroughly familiar with every detail of farm work Mr Briggs was given better advantages than many of his youthful companions, however, for a time being a student at the old college at Logansport, as well as at the Danville normal school, and when he had completed his education was well fitted to fill whatever position he might be called upon to occupy He chose farming as his life work, and has had no reason to regret his selection, for through industry, perseverance and intelligent effort, he has gained a competence and made a place for himself among the substantial men of his community At this time he is farming eighty acres of highly cultivated land, located two miles west of Clymers, on which may be found all the improvements and conveniences which mark the home of the progressive and enterprising farmer of today

On September 2, 1891, Mr Briggs was united in marriage with Miss Laura Patterson, and of their children, three survive, namely: Mabel, a graduate of the Logansport high school, who is now engaged in teaching school, Clarence, who is in his second year in the Logansport high school, and Harold, a student in the district schools. Mr. Briggs is a popular member of the Knights of Pythias, Apollo Lodge No. 62, of Logansport, and the Modern Woodmen of America. His political belief is that of the new Progressive party.

OLIVER REED. Clinton township shows some of the best regulated farms in Cass county, made so by the thrift, industry and energetic labor of their owners, who have realized the advantages of using modern machinery and methods in their farm work. One of the valuable properties of this township is the farm of Oliver Reed, a tract of 160 acres lying in sections 32 and 33, which has been cultivated into a state of high fertility through Mr. Reed's knowledge of agricultural work and his willingness to adopt modern methods and appliances to take the place of the cruder implements and hit-or-miss manner of farming of former years. Mr. Reed is a native of Clinton township, and was born August 12, 1849, a son of Michael and Sarah (Tittle) Reed. His father was born at Reading, Pennsylvania, in 1820, and his mother near Dayton, Ohio, and they were the parents of eight children, of whom six are living at this time: William D., a farmer of Cass county, Oliver, of this review, Sarah, the wife of John D. Tyner of Logansport, Clara M., who is single and lives in Logansport, Dr. John H., a well-known physician of that city, and Jacob A., who also resides in Logansport.

Oliver Reed was reared in Clinton township, and as a youth entered the district schools, which he attended until he was eighteen years of age. At that time he entered the Logansport high school, and for three years continued his studies therein during the winter months, while his summers were devoted to farm work. On completing his education, Mr. Reed chose farming as his life occupation, and after his marriage, in 1875, rented his father's farm, which he continued to operate for twelve years then purchasing his present property. He has added to his original purchase from time to time, making improvements as his finances and inclinations allowed, and his 160-acre tract is now one of the best in the township, highly cultivated, well drained and tiled and improved with excellent buildings, substantial in character and of a handsome architectural style. Politically, Mr. Reed is a Democrat, but he has never taken a great deal of interest in public matters beyond the manner in which they affect his township. He is superintendent of the Logansport and Western Turnpike, a position which he has held for some years, and in which he has served with fidelity. He and his wife are members of the English Lutheran church, and both are public-spirited and deeply interested in all that promises to be of benefit to the community in which they are such important factors. In addition to his farming operations, which are extensive, Mr. Reed devotes a great deal of attention to raising graded stock, and his cattle find a ready market at the large shipping points.

On April 22, 1875, Mr. Reed was married to Miss Mary Whalon, of Germantown, Ohio, who was born and reared there and educated in the common and normal schools, and for some years was engaged in teaching in Ohio. Five children have been born to this union: Ethel M., educated in the district and high schools single, and living with her parents, Charles E., a graduate of the State University at Bloomington

"ERCELDENE LODGE," RESIDENCE OF MR. AND MRS. JOHN W. CLARY

HISTORY OF CASS COUNTY 1027

Indiana, class of 1912, where he received the degree of Bachelor of Arts, and now a student in the Chicago Scientific School, under the supervision of Dr Taylor, and Homer L, a graduate of the Logansport high school and now a student in Purdue University Two children are dead, Omer Leroy, who died aged 12 years, and Oliver O who died in infancy

JOHN W CLARY. In the vicinity of Lucerne, in Harrison township, there is probably no more productive an estate nor more attractive rural home than that occupied by John W Clary and family Mr Clary represents one of the old families of Cass county, and was himself born in a log cabin, and was a product of the early conditions in this county He lived here when much of the land was covered by forest, and before any of the modern facilities had been instituted A railroad came when he was grown and married, and since that time every decade has witnessed a remarkable improvement in all conditions and facilities of industry and living

John W Clary was born in district number one, Harrison township, in a log house on the seventh of September, 1844 His father was Isaac Clary, and the early honors of the family in this county are given more detail on other pages of this history On February 1, 1871, John W Clary was united in marriage, in Fulton county, with Miss Lavina Marsh, a daughter of David and Anna (Hall) Marsh Mrs. Clary's father was born in Ohio, and then he came to Fulton county, Indiana The family was founded here by her grandfather, who was a soldier in the War of 1812, and later had come to Indiana from Ohio He bought land at $1 25 an acre and did much for the early development of the country Mrs Clary's father died about 1889 Mrs Clary has two parchment deeds in her possession dated June 30 1837, and executed during the administration of President Van Buren

Mr and Mrs Clary are the parents of seven children, whose names follow Cora Elsie, the wife of Isaac Emery, Jane Frances, who married Walter Ingram, David Newton, who died at the age of twelve years, William H, born April 14, 1880, Edith, born September 6, 1890, Della May, who died at the age of two years and five months, and Verdie who died at the age of fourteen months

In 1886 Mr Clary moved to his present farm in Harrison township A small frame house was the habitation which he and his family occupied, and several years later he was enabled with the fruits of his labor and management to erect a comfortable home and other buildings, which give this estate the appearance of being one of the best homes in Cass county When he first took possession all the land was cleared but forty acres, and since then he has succeeded in clearing up nearly all of the estate, so that his farm of two hundred and twenty acres is all suitable for cultivation and for the profits of agriculture

From 1872 to 1876, Mr Clary was a resident of Fulton county, this state and during that time served as supervisor of his township for about six years He and his family are members of the Presbyterian church

"Erceldene Lodge," the beautiful country seat of Mr and Mrs

John W Clary, was erected in 1911 It is one of the most modern country residences in Cass county, built of brick, with wide concrete verandas, and finished in hard woods in the most artistic manner, beautifully and comfortably furnished, and lighted from cellar to garret with a modern acetylene plant It is so large and well arranged that the host and hostess can entertain a large coterie of friends and it is well known as the abode of cordiality and friendly greeting

Mrs Clary is a gracious hostess and it is a pleasure to know her, she being of a most pleasing personality and entertaining her friends with a royal welcome

SAMUEL H SMITH From poor and obscure boyhood to a position of prominence among the agriculturists of his section and the ownership of two fine farms the career of Samuel H Smith, of Clinton township, has been replete with triumph over obstacles, pluck, determination and industrious effort, all conducing to well-earned success Mr Smith was born in Newton county, Indiana, February 24, 1870, and is a son of James H and Rebecca E (McClain) Smith

James H Smith was born and reared in Clinton township, Cass county, Indiana but as a young man went to Iroquois, Iroquois county, Illinois and subsequently to Gardner, Grundy county, Illinois, being engaged in merchandising and spending in all about ten years in the Prairie State At the end of that period he returned to Indiana, and his last years were spent on the homestead where his death occurred During the Civil war he fought for three years and four months in the ranks of the Union army, as a member of Company D, Forty-sixth Regiment, Indiana Volunteer Infantry, and was wounded in the battle of Champion Hill In his later years he was a member of the Grand Army of the Republic Mr Smith married Rebecca E McClain, who was born in Indiana, a daughter of Dr Joseph McClain a physician who came from Virginia Three sons and three daughters were born to this union, Samuel H being the only child now living in Cass county

The boyhood of Samuel H Smith was passed on his father's farm, and his education was limited to a short attendance at the district school of his locality and whatever he could pick up himself Being a keen observer, however and a man of much native intelligence, he has gained a wide and comprehensive knowledge of general subjects and is known as an exceedingly well informed man At the age of fourteen years he began to take an active part in farming and through industry, energy and thrift has accumulated $101\frac{1}{4}$ acres in Clinton township, as well as a tract of 192 acres lying north of Logansport He has always engaged in general farming, in addition to which he has carried on extensive dairying and for some years has been known as a breeder of registered cattle The same industry and energetic spirit that characterized his young manhood have marked his subsequent career, and he is known as one of his community's most progressive agriculturists one who is ready at all times to adopt modern methods and with the ability to make the most of them The old Smith homestead, on which he resides with his family has been converted into one of the most valuable farms in Clinton township, through intelligent treatment of the soil and the installing of numerous improvements and the buildings thereon are of substantial character and architectural beauty. Mr Smith's political belief is that of the Republican party, although he has not interested himself to any great extent in public matters, while his fraternal connection is with the Independent Order of Foresters. With his wife and children, he attends the Methodist Episcopal church.

On September 5, 1894, Mr Smith was married at Anderson, Indiana, to Miss Rose Snell who was born September 16, 1867, at Anderson. Mrs Smith was educated in the public schools, and the death of her parents made it necessary that she become self-supporting, she being a clerk in a general store at Anderson for several years. She and her husband have two children Reba, seventeen years of age, who has been educated in the common and high schools, and Jesse, who is now attending the country schools and assisting his father in the work of the home farm.

JAMES W LITTLE One of the old and honored residents of Clinton township, Cass county, who has spent more than seventy-three years in this section and is still connected actively with agricultural pursuits, although he has reached an age when most men would consider that they had earned a rest, is James W Little the owner of 300 acres of land, a model, progressive citizen, able agriculturist and revered veteran of the Civil war. Mr Little was born on the farm on which he now resides, July 7, 1840, and is a son of Alexander and Ann (Bowen) Little.

Alexander Little was born in August, 1802, in County Armagh, Ireland from whence he came to the United States as a young man and first settled in Franklin county, Pennsylvania. In 1834 he came overland to Cass county, Indiana, and entered land on which he erected a small log cabin, but after several years returned to Pennsylvania and married Ann Bowen, of Franklin county. After their marriage, in May, 1838, they started for the new land in the wilds of Indiana, making the entire journey of 640 miles in a wagon, the trip consuming some six weeks, and finally reached their destination and began their life in the little log cabin home in the woods along the Wabash river. There Alexander Little passed away in November, 1864, an honest, reliable straightforward man, whose life was one of unceasing industry and persistent effort. While a resident of Pennsylvania he served as captain in a military organization known as the Dragoons. He was a member of the Presbyterian church and his father was an elder in that faith in Franklin county for upwards of twenty years. Alexander and Ann (Bowen) Little became the parents of twelve children, of whom six grew to maturity, and four are still living today, namely James W, Amanda the wife of Dr Sterrett of California, Sarah, the wife of Samuel Milligan, of Waveland, Indiana, and Mrs Anna Stoutmeyer, of Onargo Illinois.

James W Little was reared on the farm on which he now lives, and received his education in the common schools, eventually securing a teacher's license and becoming an educator in the district schools. He was thus engaged at the outbreak of the Civil war and in May, 1862, enlisted in Company B, Fifty-fifth Regiment, Indiana Volunteer Infantry. After some six months of service Mr Little received his honorable discharge, on account of wounds sustained during the battle of Richmond, and at this time he is receiving a pension from a grateful government. Mr Little was known as a brave, cheerful and faithful soldier, one who gave the best of himself to the discharge of his duty, and to whom orders were as a sacred trust. He left the service with an excellent record and returned to the duties of peace, again becoming a district school teacher.

In 1866 Mr Little was married to Miss Mary Barnes who was born in Carroll county, Indiana, December 17, 1844, and educated in the district schools. Five children have been born to this union, of whom one died in infancy, the others being Flora, single and residing at home with her parents, Dr John A, who is enjoying an excellent medical practice in Logansport, Emma J, the wife of J R Colter, of Washington Iowa, and Samuel H, who is single, resides at home and assists his father in the work of the homestead place.

The members of the Little family are identified with the Associate Presbyterian church, in which Mr Little is one of the elders. He is a strictly temperate man, having never used tobacco or spirituous liquors, and has been enthusiastic in his support of all movements tending to advance religion, education, morality and good citizenship. His farm of 296 acres has been brought to a high state of cultivation through intelligent treatment of the soil, and is considered one of the valuable tracts of this section. For many years Mr Little was an adherent of Republican policies and principles, but in the campaign of 1912 his progressive ideas caused him to cast his fortunes with the young so-called Bull Moose party.

JOHN A LITTLE, M D This most accomplished gentleman, learned in his profession, a versatile devotee of science, a public-spirited citizen, as well as active and energetic in the business life of Logansport, has been in practice in this city for fifteen years, and has attained to an eminent place among medical practitioners. Like many of the successful professional men of the city, Dr Little is a product of the farm, having been born on his father's estate in Clinton township, Cass county, Indiana, November 5, 1868 a son of James W and Mary (Barnes) Little, and grandson of Alexander and Anna (Bowen) Little.

Alexander Little was born in County Armagh, Ireland. He remained in Baltimore and Philadelphia until 1834, in which year he immigrated to the newly-developed region of Indiana, where he pre-empted 160 acres of government land in Clinton township, Cass county. This land has continued in the family possession to the present time, and is now part of the home of James W Little, who has spent his life in agricultural pursuits.

John A Little was reared on the old home place and his early educational training was secured in the district schools. Subsequently, he took a high school course in Logansport, from which he was graduated in May, 1889, with all the honors of his class, and during the winters of 1889 and 1890 followed the vocation of educator teaching the Fox Den school in Jefferson township. In the fall of 1890 Dr. Little entered Wabash College to further his education, and was graduated therefrom in 1894, with the degree of Bachelor of Sciences. Later, in 1902 this same institution, for his subsequent efficient work conferred upon him the honorary degree of Master of Arts. Dr. Little took up the study of medicine in 1895, when he became a student in Rush Medical College, where he graduated in May, 1898, as president of his class in that noted institution. He immediately entered upon the practice of his profession in Logansport, and now has a large and representative clientele, which has gradually been obtained through the recognition of his high abilities. Regarded as a master of his profession, he has not been content with the knowledge which his early study gave him but has kept his eyes open to the progress of the science and has adopted every improvement that the years have brought. He has specialized in preventive measures, antiseptics, and similar branches, in which he is known as an authority. He confines himself exclusively to his practice, and has taken none other than a good citizen's interest in public matters, belongs only to the medical organizations, and has not mixed in politics.

On June 4, 1902, Dr Little was married to Miss Blanche Mitchell, of Pasadena, California, and they have had four children, namely Henrietta, Robert, Mary and Ruth. Dr and Mrs Little are members of the First Presbyterian church of Logansport, and are well known in social circles of the city.

WILLIAM A KLEPINGER. Among the pioneer families of Cass county whose members have contributed materially to the growth and development of the agricultural importance of this section, none is better known that that of Klepinger, the history of which has been commensurate with that of Clinton township during the past eighty years. A representative of this old and honored family is found in William A Klepinger, farmer and stock raiser, whose entire life has been spent here and who now occupies a foremost position among the successful agriculturists of his part of the county. Mr Klepinger was born on a farm in the southwest part of Clinton township, January 4, 1858, and is a son of Michael P and Eleanor (Lesh) Klepinger.

Henry and Mary (Miller) Klepinger, the grandparents of William A Klepinger, were born in Pennsylvania, and came to Cass county in 1833, entering land from the government in Clinton township, where they located in the woods, built a little log cabin, and there spent the rest of their lives in developing a home for their family. They were the parents of ten children, of whom six are still living. Michael P, James, William, Eliza, Susan and Elizabeth. Michael P Klepinger was one year old when he accompanied his parents to Cass county, having been born near Dayton, Ohio, May 27, 1832. His youth was spent in assisting his father to clear the farm from the wilderness, and in September, 1852, he was married to Miss Eleanor Lesh, they settling down to work on the old homestead, where they continued operations until their retirement from active life in 1909. Since that year they have lived at Burrows, Carroll county, Indiana, where they have a comfortable home and numerous warm friends. Six children were born to them of whom five are still living. Eliza J, who married John P Friend, William A, Caroline, who married W F West, George, who married Bessie Crockett, and Dennis, who married Sadie Ebbets. The members of the family are connected with the Christian church, in the work of which Mr Klepinger was active for a number of years.

William A. Klepinger was reared on the old homestead place in Clinton township and received his education in the district schools, this being supplemented by attendance in the public schools of Burrows. At the age of twenty-two years he began to give his entire time to farming and stock raising, continuing on rented property until he was thirty-four years of age and industriously saving his earnings with the end ever in view of becoming the owner of a property of his own. On May 20, 1893, Mr. Klepinger was married to Miss Minnie Shafer, who was born in Clinton township, and educated in the district schools. Mrs. Klepinger lost her parents in young womanhood and from their estate received thirty acres of Clinton township land, which formed the nucleus for the present handsome Klepinger farm of 202 acres adjoining Clymers. This property is in a high state of cultivation, Mr. Klepinger being an efficient farmer, with a thorough knowledge of soil and climatic conditions, and various modern improvements have been made, including a substantial residence and other buildings. In addition to his farming operations, Mr. Klepinger has always operated a threshing machine outfit, and has invested in 160 acres of land in the Saskatchewan country, Canada.

Mr. Klepinger is a quiet, unassuming man, and has not interested himself actively in public matters, although he votes the Democratic ticket, and supports all movements which he believes will make for good government. Through straightforward dealing and an earnest desire to assist his fellow-men in their struggle toward success, he has gained many warm friends and no man stands higher in the respect and esteem of his fellow-men. Mr. and Mrs. Klepinger have two children. Ruth, eighteen years of age, and Josephine, sixteen years old, both at home, who have been given excellent educational advantages and fitted for whatever positions they may be called upon to fill in life.

GEORGE W. SEAWRIGHT, who is one of the more prominent agricultural men of Jefferson township, was born in the same community where he now lives on September 19, 1855, and here has passed his life up to the present time. He is the son of William and Emaline (Van Atta) Seawright.

William Seawright came from Pennsylvania in the thirties, in company with his parents, and they settled in Jefferson township in the early pioneer days and identified themselves with the primitive life that obtained in that early day. They built a grist mill at Crooked Creek and this mill was operated by the grandfather of the subject for a goodly term of years, with profit to himself and great convenience to his neighbors. Emaline Van Atta, the wife of William Seawright, came to Indiana from New Jersey, her native state, settling with her parents in Jefferson township, when she was yet a young girl. She was here reared and here she married her husband, who died in 1877, leaving her with three children to mourn his departure. Of the three, George William, the subject, was the eldest; Louis is a resident of Jefferson township, and Harry is prominent in the railroad mail service.

George William Seawright was educated in the common schools and alternated his studies with work on the home farm. He remained on the home place until he attained his majority, when he launched out independently, giving his energies to farming, in which pursuit he had been well trained, and in which he has since realized a wholesome and agreeable success. He is now the owner of two hundred and eighty-six acres of splendid farm land in Jefferson township, which he operates according to the most approved modern methods, and which yields him a comfortable income from season to season. Two hundred acres of this tract is bottom land.

On November 23, 1892, Mr. Seawright was united in marriage with Miss Carrie C. Fitzer, the daughter of John Fitzer, of Clinton township. Three children have been born to Mr. and Mrs. Seawright. Ada, a graduate of Logansport high school and Winona Normal, and now teaching in Jefferson township; Fred, still in the high school, and Charles, who is attending the district schools as yet.

Mr. Seawright is a member of the Independent Order of Odd Fellows, Lodge No. 417, Logansport, Indiana, and he is politically aligned with the Republican party, in whose activities he takes an intelligent interest as a citizen. Mr. Seawright is a member of an old and highly esteemed family in this community, and he has merited and continued to share in the regard which his name has ever claimed in Cass county.

THEODORE F. PIERCE, who is engaged in agricultural operations in section 20, Jefferson township, is not a native of Indiana, but has lived here since his fourth year, and the entire period of his activity has been passed here. He belongs to that class of men who have been the architects of their own fortunes, his success being a direct result of a life of industry, energy and honorable dealing. Mr. Pierce was born in Richland county, Ohio, February 27, 1856, and is a son of Aaron K. and Margaret (Harsh) Pierce. His father, a native of Richland county, Ohio, married there Margaret Harsh, who was born in Pennsylvania, and they came to Indiana in 1860. Locating in Fulton county, near the town of Fulton, Mrs. Pierce spent the remainder of her life on a farm, while her husband died in Richland county.

Theodore F. Pierce commenced his education in the district schools of Fulton county, and at the age of thirteen years went to live with an uncle in Boone county, Missouri, whence he traveled by wagon. There he completed his studies during the winter months, and in the summers worked on his uncle's farm, thus continuing for six years. By 1874, through hard and industrious labor, he had accumulated enough to start on his own account and accordingly, returned to Indiana by wagon, accompanied by his mother and brother, and located in Jefferson township, Cass county, on a tract of land on section 19. There he resided for nine years, following which he purchased a farm north of Lake Cicott consisting of 110 acres. Seven years later he disposed of this property and bought the land which he now owns 174 acres located in sections 19 and 20. For some years, Mr. Pierce carried on diversified farming but at this time he is devoting the greater part of his attention to buying, feeding and shipping livestock of all kinds. Mr. Pierce is known as an excellent business man and has identified himself with various enterprises. He is now a stockholder and director of the Burnettsville State Bank which was organized in 1907 with a capital of $30,000, and the following officers: William Thomas, president, Ernest Thomas vice-president; J C Duffy, cashier, and Fred Duffy, assistant cashier In his political views, he is a Democrat, and for eight years has been a member of the township advisory board With his family, Mr Pierce attends the Burnettsville Baptist church, where he is a deacon trustee, and for eighteen years superintendent of the Sunday school Upright and reliable in all his dealings, he has gained and maintained numerous friendships, and is recognized as a moral influence in his home neighborhood

Mr Pierce was married in 1879 to Miss Junatta Martin, daughter of William Martin, and to this union there have been born two children Russell D, a graduate of the Burnettsville high school and Matina, who is attending that institution A man of wide and varied interests, Mr Pierce's time has been pretty fully occupied, but not so much so that he has not found time to assist in every movement calling for the betterment of his community and its people

ROBERT A STUART Stability of character and purpose and a high order of citizenship are traits which are found with a pleasing degree of frequency in the men who give their lives to the pursuit of the treasures of the soil—a fact which may be accounted for by reason of their close and continued touch with Mother Nature in their every-day life Whatever may be the possible solution, the fact yet remains and in Robert A Stuart all his life a resident of Cass county and a farmer, a splendid example is found of the open-minded and open-handed man who has lived his life in the quiet places and toiled out in the open during the greater part of his days

Born in Boone township, Cass county on March 3, 1858, Mr Stuart is the son of R F and Susan (Atkins) Stuart The father was a native of Mississippi who came to New Albany, Indiana, in about the year 1831 He was a cooper by trade There he married and settled down to farm life some five years later coming to Cass county He located in Boone township, there remaining until 1864, when he migrated to Jefferson township, and there he passed the remainder of his life He was the father of nine children, seven of that number being alive at this writing Both parents died in Jefferson township

Robert A Stuart was reared in Jefferson township and here received his schooling In due course of time he married and settled on a farm in this township, and success has attended his efforts all along the line In section 28 of this township he owns a fertile farm of one hundred and sixty acres, which has yielded most abundantly under his encouraging hand He has maintained the most friendly relations with Prosperity and is regarded today as one of the independent farming men of the township

In 1896 Mr Stuart married Miss Bertha D Eltzroth the daughter of Obidiah Eltzroth and to subject and wife four children have been born The eldest, Cloyd is sixteen years old Ralph and Roy twins are nine years of age, and the youngest born of the four is Maude, now four years old

The family are members of the Presbyterian church and they take an active part in its various departments of service, and Mr Stuart is a Republican He is a man who has acquired much of learning that

never came through schools or books A student of human nature, he finds something interesting in every chance acquaintance, and it is safe to say that this habit of observation has been of no small benefit to him in his regular business life He is an interesting conversationalist, and has read much and observed more He is known for a man of honor and integrity, whose word is as sacred as his bond, and his position in his community is one which eloquently bespeaks his many worthy qualities A man of kindly disposition and modest and unassuming demeanor, he has the most amazing capacity for attending to his own affairs, but is always ready to lend a willing ear to the man who is beset with difficulties, and a helping hand to tide him over the rough places His friends in Jefferson township are only limited by his acquaintance, and he is one of the most valued citizens of his community

WENDELL MILLER, deceased was one of the old settlers of Logansport, having come to this city from Pennsylvania in 1862 He was born in Altoona, that state, on November 21, 1840, and was there reared and instructed in the trade of blacksmithing, which he followed for some years in Pittsburg After coming to Logansport he followed his trade for a time, and held important positions at the old Knowlton & Dolan foundry and in other industrial concerns of the city Illness compelled him to relinquish his work in the seventies, and he then moved to a farm in Washington township, where he passed his remaining days, death claiming him on April 22, 1908

Always an industrious and thrifty soul, Wendell Miller was able to accumulate a goodly share of this world's goods He was able to provide liberally for his family, which was a large one, and he was known to be one of the honorable and upright men of his community Neighborly and kindly disposed toward all, he enjoyed to the utmost the respect and esteem of a large circle of friends and acquaintances He was particularly abstemious, never being addicted to the use of liquor or tobacco in any form, and his conversation was of the cleanest and most wholesome order at all times, profanity of any kind being entirely foreign to his nature or habits

On October 15, 1868, Mr Miller was united in marriage with Miss Caroline Grunsmeyer, and to them twelve children were born, of which goodly number ten were reared to years of maturity Those yet living are Dr G D, to whom a sketch is devoted in other pages of this work, Edward H Frank C, William A, Nora N and Cora B, twins, Mrs Mary Minneman, of Jefferson township, and Mrs. Joseph Lehman, of Dayton, Ohio Mrs Miller, who yet survives her husband, is living on the old home place in Washington township

DR GEORGE D MILLER Of the parentage of George D Miller, M D, further details need not be given here than to say that he is the son of Wendell and Caroline (Grunsmeyer) Miller, one time residents of Pennsylvania, later of Indiana the father being now deceased Concerning that worthy gentleman a sketch is dedicated on other pages of this work, which render further statements unnecessary at this point

Dr George D Miller was born in Logansport, Indiana, on August 7, 1873, and was reared on the old home farm He attended the district schools as a boy, and in 1893-4-5 he was busily engaged in taking preparatory course in the Manual Training High School of St Louis, Missouri In the fall of 1896 he matriculated at the College of Physicians and Surgeons, in Indianapolis, from which he was duly graduated on April 4 1901, receiving his medical degree at that time Dr Miller began the active practice of his profession in Logansport, on April 24, 1901, and he has ever since continued to exercise his professional skill and ability in the town of his nativity, where he has gained and retained the respect of the medical fraternity and of the people alike Dr Miller has been secretary of the Cass County Medical Society since 1902, and is also a member of the Indiana State Medical Society and the American Medical Association

Dr Miller is a Democrat and has served four years as coroner of Cass county, from 1906 to 1910 inclusive, an office in which he acquitted himself with credit He is identified with numerous fraternal organizations, prominent among which is the Masonic order He has attained membership in various bodies of that order, including the Knights Templar, the Scottish Rite, and the Mystic Shrine

On September 5 1897, Dr Miller was united in marriage with Maggie M Robinson They have adopted a daughter, Dorothy J, but have no other children

WILLIAM J GIBSON Among the old and honored residents of Jefferson township none is held in higher esteem than William J Gibson, former township trustee, veteran of the Civil war, and able farmer and stockman A brave defender of his flag, performing the duties of life whether in war or peace, he has been a factor in the growth and development of Cass county as a center of education, morality and good citizenship Mr Gibson was born July 22, 1841, in White county Indiana, and is a son of R P and Sarah (Tam) Gibson The former was born in Tennessee and the latter in Pennsylvania, and both came in youth to White county, Indiana, where they spent the remainder of their lives on a farm in Jackson township

William J Gibson was reared on the home farm in Jackson township, and as a youth entered the district schools, which he was attending at the outbreak of the Civil war He enlisted from Deer Creek township, Cass county, in 1864, in Company B, One Hundred and Forty-second Regiment, Indiana Volunteer Infantry and served for nearly a year, or until the closing of the war, when he returned to Cass county, was mustered out of the service, and given his honorable discharge On the close of his military career, Mr Gibson resumed farming on the home place and was so engaged up to the time of his marriage, March 29, 1866, to Miss Mary E Fry, who was born near Dayton, Ohio, September 5, 1842, daughter of Ephraim Fry Mr Fry was born in Maryland and his wife in Virginia, and were married in Ohio from which state they came to Indiana in 1842 locating in Carroll county Subsequently they moved to Cass county, and there both died

To Mr and Mrs Gibson there were born eleven children nine of whom are living, and except the oldest child all are married, and all living in Cass county Mrs Gibson is a member of the new Dunkard church at Lockport, Indiana Mr Gibson is a Democrat in his political views, and from 1869 to 1873 was trustee of Jefferson township, his service lasting four years and two months He is regarded as one of the wheel-horses of his party in this section, and has numerous influential friends in political life. Mr Gibson, by reason of his services during the Civil war, receives a pension from the government Ever since his marriage he has been engaged in agricultural pursuits on his present property, where he has accumulated 280 acres, a part of which is in Jefferson township, Cass county, and a part in Jackson township, White county His land is well cultivated, his improvements of a modern character and his residence, barn and outbuildings are substantially built and in good repair, and the whole appearance of the property gives evidence of the presence of thrift, industry and able management In addition to general farming, he has carried on stock raising, and his ventures have been uniformly successful because they have been directed along well-defined lines and pushed with energy and perseverance. Mr Gibson takes a keen interest in all matters that affect his community, and as a consequence is known as a good and public-spirited citizen

WILLIAM BANTA In writing of the agricultural men of Cass county who have made distinctive progress in their particular line of industry, it is peculiarly fitting that mention be made of William Banta, one of the well-to-do farmers of Jefferson township, now retired from the activities of farm life A veteran of the Civil war, in which he fought with characteristic fervor and gallantry, Mr. Banta may well be said to have done well his part on the stage of life thus far He has contributed in no small measure to the growth and development of his native township along industrial lines, and has assumed his full share of the civic burdens in the community He is undeniably entitled to his well-earned rest and recreation in his present capacity of retired farmer

Born in Jefferson township, Mr Banta has been one who realized that far off hills were not always greenest, and he has remained in his native town and township, content to realize upon the opportunities that district offered him He was born on the farm which he owns today on New Year's Day, 1846, and is the son of Beauford and Elizabeth (McNay) Banta He was the youngest of the children of his parents, and he remained on the old home place long after the other members had gone out into the world to make homes of their own and take up the burdens of independent life The common schools of his native community afforded him such book learning as he received, and his schooling was terminated at the age of eighteen by his enlistment in Company K, of the Ninth Indiana Volunteers He was in General Howard's army and was with Sherman at Atlanta At Lovejoy station he was wounded for the second time, but recovered and rejoined his regiment both times He was discharged in Texas on September 28, 1865, at the close of the war, whereupon he returned to his Indiana home again and took up the more quiet activities of farm life

In the course of time he began farming on his own responsibility, and his labors were from the beginning rewarded with a reasonable degree of success Years of sturdy effort in his own fields have brought him a place of independence and importance in his community and he is known today for one of the financially independent men of his section.

He is the owner of farm land in Cass county aggregating three hundred and fifty-three acres, in two farms, with other holdings in and about the county, so that his retirement from active business came as the natural result of his well-spent labors

On March 28, 1872, Mr Banta married Maggie D Zinn, the daughter of John Zinn, a native Pennsylvanian who came to Indiana in 1854 He settled in Carroll county and there passed the remainder of his life. Mrs Banta was born in Butler county, Ohio, on September 8, 1847, and was reared in Carroll county Mr and Mrs Banta have two sons: Charles and Ira E. The first named was born on May 13, 1873 He has been married and widowed, and is now engaged in running the old farm which was his birthplace and the birthplace of his father as well. Ira E , the second son, was born on May 20, 1881 He has been married, but like his brother, he is also a widower He lives on a farm in Clay township, and is successfully engaged in carrying on the work for which he is so well fitted by nature and training

Mr Banta, as might be expected, is a member of the Grand Army of the Republic and affiliates with Logansport Post No 14 He has always been a Republican, but in 1912 he cut loose from the old party and voted the Progressive ticket He has taken a leading place among the citizenship of Jefferson township and has lived a life of the utmost beneficence from every standpoint He and his wife are known and appreciated throughout the community for good friends, pleasant neighbors and thoroughly reliable and honorable citizens

JETTHA M MARTIN The life history of Jettha M Martin is closely identified with that of Jefferson township, where he has been engaged in agricultural pursuits for many years His life has been one of untiring activity, and has been crowned by a degree of success reserved for comparatively a few He is of the highest type of agriculturists, and none more than he deserves a fitting recognition among the men whose labors and abilities have achieved results that are most enviable and commendable Mr Martin was born November 1, 1861, in White county, Indiana and is a son of William and Malinda Jane (York) Martin

William Martin was born August 22, 1831, in the city of Belfast, County Down, Ireland and came to the United States with an aunt and uncle, landing in New York City December 5, 1839, and going thence to Philadelphia He remained in that city until 1843, at which time he went with Jesse McClure to East Waterford, Juniata county, Pennsylvania, there working at the blacksmith trade for some time Commencing work February 18, 1844, he remained until the fall of 1848, when he returned to Pennsylvania and remained for one year at Pine, then going to Juniata county, where he stayed until 1850 In that year Mr. Martin came to Indiana, settling first in the city of Madison, later going to Tippecanoe county, thence to Delhi and on to Logansport, and then settling at Camden, Carroll county, where he remained until the spring of 1853 At that time Mr Martin located in White county, working there until the spring of 1854, when he went to Iowa, and following this was at various places in the West, but finally returned to Burnettsville, White county, Indiana On November 11, 1858, he was married to Malinda Jane York, and they resided in Burnettsville until 1867, on

April 15th of which year Mr Martin purchased a farm on Lake Cicott, in Jefferson township, Cass county, Indiana, where they spent the remainder of their lives Mr. Martin was a liberal supporter of religious bodies, and was known as a kind friend and exemplary citizen His political faith was that of the Democratic party, although he was never an office-seeker He was the father of seven children, of whom five are alive at this time Jennie, who is the wife of Frank Pierce, Jettha M , Henry, who makes his home in Montana, Flora, the widow of Harry Spence, and Earl, living in Kansas

Jettha M. Martin was about five years of age when he accompanied his parents to Jefferson township, and here he attended the district schools until he was nineteen years of age He then began farming on the old homestead, and at the death of his parents he purchased this tract, where he now has one hundred acres in a high state of cultivation This land, located on section 27, is devoted to general farming and stockraising, and the fine crops raised as well as the appearance of the stock proves Mr Martin's unquestioned title of able agriculturist Politically he is a Democrat, and at this time is efficiently serving in the capacity of Jefferson township trustee His religious belief is that of the Baptist church, while fraternally he is connected with Logansport Lodge, Tribe of Ben Hur

On June 15, 1882, Mr Martin was married to Martha J Byers, who was born in Carroll county, Indiana, July 2, 1862, and there educated in the public schools Two children have been born to this union Fred B , educated in the common schools of Logansport, married Lizzie Burkett, of Burnettsville, and has one son—Clyde, aged four years, and Elsie C , born September 27, 1894, a graduate of the public schools, who is now attending Burnettsville high school Mr. and Mrs Martin also reared an orphan, Pearl Young, from the time she was five years of age until her marriage to Ross Prescott, since which time she has resided in Logansport

WILLIAM R GRAY All his life William R Gray has passed thus far in the vicinity of his present residence in Jefferson township, and his record has been one sufficient to win for him the high regard and straightforward friendship of all who have shared in his acquaintance during those years Born in Jefferson township, Cass county on a farm about a mile distant from his present home, Mr Gray claims November 14 1873, as the date of his nativity, and he is the son of James A and Rebecca W (Rogers) Gray

James A Gray, also a native of Jefferson township, was born here on September 28, 1836, and was the son of Alex and Elizabeth (Blight) Gray, both of whom were Pennsylvanians by birth, and pioneer settlers of Jefferson township, arriving here in about the year 1836 Both finished their lives in this township and here were well known and highly respected by all who knew them They were true pioneers, and lived in primitive fashion, rearing their children in simplicity and honesty, and training them well in the simple but vital things of life Their son, the father of the subject, settled in Jefferson township and there died He married Rebecca W Rogers and they became the parents of two children—Harrison L , a farmer who lives in this township about a mile from the home of his brother, Milton R, who is the immediate subject of this review.

Milton R Gray was reared on the old farm in Jefferson township and in connection with the work of the home place, he received such rudimentary education as the schools of his native community afforded. He continued in attendance at the district schools until he was twenty years old, after which he gave his exclusive attention to farming, a business in which he has since continued with a pleasing degree of success and prosperity Today Mr Gray owns a farm of some one hundred and twenty acres in section 14, this township, and general farming and stock raising occupy his attention He gives close and careful study to the subjects which occupy him, and his diligence has been rewarded accordingly

On September 5, 1904, Mr Gray took upon himself the responsibility of a wife and was then united in marriage with Miss Goldie M Mickel the daughter of Jonas and Sarah Mickel She was born in Pulaski county, Indiana, on the 4th of September 1883, and was educated in the schools of her native community Two sons have been born to Mr and Mrs Gray Ormus, born September 29, 1905, and Leo E, born March 27 1911

Mr Gray and his good wife are members of the Pisgah Presbyterian church of Jefferson township, and Mr Gray is fraternally affiliated with the Eel River Lodge, No 417 Independent Order of Odd Fellows Politically, he gives his allegiance to the Democratic party, but has not been active beyond the demands of good citizenship

ANDREW THOMPSON Among the many well known and estimable men of Boone township it is safe to say that none have a wider acquaintance or a better standing in the township than has Andrew Thompson, a native of this community, where he was born on January 15 1861 He is now the owner and operator of a fine farm in section 21, Boone township, and is enjoying a pleasing degree of prosperity in his chosen vocation He is the son of Kendall E and Naomi (Thompson) Thompson, concerning whom the following brief facts are here set forth

Kendall Thompson was born in Sussex county, Delaware, as was also his good wife When they were children their parents, with a party of other homeseekers, left their Delaware associations and connections and sought the wilds of Indiana where they established homes and took prominent parts in the development of Cass county Jefferson and Boone townships received the majority of them and here, taking up government land according to the Homestead act, they became land owners and home builders The parents of Kendall Thompson secured land with the others, settling in Boone township At that time Kendall Thompson was a child of seven years He was reared in the primitive home of his parents, became inured to the hardships of pioneer life and the rugged work of the farm, and in his young manhood married Naomi Thompson, who had migrated from Delaware with her parents in like manner as he had done To them were born seven children, of which number five are still living They are named as follows Emma, the wife of Phelix Kistler, of Cass county; Joseph, a resident of Logansport Andrew, the subject of this review, Martha, the wife of Rich B King of White county, Indiana,

Carrie E., who married Charles Kistler, and lives in this county, Jane and Nettie are deceased

Andrew Thompson was reared in his father's household and aided him in the work of the farm He owned a place of two hundred and forty-two acres in Cass county, and one hundred and sixty acres in White county, and his total holdings required a deal of attention and care, so that the assistance of his son Andrew was of great value to him Such advantages as the common schools of the community offered, Andrew Thompson embraced and he finished with the elementary and graded schools of Burr Oak, after which he turned to the farm again

When Mr Thompson married in 1886, he became the owner of a fine farm of one hundred and twenty acres in sections 20 and 21, and he has carried on a general or diversified farming business independently since that time, experiencing a pleasing measure of success in his operations, as becoming to one who was so well versed in matters of agriculture in the service of his father

On March 4, 1886, was solemnized the marriage of Andrew Thompson with Emma Reed, of White county. She is the daughter of Charles Reed, who was a native of Scotland, and who came to Canada in his young manhood, thence to Ohio and later to White county, Indiana He was a cooper by trade and has long been occupied in that work He married Susanna Glazek, whose parents died while she was yet very young Mrs Thompson was born in White county, and there reared Six children have been born to Mr and Mrs Thompson, one son and five daughters, brief mention of them being made as follows Nora Pearl is the wife of Fred Tickfer, of Logansport, she was born in November, 1886, and attended school at Royal Center and Marion Fred E, born August 4, 1888, married Opha Bird Iva, born September 15, 1893, is at home with her parents Bertha born November 17, 1895, also at home, is attending the high school of Royal Center May Thompson, born July 6, 1898, is also in school Fern born July 29, 1900 and the youngest of the six, is attending school in Burr Oak

Mr Thompson is a Republican in his political proclivities, but not more than ordinarily active He is recognized as one of the substantial citizens of the community, and enjoys a wide circle of friends in the county

WILLIAM HOLLIS, long and prominently known in Boone township, Cass county, Indiana, as one of the well-to-do farming men of the community, is a native son of the township and county he now calls his home, and has passed his life within the confines of the county He was born on May 10, 1869, and is the son of Joseph and Elizabeth (Giddings) Hollis.

Joseph Hollis was born in Wesbadge, Lincolnshire, England and came to America when he was in his early manhood He came almost directly to Cass county, and secured work at whatever he could lay his hands to that offered honest employment until he became sufficiently forehanded to buy a farm He then married and settled down to farm life, in which he continued as long as he lived His wife, Elizabeth Giddings, came to Cass county with a party of friends when she was in her young womanhood, soon after which she met Joseph Hollis Their acquaintance terminated in their marriage and to them thirteen children were born, of which goodly number ten are yet living They are here named as follows. Robert G, living in this township; Mary, married Saul Mathewson, and lives in Jefferson township Joseph, also a resident here, John, living in Royal Center, Lizzie the wife of George Wesley, of New Plymouth, Jane, married Thomas Wesley, of this community, William, of this review, James, living in Mississippi, Thomas, living in this vicinity, and Frank, a resident of Minneapolis, Minnesota

William Hollis remained in the parental home until he married in 1896, after which he established an independent rooftree and became a farmer on his own initiative. After his marriage he settled in Monon, in White county, where he continued for four years, later moving about from time to time until he located in his present place in Boone township, which he had occupied in previous years. He has a farm of forty acres which under his careful supervision yields abundantly, and he is recognized as one of the successful farmers in the township

On October 26 1896, Mr Hollis married Dora Kerns, the daughter of Edward and Annie (Kerns) Kerns, both of Virginia parentage and birth Five children were born to Mr and Mrs Kerns, of which three are now living Ada, the wife of Thomas Balty, of Royal Center, Otha Allen Kerns, of Harrison township, and Dora, the wife of the subject. One child was born to Mr and Mrs Hollis, Lucy Esther at home with her parents

JAMES W STEWART, M D, of Logansport, Indiana, is a native of Carroll county, Indiana, born on the Cass county line on May 27, 1857, and has made his home in Cass county practically all his life. He is a son of James Stewart and his wife, Elizabeth Cook, Pennsylvanians by birth, who were the parents of five children, and who moved from their native state to Indiana in 1850 and located on a farm The father was a farmer all his life, and died in Carroll county in 1867 Two children were born to these parents after their location in Carroll county, the subject and one other who was the youngest of the five

Dr Stewart was reared after the manner of the average country youth of his day and age, and he was early initiated into an intimate knowledge of the many tasks incident to farm life, while he attended the district schools with tolerable regularity, eventually completing the course of study in the Delphi schools at the age of seventeen In June, 1875 he entered the Louisville Medical College, at Louisville, Kentucky, and in 1876 he was graduated from that institution, after which he entered the College of Physicians and Surgeons at Indianapolis, which granted him his addendum degree in 1877 Following this he served a year as interne at the city hospital in Indianapolis, completing his term in 1878, when he was twenty-one years of age, a splendid record for the country youth

Dr Stewart located at Burrows, Indiana, and was for six years engaged in practice at that point, whereupon he moved to Rockfield and there practiced for ten years In 1894-5 he took a post graduate course at the New York Polyclinic, and in 1895 he came to Logansport, which he has since made his home and the center of his professional activities. Until of late Dr Stewart has been engaged in general practice, but giving

JAMES W. STEWART

especial attention to surgery. His specialty now is internal medicine and surgery, and his ever growing office practice practically precludes any outside practice. He has taken a number of special courses on internal medicine and surgery at London, Edinburgh, Vienna, Berlin and Berne, and is considered an authority on that subject.

Dr. Stewart is a Mason and a member of the Country Club. His chief recreation is golf and chess, at both of which he is something of an expert.

SAMUEL P. HOFFMAN. In looking for a prosperous and progressive farmer who adheres largely to scientific methods in his operations, one might "go farther and fare worse," as the old saying has it, than the place of Samuel P. Hoffman. Farm life has ever been an attractive one to him, and he has made distinctive and praiseworthy progress in his agricultural activities with the passing years. His son, Ferdinand L., who assists him in the operation of the home farm, took a course in scientific farming at Purdue University, and is the able assistant of the subject. Mr. Hoffman was born in Pulaski county, Indiana, on March 26, 1863, and is the son of Charles and Susan (Hoffman) Hoffman. The father was a native German, born in that country in 1812, who came with his parents to America in 1824 and located in Seneca county, Ohio, where he was reared to young manhood. He came to Indiana while yet young in years, in about 1840, and in Fulton county he married a Miss Cox, and by that union had two children. Wm. H. Hoffman and Mary, the wife of Lewis Strahlem, of Logansport, Indiana. The wife and mother died and in later years Mr. Hoffman married for his second wife Susan Smith. Five children were born of this latter marriage. Isabella now deceased, Sarah, the wife of Eli Fink of Logansport, Indiana, where he is employed as a passenger conductor on the Pan Handle Railroad.

Samuel P. Hoffman was six years old when he came to Cass county to live. He was educated in the public schools up to the age of twenty years, after which he took up farming as his life work, to which he has ever since adhered and in which he has attained a pleasing prosperity. He has a farm of eighty acres three miles southwest of Royal Center, his place being one of the best drained and improved farms in the township. He has for some years specialized in thoroughbred Norman horses, and is generally admitted to be one of the wide-awake farmers in the township.

Mr. Hoffman married Alice Berkshire, the daughter of William Berkshire of Boone township on December 12, 1882. She was reared in Boone township and received her education in the common schools. Two children were born to them: Ferdinand L. and Manford B. Hoffman. The eldest son, who is unmarried, is engaged in farming with his father and as was previously mentioned, has made a scientific study of agriculture. He is one of the most capable young farming men of his day in this township and it is expected that he will make a signal success of the business of farming should he continue in it. Manford B. Hoffman deceased January 30, 1913, was educated in the common and high schools of his native community, and was married to Pearl S. Schlegelmilch.

Mr. Hoffman is a member of the Christian church as are also the members of his family, and he has served in that body as elder and trustee, and has been for some time chorister in the church, as well as taking an active part in the Sunday school. His politics are those of an uncompromising Prohibitionist He has never been active in the political affairs of the town, but has ever performed well his part as a citizen of genuine worth in the community which has so long been his home and the center of his activities

IRA A. KISTLER As cashier of the Citizens State Bank of Royal Center, Ira A Kistler occupies a position of prominence in Royal Center, one to which he is well entitled by reason of his native ability and accomplishments A native son of Cass county, he has not felt it necessary to fare forth into the unknown world to achieve a measure of success, but has realized his business success in the identical township in which he was born

Ira A. Kistler was born in Boone township Cass county, Indiana, on Christmas Day, in 1876, and is the son of Martin L and Sarah (Fultz) Kistler The father, who still lives was born in Boone township and at present lives at Bass, Indiana The mother was a native of Findlay county Ohio They became the parents of nine children seven of that number being yet alive in the year 1912

Of the seven living children of his parents, Ira A Kistler is the second oldest He was born and reared on the farm which represented the family home in Boone township, and received his education in the district schools, after which he taught in the rural districts of Pulaski county, Indiana, for five years In November, 1901, he married Adria J. Fultz, a daughter of Boone township who was educated in the public schools of Royal Center Two children were born to them Dowania, born in 1903, and Dortha, who was born in 1908

In November, 1911, Mr Kistler was appointed cashier of the Citizens State Bank, a position which he has since continued to occupy, with all of satisfaction to the bank and its patrons The bank was incorporated under the laws of the state of Indiana on the date above mentioned, with a capital stock of $25,000, and its official personnel is as follows A Ross Beckley, president, J J Schmidt vice president, J A Kistler, cashier The directors of the bank are George S Kistler, A M Dell, A Ross Beckley, Beecher House, Ira A. Kistler, E D Baughman, J. J Schmidt

Mr. Kistler is an adherent of the Progressive party, and is at present trustee of Boone township He holds a high place in the regard of his fellow citizens, and is a man of many fine traits of character which have contributed in a great measure to his establishment in popular confidence and esteem He is the owner of a fine little farm of eighty-two acres in section 25 in Boone township, which he farms indirectly, and has other property interests in the community He is a member of the Independent Order of Odd Fellows and is the present chancellor of the Knights of Pythias Lodge No 462 of which he is also a member Mrs Kistler is a member of Grace Evangelical church, as are also her children

THOMAS J. KISTLER The name of Kistler is one that has been accorded an honored place upon the rolls of the pioneer history of Cass county since 1835, and many of that name have given praiseworthy service in the development and upbuilding of the county in the years that have passed. It is safe to say, however, that none has occupied a higher place in the county or has been more greatly esteemed than is Thomas J Kistler, the subject of this brief review. Born in Boone township, Cass county, Indiana, on the thirtieth day of June, in 1863, he is the son of Jonas and Amelia (Simmons) Kistler, both now deceased.

Concerning the parentage and family of Mr Kistler it may be said that the father came into the state when he was a lad of ten years, and there passed the remainder of his long and useful life. He was born in Fairfield county, Ohio on the 9th day of September, 1825, and was the son of Jacob and Catherine (Mishamoor) Kistler, natives of Pennsylvania. Jacob Kistler like his worthy father before him, was a miller by trade, and he migrated from Ohio to Indiana in 1835, locating on a farm in Cass county, Indiana. There Jonas Kistler spent the years of his youth from the age of ten to twenty-one, and when he set out in independent life for himself he still continued in that business, one which occupied him all his days and in which he achieved signal success and prosperity. He was ever the advocate of progress and advancement in the county and actively participated in the development and promotion of the district which has eventually made Cass county on a par with the older counties of the state. Four times did Jonas Kistler venture onto the sea of matrimony. He married Lydia Kistler, a native of Boone township, on the 16th of January, 1847, and she died on April 1 1857, leaving four children George N, Lewis, Sarah M, another who died in infancy. On August 10, 1857, Mr Kistler married Amy Simmons and to them seven children were born. Andrew J, Jacob, Thomas J Elizabeth William H, Cordelia A and James. The wife and mother died on April 27, 1873. On October 1, 1873, Mr Kistler married Ann E Simmons, who died on March 9, 1877. On September 20th of that year, Mr. Kistler married Mary Kistler whose death occurred on January 9 1898. Mr Kistler died in 1902, at the age of eighty-seven years. Of the marriage of Amy, or Amelia, Simmons and Mr Kistler, four children are yet living Thomas J, Jacob, William H and Cordelia, the wife of William H Walters.

Thomas J Kistler was reared on the home farm to the age of thirteen years, and divided his time between the duties incident to farm life and the country school which his town afforded. When he was thirteen he left home and went to work on a nearby farm, where he earned his board and clothes and attended school in the winter seasons in exchange for what he could do about the place. He remained thus until he was seventeen, when he launched out in farming for himself. He continued the life of a farmer until he married on May 7, 1900, Carrie D Kistler (not related) becoming his bride. She was born and reared in Boone township, and is one of the most esteemed women of the community.

After his marriage Mr Kistler engaged in the hardware business, and he is the owner of the hardware stock on Chicago street, in Royal Center, there carrying on a general hardware business. He has experienced a pleasing measure of success in the business and enjoys a comprehensive trade throughout the township.

Mr and Mrs Kistler are earnest members of the Baptist church in Royal Center, and he is a trustee of the church. His political affiliations are with the Prohibition party, whose firm adherent he has long been.

He is one of the stable and dependable citizens of the town and township, and enjoys the respect and esteem of a wide circle of friends in the community where he has spent all his life thus far. Affable and friendly, he is more than ordinarily popular, and his upright and honorable character has secured him a place in the public mind which is in every way worthy of him and his always estimable family.

WILLIAM D LUTES Farm life and merchandising constituted the business of William D Lutes for a good many years, until in 1903, when he was appointed postmaster at Royal Center, an office which he has continued to fill in a manner most satisfactory to all concerned. His whole life has been spent in Cass county, and no more loyal citizen will be found within its borders than he

Born in Fulton county, Ohio, on October 7 1837, Mr Lutes is the son of Henry and Mary (Donut) Lutes. The father and mother were both natives of Pennsylvania, and they came as children to Wayne county, Ohio, where they grew to years of maturity, and it was there they were married. Soon after their marriage they settled in Williams county, Ohio, later moving to Fulton county where they established their home in German township and lived there for twenty-three years. Late in life they moved to Kosciusko county Indiana, where they passed their remaining days. Henry and Mary Lutes reared a family of four children three of whom were living in 1912. William D the eldest is the subject of this review, Eliza J is deceased, M W is engaged in farming in Kosciusko county, Indiana, and Ellen is the wife of Simon Wheltstone of Kosciusko county, Indiana

William D Lutes was reared on a farm in Fulton county, Ohio, the home of his parents at that time, and there he attended the district schools. He later became a student in the high school of West Unity, after which he engaged in teaching and continued to be occupied with that most laudable branch of public service for four years thereafter. On April 14, 1859, the young man was united in marriage with Miss Mary Peddcoard, of Fulton county, Ohio, where she had been born and reared her natal day being December 22, 1841. They came to Indiana in April the same week in which their marriage was celebrated, and established their new home in the state which has since been the scene of their activities. They first located in Harrison township some six miles west of Warsaw, and there they bought land and began to farm. For six years they remained on that place, after which they sold out and moved to Atwood, Indiana, where for ten years Mr Lutes was engaged in the merchandise business with more or less success. He then sold his stock of goods and returned to the farm, locating in Boone township and continuing for four years. In 1879 he moved to Royal Center, and in 1896 he gave up his farming activities for a second time and turned his attention to the boot and shoe business. He was successful and prosperous in that business and continued in it until 1903 which year marked his appointment to the position of postmaster at Royal Centre. His work in this respect has been all that could be desired, and the department has been well kept up under his regime. He is assisted in the work of the office by his daughter, Lida

Six children were born to Mr and Mrs Lutes, concerning whom

mention is made as follows John W is engaged in the merchandise business at Logansport, Indiana J O is a farmer, and is located in Wisconsin Lillian is married to Charles Fry, of Star City, Indiana N F is also engaged in farming in Wisconsin, Lida, as mentioned above, is assistant postmaster at Royal Center She is a graduate of the commercial department at Valparaiso, Indiana William H is assistant cashier of the Thomas State Bank of Royal Center

The Lutes family are members of the Methodist Episcopal church, and Mr Lutes is a trustee of that body His fraternal affiliations are with the Masons, and he is a member of Royal Center Lodge No 585, A F & A M, in which he is past master He is also a member of the Independent Order of Odd Fellows, Lodge No 694, at North Judson, Indiana Politically, he gives his support to the cause of Republicanism, and he has always been active in the ranks of the party in his district

Mr Lutes has acquired a considerable property in and about Royal Center and Hammond Indiana, and is regarded as one of the well-to-do men of this community He enjoys the confidence and esteem of a large circle of friends and acquaintances in his home town, and his acquaintance extends well through the county as well, where his many excellent traits of mind and character are appreciated and acknowledged.

W J GOODRICH conducts a lumber, tile and cement business in Royal Center, in which place he was born on April 3, 1876 He is the son of Hiland E and Mary Jane (Vickers) Goodrich The father was born near Washington, Ohio, in the vicinity of Columbus, on a farm, and was there reared. The mother was born in Maryland, near Harper's Ferry, and is the daughter of English parents, who came from Maryland to Indiana, bringing their daughter with them They made the trip by canal, and settled on a farm near Star City In this community Hiland and Mary Jane (Vickers) Goodrich were married, and they spent their lives within the county They became the parents of six children, three of whom are now living The names of the six, in the order of their birth, with brief comments concerning them are as follows Alice O the wife of J J Schmidt, living in Royal Center, Hiram E, in Boone township, W J, the subject of this brief review, Alba, who died at the age of four years, Dudley, who died at the age of twenty-one, and George, who died when twenty-seven years old

W J Goodrich received a common school education, finishing with the Park high school, after which he took a course in a business college in Logansport, Indiana After finishing his business training he went to Florida, remaining there for six months, after which he returned home and remained on the farm until the death of his father two years later, in 1899 He still continued to make his home at the old place, remaining with his mother until she died in 1909, aged seventy-seven years, secure in the regard and esteem of all who knew her

On February 14, 1910 W J Goodrich was married to Miss Anna H Frimel the daughter of Frank Frimel of Jefferson township, in Cass county, and to them one child has been born Wilma Jane Goodrich

Mr Goodrich is a member of the Knights of Pythias Lodge No 62, and he is a Democrat in his political faith He is president of the town council, and takes an important part in all the activities of the community which tend to its growth and advancement

He owns sixty-two and a half acres of land in Boone township and has twenty acres in Royal Center, in what is known as the Goodrich addition His activities in the lumber, tile and cement business are carried on quietly and steadily, and constitute one of the leading industries in Royal Center

ANDREW J CONN, well known in Royal Center Indiana, as a farmer and in the operation of a buggy and harness business, was born in Boone township, Cass county, Indiana, on June 19, 1862, and in the vicinity of his present home has passed his life thus far He is the son of George and Helen (Hendee) Conn, the father a native of Pennsylvania from which state he migrated to Indiana in its early manhood The mother was a native Canadian and came from that country with her parents George Conn was in some respects a pioneer of Cass county, and he it was who ran the first sawmill in Boone township, which he operated with oxen He died when the subject was a lad of three years He had been three times married, and was the father of thirteen children, ten of them being the children of Helen Hendee, the mother of the subject Seven of the number are living today, and they are here named as follows Jess, living in Rushville, Indiana Lawrence, of Boone township, Reuben in Long Beach, California, Eunice, the wife of William Batty, living in Pulaski county, George a retired farmer of Royal Center, Andrew J, of this review, and Hannah, the widow of William Kramer, of Royal Center.

Andrew J Conn was educated in the district schools and remained at home until he married He was twenty years old when he took upon himself the responsibility of a home and family and on January 4, 1882, he married Anna C Humes the daughter of William and ——— Humes For three years he remained on a farm and then gave up agricultural life to engage in the mercantile business in Royal Center, where he continued for twenty-five years At the end of that time he retired from active business, sold out and invested in farming property in and about Royal Center He is the owner of a goodly portion of town property, and has five hundred and twenty acres of land, with one hundred and sixty acres lying about a half mile south of Lucerne He also has one hundred and twenty acres in Van Buren township, in Pulaski county, and two hundred and forty acres near Winnemac, also in Pulaski county These properties are the fruits of his quarter century of unceasing toil and they have been acquired, not in a day nor a year, but little by little, each passing year adding something to his accumulations What he has done has been accomplished without aid from any source whatsoever only his native industry and business wisdom contributing to his ultimate success

Mr Conn is the father of eight children, of whom mention is made briefly as follows Mabel, the wife of Verne Seward, of Royal Center, Alice, living in Logansport, Indiana, Maggie, the wife of Clarence Fultz, of Boone township, Jesse, a railroad man, living in Logansport Andrew J, Jr at home, Forest, a baker in Royal Center, and Marr, living at home

"BROAD LANDS GRANGE," RESIDENCE OF MR. AND MRS. MELVIN TUCKER

Mr Conn is a member of the Benevolent and Protective Order of Elks, Lodge No 66, and of the Knights of Pythias, No 462, Royal Center He is a Democrat in his political faith, but is not more active than the demands of good citizenship require He occupies a position of prominence and popularity in his native community, where he has long been known for his sterling character and many splendid traits that have contributed so much to the prosperity of the town and township of which he has long been a resident.

MELVIN TUCKER Since the year 1845 the Tucker family has been residents of Cass county During this period of nearly eighty years, the members of three generations have contributed their industry and their character to the material development and the civic welfare of this section of Indiana The family have been chiefly identified with agriculture, and it was on the land that they have depended for their material prosperity

Mr Melvin Tucker, who represents the third generation in the county, is present trustee of Harrison township, and has spent practically all of his life in his present home vicinity He began his career without any capital to speak of, and through his own good management has acquired a prominent position in Harrison township

Melvin Tucker was born in Harrison township, Cass county, June 10, 1862 His father was named Abraham and his grandfather was Michner Tucker The maiden name of his mother was Margaret Witters, a daughter of David Witters The grandfather with his son Abraham, and other members of the family came to Cass county in 1855 His first settlement was on what is known as the Jacob Yantice farm Land was to be had then from the public domain by paying the government price of about $1 00 per acre, and the grandfather acquired a large amount of land either from the government or private purchase Through his own industry and that which he hired, he was instrumental in clearing up a large tract and putting it in condition for agriculture Abraham Tucker the father, spent all of his life as a farmer in this county, and died in September 4, 1903, after nearly seventy years of residence in Cass county The mother passed away in October, 1895, and both parents now rest in Zion cemetery of Harrison township

Melvin Tucker was reared in Harrison township, where he attended the public schools, and there by practical experience he prepared himself for an active career as a farmer On the twenty-second of March, 1887 he married Miss Anna Backus, a daughter of Richard and Rose (Fitzsimmons) Backus Her father died about 1874 and her mother in 1892 Mr and Mrs Tucker are the parents of one child, Mollie, who was born November 26, 1888, and who is the wife of Harvey Clary In 1889 soon after their marriage, Mr and Mrs Tucker moved to the farm which they still occupy They found the land with practically no improvements, and a number of years in their early married life were devoted to the hard industry which makes successful farming There were no buildings on the place when they came to it, and the present equipment of home barns, fences and drain field, and all other facilities are the result of the good management and effective work of Mr Tucker, who has always been loyally aided by his wife. Their homestead consists of one hundred and forty-one acres.

Mr and Mrs Tucker, coming from one of the pioneer families, have in their possession three of the old parchment deeds which were executed under the hands of President Martin Van Buren and they bear the following dates March 30, 1837, April 10, 1837, April 10, 1837, and these old souvenirs are valuable heirlooms in their home.

Fraternally Mr Tucker is affiliated with Royal Center Lodge, No. 585, A F & A M and has passed through all the chairs of Lucerne Lodge, No 680, I. O O. F His fellow citizens have honored him with the office of council trustee, a place of responsibility, which he is filling with characteristic ability and efficiency.

Mr and Mrs Tucker's beautiful estate is called "Broad Lands Grange" and lies fronting the south, and this home is ever open to their many friends.

WILLIAM H FELTIS Among the well known, prosperous and highly esteemed citizens and farming men of Boone township, none enjoys a more pleasing status in the eyes of the community than does William H Feltis, a native Ohioan but a resident of Cass county, Indiana, since 1884 Mr Feltis was born in Crawford county, Ohio, on January 13, 1860, and is the son of Edward and Eliza (Cassady) Feltis

Edward Feltis was born in Wexford county, Ireland, and was the son of William Feltis, a native Scot, who settled in Ireland Edward Feltis came to the United States and located in Crawford county, Ohio, and from there he moved to Wyandot county, where he passed his remaining days, death claiming him in 1872 He married Eliza Cassady in Crawford county, Ohio, and she died at the home place in Wyandot county on December 8, 1903 Six children were born to the worthy people mentioned above, five of that number yet living They are: William H, of this review, John J, of Wyandot county, Ohio, Nettie, the wife of Lewis Muncie, Jennie who married John Williams, and Cora, the wife of Joseph Eckelbery

William H Feltis was reared on the Crawford county farm and educated in the district schools, in which he continued until he was eighteen years of age, or thereabouts. He then worked on the farm by the month, and in 1884 he came to Cass county Indiana, where he again secured work as a farm hand In 1885 he went to Benton county, Indiana, there working at farm work for the space of four years, his identification with that county covering a period of something like fifteen years On June 1, 1901, Mr Feltis moved to the farm which he now occupies, and he has a farm of one hundred and forty acres, devoting himself to general farming and stock raising

On March 25, 1891, Mr Feltis was united in marriage with Miss Sarah A Goble, who was born in Hancock county, Indiana, on April 21, 1869 She was educated in the district schools of her native county and came to Jasper county, Indiana, in company with her parents in 1884 She is the daughter of F M and Emily (Winslow) Goble, the former of whom was born in Henry county, Indiana, on December 6, 1833, and died in August, 1910 The mother died on September 7, 1905 She was born in North Carolina in 1842 and came to Indiana when she was a girl, locating in Henry county She was married in Raysville county, Indiana, soon after which her husband enlisted in the Twenty-second Indiana Light Artillery and served to the close of the war He was a member of the G. A R. Mrs. Feltis was one of the eight children of her parents, the others being Martha; Flora, the wife of William Hammond, of North Dakota, Mary who married John Thornton Tina, the wife of John Blaze, Edward, Albert; Louie, the wife of Oscar Hurley, of North Dakota

Mr and Mrs Feltis became the parents of seven children, as follows Murle M , born July 10, 1893, a graduate of the common schools, Gladys M , born July 13, 1895, Leona M , born on March 7, 1897, George D , born on January 1, 1899, William H , born April 11, 1900, Jerry O , born October 3, 1903, and Junie A., born on June 16, 1905

Mr Feltis is progressive in his political tendencies and is one of the leading citizens of his town and township His family is one that is highly esteemed in the community it claims as its home, and all are giving promise of filling useful places in society as they come into the duties of life

SAMUEL A WILLIAMSON Royal Center has numbered among her citizenship more than a few wealthy retired farmers who have settled down to enjoy the remainder of their lives, content with what they have been able to accumulate in the earlier part of their careers Among such wise and happy men may be mentioned Samuel A Williamson one of the well-to-do men of Boone township, in which he made his home for a number of years He was born in Boone township on September 28, 1858, and is the son of Moses T and Mary J (Callahan) Williamson

Concerning the father of the subject, it may be said at this point that Moses T Williamson was born in the vicinity of Dayton, Ohio, in the year 1816, and came with his father, Samuel Williamson, into Carroll county, Indiana, in 1829, and there his parents passed their remaining days Moses T lived with them until he had reached man's estate, and in 1840 he determined to start out upon an independent career He accordingly entered a piece of land from the government, with his brother taking up one hundred and sixty acres. This bit of government land formed the nucleus of a much larger holding in later years, and at one time he owned more than a section of land in Cass and White counties, all but eighty acres lying in Boone township He passed his life on his farm, and was one of the well known men of the county He was a stanch Republican, always up and doing in the interests of the party, and took a prominent part in its activities all his life Five children were born to these parents, all of whom still survive, and concerning whom the following brief mention is made. Joseph E. is engaged in farming in Idaho, Elizabeth A is the wife of John F. Troutman, of Logansport, Indiana, James E is engaged in teaching in California, and William Andrew, a Kansas farmer Samuel A , the subject of this review, is the youngest of the five

The common schools of Boone township gave to Samuel A Williamson such education as he received, and he remained at home with his father until he had reached man's estate He tried his skill at school teaching and was thus engaged during one term in Miami township and one in Boone but he found farm life more pleasing to him and gave up teaching, returning to the farm with his father On April 5, 1888, he was married to Miss Rosella J Hughes, the daughter of William and Mary E Hughes The young man erected a dwelling house on the farm of his father, and there he and his family lived until five years ago, when he moved into town, since when they have made their home in Royal Center Mrs Williamson was born in Jefferson township, near Lake Cicott, and her parents were natives of Ohio and Pennsylvania They were farming people and gave their lives to that industry The father died some years ago. They were the parents of six children, of which number five are now living, as follows Josephine, Ella, Mrs Williamson. John Schuyler, who lives with his widowed mother, Etta, who died single, and William

To Mr and Mrs Williamson were born six children, four of whom are yet living Arthur C is at home on the farm Grace E is dead, as is also Edna M , Iva L is the wife of J Marcus Bliss, of Logansport, Indiana William M is in the high school, and Ruth O, a student in the common schools of the home community Edna M married Lloyd P Plotner, of Royal Center, and they had one child, Grace C , who makes her home with the subject, Mrs Williamson Mrs Plotner died November 30, 1907

Mr Williamson is the owner of some especially valuable farming property in the township, aggregating about three hundred acres as well as considerable other property in Royal Center He took the census report of 1910 for Royal Center and for the twelve northeast sections of Boone township. Mr Williamson is a Republican in his political faith, and his churchly affiliations are with the Methodist Episcopal church in which he is a trustee, and of which his wife is also a member, as well as others of his family

JOHN W CLINE, well known among the residents of Boone township, in Cass county, was born in Pickaway county, Ohio, on September 30, 1860 and is the son of Joshua and Matilda (Glick) Cline When John W Cline was six years old his father died, and his mother married a second time, in September, 1875 Conditions in the home were not the most favorable to the young lad after the advent of a second father, and he was but little more than seven when he began to make his own way, working for his board and clothes He went to school some, but his education was of a most meager character, and when he was seventeen years old he began to draw wages, after which he continued to work on a farm until he was twenty-five years old When he was twenty-seven, in 1887, Mr Cline married Laura A Boyer, of Fairfield county, Ohio They lived in Ohio for a year after their marriage, then came to Cass county, Indiana, and some little time later Mr Cline made the purchase of an eighty-acre farm He went in debt for the place, but with the help of his faithful wife they were soon able to clear away the indebtedness, and they eventually made a fine place of the farm

Mr. and Mrs Cline have one son, George W , born on November 12, 1892 He is a graduate of the Royal Center high school They are members of the Methodist Episcopal church of Royal Center, and Mr Cline is a member of Royal Center Lodge No 585, A F & A M, in which he is past master. He is also a member of Myrtle Lodge No 567, Independent Order of Odd Fellows, of which he is master, past grand, and a member of the grand lodge. He is a Prohibitionist in his political faith, but has never been an office holder. General farming and stock raising occupy his attention for the most part and he is regarded as one of the most wholesome and substantial citizens in his community.

WILLIAM H BINGAMAN The business interests of Royal Center have in a number of ways felt the influence and activity of William H Bingaman in recent years, and he is today regarded as one of the successful men of the town, wherein he has conducted a hardware business since 1890. It is true, he established himself in his present connection in a time when he possessed neither money nor a great deal of credit, but his careful methods, progressive ideas and general steadfastness of character have placed him in a position where he today can command an ample supply of both those commodities.

A native son of Boone township, Cass county William H Bingaman was born in December, 1860, and his parents were Jacob and Emily (Kistler) Bingaman. The father was a native of Carroll county, Indiana, and the mother was born and reared and passed her life in Boone township. When Jacob Bingaman was a boy he came to Cass county, and here he grew to young manhood and married. He was ever a quiet and home loving man, but one who never shirked his civic duty, and he served Boone township as trustee for three terms giving praiseworthy service in that office as long as he was associated with it. He was a member of the Independent Order of Odd Fellows, and derived a deal of quiet pleasure from his identification with the lodge and his association with his fellows as a result of his membership. He died on July 4, 1910, his good wife having preceded him some time before. They were the parents of two children, John M and William H, the subject of this brief review. The former died on April 30, 1912, in the state of Pennsylvania, where he had made his home for the past twenty years. He married and had a family.

William H Bingaman was reared to farm life on the home place in Boone township, and when arriving at school age, he was sent to the district school, and later to the schools of Royal Center. He continued in attendance there until he was about seventeen years of age, after which he gave his attention to the work of his father's farm. He was twenty-one when he decided to leave home, and he accordingly became a clerk in a general store in Royal Center, where he was employed for two years. He then returned to the farm and was thus occupied until he engaged in business here in 1890. He was entirely without capital, but he managed to place a small stock of goods and by the most careful and shrewd manipulation of his stock and the proceeds from the business for a few seasons he was soon able to branch out considerably. Today he carries a complete stock of hardware, stoves and implements and enjoys a most gratifying patronage from all parts of the township. He erected his present place of business in 1911, at a cost of about $10,000. He is a member of the directorate of the Royal Center State

Bank as well as of the local electric light plant, of the latter of which he is secretary, and is likewise interested in a telling manner in other industrial and financial concerns in and about the town

Mr Bingaman is inclined to the progressive view in politics, and took the side of the new party in the campaign of 1912 He is a member of the Baptist church of Royal Center, with his wife, and he also has membership in the Masonic Lodge No 585 the Knights of Pythias Lodge No 462, and the Independent Order of Odd Fellows, in the latter of which he holds the office of past grand

In 1889 Mr Bingaman was united in marriage with Miss Ida Washburn, who died without issue in 1906 He married Nora Lawhead in May, 1908

WILLIAM O BLISS holds a prominent place among the prosperous farmers and stockmen of Boone township, and enjoys in generous measure the esteem and confidence of a wide circle of friends and acquaintances He occupies today the farm on which he was born on the 26th day of August, 1853, and which was then the property of his parents, Horace N and Sarah (Dritt) Bliss

Concerning the parentage of the subject it may be said that Horace N Bliss was a Pennsylvanian by birth and ancestry, as was also his wife They were married in their native state and came to Indiana in their young days, being rightfully regarded as among the pioneer citizens of the state and of Cass county Mr Bliss was a man who long occupied a foremost place in his community He was a capable and energetic farmer and succeeded beyond the status of the average farmer of his day, and his activities extended to civic and public life as well He served Cass county as its county clerk for eight consecutive years, and was for four years the incumbent of the office of county recorder Both those offices he filled with credit to himself and the county, and his services were of an order eminently satisfactory to his constituency He continued to conduct his farm in conjunction with his official duties, and was all his life one of the busiest men in his township. He was a Democrat and was ever active in the ranks of that party He died in about 1887, the father of five children, two of whom are yet living, Andrew D, concerning whom specific mention is made in other pages of this work, and William O Bliss, the subject of this necessarily brief review

William O Bliss was reared on the home farm and educated in the public schools He was well trained in the work of the farm and early learned the benefits to be derived from a careful management of a choice farm In consequence of this knowledge he elected to follow in the footsteps of his father when choosing a vocation and he may be found today busily engaged in carrying on the work of the fine old farm upon which he was born sixty years ago His holdings in Boone township aggregate six hundred and fifty-three acres and general farming and stock raising constitute his industry

Mr Bliss, like his father, is a Democrat, active, in a measure, in the work of the party in his district, but not an office holder He has never married

ORVILLE M MCCOMBS, prominent in Royal Center as a merchant, contractor and lumber dealer, has been a resident of this place all his life, and was here born, reared and educated He has been a school teacher, drug clerk, merchandise clerk, and was for four years with the Sweet Brothers in their elevator business Altogether his business career has been a varied one The past eighteen years of his life have been devoted to the lumber business with contracting and merchandising, and he has acquired a leading place in the ranks of the business men of this city He has acquired an interest in many of the leading industries and financial concerns in and about Royal Center, and is properly regarded as one of the leading business men of the community

Born near Royal Center on a farm on March 25, 1873 Orville M McCombs is the son of Albert and Mary (Mason) McCombs The father was born in Royal Center on August 6, 1844, and was a son of John McCombs, who came here from Pennsylvania, his native state, soon after his marriage, and here entered land from the government, the town of Royal Center standing on the land he so acquired The patent to his land bore the signature of John Tyler, then president of the United States, and he engaged in farming here when Cass county was in a most primitive state, indeed. A pioneer, every inch of him, John McCombs lived and died on the land he secured as the right of a United States citizen, and he saw the outlining and early development of what was destined to become one of the wealthiest and most prominent counties in the great state of Indiana He passed the best years of his life here and death claimed him when he had reached an advanced age after a life of the utmost usefulness in his necessarily circumscribed sphere of activity.

Albert McCombs, his son, and the father of the subject, was reared on this old farm, and here he attended the schools of the day When he reached manhood, he married Mary Mason and settled in Boone township, where he passed the remainder of his life Two children were born to Albert and Mary McCombs Emma, the widow of W. R. Thompson of Royal Center, and Orville M, the subject of this review

As a boy in Royal Center, Orville M McCombs attended the schools of his native town, and later was privileged to attend the Danville (Ind) Normal School He taught one term of school in Boone township, after which he secured employment in a drug store, and later took a clerkship in a general store He remained something like a year in the latter position, after which he took service with Sweet Brothers in the elevator business This work won him a most extended acquaintance in the four years of his connection with Sweet Brothers, and he then started up in the lumber business It is eighteen years since Mr. McCombs set out to run a business of his own, but the passing years have proved the wisdom of his venture He has increased his interests from time to time, adding other branches, and he now has a general store in Royal Center and conducts a contracting business in connection with his lumber operations He is a stockholder and a member of the directorate of the Royal Center State Bank and is a director of the Royal Center Electric Light Company, Inc

Mr McCombs has not withdrawn himself from public service, but has ever shown himself willing to bear his full share in the village government He has served as a member of the village school board and of the village council, and has been president of both bodies, at all times proving himself a capable and wise official and executive He is president of the village school board at this time Fraternally Mr McCombs is a member of the Masonic order, the Knights of Pythias, the Independent Order of Odd Fellows, the Knights of the Maccabees, and the Benevolent and Protective Order of Elks, with membership at Logansport He is a Progressive in his political faith and activities

In 1891, Mr McCombs was united in marriage with Miss Ella Pherson, a native daughter of Cass county, where she was reared and educated Four children have been born to them. Howard, now nineteen years old, and a graduate of the high school, Vivian aged sixteen, a student in the high school, Thelma, twelve years old, attending the public schools, and John A, two months old at this time (December 1912)

The family are members of the Baptist church of Royal Center and Mrs McCombs is actively identified with the work of its various departments

Mr McCombs enjoys the respect and confidence of a wide circle of friends and acquaintances in and about Cass county, where he is prominently known in a business and social way His genial and kindly nature has brought him innumerable friends, as have the other sterling qualities of his nature, and he is regarded as one of the valuable citizens of the community

HARRY CHARLES JOHNSON, M D. Among the medical practitioners of Cass county who have won financial success and professional prestige are found many who are practicing in the place of their birth, and in this class stands Dr Harry Charles Johnson whose home has always been in his present field of endeavor, the city of Logansport Dr Johnson was born August 18, 1880 in this city, and is a son of Samuel F Johnson who, in point of continuous service, is probably the oldest railroad employe in Logansport, and the present trainmaster of the Pennsylvania lines at this place

Samuel F Johnson was born at Richmond, Indiana, August 20, 1857, a son of Hon Calvin R Johnson, a prominent journalist of Indiana who was identified with the press of Richmond for nearly a half a century The latter was born near North Vernon, Indiana, in December 1823, and it was largely in the printing office that he received his training and equipped himself for life's duties His early work as a printer was in Indianapolis, from whence he went to Richmond, and in the latter city published its first newspaper, known as the *Broad-ax of Freedom* In addition to being connected with nearly every newspaper of importance published in Richmond, he served through the Civil war as lieutenant in the One Hundred and Twenty-fourth Indiana Volunteer Infantry, and for many years was prominent in Republican politics He married Miss Sarah Lewis, a daughter of one of the prominent merchants of Richmond, whose ancestors were Virginians and who was a devoted and well known member of the Society of Friends, of Wayne county Seven children were born to Dr. Johnson's grandparents, Samuel F being the fourth in order of birth

Samuel F Johnson was reared to manhood in his native place, and there received his education in the public schools and taught the dignity and value of hard labor. When he was but a lad of ten years he showed his self-reliance and industry by earning money as an office boy for Dr. McIntyre of Richmond, and when he was fourteen entered upon his railroad career He continued as a brakeman on a freight train from his fourteenth to his eighteenth year, was then made freight conductor, a position which he held until he was twenty-four, and was then made conductor of a passenger train In 1872 he located in Logansport as his home and in November, 1892, he was made assistant trainmaster at Logansport, from which position he was called to that of trainmaster in 1903 On April 2, 1877, he was united in marriage with Miss Mattie Kendall, and they have two children Harry and Eva

Harry Charles Johnson was educated in the public schools of Logansport, and graduated from the high school in 1900 When still a student in the latter institution, he commenced his medical studies under the preceptorship of Dr E M Hatch. In 1900 he matriculated at Hahnemann Medical College, Chicago, from which, after a course of four years, he was graduated in 1904 Succeeding this, he at once engaged in the practice of his profession in his native city, and here he has since continued, having gained a large and representative clientele. He is known as an able physician, and his success in a number of complicated cases has served to establish him firmly in the confidence of his patients and the respect of his confreres.

On June 6 1905, Dr Johnson was married to Miss Grace A Green, and they have one child Grace Alice

ANDREW D BLISS has achieved considerable distinction as a progressive and successful farmer in Boone township which has represented his home since his young boyhood, sixty-three years representing his actual residence in this place He was born in Lancaster county, Pennsylvania, on April 21, 1847 and is the son of Horace M and Sarah (Dritt) Bliss

Horace M Bliss was born in Massachusetts, in March, 1808, and went to Pennsylvania when he was a youth of eighteen years He received his education in the schools of Massachusetts and Pennsylvania, and was admitted to the bar at Lycoming county, Pennsylvania, where he practiced law at the county seat for several years He married Sarah Barnfield and two sons were born to them, Edward and Simon, deceased Subsequently he married Sarah Dritt, a native of Lancaster county, that state, and they came to Indiana in 1849, locating in Boone township in September of that year Here Horace Bliss became an extensive land owner and farmer and was well known as one of the most successful men of his day in Cass county He was a Democrat of strong convictions and he served his party in varied ways in the county He was county clerk of Cass county for eight years and recorder of the county for half that length of time, and he carried on his farm work in conjunction with his official duties When he finally retired from public life, he devoted himself entirely to farming activities

Mr. Bliss died in 1883 and his wife preceded him in 1880 They were the parents of three children—Andrew D, John M and William O Bliss John M Bliss was reared on the farm in common with his brothers, and educated in the public schools He married Minnie Potter in Logansport He served Cass county for four years as clerk, and died in 1903 Concerning William O, detailed mention is made in another article devoted to him in this work

Andrew D Bliss was reared on the old home farm, and educated in the public schools of the community, as well as receiving some training in a private school He turned his attention to farming when he settled down to establish a home of his own and has gained a pleasing prominence in that field of activity, as have other members of his family in Boone township

In 1874 Mr Bliss married Lucinda Berkshire, the daughter of Solomon Berkshire She was reared in Boone township, in which she was born in June, 1853, and was educated in the public schools They have eight children, concerning whom brief mention is here made Horace M is living in the West, Sarah is the wife of Clarence Julian, Jennie married Bert Anderson, William is unmarried, Rebecca married Jesse C Julian, Lucinda is the wife of Howard Clapp, Alice is a teacher in the public schools, and John M is a fireman on the Panhandle railroad

Mr Bliss is a member of Royal Center Lodge No 585 A F & A M, and is a Democrat in his politics, like all his family He has been active in the work of the party in Cass county and in years gone by when his father was active as a county official, he served as his father's deputy in the office of county clerk

Mr Bliss and his family enjoy the hearty friendship of a large circle of people in Boone township who have known them all their days, and they are everywhere regarded as among the leading citizens of the community

WILLMONT L FERNALD While Mr Fernald has been a resident of Logansport for the last thirty-eight years, and among this city's most enterprising and substantial citizens, his business interests have been so extensive and widespread as to entitle him to claim identity with the great Middle West During this time he has been connected with the lumber interests of several states, and for thirty years one of the most extensive manufacturers and largest dealers in hardwood lumber among the many enterprising men whose vigor and energy have made that one of the leading industries of this section His career adds another to the many illustrations which Logansport has furnished, of the grand results which are attained by intelligence, tact and perseverance, when applied to the building up of a great business under the favoring conditions which have, for nearly half a century, attended all the city's enterprises It is true that during this period unusual business opportunities have opened to business men, but they have only yielded the meed of great success to those who have had the sagacity to perceive them and the boldness to push them to their best results

Willmont L Fernald comes of good old New England ancestry, and was born in Penobscot county, Maine, October 21, 1855, there being reared to manhood and receiving, in most part, his education At the age of nineteen years, he began life on his own account as a farm hand, receiving for his services a salary of sixteen dollars per month. In

1875 he came to Logansport, Indiana, and secured employment with the old lumber firm of Tucker & Howe, the junior member of which was his uncle, Samuel E Howe, and here also, he completed his schooling For a period of about eight years he worked for Tucker & Howe, and since that time has been engaged in business on his own account Both of the original members of this old and honored concern have passed to their reward, but the business continues to be carried on by Mr Fernald and the Messrs W H and O D Howe, under the corporate name of the Howe Lumber Company The firm's establishment at Wabash, Phillips county, Arkansas, is in charge of W H and O D Howe, while Mr Fernald takes care of the Logansport end of the business, which is the buying of hardwood timber lands and the manufacture of band-sawed hardwood lumber, plow and wagon stock and railroad material Although one of the quiet and unassuming business men of Logansport, Mr Fernald is also one of its most influential citizens Amidst his active business life he has found time and manifested an inclination to perform all the duties of good citizenship, is alive to all the demands which the exigencies of a great and growing city cast upon its leading men, is broad-minded and intelligent on the questions that interest the public, and appreciative of all the interests that affect the community, yet he has not sought personal preferment nor entered actively into the contests of the political arena However, he is not indifferent to the amenities of social life, and also takes a keen and intelligent interest in the work of the Cass County Historical Society, of which he is a valued member

In 1882, Mr. Fernald was married to Miss Emma F Hoover, whose people were among the first of the pioneers of Cass county, and appropriate mention of whom is made elsewhere in this work

DUGAL CAMPBELL was the second of the family to settle in Logansport, Indiana, and his association with this city began as long ago as the year 1848, when in May he came here from Stark county, Ohio, via wagon train and canal He bought land and made a home for his family, but his life in this community was all too short, death claiming him within three years after he settled in Logansport Mr Campbell was born on June 10, 1803, in Washington county, Pennsylvania, and there is something of Scotch blood in the ancestry of the man, as the name plainly evidences He was a young man when he migrated with his parents and others of the family to Stark county Ohio, at a time when it was virtually an unbroken wilderness Here the pioneer spirit was strongly manifested in this man and in others of his immediate family, and like many another of his day, he experienced all the hardships of the pathfinder or the homemaker in a wilderness He married Mariah Carr, a girl of German-Irish parentage, and with this companion settled on a woodland tract their home a tiny log cabin, furnished in the most meager style with the barest necessities A puncheon floor was a feature of the little home, but as Mr Campbell had learned the trade of a carpenter and cabinet maker he was able with the passing of time to greatly enhance their condition by the work of his hands He gave much of his time, however, to the cleaning up of their potential farm, and as time passed his unremitting toil began to give shape and semblance to their home, and a fine farm was eventually evolved out of the forest

His family grew with the passing years, and the parents, ever remembering the benefits that schools could give, concluded that it might be better to move to a district where there would be greater advantages for the children. Thus it was that in 1848 Dugal Campbell sold the place where he had passed so many years, and where he had experienced so much of the joys and vicissitudes of life. He secured the then phenomenal price of $40 an acre for his land, and moved to Cass county, Indiana, where he had a brother-in-law living, and on May 20, 1848, he found himself in Logansport, Indiana. He found suitable land in Clay township and there bought one hundred and ninety acres, paying twenty to twenty-five dollars the acre for the land, and settled down to enjoy the benefits that might be derived from life in the newer community. Three years later, however, he died at his home, his widow surviving him for eleven years, her death occurring in 1863. Nine children were born to these parents, of which goodly number only two are living today. One, a daughter, makes her home in Franklin, Indiana, and the son, Hon. Benjamin Franklin Campbell, who has gained something of distinction in Cass county, and of whom extended mention is made in another sketch appearing in this biographical and historical work.

Mr. Campbell was a consistent member of the Friends church, and his entire life and experience was in accord with the kindly Christian spirit of that sect. His wife was a member of the Methodist Episcopal church, and was equally faithful and consistent in her everyday life. They were worthy and honorable citizens, esteemed of all who knew them and beloved of many for their splendid character and the manifold qualities of generosity and kindliness which illumined their plain and homely lives. Their children were named: William C., John T., Eva Margaret A., Benjamin F., Harriet Amanda J., Rachel, Mary and Robert C. As mentioned previously, all but two of these are deceased.

HON. BENJAMIN FRANKLIN CAMPBELL, a man who has gained much of prominence and position in Cass county in the field of politics, as well as in the more prosaic industry of farming, was born in Stark county, Ohio, on March 4, 1835. He is the son of Dugal and Mariah (Carr) Campbell, of whom detailed mention is made in another article devoted to them, to be found elsewhere in this work, thus obviating the necessity for further details in regard to the immediate family of the subject.

When B. F. Campbell was a boy of thirteen years the family moved from Stark county, Ohio, to Cass county, Indiana, and here Mr. Campbell has made his home continuously since that time. He was reared amid scenes of rural life, both in his earlier home in Ohio and in Clay township, Cass county, and received the somewhat limited educational advantages of the district schools of his day and age. Though his training was thus not of great scope it is a significant fact that Mr. Campbell was able to supplement such schooling as he did receive in a large measure by careful reading of his own choosing, so that he has ever been regarded as a man of no little learning, and one whose information covers a wide field, a broad general knowledge being his. He devoted himself to farm work and remained at home and when his father and mother passed away, he continued on the old home place, there bringing his bride when he married in 1861. For forty-eight years Mr. Campbell made the old farm his home, his removal to Logansport coming in 1896 at a time when his political prominence made it imperative that he give up his rural life and make a home in the city.

Although today Mr Campbell is prosperous, and has been for many years, it must be remembered that he bore his share of early privations and the burdens that the death of his father and elder brother placed upon him when he was yet a lad. The family was not a small one numbering nine children, and when Dugal Campbell died, Benjamin F. was but seventeen years of age. Thus as the eldest son of the household, responsibility of no small order fell upon his young shoulders.

In 1878 the influence and strength of Mr Campbell as a man among his fellow men began to be recognized and he was elected representative from his district to the state legislature, and while there was a member of the committee on elections and canals. He introduced three bills into the assembly, one for the relief of one Mrs Lyon from the bond of a defaulting trustee, one for the relief of the town council of Walton, to legalize its acts, and one for the abolishment of the superior court of Cass county. The two first mentioned passed through. In 1896 Mr Campbell moved to Logansport, and in the following year he was appointed by the governor of Indiana to represent the eleventh congressional district in the National Road Parliament held at Nashville, Tennessee. In 1898 he was president of the Farmers' Institute, held at Nashville, Tennessee, and he has ever been a leader in all movements tending toward the advance of agriculture and its methods. All public enterprises of a worthy nature have found in him a generous support, and he has left his mark upon many a movement and industry that has had its inception in Cass county in the past quarter century. Mr Campbell was president of the County Agricultural Society and he assisted in the organization of the Citizens Coal Company of Logansport, of which concern he was the first president. He was a director of the Board of Charities for two years, and did excellent work in that connection. He is a man of strong religious tendencies, reared in the atmosphere of a Quaker home, but in recent years a member of the Baptist church. He has served as president of the County Sunday School Union, and has been actively identified with the work of the church in other ways.

On January 7 1861, Mr Campbell was united in marriage with Margaret, the daughter of William South. Mrs Campbell passed away in 1895, leaving two children—Robert Atwood and Blanche Edith, now Mrs Charles Richardson. Three years after the death of his wife, Mr Campbell married Mary E Kimbrough, the daughter of Joseph Brower and the widow of James M Kimbrough. Mr Campbell is fraternally associated with the Masonic order, in which he takes a hearty concern, and is also a member of the Cass County Historical Society.

JOHN A NEWBY has been a resident of Logansport for the past forty-three years, thirty-five years of which have been passed in the florist business. He is a native of Yorkshire, England, and when eighteen years old came to the United States, bringing with him his mother and grandfather. He began working for Judge Whiteside in his greenhouse, having learned horticulture with some degree of thoroughness as a boy in his native land, but did not continue in the business more than a short time with Judge Whiteside, chiefly because the demands of the trade in Logansport did not warrant such continuance. He engaged in railroad work, in which he continued for some time, but in 1877 he saw an opening for a florist in Logansport, and began an independent business though necessarily in a small way. His first greenhouse was 10x50 feet in size, but as time passed and his trade steadily increased, his capacity gradually assumed more generous proportions so that today he has about 30,000 square feet of glass covering. The old brick heaters have been replaced by modern methods of heating, and new systems have been introduced throughout, while new varieties of flowers and foliage have been constantly added until today Mr Newby has one of the most modern and up-to-date establishments of its kind in Cass county. His business has now outgrown the bounds of Logansport and he supplies neighboring cities and towns as well. His business methods have ever been of that high order which has won him the confidence and good will of his wide and rapidly growing patronage, and he is accounted one of the substantial and dependable business men of the city and county.

CHARLES H MAIBEN Twenty-one years ago Charles H Maiben invested all his available capital, consisting of one hundred dollars, in a hand laundry business in Logansport. Today he leads in the laundry industry of the city. The modest equipment and quarters which were his when he launched out in the business world upon his own resources have with the passing years doubled, trebled and quadrupled themselves many times, and as one of the leading business men of Logansport and a man who has built up an immense industrial enterprise with the slender means at his command, he is manifestly entitled to a place in this historical and biographical work, for it is the biographies of such men as he which ever has and ever will go to make up the history of a given city, or county, or commonwealth. Born in Logansport, Indiana, on January 14, 1864, Charles H Maiben is the son of John T and Margaret (Johnson) Maiben, and of the father it is fitting that more than a cursory mention be made in this biography of his son, who has attained so prominent a position in the city of his birth.

John T Maiben was of Irish birth and parentage, born in County Sligo, Ireland in 1822. He was there reared and educated, and in his boyhood learned the trade of a cabinet maker. He was twenty-two years of age when he came to America, and after arriving in New York he remained in that city for some years, finding ample employment at his trade, and becoming a full-fledged citizen of the United States. In New York he met and married Margaret Johnson, and it was not until the early fifties that he came to Indiana. He located in Logansport straightway, the city then being in its infancy, and here he began working at his trade for one of the early undertakers of the county, Mr Manley by name. In those days caskets were made entirely by hand, and while Mr Maiben was in the service of Mr Manley his entire time was spent in casket making. He was subsequently employed in a similar capacity by other representative dealers in furniture and undertaking supplies, and continued in varied branches of the cabinet maker's trade until his death, which occurred in 1902 Mr Maiben was one of the quiet, industrious men, who seldom make a great show of accomplishment but are continually achieving He devoted his time chiefly to his own affairs, and as a result retained to the last the unfailing confidence and esteem of all who shared in his acquaintance He, was an Episcopalian reared in that faith in his native land, and politically he was a radical Democrat It is significant, however, that with the passing years as he became broadened and softened by years of contact with the world, he became much more liberal in his views He was for years a member of the old west side fire department, which is yet green in the memory of old Logansport settlers Mr. Maiben was an enthusiastic Odd Fellow and was ever an enthusiastic worker in the order. He was generous and charitable, and his benevolences were many, although performed in the quiet manner which characterized the everyday life of the man Mr and Mrs Maiben were the parents of eleven children Of this number three died in infancy while the family were yet residents of New York City Six died in Logansport and four grew to maturity Two sons, Charles H of this review and Walter, both make their homes in Logansport The wife and mother died in 1898, mourned by all who knew her

Charles H Maiben has always regarded Logansport as his home, and indeed, practically all his life has been spent in the city of his birth He was educated in the public schools of the city and for a short time clerked in the store of Wiler & Wise in the days when that well-established firm was conducted by the original founders of the house, of whom extended mention is made in other pages of this work He was also employed as a clerk with Marshall Field & Company of Chicago, but did not long continue in that connection In 1889, or thereabouts, Mr Maiben embarked in the fish and oyster business on Market street, but only remained in that business about a year He entered the laundry business on Third street in the year 1892, and this venture represented the investment which has resulted in his present successful position in the business world of Logansport

The initial investment on the part of Mr Maiben represented an outlay of one hundred dollars, or all his worldly goods, and he began by operating a small hand laundry For six months he continued with his hand laundry, when he had prospered sufficiently to make possible a little expansion He accordingly built a wooden structure at the back of where his present establishment is located, and here he changed from the hand system to the steam process He secured an old steam boiler and advertised his place as a steam laundry, and the work went merrily on The growth of this now mammoth plant has not been of a spasmodic order but has continued sanely and surely, every year marking a growth that warranted new expenditures, more modern equipment and expansion in all departments, and practically every two years since he began in business has Mr Maiben felt it necessary to bring about radical improvements in his equipment and enlarge his capacity in accordance In the summer of 1911 he began the erection of an entirely new plant at his present place, 116-118 Cicott street, and on January 1, 1912, moved into the finest electric process laundry to be found in the country, in point of completeness, modern appliances and facilities for the performing of all classes of work of this nature. The building is a single story and basement brick structure 70x165 feet, and is equipped with a complete line of modern laundry machinery, operated by electric power, with nineteen motors, of capacities ranging from one and a half to ten horse power. He has added a modern and complete dry cleaning, pressing department, also a shoe repair department, and the plant, in all its departments, gives employment to about fifty persons. All this, from an investment of one hundred dollars, twenty-one years ago. The same alertness and progressiveness which have marked the business activities of Mr. Maiben in this project have characterized his life as a citizen, and he has earned a reputation for civic pride and public-spiritedness that is well merited and highly indicative of the many splendid traits which are inherent within him.

Mr. Maiben is an Independent Democrat in his political faith, and fraternally is a member of the Knights of Pythias, the Benevolent and Protective Order of Elks, and the Fraternal Order of Eagles, in all of which he is active and prominent. He was married in 1904 to Miss Mary Shuman, and they have two children—Bessie and Thomas Maiben.

MARION E. CALLENDER. It is not always the men of a community who make the greatest noise and who take the most prominent places who contribute the most to the solid growth and advancement of that community. Rather it is an indisputable fact that some of the quiet, steady-going and persistent men have left more indelible marks upon their home towns than the most showy and prominent individuals, and Marion E. Callender, farmer and citizen, is entitled to consideration in this work because of his membership in this class of reliables.

Marion E. Callender was born in Clay township, Cass county, on July 26, 1853, and is a son of Collins and Elvira (Sisco) Callender, both of whom were natives of Ohio, and of German and English ancestry respectively. The death of Marion Callender's father when he was yet a mere boy, caused the subject to early begin to make his own way in the world, and from the age of nine years he was without the guiding hand of a father, beginning as it were, at the bottom of the ladder of life, Collins Callender having passed away in 1862. It may thus be assumed that the boy secured the most limited sort of an education. His early life was spent in farm work, and when he married in 1878, he and his estimable wife settled down to farming on their own responsibility, continuing ever since in that worthy industry, and experiencing a pleasurable degree of success. His first place was a fifty-acre farm, which possessed a small three-room dwelling house. This little place sheltered the family for six years, when the home was destroyed by fire. Mr. Callender then moved with his family to a rented place some two miles distant, and for nineteen years they lived there, the farm being one known as the Joseph Chestnut place. From there they moved to their present place in Bethlehem township—a fine improved farm of eighty acres which Mr. and Mrs. Callender have acquired the ownership of. In addition to this well developed place, they also have another farm of forty acres located two and one-half miles distant from the home place. Since the Callender family took possession of their present

"ALPINE LODGE," RESIDENCE OF MR. AND MRS. MARION E. CALLENDER

home, the place has taken on a decidedly home-like appearance, and shows the results of much well-placed labor. The house has been practically re-built, and in many ways shows the enterprising nature of the family. General farming occupies the attention of Mr. Callender and he is regarded as one of the most capable and successful farmers in Cass county, where he has been well and favorably known all his life.

The principles of Mr. Callender have always been of the most stable order, and they find expression in his every-day life, not being reserved for special occasions. He has always been a Republican and voted the ticket consistently, until recent years, when he began to show a growing tendency to favor the platform of the Prohibition party—the subject of prohibition being one in which he has long held a hearty interest.

It was on September 22, 1878, that Mr. Callender was united in marriage with Miss Mary J. Conrad, the daughter of John S. and Artelia R. (Conrad) Conrad. Mrs. Conrad was a pioneer of pioneers in this part of Indiana, having settled here in about 1837, her family being an old North Carolina one and having come direct from that state to Indiana. She was a daughter of John and Susan (Atwood) Conrad. Mrs. Callender was born in Cass county on July 16, 1858. She received a good education considering her time and place, and in the schools of Logansport finished her educational training. The following children have been born to Mr. and Mrs. Callender: Myrtle A., the wife of George F. Hopkins, resident of Adams township, an agriculturist and they have six children: Russell G., Gertrude L., Marion D., Josephine F., Mary Jane and Edith E. Mrs. Hopkins was educated in the township schools and she is a member of the Christian church. Frederick S., a resident of Chicago, and is a civil engineer for the Chicago, Milwaukee & St. Paul Railroad, and at present is engaged in Montana. He wedded Miss Edith Long. He is a member of the Methodist Episcopal church. He received a good common school education and spent two years in the Logansport high school and was a student at the Marion Normal and taught one year in Bethlehem township and the Metropolitan Business College, and then took a full course in civil engineering. Harriett A., the wife of George C. Kingery, a resident of Logansport, and connected with the Pennsylvania Railroad Company. Mrs. Kingery was educated in the schools of her home county. They have one little daughter, Crystal M. Mrs. Kingery is a member of the Christian church. Bertha E. is the wife of Earl E. Ingonire, a resident of Clay township and an agriculturist. Mrs. Ingonire spent one year in high school besides attending the public schools and both she and husband are members of the Christian church. Frank M. is a pharmacist in Kokomo, Indiana. He took a preparatory course at the Tri-State Normal at Angola, Indiana, and is succeeding in his chosen vocation. Catharine F. completed the eighth grade of the public schools and has also taken instrumental music and is a member of the Christian church. John M. received his diploma from the public schools in the class of 1909 and then graduated from the Meta high school in 1913, and he is also a member of the Christian church. Donald G. received his diploma from the common schools in 1911 and has been a student in the Meta high school two years. He is the youngest child.

As it is noticed Mr. and Mrs. Callender have given their children the benefits of good educations as well as God-like teachings in the home Mrs Callender, the wife and mother, was reared in Cass county and is a lady of more than ordinary merit and one possessed of social faculties that give her a cordial welcome to all She is one of the active members of the Christian church and is now vice-president of the Ladies' Aid Society and was its president four years. She is also president of "The Spring Creek Cemetery Association," one of the most beautiful cemeteries in the county and this was perfected by the tireless work and care exerted by Mrs Callender She has a Masonic apron that is now over a century old and it was worn by her maternal grandfather, John Conrad, and the Callenders have one of the old parchment deeds executed under the hand of President John Tyler, and is one of the valuable heirlooms in the family The beautiful farmstead of Mr and Mrs Callender is known as "Aldine Lodge," and it is one of the pleasant and happy homes of the county

The Callenders enjoy the hearty goodwill of all who have known them, and a large circle of friends in and about the township and county hold them in the highest esteem

JULIUS F LIENEMANN The title of Julius F Lienemann to prominent position on the roster of Cass county's progressive and successful men rests with his long residence, his connection with large business affairs and his identification with public life As a citizen he has done his full share in promoting his community's welfare, his business has added to Logansport's commercial prestige, while his signal public services have won him the respect and esteem of his fellow citizens in no small degree Mr Lienemann has been a resident of Logansport since 1865 His parents, Edmund and Katerina (Wurstner) Lienemann, were natives of Baden and Wurttemburg, Germany, respectively, and his father was a tailor by trade Edmund Lienemann came to the United States in 1852 and first settled at Dayton, Ohio, then removing to Delphos, Ohio, where he was married After coming to Logansport, in 1865, he took up his trade and here continued to spend the remainder of his life, passing away November 3, 1906, while his wife died September 4, 1895 Mr Lienemann was originally a Republican, and cast his first vote for Abraham Lincoln, continuing to support that party's principles and candidates until the administration of Grover Cleveland, when he voted the Democratic ticket He was a Roman Catholic in his religious belief He was unusually well read in literature, especially in American and European history, and was an ardent admirer of the writings of Schiller. A representative of the best class of German-Americans, honest, industrious and frugal, his word was known to be as good as his bond, and his death lost to his community one of its leading citizens

Julius F Lienemann was born at Delphos, Ohio, April 29, 1856, and came with his parents to Logansport, when he was nine years old He secured his education in the public and parochial schools and at Hall's Business College, and learned the trade of tailor with his father In 1879 he established himself in business as the proprietor of a tailoring enterprise, and with the exception of four years has since continued in that vocation A Democrat in his political views, in 1898 he was elected clerk of the courts of Cass county, taking office two years later and serving in the position for four years In 1910 he was elected to the board of county commissioners, a position which he still occupies Mr Lienemann has proven himself a faithful, conscientious and able county official, his long business experience being brought into play in discharging his duties He is known as absolutely trustworthy, and is esteemed by his associates and has the full confidence of the people at large He has been the architect of his own fortunes in the business field, and the establishment that now bears his name is well worthy a place among the business houses of a growing and flourishing city like Logansport.

On October 7, 1879, Mr. Lienemann was married to Magdalene Hoover, and they have had five children, namely: Gertrude, who married Ben Porter, of Logansport Oscar, who died in 1906, at the age of twenty-three years, Eva, who married Andrew Angemeier, and Hugo J and Marie, who live with their parents

DR JOHN WILLIAM BALLARD was for many years one of the best known physicians who ever practiced medicine in Cass county He was a native Indianian his birth occurring in Carroll county on February 28, 1855, and he was the son of Anson and Mary J (Hornbeck) Ballard The father was a native of Hamilton county, Ohio, and was of French descent, while the mother whom he married in Fountain county, Ohio, was also a native of that state and was of Scotch-Irish descent. Anson Ballard was a leading citizen of his community in his day, and held many positions of public trust in his county

After attending the common schools of his native community, John W. Ballard, at the age of seventeen years, entered Purdue University, from which he was graduated in 1876 In order to secure the necessary means to prosecute his studies in medicine having already decided upon his life work, the young man taught school for several terms, at the same time reading medicine under the direction of Drs Smith and Beck, at Delphi In 1877 he matriculated in the Medical College of Ohio, from which institution he received his degree two years later For a short time thereafter the young doctor practiced in Lockport, Carroll county, and in 1881 he located in Logansport. In the course of time his practice began to assume pleasing proportions, and there were comparatively few localities in Cass county that were not frequently visited by him in his professional capacity. At all hours of the day and night, in sunshine and shower, midst the biting blasts of wintry wind, contending with bad roads and worse weather, Dr Ballard's was a familiar face to be encountered His memory is revered by many because of his work among them, and he will long be recalled among the men who lived lives of unselfish devotion to their work and to their people

Dr Ballard served as county coroner for three terms He was a member of the Masonic order, Tipton Lodge, A F & A M, and also of the Independent Order of Odd Fellows and of the Tribe of Ben Hur On November 4, 1876, Dr Ballard was married to Ellen Milroy, of Delphi, Indiana, and four children were born to them Samuel Milroy, a mining engineer, Bruce Milroy, who died in infancy; Charles A, mentioned below, and John W, attending the University of Southern

California Dr Ballard died on September 9, 1911, and his work is being ably carried on by his son, Dr Charles A. Ballard

Dr Charles A Ballard was born in Logansport, Indiana, on September 12, 1882, and was here reared and received his early education He graduated from the high school in 1903, after which he entered the State University at Bloomington, Indiana, attending there for two years and giving special attention to the studies pertaining to physiology, anatomy and chemistry In 1905 he entered the College of Physicians and Surgeons at Chicago, and was graduated therefrom with the degree of M D in 1907 Following his graduation he served some six months as interne in the Illinois State Insane Asylum at Elgin, after which he came to Logansport and here he has since been engaged in the active practice of his profession He was associated with his father until the death of the latter, and since then has conducted practice alone. He is a general practitioner and a prominent physician In politics he is a Democrat, and in the line of his profession he is affiliated with the American Medical Association and with the County and State Medical Societies

Dr Ballard was married on June 15, 1909, to Miss Nina Douglas a teacher in the high school of Logansport. One son has been born to them, Charles Douglas Ballard

JOHN H ROHRER One of the particularly substantial and prosperous farmers of Bethlehem and Clay townships is John Rohrer, who owns valuable farming property in both these townships, and is known in both as a man of splendid capabilities in an agricultural way, with excellent business faculties as well The Rohrer family is one of Swiss and German ancestry, and is one that has long been identified with the agricultural activities of the state in various sections

John Rohrer was born in Wayne county, Ohio, on December 26 1844 and is the son of Joseph and Maria (Kampf) Rohrer, the father was a son of John Rohrer and the mother daughter of Anthony Kampf both natives of Pennsylvania The subject came to Cass county in 1851 in company with his parents, and they settled first in Clay township, where they spent the remainder of their lives The mother died in 1853 and the father survived until 1906 They were the parents of two children, namely John, whose name initiates this review, and Simon who married Edith Conger, and lives in Buffalo, New York In 1854 Joseph Rohrer married Susan M Tweed, born in 1834, and died in 1912 Of this union were born two children—Lee who died in infancy, and Ella, who died at the age of fourteen years It was in 1902 that Mr Rohrer moved to his present farm in Bethlehem township, from the old farmstead in Clay township on which he had been reared The log house that his father first occupied when he moved there years before had been replaced five years later with a concrete dwelling and other suitable buildings John H Rohrer remodelled his present residence in the most approved fashion when he came into possession, and the farm has taken on an appearance of fruitfulness and cultivation that is well in accordance with the activities and policy of the owner In addition to this fine place of two hundred acres, he has a farm adjoining of one hundred and sixty acres in Clay township that is equally prepossessing in appearance, and his farm holdings in the aggregate mark him as one of the successful and substantial agricultural men of the county

It is a fact that aside from his meritorious career as a farmer, Mr. Rohrer has also had a brief career as a preacher, having served for seven years in the ministry of the Christian church He also gave three years to the teaching profession and in 1863, when in the first years of his young manhood, he served eight months in the Civil war with the One Hundred and Eighteenth Indiana Regiment He is a college man, his higher education having been gained at Alliance, Ohio, and at Indianapolis, where he attended some of the best colleges, and he was prior to that a graduate of the Westville high school, in Westville, Laporte county, Indiana

On October 12, 1880, Mr Rohrer married Cecelia M Williamson, born October 1, 1850, the daughter of Samuel A and Temperance (Conrad) Williamson, people of Scotch-Irish and German ancestry, respectively They were married in Bethlehem township, and much of their wedded life has been spent here and in Clay township They have one child, Clark Rohrer, born on August 3, 1881 The son was married on May 1, 1912, to Miss Grace Horney, born December 7, 1889, the daughter of George and Lucy Horney of Bethlehem township, and they make their home in Bethlehem township, where Mr Rohrer is engaged in the agricultural industry, in which he received an excellent training at the hands of his father, and in which he is making splendid progress, having the reputation of being one of the most progressive and successful young farming men of the community.

The Rohrers are among the most successful and prominent people in the township where they have long resided, and they enjoy to the fullest extent the hearty regard that is accorded to them by a large circle of friends and acquaintances, who hold them in high esteem because of their many pleasing qualities of heart and mind They are citizens of the highest order, and have a genuine and wholesome interest in all that leads up to a betterment of social and business conditions of their district

WILLIAM SEARIGHT was born in Cumberland county, Pennsylvania, on June 17, 1819, and was a son of Alexander and Elizabeth (Lobaugh) Searight The Searight family is one descended from William Searight, who came from Londonderry, in the north of Ireland, in the year 1740, or thereabouts, and settled in Lancaster county, Pennsylvania Alexander Searight was born on December 29, 1776, and he married Elizabeth Lobaugh November 15, 1804 In 1838, in "Conestoga" wagons, he drove across the country to Indiana and settled in the dense woods of Jefferson township, in Cass county There he built a two room log cabin, into which the little family moved, and there began the work of cleaning up their farm In later years Mr. Searight erected a sawmill on Crooked Creek, their mill being one of the first in that locality It provided lumber for the building of the frame houses built in their community for years, and was a source of considerable profit to its owner On February 12, 1848, Alexander Searight died. Prior to his death the family built a flouring mill on Crooked Creek, which became famous for the grinding of grain throughout a wide area of the new country The mill was burned in later years, its destruction supposedly being of incendiary origin, and this misfortune crippled the financial resources of the Searight family. Alexander Searight and his wife were the parents of nine children, William of this review, being the seventh born of that number. After the burning of the mill, William Searight and a brother, Alexander, went via the Isthmus of Panama to California in 1849. There he was engaged in teaming and freighting goods to the mines, this business resulting in a profit of a nice order, until in 1852 when he returned to the states, making the return trip via the Overland-Southern-New Orleans route. He was engaged in farming and lumbering until 1864, then removed to a farm, where he died on September 25, 1877. Mr. Searight was married on April 6, 1854, to Emily Vanatta, a native of Warren county, New Jersey, and they became the parents of three children as follows: George W., William L., and Harry A.

HARRY A. SEARIGHT was born in Cass county, on September 21, 1860, and is the son of William and Emeline (Vanatta) Searight. Concerning the former, appropriate mention is made in the preceding article dedicated to William Searight, so that further details as to the family and ancestry of the subject are not required here.

Harry A. Searight received his education in the district schools and Logansport high school, and began teaching in the rural districts when he was nineteen. He continued his work in this line for eleven years. In 1889 he became superintendent of the schools of Cass county, serving one term of two years in that office. He entered the government railway mail service in 1891, in which line of work he has ever since continued.

On December 24, 1889, Mr. Searight was united in marriage with Miss Disa Gorden, daughter of William M. Gorden, one of the early settlers and well known men of Cass county, and to their marriage four children were born, as follows: William H., Grace G., Anna M., and Margaret E.

Mr. Searight and his family are members of the First Presbyterian church of Logansport.

JOHN DODT. One of the prosperous and progressive business men of his community is John Dodt, who was for years engaged in business in Lucerne. On March 1, 1913, he changed location to Hamlet, Indiana, to engage in the implement and garage business. He has made good in the business and is the owner of a nice farm in Jefferson township, in addition to his valuable property in Lucerne. He is a man who has proven his worth to the community as a citizen in no uncertain terms, and it is the men of his stamp and order who have done much to further the best interests of their communities, wherever they have been found.

John Dodt was born in Cass county, in 1861, the 26th of April being his natal day, and is the son of Henry and Katherine Dodt. He was one of the eight children of his parents, the others being as follows: Henry, William, Charles, Frederick, Daniel and Andrew. He was reared on the home farm and when he reached years of young manhood engaged in business in the grocery line in Lucerne, in which he

THE FRUSHOUR FAMILY GROUP

continued with a due measure of prosperity until ten years ago That period marked the change in his business from a grocer to a dealer in farming machinery and implements With the passing years Mr Dodt acquired some property in Lucerne, as well as a fine farm of seventy-five acres in Jefferson township, which yields him a nice income annually Mr Dodt has given valuable service in public offices in his town, and has been a member of the advisory board of the Harrison township, and is now serving his second term in that office He served as supervisor of roads for something like eight years, or two terms, and has also been justice of the peace A Democrat, he takes an intelligent and interested part in the activities of the party in his district, and is a member of the Presbyterian church, of which his parents also were members

On February 18, 1886, Mr Dodt was united in marriage with Miss Carrie Johnson and they have a family of seven children Charles, the eldest, was born on December 6, 1886, he is married to Miss Lillie Ream, the daughter of William Ream Their marriage was celebrated on April 15, 1908 Bertha is married to Fred Erwin Harry married Miss Bertha Meyers Florence married Clark Stevens The three youngest children, Mary, Elsie and Alice are unmarried, and share the parental home

The Dodt family is one that has long enjoyed the friendship and high regard of the best people of the community which has represented their home for so many years, and they are in every detail worthy of the high place they occupy in popular confidence and esteem.

MRS. ETTA FRUSHOUR was the wife of the late William Frushour, a man who was all his life a resident of this township, and who passed his life on the farm on which he was born and where his death occurred, and one of the substantial citizens of Bethlehem township His widow occupied that place, and like him, was regarded as one of the most estimable and honorable of people She maintained her high place in popular confidence and esteem and was prominent in every good work that found expression in her community

Born in Missouri, April 25, 1859, Mrs Frushour was the daughter of Paul and Ellen (Long) Gundrum Paul Gundrum was a native Indianian, who came from Winnimac, Indiana, in 1869, and settled in Cass county, where Mrs Frushour, his daughter, was reared He died on March 2, 1912, after having passed a life devoted to farming and kindred activities They were people of German ancestry and descent The mother died on the 8th day of April, 1912, surviving her honored husband by but a very brief period as will be seen Etta Frushour was their only child

In her young maidenhood Mrs Frushour married William Frushour, the date of their marriage being October 21, 1880 He was a son of old pioneers of Cass county, and he was born on the farm where he passed his life and died, and where his widow also died His father came here in a most primitive period and located a farm putting up a rude log house and settling down to farm life in a new and untaught country Heavy timber growths covered the land at that time, and this was gradually cleared away and the farm came to take on an aspect of homelikeness that has been only intensified with the passing years. Indians were not strangers to the settlers of that time, and trying times were experienced by the sturdy family who settled in the wilderness. The farm as it originally stood comprised one hundred and twenty acres of land, but the pioneer father and his sturdy sons continued to add to their holdings by purchase, until at the time of the death of William Frushour, the home place aggregated some eight hundred acres of the most arable land in Cass county. Building work has been kept up on the place from year to year, and the dwelling and other buildings are of the most modern and approved type in all that makes for comfort and convenience.

William and Etta Frushour had three children. The eldest of these, Essie, married Edward Johnson, and they had two children,—Russell, born April 22, 1902, and Mary Hazel, born August 6, 1906. For her second husband Essie wedded Francis M. Bolton, September 25, 1912. Mr Bolton is a native of Cass county, Indiana, born July 6, 1873, and educated in the common schools. He is an agriculturist and belongs to the Gleaners. Mr and Mrs Bolton reside in Bethlehem township. Frank was the second child of his parents. He was born in 1884, and died on January 17, 1912. Cecil, born in 1895, died on November 12, 1912.

Mrs Frushour and her family were members of the Presbyterian church of Bethlehem township for many years and she maintained an active position in the various departments of the activities of that body. She was a woman of the most excellent traits of mind and heart, and was a leader in thought and action in her community, where her accomplishments gained her an enviable position in the esteem of her many friends and acquaintances.

Mr Frushour passed away at his home on December 7, 1909, at the age of fifty-five years, and his death is still felt in a community that had known him intimately all his life and which recognized his many splendid qualities and his worthy and consistent life. Mrs Frushour departed this life January 19, 1913, and she was interred in Mount Hope cemetery Logansport, Indiana.

JOHN J HELMS One of the well improved and prosperous farms in this state in northeastern Cass county near Hoover is that owned by John J. Helms, who has been identified with this part of Cass county for the past quarter of a century, and who has acquired a liberal share of material goods, and at the same time has won a place of high esteem in the community. Both he and his wife represent old Indiana families, and Mrs Helms' people were pioneers of Cass county.

John J Helms was born in Hamilton county, Indiana, December 30, 1857. His parents were Calvin Fletcher and Priscilla (Woods) Helms. There are two brothers of John J Helms, namely William J who married Lydia Wiseman, and Elworth, who married Claire Lamb. All the family were born and reared in Indiana and its members have lived in the state practically from the pioneer time.

On the ninth of January, 1888, Mr Helms was united in marriage with Miss Sarah Crook. Mrs Helms is a native of Cass county, and her parents were Patrick and Nancy (Stevens) Crook. Her father died in March, 1885, while her mother is still living and resides at her home Her father had come to Cass county from Wayne county, settling in Clay township, and later moving to his permanent home farm, where he bought one hundred sixty acres At the time of his settlement the land was covered with woods and it required all of the labor of a pioneer to clear it off for cultivation. There were no railroads, and the only means of travel was by wagon or horseback, and in making the trip from Wayne county they were on the road for one week The Crook family has been well known for many years in Cass county, and Mrs Helms has six brothers and one sister, whose names are as follows Charles, who died in 1896, William, who married a Miss Eliza Young, Margaret, who died in 1862, Jacob wedded Elizabeth Young, Ashford, James, who died in 1888, and Willard, who married Mary Rush.

Mr John J Helms came to Cass county in 1888, settling upon the farm which he still occupies The place at that time was unproved with a small frame house, and barn, and with his subsequent thrift and prosperity he has remodeled both of them and not only made them modern but representative of the thorough business-like conditions which are maintained all over the estate He is the owner of one hundred and fifty-five acres and cultivates it practically all himself He and his wife have labored together to effect a comfortable prosperity and to create a good home for their children, and their work has been entirely successful Mr Helms is a member of the Christian church, and in politics is a Republican He and his wife are the parents of five children Herman Clifford, born November 4, 1889; David Ross, born July 18, 1891, Ruth, born September 6, 1892, Laura, born June 15, 1895, Anna, born September 29, 1899 The son Herman married Lola Leffel and the daughter Ruth married Hubert Moss

GEORGE L. BEECHER Of Cass county farmer citizens who began their careers with practically nothing and have used a splendid industry to make a modern homestead out of the wilderness of brush, and against all the obstacles of nature, one of the best examples lives in Adams township, Mr George L Beecher Mr Beecher's address is R F. D 12 miles No 21 It is at that point on the rural free delivery route that his present homestead, with all its excellent improvements is located Some twenty-three years ago Mr. Beecher took this place when it was covered with woods and brush, and much of the land was under water during the seasonal part of the year, and his first home was a log cabin, which existed there at the time of his removal All these things have given way to a modern system of cultivation and he is now one of the most progressive and prosperous farmers of Adams township

George L Beecher was born in Peru township, Miami county, Indiana, September 22, 1862 His parents were William V and Julia A (Beecher) Beecher The family were originally from Pennsylvania, and the name of the paternal grandfather was Benjamin Beecher and of the maternal grandfather William Beecher. The father, during his early life, moved from his native state to Ohio, locating first near Columbus, where he was married, and where he lived for about four years and was engaged in his trade as carpenter Later he moved to

Indianapolis, where he followed the same occupation, and then came to Peru township in Miami county, Indiana. This last removal occurred in 1860, and in Miami county he became a settler upon a farm, which was his home until 1871. At that date he bought a home in Jefferson township, of the same county, and there continued his quiet occupations of a farmer and substantial citizen, up to the time of his death, which occurred on the twenty-third of September, 1900.

George L. Beecher remained at home until he was twenty-one years of age, and in the meantime had acquired a fair education in the district schools, and by the work and responsibilities of the home farm had developed good physical powers and a knowledge of the business of farming. Beginning for himself, without any capital, he first rented a farm in Adams township of Cass county, but a year later returned to Miami county where he lived as a renter for five years. After this he came to the homestead which he still occupies. It was eighty acres of land, but of this quantity only twenty-five acres could be worked since all the rest was covered with brush and timber and water, and it was by dint of hard labor and close and thrifty management that he cleared up the land and tiled it until now the entire farm is productive and cultivatable. Besides the lack of other improvements, the farm had only a log house, and a rough barn, and these two have long since yielded to a comfortable and attractive residence, and first class improvements in barns and outbuildings.

Mr. Beecher was married March 2, 1884, to Miss Sarah E. Fisher. Their five children, with dates of birth as follow: Clinton E. born February 9, 1885; Lyman E., born December 13, 1886; Wreathe Fern, born December 29, 1886; Walter V., born November 19, 1895, and Truman, who died in infancy.

Clinton E. received a common school education and one term in the Twelve-Mile high school and two terms in Marine Normal. He wedded Miss Grace H. Condon, second child of Merrill Condon and Mary Elrine. Mr. and Mrs. Beecher are members of the Brethren church. He is a Republican, a resident of Fulton, Indiana, and a carpenter. Lyman E. also received a common school education and is a resident of Minneapolis, Minnesota, employed in a department store. He married Lorina Jamica. Wreathe Fern is the wife of Rev. Charles W. Ronk, of Bridgewater, Virginia, a finely educated man. They have one little daughter Mildred Christine. Truman died aged 15 months. Walter V., the youngest, graduated from the public schools in the class of 1910 and did two years high school work in Twelve-Mile school and is a great lover of mathematics.

Mrs. George L. Beecher is a native of Miami county, Indiana born July 9, 1858, and she is the fifth born in a family of nine children, five sons and four daughters born to Benjamin and Elizabeth (Rush) Fisher. Six of the children are residents of Indiana and two brothers Abram and Isiah are residents of Michigan. Mrs. Beecher's father was of German lineage and the name "Fisher" was originally spelled "Fischer" in the German.

The Beechers have a five-passenger touring car of the Ford make and their estate is called "The Crescent Stock Farm."

C T KINZIE The last sixty years have brought many and marked changes to what is now Cass county Half a century or more ago there were large areas of land, extending for miles in unbroken forest, a few settlements having been made along the streams, but practically all that part now included in Adams township could be secured for homesteads from the government by those in search of permanent homes, by the payment of a very small amount of money It was at a time when people spoke of a dollar as made up of one hundred cents and dollars were scarce with the pioneering class, and when Abraham Kinzie paid for a claim of 160 acres of virgin land, his capital was about exhausted although this land, now worth hundreds of dollars, was secured for thirteen dollars an acre The Kinzies came to Indiana from Virginia, a vigorous, enterprising family, members of which have ever since been identified with the development of Cass county C T. Kinzie, who may almost call himself a native of Cass county, having been brought to this section in his infancy and spent sixty-one years here, is one of the respected citizens and prosperous agriculturists of Adams township, his 276 acres of fine land representing two separate farms He was born January 1 1852, in Franklin county, Virginia, and is a son of Abraham and Charlotte (Shawalton) Kinzie, and a grandson of Abram Kinzie and George Shawatter.

C T Kinzie was brought as an infant to Indiana, the trip from Virginia made by wagon, taking six weeks The family first settled on the old Tabor farm, a tract of 160 acres, where a two-room log house and small log barn were built, and this land was subsequently cleared by the father and his sons and. is now the property of Mr Kinzie's brother Here Mr Kinzie was reared to manhood, his education being secured in the primitive schools of his day and locality, and he was thoroughly trained in the rudiments of farming and taught to respect the honor and dignity of hard labor, thrift and industry After his marriage, he settled on the John Leffel farm, where he resided for fifteen years, working this land in conjunction with his brother and building good structures on his half of the property Later he traded his land for 144 acres in Adams township on which there was a log house and barn, and there spent six years, greatly improving this farm In the meantime he secured two hundred acres in Miami township, south of the river, and also his present farm in Adams township, a tract of thirty-three acres, which he has continued to cultivate to the present time, and on which he now resides He is an able agriculturist, taking advantage of all the aids that invention discovery and science have made, and his success has been commensurate with his hard and faithful labor

In 1872 Mr Kinzie was married first at New Waverly Indiana, by Dr Quick, to Miss Mary Moore, and they became the parents of nine children, as follows Ida, who married Amos Eller, Lottie who became the wife of William Kinger, Noah, who married Clara Moss, Elsie, who married Charles Angle Laura, who married Ray Movtz, Maggie, who married Harry Miller, Marian, who married Elva Wagner, Martha, who married Irvin Angle, and Teresa, who became the wife of Emmett Buskirk His first wife died in 1897 and he was married second to Miss Lillie Harris His third union occurred in 1902, when he was married to Mrs Fannie (Altice) Dillon and she died in March 1909 having been the mother of three children, Claudine, who was born in March, 1903, Cecil Abraham, born in October, 1904, and Sarah, born in October 1907 Mr Kinzie is a consistent member of the old Dunkard church, and he is a Republican in politics

WILLARD AULT The title of Willard Ault to a position among the representative men of Cass county lies not only in the fact that he has resided here for more than a quarter of a century, but also as one who has contributed in no small degree to the growth and development of his section Mr Ault's present handsome farm in Adams township was but a worthless stretch of timbered ground devoid of any improvements save several primitive log buildings, and the property bore little resemblance to the present Maplehurst Farm, which, with its stately structures, its well-kept fields and its herds of sleek cattle, presents an air of prosperity that at once assures the visitor of Mr Ault's ability as an agriculturist He was born March 11, 1866, in Miami county Indiana, and is a son of John and Elizabeth (Price) Ault, and a grandson of Frederick Ault and Charles Price Mr Ault's father died in 1883, while his mother still survives and lives in Adams township

Willard Ault received his education in the district schools of his native locality, and in 1885 located on his mother s farm in Adams township, on the Cass county-Miami county line There he continued to be engaged in agricultural pursuits for five years, and in 1890 came to his present farm, a tract of one hundred acres, on which stood a little log stable and a shack which passed for a house Here Mr Ault settled down to clear his land, and soon replaced the primitive buildings with others of a more substantial character As the years passed, he put more and more of his land under cultivation, and his equipment and improvements increased as his finances would permit Maplehurst Farm is now one of the valuable properties of Adams township made such through hard and intelligent work, and in addition Mr Ault owns thirty-five acres located one mile east of his home, which is a beautiful location Although he has been busily engaged in agricultural pursuits, Mr Ault has found time for other activities, following contracting with a large measure of success and being the builder of all of his own buildings as well as those of a number of his neighbors He is recognized as a business man in whose word the highest confidence may be placed, and his integrity and honorable dealing have attracted to him a wide circle of friends While a resident of Miami county, prior to coming to Cass county, he taught school for fourteen years, and became a well known and popular educator Although not an aspirant for public preferment, Mr Ault takes a keen and intelligent interest in political matters, and has always given his hearty support to the policies and candidates of the Democratic party His religious affiliation is with the Christian church

On March 28, 1890, Mr Ault was married in Howard county. Indiana to Miss Kathryn Morrison, daughter of Enoch and Sydney (Snyder) Morrison, farming people of Howard county and to this union there have been born two children · Ina M, born November 16, 1891, who resides on the home farm, and Elizabeth, born March 23, 1893, who married Dwight M Kime Probably no family in Adams township is better known or more highly esteemed, and the name has always stood for business integrity, public spirit and good citizenship

WILLIAM CARSON. The general citizenship of Adams township is made up of people of sterling character, good morals and a pleasant friendliness which fine schools and many church privileges encourage. Many of the substantial families have been known here for years and the present heads of some of them are not only residents but also natives of Indiana. They are largely agriculturists and their well-cultivated fields and herds of sleek cattle and healthy looking stock proclaim that many of them lead particularly pleasant and profitable lives amid prosperous surroundings. William Carson, whose valuable farm of eighty acres lies in a very desirable section of Adams township, has not, however, always been a farmer, for three long years and three months of his early manhood were given to the service of his country when secession raised its gory head during the dark days of the Civil war. Mr. Carson is a native of the Hoosier state, having been born in Jennings county, September 10, 1841, and a son of John and Julia (McCammott) Carson. His paternal grandfather, William Carson, died January 12, 1841. Mr. Carson's father was born January 12, 1818, and his mother July 17, 1818, and they came from Rutherford county, North Carolina at a very early day, locating in Jennings county, where they spent the remainder of their lives in agricultural pursuits.

William Carson was reared in Jennings county, and there received his education in the public schools. He was engaged in work on his father's farm, when the Civil war broke across the country, calling all classes and conditions of men to the defense of the flag. Mr. Carson, with youthful patriotism, offered his services and was accepted as a member of the Sixth Regiment, Indiana Volunteer Infantry. Perhaps it was the military blood of his ancestors stirring within him, for his grandfather and great-grandfather had both been valiant soldiers in the American army during the Revolutionary war and the War of 1812-14. At any rate he made a brave and faithful soldier, and during the three years and three months in which he fought under the Stars and Stripes, he gained commendation for his bravery and respect for the cheerful manner in which he performed every duty assigned to him. When he had completed his long and arduous service and had received his honorable discharge, he returned to the quiet occupations of peace, which he resumed with added zest and self-reliance. Not long thereafter he made his advent in Cass county, settling first in Noble township, where he spent three years, and then coming to Adams township, where he rented land from Paul Taber for some years. Finally he purchased his present tract of eighty acres, on which he has since made his home. At the time he purchased it there was considerable timber still on the property, the buildings were of a mediocre order and the land was without fencing. The timber has been cleared away, the farm thoroughly and neatly fenced, and the old buildings replaced with new ones of architectural beauty and substantial character. This work has consumed years, but the present value of the farm repays in full the labor expended upon it. Mr. Carson is known as an excellent farmer, thoroughly conversant with every detail of his vocation. He has not devoted his entire attention, however to agricultural matters, as he has been identified with the Twelve-Mile State Bank since its organization in 1911 as a director and holds a like position with the Twelve-Mile Telephone Company, an enterprise which has been successful since its organization in 1903. Among his associates, Mr Carson is known as a shrewd, far-sighted man of business, whose word is as good as his deed. His religious connection is with the United Brethren church, to the movements of which he has been a liberal contributor. In politics a Republican, he has served as a member of the board of trustees of his township for six years. Mr Carson has been interested to some extent in fraternal work, and since 1867 has been a member of the Masons.

On January 12, 1870, Mr Carson was married to Miss Elizabeth Hicks, daughter of James Hicks, and to this union there were born five children, as follows: Joseph A., born July 4, 1871; Frederick, born July 26, 1875; Jessie, born October 17, 1879. and two who died in infancy. Mr Carson was married (second) February 23, 1888, to Miss Lorinda Leffel, daughter of William and Catherine (Haney) Leffel, of Cass county, and they have one daughter—Inez, born March 1, 1889, who married Hugh Skinner and lives in Adams township.

Mr Carson has one of the old parchment deeds, which is a valuable heirloom in the home. This is the eighth deed found in the county and bears the signature of President Van Buren. His great-grandfather was a soldier in the Revolutionary war and this gives Mr. and Mrs Carson and children place in the Sons and Daughters of the Revolution.

Mrs Carson was born in Cass county, November 17, 1857. Both her parents are deceased. She was reared and educated in Cass county and she is a member of the United Brethren church. Mrs Carson is of German and Mr Carson of Irish descent.

DANIEL R CARSON, general farmer, who owns seventy-two acres of some of the best land lying in Adams township, has been a resident of Cass county for a number of years and is identified with all that goes to make up its best citizenship. He was born on a farm in Jennings county, Indiana, May 4, 1857, coming from ancestry largely agricultural in its vocation but not lacking in patriotism when called on, for both his grandfather and great-grandfather took part in the War of 1812 and Revolutionary war, while his brother, William Carson, served gallantly in the Union ranks during the War of the Rebellion. His paternal grandfather, William Carson, of Rutherford county, North Carolina, died January 12, 1841. His parents were John and Julia (McCammott) Carson, the former of whom was born January 12, 1818, and the latter July 17, 1818. From Rutherford county, the family came to Jennings county, Indiana, and here the parents of Mr Carson spent the remainder of their lives in agricultural pursuits.

D R. Carson received his education in the district schools of Jennings county, but as a young man came to Cass county and first located on the Taber section in Adams township. His first dwelling was a house made of rough boards, in which four of his children were born. Mr Carson continued to rent on the Taber section for a period of fifteen years and then purchased his present tract of seventy-two acres in 1903. Here he erected almost all of the buildings, put up new fencing,

"COUNCIL CREST," RESIDENCE OF MR. AND MRS. GEORGE H. SHIREY

graded and drained the land, and made numerous other improvements, all of which have served to enhance its value. He is an able agriculturist, bringing to his work the knowledge gained during many years of experience in his vocation. His standing among the citizens of his community is high, and his transactions have always been marked by strict integrity. Mr Carson is a member of the Odd Fellows, in which he has many friends, and his political faith is that of the Prohibition party. With his family, he attends the United Brethren church, of which he is a member of the board of trustees

On January 13, 1881, Mr Carson was married to Miss Lucy McCassline, daughter of George McCassline, and to this union there have been born six children, as follows: John McCassline, Fred D, Doris, who married Walter McGuire, Everett; Ovie, and Ernest, the eldest, who died at the age of five years.

GEORGE H SHIREY. The quality of a man's usefulness in his community is in no wise impaired by the fact that he leads a quiet and unpretentious life, is seldom seen in public places and takes little part in the political activities of his district. If he goes on in a straightforward manly and enterprising way, giving his best energies to the work before him and performing his share in matters of civic responsibility, he proves the quality of his citizenship as forcibly as does the most prominent individual. George Shirey is one of those plain and unpretentious characters who find their chief interest in their own private affairs, and he has made his home in this township and community for the past eight years, in which time he has added his full quota to the products of the township as the seasons come and go.

Born in Roanoke county, Virginia, on June 3, 1851, George Shirey is the son of John and Leannah (Miller) Shirey, who died in 1885 and 1882, respectively. They were the parents of four children,—those besides the subject being William R, Walter G and Emma (deceased).

Mr Shirey came to Bethlehem township in 1895, and eight years ago acquired his present farm, which is a representative place of one hundred acres, handled by himself, without any other help. He is prosperous and comfortable, and plays the part of a good citizen in the varied activities of communal life in his own unassuming and quiet manner. He is a member of the Presbyterian church, as is also his wife, and his politics are those of a Republican.

Mr Shirey wedded Miss Addie L Montgomery, September 12, 1883. She was born in Bedford county, Pennsylvania, July 26 1854, the second child in a family of eight children, one son and seven daughters, born to James H and Mary E (Brindle) Montgomery, and five of the children are living. Father Montgomery was a well educated gentleman and was a school teacher by profession. He was one of the valiant men who went from the old Keystone State of Pennsylvania in defense of the Union and served his country nobly and received his honorable discharge. Politically he was a Democrat. Both he and his wife were members of the Methodist Protestant church. Mr Montgomery died September 3, 1912, and his wife died August 31, 1889.

Mrs Shirey was educated in the common schools and she has nobly performed her part in counsel and advice with her husband. Mr and

Mrs Shirey have a beautiful home situated near the Michigan pike and it is known as "Council Crest" Mrs Shirey's brother, Strock Montgomery, makes his home with them Mr Shirey is a gentleman who dearly loves good driving horses, and has been the owner of many They have a fine five passenger touring car and take great comfort in life They made a pleasure visit to the Pacific coast recently Besides their fine property in Bethlehem township they have 240 acres in Gray county, Kansas

L C MILLER, M D There is no profession to which men devote themselves more dignified in its ethics or more reasonably helpful to the world than that of medicine Similar claims are made by the church and by the law, but they, while essentially true enough, are based on other foundations The healing art demands of its real followers that natural reverence for the dignity of the human body that commands the exercise of all the skill that years of study and training have brought to them; to cure its ills even when they well know their services will receive no monetary reward Where or when does a real physician refuse to give help, and to what other body of men does the world owe so much? Its scientific discoveries have not only eased the bed of former torture but have found the cure for almost every bodily affliction Justly is this noble profession in the fore-front Methods may differ, systems may not be quite alike, and personality counts for much, but the aim and principle remain the same Among the members of the medical profession well known in Cass county is Dr L C Miller, whose skill and faithfulness, together with his determined hopefulness and cheerfulness, have made his presence valued in many households during the last eighteen years, which period has covered his residence at Twelve-Mile Dr Miller was born at Alliance, Ohio, March 24, 1869, and is a son of Levi and Alma (Lazarus) Miller, grandson of Samuel Miller and George Lazarus, and great-grandson of John Craig

Dr Miller was reared at North Benton, Ohio, at the home of an aunt on his mother's side, Anna Lazarus who gave him excellent educational advantages On determining upon a medical career the young man went to Ann Arbor, Michigan, and entered the University of Michigan, where he was graduated from the medical department and received his degree of Doctor of Medicine. In 1895 Dr Miller came to Twelve-Mile, and purchased the practice of Dr Harding, who is now located at North Manchester, Indiana Here he has remained ever since, his practice being a large and lucrative one and extending out into Adams township for a number of miles He keeps fully abreast of the new discoveries and inventions by subscription to a number of the leading medical periodicals, and takes a deep interest in the work of the various medical organizations of which he is a member. It is not alone as a physician, however, that Dr Miller is well known, for he has identified himself with every movement that has affected his community, and is at this time connected with several of the leading business enterprises of this place In 1911, when the Twelve-Mile State Bank was organized, he was chosen president, a position he has held to the present time, wisely directing the institution's policies and popularizing its coffers A new, one-story bank building has been completed, furnishing a handsome home for this enterprise In 1903 the Twelve-Mile Telephone Company was organized, and since that time Dr Miller has acted in the capacity of secretary. He is recognized by his associates as a shrewd, forceful man of business, with high ideals and possessed of the strictest integrity His connection with any enterprise is a warranty of its legitimacy, and he firmly holds the confidence of the people among whom he has lived for so long He has taken an interest in fraternal work, belonging to the Modern Woodmen of America, the Masons and the Odd Fellows, and for a number of years was treasurer of his lodge in the latter order With his family, he attends the Twelve-Mile United Brethren church

Dr Miller was married in 1897 at Deedsville, Indiana, to Miss Mary J Snider, daughter of Solomon Snider, and they have three children, as follows Galen, born April 28, 1898, Alma, born June 23, 1905, and Donald, born August 29, 1907

WILLIAM H DILLMAN. One of the oldest families of Cass county is represented by William H Dillman of Adams township, whose postoffice address is Hoover No 20 The Dillman family have been residents in this vicinity on the present farm just mentioned since 1840, a year which was not removed from the period of first settlement, and at which time the present Dillman farm, as well as nearly all the rest of the country was almost in a condition of primitive wilderness The present proprietor of the well improved and profitably managed place, was a mere child when the family came to this location The various members of the family have been well known, have been industrious workers, and substantial citizens, and have borne the responsibilities of their relations with man and God in a way that is deserving of a permanent place in the record of Cass county

W H. Dillman was born in Preble county, Ohio on the ninth of October, 1839, a son of Daniel and Elizabeth (Aukerman) Dillman The maternal grandfather was John Aukerman Daniel Dillman, the father, was born in 1804 and was a Virginian, from which state, when quite young he came to Ohio and was married there, and several years later in 1840 moved to the present homestead in Cass county His death occurred here in 1875, and his remains now rest on the home farm in Adams township At one time he served as trustee of the township, and was also a justice of the peace The wife of this venerable pioneer was born in 1808 and died March 21, 1859

W H Dillman was the fifth in a family of eleven children. The others being as follows Mary, John H born February 19, 1832, Aaron A, born October 5, 1834, and died April 16, 1837; Elizabeth C, born July 16, 1837, Maria V, born June 15, 1841 Solomon F, born February 20, 1843, Eliza L, born April 26, 1845, Lovina E, born May 20 1847, Isabelle H, born August 7, 1849; Margaret A, born June 6, 1852

Reared in Cass county, where he received his education from such schools as existed during his youth, and growing to manhood Mr Dillman assumed the responsibilities of farm life He and his brother conducted the farm for some years, until they finally divided the farm, and he has ever since been proprietor and manager of this estate, which has been in the family possession almost since the earliest period of settlement. At the time his father came here, the entire tract of land was covered by woods and a small log house was the first habitation for the family. Father and sons worked together to clear up the land, and in time it became a very productive homestead, which it still remains. The father, during his life time, built a very fine barn, and it is still standing, but Mr Dillman has erected the present home.

Mr W H Dillman was married April 21, 1895, to Miss Elizabeth Teel, a daughter of Joel H and Elizabeth (Kenzie) Teel. Her people came to Indiana from Virginia. Her father died when she was quite young, and her mother brought the family to Cass county. Mr and Mrs Dillman became the parents of three children, namely Gale Marie, born October 14, 1896, Carl Teel, born January 16, 1899, Daniel R, born June 6, 1901

The pretty home of Mr and Mrs Dillman is known as Pine Lodge ''

GEORGE W McCoy As a merchant, George W McCoy is one of the enterprising men in the little town of Galveston, the metropolis of Jackson township. Mr McCoy is a native of Indiana, has spent all his life in this state, received only a district school education, as preparation for a practical career, but has used such energy and thorough business ability in his endeavors, that he has for a number of years been marked as one of the successful and prosperous men of his community.

George W. McCoy was born in Ripley county, Indiana, October 21, 1870. He is a son of Robert W and Lutetia (Scothorn) McCoy. The father passed away in 1906, and the mother in 1884. Mr McCoy received his early schooling in Ripley county, though only in the district schools. He was reared in the influences of a good home, and his parents were both people who gave him all the advantages they could afford. His father, during the war, had served as a homeguard, though never going to the front for service.

In February, 1896, Mr McCoy married Miss Laura B Harness, a daughter of A J and Jane (Rosberry) Harness. Mrs McCoy is a native of Cass county, and her father's people were among the oldest settlers. Her great-grandfather, George W Harness had come here during the pioneer period, and he lived to the very unusual age of 108 years. The four children of Mr and Mrs McCoy are as follows Ivan R, born October 23, 1897. Russell Morton, born October 15 1899, Robert Loran, born November 6, 1901, and Frederick Damon born October 5, 1905, all the children reside at home.

Mr McCoy has been a member of the board of trustees of the Methodist church in his locality, and his fellow citizens have also shown their confidence in his judgment and capacity by choosing him to the school board. He has been a resident of Galveston, since 1900. Previous to that time he had followed farming to some extent, and in 1900 entered upon his mercantile career. He established a business here in partnership, but after its existence for about a year, his partner died, and he then bought out the other interest, and has since conducted a very flourishing grocery business. In politics, Mr McCoy is a Republican

WILLARD BURROWS Three generations of the house of Burrows have lived on the old farm that came to be the property of the grandfather of Willard Burrows of this review many years ago in Deer Creek township, and which was then a virgin wilderness The axe of the pioneer had not as yet penetrated the dense forest region, and the man who first settled on the farm that is today one of the fine productive tracts of the fertile Cass county, proved his hardihood and courage in no uncertain terms when he fared forth on his home seeking expedition and located in a wilderness. But those were the dominant characteristics of our ancestors, and it was qualities of that order that made possible the race that has brought forth so much in the way of achievement in the present generation

Willard Burrows was born in Deer Creek township on March 4, 1883, and is the son of John T. and Susan A. (Lenon) Burrows, the father being the son of Joseph Burrows, who established the family in Indiana He was a native of the state of Ohio, and soon after his marriage came to Cass county, where he settled on the farm, mentioned above, and which is now owned by the father of the subject There the old pioneer passed his life, leaving the place to his son when he passed on He brought about many improvements of no mean order, and the buildings which stand there today are those that he erected in the years of his activity upon the place

Logansport, in those early days, was a mere trading post, and the wildest and most primitive conditions prevailed on every hand The old pioneer came to be the owner of some five hundred acres of land and was regarded as one of the prosperous men of his day John E Burrows was reared there and since the passing of his father, retains the old homestead, and carried on the work of the place in a worthy manner, up to 1905, since when he conducts a drayage business with good success

Willard Burrows is one of the two children of his parents, the other being Mabel, who married Herbert A. Keller In recent years Mr Burrows engaged in the grocery business at Galveston and has enjoyed a pleasing measure of success in that industry. He is one of the prominent and popular men of Galveston, and takes an active part in the best social and civic activities of the place He has long been a member of the United Brethren church, in which he is a trustee, and treasurer of the church as well He is a Mason, affiliating with the Eastern Star and Galveston Lodge A F & A M, No 244, as well as the Knights of Pythias, Amity Lodge No 262 Politically, he is a Prohibitionist and is enthusiastic on the subject of prohibition

In 1905 Mr Burrows married Miss Katherine E Novinger the daughter of John H and Adeline (Storer) Novinger Mrs Burrows was one of the three daughters of her parents, the others being Lura and Della, the latter of whom married Joseph Kroeger. One child has been born to Mr. and Mrs Burrows, Thelma May, who died in infancy

CHARLES F THOMAS Galveston, in Cass county, Indiana, has known the business activities of Charles F Thomas and others of his family since 1865, and the years that have passed have witnessed his progress in merchandise and other lines in a most pleasing degree He was born in Afton, Minnesota, on February 2, 1856, and is the son of Meredith H and Harriet A. (Knowlton) Thomas. The mother was the daughter of Artemas B Knowlton, and the father a son of H L Thomas Meredith Thomas came to Indiana with his father's family in 1850 He was a leader in church circles and was treasurer of the local Baptist church for ten years and clerk of the church for a similar period. He served two years in the city council and was in many other ways active in the best interests of the place He was engaged in the mercantile business in Logansport, Indiana, from 1850 to 1854. after which he returned to Minnesota, and came to Cass county again in 1865 when he engaged in the general merchandise business with his brother-in-law, M. B Knowlton This partnership endured for a few years, after which the father of the subject continued alone until 1875 The senior Thomas also established the grain elevator in Galveston, and continued in its operation until 1895, when he established the bank at this place, continuing to be identified with it up to the time of his death, which took place in 1899.

Charles F Thomas received his early education in the schools of Galveston, and during the years when his father was occupied in the merchandise business in this place he assisted him in the work of the establishment, there learning much in the way of operating and managing such a business which he put to good use in later years on his own responsibility He at one time, with his brother, operated a general merchandise store in Galveston, but by mutual consent they dissolved partnership, and he started a store across the street from his brother This he conducted until the place was destroyed by fire, since which time he has been engaged in the real estate business, in which he is conducting a nice business at the present writing

In 1880 Mr Thomas was married to Miss Laura L Armstrong, the daughter of Charles Laban and Elizabeth (Lease) Armstrong, and they have six children, namely Harry B , who is married to Maude Sharp, Nellie B , the wife of Charles Stewart, Sarah, married to Elbert E Day, Bernard C , who married Mamie Cooper, Meredith H , single, Daniel H , also single

Mr Thomas is a member of the Baptist church, in which he is active and prominent, as well as others of his family, and a progressive Republican in his politics He is a member of the Knights of Pythias and the Modern Woodmen, and is active and interested in the work of the societies, as well as in all work pertaining to the general welfare

WILLIAM B. LAKE It has been well said that history treats of those men who have been foremost in the political and military activities of a nation, while biography goes further, and deals with the individuals who have devoted their lives to the tilling of the soil and the quiet growth and development of the nation along those lines This being the fact, it is most fitting and proper that a man like William B Lake, who is the subject of this necessarily brief review, and one of the well known farmers of the county, should find place within the pages of this work

William B Lake was born on the 13th of November, 1842, and is the son of Isaac and Laura (Viny) Lake The father came from New Jersey in young manhood, settling in Marion county, this state, later

"GLENDALE FARM," RESIDENCE OF MR. AND MRS. NOAH SULLIVAN

settling in Carroll county, where he passed away in 1871. He was the father of nine children, of which number William B. was the sixth born.

William B. Lake was born in Carroll county, on the old homestead of his father, and in the common schools of that community he received his early education. In 1879 he came to Cass county, here acquiring his present farm, and he has continued to live in the vicinity of Galveston through the ensuing years. In 1867, on the 3d day of October, he married Lydia Jane Wright, the daughter of Isaac and Susanna (Cline) Wright, and six children have been born to them three of whom are deceased. The others are Laura B., who married Val Cunningham, and has three children—Ellis, Everett and Otis, Lenora, married to Walter Robinson, has two children—Truman and Raymond, and Clarence, who married Dora Tilley, has three children—Russell, deceased, Glenn and Elsie Imogene. The first, third and fourth born of the children of Mr. and Mrs. Lake are dead, they being Estella, Luella and Clara.

Mr. Lake has lived a life of usefulness in the state and nation, and as a soldier in the Forty-sixth Indiana Infantry did his full share to preserve the integrity of the Union in the years of 1861-65. He gave gallant service in the Army of the Potomac and in General Sherman's army, and saw much of the most strenuous fighting of the whole conflict. When the war was ended, he turned his attention to the farm once more, and has continued in that industry without interruption since that memorable time. He is known for one of the sturdy and stable citizens of his community, bearing a most excellent reputation wherever he is known, and with his wife is a member of the Baptist church of Galveston. They have been residents of Cass county for thirty-three years.

NOAH SULLIVAN, the present trustee of Adams township is one of the respected and substantial men of Cass county, who have spent their lives in farming, and who, in addition to acquiring a good stock of the substantial things of life, and in providing well for their families, have also given public service to the community in which they reside, and have borne well the responsibility of citizenship.

Noah Sullivan was born on the twenty-fifth of February, 1854, in Miami county, this state. His parents were Phillip and Rosanna (Long) Sullivan. He was reared in Miami county, where he attended the schools and at an early age took up the practical work of farming, which he has followed practically all of his life. On the sixteenth of August, 1878, he married Miss Melissa Parks. Her father was Joseph Parks, a resident of Miami county. The six children of Mr. and Mrs. Sullivan are as follows: Milo, Grover, Mary, Ruth, Nellie, and Enid.

Mr. Sullivan and his family came to Cass county in 1900 from Miami county, and bought eighty acres of his present homestead in Adams township, and near the Twelve-Mile postoffice. Since the first purchase he has added twenty acres to his estate and it is on this little homestead of twenty acres that he makes his present home. His son, Milo, lives on and is active manager of the eighty-acre farm. Michael married Miss Cora Black, and they are the parents of one child, Mabel, age five years. The family are members of the United Brethren church, and in politics Mr Sullivan is a Democrat. As a man who had given many years of his life to farming, and who had always borne a high reputation for integrity in the community, he was honored by his fellow citizens in Adams township with the office of trustee, the duties of which he has been efficiently performing since his election

EMERSON KITCHEL Cass county is rich in her farming industry and in her innumerable sturdy and stanch young men who are devoting their energies to the tilling of the soil and to the development and continued cultivation of one of the most fertile spots upon the globe Not the least of these men is Emerson Kitchel, the owner of a fine little farm of recent acquiring, and the manager of another which is the property of his father Emerson Kitchel was born in 1871 in Deer Creek township, on the old Kitchel homestead, and is the son of Daniel and Ellen (Babb) Kitchel The father came from Union county, Indiana, in his young manhood, and practically all his life has been devoted to farming activities He is a veteran of the Civil war having fought in the Eighth Indiana Infantry He reared a family of ten children, as follows Emerson, Lauana, Jacob, Harriet, Alvin, Nellie, Everett, Edgar, Charles and Nettie This family were schooled in Young America, Cass county, and all attended the schools of Terre Haute Everett is a student of Purdue University, and Charles and Nettie attended college in Marion Five of the children taught school in Cass county, and gave excellent service in an educational way while they were thus employed

Emerson Kitchel worked on the home farm between school periods and finished in the Young America high school He later taught school and saved enough money from his earnings to buy his present farm, which he has been most successful in operating General farming and stock raising claim his attention, and in addition to his own place he rents the farm of his father near Walton which he operates in conjunction with his own place

Mr Kitchel bears a most excellent reputation in the community and enjoys the high regard of all who know him He is a member of the Sons of Veterans, and he and his family are members of the Methodist Episcopal church

On March 15, 1900, Mr Kitchel married Miss Nellie Bell, the daughter of James and Susan (Knock) Bell, and she was a teacher in Galveston for twelve years Mr Bell came to Cass county with his parents, and there has continued to make his home to the present time, although he is now retired from active business and is leading a quiet life of rural content at his home in Galveston Mr and Mrs Bell had three children, those in addition to Mrs Kitchel being Elizabeth, now Mrs Davis and Harvey, who lives in Galveston Mr and Mrs Kitchel have four children—Mary, Pauline, Frances and Edwin The three first named are attending school in Galveston

D C BARNETT, M D One of the oldest and best known physicians of southern Cass county, Dr Barnett has practiced his profession for upwards of half a century, and has rendered an aggregate of service to humanity which could not be described in any fitting manner represented as it deserves Dr Barnett represents one of the old families of

Cass county, and is himself one of the oldest living native born residents

D C Barnett was born in Georgetown, Cass county, February 14, 1839, a son of Joshua and Jane (Voorhees) Barnett Joshua Barnett came to Indiana from Ohio, and was one of the pioneer settlers in Cass county, having located here before the wilderness was cleared up, and he himself contributed no unimportant share to the labors of the pioneers

Dr Barnett received his early education in Howard county, and in the city of Kokomo He read medicine at New London in Howard county, and first began practice at Young America, in Cass county. When he was twenty-three years of age he went into the army as a member of Company D of the Eighty-ninth Indiana Infantry, under Captain John E. Williams of Kokomo He was at the front for two years, and was wounded in the battle at Pleasant Hill, Louisiana, and at the engagement of Sabine Crossroads he was captured and kept a prisoner of war for sixty-five days. Then being paroled he came home in July, 1864, and was mustered out of service in December following.

Dr Barnett was married in 1861 to Miss Virginia Stewart, a daughter of Edward and Elizabeth (Williamson) Stewart The six children born of their marriage are as follows Mrs Carrie Duncan, who is the mother of six children, Frank, who married Margaret Vance, and who has seven children, Lola, who is married and has one child named Olive, Harry, who married Nora Garr, and has two children named Paulme and Rosaline, Fred, who married Elizabeth Williams, and has four children named Thelma, Earl, Vera and Areline; Edward, who married Dora Alexander and has two children The doctor is affiliated with the Grand Army post, and his wife is a member of the Methodist church

CHARLES S. SARIG is one of the prominent and prosperous young farmers of Cass county, of which he has been a resident for a number of years He was born in 1856 in Berks county Pennsylvania, and is the son of Daniel and Katherin (Sassaman) Sarig, of German ancestry The parents were born in Berks county, and was there reared, being one of the prominent citizens of the district, in which he was widely known as a prosperous farmer He reared a family of eight children, named as follows Charles, of this review; Ellen; Sarah, Emma, Salena, Ellis, Wilson, and Albert The father died in 1909, and the mother is still a resident of the old Pennsylvania home in Berks county.

As a boy Charles Sarig attended the public schools and did his full share of the work of the farm, in connection with his school work He learned the carpenter's trade in his native community, and when he was in early manhood left his country home and came to Indiana He had an uncle living in Kokomo, and he settled there, for two years giving his time to carpentering He later turned his attention to farming, and acquired a fruitful farm of eighty-six acres in Jackson township, about three and a half miles from Galveston Here he has continued to farm in the most approved fashion, and is rapidly coming to be known as one of the successful farming men of the county.

On February 24, 1887, Mr Sarig married Miss Adie Bell Winters, and they have three children J D Harry E and Minnie B The eldest son is married to Lela Timmons, and they live in Walton, Indiana.

Mr Sarig affiliates with the Democratic party and is a member of the advisory board of the township.

JAMES A HENRY Long years of active and successful farming in Cass county have won for James A Henry a reputation for efficiency, skill and far-sightedness in his work that extends throughout the length and breadth of the county and established him in all fixity in the ranks of the leading agricultural men of the district He has demonstrated most unequivocally his prowess as a tiller of the soil, and his achievements in the stock-raising industry have been no less praiseworthy Diversified farming finds its ultimate success in Cass county, and none has done more to establish the fame of the county along those lines than has Mr Henry As the owner and manager of a fine farm of some two hundred acres near Galveston, his name stands for much that is praiseworthy in agricultural circles, and it is eminently fitting that some mention, however brief it must be, shall be made of him and his accomplishments in a work of the nature of which this publication partakes

James A Henry was born on the 11th of December, 1842, in Carroll county, in Burlington, Indiana, and is the son of William and Jane (Gunn) Henry The father came from Pennsylvania, of the vicinity of Harrisburg, in his early manhood and settled in Indiana He was reared to the trade of a cabinet maker, although born on a Pennsylvania farm, and when he came to Indiana he forsook the cabinet maker's art and turned his attention to farm life, for which he possessed a natural fondness, and in which he had received a judicious training in his boyhood at home He amply demonstrated the wisdom of his choice, gaining a prominent place in farming circles, and ending his days in the occupation of a farmer He and his wife reared three children: Samuel A, Malinda Jane, and James A. Henry, whose name initiates this brief review

James A Henry settled in Cass county in his young manhood, and here he acquired a tract of farming land, settling down in a home of his own after his marriage with Miss Jane H Millman Eleven children were born to them, ten living named as follows Elisha, Alma, Lily, Maud Ruth, Myra, Bernice William R, Paul J, and Clinton B all of whom are today living lives of usefulness in the various communities in which they have settled with the coming of years of maturity and responsibility

Mr Henry, naturally enough, has in his time experienced certain of the hardships of the agricultural man, but he has, in the main, prospered agreeably, and is today regarded as one of the well established and wholly successful men of his community He is still active and prominent in the farming industry, diversified agriculture and stock raising claiming his interests

Fraternally Mr Henry has membership in the Masonic order and in the Independent Order of Odd Fellows, and the churchly relations of him and his family are with the Baptist church of Galveston

JOHN F STANLEY. Another of the sons of pioneers who have given their lives to the upbuilding and development of Cass county, is John F. Stanley, a resident of this community from his birth, and the son of a man who was born in Galveston, his father having pioneered to these parts in the days before county lines existed, and when farming was at its earliest state of development The old Stanley farm is one that stands for much in the way of growth and development in this community today, three generations of its men having derived their sustenance from its broad acres and built it up to its present state of agricultural perfection John F Stanley, whose name introduces this sketch, all too brief to do justice to the family, was born on the old Stanley farm, on November 16, 1879, and he is a son of William F and Sarah (Emery) Stanley, the former of whom was also born in Galveston, Indiana

John F Stanley received his education in the schools of Galveston, and early turned his attention to practical farming, with the intention and expectation of giving his life to that work, in which he had been thoroughly grounded by his father, a successful and well known farmer of the community Mr Stanley is now the owner of a fine farm of about two hundred acres, his place being one of the most productive among the better farms of Jackson township

Mr Stanley has shown himself to have profited well by the training he received in his youth, and he has supplemented that training by actual experience gained from his own activities, so that he is today reckoned among the most capable farming men of the township

Mr Stanley, it may be said here, is the sixth child of his parents, and the youngest as well, the others being Jesse; Emma, George, a resident of Galveston, Pearl, a well known and successful school school teacher, and Dolly.

On Christmas day, in 1903, Mr Stanley was united in marriage with Eva Stafford, and they have had three children William H, the first born, is dead, as is also Burl F, who died at the tender age of two years, Wilber Floyd, the youngest of the trio remains to brighten the home of his parents Mrs Stanley is a daughter of Henry Stafford, a native and resident of Lincoln, in Cass county The Stanley family are members of the Baptist church of Galveston, and participate actively in the good works of that body They are people who enjoy the genuine friendship of a host of good people in their community, and none are better deserving of that regard than are they

JAMES S MCWILLIAMS In a community where farming has reached a point where it is conducted along scientific lines and is the principal business of the residents, interest must inevitably attach itself to the activities and accomplishments of any one of the devotees of that enterprise James S McWilliams, who is especially prominent among the farming men of Jackson township, is one who is especially worthy of mention in this historical and biographical work His fine farm of two hundred and forty acres is one of the show places of the community and manifests in the most telling manner the character and calibre of the man Mr McWilliams was born in 1844 in Decatur county, Indiana and is the son of Robert and Sarah (Graves) McWilliams They were natives of Bartholemew county, Kentucky, and came to Galveston,

Indiana, in the early fifties, where they made their home during the remainder of their lives. They were the parents of two children—James, of this review, and Mary, who is now deceased.

When he was a young lad James S. McWilliams came from his native community with his parents and settled on the farm that is today the property of the subject. Mr. McWilliams attended the common schools of the community, there gathering the rudiments of an education, to which he has supplemented in an admirable manner with the passing years through reading and observation, so that his education compares favorably with that of men who had greater advantages in youth. He remained at home until he was twenty-two, then started out for himself, and he has been successful and prosperous in all his undertakings. Mr. McWilliams was not lacking in a thorough training in the agricultural business, for his father was a man who farmed intensively and did not slight the education of his son in the lessons that he had learned through years of experience. In 1869 Mr. McWilliams married Martha Logan and they have reared three children, named as follows: Minnie, the wife of Robert Hyatt, who is the mother of one child—Russell Hyatt; Mary E., who is the wife of William R. Hyatt, and they have one son, Clarence C., and George E., who married Grace Hoover, and is the father of two children—Everett H. and Marie Helen.

In due time Mr. McWilliams succeeded to the old home place, and here he has since enjoyed a high degree of prosperity and a generous measure of content and happiness. He is undeniably one of the well established men of the township in a material way as well as in the sincere esteem of his fellow men. They are members of the Baptist church, and his fraternal relations are with the Masonic order, of which he has long been a member. The entire family is one that has earned and retained the high regard and confidence of all with whom its individual members have come into contact and in their respective homes and communities are securely established in the hearts and minds of their fellows.

EDMAN A. LEFFEL. Instances are not lacking in Cass county of men who born to the soil, have spent some years in other pursuits only to find the call of the land too strong to resist and have therefore returned to the occupation of their forefathers. In this category stands Edman A. Leffel, of Bethlehem township, who for the past seventeen years has lived on his present property, a well-cultivated tract of 190 acres, which he has brought to a high state of cultivation, and which has been in the possession of the Leffel family for many years. He was born in the town of Bethlehem, Cass county, Indiana, April 27, 1863, and is a son of Arthur and Nancy (Tilton) Leffel.

The educational training of Mr. Leffel was secured in the public schools of Bethlehem, following which he went to Logansport, and for some years was engaged in various occupations, but eventually in 1896 returned to the homestead in Bethlehem township, where he has since carried on general farming. He has made numerous improvements on this property, has a handsome, modern residence situated on Twelve-Mile Rural Free Delivery Route No. 21, and is considered one of his community's enterprising and progressive citizens, and one who is at

"THE PINES," RESIDENCE OF EDMAN A. LEFFEL.

all times ready to adopt new ideas and methods He believes in the use of modern machinery in his work, has a thorough knowledge of the rudiments of his vocation, and is an acknowledged judge of livestock Essentially a farmer, he has never cared to enter public life, but has been content to follow the peaceful occupation of tilling the soil, but can be depended upon to support all measures that promote good government or make for the betterment of his community

On October 13, 1886, Mr Leffel was united in marriage with Miss Mollie Krider, and they had four children, namely Teresa and Roy, mentioned below, Zola, who died at the age of fourteen months, and Floyd, who died when thirteen months of age The daughter, Teresa, is the wife of Russell Conrad and resides in Bethlehem township, where he is an agriculturist Mrs Conrad received her diploma from the public schools in the class of 1898 and spent one year in the Twelve-Mile high school She attended musical institutions in Logansport and has taught instrumental music for two years She is a member of the Bethlehem M E church and a member of the Ladies' Aid Society The son Roy, has completed the public school course in the class of 1913, and is at home with his father

Mrs Leffel, daughter of Isaiah W and Martha T Krider was born in Fulton county, Indiana, September 26, 1864 She removed with her father's family to Cass county when four year sold, where she lived continuously until her death, excepting three years spent in Logansport She was educated in the country schools and at the old Fort Wayne College and De Pauw University She was married to Edman A Leffel October 13, 1886 For three years she fought a courageous battle with disease but the grim monster at last was conqueror and at 8 15 o'clock on the morning of October 28, 1907, her redeemed spirit left the emaciated body and went home to heaven

Mr Leffel and his son reside in their beautiful home, which is known as "The Pines " Mr Leffel is a member of the Masonic order at Twelve Mile, Lodge No 673 He attends the Methodist church, as did also his wife, and he is a liberal contributor to religious and charitable movements

ROBERT C HYATT is one of the well known farmers of Galveston, Indiana, where he has lived practically all his life He is the son of William Henry and Mary J (Jackson) Hyatt, concerning whom further mention is made in the sketch of William R Hyatt, the brother of the subject of this review

The district schools of Galveston and vicinity furnished practically all the schooling that Robert Hyatt received He alternated his school attendance with the regular work of the farm as a boy, and so well did he utilize his opportunities for study that he was able to teach in the country schools of Howard and Cass counties He gave up the work to devote his entire time to farming and has since then been making splendid progress in that line of industry His farm is a fertile and well developed place of some eighty acres, and yields him under his careful management, a bountiful income It is located on the Graves road, about a mile north of Galveston, and is one of the well-kept places of the township

Mr Hyatt is still a young man, his birth having occurred in Ripley county, Indiana, on January 23, 1870, and his accomplishments thus far are well worthy of him He was postmaster in Galveston for six years, in which office he gave the most efficient service to the patrons of the department In his farming he gives the preference to stock raising, in which he has been very successful

Mr Hyatt was married on Christmas day, 1895, to Minnie McWilliams, and they have one child—William Russell The political affiliations of Mr Hyatt are with the Republican party, and fraternally he is a member of the Knights of Pythias, and also a member of Galveston Lodge No 244, F & A M He and his wife are members of the United Brethren church

PLINY A GRAVES occupies one of the fine farms of Cass county, situated some two and a half miles north of Galveston on what is known as the Graves road, and comprising one hundred and thirteen and a half acres of the most fertile and productive soil in the county He has lived all his life in this community, his birth having taken place on his father's farm about a half mile distant from his present property He was born on the 12th day of November, 1870, and is the son of James F. and Rebecca (Stanley) Graves The father was born in Decatur county, on the 3d of July, 1837, and came to Cass county with his parents in 1849, and in 1856 located on the land where his son, Pliny A, now lives. He later bought a farm of his own and married, establishing a home there, and he and his wife became the parents of four children, of which number the two eldest—Charles and Lenora—are deceased

Pliny A Graves the youngest child of his parents, attended the Graves school, so called, and later finished his schooling at Galveston He worked on the farm with his father between schools seasons, continuing at home until he married in 1896, on the 26th of February He married Eva the daughter of Joseph and Almena (Misener) Lutz, who came from Pennsylvania, and were of Dutch ancestry The father was a mere boy when he came from his native state to Indiana, and here passed the greater part of his life, devoted to farming He was born on January 7, 1827, and died in 1903 Mr Lutz came to Cass county in 1856, took up forty acres of government land and set about clearing it In 1859 he moved on his own farm To this worthy pioneer is accorded the credit for making one of the first roads ever built in this township He built a cabin in the forest for his family, performing all the work himself, and lived a life of usefulness in Cass county until the day of his death He was the father of eight children, as follows: Lucinda, Mary E, Elizabeth, Frank J., Stephen A, Valla, deceased, William C, Eva M, and Minnie

Mr and Mrs Graves have three children, of whom brief mention is here made Nina, the eldest, died at the age of fourteen years, and is buried at Galveston; she was born on February 17, 1897, Carmen, born August 9, 1905 and Josie R, born March 14, 1907

Mrs Graves is a member of the Methodist Episcopal church, in which she is especially prominent and active in all departments of its work

Mr Graves is known for one of the substantial men of the community, and is most successful as a farmer and stock raiser, enjoying the friendship of a wide circle of acquaintances in and about Galveston, and occupying a secure place in the confidence and esteem of the community at large, in which he was born and reared.

WILLIAM E COUNTRYMAN for a number of years past has successfully engaged in raising the general crops of the locality and in producing a number of cattle and other live stock His record in business and in citizenship has been marked with a most solid integrity, and honorable in his dealings and esteemed among his fellow citizens, he is one of the foremost men of Jackson township.

William E Countryman was born on the homestead farm in Jackson township, section 13, on November 9, 1860, the son of Isaiah and Sarah (Crull) Countryman His father came from Highland county, Ohio, being eighteen years of age when he located in Jackson township The four children in the parents' family were named Lucetta, now deceased, John A, William E and Jennie Gore

The schooling with which Mr Countryman was prepared from first to last was received in the Cass county schools, after which he took up the work of the farm and was his father's assistant for some years Since then he has acquired proprietorship of the old J T Howard farm, section 9, Jackson township, and is now conducting it successfully for the raising of stock.

Mr. Countryman was married June 26, 1861, to Miss Sarah Haward, a daughter of J T and Elizabeth (Bickell) Haward Her father came to Indiana from Clarke county, Ohio, where he was born and reared Mr and Mrs Countryman are the parents of two children Maud is a graduate of the grade and high schools and has been a successful teacher, she now resides at home, Claude H is also through school and is still with the home people Mr Countryman is affiliated with the Knights of Pythias and is a member of the Universalist church

DAVID A AMAN, one of the best known farming men in Cass county, in which he has lived for the past sixty years, was born in Ohio, in December, 1847 and is the son of Andrew and Elizabeth (Myers) Aman The father, Andrew Aman, came from Germany with his wife, where both were born and reared, and settling in Ohio, they reared a family of eight children, all of whom are now deceased with the exception of the two youngest born, John and David of this review. The others were named Jacob, Michael, William, George, Andrew and Mary E.

When David Aman was about four years old the family migrated to Logansport, Indiana, and there they made their home The father rented land in Washington township and occupied himself with farming for the remainder of his life David Aman attended school when he might, but the greater part of his time and energies were devoted to the farm during his boyhood days, and when he reached man's estate he took up farming upon his own responsibility When he married he acquired a farm of some ninety acres, upon which he lived during the years in which he was rearing his family and when his five children had reached years of maturity he sold that place and divided the proceeds among them. Later he bought his present ninety acres upon which he is spending the closing years of his life. He has all his life been accustomed to toil and has lived a quiet, wholesome life, but one that has been characterized by an influence for good that is always to be found in the unpretentious activities of a man of his stamp.

In 1871, April 11th, Mr. Aman married Mary E. Hunter, and to them five children have been born. Rose, the eldest died as the wife of Frank Kerry, leaving one child Olliver Kerry. Hattie married Walter McKibben and they became the parents of two children, Ethel and Everett, she at present time is the wife of Harvey Gotschall. Ella, the third born child of David Aman and his wife married Edgar Phillip, and they had two children, Edith and Russell. Alvin W. married Grace Sperry, and they have four children. Bessie is the fifth born child of the Aman family, and is the wife of Harvey Snyder.

JOHN GALBREATH is one of the old established farming men of Galveston, where he has lived for twenty-eight years. He is the owner of a well cared for and productive farm of eighty acres which has represented his home here for many years, and he is regarded as one of the substantial farmers of the township.

Born on December 11, 1834, in Darke county, Ohio Mr. Galbreath is the son of Joseph and Eliza (Bricker) Galbreath. The father came to Indiana from Ohio, his native state, in 1839 and settled in the vicinity of Warsaw, bringing with him his family. He reared ten children in his home, the first in order of birth being John, the subject of this review, the others are Martin, Charlotte, Nancy, Jane, William, Frank, Samuel, Lafayette and Byron.

John Galbreath was reared on a farm and attended the country schools in his boyhood. While yet in his teens he was occupied for some time in teaching in the district schools of his county but when he was thirty-four he married and returned to farm life. He married Annie Wagner, who was born on March 15, 1840, near Bellefontaine, Ohio, where she lived until her marriage. She was the daughter of Isaac and Nancy (Firestone) Wagner, the father a native of Xenia, Ohio, and the mother of an old Virginia family. Isaac Wagner passed his life in Bellefontaine as a farmer.

Four children were born to John Galbreath and his wife, of whom the following mention is made. Fay, the first born, married Philip Noel, and they have two children, Claude and Vivian. Ida is unmarried and is engaged as a teacher in the public schools of Columbia City. Ada is the wife of Louis Graham, and to them four children have been born: Victor L., Wahnita, Helena and Ruth. Minnie, the fourth born and youngest of the family, is the wife of John Burrows now deceased.

Mr. Galbreath has been a member of the Masonic fraternity for many years, and affiliates with the Universalist church. He is a man of the most estimable character and one who has won and held the confidence and high regard of all who have come to know him in the years which he has passed in Jackson township as a citizen and farmer.

WILLIAM A. PATTERSON, who has gained some prominence as a farmer and stock-raiser in Jackson township, was born on the old Patterson homestead in Jackson township, Cass county, on the 23d of February, 1849 and is the son of James and Catherine (Sprinkle) Patterson. The father, James Patterson, came from Pennsylvania to Kentucky, in 1841 and later made his way to Cass county, where he passed his remaining days. He was a farmer and reared a family of six children, as follows: Mrs. Amanda Weaver, William A. of this review, Elmyra, now deceased, Benjamin, also dead, Mrs. Louisa Steward, who has three children Sadie, Oney and Mary, and George W., who married Mary Crull lives in Galveston, and they have six children, as follows Frank, Reed, John, Pearl, Myrl and Burr.

William Patterson worked on the home farm during these years in which he attended the country schools, and when he was eighteen years of age he commenced to "shift for himself," as the old familiar saying has it. He was without capital at that time, and as he resolved to farm, he rented a place, which served him well until he was able to purchase a place of his own. He now has a fine place of one hundred and twenty acres of the most fertile land in Cass county, as well as another place of some one hundred and fifty acres of equally desirable land. He has prospered with the passing years, and is regarded as being a wise and skillful farmer.

In 1875 he married Miss Juniatta Van Buskirk, the daughter of Elisha and Martha (James) Van Buskirk. Six children have been born to Mr. and Mrs. Patterson. Harry, the eldest is deceased, Benjamin Sarah, the wife of B. F. Conwell, Anna, married William Stine, Grace, living at home, and Charles O., who married Miss Edith Shope, and has three children, Edgar, Felma and Elma. The Pattersons have no church affiliations being rather inclined to the attitude of free thought and subscribing to no set religious belief. They are highly esteemed among the best citizens of the community and are in every way worthy of the position they hold.

GEORGE W. SEYBOLD, directing head of the great mercantile establishment of Seybold Dry Goods Company, has been connected with the dry goods business in Logansport for more than forty years. Commencing in the humblest position, he mastered its many details, and continued in the business until he attained at length a commanding position among the enterprising dealers in Logansport, and has been able to hold it amid the strong competition which increasing capital and trade has brought to the city. His success has been due alone to his energetic character and business capacity, for he began life without pecuniary assistance or the aid of family or other favoring influences. Mr. Seybold was born at Dayton, Ohio, April 30, 1850, and is a son of John G. and Ursula (Munger) Seybold, and a grandson of John G. and Jacobenia (Fulmer) Seybold.

John G. Seybold, the father was born September 11, 1824, in Montgomery county, Ohio, near the city of Dayton, and was there reared to manhood. Early in life he turned his attention to agricultural pursuits, and this has been his vocation throughout life, with the exception of four years when he was engaged in the brewing business in

Dayton He was married July 19, 1849, to Ursula Unger, and in 1864, with his family, came to Cass county, Indiana, locating on what is known as the Seybold farm, south of Logansport There he owns 300 acres of finely improved land, and no citizen in his section stands higher in general esteem Mr Seybold has always ardently supported Republican principles His wife was born in Germany, and as a young woman accompanied her parents to the United States, the family settling in Ohio. where she met and married Mr. Seybold Eleven children were born to this union, namely. George W., Sarah J, Rosetta, J. Byron, Mary A, Joseph A, Henry Sylvester, Charles, Oscar M Ira and Clara

George W Seybold was one year old when his parents removed to Darke county, Ohio, and when fourteen years of age was brought to Cass county, Indiana Here he spent several months in the district schools to complete his education, and also attended Hall's Business College, after graduating from which he returned to the home farm in Washington township there assisting his father until he was twenty-two years of age At that time he became a clerk in the store of Jacob Wiler, at a salary of $3 50 per week, and, as his board was $4 50 per week, he was compelled to use a part of his scanty savings while learning the business Coming to the store a country boy, unsophisticated and unlearned, with a knowledge of naught but hard work and close attention to business, he was derided by his fellow-workers for his countrified ways, and laughed at for the hard work he made of everything The youth was possessed of good common sense, however, passed these criticisms by for what they were worth, and at the end of the first year had the satisfaction of seeing the vindication of his labor, for his wages by that time had grown to $50 00 per month He continued four and one-half years with Mr Wiler, and then went to LaFayette as manager of the branch store of Wise & Wiler, where he remained seven months, then returning to Logansport to enter business on his own account With a carefully saved capital of $900, the country youth of but five years before managed to secure $4,000 worth of goods on credit, and with this established himself in business as the proprietor of a dry goods store in November, 1877, at No 313 Market street During the seven years that he remained there he entered so deeply into the confidence and esteem of the people that his little place of business became one of the most popular in the city In 1884 he admitted one of his brothers, J Abner Seybold, to a working partnership, and in that year the business was removed to 317-319-321 Market street, where it has continued ever since This has become the most important store of its kind in Logansport, and one of the leading ones in northern Indiana. It is operated as a department store, occupying three stories and a basement, the latter as a storeroom, this department feature having been inaugurated in 1897 About the year 1888 Oscar M Seybold, another brother, was admitted to partnership, and he continued to be connected with the firm until his death, June 6 1911 A stock valued anywhere from $30,000 to $100,000, in dry goods, carpets, house furnishings, etc, is carried, and a business of approximately $225,000 is done annually In January. 1904 the business was incorporated under the style of Seybold Dry Goods Company with a capital stock of $60,000 Mr Seybold has never known the time, from when he first entered business, that he has not been able to meet his obligations as they have matured, and never has his credit been questioned The rules that have spelled for success in his case have been hard work, intelligently directed good native business qualifications and the mastering and constant attention to the many details of his business It is but natural that this business, being of his own creation, should enlist the greater part of his attention, but a man of such abilities cannot escape being drawn into other large enterprises, and it has been so in Mr Seybold's case He was one of the organizers of the Logansport State Bank, and on its establishment, in May, 1893, was chosen its president, a capacity in which he acted for four years, when he retired to accept the vice presidency, as other business interests would not permit him to give his attention to the office He directed its policies in such an able manner that he popularized its coffers, won the confidence of the banking public, and made the institution one of the foremost in northern Indiana He also belongs to the Knights of Pythias fraternity and in politics may be said to be a Republican with progressive tendencies

Mr Seybold was married August 30, 1882, to Miss Alice R Whitmore, of Logansport

Henry Sylvester Seybold was born in Darke county, Ohio, son of John G and Ursula (Unger) Seybold, August 23, 1862 He accompanied his parents to Cass county in 1864, and was reared on the home farm, securing his education in the district schools and Hall's Business College When twenty-one years of age he started helping his father on the farm for wages, but after six years, in 1891, became a clerk in his brother's store in Logansport, and in 1904 was admitted to partnership in the business with which he has since been connected He was married June 26, 1895, to Miss Nellie Bevan, and they had two children Theresa, who died aged two and one-half years, and Howard

FRANK R MORRISON One of the best known and most popular men in Galveston is Frank R Morrison, postmaster here for the past eight years, and actively engaged in the painting business His genial and wholesouled nature has won him innumerable friends in the years of his residence here, and his position in the community is one of the most pleasing order He is a native son of the state of Wisconsin, born in Richland Center, Richland county, that state, on the 28th of July, 1872. and is a son of F M. and Maria (Hoskins) Morrison, the former of whom was born in Darke county, Ohio They have reared a fine family of four children, namely: Mrs Aura Shelley, Frank R of this review, Mrs Anna McKibbin, and Mrs Mabel Armstrong

Frank R Morrison in his boyhood and youth attended the common schools of his native community, after which he was employed as a clerk in a store for some years When he was about twenty-two years old the calm and quiet of his country existence began to pall upon the man, young and vigorous and full of fire and life and he went to the western states, spending something like two years in the strenuous life of the ranchman, after which he returned to Galveston, where he had become established prior to his departure for western adventures, and here he became engaged in the painting business Trying it out as a venture, Mr. Morrison found the enterprise a lucrative one, and he continued to conduct a thriving trade in the work Mr Morrison was appointed postmaster at Galveston, receiving his appointment under President Roosevelt, and he is still in charge of that office, the duties of which he has discharged in the most painstaking and efficient manner, and winning the confidence of all who know him in his official capacity

On May 30, 1900, Mr Morrison married Miss Gertrude Doran and they have one son, Harry Mr Morrison is a member of the Masonic fraternity, the Independent Order of Odd Fellows and the Knights of Pythias, while he and his wife are members of the Methodist church The family is one that is both popular and prominent in local social circles, and their home is a center of hospitality in Galveston

JOHN MARTIN Any history of Cass county would indeed be incomplete that did not make mention of John Martin, who has passed the eighty-fourth milestone on life's journey, and who for many years was identified with the agricultural interests of Deer Creek township Mr. Martin's career has ever been one in which business activity has been blended with unbending honor and unflinching integrity, and success has come to him as the result not only of indefatigable industry but also of honorable and straightforward dealing His career is one worthy of emulation by aspiring youths who would reach positions of independence in a material way and justly command the respect of their fellow men Although now living retired from active pursuits enjoying the fruits of his years of labor, Mr Martin still displays a lively interest in the welfare of his community and contributes in no small manner to the advancement of Deer Creek township

John Martin was born June 13, 1828 in Butler county, Ohio, near Hamilton, and is a son of John and Margaret (Ward) Martin His father, a farmer by vocation brought the family to Carroll county, Indiana, there being ten children, of whom John is the only survivor John Martin secured his education in the common schools of Carroll county, and assisted his father until the latter's death at which time he embarked upon a career of his own He came to Cass county in 1844, settling in Deer Creek township, where he bought a small tract of land, and to this he added from time to time until he was the owner of 150 acres This he continued to operate until his retirement, in 1906, since which time he has lived in his comfortable residence at Galveston. Mr Martin was successful in his general farming and stock raising operations, and his success was gained through no questionable methods On the contrary, he was known as a man who would never take advantage of another's needs but having succeeded himself, was ever ready to lend to others an assisting hand Highly esteemed by all who know him, the uniform regard in which he is held is a tribute to an upright life For years he has been a valued member of the Masonic fraternity, and is connected religiously with the Methodist Episcopal church the movements of which he has always liberally supported

On September 30, 1850, Mr Martin was united in marriage with Miss Mary Campbell daughter of James and Martha (Bryant) Campbell One child has been born to this union· Lamartine, residing on the old homestead, which he manages, he married Mary Smith, and has one son Bruce. The latter married Elizabeth Emrick, and has two children, Emerson and Esther.

H B SEAWARD One of the leading industries of Cass county is that pertaining to the handling of grain, and the town of Galveston, situated in the midst of a great agricultural community, and possessed of admirable transportation facilities, is an important point in the activities being carried on in this line. Here is situated the Galveston Grain Company, an enterprise which has shown a steady and continuous growth during the past several years, the general manager of which H B Seaward, is numbered among the energetic and progressive young business men of his part of the county. Mr Seaward has risen to his present position of prestige through the medium of his own ability and persevering effort, as he started his career at the bottom of the ladder without influential friends or capital, and has gained success by steady application along well-directed lines.

H B Seaward was born March 6, 1882, in Howard county, Indiana, and is a son of C F and Dora A (Hansell) Seaward. His father, an agriculturist by vocation, carried on operations for many years in Howard county, where he attained a fair measure of success. He had five children H B, E B, R P, Madella and Mildred. H B Seaward was educated in the district schools of his native vicinity, and during the summer months in his boyhood assisted his father in the various duties of the homestead, it being his parents' intention that he should follow in the footsteps of his father and take up agricultural work. The young man had different ideas, however, believing that he could better make use of his abilities in other lines than tilling the soil, and when he was nineteen years of age he left the parental roof and secured a position with the Kokomo, Marion & Western Street Car and Electric Light Company. In this capacity, however, he remained only a short time, subsequently turning his attention to the grain business. He has had no reason to regret his choice, for within a few short years he has risen to the management of a flourishing enterprise, which carries on a trade that covers a wide contiguous territory in Cass county and the business of which is steadily increasing under his efficient direction. He is able, alert, shrewd and possessed of much acumen, but his transactions have been carried on in such a manner that his integrity has been unquestioned, and among his associates he has gained wide confidence and respect. He has been too busy with the management of his personal affairs to think of entering the political arena as a seeker after public preferment, but has not been indifferent to the duties of citizenship and has at all times shown an active interest in all matters that pertain to the welfare of his adopted community, and has endeavored to assist in forwarding good government and good citizenship. His fraternal connection is with the local lodge of Masons in which he numbers numerous friends. With his wife, Mr Seaward attends the Methodist Episcopal church.

On March 21, 1901, Mr Seaward was united in marriage with Miss Minnie R Morris, daughter of Thomas and Sarah Morris, and to this union there has been born one child · Esther.

FRANK H THOMAS As proprietor of the largest general merchandise store in Galveston, Mr Thomas has a place of recognized leadership in this section of Cass county, and by his own career has maintained and increased the high prestige belonging to the Thomas family in Cass county since the earliest time He is representative of the third generation of the Thomases in that part of the state

Mr Frank H Thomas was born in the city of Logansport, April 15, 1853 He is a son of Meredith H and Harriet A (Knowlton) Thomas The history of the Thomas family in Indiana begins with Minor Thomas, who was a native of Connecticut, and of Welsh origin In 1819, with his wife, he migrated to Indiana and settled in Fayette county, where he was especially well known as a Baptist minister, though he also owned a farm It was on this pioneer homestead in Fayette county, that his son Hewitt L Thomas, grandfather of the Galveston merchant, was reared. Hewitt L Thomas was born in New York state April 27, 1805 During his youth he managed to get some college training and followed teaching and farming for a number of years In 1836 he came from Fayette county to Clinton township in Cass county, where he made his home until 1853, at which time he moved to Noble township in this county From 1855 to 1865 he was engaged in the lumber business and as a merchant in the state of Minnesota and then returned to Cass county and was a resident of Galveston for many years He was in the insurance business during most of the time and was prominent in local affairs He married in 1826 Charlotte Helm, who was born in Kentucky August 26, 1808, and was of Scotch and English descent Her father had been a soldier under General Harrison during the war of 1812, and had been one of the early settlers of Kentucky who had to contend against the difficulties of nature and against the hostilities of the Indian tribes Hewitt L Thomas, who with his wife, was a devoted member of the Baptist church was one of the organizers of that church at Galveston and served as its sexton for twenty-two years A Republican in politics, he served as justice of the peace and for ten years was associate judge, was a township trustee, and during his residence in Minnesota was state senator He was president of the first agricultural society organized in Cass county, and had numerous places of trust and responsibility thrust upon him during his useful and influential career His death occurred October 23, 1895 His wife survived until July 3, 1898, passing away at the age of ninety years They were the parents of three sons, Meredith H. Minor T, and William H The second son became a distinguished officer of the Civil war, joining the Union army in Minnesota, being chosen second lieutenant, and then advanced to first lieutenant, serving on the frontier during the Indian troubles in the Northwest, and after his troops were transferred to the main scene of conflict, he was promoted to colonel of the Eighth Minnesota In the latter part of the war he commanded an expedition into the far Northwest among the Indians of the upper Missouri, but returned south in time to accompany General Sherman on his march through the Carolinas At the close of the war he was commissioned a brigadier-general The other son William H Thomas, was also a captain in the Union army, and subsequently for many years a prominent physician in Indianapolis

Meredith H Thomas father of the Galveston business man, was born in Fayette county, Indiana, November 20 1826, and was reared in Cass county. He began his career in 1845 in a general store at Logansport, but in 1855 accompanied the family to Minnesota, where he became identified with lumbering and merchandising. In 1865, on his return to Cass county, he located at Galveston, where he had a general merchandise store up to the time of his death. On January 14, 1896, he also established the Galveston Bank, an institution which has an important part in the commercial history of this town. A large grain elevator was erected by him in 1879. His career was of the kind which is not only successful from a private point of view, but adds to the general prosperity of the community. During the Civil war he had offered his services but on account of physical disability they were rejected. In politics he was a Whig then a Republican, and for some years prior to his death was a Prohibitionist. He was also one of the organizers of the Baptist church of Galveston, and from the beginning had served as deacon. His death occurred at his home in Galveston, July 24, 1898. He was married October 16, 1851, to Harriet A. Knowlton. Their five children were as follows: Frank H., Charles F. and Daniel W., twins born February 28, 1856, Claudia B., born May 13, 1866, and Mary B., born September 10, 1869.

Mr. Frank H. Thomas was about two years old when the family moved to Minnesota and he was brought up on the Northwest frontier, where he attained his early education in the public schools. After the return of the family to Cass county he continued his education in the Logansport high school, and in 1874 was taken into partnership by his father. The other sons were subsequently admitted to the firm and the firm of M. H. Thomas & Son continued until July, 1882, at which time the partnership was dissolved and Frank H. and Charles F. remained as proprietors of the general store. In 1898 Mr. Frank H. Thomas bought out his brother's interest, and has since been sole proprietor. He has three floors devoted to a general merchandise stock, which comprises every commodity used by the people of this vicinity. He has employed first-class methods of merchandising, and has always been known, as have other members of this family, for a sterling integrity and reliability which has enabled them to command a large business year after year. After his father's death, Mr. Thomas served as president of the Galveston Bank, up to the time it was sold to the First State Bank, an institution of which Dr. Z. U. Loop is president, and H. Z. Carey, cashier.

Mr. Thomas was married September 8, 1875, to Miss Virginia Forrest who was born in Logansport, December 11, 1855, a daughter of John M. and Rebecca (Longstreth) Forrest. Her father came to Cass county in 1849 by way of canal and was for many years head miller in the old Wilson mill at Logansport. Mr. Thomas and wife are the parents of one child Elsie M. who was born September 3, 1878, and who is the wife of H. H. Miller, M. D. Dr. Miller and wife have one son, Forrest Thomas Miller. Mr. Thomas is one of the charter members of the Knights of Pythias lodge in Galveston and he and his wife are active members of the Baptist church. He has served as township trustee, has been president of school board of Galveston since the incorporation of the town and is one of the most public-spirited and influential citizens of this county

HENDERSON FICKLE One of the oldest families in southeastern Cass county is represented by Mr Henderson Fickle, who is himself a native son of the county and has for many years been well known as a substantial farmer and as a public-spirited citizen, who has given his service in the office of county commissioner and has assisted in every movement for the general improvement and upbuilding of this community

Mr Fickle is now retired from the active life of agriculture, but owns a farm of eighty acres in Jackson township He was born in Jackson township, Cass county June 3, 1849, and was a son of David T and Rebecca (Engler) Fickle David Fickle came from Marion county, Ohio, when a young man, and in company with his father Daniel Fickle Daniel Fickle, the grandfather, was the founder of the Fickle settlement in Jackson township of Cass county David Fickle was the father of nine children, whose names are as follows Amanda, Mannington, Jane, Emeline, Wilson, Henderson, David, Arminta, and Nora

Mr Henderson Fickle was a scholar in the first public school at Galveston and he finished his education in the new academy of that town During his early youth he worked on the farm and farming has been his occupation throughout his career At the age of twenty-seven he began his independent career as a renter and finally accumulated enough, as a result of his industry and good management, to buy a small tract of land in this township From that time he has progressed in prosperity and has always enjoyed a secure position in this community The confidence of his fellow citizens was well shown when they elected him to the office of County Commissioner, and he has held several other minor positions indicative of their trust in his ability

In 1876 Mr Fickle married Mary A Kelly The six children born to their marriage are as follows Jesse, now deceased, Fannie, who married Charles Haynes, now deceased, and has one child Margaret, Charles, who resides on his father's farm Elizabeth, who married David Davis and has one child Helen, Lola, the wife of Walter King, and the mother of two children Harry and Bernard and Marie, who is single Mr Fickle and family are members of the Catholic church, and he is affiliated with the Knights of Columbus

HARRY GRAY Another of the young men of Galveston, Indiana, who have made good in the farming industry in this section is Harry Gray, whose fine place of something like two hundred acres is known as the Joseph Gray home farm It is situated in the northeast quarter of section twenty-five, in range two east, and is known for one of the finest places of the township Mr Gray was born on May 2, 1878, on his present farm, and is the son of Joseph and Mary A (Neely) Gray, the father a native of Butler county, Ohio, and the mother a native of Juniata county, Pennsylvania

Joseph Gray was born in Butler county, Ohio, on December 20, 1830, and came with his parents to Carroll county, Indiana, in 1831 His parents were James and Ruth (Merritt) Gray and James Gray's

father, James, was the first of the name to leave Ireland and come to America

Harry Gray attended the common schools of his native community, later entering Indiana university, and he was graduated from that institution in 1902, in the literary department Thereafter he taught school and for one year was principal at Lucerne, Indiana

He was married on December 30, 1903, to Miss Cora Herd, the daughter of William and Martha (Callahan) Herd William Herd was an Englishman, and was occupied in farming in Harrison township. Mrs Gray was educated in Logansport, Indiana, high school and Marion (Ind) Normal, finishing in Indiana University After the death of his father, Mr Gray made his home on the old home farm for a time, but has since given up the place, renting it, since the death of his wife, which occurred August 12, 1912, she being struck by lightning Mr and Mrs Gray have two children Jeanette and Virginia

Mr Gray is recognized as one of the most valuable citizens of Galveston, and a man who has considerable pride in his community, being public spirited in a high degree, and always willing to aid in any cause promoted in the public welfare

W E LYBROOK, M D Few citizens of Young America, Indiana can lay claim to greater prestige either in length of residence, or position attained in professional, business or social lines, than Dr W E Lybrook, who for thirty-five years has been numbered among the leading medical practitioners of Cass county His high attainments and acknowledged ability have brought him before the public in various positions of responsibility and trust, in all of which he has given evidence of a profound respect for the duties of citizenship, while his personal character is such that he has gained a wide popularity Dr Lybrook is a native of the Hoosier state, born in Union county, February 16, 1850, a son of Daniel and Magdalene Lybrook, natives of Ohio, of German lineage In 1854 they removed to Cass county, locating on a farm, where Dr. Lybrook spent his boyhood days, frequently assisting in the cultivation of the fields and in other labor connected with the planting and harvesting of crops His early education, acquired in the common schools, was supplemented by a course in the National Normal School, at Lebanon, Ohio, which he attended two years, succeeding which he began teaching school in Cass and adjoining counties in Indiana After following that profession with a large measure of success for some time, Dr Lybrook entered upon the study of his chosen profession, that of medicine, which from early manhood he had decided upon as his life work Accordingly, in 1874, he entered the office of Dr. J W Powell, of Rockfield, who became his preceptor, and under whose direction he studied for two years On the expiration of that period he matriculated in the Kentucky School of Medicine, at Louisville, where he was graduated in 1879 with the salutatory honors of the class and his oration was such a masterly effort that the class rendered him a vote of thanks therefor

On his return to Young America, Dr Lybrook began the practice of his profession in the vicinity of his old home, and his success in a number of complicated cases soon won the young physician recognition and professional business, and as the years have passed his practice has enjoyed a steady increase until he is now rated among the leading physicians of his part of the county. He subscribes to the leading medical journals of the day, keeping fully abreast of the various advancements and discoveries of his profession, and also takes a keen and intelligent interest in the work of the various medical organizations. A Democrat in his political views he has taken a prominent part in public life. In August, 1883, he was appointed township trustee by the county commissioners to fill a vacancy caused by the resignation of Thomas Henry, and at the close of that term was elected to the office, the duties of which he discharged with signal ability and promptness. He took particular interest in the improvement of the public highways in his township, and was instrumental in extending the length of the school term from four and one-half to eight months. He was elected to the trustee's office again in 1886, and served for four years. Dr. Lybrook has been interested in fraternal work to some extent, and is a member of Young America Lodge No. 534, A. F. & A. M., and Logansport Chapter, R. A. M.

On March 19, 1878, Dr. Lybrook was united in marriage with Addie F. Hewitt, who was born in Carroll county, Indiana, September 15, 1861, daughter of Elias and Elizabeth A. Hewitt, and to this union there were born seven children: Ross E., Mary E., Bessie M., Rolland V., Daniel E., Bud and John C.

It is not every son of an industrious father who may gain success in the same field of endeavor which the elder man graces, but it would appear that such has been the case with Dr. Daniel E. Lybrook, son of Dr. W. E. Lybrook. Born December 25, 1884, in Young America, Indiana, he here received his early instruction in the common schools, subsequently attending the high school, where he was graduated. In 1908, he received the degree of Bachelor of Arts from the Indiana University, following which he entered upon a medical course in the Indiana School of Medicine, at Indianapolis, where he received his degree in 1910. Since that time he has been engaged in a successful practice at Young America with his father and is making rapid strides in his chosen profession.

Dr. Lybrook was married September 27, 1910, to Miss Matilda Brown, of Marion, Indiana, daughter of William and Matilda (Peterson) Brown, and to this union there has been born one child, Elizabeth. Like his father, Dr. Lybrook is a member of the Masonic fraternity, where he has numerous friends. He is respected by his professional brethren, is popular in social circles and highly regarded as a public-spirited citizen who takes a great interest in the welfare of his community and its people.

ROBERT H. ROSS, M. D., of Galveston, Indiana, was born in Rockingham county, Virginia, and is the son of David and Eliza (Whitsell) Ross, the former of whom was born in Virginia and was of Scotch-Irish ancestry. He was a United Brethren minister and moved to Indiana in 1861, continuing in the ministry up to the time of his death. He was a presiding elder in the church and was a trustee of Westfield College in Illinois, his declining years being passed in Westfield, where he died on July 3, 1879 His faithful wife died in Edgar county, Illinois, some time previous These worthy people were the parents of eleven children, of whom the following brief mention is made Rev Samuel H, a minister of the United Brethren church, now deceased, Dr John H, a prominent physician of Kokomo, Indiana, William H, who also became a physician and is now deceased, Elizabeth, the wife of William Devore, David H, graduate of Westfield College, one time teacher and now in the commercial business at Terre Haute, Indiana, George H, Sally, who married John Woods of Westfield, now deceased, Dr Robert H, of this review, and Peter After the death of the mother of these children, Mr Ross married again, and two daughters were born to him, Ella and Ida both married

Robert H Ross passed his boyhood days upon the home farm and in attendance at the schools of his native community When he was seventeen years old he attended Westfield College in Illinois whither the family had removed in recent years He then commenced the study of medicine, in which his brother John had already engaged in the practice of, and under the tutelage of Dr John Ross the subject received excellent training in his chosen work In 1877 he matriculated in the Indiana Medical College at Indianapolis, which in the following year became the medical department of Butler University, and two years after, in 1879, he was graduated and settled at Bennett's Switch, where he engaged in practice He was located at that point for six years, during which time he played an important part in the varied life of the community He was identified with the only drug business in the community and filled the office of notary public at the same time, so that his services were in demand from many angles of life's activities In 1887 he went to Clinton county, remaining two years and then locating in Cassville, where he continued until 1908, with the exception of a three-year period when he was engaged at Kokomo as surgeon with the Plate Glass Company at that place Since 1908 Galveston has been the headquarters of Dr Ross, and he is accorded the highest regard in his professional capacity and as a citizen in this community

Dr. Ross is a member of the County, State and American Medical societies, and maintains a number of memberships in fraternal societies as well In addition to his professional interests, Dr Ross is the owner of a fine farm in the county, which has claimed a goodly share of his attention in recent years, and marked him as a man of some versatility.

In 1879 Dr Ross married Miss Josie I Shafer, the daughter of an old and honored family of Indiana Her father, who was John A. Shafer, a native of Indiana, was for many years a prominent merchant of Cassville, filling the office of postmaster for years, as well as other positions of public trust Mrs Ross was one of the five children of her parents

Three children were born to Dr and Mrs Ross, one of whom died in infancy The others are Dottie and Lulu

In 1908 Dr Ross was married a second time, when Mary Campbell, the daughter of John and Rebecca (Spencer) Campbell became his wife No children were born of this latter union Dr and Mrs. Ross are members of the United Brethren church

EDWIN A. RUTENBER has achieved distinction in the designing and manufacturing of the first four-cylinder gasoline engine produced in America, and the "Rutenber" motor has a world-wide reputation. Born at Sadorus, Illinois, on August 10, 1876, Mr. Rutenber is remotely descended from German ancestry. He is the youngest of five children born to Darwin and Zelia A. Rutenber, all of whom are living. The father was a carriage maker by trade.

In boyhood Edwin A. Rutenber of this review attended the public schools and college.

He learned carpentering from his grandfather and carriage making from his father, and it is beyond question that he inherited a taste for mechanics from both. He made a study of mechanics, learning the machinist trade thoroughly, and in 1892 or thereabouts, invented a single cylinder motor. This but fathered an ambition within him to devise a four cylinder motor of commercial value, and for a number of years he worked with that object in view. In 1898 he produced his first four cylinder gasoline motor, also the first to be manufactured in the United States and the fame of the design spread to foreign parts as well as throughout his native land.

In June, 1902, the Rutenber Manufacturing Company was moved from Chicago to Logansport, and from that time Mr. Rutenber has been a resident of the latter city. The name of his company was later changed to the Western Motor Company, but since July, 1912, it has been the Rutenber Motor Company. At the last mentioned date, Mr. Rutenber disposed of his holdings in the corporation, since which time he has devoted his energies to the manufacture of electric appliances in connection with his other activities.

Since becoming a resident of Logansport, Mr. Rutenber has become identified with its commercial success, and has taken a leading part in the industrial activities of the city.

On October 3, 1900, Mr. Rutenber was married to Miss Edna L. Rolley, of Morris, Illinois, and they are the parents of three children Garnet M., Ellwood R. and Bradley A. Rutenber. Mr. and Mrs. Rutenber are members of the Broadway Methodist Episcopal church.

FRANK DAY. It is sometimes interesting to note the aptitude with which men untrained in a specific line of enterprise will turn their attentions thereto and evolve a brilliant success from conditions that the more experienced man would regard as offering only defeat to the novice. Frank Day, a telling example of this fact, operates one of the finest farms on the Marion and Delph pike, which is owned by his mother, and in its management has proven himself to be a farmer of no mean ability. He was not reared to farm life, but turned his attention to that work after the death of his father, and his success has been of a particularly high order such as to place him in the front rank with the able agricultural men of the district.

Born on September 10, 1884, in Logansport, Indiana, Mr. Day is the son of Nicholas and Catherine (Keel) Day. The father came from Germany, his native land, when a young man, and his parents never left that country, but ended their days in the region where they were born and bred. Settling in Logansport, Mr. Day engaged in the saloon and barber shop business and in the latter enterprise he was sufficiently prosperous to make possible his investment in farming property in Jackson township, the property which his son now operates so successfully While the senior Day began in Logansport a poor man, dependent upon his daily earnings, he had reached a comfortable state of independence before he passed to his reward, and with a goodly accumulation of this world's goods, was known for one of the successful men of the city He died in July, 1909, and is buried in Logansport

The schools of Logansport contributed to Frank Day such education as he received, and when his father died, soon after engaging in farming activities, Mr. Day took up the management of the farm which had become the family home, and has since continued in that work, with a degree of success that has already been intimated in an opening paragraph Mr Day has gone into the work in a whole-souled and energetic manner, and has been quick to see and appropriate new ideas in the matter of up-to-date and scientific farming

In 1906 Mr Day was united in marriage with Miss Frances Emery, the daughter of George and Mary (Davidson) Emery Three children have been born to them, as follows Walter, Josephine and Mary Catherine Mr and Mrs Day are members of St Joseph's Catholic church in Logansport, and Mr Day is a stanch supporter of the principles of the Democratic party The family is one that has the most excellent standing in social and other circles of the community and their roster of friends is coincident with that of their acquaintances

DR J FRANK CORNELL The duties of a physician in the small town and its outlying districts are seldom anything short of the most arduous, and entail upon the part of the practitioner a generous fund of sympathy, courage and energy, as well as their indispensable fellow, skill

Dr Cornell is a native son of Cass county, born in Deer Creek township on February 9, 1870, and is a son of Benjamin D and Sarah (Bunnell) Cornell Benjamin Cornell was born in Butler county, Ohio, and he came to Cass county in 1847 He was one of the old time school teachers, and it is possible that Dr Cornell drew something of his aptitude for his present educational work from the fact of his father having been interested in the same work years gone by The senior Cornell was one of the old time school masters, and like others of his day and age, he interspersed his teaching seasons with other seasons devoted to the tilling of the soil, in both of which branches of activity he enjoyed a success commensurate with the most prosperous of his day He died in 1907 and the wife and mother passed away in 1901

J Frank Cornell attended the district schools of District No 1 so called, and then attended the Normal school at Logansport for a time, after which he spent a term and a half at Valparaiso, Indiana He later attended and graduated in scientific course in the Marion Normal at Marion Indiana and was graduated from the medical department of the University of Illinois at Chicago in 1902 Dr Cornell established himself for practice in Galveston where he has been actively engaged since 1902, and where he has experienced a pleasing degree of success in his chosen field of activity His work in the educational field has been all that could be desired, and has borne fruit in the school system of the county that amply justified the choice of the people, as he was twice elected county superintendent of schools and serving as a member of school board of Galveston of which he is acting secretary

Dr Cornell was united in marriage in 1900 to Miss Lena Williams, the daughter of George and Hannah J Williams They have three children Sarah E, George B and Wendell The two first named are attending school in Galveston

Beyond his membership in the Knights of Pythias, Dr Cornell has no fraternal affiliations He has never outgrown his fondness for farm life and now, in the days of his professional activity, he still finds time to look after a fine farm of one hundred acres of which he is the owner in Deer Creek township, and which thrives most abundantly under his direction The Doctor and his wife are prominent socially, and number as their stanch friends all with whom they have acquaintance in and about the township

WILLIAM R DARLAND, a native son of Cass county, Indiana wherein he has always lived and carried on his various business affairs, was born on the 15th day of June 1863, and is the son of Samuel and Elizabeth (Clark) Darland Of these worthy parents for many years prominent among the best citizenship of Cass county it is eminently fitting that more than mere cursory mention be made, but a dearth of information regarding them and their lives makes expansion impossible at this juncture It may be said, however, that Samuel Darland was born in Ohio, in the year 1825 In his young manhood he moved to Indiana from his home state and settled in Clinton county, his removal to Cass county taking place in 1854 Here he had purchased land from the government as early as 1849 anticipating his later residence in the county and in 1854 the family moved to this new and untried district, cleared a bit of space in the heart of the woods and built a log cabin home The land he settled on then came to be with the passing years, and because of his untiring labors upon it, a valuable and fruitful spot, which maintained him and his family comfortably all his life He had the true pioneer instinct, and was a leader in every project calculated to redound to the good of his community Ever a public-spirited and aggressive character, he helped to lay out the township roads, organize the school districts and to build proper schoolhouses in his township, so that his whole life was fraught with good and permanent works in the best interests of his adopted county He died in the year 1880, December 22d having given a quarter of a century of his life to Cass county in his capacity of citizen in which capacity the highest qualities of his nature were brought to bear upon the growth and development of his community and the county He was the father of five children: Martha A David, John A William R of this review, and Albert

William R Darland attended the district schools of his community as a boy and spent his summers in the work of the farm, in which he gained much proficiency under the able instruction of his energetic father He remained at home until he reached the age of twenty-one, when he married and established a home of his own He gave his time and attention at first to farming and enjoyed a pleasing success but he did not continue to confine himself to that industry. In later years he took up the tile industry, and today he is the sole proprietor of the Darland Tile Factory, the only plant of its kind in the county. The plant is complete in all its details and has a capacity sufficient to meet the demands of the farming interests of the community. Mr Darland owns and continues to operate his very attractive and fertile little farm of sixty acres, where his home is maintained, and which is located a mile from the home of his boyhood.

Mr Darland has been twice married. His first wife was Clare Winegarden, who died, leaving two children, Frank and Elizabeth. The former married an Ohio girl and lives at Struthers, Ohio. They became the parents of three children, Frances, Leo and Clara. Elizabeth became the wife of George Shedron and they have three children also, Robert, Bond and Milford. The second wife of Mr Darland was Jennie Kantner, and five children have been born to them, Willard A, Edward B., Albert A, Alta L, and Orene, deceased.

The family attend the Methodist Episcopal church, and are among the most highly esteemed people of Lincoln, where they have made their home for so many years.

WILLIAM R. HYATT. To have been prominently identified with the carrying on of the development of any given section of the country is an honor to which any might aspire with credit, and to have a hand in the bringing about of a high standard of prosperity in one's own community is an achievement indeed, and one that marks a man among his fellows, wherever found. William R Hyatt has been an indefatigable worker in Jackson township, where he has carried on farming operations for a number of years, and a fair and honest share of the credit for the growth and development of the town is his meed.

William R Hyatt was born in Decatur county, Indiana, on November 2, 1872 and he is the son of William Henry and Mary J (Jackson) Hyatt. The father came from Ripley county, Indiana and located in Irvin township, Howard county, just across the line, there establishing a home. He married in early life and a goodly family of nine children were reared under the care of himself and his wife. Eight of that number are yet living, and the names of the children are as follows Flora, who married a Mr. Caldwell, Ora, deceased, Robert, a resident of Jackson, Newton, living in Galveston, William R of this review, Mrs. Maud Hauser, Lola Leona, the wife of a Mr. Nutter; Gertrude who married Walter Stout, a farmer near Connersville, Indiana, and Mrs Pearl Harrison.

William R Hyatt was reared on the home farm and his training was much on the order of the youth of his community, consisting of the usual district school advantages, and an excellent home training. His schooling came to him in the seasons when farm work was not flourishing, and did not permit of any great regularity. He was twenty-two years old when he left home and established an independent domicile following his marriage on August 5 1904, to Miss Mary McWilliams the daughter of James and Martha (Logan) McWilliams One child has been born to them, Clarence Clermont Hyatt.

Mr Hyatt has acquired a fine farm of his own of one hundred and sixty acres near the town of Lincoln, and is accounted one of the financially independent men of the community wherein he resides. He has carried on his own farming operations with the same vigor and vim that characterized his long connection with his father's home place, and his farm shows all the evidences of thrift and capitalized energy.

Socially, Mr. Hyatt and his family are prominent and popular, and they are members of the United Brethren church of Galveston, Indiana. Mr. Hyatt is fraternally identified by his relations with the Masonic order, Lodge No. 244 of Galveston, and of Amity Lodge No. 362, Knights of Pythias of Galveston.

GEORGE W. BURKET. Some fifty years or more ago, thousands of men and boys marched away from comfortable homes and loved ones to offer up their lives on the altar of patriotism. Some dyed that altar with their life blood and never returned; others came back, but have borne through the succeeding years the indelible imprint made by a soldier's hardships. Those who did return found hard conditions awaiting them. After years of strenuous endeavor, when each minute might be their last, when a nation's life hung upon their bravery and endurance, it was extremely difficult for them to resume the ordinary occupations of life, to take up the prosaic duties of peace, and again to settle down in the rut of every-day existence. Yet thousands did this very thing, and developed into magnificent men, sound of principle, possessed of high moral courage as well as physical, and with the valuable discipline that army training gives have rounded out useful lives and have fought the battles of peace in the same courageous manner that marked their struggles during the dark days of the War of the Rebellion. Cass county sent its full quota of volunteers to the front in 1861, and among these was George W. Burket, who served for more than four years in the Union ranks and who has spent many years in farming on the Walton road where he is the owner of 120 acres of land. Mr. Burket is a native of Cass county, having been born on a farm in Jefferson township, November 28, 1841, a son of James and Barbara (Small) Burket. His grandfather, Solomon Burket, was one of the pioneer settlers of Cass county, where he was engaged in agricultural pursuits for a long period, as was also James Burket, who had come to Jefferson township as a lad.

George W. Burket was educated in the district schools, and divided his boyhood days between securing his education and assisting his father in the duties of the home farm. At the outbreak of the Civil war, with other patriotic and adventurous youths of his neighborhood, he enlisted in the Fifteenth Regiment, Indiana Volunteer Infantry, Company G, under Col. D. D. Wagner. With this organization he served three years and twenty-five days, then re-enlisting in the Sixteenth Regiment, Indiana Mounted Volunteer Infantry, but after seven months was transferred to the Thirteenth Indiana Volunteer Cavalry with which he completed his military career, being honorably discharged after a service covering four years and twenty-eight days. He was a brave and gallant soldier, earning the admiration of his comrades and the respect of his officers, and participated in numerous hard-fought engagements. On his return to civil life, he engaged in agricultural pursuits and one year later moved to Deer Creek township, where he has since accumulated a

MR. & MRS. GEORGE W. BURKET

farm of 120 acres, located on the Walton road. Here he is still engaged in general farming and stock raising, having met with a full measure of success in all his operations. His land is well improved and furnished with good buildings, and he is known as a good practical farmer and an excellent judge of cattle and horses. Essentially a farmer, he has not cared for public life, but has not been indifferent to the duties of citizenship, and every call made upon him in behalf of public-spirited movements has met with a prompt and hearty response. He is a valued comrade of Dan Piatt Post, Grand Army of the Republic, in which he has many friends.

Mr. Burket was married first to Elizabeth Boucher who died without issue. His second marriage was to Margaret M. Bowlan. They have no children.

CHARLES DAGGETT. Forty years have elapsed since Charles Daggett came with his parents from their old home in Ohio, where the Daggetts had long been established, and settled in Cass county with them, and his home has been here located ever since. They were worthy and ambitious people, and the labor they expended in the cultivation of a farm in their community brought forth abundant fruit and prospered them beyond the lot of the average farming family. To their son they unconsciously bequeathed the same spirit of progress and the will to accomplish that was theirs, and he has experienced in his own life a degree of success most pleasing to behold.

Charles Daggett was born on September 27, 1857, and is the son of Freeman and Carolina (Fickel) Daggett who migrated to Indiana from Ohio in 1872. Charles Daggett was then fifteen years of age and he was the third child in a family of seven born to his parents, the others being Daniel Ladoska, Clinton, Anna Hattie and George, the two last named being now deceased.

As a youth in his new home Charles Daggett attended the Rodebaugh school, in which he finished what must be called his education. Up to the time when he reached the age of twenty-one years, he gave the greater part of his time to the performance of the regular duties of the farm. He then rented the old home place and continued to operate it on his own initiative and responsibility, giving something like three years to the work, after which he came to his present place, known throughout these parts as the old Samuel Parks farm. Here he has carried on a thriving business in farming and stock raising, and is, ranked among the leading operators of the district. His success has been one well worthy of the name, and entirely justified by his activities and energies as applied to the care and conduct of his place. It is a well improved and well kept place, reflecting on every side the character and calibre of the owner and operator, and Mr. Daggett may be justly proud of his success in his chosen field of activity.

Mr. Daggett has been twice married. His first wife was Callie Fickel and in 1884 he married Lillie Chadwell, the daughter of William and Fannie (Layhue) Chadwell. The ceremony took place on the 29th day of December in that year, and to them have been born four children. Gertrude, first born, is the wife of Irvin Kern; Freeman, the second born of the five is deceased; Laura married Clyde Babb and they have two children Hilda and Robert, Clarence, the youngest of the family, was born on the farm on February 5 1892

Mr Daggett is a Democrat in his politics, and though an admirable citizen, is not especially active in the work of his party He has always upheld his share in the burden of civic responsibility in the community, and realizes full well the duties of citizenship

LAWRENCE L McDONALD As manager of the Indiana Lumber Company at Galveston, Indiana Lawrence L McDonald occupies a position of prominence in his community, of which he has been a resident for twenty-four years He began with the Indiana Lumber Company in his early manhood and has worked his way from a humble position with the company to his present advanced place Mr McDonald was born on the 6th day of April, 1876, in Darke county, Ohio, near Greenville, and is the son of Aaron and Sevilla (Geeting) McDonald

Aaron McDonald was born in Darke county in the vicinity of Greenville and there he was reared and passed his life until he came to Indiana in 1879, bringing his family with him He took up his residence in Howard county on a farm and he and his wife still make their home on that place, which is one of the finest in the county Ten children were born to Mr and Mrs McDonald, named as follows Joseph Lawrence the subject of this review, Charles, now deceased, Essie, Lahman, Anna, Ira, Edith, Earl, and Mark

The common schools of Clay township afforded such education as Lawrence L McDonald received his attendance being at the Macedonia school and during his vacations he worked on the farm at home He continued with his parents until he was twenty-one years old, and then started out for himself, determined upon an independent career He at first worked on a farm by the month, receiving a monthly wage of eighteen dollars, and for a time he was engaged in carpenter work, which he thought of learning He gave up the work, however, to take a position with the Indiana Lumber Company He began in a humble way but he advanced rapidly, and soon had worked himself up to the position of manager, which he still retains He is a stockholder in the company as well as its manager

On June 18, 1907, Mr McDonald married Miss Minnie Persinger, and they have one child, Frank McDonald

Mr McDonald is a member of the Masonic fraternity and the Knights of Pythias and he and his wife are members of the United Brethren church

EVERETT R GORE A genuine talent for the agricultural industry is one that may not be despised in summing up the various qualities that go to make for valuable and useful citizenship, and especially is this true in Cass county where the fairest wealth of the district lies in her bountiful farming lands Those men who have applied themselves to the work of developing the splendid natural resources of the county and converting it into the wonderfully productive region it is today have done as much for their country as have those in higher places and wielding a wider influence They have done what they could, and of none is more required Everett R Gore is one who has amply earned the distinction of coming into this class of men by his achievement in the farming line, and he is today the owner of one of the fine show places of his community, though it may be said that when he married and began life independently he established himself on a rented farm He has been devoted to the work of the farm all his life, and is a practical, far-sighted and successful farmer

Everett R Gore was born in Shelby county January 15, 1860, and he is the son of James Wesley and Martha (Bradley) Gore The father came from Virginia, his native state, to Wayne county, Indiana and later removed to Cass county, where he passed the remainder of his life He devoted his years to farming and was fairly successful in the work, and was one who was prominent in his community all his days To him and his wife three children were born, namely Mary J, who married a Mr Grusmeyer, Willard, living in Lincoln, and Everett R, whose name heads this necessarily brief review

Everett R Gore came up through boyhood years as an attendant upon the schools of Shelby and during his vacation seasons worked on the home farm He later applied himself to the trade of a carpenter for some time, but the work was not entirely congenial to him, and when he married in 1891 he reverted to farming and farm life once more, for which he had a natural talent and a genuine liking, the qualities undeniably, that have made him successful in his enterprise Being without capital, Mr Gore rented a place from his father-in-law which he operated until he had prospered sufficiently to purchase one of his own Mr Gore married Jennie Countryman, the daughter of Isaiah and Sarah (Crull) Countryman, and three children have been born to them Ina, the eldest, being a student in the local high school, and Elma and Pansy attending grade school

The family are members of the Baptist church, and assume their just share of the duties and responsibilities attendant upon the work of that body They are popular in their home community and number their friends in generous measure Mr Gore is a man who lives quietly, taking no undue interest in affairs of a political nature, but giving his support to the Democratic party Though he has considerable influence among his fellows, he is not one who has ever been an office seeker

DICK ALFORD ZEHRING is the son of an old and honored Indiana family, and a most interesting history attaches to the name In this connection it is impossible to more than briefly cite a few facts relating to the ancestry of the subject, lack of space making a detailed statement impossible Mr Zehring was born on the 12th day of November, 1873, and is the son of William I and Lydia (McIlwain) Zehring Beginning with the first of the name of whom a record has been established Christian Zehring, the great-great-grandfather of the subject, was born in Lebanon county Pennsylvania, of Dutch origin as the name and the location would indicate He was the son of a pioneer farmer and blacksmith of that county He married Mary Rauch, who was like himself a native of Lebanon county, and there he continued to live, following the calling of a blacksmith, in which trade he had been trained by his worthy parent Christian and Mary Zehring reared a goodly family of twelve children named as follows Henry, John, Catherine

Christian, Philip, William, Bernard, David, Peter, Susan, Mary and Martha. Three others died in infancy. He moved to Ohio in the year 1818, and settled in Warren county where he became the owner of a fine farm and there passed his remaining days, living to reach the age of seventy. He was a man of splendid character, and was a power for good in his community to the day of his death. Of his family, William, born in Lebanon county, Pennsylvania, engaged in agriculture in Dauphin county, that state, and was thus occupied for some little time. He married Elizabeth Garst and soon after that event, in 1818, moved to Ohio and settled on fifty acres of land in Butler county, near the town of Middletown. He passed his remaining days in Ohio and was one of the well known men of his time. His children were John William, Christian, Lydia and Barbara. He died in September, 1872 and his widow survived him until 1885.

William Zehring, his second born son, the father of William I. Zehring and the grandfather of Dick Alford Zehring of this review, was born in Butler county, Ohio, on May 3 1821. He received a common school education and was early instructed in the art of farming, a business which occupied his attention to the time of his death. He married Susan Feagler, a daughter of John and Susanna (Cullers) Feagler, and she was one of their seven children. After his marriage Mr Zehring settled on his father's farm in Montgomery county, and in later years moved to Preble county, Ohio, where he continued until 1857 when he made his way to Indiana, locating in Deer Creek township, Miami county, and this state has since then been the home of him and his family. He purchased a quarter section of land, fifty acres of which were under cultivation the remainder being covered with a thick timber growth. He improved this place and added to it until he finally owned two hundred and eighty acres in the township, besides an additional hundred acres in Cass county. Mr Zehring was a man who always occupied a high place in public esteem, wherever he found himself. He was a Democrat and stood high in the party. Eight times he was elected township trustee, and he was county commissioner for six years. In 1856-7 he was a member of the state legislature, for two terms he was road commissioner of his township and was on one occasion assessor of his town. He was chosen as administrator for various estates, fifteen in all, and was appointed guardian for the children of two different families. Mr Zehring was twice married. His first wife died in February, 1865, leaving six children Josiah, William I. the father of the subject Benjamin F. John Edgar A and Elizabeth. She was a devoted member of the Lutheran church from her earliest girlhood and a woman of the most exemplary character. On March 16, 1869, Mr Zehring married Mrs Lucinda (Burtner) Wilson, a widow, and their remaining years were passed in delightful companionship.

William I. Zehring was reared in Miami county, in Deer Creek township, and there attended school in his boyhood days. He was trained to farm life and in his young manhood became the owner of a fine farm in his native town. He early married, Lydia McIlwain becoming his bride, and they passed their lives in the quiet of their country home, where they reared their family and gave them such education as their means and the schools of the county afforded.

Dick Alford Zehring, the second child of his parents and a representative of the fifth generation of Zehrings since the time of Christian of that name, of Pennsylvania birth, was reared on the farm in Deer Creek township. He attended the schools of Galveston, and when his education was finished he gave his attention to teaching, and was occupied in that worthy work in both Cass and Howard counties for a number of years. Ten years ago Mr. Zehring decided to take up farm life, in which his family had been successful and prosperous for a number of generations, and for which he was fitted by ability and inclination, and he now has a fine farm of one hundred acres about eight miles north of Kokomo, Indiana.

Mr. Zehring was married on August 2, 1902, to Mabel Gray Campbell, the daughter of George Wilson and Agnes (Tyner) Campbell. Two children have been born to Mr. and Mrs. Zehring: Margaret Janice, born December 7, 1909; Ruby Marcella, born February 25, 1913. Mr. Zehring is a member of the Knights of Pythias, and has been through all chairs in the order. The family are members of the Methodist church, and are active in the benevolent and other work of that body.

BENJAMIN B. RICHARDS. For more than thirty years a member of the bar, Mr. Richards has had a busy and influential career in Howard and Cass counties, and for the last twenty-five years has been located in practice at Galveston. Mr. Richards stands high in local citizenship, and is one of the men whose influence is counted as important in the promotion of any local public enterprise.

Benjamin B. Richards was born in Ripley county, Indiana, September 13, 1847, a son of Benjamin and Eliza (Marquis) Richards. Benjamin Richards' father had a somewhat remarkable career. He was born January 1, 1798, in Bourbon county, Kentucky, and when fourteen years of age enlisted with the Kentucky Volunteers in the regiment under Captain Crogan for service in the War of 1812. His company marched the entire distance from the Ohio river to Detroit, where he and his comrades with other parts of the army fought for the American cause until the war closed. After the war he returned to Kentucky and at the age of twenty-five moved to Madison, Indiana, on the Ohio river. During his residence there he was a brick manufacturer, and he had the distinction of building the first railway station in Indiana at Madison, for the old railroad which began at Madison and which was the first piece of railway construction in this state. He and his wife were the parents of seven children, named as follows: Angeline, deceased; David, Anna, Olive, deceased; Samuel, deceased; Benjamin B. and Morris, deceased.

Benjamin B. Richards at the age of five years accompanied his parents to Decatur county, where he was reared to manhood on a farm. In 1865 he entered Hartsville University in Bartholomew county, where he took a three years collegiate course. In the autumn of 1867 he began teaching school in Howard county, and was connected with school work there for five years. Then for two years he was engaged in the harness business at New London, and for eight years manufactured harness at Russiaville. In 1881 he was admitted to the bar after having carried on his studies in leisure intervals for several years, and after beginning practice for several years he also edited the *Russiaville Observer*. In 1887 he removed to Kokomo, and then in the fall of 1888 came to Galveston where he has since had his office for general law practice, and has also done considerable business in the settlement of estates. Mr. Richards is a Republican in politics and has served as a justice of the peace. Fraternally he is affiliated with the Knights of Pythias and the Independent Order of Odd Fellows, and his church is the Methodist. He was married on May 10, 1870, to Miss Rebecca Gossett, who belonged to a Howard county family. They are the parents of two children, Ollie and John O. Ollie is the wife of W. A. King, and has two children Walter, and Lena, the latter being the wife of Chester Purdy, and the mother of one child Benjamin R. Purdy. Walter King married Lulu, daughter of Henderson Fiekes and is assistant trainmaster in the Pennsylvania office at Richmond, Indiana. John O. married Emma Goldsberry and they have one child Rebecca.

JAMES MOORE BUCHANAN. When James Moore Buchanan first located in Bethlehem township there were not more than ten acres of cleared land on the farm. He came to Cass county with his family from Blair county, Pennsylvania, to Terre Haute, Indiana, in 1838 and after spending one season there with his family moved on to Cass county where the Buchanan family has ever since been represented. They arrived in Cass county on April 5, 1839 stopping on their first night in the county at a tavern located on the present site of Heppe's soap factory, then moving to Bethlehem township. The house the family occupied here was a mere cabin, built of round logs covered with a four-foot clapboard roof held down by two poles laid longitudinally across it. A cabin adjoining it was connected by a covered hallway, and in later years another cabin was built fronting the hallway. The fireplace in each cabin was of mud and stick construction. In one of these cabins James Buchanan and his family lived, and in the other was found shelter for his hired help. The family consisted of the father and mother and one son, James also the grandfather, James Buchanan by name, and two unmarried sons of the elder Buchanan, Blair and William by name. Blair Buchanan married Sarah Houck and they lived on his farm in Jefferson township until his death on October 7, 1878. He was a man of note in his day and served as county commissioner of Cass county for several terms. William never married. He enlisted in the Mexican war and died in the service of his country near the mouth of the Rio Grande river on September 20, 1846.

James Buchanan was born in Hagerstown, Maryland on May 4, 1784. He married Pleasant Moore, who died on May 16, 1833, and they were the parents of four sons and two daughters. He later married Mary Wilson, who died at Terre Haute, Indiana, on September 13, 1838, without issue. He was a farmer and in Pennsylvania operated a line of stage coaches and a store and hotel, and during the War of 1812 he and a brother made guns for the American government, carrying on the work in Maryland. He died on June 14, 1860. His son James Moore Buchanan, who pioneered into Cass county in 1838 was born on November 14, 1810. He early gained prominence in his community, and for seventeen years he was the postmaster at Metea

HISTORY OF CASS COUNTY 1117

On May 2, 1837, he married Mary A D Gourley, who was born on February 28 1814, in Gettysburg, Pennsylvania They became the parents of five children, who grew to maturity. James, Samuel M, Martha Jane, who died young George W, John G and Edwin Boyd The father, James Moore Buchanan, died on March 23, 1897, and his widow survived his passing just a month, her death occurring on April 27, of the same year They were Presbyterians, and of Scotch ancestry, as the name plainly indicates

JAMES BUCHANAN, the son of James Moore and Mary A D (Gourley) Buchanan, was born in what is now Terre Haute, Indiana, on October 3, 1838, and in the year following he was brought to Cass county where he was reared and has spent his life thus far The preceding article gives complete details concerning the early family history of the Buchanan family, and the life of the parents of the subject so that further mention of those worthy people is unnecessary at this juncture

Such education as James Buchanan received up to the age of ten years was given him by his mother, and it was about that time that his father and certain of the neighbors united in building the log schoolhouse known as the Harmony school Here the subject attended for some three or four terms, later having one term at the Logansport high school

On December 11, 1862, he married Mary C Buchanan, a second cousin, and following this event they took up farm life in Bethlehem township, on the farm which is to this day called the Simon Farm Here the property was one hundred and forty feet above the level of Logansport, but it was flat and unprovided with a drainage outlet, but by persistent effort on the part of Mr Buchanan the land was eventually drained, but not until numerous law suits had been brought Today this land is recognized as among the most valuable in Cass county To his original tract Mr Buchanan added from time to time, once he owned three hundred and thirty-three acres there but today has only two hundred and thirteen acres In October, 1903, he moved to Logansport and has since lived a retired life

As previously mentioned, Mr Buchanan, in 1862, married Mary C. Buchanan, the daughter of Thomas Blair and Mary McKillip Buchanan, and they became the parents of seven children, named as follows: Martha Pleasant, is now the wife of William Randall, of Ambia, Indiana, Thomas Blair, died when one year old, Clarissa Williams, married William Sharpe, of Wellington township, Cass county, Edward Bowman, married Hattie Brown, and is a farmer of Fulton county, Indiana, George Chester, married Edna Peter, and they live at Burnett's Creek, Indiana, James Judson, married Frances Davis, and lives at Burnett's Creek, Indiana, and Rea, married Lura Aline Reed, and is a practicing physician at Lincoln, Nebraska

Mr Buchanan is a Democrat in his political faith and in 1882 he was elected a member of the board of county commissioners He was reelected to the office, and has served seven years in all in that capacity He also served one full term as a member of the county council, and served by appointment one unexpired term in the same office

Mr and Mrs Buchanan were members of the Bethlehem Presbyterian church for forty years, but are now members of the First Presbyterian church of Logansport, and are active and prominent in the work of that body.

ALLEN PRICE   Too many men who give their earlier years to the toil and struggle incident to the acquiring of a competency find it impossible, after they have reached the goal of their ambition, to settle down and enjoy the fruits of their labors   Allen Price is not one of these   Hard work and close application to the business in hand have marked his career from its inception but he has reached the place in life where he finds it possible to leave off the cares of business, and with his family, he is now enjoying to the uttermost the results of his leaner years of toil   As a successful farmer and drover, he has long been prominent in Jefferson township but the greatest and the best part of his popularity is the result of his sterling character and his kindly and genial disposition, which will always win friends for him, in whatever station in life he may find himself

A native of the Keystone state, Allen Price was born in Bucks county, on September 2 1847, and is the son of Smith and Harreetta (Opp) Price   These worthy people were born, reared and educated in their native state, Pennsylvania, and there they met and married and settled down to quiet rural life, ending their days in the county in which they were born   They were the parents of three children, Allen Price being the only survivor   A brother of the subject, was a veteran of the Civil war Valentine by name, died in the Mountain Branch (Tenn) Home for Soldiers, in 1912, and a sister died at the age of three years

Allen Price was reared to manhood in his native state   He came to Cass county in 1872   He was twenty-five years old then but unmarried, and had devoted himself to the care of his parents in the old home until that time   His only possession was cash to the amount of $150   He set himself to learn the miller's trade when a boy and was employed for about nine years at the Banta Mills   One year after his advent into Cass county he married Sarah E Barr, and she was reared in Cass county and educated in the district schools of her native township   They have one child, Etta, who became the wife of S C Waters of Jefferson township

Mrs Price was born in Jefferson township July 13, 1851, a daughter of William and Sarah (Gray) Barr   The mother was from Pittsburgh and the father was born in Scotland in 1800   He came to Cass county in 1840   He was a devout Christian and a very prominent old settler of the county   He died March 3 1867

Mr Price with the passing years, turned his attention to farming and gave up the milling business   He acquired some fine farming property, and is now the owner of two hundred and twenty-three acres of the most productive farm land in Jefferson township, where he makes his home   He did not confine himself to farming alone, but added sheep and cattle raising to his operations but specialized particularly in sheep and that branch of his activities yielded him a bigger cash return than all his other departments   He has always kept a quantity of high bred

MR. AND MRS. ALLEN PRICE AND DAUGHTER

sheep on his place, and, in addition, made a practice of going up into the lower peninsula of Michigan during the winter months and buying up droves of sheep, which he would send to his farm, feed for a time and dispose of them at a nice profit. His operations have made it possible for him to accumulate a competency sufficient to permit him to retire from active business and enjoy his home and the remaining years of his life, without thought for the morrow, and his home which is one of the finest in the township, is the center of many pleasant social events.

Mr Price and his family are members of the Center Presbyterian church, which was erected on a portion of his farm, and he is most liberal in its continued support. Not only is he generous in the way of church matters, but he may be depended upon to give liberally to any cause or movement that has for its purpose the ultimate good of his community. His politics are those of the Progressive party, and he has served his township during two terms as trustee. It is safe to say that there are few people, if any, who enjoy to a greater extent the respect and confidence of their fellow citizens than do Mr Price and his good wife in the community which has so long represented their home, and where they have been known all their lives.

HARVEY A SPENCER, well known in Logansport as the proprietor of the Spencer Transfer & Storage Company was born in Harrison township, on March 4, 1882. He was reared on a farm, but his boyhood was for the most part spent with his grandfather, S M Cogley, his mother having died when he was a boy of about eight years. He attended the district schools of Noble township, in which his grandfather had his home, and received a diploma from the school in the common branches. He thereafter attended the Logansport high school for one year, which was followed by a course in the Logansport Business College. For a number of months after he finished his schooling and started out for himself he was variously employed in Logansport, and managed to save from his earnings one hundred and fifty dollars, which he invested in a span of bronchos. He bought a wagon on his good name, and thereupon started out in the draying business, doing teaming and general hauling. His first year did not show a profit, but as he had not lost money he was emboldened to continue, and decided that by increasing his capacity by another teaming outfit he would do better. He accordingly did so, and the wisdom of his plan was soon apparent. Since that time the young man has added a teaming outfit to his equipmment each year. As a natural outgrowth of the draying business, he gradually drifted into the storage business and since 1907 this has been one of the principal features of the business. Mr Spencer now has 18,600 feet of floor space, covering three floors, and the business furnishes steady employment to twelve men.

Mr Spencer began his business career in Logansport without a dollar, and the present establishment and business of which he is now the head is the direct result of his applied business sense and all around efficient business methods. The Spencer Transfer & Storage Company does an annual business of about $30,000, and is constantly increasing and making necessary further expansion on the part of its management.

Mr Spencer is a Republican of progressive tendencies and is a member of the Commercial Club of Logansport. He is a Pythian Knight, but beyond that has no fraternal affiliations.

On March 23, 1910, Mr. Spencer married Miss Martha L. Campbell and they have one daughter, Amy Louise Spencer.

WILLIAM A. HOLLOWAY, M. D. A resident of Logansport since 1893, during which time he has achieved marked success in the practice of his profession, Dr. William A. Holloway holds prestige among the medical men of his adopted city, and is fully entitled to the confidence and respect that are his. He was born in Boone county, Indiana, September 23, 1870, and is a son of Park and Mary (Dukes) Holloway.

Dr. Holloway was a small lad when he was taken by his parents to Clinton county, Indiana, and there he grew to manhood on his father's farm. After going to the usual district schools in boyhood, he commenced attendance at the state university, at Bloomington, for two years, succeeding which he taught school for one year. Dr. Holloway read medicine under the preceptorship of Dr. Joseph D. Parker of Colfax and in 1889 entered Miami Medical College, Cincinnati, Ohio, where he continued his studies two years, then becoming a student in Bellevue Hospital Medical College, New York, from which noted institution he was graduated in the spring of 1893, receiving therefrom his degree of Doctor of Medicine. Since that time he has been continuously engaged in the practice of his profession in Logansport. In 1889, he took a post-graduate course at the New York Post-Graduate Medical School and Hospital, and in 1912, attended a similar course at the New York Polyclinic Medical School and Hospital.

Dr. Holloway is a member of the Cass County Medical Society, the Indiana State Medical Society and the American Medical Association. A student, he has advanced in his profession along with the progress made in the science of medicine and surgery, subscribing to the leading journals of his profession, and being greatly interested in various lecture courses. He is a thirty-second degree Scottish Rite and Knight Templar York Rite Mason, a Pythian Knight, a member of Mystic Shrine and a member of the Benevolent and Protective Order of Elks. Like other prominent and public-spirited citizens, he has given his interested attention, and when opportunity has offered his support and co-operation, to those movements which have to do with the welfare of his community, and in all walks of life is held in the highest esteem.

On December 27, 1893, Dr. Holloway was married to Miss Myrtle Treen, of Clinton county, Indiana. Mrs. Holloway is a member of the Methodist Episcopal church.

S. G. THOMAS. One of Cass county's native sons who has attained well-merited success in the vocations of farming and stock raising and who is now a highly esteemed resident of Tipton township, is S. G. Thomas, the owner of 160 acres of good land located on the Lewisburg road, about twelve miles from Logansport. The family has been identified with agriculture in Cass county for more than three-quarters of a century and has furnished Tipton township with some of its best citizenship, men who have taken an active interest in the material growth and development of their community, and as a worthy representative of the name Mr Thomas is held in high esteem by his fellow-townsmen He was born January 16, 1850, on the Lewis Little farm in Tipton township, and is a son of W P and Margaret (Stafford) Thomas

W P Thomas was the first white child born at New Carlisle, Clark county, Ohio, and was there educated and reared to the occupation of a farmer In young manhood he migrated to Cass county, in 1838 But after remaining here about a year he returned to his native state and was there married Shortly thereafter he returned to Cass county with his bride, and they continued to spend the remainder of their lives in clearing the land, cultivating the soil and making a home for their children, of whom there were seven in the family Giles S, who now resides in Nebraska and is engaged in farming, George W, a resident of Miami county, Indiana, Martha, who is deceased, S G, W R, who lives on his well-kept farm in Tipton township, J C, who is the owner of a farm in Clay township, Cass county, and Nettie, who married D S Bailey and resides in Minneapolis, Minnesota

S G Thomas received his early education in the old Crossroads school in Tipton township, and like other farmers' sons of his day divided his boyhood between the farm and the schoolhouse, attending the latter during the short winter terms He continued to work with his father until he reached his majority, at which time he determined to test the accuracy of the reports concerning the great opportunities offered in the state of Nebraska for ambitious young men Accordingly he journeyed to that state, but after a short period returned to Indiana and took up land in the vicinity of his birth-place, where he has continued to reside to the present time, with the exception of the seven years in which he lived in Logansport Since his return he has devoted himself to general farming and stock raising, with what degree of success may be gathered from a visit to his well-cultivated farm, with its substantial buildings, neat fences, well-fed cattle and general air of prosperity A firm believer in scientific methods and modern ideas, he uses the latest machinery and tills his soil in the most approved manner, constantly keeping abreast of the times in his vocation and being at all times ready to experiment with new ideas He has not cared for public life nor has he been affiliated with fraternal societies, his farm and his home satisfying all of his ambitions

In 1878 Mr Thomas was married to Miss Sarah Panabaker, and to this union there have been born two children namely Owen, who married Frances Miller, of Pittsburg, who have one son, Samuel G, and Jennie, who is the wife of Charles A Wright With his family Mr Thomas is a faithful member of the Methodist Episcopal church

JOHN MYERS was among the earliest pioneers of Cass county, Indiana, the date of his location in Clinton township being in 1833. He was born in Franklin county, Virginia, on September 3, 1808, and was descended from Dutch Huguenot ancestry His father was a soldier in the War of 1812 and his grandfather served in the American Revolution and was under General Washington at the defeat of Braddock In 1814 his parents moved to Montgomery county, Ohio, and until he was nineteen years old he worked on the home farm. He learned the blacksmith's trade, at which he worked five years In 1830, in Preble county, Ohio, he married Ann Swisher, and upon his arrival here in 1833 he bought two hundred and forty acres of heavily timbered land which he at once began to clear and improve. He participated in all the hardships and privations incident to pioneer life, and died in Logansport on September 7, 1890. He and his wife became the parents of four children, Isaac N., Henry C., Mary A. and Alfred B. The wife and mother died on February 26, 1877.

Isaac Neff Myers, the oldest son of John and Ann Myers, was born in Preble county, Ohio, his birth occurring on September 10, 1831. He was but two years old when he was brought to Cass county by his parents, and his early life was passed after the manner of the farmers' boys of those days, in clearing, grubbing, planting and harvesting, and, to a limited extent, attending school in the old log school house which was an adjunct to practically every country neighborhood in his day. His life was an uneventful one. He followed farming and stock raising as his chief employment and for about fifteen years operated a sawmill somewhat extensively, furnishing the Wabash and the present Pennsylvania railroads with the heavy timbers entering into the construction of these lines in this vicinity. Upon the breaking out of the Civil war he recruited a company for the Forty-sixth Indiana Volunteer Infantry, of which he was elected captain. Eleven employes of his farm having enlisted, Mr. Myers did not himself go to the front but took upon himself, at their request and his promise, the maintenance of the families of those of his employes, five in number, who did, which promise he faithfully kept. He was first a Whig in politics and later a Republican, and he was twice the nominee of his party for the office of county sheriff, but was defeated because of the strongly Democratic tendency of the county at the times. On December 4, 1851, he married Rosanna Justice, second daughter of James Justice, a pioneer of Clinton township. They became the parents of five children, three of whom survive. Mr. Myers died on June 2, 1905, preceded by his wife on May 5, 1898.

Quincy Alden Myers, justice of the supreme court of the state of Indiana, is the eldest son of Isaac N. and Rosanna (Justice) Myers. He was born on September 1, 1853, on what is now known as the Hugh Fitzer farm, in Clinton township, Cass county, Indiana, and was reared to manhood in that township. His early education was in the neighboring district schools. He prepared for college at the old Presbyterian Academy, in Logansport, from which he was graduated in 1870, after which he entered Northwestern Christian University, now Butler College, at Indianapolis. Owing to failing health he was compelled to relinquish active school work after a year of attendance there, but continued his studies under a tutor and was enrolled as a pupil at Smithson's College in Logansport. In 1873 he matriculated at Dartmouth College, New Hampshire, from which he was graduated with the degree of Bachelor of Arts in June 1875. Following this he read law at Logansport, under the direction of DeWitt C. Justice and Judge Maurice Winfield, and in September, 1876, entered Albany Law School, Union University, at Albany, New York. In June, 1877, he received his diploma, graduating as valedictorian of his class. After his graduation he returned to Logansport, and was associated with Judge Winfield, his former preceptor, in the practice of his profession, until the election of his partner to the circuit court bench in 1882. He then formed a partnership with Judge John C. Nelson, which continued until 1903, when Charles E. Yarlott became a member of the firm. The retirement of Judge Nelson in 1906 brought about the firm of Myers & Yarlott, which continued without interruption until January 1, 1909. In 1908 Mr. Myers was elected to the Indiana state supreme bench, and he has since filled the duties of that high office.

Judge Myers is a Republican in politics, a Knight Templar Mason, a member of the Benevolent and Protective Order of Elks and a Methodist in his religion. He is a trustee of De Pauw University, has been city attorney of Logansport, county attorney of Cass county and was for thirteen years a trustee of the city schools of Logansport.

On March 3, 1886, Miss Jessie D. Cornelius, eldest daughter of the late Edward G. Cornelius a leading merchant of Indianapolis, became the wife of Judge Myers and to them have been born two daughters: Melissa, now the wife of Joel Whitaker, a leading physician of Raleigh, North Carolina, and Marie Rosanna, who died on November 6, 1910, when in the twenty-first year of her life. Mrs. Myers is a member of the Presbyterian church and an active and efficient member of the board of managers of the orphans' homes of Logansport and Indianapolis and of the Home for Aged Women in the latter city.

H. H. MILLER M. D. A graduate from medical college in 1897, Dr. Miller has since been engaged in the practice of his profession at Galveston, in Jackson township. He is one of the young and vigorous doctors of the county and being a product of the modern school his methods have made a very successful record and he is prominent socially in his home community. Dr. Miller was born in Brooksburg, Indiana, November 4, 1871, and is a son of William and Augusta (Johnston) Miller. The father was a native of Pennsylvania, whence he came to Indiana as a young man and has for many years engaged in farming in this state. His early education was received in Pennsylvania. The old farm where the father lived and died is now the home of the mother and some of her children. There were eight children altogether in the father's family, and the six who are living now are named as follows: Evan C., Charles A., Sarah F. Ella, Harry E. and Dr. Harley H.

Dr. Miller was an attendant at the common schools near his home vicinity, and was engaged in farm work at the intervals of his schooling. Before beginning his studies for his profession he taught school and from this and other sources he earned practically all the money with which he prepared himself for his profession. He was a student of the State Normal College at Terre Haute and afterwards entered the Louisville Medical College, where he earned his way and was graduated with the degree of M. D. in 1897. His practice is principally in general medicine, but he has a recognized skill in surgery. Dr. Miller is a member of the Cass county and the Indiana State Medical societies, and in social circles in Galveston he and his wife play a very prominent part. He was married July 3, 1892, to Miss Elsie M. Thomas, and they are the parents of one child Forrest Thomas. The doctor and his wife are members of the Baptist church and he is affiliated with the Independent Order of Odd Fellows.

WILLIAM ERROL PACKARD One of the younger generation of enterprising Cass county farmers Mr Packard was born and reared in this county, and with a substantial training in both the practical details of his vocation and with school advantages appropriate for his career, he has already gained recognition as one of the prosperous and prominent young men in the rural activities of this county

William Errol Packard was born on the old D K Smith farm in Cass county on the seventeenth of February 1878 He is a son of Frank P and Marietta (Snyder) Packard His father, whose life is sketched on other pages of this work, is one of the best known citizens of Tipton township The Packard family was established in this part of Indiana by the grandfather, and Frank P Packard was born and reared in Miami county, where he was trained to the occupation of farmer, and since attaining manhood has passed practically all his career on farms in Cass county He is now a retired resident of Onward He has also taken an active part in public affairs of his township and county, and is one of the thoroughly esteemed men of this vicinity

Mr W E Packard now farms and owns eighty acres of fine land in Tipton township and has improved his place and brought it up to the highest standard of agricultural efficiency He was reared in Cass county received his education in the common schools, and throughout the time that he was a student, he was also acquiring practical experience on the home farm He is a young man who has given his full attention to his business and has formed no marriage relations

He began farming for himself in 1896 and in 1905 he bought the farm he now owns and lives on

GEORGE W WEYAND Success, in no uncertain degree, has attended the efforts of George W Wevand, the untoward circumstances of his early manhood and his lack of worldly advantages notwithstanding He established himself in the farming business in the vicinity of Royal Center after the close of the War of the Rebellion, through which he had served valiantly from first to last and there he continued until 1900, since which time he has been retired from active business life Born in Boone township, Cass county Indiana, January 31, 1844 Mr Wevand who has ever been a resident of his native town, is the son of Daniel and Eliza (Beckley) Weyand, concerning whom the following brief data are here incorporated

Daniel Weyand was a native of Bucks county, Pennsylvania, as was also his wife They came to Indiana in 1836 and settled quietly in Boone township, where the father of the family secured a farm and set about the business of farming In that early day Indians infested the country, and he carried on his work at the risk of his life subjected to the many annoyances of the tribes that were more or less hostile to the white invaders of their territory Daniel Weyand served as the first postmaster of Royal Center He was a stanch and true Democrat and was ever active in the ranks of the party He served his township as trustee for years, and was long a prominent man in the town and county He and his faithful wife became the parents of a family of seven sons, of which number two survive at this time Enoch, now a

resident of the state of Missouri, and the subject   The father died in March, 1896

George W Weyand was reared on the home farm and attended the public schools   He was yet a boy in his teens, busy with his books, when the call to arms in '61 put an end to his quiet humdrum life on the farm and in school, and he enlisted on November 23, 1863 in Company F, Twentieth Indiana Volunteer Infantry   He, with his regiment became a part of the Army of the Potomac, with Generals Grant, Hancock and Meade in command, and he served until the close of the war   He saw much of active service, and participated in the Battle of the Wilderness, the battle of Cold Harbor, Appomattox and others of equal importance   The war at an end, George Weyand returned to Royal Center and there took up the business of farming   He came to be one of the prosperous farmers of the township and when he retired from active farm life in 1900 was known for one of the well-to-do men of the community   He owns today one of the finest homes in Royal Center, with other property in the township, and is a stockholder in the local electric light plant

Fraternally Mr Weyand is a member of the Independent Order of Odd Fellows, in which he is treasurer of the order and past grand master   He is a Democrat and has always been active in the ranks of the party   As trustee of Boone township for six years, he gave most praiseworthy and valuable service to the township, and he has been a member of the local school board since 1905, and is secretary of the board at present   He and his good wife are earnest members of the Christian church in Royal Center.

In December, 1866 Mr Weyand was united in marriage with Miss Mina Kramer, who was born and reared in the state of Ohio   She came to Indiana in 1864, when she was about nineteen years of age, and there met and married her husband   Of the five children born to them, two are now living —Morris A , a member of the firm of Weyand & House, and Addie, the wife of James M Winn of Harrison township, Cass county, Indiana

Mr and Mrs Weyand occupy a secure place in the regard of the best people of Royal Center and vicinity, and as honorable, upright and earnest people are peculiarly deserving of the position they hold

JOHN E SHEETZ, a prominent farmer in Jefferson township, and long a resident of Cass county, was born in Dolphin county, Pennsylvania, on March 6, 1864, and is the son of Josiah and Salome (Lankert) Sheetz

Josiah Sheetz was the son of William and Barbara (Zimmering) Sheetz both born and reared in Pennsylvania   The father William was orphaned when yet a small boy, and he stayed at home with his widowed mother and helped her in paying for a farm   When he was of age he married and later bought the farm from the heirs of his mother On that farm William and Barbara Sheetz spent the rest of their lives, and there reared their family   He died in June, 1906   Josiah and Salome Sheetz lived on a farm which their parents gave them when they married   He was one of the eleven children of William and Barbara, and to each of their sons they gave a farm   All their lives were spent in Dolphin county, Pennsylvania, the mother dying there in May, 1885

John E Sheetz came to Indiana in December, 1884, when he was twenty years of age He came directly to Cass county, and began work at the trade of a carpenter in Cass county, in which he expected to continue, but when he arrived at Logansport he change his mind and turned his attention to farming For four years he worked on the farm for wages but he married about then and his new responsibilities gave him an incentive to greater accomplishments, so that he found himself soon the owner of a forty acre farm In later years, when his prosperity on the farm made possible another venture, he bought some property at Ford's Crossing and established a store there He remained in business at that stand for seven years and during that time was post master and station agent at the place He sold out after seven years and bought a farm in Jefferson township He started to build a house on the place, but before it was completed sold the place and bought his present home He has a tract of forty acres at his present location, with other holdings sufficient to make fifty-eight acres in all

On March 6, 1889, was solemnized the marriage of Mr Sheetz to Jennie Cotner, the daughter of Easten and Mary Jane (Rector) Cotner Easten Cotner was the son of Elia Cotner, who came to Indiana from North Carolina and his wife was a daughter of the Logansport family of that name Mr and Mrs Sheetz are members of the Christian church at Crooked Creek and he is fraternally associated with the Independent Order of Odd Fellows at Royal Center, in which he is Past Grand Master, and has passed through all chairs in the order. Both are members of Purity Lodge No 127 at Logansport Mr Sheetz is a Democrat, and has been a member of the advisory board of the party for four years

CHARLES E TONLY Here is another of the enterprising and progressive young farmers of Cass county, Indiana, whose rise in the world has been brought about through personal effort and whose career is illustrative of the success to be gained through the application of well-directed industry combined with strict integrity in all business matters From early boyhood Mr Toney's life has been filled with persevering effort and laudable ambition, and that his labors have borne fruit is testified by his present farm, a well-cultivated tract in Deer Creek township, which, under his skillful management is yearly growing more valuable Mr Toney has the added prestige of being a native son of Cass county, having been born on his present farm October 28, 1879 a son of William S and Mary (Moss) Toney His father, a native of Union county, Ohio, came with his parents to Cass county when a young man of twenty-two years, and subsequently went into debt for his farm, which was then covered with a heavy growth of timber and was entirely devoid of improvements Settling down in a little log cabin, he started the clearing of the land from the wilderness, and as the years passed added improvements as his finances would permit until he owned one of the best farms of his locality He continued to engage in agricultural pursuits throughout the remainder of his life, along with work in the ministry and heading a Mutual Insurance Company He was a well known and highly esteemed citizen of his community He and his wife became the parents of six children, namely. Frank H and Elma O,

May, who married a Mr Dutchess, Charles E, Sylvia, who became the wife of a Mr Bowman, and Wilbur E

Charles E Toney received his education under the preceptorship of John R Babb, at the Babb school, subsequently attending the Young America High school and an institution at North Manchester, Indiana, where he completed his studies During this time he had been assisting his father in the work of the home farm and receiving training and practical experience that has aided him greatly in his later life On attaining his majority, he began working for wages, which were carefully saved, and eventually, when he was twenty-seven years old, he purchased his present farm of eighty-four acres in addition to which he rents other land and now operates in all 314 acres He has devoted his attention to the cultivation of the soil raising diversified crops, and has also had a full measure of success in his stock raising activities He has added materially to the improvements on his land and the general appearance of his property denotes the presence of able management and thrift Among his neighbors he bears the reputation of being an industrious, hard-working farmer, who is rapidly gaining a place of independence in his chosen calling

On January 18, 1904, Mr Toney was married to Miss Maud Pierson, daughter of M H and Mary (Jeaness) Pierson and to this union there have been born children as follows Clarence O, Geraldine V and Ernest W Mr Toney is a member of the German Baptist church

BENJAMIN F CROCKETT The visitor to Cass county, viewing for the first time its well regulated farms, fertile fields of flowing grain, herds of sleek, well fed cattle, modern residences and other buildings, finds it hard to realize that only a comparatively few years ago this section was practically a wilderness, its land largely covered by timber for a large part and its excellent resources entirely wasted Yet such is the case, and the present prosperous condition of the county has only been attained through the untiring labor and persistent endeavor of men of energy and perseverance, whose lives have been devoted to the development of the interests of this part of the state Probably no other family within its limits has contributed in greater degree to the material welfare of Cass county than that of Crockett, members of which have here tilled the soil for years Among those bearing that name, a worthy representative of the younger generation is found in Benjamin F Crockett, of Tipton township, who is conducting the eighty acre farm belonging to his father-in-law, Matthew H Pierson Mr Crockett was born August 2, 1878, in Miami county, Indiana, and is a son of Henry and Catherine (Knight) Crockett

Henry Crockett was born September 13, 1849, in Deer Creek township, Cass county, Indiana a son of Asher and Susannah (Plank) Crockett Asher Crockett was a farmer and was born near Greenville, Ohio, whence he migrated to Miami county in 1831, and to Cass county, Indiana, in 1840, and in the latter spent the remainder of his life Asher Crockett was the father of five children Henry, Jane, Eliza, Sarah and James

Henry Crockett received his education in the common schools of Cass county and Miami county, and has spent his entire life in agricultural pursuits, now being the owner of eighty acres of land on the Crockett and Richeson road. He is known prominently among his fellow citizens, and is serving in the office of justice of the peace. With his family, he belongs to the Christian church. He was married January 15, 1876 to Miss Catherine Knight, and to this union there have been born eight children, namely: Carrie, who lives with her parents; Benjamin F., of this review; Harvey, who married Ethel Hymon and has one child, Opal; David and Laura, residing at home; Mae, who married Daniel Brunner and has three children, Wilmer, Florence and Velma; Chester, who married Hannah Pippinger, and June, who lives with her parents.

Benjamin F. Crockett was reared in Cass county, dividing his time between attendance at the district schools and work on his father's farm until fifteen years old and then worked on other farms until his marriage, and since that time has been carrying on operations on the farm of his father-in-law. He has won success, not only in material manner, but in gaining the confidence and friendship of the people of his community. Mr. Crockett was married in 1904 to Miss Mae Pierson, a daughter of Matthew H. and Mary Jenness Pierson, whose sketch will be found in another part of this work. Two children have been born to this union, namely: Gilbert Pierson and Herbert Landon.

Fraternally Mr. Crockett is connected with the Modern Woodmen of America. With his family he attends the Rock Creek Valley Christian church.

CARL S. WISE. The firm of Wiler & Wise was established in Logansport in 1878 by Joseph Wiler and Sol Wise, the fathers of the present members of the firm. The business was organized in 1867 by Jacob Wiler & Joseph Wiler. The style of the firm was changed in 1878 to Wiler & Wise and in 1906 to Wiler & Wise, Inc. The business has been continued uninterrupted by the family to the present time. Of these gentlemen, both now deceased, it may be said that Joseph Wiler came from Germany, his native land, in 1867, and was for a time associated with his brother, Jacob in the dry goods business on Market St. Following the accidental death of the brother, Joseph Wiler in 1878 associated himself in business with Sol Wise. Sol Wise was not only of German parentage, but was born in Landau, Germany and came to America in 1860. He returned to Germany in 1862, where he was married on September 10, 1862, to Miss Caroline Wiler. He came to Logansport from Toledo, Ohio. The firm was known as Wiler & Wise, and it is of interest to know that these names were originally spelled "Weiler" and "Weise," but that the almost invariable failure of Americans to give the words the proper pronunciation resulted in each of them dropping the superfluous letter "e" from the names, the present form being the result.

Wiler & Wise began business at 213 Fourth Street and after nearly a quarter of a century of established trade at that point, they moved to No. 409-11 Broadway, and finally to their present location at 412-414 Broadway.

Joseph Wiler was undeniably the foremost merchant of his time in Logansport. He was a man of superior business ability and he radiated hearty good fellowship wherever he was seen, so that to be numbered among his friends was an unqualified pleasure. The present business men of Logansport remember him with feelings of the kindliest affection and respect. He died on November 24, 1906. His long time partner Sol Wise, was no less a credit to the community where he so long resided. He was a man more retiring in his relations with the public than was Mr. Wiler, but his indomitable energy, sterling integrity and keen business sagacity had much to do with making the firm name synonymous with probity and success. He died September 28, 1897.

Following the death of these gentlemen the firm was incorporated as Wiler & Wise, Inc., the principal stockholders being the sons of the founders. Carl S. Wise is the president, Victor S. Wise is vice president and treasurer, and Carl J. Wiler is secretary. These men are carrying on the business established many years ago by their worthy fathers in a manner that is wholly creditable to them as the sons of such fathers.

Carl Solomon Wise was born in Lafayette, Indiana, November 1, 1869, a son of Solomon and Caroline (Wiler) Wise. Besides Carl S. there were two brothers, Victor and Louis, who died in Cincinnati, Ohio, August 14, 1885, also two sisters, Bertha and Amelia. Carl S. Wise has been a resident of Cass county and Logansport since September, 1878. His education was acquired in the local schools of Logansport, and also at Toledo, Ohio. At an early date he became familiar with the business conducted by his father, and is one of the leading merchants of the present city of Logansport. Mr. Wise is president of the Logansport Commercial Club, is a trustee of the Home for the Friendless, belongs to the state executive committee for the Business Form of Government, is on the executive committee of the State Board of Charity and among other business interests is treasurer of the Logansport Heating Company. In politics he is a progressive.

Mr. Wise married Corunna M. Stettiner at Toledo, Ohio, March 6, 1901. Her father was Samuel Stettiner, a wholesaler in Toledo. To their marriage has been born one son, Jack S. Wise, on February 12, 1907. Fraternally Mr. Wise is affiliated with the Masonic Order and with the Benevolent and Protective Order of Elks.

DENNIS UHL. One of the old and honored residents of Logansport, whose identification with the business interests of Cass county extends over a period of more than half a century, is Dennis Uhl, proprietor of one of this section's best known milling enterprises. Born in Allegheny county, Maryland, March 26, 1840, he is a son of Joseph and Naomi (Lenhart) Uhl, the latter of whom died when he was a small child, and his father subsequently remarried and in 1851 brought his family West, locating on what is now known as the Jesse Martin farm in Washington township, Cass township, Indiana.

The Uhl family originally emigrated to America from Holland, settling on Manhattan Island, then known as New Amsterdam. When the Duke of York changed the name of the Island to New York and drove many of the early settlers away by his heartless persecution, the Uhl family located along the Hudson river, and members thereof subsequently went to Pennsylvania and Maryland. It was in Somerset county, Pennsylvania, near the Maryland line and adjoining the city of Wellersburg, that Joseph Uhl, the father of Dennis, was born and where he married his first wife Noami Lenhart was a daughter of a seaman, and of Scotch ancestry, who was supposed to have been lost at sea, while her mother died in giving her birth, the latter being of German ancestry Naomi was reared in the family of early settlers of Pennsylvania where she met and married Mr Uhl, they having four children After her death, Mr Uhl married Caroline Miller, in Clarion county, Pennsylvania, and they became the parents of eight children Joseph Uhl was a millwright by trade, and sawed the timber in the place known as the "Shades of Death," where Gen Washington had assumed charge of the Colonial army, this timber being used in the construction of the Baltimore & Ohio Railroad After coming to Cass county, he worked at farming for a season in Washington township, and then, in 1852, built an overshot water wheel flour mill on Minnow Creek about four miles southeast of Logansport This mill has long since been razed Mr Uhl continued to follow his trade, operating a mill trading in land and building business blocks and other structures in Logansport and elsewhere until his death in 1892 He was a Democrat in politics all of his life and for a term of years acted in the capacity of county commissioner

Dennis Uhl was eleven years of age when brought to Cass county, and his education was secured in a log school house during winters until he was thirteen years of age, this comprising his entire schooling His youth and early manhood were passed in assisting to operate his father's mill on Minnow Creek, and when twenty-one years of age he rented the mill there and began operating it on his own responsibility, his father having built the mill in Logansport during the previous year He was there eighteen months, following which he became a partner in the Logansport mill under the firm name of Uhl Cheney & Company and his connection with this mill has continued to the present time In 1866 he became a third-owner in the enterprise and after his father's death he became the sole owner His partnership with his father covered a period of thirty-eight years and about 1900 the mill was incorporated, the stock being all owned by Mr Uhl and his immediate family Mr Uhl is a Democrat in politics, and for seven years served as county commissioner of Cass county He also for fifteen years, was a member of the county board of equalization was for ten years a trustee of the State Insane Asylum at Logansport and for a term of years was one of the three members of the water works committee of the city of Logansport, and during this time erected the present water works and installed the system

In 1864 Mr Uhl was married to Miss Sophia Jane Croll, of Cass county and to this union there have been born ten children William C , Walter J , Naomi who died when two years of age , Catherine, who died in 1872, Clara who married Joseph Herman , Chas Harry Uhl associated with him in the mill Florence Geneva Leonora who married Delbert Flynn , and one child who died in infancy The family attend divine worship at the Presbyterian church Mr Uhl is a valued member of the Masons and the Benevolent and Protective Order of Elks He has lived a long and useful life, and can look back over an honorable career, secure and content in the knowledge that no stain or blemish mars his record

FRANK B. WILKINSON is a comparatively recent resident of Logansport, but notwithstanding this he has figured prominently during the past decade in the commercial development of the city. He was born in Belmont county, Ohio, on the 28th day of May, 1856, and was one of the family of ten children born to William Wilkinson and Mary Ann Leckliter. Until he was twenty-six years of age Frank B. Wilkinson lived on the home farm. He received his preliminary education in the district schools, his later training being represented by one term at the famous normal school at Lebanon, Ohio. For a time thereafter he taught school and three years later completed a course in the Chicago School of Pharmacy, after which he engaged in mercantile activities and for a number of years was thus occupied at Belmont, Ohio, of which town he was postmaster as well as the leading druggist. He became secretary and treasurer in 1891 of the Indiana Window Glass Company at Pendleton, Indiana, and of the Bell Window Glass Company at Fairmount, Indiana, both corporations being controlled by one concern. Upon the absorption of both firms by the window glass trust in 1889 Mr. Wilkinson, in the following year, came to Logansport, Indiana, and purchased a one-half interest in and served as secretary and treasurer of the Logansport Foundry Company, and this city has since represented his home. In 1904 the consolidation of the Logansport Foundry Company and the Rutenber Manufacturing Company created the Western Motor Company. Mr. Wilkinson became president of this corporation in 1906, and served in that office until 1912, since which time he has not been actively engaged in any particular line of enterprise. He is a stockholder and a director in the Logansport Loan and Trust Company and of the City National Bank, and is the second vice president of the first named institution, also a stockholder and director in the American Mortgage and Guarantee Company of Indianapolis.

For many years Mr. Wilkinson has been actively identified with the Methodist Episcopal church as a member, and has been superintendent of the Sunday school in Logansport with excellent results. In many ways he has been closely identified with the growth of the moral, social and commercial welfare of the city, and is justly accounted one of its most valued citizens.

Mr. Wilkinson married Miss Julia E. Lewis of La Mira, Ohio, and two children have been born to them, Charles H. and Grace Anna, the latter of whom is now the wife of Allen E. Nelson, of Logansport.

JAMES L. ALLISON, M. D., a well known physician and surgeon of Cass county, with residence in Royal Center, Indiana, has been engaged in the practice of his profession since 1891. He came to Royal Center in June, 1910, and in the two and a half years that have elapsed since then has built up a pleasing practice in and about the village. He is the descendant of an old and highly esteemed family, and was born in Madison, Wisconsin, on September 17, 1862, the son of Rev. Daniel P. and Mary L. (Pitzer) Allison.

Reverend Allison was prominent in the ministry of the Christian church in his day, and was a man of excellent educational attainments. He also was prominent in politics, and was active in the political circles of the state of Wisconsin, where he held a number of important offices in Wayne county. He was born in the Old Dominion state and educated in her schools and his wife was an easterner, born in the Empire state. After their marriage they went to Wisconsin, where Reverend Allison's work called him and he occupied a pulpit in the Christian church of Madison, Wisconsin, for several years. It was in Madison that the subject was born.

James L. Allison was brought to the Hoosier state at an early age, and he received the advantages of the public schools until he finished the high school, then entered Wabash College in Indiana, where he took a literary course, preparatory to a course in medicine, upon which he was already resolved. He later entered the School of Homeopathy, from which he was duly graduated, his course including a year and a half as house physician in St. Luke's Hospital at Chicago. Dr. Allison was a close student in his college days, and he has never rid himself of the habit of study, but has kept closely in touch with the advance of science as it affected his profession. He has been engaged in practice in Indiana for twenty-one years, having commenced in 1891. He was physician and surgeon at the Harrell Hospital, Noblesville, Indiana.

Dr. Allison is a prominent member of the Masonic order, of the Knights of Pythias and of the Red Men.

In 1881 Dr. Allison was united in marriage with Miss Viola Jarrett of Tippecanoe, Indiana, a lady of refinement and splendid characteristics. She was educated in the public schools of Indiana, where she was reared. Dr. and Mrs. Allison have two interesting daughters, Pearl, a graduate of the Monticello high school, and now the wife of Merton Hinsley, of Fulton county, Indiana, and Ruby, who is unmarried. Mrs. Allison is a devoted member of the Methodist Episcopal church, and is an earnest worker in its various departments of activity.

ANTHONY GRUSENMEYER is a native of Alsace, France, now Alsace, Germany, since the Franco-Prussian war of 1870. He was born on May 27, 1832, and is the son of Valentine and Katherine (Schwartzman) Grusenmeyer. The father who was a shoemaker by trade, died on February 3, 1850. Ten children were born to these parents, only two of which number are now living, Anthony of Logansport and Mrs. Magdalena Leppert of Dayton, Ohio. One son, Joseph, came to the United States in 1835 and was occupied in blacksmithing in Buffalo, New York. He came to Indiana in 1852 and located in Logansport, where he passed the remainder of his days. Two others of the children, Michael and Katherine, came to America in 1846, locating at Dayton, Ohio. In August 1850 following the death of the father Michael returned to Alsace and brought the remainder of the family to America. They left their home in Alsace on the 26th day of August, 1850, by wagon for Havre, from where they embarked on the *Arcadia*, a sailing vessel bound for the United States, their port being New Orleans. After a voyage of four weeks, a storm arose and damaged the vessel to such an extent that they were compelled to put into St. Thomas, West Indies for repairs. They landed at St. Thomas on the 26th day of October, 1850 and was ready again for sailing on the 6th of December, 1850, and resumed their journey to New Orleans where they arrived on the 23rd of December, and left New Orleans December 25, by steamer for Cincinnati, Ohio, where they landed on January 6, 1851, their departure from Havre having taken place on September 13th previous. From Cincinnati the mother at once moved to the vicinity of Dayton, where they arrived on the 9th of January, 1851, and buying fourteen acres of land, expected to go into the gardening business. She died on September 9, 1851, less than a year after her arrival in this country.

Anthony Grusenmeyer received a good common school education in his native land, and after coming to America he lived at Dayton until March, 1853, when he made his way to Logansport, Cass county, Indiana, by stage, the prevailing mode of travel in that time. He set about learning the blacksmith trade at once with his brother in Logansport, and he served an apprenticeship of two years with him, then worked for him six years as a wage earner. In that time he accumulated sufficient means to enable him to go into the business for himself, and he continued in the blacksmith business here for thirty-two years, that period including the time he spent while learning the trade, and in the service of his brother. During the passing years he perfected his knowledge of the English language, and acquired a wide acquaintance in the county. He became a Democrat, and in 1884 he was nominated for the office of county treasurer, and elected. He served one term of two years and succeeded himself in the office, his total service covering a period of four years. He also served one term in the City council of Logansport, from 1872 to 1874. Some two or three years after the expiration of his second term as county treasurer Mr Grusenmeyer embarked in the grocery business, in company with his son, Charles X , who is now deceased. Upon the death of Charles, another son, Frederick M , by name, became interested in the business, and Frederick M and his son, Anthony, are still engaged in the business here. Mr Grusenmeyer retired from the business in 1900, since which time he has given his attention to his private interests.

On February 24, 1857, Mr Grusenmeyer was united in marriage with Miss Elizabeth Schakome, of Logansport, Rev Father Wm Doyle officiating, and nine children were born to them. Mary C , the wife of William Bronson of Detroit, George F now deceased, Frederick M , in business in Logansport, Charles X , deceased, Leonore C , also deceased, Elizabeth J , the wife of Jacob Graf, of Logansport; Joseph V , Emanuel A , and William H , all deceased.

Mr and Mrs Grusenmeyer are members of the St Joseph's Roman Catholic church, and are enjoying the very best of health.

FREDERICK GUY NEEL. Among the younger men who have chosen educational work as their vocation in Cass county Indiana, Frederick Guy Neel is making rapid progress and it is expected that he will be heard from at no far distant date in his particular field of endeavor. In these days of materialism it is particularly pleasing to find a young man with an inclination for the duties of the educator, and who realizes the importance of his vocation and the possibilities for wholesome good that it holds out.

Born in White county, Indiana, on August 14, 1886, Prof Frederick Guy Neel is the son of James H and Susan (Cromer) Neel. The father was born in the vicinity of Idaville, in White county, on October 12, 1855, and the mother, also a native of that county, was born on November 27, 1864 Both received somewhat limited educations in the district schools of their immediate vicinities and the father early learned the carpenter's trade, and when he reached man's estate, gave himself to the contracting and building business He came to be a resident of Royal Center, in Cass county, in 1911, there engaging in that business, and he is still so occupied Both of these worthy people are devout members of the United Presbyterian church, and they are highly esteemed and respected in the town which represents their home Six children were born to them Frederick G. being the eldest of that number, and the others being Elizabeth G, Mamie B, Vance, Reed and Lucile

Frederick G Neel received his preliminary educational training in the public schools of Idaville, Indiana, and he was later graduated from the high school of Monticello, Indiana, that event taking place in 1905 He then gave his attention to teaching and for two and a half years he taught school in White county It was thus that he earned the money which secured to him the best part of his college education. He was graduated from the scientific department of the university at Valparaiso, Indiana, and was a student for some time at the University of Indiana at Bloomington In January, 1908, he accepted a position as teacher in the schools of Royal Center, and so well did he succeed in his work that in 1911 he was elected to the superintendency of the schools, which position he now holds He is making rapid advancement in his work, and has placed the work of the schools of Royal Center on a par with that of the schools of much larger places

On June 19, 1909, Mr Neel was united in marriage with Miss Lottie G Vernon a native of White county, where she was reared and educated Two children have been born to them James Robert, aged three years, and Wilma Vivian, now one year old

Mr Neel is a member of the A F & A M and affiliates with Royal Center Lodge No 585 Both he and his wife are earnest members of the Methodist Episcopal church of Royal Center, and he is one of the trustees of that body as well as having served as superintendent of its Sunday school

OLIVER H BINNS The Casparis Stone Company has found in Oliver H Binns from its earliest inception an able and efficient manager and general superintendent, and in giving a summary of the life of Mr Binns, it is entirely in keeping with the general fitness of things that the history of the Casparis Stone Company be outlined more or less briefly This flourishing concern was organized in 1892 with a capitalization of $100,000, under the laws of the state of Ohio, and the stock was subscribed for by Ohio people, in the main The primary object of the company was to quarry limestone, the demand being from manufacturing centers for blast furnace purposes The company originally purchased three hundred and sixty-eight acres of land in Noble township, Cass county, since which time it has added five hundred acres to its holdings. The work was begun soon after incorporation, and a plant was erected at a cost of $50,000, Oliver H Binns, the subject of this review, being appointed superintendent in charge of the erection of the plant, and upon its completion he became general superintendent. The firm found no difficulty in securing a market for its product, and they experienced a steady increase in sales from the outset In 1897 the capital stock was increased to $500,000 and has so continued up to the present time The present output aggregates one million tons per annum and the principal markets are South Chicago, Indiana Harbor and Gary. Aside from these points, their product goes largely into road construction throughout northern Indiana The plant employs an average of two hundred and fifty men, and is run at capacity the year around Since the erection of the original plant, a practically new one was built in 1902 to take the place of the old one, which was no longer adequate to the demands of the constantly growing business

Oliver H Binns, the capable superintendent in charge of this splendid enterprise, was born in Harrison county, Ohio, in 1860. When he was twelve years old he moved to Columbus with his family and was there reared and educated in the public schools His graduation from the high school of that city took place when he was seventeen years old soon after which he entered the employ of a railroad contractor, and for two years he continued to be thus occupied, learning much of mechanical and constructive work that destined to be of great value to him in later years His employers gradually drifted into the stone business, and Mr Binns continued with them, coming to Logansport in 1892, which city has ever since represented his home and the scene of his business activities

In 1894 Mr. Binns married, and he maintains a home in Logansport, although his work at the quarries keeps him there a goodly part of the time Mr Binns is a director of the First National Bank of Logansport, and is recognized as one of the substantial business men of the city. He is a Republican, but not active as an office holder or seeker, and he is a member of the B P O E

MAJOR W H SNIDER Now living retired in Logansport, after a long and successful career as a merchant of this city, Major Snider is a native of Indiana He was living in Ohio when the War of the Rebellion broke out, and was one of the honored and valiant soldiers from that state during the struggle, but for more than forty-five years has been identified with Cass county, Indiana

William H Snider was born at Centreville, in Wayne county, Indiana, and is of good old American stock His parents were Frederick V and Mary (Smith) Snider, his father a native of Virginia and the mother of Ohio The father was a cabinet maker by trade and died in Centreville Besides Major Snider there was one son and two daughters in the family

In Wayne county, Major Snider spent his boyhood and completed his education in the Whitewater seminary at Centreville He was a boy when the war came on, and in July, 1862, enlisted in the Ninety-fourth Regiment of Ohio Volunteers He was promoted to lieutenant of Company F, and in February, 1863, became captain In January, 1865, he was made major of his regiment His military record includes active participation in campaigns and battles from the early months of the war until its close, and the more important are mentioned as follows

Battle of Perryville, Kentucky, Stone River and Murfreesboro, Tennessee, the campaign after Chickamauga, leading up to the siege of Atlanta, in which he fought at Resaca and Peachtree, in Georgia, at Jonesboro, Georgia, and the various engagements about Atlanta, he was with General Sherman on his march from Atlanta to the sea, participating in all the engagements of that campaign, then was in the Sherman campaign from Savannah north to the Carolinas, to Richmond, Virginia. He was mustered out with his regiment at Washington, D C, after the war had closed

With this rank and experience as a soldier Major Snider returned home, and in May, 1867, arrived in Cass county, having been a resident of Logansport ever since. From 1867 until 1910 he was engaged in the crockery business at Logansport. Major Snider in November, 1871, married Miss Mary Jerolaman, a daughter of George M and Mary Jerolaman. Major Snider is a member of the Presbyterian church, and has taken an active part in social and civic affairs. He is a Knight Templar Mason, is a member of the Loyal Legion military organization, comprising the officers of the late war, the Tuesday Night Club and the Deutscher Verein

WILLIAM HEFFLEY Although making his home in the city of Logansport, William Heffley is reckoned among the successful farming men of this region. He owns a fine farm of about eighty acres in Miami township, where he was reared and educated, and this place is now operated by a man who is hired by Mr Heffley for that express purpose.

Born in Cass county on January 1, 1864, William Heffley is the son of Simon P and Mary E (Kline) Heffley, who came to Indiana in their young lives, settling in Montgomery county first, and later coming to Cass county. The father settled on a farm in Miami township, and there reared his family and ended his days. It was a wild and untouched bit of land, heavily wooded and utterly unfit for the production of a crop until a vast amount of toil had been expended upon it, but the sturdy countryman brought out of it a productive little farm—one that sustained him in his later years and now adds considerably to the income of his son. Since William Heffley came into ownership of the place, he has added something to it in improvement as well as in acreage, and the place of seventy acres is more expansive now by some twenty acres. He has improved the building in many ways, and made of it a prosperous and well kept place

Mr. Heffley owns a fine residence in Logansport, which he built himself, as well as having erected the buildings on his farm. He attends the Methodist Episcopal church and politically he gives his aid to the Republican party

On November 25, 1908, Mr Heffley was married to Mrs Elizabeth Potthoff Miller, the daughter of John and Fredericka (Eberlein) Potthoff, who were early settlers in Cass county

CHARLES A ENYART Charles A Enyart has for the past twenty-five years been continuously engaged in carrying mail in Logansport, in which city he was born, reared and passed his days thus far. He is the

son of Pearson and Martha J (Gearhart) Enyart, and the grandson of Benjamin and Sarah Enyart

Pearson Enyart was born in Hamilton county, Ohio, on December 28, 1828, and when he was six years old accompanied his parents to Cass county In those early days the region was infested with Indians and wild animals, and the lives of the sturdy pioneer settlers were much harassed by the unwelcome attentions of these older inhabitants of the country Pearson Enyart was reared in a log cabin on the old place in Clay township, and his boyhood days were passed for the most part in the strenuous toil of grubbing and clearing up the wilderness farm and assisting in the cultivation of such crops as were practicable under the conditions In young manhood he married Martha Gearhart and soon thereafter moved to Logansport, where he began working at the trade of a plasterer and mason Thus he continued until 1893, when he moved to Medford, state of Oregon, and there he now resides With the exception of a four-year period, from 1872 to 1876, when he lived in Indianapolis, he has made his home in Logansport after he married and settled there, and much of the work in his line which has been done in the city is the work of his hands Mr Enyart is a Republican, stanch and true, and his religious belief is that of a Methodist, as is that of his wife They became the parents of two children—Charles A and Jesse E Enyart

Of the immediate family Charles A Enyart is the only one now making Logansport his home, and he was born and reared here, and regards the city as his real home In his boyhood Mr Enyart worked with his father a considerable time, and for some years worked with his cousin in the bottling business It was in 1888 that he first entered the employ of the government as a substitute letter carrier, and he was thus employed for three years He was then regularly appointed and for the past twenty-one years has been engaged in the government service as a mail carrier

Mr. Enyart has lived quietly and has been able to save considerable from his salary, which has been carefully invested, so that he is now the owner of a nice home, new and of his own designing Mr Enyart is a Mason of the Knight Templar degree and also a Knight of Pythias He is a Republican in his politics

On May 10, 1882, Mr Enyart was married to Miss Carrie C Fiddler, the daughter of Frederick and Margaret (Hager) Fiddler The Fiddler family is of German ancestry, the name at one time being rendered "Fieddler" One daughter has been born to Mr and Mrs Enyart— Ethel B The family are of the Methodist Episcopal church in their religious faith, and Mrs Enyart and daughter are active and enthusiastic members of the Eastern Star

WATERMAN G SWEET The great state of Ohio has contributed many of her sons to the growth and development of her sister state, Indiana, and Cass county owes much to the new life and blood that has become a part of her through migration from Ohio Many of the leading men, farmers, merchants, mechanics, followers of the professions, etc , who have made names for themselves in all these varied fields of activity in Cass county, have had their origin in Ohio and there received their early training One of these is Waterman G Sweet, born and reared in Lorain county Ohio

The natal day of Waterman G Sweet was May 12, 1858 and he is the son of Colvin and Bricena (Chadwick) Sweet The father was a New Yorker by birth, born there in about 1812, and came to Ohio when a boy. He received the best part of his education in the schools of his native state and after reaching man's estate he married in Ohio, and there passed the remainder of his life. He was a farmer and gave his life to that business Eight children were born into this home, and of that number four are living at this writing (1912) Bricena Sweet is unmarried; Mary M is the wife of Clement B Snow; Waterman G. of this review, and Charles D, who lives on the old home place in Ohio. The four who are now deceased are Theodore P, Luther A, William E and Calvin M

Waterman G Sweet was reared in Lorain county, Ohio and as a boy of eighteen years he migrated in 1876 to Indiana, and located in Cass county He was engaged as a clerk in Royal Center, and continued to be connected with mercantile work for something like twenty years He saved some of his earnings regularly, and in 1896 he embarked in business upon his own responsibility entering into a general merchandise business with grain and live stock dealings as a side line He has experienced a pleasing degree of success in all departments of his business, his long mercantile experience as an employee giving him a thorough education in mercantile principles, and his own natural ability making it possible for him to succeed as a dealer in grain and live stock He has gradually assumed other business relations, and is a director and stockholder in the State Bank of Royal Center, and the president of the Royal Center Light Company

In June 1888, Mr Sweet was married to Miss Laura E Thomas, the daughter of Dr James Thomas Two sons have been born to them — Theodore T, who is now a student in the Wabash College, and Garold G, a graduate of the Royal Center high school and also a student at Wabash College The family are members of the Baptist church Mr Sweet is a Republican and takes an active part in the workings of that party in his district

A man of few words but ever up and doing, Mr Sweet, in the twenty years of his clerkship in Royal Center established a reputation for veracity, faithfulness and general business integrity that made it possible for him to step into a new business of his own establishing without passing through a preliminary try-out period in the community So well had he become known as a business man who was in every way reliable that his success was made when he embarked in business on his own initiative He stands high in the regard of all who know him, and he has proven himself to be worthy in all the relations of life

JOHN L. LEONARD was born at New Castle, Henry county, Indiana, on October 14, 1857, and was one of the six children of Zephaniah and Elizabeth (Rogers) Leonard, two of that number now being deceased Both families are of American birth and ancestry, dating back for several generations in the history of America The father of

Zephaniah Leonard moved to Henry county when that locality was yet in a most primitive condition, and there he battled with the unpierced forests, brought his family up after the manner of those pioneer times, and reared them in the knowledge of good, hard work and its many benefits, and in the doctrine of the Methodist church. He settled on the Blue River valley bottom and there, through his hard work and incessant economy, prospered beyond the average man of his time. As his children grew up and married, he gave to each an eighty-acre farm. Zephaniah Leonard, his son, lived in Henry county, Indiana, practically all his life. In 1877 he and his family moved to Logansport and there he conducted a garden on Orphan's Hill for some years. Both he and his wife are now dead.

John L. Leonard was twenty years old when he came to Cass county. He had been reared on the home farm, and in the district school acquired what education he possessed. After coming to Logansport he spent two years in the employ of Sanderson & May in the marble business, then clerked for a year for Michael McCaffrey in his grocery store. His next position was with the Adams Express Company, and for almost eleven years he was employed as a messenger on the Panhandle Railroad. It was in 1890 that he established the grocery store in Logansport which has proved so successful to him. He began in a small way in one room at his present location, and by close and careful attention to the wants and requirements of the public, as well as the application of safe and sane business methods, he has prospered through the passing years, and his is now one of the largest retail groceries in Logansport.

Mr. Leonard is a Republican in his political views, but he has never aspired for office, preferring to devote his entire attention to his personal business. He was once nominated, without his consent, for the office of councilman, but much to his satisfaction was defeated, although without any effort on his part he reduced the usual Democratic majority from a nominal one hundred and fifty to about forty. Mr. Leonard has no fraternal affiliations beyond his membership in the Knights of Pythias.

On May 25, 1885, Mr. Leonard was married to Miss Dora Busjahn, and they have one son, Russell Leonard. The family are members of the German Lutheran church.

CHRIST BABER. A native of Ohio and a member of a family well known in the Buckeye state, Christ Baber came to Cass county some twenty years ago, and since has been engaged in agricultural pursuits. He belongs to that class of successful men who prize their success the more because it has been self-gained, for since attaining his majority he has been the architect of his own fortunes, and the position he now holds warrants him in taking a pardonable degree of pride in the title of self-made man. At this time he is the owner of an excellent farm of 285 acres, in the accumulation of which his dealings with his fellow men have always been of an honorable nature, thus winning him the respect and esteem of all with whom he is acquainted. Christ Baber was born February 20, 1864, in Fayette county, Ohio, and is a son of James and Elizabeth (Hanawalt) Baber. The family first came to Indiana during the early 'fifties, Mr. Baber's father following farming here, but later went to Illinois, from whence they returned to London, Ohio, and there a number of people of the same name are to be found today There were ten children in the Baber family John, William, Christ, George, Alfred, Andrew, Eliza, Melissa, Ella and Alice

During his school days in Ohio Christ Baber assisted his father in the work of the home farm, and on attaining his majority embarked upon a career of his own Sober, thrifty and industrious he carefully saved his earnings, purchased a team, and eventually became the owner of land in Ohio, which he disposed of at a profit when he left, in 1894, to come to Cass county Here he purchased a tract of land, to which he has added from time to time, and he now has 285 acres of fertile soil, which he devotes to general farming and stock raising His operations have proved uniformly successful, and each year finds new improvements on the place, his buildings being of modern architecture and substantial character, and modern conveniences and comforts have been installed He uses the latest machinery and methods practicing scientific farming, and is recognized as an excellent judge of live stock

In 1887, near Danville, Illinois, Mr Baber was married to Miss Sarah Fyllington and to this union there have been born eight children as follows William, who married ——————— Woodruff has two children, Orville and James E , and is engaged in farming, Bert, who is single and resides with his parents, Carrie, who married Wilsie Ramer and has three children—Marie, Mayne and Janice, Edward, who married Nellie Brown, Bud who married Emma Sheets and has two children—Leonard and Milburn, Frank, who married Elsie Crane; Stella, who became the wife of John Maynes and Effie, who married Len Shaft and has one daughter, Josephine Mr Baber has not mixed in politics, his time having been entirely engaged with his farm work Nevertheless, he has not been indifferent to the duties of citizenship and has staunchly supported these men and movements which he has believed desirable for the community During his long residence here he has formed a wide acquaintance, in which he numbers numerous friends

JACOB W DELAWTER Farming is a business that has always paid well in Cass county, and people have been attracted to this locality from other parts of the country because of the fertile soil and excellent climatic conditions One of the older agriculturists of the country, who was brought here in babyhood by his parents, is Jacob W DeLawter, a prosperous citizen and owner of eighty acres of land located on the Seven-Mile road, about nine miles from Logansport, in Tipton township Mr DeLawter was born December 14, 1850, near Eaton, in Preble county, Ohio, and is a son of Ezra and Sophia (Heck) DeLawter His father, also a native of Ohio, came to Cass county in 1853 and here spent the balance of his career in agricultural pursuits, becoming one of his community's substantial and highly esteemed citizens

Jacob W DeLawter was only three years of age when he was brought to Cass county by his parents, and here he received his education in the country schools, in the meantime being reared to agricultural work and trained to habits of honesty, integrity and industry When he was twenty-one years of age he decided to engage in farming on his own account, and accordingly settled on a tract of forty acres, for which he went into debt During the first few years he encountered many obstacles and discouragements, but continued ambitious and persevering, and his unflagging industry and determination soon brought him to a position where he was able to make a number of improvements and to add to his original purchase He now has eighty acres of well cultivated land, which he devotes to general farming and stock raising, and has earned the right to be numbered among his town's substantial men

On April 9, 1872, Mr DeLawter was united in marriage with Miss Indiana McDonough, daughter of Enoch and Sarah (Cathire) McDonough Her father, a farmer died when still a young man, and she was brought to Cass county when seven years old by her mother, being accompanied also by her brother, Hugh, who is now a resident of Marion, Indiana Mrs DeLawter was reared in Cass county, and here attended the country schools. She and her husband have been the parents of five children as follows Jesse B, an agriculturist of Cass county who married Jeanette Cherry and has two children—Jesse Jr and Nellie, Perry Franklin, also of Cass county, who married Catherine Casky and has two children—Florence and Esther, Sadie S, who is the wife of Charles Black and has one child—Pauline, Agnes, who married J C Hahn, and has three children—Dorothy, Alice and William, and Nellie, who is the wife of Charles Little

Mr and Mrs DeLawter and their children are members of the Christian church, in the work of which they have always taken an active interest Mr DeLawter has not cared for public preferment, but is ready at all times to support good government, and shows himself especially active when the welfare of his community is at stake

JOHN JAMES GUGLE A thorough and comprehensive knowledge of the multitude of subjects upon which a good farmer must be informed in order to meet with a full measure of success in his vocation, an energetic and enterprising nature and an inherent business ability that is his heritage from a line of thrifty, industrious German ancestors, have made John James Gugle one of the leading farmers of Tipton township, where he is now the owner of 160 acres of well cultivated land on the Peru road, about one mile west of Lewisburg Although not a native of Cass county Mr Gugle has lived here since boyhood was reared on a Cass county farm and educated in the district schools, and his entire business activities have been carried on within its borders He was born September 17, 1851, in Ohio, and is a son of Jacob and Mary Ann (Essiek) Gugle

Jacob Gugle was born in Germany, and as a young man left the Fatherland for the United States, settling first on the lower Sandusky, in Ohio From that section he enlisted for service in the Mexican war some time after the close of which he came to Cass county, Indiana, where the remainder of his life was spent in agricultural pursuits He and his wife were the parents of nine children, of whom five are still living· Christina, who married a Mr Rush, Katie, who became the wife of a Mr. Lutmon, Louisa, Sarah and John James.

Like most of the farmers' sons of his day and locality, John J Gugle divided his boyhood between work on the homestead in the summer months and attendance at the district schools during the short winter terms He was reared to agricultural pursuits, in which his entire life has been passed, and his home training was such as to make him thrifty, industrious and honest At this time his handsome farm, a tract of 160 acres, shows the presence of good management, being well cultivated, neatly fenced, drained and graded, and improved with buildings of modern architecture and substantial character Mr Gugle devotes the greater part of his time to general farming, although he has also successfully experimented in cattle raising Among his neighbors and business associates he bears a high reputation for integrity and honorable dealing, and as a citizen he has at all times been ready to contribute of his means and time to the advancements made in his community

On March 25, 1877, Mr Gugle was united in marriage with Miss Mary Smith, the estimable daughter of Michael and Rachael (Collier) Smith. Michael Smith was about forty years of age when he migrated from his home in Dalton county, Pennsylvania, to Cass county, Indiana, and here settled on a farm in Clinton township, on which he spent the remainder of his life Mr. and Mrs Smith had three children Catherine and John, who are both deceased, and Mary, who married Mr Gugle Mr and Mrs Gugle have been the parents of three children—Fannie, who became the wife of John Baines Harley, and Gertrude With his family, Mr Gugle attends the Methodist Episcopal church

FREDERICK H KLINSICK, well known and successful as a boot and shoe merchant in Logansport, is a native born citizen of this place, born here on March 1, 1866, and the son of Henry and Minnie (Alfield) Klinsick The father was a native born German, and he emigrated from his native land to America in the year 1844, four years later establishing himself in the blacksmith business in Logansport—a trade which he had learned in his youth at home He followed that business practically all his life and ended his days in Logansport, death claiming him in 1873

As a boy Frederick H Klinsick attended the German Lutheran parochial schools and the public schools of Logansport after which he took a commercial course in Hall's Business College He was a mere youth when he set out to make his own way in the world, being but fourteen years of age, and he began as a clerk in the store of Murdock, Vigus & Co , beginning with that well-known firm on June 1, 1881, and continuing with them without a break until February 2, 1892 It was then that he branched out in an independent business and entered a partnership with one Charles Stevenson, under the business appellation of Stevenson & Klinsick They opened a boot and shoe store at No 403 Broadway, and their venture proved a prosperous and successful one, so that they made very material progress in the business life of the community On July 1, 1901, Mr Klinsick saw fit to take over the interest of his partner in the business, and since that time he has been the sole proprietor of the establishment, which is today one of the leading places of its kind in the city With the passing years Mr Klinsick has won an excellent reputation for business integrity and clean and wholesome methods, and is rightly regarded as one of the staple and dependable business men of the city. His enterprise represents a steady and conservative growth, the business being founded upon the most praiseworthy principles, and its able proprietor has in every way proved up his claim to the title of business man.

Mr Klinsick is a member of a number of fraternal organizations, among which are the Benevolent and Protective Order of Elks and the Knights of Pythias He is a Democrat ordinarily, but is one who is inclined to assume an independent attitude when matters of a political nature are under consideration

On September 22, 1903, Mr Klinsick married Miss Emma H Elliott, daughter of William H Elliott, of Logansport

JAMES DELAPLANE One of the handsome farming properties of Cass county is that known as Sunny Dale Farm, a tract of 112 acres, located on the Cass-Carroll county line, about ten miles south of Logansport the owner of which, James Delaplane, is one of his locality's practical agriculturists and sterling citizens He has been a resident of Cass county for upwards of thirty-eight years, and although he is now retired from active pursuits, his sons looking after the farm, he still takes a keen interest in the welfare of his community, demonstrating his public spirit on every possible occasion Mr Delaplane was born July 17. 1856, in Butler county, Ohio, and is a son of William and Sarah E (Zinn) Delaplane, and a grandson of James Delaplane, who was born in Maryland and emigrated therefrom to Ohio, where William Delaplane was born. The latter was a farmer and stock raiser for many years and during the Civil war did a large business in the latter capacity with the government in supplying meat for the Union troops In 1875 he brought his family to Cass county, where he took up a farm, and here spent the remainder of his life He and his wife were the parents of seven children, of whom five survive Mary, who married a Mr Yeider Margaret, who became the wife of a Mr Coons, Bertha L, who married Mr Cook, John, who resides in Carroll county, and James

James Delaplane commenced his education in the common schools of Butler county Ohio, which he attended until he was eighteen years of age, and at that time entered the normal school at Valparaiso and took a short course there. On the completion of his studies he turned his attention to the cultivation of the soil, in which vocation he had been reared, and in which he continued to the time of his retirement, since which he has lived quietly, merely superintending operations on the home property This tract, a part of which lies beyond the line in Carroll county, has been brought to a high state of cultivation Its buildings are large and substantial and its improvements modern and valuable, and to the visitor there is at once given the impression of the presence of thrift, ability and industry Mr Delaplane had led an active and useful life, and the success which has rewarded his efforts is but the result of well-applied energy His business dealings have given him a widespread reputation for integrity and honorable methods and his public spirit has given him high place as a representative citizen

On March 24, 1886, Mr Delaplane was married to Miss Belle Borges. daughter of Ferdinand and Mary (Kerlin) Borges Her father, a native of Germany, was educated in that country, and emigrated in young manhood to the United States, subsequently serving in an Indiana cavalry regiment during the Civil war. After the close of that struggle he located in Logansport, and there for many years was engaged in the drug business. Mr. and Mrs. Delaplane have had a family of three children. William, a graduate of the agricultural department of Purdue University, Lafayette, who resides at home and assists his brother in conducting the home farm; Worth L., who is a graduate of the public schools of Young America, assisting his brother, and Robert, also at home, a student in the graded schools.

HOMER LYTLE, who has all his life been a resident of Boone township, and an occupant of the farm where he now resides, is one of the many prosperous and highly esteemed farming men in this community. He has lived a worthy representative of that fine old family which has been identified with this township since the year 1845, when his father, William Lytle, was born here, and which made for itself a good name and an enduring reputation in Cass county.

William Lytle, the father of Homer Lytle of this review, was born in Boone township, on May 4, 1845, and was the son of David and Mary (Burton) Lytle, the former of whom was born in Ohio, and became an early settler of Boone township in Cass county, where he lived until his death. He married into one of the oldest and most highly esteemed families of Boone township, from which Mary Burton, his wife, came, and they became the parents of four sons: George, John, Joseph, William. John Lytle is still living at this writing.

William Lytle married Amelia Dye on April 5, 1863. She was a daughter of Cornelius and Catherine (Copic) Dye, who came to Indiana from Ohio. Amelia (Dye) Lytle was born on March 17, 1850, and when she was seven years old her mother died, so that she was from that time on reared in the home of John F. and Rebecca Fultz. William and Amelia Lytle became the parents of ten children, of which number nine are yet living. Concerning them the following brief mention is made at this juncture: Edward is a resident of Royal Center; Florence is the wife of James Fuller; Anna married George Schlegenmitch; Stephen is a farmer in Tippecanoe county, Indiana; Effie married Warren Harvey, of Logansport, Indiana; Gertrude is the wife of W. P. Wray, of Logansport; Homer, the subject of this review; Fred is a resident of Anderson, Indiana; Gilbert, of Boone township, with his mother.

Mrs. Lytle is a member of the Evangelical church of Royal Center, and is active and prominent in the work of the various departments of that body with which she has long been identified in a praiseworthy manner. She is the owner of a fine farm of one hundred and forty-three acres of land in Boone township, upon which she is living at the present time, the same being operated by her sons, Homer and Gilbert.

Homer Lytle is a member of Royal Center Lodge No. 462, Knights of Pythias, and he is a stanch Democrat in his political adherence. Gilbert Lytle is a member of Royal Center Lodge No. 585, A. F. & A. M., and has served one year as senior deacon of the lodge. Both brothers are prominent and popular in the community which has long represented their home, and have the esteem and confidence of all who know them.

WILLIAM LYTLE

BRUCE E BUTZ Without any but the meagrest education, without business training, business influence or financial backing, Bruce E Butz has arisen above the material difficulties that beset the path of the young ventured into commercial and manufacturing waters and established himself safely and soundly upon the rock of success Today the lumber business he managed and helped establish in Walton, known as the Walton Lumber Company, is one of the prosperous and rapidly advancing young business concerns of the county, and its proprietor is part owner and manager of the establishment His career has not been without its ups and downs, but such has been the courage and integrity of the man that he has been able to reach his present place of security despite the difficulties he has encountered

Bruce E Butz was born on December 15, 1884, in Deer Creek township, Cass county, on the old Snider farm, near Young America He is the son of Charles H L and Jennie (Snider) Butz, the father a native of Allentown, Pennsylvania, and the mother of Deer Creek township, where she was born and reared, the daughter of pioneer parents of this section Charles H Butz came from his native state to Indiana in 1876 and here, after his marriage, engaged in agriculture and like pursuits They reared a family of five children, named as follows Harry W , Ora E , who is the manager of the Indiana Business College in Logansport, Kokomo and Marion, Indiana, Bruce E , of this brief review, Anne, the wife of Howard Bone, and Frank, who married Ressie Rife.

Bruce Butz as a boy in his native community attended school in District No 4 of Deer Creek township. He finished his education in District No 5, and then gave his entire attention to the work of the home farm until he reached the age of twenty years At that age he started working for the Galveston Lumber Company and as an employe of that concern he learned the lumber business in all its varied details In 1906 he came to Walton and took management of the Walton Lumber Company, of which he is the head and he has since conducted a successful lumber business in this place He is the only man in Walton who has a financial interest in the firm, the capital stock of the corporation being subscribed by outsiders

On Christmas day, 1907, Mr Butz married Audrey Murphy, a daughter of Charles and Maggie (Ault) Murphy, and they have two children Charles D and Creston B Butz

Mr Butz is a member of the Knights of Pythias and the Masonic fraternity, and his churchly relations are with the United Brethren at Galveston He is active in the work of the church and prominent in all its concerns as is also his wife Mr and Mrs Butz are highly esteemed in Galveston and enjoy the friendship of the best people of the community

JARED B RICE Cass county is admirably located for the successful prosecution of farming, for the soil is exceedingly fertile, the climatic conditions almost ideal, and transportation facilities unsurpassed However, although the agriculturist here has these advantages he cannot compete successfully with others unless he carries on his operations according to modern ideas and uses improved machinery in his work

That the majority of the farmers are progressive is proven by the number of finely developed farms to be found all over the county, a fact that has very materially raised the standard of excellence here and placed Cass among the leaders in agriculture in Indiana One of the men who has assisted in bringing about this desirable condition is Jared B Rice, of section 17, Clinton township, who, alone and unaided, has brought his present farm of eighty acres to a state of high cultivation, although when he first settled here, a quarter of a century ago, this land was entirely covered with heavy timber

Jared B Rice was born in Washington township, Carroll county, Indiana, July 30, 1862, and is a son of Solomon and Hannah A (Pittman) Rice, the former a native of Pennsylvania and the latter of Indiana Solomon Rice came to Indiana in young manhood, and settled in Carroll county, from whence he enlisted, in February, 1863, in Company K, One Hundred and Twenty-eighth Regiment, Indiana Volunteer Infantry, for service in the Civil war He had a long and honorable service, receiving his discharge in September, 1865, when he returned to agricultural pursuits, in which he was engaged until his retirement, and is now a resident of Logansport He and his wife had nine children, of whom eight are now living, William H , who is married and a resident of Logansport, Jared B , Martha A who is deceased, John C , married, rural carrier R F D No 33, Clymers, Emma, who is the wife of Harry Yost, of Logansport, George E , married, a farmer of Clinton ton township, Solomon, Jr , a resident of Clymers, Indiana , Anna, the wife of Hiram Isaacs of Clymers, and LeRoy E , who is carrying on operations on the old homestead place

Jared B Rice was reared on the homestead farm in Clinton township and attended the district schools until he was about seventeen years of age, at which time he began farming on his own account, although he continued to live under the parental roof In December, 1887, he was married to Miss Mary E Yeakley, who was born in Cass county, Indiana, and to this union there have been born two children Julia, born in March, 1889, a graduate of the Logansport Commercial College and now bookkeeper for H G Reed, at Clymers, Indiana, and Agnes, born September 18, 1893, a graduate of the Logansport high schools, who makes her home with her parents A pleasant, outspoken man, true to his word, and with the courage of his convictions, he has thoroughly established himself in the confidence of his neighbors and associates, and his title of "self-made man ' has been won by perfectly legitimate methods His farm of eighty acres is well cultivated, bears heavy crops and shows, in its prosperous appearance, the presence of able and thrifty management While the greater part of his time is given to general farming, he has also devoted considerable attention to the breeding of stock, and his pure Duroc hogs have attracted attention at a number of live stock fairs

WALTER A HOUSE Much of the wealth of Cass county lies in her splendid farming districts, represented by innumerable well-kept and bountifully productive estates that had their inception, insofar as present-day conditions extend, in the labor and initiative of those hardy pioneers who sought out this region many decades ago How well they wrought and how successful they were is a story that may only be touched upon in passing here but that they built up sturdy foundations on which their numerous progeny might rear the fair structure of prosperity is a fact that is obvious to all Today the prosperous and thriving farms conducted along both general and specific lines of agriculture, constitute a happy feature of Cass county, and the men who are carrying forward the work then begun are worthy successors of their worthy ancestors Walter A. House, owner and manager of the Plain View Stock Farm, is a striking example of men of this type

Born in Cass county, Indiana, on the 24th day of January, 1872, Walter A. House is the son of Simeon A and Elizabeth (Adams) House. The father was a native of Preble county, Ohio, whence he came to Indiana when he was a young man of twenty-five and settled in Jackson township Here he married a native daughter of Cass county Elizabeth Adams, as has been mentioned, and to them were born seven children, named as follows Jessie B, Walter A, Nola, Luther, Orba, Pear and Ernest

Walter A House attended the common schools of his native community as a boy and finished his education at Schyenne school, there receiving educational advantages somewhat better than those accorded to the average country youth of his district He was well trained in the work of the farm as a boy at home, it is needless to say, and up to the time when he was twenty-two years of age he remained on the home place as the principal assistant of his father In 1894 he married Nellie Eckley and established a home of his own She was a daughter of John and Amanda Eckley, and to them four children have been born Earl, Edna, Cressa and Alta

Plain View Stock Farm, comprising one hundred acres of the finest land in the county, came to Mr House through his own well applied energies and his success today represents the sturdy labors of his earlier years The place is located four miles due north of Galveston, and is one of the fine and showy places of the township

The House family are members of the United Brethren church, and Mr House further manifests interest in affairs of this nature by acting as superintendent of the Sunday school, in which he has done excellent work among the young of his community He has prospered specifically in his stock-farming, always keeping in view that the best is none too good, buying and raising pure bred stock whenever circumstances will permit, and he is freely regarded in the township as one of the most intelligent and successful stockmen in the community Not only as a source of profit but to maintain the fertility of the farm

HENRY N MILLER was born in Greene county, Ohio, March 30, 1842, and is a son of John E and Catherine (Minnick) Miller His father, a native of Franklin county, Pennsylvania, migrated to Ohio in young manhood, and later, in 1844 came to Cass county, Indiana, where he spent the remainder of his life in the cultivation of the soil He became one of the prominent agriculturists of his day and locality, was successful in his operations, wielded a wide influence among his fellow-townsmen in matters of general importance, and at his death left a wide circle of friends to mourn his loss He and his wife became the parents of ten children, of whom six still survive, as follows Elizabeth, who married a Mr Neff, Henry N, Eliza, who married a Mr Britton, Caroline, who married a Mr Toney Jane, who became the wife of a Mr Wilson, and Harriet, who married Dr Delzell

Henry N Miller grew to manhood in Deer Creek township, his education being secured by attendance during the winter terms in the old Miller school During the summer months he assisted his father in plowing, in clearing and in grubbing, and in the various other employments incidental to the planting and gathering of crops He was about twenty-one years of age at the time of his father's death, and at that time he took over the home farm and assumed the responsibility of caring for the family

In 1866 Mr Miller was married to Miss Alice Riggle, who died leaving five children, John, William Oscar, Belle who married a Mr De Haven, and Harry In 1886 Mr Miller was married again, when occurred his union with Josie E Baughman, daughter of Oliver E and Matilda (Nabors) Baughman, of Fairfield county, Ohio who migrated to Carroll county, Indiana and became prominent farming people Four children were born to this union, Leah, who married a Lybrook, Carl, who resides at home, and Ruth and Arthur, deceased

EDGAR C. CRIPE Among the younger generation of agriculturists of Cass county, one who has spent his entire life within its limits is Edgar C. Cripe, of Deer Creek township, who is ably managing operations on his father's farm of eighty acres Mr Cripe was born on this farm November 11 1889, and is a son of Jacob and Sarah (Smith) Cripe His father a native of Clinton county, Indiana, was only eighteen years of age when he came to Cass county, and here he has since resided, now being retired from active pursuits He has been closely identified with the agricultural interests of the county and has, as well, gained a position of confidence in the regard of his fellow citizens He and his wife have had five children Lyna, who married a Mr. Burroughs, Effie, who became the wife of a Mr Wolf, Eunice, who married a Mr Hoover; Frank and Edgar C

Edgar C Cripe was given good educational advantages, attending first the common schools of Deer Creek township, later the Young America high school, and finally the institution at Manchester, Indiana, where he passed one year During all of this period he was engaged in assisting his father in the work connected with the home farm, was reared to habits of industry and integrity, and thoroughly trained in the duties with which every good farmer should be conversant At the time of his marriage he took over the management of the home place, which he has since conducted for his father The excellence of his early training has been shown by the able manner in which he has carried on the business of the farm, his land yielding large and abundant crops and his cattle being sleek and healthy and bringing top-notch prices in the markets His entire attention has been devoted to his farm and his home, and he has found time for neither politics nor fraternal work Among his associates he is known as an industrious, enterprising young farmer, possessed of progressive ideas and the ability to carry them out He has many friends who have followed with gratified approval his rise in the agricultural world.

HISTORY OF CASS COUNTY

In 1908 Mr Cripe was united in marriage with Miss Nellie Turnpaugh, and they have had two children: Robert and Keith.

JOHN WISSINGER, whose connection with a combination of business enterprises has made him one of the leading and substantial men of Onward, Indiana, owes his success in life to hard work intelligently directed, to inherent ability of a versatile nature, and to a perseverance that has kept him steadily at whatever task he has found himself until it has been ended in successful accomplishment He has been farmer, sawmill operator, lumberman, cider manufacturer and threshing machine owner in turn, bringing to each venture an enthuisasm and progressive spirit that would admit of no defeat, and in the midst of these multitudinous activities has always found time to give to the promotion of his community's welfare Mr. Wissinger is a Hoosier by birth, having been born May 7, 1858, in Washington township, Miami county, and is a son of Isaac and Mary (Straup) Wissinger His father, a native of Ohio, grew up near the city of Dayton, from whence he came to Indiana in young manhood, settling in Miami county, where he continued to spend the remainder of his life on a farm which he had purchased in Washington township He and his wife became the parents of four children, as follows. William, John, Elizabeth, who married Mr Cripe, and Sarah, who married Mr Metzgar

John Wissinger grew to manhood on the old home place in Miami county, and there attended the country schools of Washington township, in the meantime being reared to agricultural pursuits and to habits of industry sobriety and honesty He continued to assist his father until he reached man's estate, at which time he began renting land, thus being able to accumulate enough means to purchase his first property, which he still owns On this land he earned the capital with which he bought his present valuable town property, and after some years spent in farming he entered the sawmill business, which he has built up to large proportions, his trade extending throughout the surrounding country Later, Mr Wissinger became the proprietor of a cider business, and at this time he is distributing the famous Wissinger cider to the wholesale trade throughout Indiana In addition to these enterprises, he has operated a threshing outfit for the past twenty-two years, traveling all over Cass county From the foregoing it may be seen that Mr Wissinger is a man of progressive spirit commendable industry and unflagging energy In his various and varied enterprises he has ever been known as a man of the highest integrity, and his transactions have always been of a strictly legitimate nature He has cared little for politics, and has never sought public preferment on his own account, although he has been a staunch supporter of good government and takes a pride in furthering the interests of his adopted locality

Mr Wissinger was united in marriage with Miss Sophia Tillett, daughter of Michael and Susanna (Smith) Tillett and to this union there have been born seven children, as follows. Susanna, who is married and has three children—Paul, Bernie and Margaret; Charles, who married Laura Rose, and has five children—Donald, Bady, Nancy, Lawrence and Lester, Millie, deceased. who was the wife of Harley Linderman, Pliny, the wife of L Kesling, who has one child—Walter,

Bessie, who married a Mr Bird, and has one child—Marie, and Lloyd and Sylvia, who are attending school. Mr and Mrs Wissinger are members of the Baptist church, in the work of which they have been commendably active

CHARLES D CARPENTER M D Probably there is no learned profession that demands so much of its members as that of medicine The conscientious physician of today has little rest, as when he is not ministering to the sick he must spend a great deal of time in study along the lines of his profession in order to keep in touch with the discoveries that are constantly being made The physician in general practice has to give more of himself in his work than those who confine themselves to specialties or to office consultation, as regardless of personal inclination he must fare forth at all times and in all degrees of weather to answer the calls of those dependent upon him Cass county knows of many of these self-sacrificing men, who regard their work as a sacred duty, and none enjoys a larger amount of good will in his community than Dr Charles D Carpenter, of Walton

Doctor Carpenter comes of a line of physicians. His grandfather, Eber Carpenter, M. D, was an old New England physician, and his father, Dr George H Carpenter, was also engaged in practice for many years The latter was born in 1820, at Alstead, Cheshire county, New Hampshire, and there received his common school education, reading medicine in the office of his father In 1842 he came to Athens, Ohio, the journey from Buffalo, New York, being made by stage coach, as the railroads had not yet extended their lines that far west During the Civil war he enlisted in the Ninety-first Regiment, Ohio Volunteer Infantry, of which he was for a time surgeon, but failing health caused his retirement from the service For some years he practiced in Boston and other large cities, but eventually was forced into permanent retirement Doctor Carpenter married Miss Mary Welch, daughter of Judge John Welch of Athens, Ohio Judge Welch at one time was chief justice of Ohio and was thirteen years on the Supreme bench and a member of Congress from the fifteenth district Two children were born to Dr and Mrs Carpenter Charles D, and Helen B., a graduate of the New York College who is now living in Seattle, Washington

Charles D Carpenter attended the common schools of Athens, Ohio following which he spent some time in Keene, New Hampshire, and on his return took his first course in medicine in Cleveland His medical studies were completed in the Ohio Medical College, from which he was graduated on March 1, 1872, and at that time he became his father's associate in practice In 1877 he became a member of the first board of the Columbus Hospital for the Insane but resigned from that position to return to private practice Doctor Carpenter has been an extensive traveler His first location was Marysville, Ohio, but several years later he went to Chicago and engaged in practice there Subsequently he moved to Belvidere, Boone county, Illinois, and later to Carthage, Missouri Since 1899 Doctor Carpenter has been in continuous practice at Walton, where he has secured a large and lucrative professional business Wherever he has been located he has gained universal esteem and has steadily won friends by his reliability and warm sympathy Unsolicited, he has received many testimonials to his skill and kindly interest in his patients He is a close student, an able physician, and a steady-handed surgeon The services of such a man are a valuable boon to any community and the people of Walton manifest their appreciation of the service rendered by Doctor Carpenter in choosing their community as the field of his labor

In 1882 Doctor Carpenter was married to Miss Rena Vlereborne, of Pickaway county, Ohio a member of an old and prominent family. Two children were born to this union Rosalie, who married C C Bumgarner, and Dorriss, a graduate of the Walton high school, who is now in her freshman year at the University of Indiana

Doctor Carpenter is fraternally connected with Lodge No 423, of the Masonic order, of which he has served as master, and Walton Lodge I. O O F, and Logansport Lodge No 66, B P O E For four years he was chairman of the pension board at Belvidere Illinois. He has identified himself with all movements that have made for progress and has done his share as a citizen in promoting good government

LEANDER MCFADDEN With supreme faith in the future of Walton, with the ability to profit by present conditions and with the desire to aid others to do so, Leander McFadden, proprietor of the Walton elevator, is one of his city's representative business men, and through precept and example has encouraged the advancement of good citizenship A self-made man, who appreciates the value and dignity of hard labor, in that it was the medium through which he attained independence and position, Mr McFadden has steadily forged upward, his activities being of benefit not only to himself but to his community as well Mr. McFadden was born in Ashland county, Ohio, and is a son of Alfred and Elizabeth (Richards) McFadden His father, a farmer by occupation, spent his early life in Wayne county, Ohio, but later made removal to Ashland county, where he established the McFadden home, and there spent the rest of his life in tilling the soil He was the father of five children, as follows Diana, who married a Mr Simmons, Franklin P and Oliver, living in Cass county, Leander, and Essie, who married a Mr Rickett.

Leander McFadden spent his boyhood much the same as other farmers' lads of his day and locality, pursuing his studies during the winter months and devoting his summers to assisting his father in the work of the home farm On reaching manhood, he began farming with his father on shares, and then for five years rented his father's farm of 115 acres At the end of this time he became interested in the lumber business at Twelve Mile, Cass county, in company with his brother, Franklin P. McFadden, an association that proved eminently satisfactory. For a number of years he was in business in Allen county, Indiana, and still retains a half interest therein For the past eight years Mr McFadden has devoted his attention to the grain business, and in 1910 came to Walton and purchased his present elevator Through the exercise of good judgment natural ability and constant industry, he has made a success of his numerous ventures, and is today justly considered one of his adopted city's reliable business citizens He has never taken more than a passing interest in matters of a political nature, preferring to confine his energies to the field of business rather than to the public arena Movements tending to advance the community or its

children, of whom six still survive, as follows Elizabeth, who married a Mr Neff, Henry N, Eliza, who married a Mr Britton, Caroline, who married a Mr Toney Jane, who became the wife of a Mr Wilson, and Harriet, who married Dr Delzell

Henry N Miller grew to manhood in Deer Creek township, his education being secured by attendance during the winter terms in the old Miller school During the summer months he assisted his father in plowing, in clearing and in grubbing, and in the various other employments incidental to the planting and gathering of crops He was about twenty-one years of age at the time of his father's death, and at that time he took over the home farm and assumed the responsibility of caring for the family

In 1866 Mr Miller was married to Miss Alice Riggle, who died leaving five children, John, William Oscar, Belle who married a Mr De Haven, and Harry In 1886 Mr Miller was married again, when occurred his union with Josie E Baughman, daughter of Oliver E and Matilda (Nabors) Baughman, of Fairfield county, Ohio who migrated to Carroll county, Indiana and became prominent farming people Four children were born to this union, Leah, who married a Lybrook, Carl, who resides at home, and Ruth and Arthur, deceased

EDGAR C. CRIPE Among the younger generation of agriculturists of Cass county, one who has spent his entire life within its limits is Edgar C. Cripe, of Deer Creek township, who is ably managing operations on his father's farm of eighty acres Mr Cripe was born on this farm November 11 1889, and is a son of Jacob and Sarah (Smith) Cripe His father a native of Clinton county, Indiana, was only eighteen years of age when he came to Cass county, and here he has since resided, now being retired from active pursuits He has been closely identified with the agricultural interests of the county and has, as well, gained a position of confidence in the regard of his fellow citizens He and his wife have had five children Lyna, who married a Mr. Burroughs, Effie, who became the wife of a Mr Wolf, Eunice, who married a Mr Hoover; Frank and Edgar C

Edgar C Cripe was given good educational advantages, attending first the common schools of Deer Creek township, later the Young America high school, and finally the institution at Manchester, Indiana, where he passed one year During all of this period he was engaged in assisting his father in the work connected with the home farm, was reared to habits of industry and integrity, and thoroughly trained in the duties with which every good farmer should be conversant At the time of his marriage he took over the management of the home place, which he has since conducted for his father The excellence of his early training has been shown by the able manner in which he has carried on the business of the farm, his land yielding large and abundant crops and his cattle being sleek and healthy and bringing top-notch prices in the markets His entire attention has been devoted to his farm and his home, and he has found time for neither politics nor fraternal work Among his associates he is known as an industrious, enterprising young farmer, possessed of progressive ideas and the ability to carry them out He has many friends who have followed with gratified approval his rise in the agricultural world.

HISTORY OF CASS COUNTY 1149

In 1908 Mr Cripe was united in marriage with Miss Nellie Turnpaugh, and they have had two children: Robert and Keith.

JOHN WISSINGER, whose connection with a combination of business enterprises has made him one of the leading and substantial men of Onward, Indiana, owes his success in life to hard work intelligently directed, to inherent ability of a versatile nature, and to a perseverance that has kept him steadily at whatever task he has found himself until it has been ended in successful accomplishment He has been farmer, sawmill operator, lumberman, cider manufacturer and threshing machine owner in turn, bringing to each venture an enthuisasm and progressive spirit that would admit of no defeat, and in the midst of these multitudinous activities has always found time to give to the promotion of his community's welfare Mr. Wissinger is a Hoosier by birth, having been born May 7, 1858, in Washington township, Miami county, and is a son of Isaac and Mary (Straup) Wissinger His father, a native of Ohio, grew up near the city of Dayton, from whence he came to Indiana in young manhood, settling in Miami county, where he continued to spend the remainder of his life on a farm which he had purchased in Washington township He and his wife became the parents of four children, as follows. William, John, Elizabeth, who married Mr Cripe, and Sarah, who married Mr Metzgar

John Wissinger grew to manhood on the old home place in Miami county, and there attended the country schools of Washington township, in the meantime being reared to agricultural pursuits and to habits of industry sobriety and honesty He continued to assist his father until he reached man's estate, at which time he began renting land, thus being able to accumulate enough means to purchase his first property, which he still owns On this land he earned the capital with which he bought his present valuable town property, and after some years spent in farming he entered the sawmill business, which he has built up to large proportions, his trade extending throughout the surrounding country Later, Mr Wissinger became the proprietor of a cider business, and at this time he is distributing the famous Wissinger cider to the wholesale trade throughout Indiana In addition to these enterprises, he has operated a threshing outfit for the past twenty-two years, traveling all over Cass county From the foregoing it may be seen that Mr Wissinger is a man of progressive spirit commendable industry and unflagging energy In his various and varied enterprises he has ever been known as a man of the highest integrity, and his transactions have always been of a strictly legitimate nature He has cared little for politics, and has never sought public preferment on his own account, although he has been a staunch supporter of good government and takes a pride in furthering the interests of his adopted locality

Mr Wissinger was united in marriage with Miss Sophia Tillett, daughter of Michael and Susanna (Smith) Tillett and to this union there have been born seven children, as follows. Susanna, who is married and has three children—Paul, Bernie and Margaret; Charles, who married Laura Rose, and has five children—Donald, Bady, Nancy, Lawrence and Lester, Millie, deceased, who was the wife of Harley Linderman, Pliny, the wife of L Kesling, who has one child—Walter,

people have always found him heartily in sympathy, however, and he is never too busy to lend his aid to enterprises of this nature

Mr McFadden was married in 1893, to Miss Estella Markel, daughter of Jacob Markel, and they have had five children, namely · Walter, Osa, Fleece, Lucille and Pearl, all of whom are attending school in Walton Fraternally Mr. McFadden has identified himself with the work of the Masons and the Independent Order of Odd Fellows, in which he numbers many warm friends With the members of his family, he is an attendant of the Methodist Episcopal church.

CHARLES STEWART ALBERTSON, M D It was Robert Louis Stevenson who made the assertion that when posterity came to study the present age it would find that its noblest figure was the doctor The physician's role, whether in city or country, in the sickroom, on the lonely road or the deserted street, calls for a high order of courage as well as high ideals of service to mankind Here is found the spirit which has made the advance of modern science resemble the advance of a new religion There has been the same devotion to an ideal, the same abandon of self, and the only reward held out has been the welfare of generations yet unborn It is for these reasons that the profession is held in such high esteem, that its devotees are ranked among the leading men of every community Among the medical men of Cass county who have reached high positions as practitioners, Charles Stewart Albertson, M D, of Walton, is known as a man who has responded to every duty imposed upon him by the ethics of his calling Although still a young man, his abilities have gained him a place in the confidence of the men of his vocation in his adopted locality, as well as of a wide and representative clientele Doctor Albertson was born in 1881, in Walton, Indiana, and is a son of E F Albertson, a minister of the Methodist Episcopal faith, belonging to the Eastern Conference He was sent to this section by his church, and for many years labored faithfully in the service of his Master

The oldest of a family of five children, Doctor Albertson early attended the public schools of Walton, but as his father's vocation called him to various points the family stakes were not driven in one place for very long. Following his removal from Walton, the doctor lived for different periods at Bunker Hill, Goshen, Ligonier and Columbia City, Indiana, Buffalo, New York, and Fort Wayne, Indiana, and in the latter place graduated from the high school At that time he took up his medical studies, entering Jefferson Medical College, Philadelphia, and later entered Indiana Medical College, at Indianapolis, from which institution he received his degree Succeeding this he entered upon the practice of surgery in Fort Wayne, as assistant to Dr McBeth, and after a short period he went to South Whitley, Indiana, where he continued in practice for five years In Walton his years of diligent study and critical and careful observation have borne fruit in the shape of recognition His knowledge of his profession is broad and comprehensive, and he is quick to grasp the principles of every advancement or innovation which comes to his notice For two years he has acted in the capacity of secretary of the Cass county board of health, where his abilities were made manifest in numerous ways Keeping full abreast of the times by his subscription to the leading medical journals, he also takes an interest in the work of the leading organizations of the profession, and is a valued member of the Cass County Medical Society the Indiana State Medical Society and the American Medical Association. He also holds membership in the Masons, the Knights of Pythias and the Modern Woodmen of America, in all of which he numbers many friends,

In November, 1907, Dr. Albertson was united in marriage with Miss Maud Robbins, of South Whitley, Indiana. They have had no children

J. E HEINMILLER. For a number of years Mr Heinmiller has been identified with the little town of Young America. He has the only undertaking establishment in this vicinity, and as a business man of fine principles and thorough ability, he enjoys a large patronage and the respect and esteem of his fellow citizens

Mr. Heinmiller was born in Ervin township, Howard county, Indiana, November 11, 1862 His parents were John and Susannah (Cupp) Heinmiller The father was born in Germany and came to America with his parents, his father being also named John, and from New York City moved to Pennsylvania where the grandfather was for many years a farmer John Heinmiller, the father, was a young man when he came west to Carroll county Indiana, and a few years later bought land and was actively engaged as a farmer there for many years There were seven children in the family of the parents, namely William, John D, George W, Moses, J E, Anna, deceased, Luther, deceased, and Rettie

J E Heinmiller during his boyhood lived on a farm in Howard county, and attended the common schools in that vicinity At the age of twenty-one he began his independent career, and with some help from his father was able to fit himself for the undertaking business He studied in the Barnes College of Embalming at Chicago, and on graduating from that institution came to Cass county and established himself in business in the little town of Young America

Mr Heinmiller was married in 1889 to Miss Lilly Williams, a daughter of John Williams One child was born to their marriage, but is now deceased Fraternally Mr Heinmiller is affiliated with the Knights of Pythias and the Masonic order, and belongs to the United Brethren church

FRANK HARNESS Many of the leading agriculturists of Cass county are specializing in the raising of cattle, finding that in this branch of agricultural work they were able to achieve a greater measure of success than if their energies were devoted to diversified farming. Frank Harness, one of the enterprising young farmers of Deer Creek township, who owns fifty-five acres of good land and oversees 400 acres belonging to the Harness estate, is engaged in raising Hereford cattle, and since his eighteenth year has been an acknowledged judge of livestock Mr Harness was born in Howard county, Indiana, just across the road from his present property, in 1881, and is a son of G W and Lucinda (Lowry) Harness

The education of Mr Harness was secured in the public schools of Cass county, whence he was brought as a lad, and during his entire school period was engaged in assisting his father on the homestead place. An energetic, ambitious youth, at the age of eighteen years he entered the cattle business, and the success which has rewarded his efforts is ample proof of his ability in his chosen line. His standard bred Hereford cattle have always brought top-notch prices in the markets and have made a creditable showing wherever exhibited. His entire time is devoted to his farm and his home, and he has found no leisure to engage in politics, his only interest in public matters being that taken by every good citizen. In business circles he is known as a shrewd competitor, but one who has never stooped to use other than legitimate methods, and as a result he has the confidence and esteem of his associates. He has shown some interest in Masonic work, and has numerous friends in the local lodge of this fraternal order, as he has in business and social circles.

In 1902 Mr. Harness was united in marriage with Dora Swafford, daughter of William and Jane (Hinkle) Swafford, and to this union there have been born two children: Herbert and George W.

BENJAMIN F. SHARTS. Cass county has no more honored family than that bearing the name of Sharts, members of which have been identified with the agricultural, commercial, financial and military history of this section for approximately sixty-five years. Among those who are entitled to consideration as worthy representatives of the name are Abiah J. and Benjamin F. Sharts, father and son, the former a Civil war veteran and highly respected farmer of Tipton township, and the latter president of the Fenton Investment Company. Both have identified themselves vitally with the best interests of Cass county, where they have been known as useful and public-spirited citizens.

The Sharts family originated in Hagerstown, Maryland, from whence George P. and Frances (Bear) Sharts removed to Preble county, Ohio, at an early day. Settling near Germantown, George P. Sharts erected a grist mill and carried on operations for several years, but in 1848 came to Cass county and settled on what is known as the N. B. Richeson farm, the family home during the first few years (or until it was replaced by a frame house) being a log cabin. There George P. Sharts died in 1853, at the age of fifty-two years, while his wife survived him until 1875, and was seventy-two years old at the time of her demise. They had a family of eleven children, namely: Mary M., Rose Ann, Elizabeth, Catherine, Abraham, John, Eliza J., George P., William O., Abiah J. and Caroline.

Abiah J. Sharts was born October 24, 1845, in Preble county, Ohio, and passed his boyhood days on the home farm in Cass county, whence the family had come when he was four years of age, and where he secured his education in a log cabin school. When he was but fifteen years of age he started out to make his own way in the world, and early took charge of the home farm, which he operated until 1879, at that time moving to his own farm which joins the other on the south. In June, 1863, he became a member of Company F, 116th Regiment, Indiana Volunteer Infantry, and was mustered into the service at Indianapolis, subsequently participating in a number of engagements during the Civil war, including Knoxville, although the greater part of his military service was passed in doing guard duty at Cumberland Gap, Greenville

Benjamin F. Sharts
President
Fenton Investment Co.

and Tazewell, Tennessee He received his honorable discharge at Lafayette, Indiana, in March, 1864, after a brave and faithful service, and once more returned to the duties of peace In 1867 he was married to Ellen Alice Wilson, daughter of Andrew Wilson, one of Cass county's old pioneers, and they have had six children, namely Harry, who is deceased, Benjamin F.; Elmer, Walter, who is deceased, Blanche and Charles Mr Sharts still lives on the old home farm on section 11, Tipton township, a tract of 154 acres of well-cultivated land Although advanced in years, he still is engaged actively in the work of tilling the soil, and also takes a keen interest in Republican politics. He is a member of the Odd Fellows and the Grand Army of the Republic, and attends the Seven-Mile United Brethren church, of which Mrs Sharts is a member

Benjamin F Sharts was born on the old home place, December 12, 1871, and was reared after the manner of the farmers' sons of his day, attending the district schools during the winter months and spending his summers on the home place During the fall of 1888 he went to Topeka, Kansas, where a relative was living, and while there attended the high school for three years, each year carrying off the honors of his class When he was twenty years old he returned to Indiana and began teaching at his old home school in Tipton township, where he remained one year, subsequently spending one year at the Boyer school, one mile east of Walton, and two years in the Woodling school in Washington township During the summer of 1895 he gave up the educator's profession to accept a position in the county treasurer's office One year later, in May, 1896, he entered the Logansport State Bank in the capacity of messenger and bookkeeper, and there his faithful discharge of his duties, his constant attention to business and his general native ability won him advancement to the position of teller In May, 1906, he became cashier of this institution, one of the most solid and substantial in northern Indiana, and he continued to hold the same office until recently During the early months of 1913 Mr. Sharts received a proposition to take over the management of their extensive mortgage, loan and investment business, fostered and created by the late C O Fenton (whose sketch appears elsewhere in this volume) After due consideration he accepted same and resigned his position as cashier of the Logansport State Bank, to take effect June 1, 1913 He is at present president and manager of Fenton Investment Company, 218 Fourth street. Mr. Sharts' rise has been rapid and continuous, but it has been deserved and no element of chance has had anything to do with his promotion Rather it has come through a steadfast determination to succeed, an ambition before which all obstacles have been swept aside.

On October 3, 1900, Mr Sharts was married to Miss Pearl McManus, and they have had two children Victor Benjamin and Robert Wilson. In politics Mr Sharts is a Republican He has been prominently connected with fraternal matters, being a member of Tipton Lodge No 33, F & A M, Logan Chapter, R A. M, Logan Council No 11, R & S M, and St John Commandery No 24, K. T., all of Logansport, and in 1907 served as eminent commander of the latter He also holds membership in the Cass County Historical Society, and is its present treasurer

EDWARD E MILLER. The success which Edward E Miller has attained is due to his enterprise, strong determination and business ability, and he is now classed with the representative farmers of Deer Creek township, where he owns and operates a farm of sixty-two acres Belonging to the modern school of agriculture, Mr Miller carries on his operations according to the most approved methods, thereby achieving enviable results, personally, that his life has been honorable and straightforward is shown by the fact that among his stanchest friends are many who have known him from boyhood Mr. Miller is a native of the Hoosier State, a son of Isaac and Sarah J (Ewing) Miller. His father, who was formerly a farmer of Fayette county, Indiana, migrated to Cass county in 1868, and here continued to carry on agricultural pursuits during the remainder of his life becoming a substantial farmer and well known citizen The mother of Edward E Miller was born and reared on the farm on which he is now operating, but as a young woman moved to Fayette county with her parents, and there met and married Isaac Miller, with whom she returned to Cass county She also is deceased She and her husband became the parents of two sons. Alvin, who died when he was ten years of age, and Edward E

The boyhood of Edward E Miller was filled with hard work, as being the only son left to his parents, he was relied upon as his father's assistant in the work of the farm Clearing, grubbing, plowing, planting, harvesting, and the thousand and one other duties that fall to the farmer's lot, all had a place in the youth of our subject It is not to be supposed that he had much time for his studies, but they were not neglected, and being an ambitious and enterprising youth, and quick to learn, he made the most of his opportunities and gained as good an education as many who had far better chances His first schoolroom was in the old Hubler school in Deer Creek township, but he completed his studies in Young America, following which he turned his whole attention to his farm work On attaining his majority, he embarked upon a career of his own, and so faithfully has he labored that his sixty-two-acre tract is now one of the most valuable of its size in the township A friend of progress along all lines, Mr Miller has introduced modern methods, ideas and machinery into his work and his well-tilled fields yield him a golden harvest for the work expended upon them, while the fine condition of his stock shows what may be accomplished along that line by the man of ability, industry and perseverance He has had no reason to regret, his choice of callings, for in addition to having won material success, he has also gained and retained the esteem and respect of his fellow citizens and the warm regard of a wide circle of personal friends

In 1896 Mr. Miller was united in marriage with Miss Nellie Beamer, daughter of John and Margaret (Bell) Beamer, the former a retired merchant of Walton They have no children Mr Miller has been prominent in fraternal matters as a member of Young America Lodge No 346, in which he has passed all the chairs He holds the office of past chancellor of Knights of Pythias, and has represented his lodge in the Grand Lodge of the state, at Indianapolis

ORMUS L HARRINGTON As a professioanl photographer Mr Harrington has a reputation not only through Cass county, but is one of the ablest men in his work in the state of Indiana In the photographic competition he won the state honors in 1906, 1907 and 1908, and won the state honors in Illinois in 1912

Ormus L Harrington was born July 2, 1868, in East Alburgh, Vermont, and is of an old American family. His parents were Hardy Warner and Anne Stuart (Thompson) Harrington His father was a native of Alburgh Springs, Vermont, and the mother of South Hero, Vermont The father is now living retired in Wilmette, Illinois

Mr. Harrington received his early education at Burlington, Vermont, and has lived in Cass county, since 1889, his home since that date having been in Logansport He learned his business as a photographer at Albany, New York, and his studio in Logansport has for many years been recognized as the place where could be obtained the most artistic and satisfying work in Logansport and Cass county.

At Butler, Indiana, August 11, 1892, Mr Harrington married Mae Robinson, a daughter of John James and Louie Elizabeth (Callaway) Robinson, well known farming people of Cass county Mrs Harrington is a member of the Christian church of Logansport. Fraternally Mr Harrington affiliates with the Masonic order, being a Knight Templar, and also with the Knights of Pythias, the Benevolent and Protective Order of Elks, and the Independent Order of Foresters

T. EDWARD MINNICK A brother of the present county treasurer of Cass county and one of the leading farmers of Tipton township, Edward Minnick is a life long resident of Cass county, and belongs to that substantial and honored family which has been resident here since the close of the Civil war

Mr Minnick's grandfather was Conrad Moench, according to the German spelling of the name, and was born in Hesse-Cassel, Germany, whence he came to the United States during young manhood and settled in Pennsylvania. It was in Pennsylvania that Elias Minnick, the father of Edward, was born in 1843 Educated in Pennsylvania and acquiring the trade of a blacksmith he was nineteen years of age when the Civil war came on, and he enlisted in Company K of the Ninth Indiana Infantry, his enlistment having been made at La Porte, Indiana He went through the war as a member of the eastern army, and subsequently of the Army of the Cumberland, and fought at Corinth, Iuka, Murfreesboro and Pittsburg Landing, at the battle of Chickamagua where he was captured and for several months incarcerated at Andersonville, and finally released from this Confederate prison to receive his honorable discharge from the army After the war Elias Minnick settled in Tipton township of Cass county, and the remainder of his life was devoted to the quiet pursuits of agriculture He was a Democrat in politics, but never entered public life, and he held no desire for an official position. For many years he was one of the popular members of the Grand Army of the Republic, and his church was the Christian, in which faith he died on April 14, 1892 His widow still survives and makes her home at Walton Before her marriage she was Miss Elizabeth A Lindesmith.

A son of Elias and Elizabeth Minnick, Edward Minnick was born on the farm where he now resides, and which had been the homestead of his father, on the eighteenth day of July, 1869. He attended the local schools and was reared in this neighborhood, where after the period of boyhood he took up the sterner responsibilities of life as a farmer. His present estate consists of about eight acres of land, and is located some ten miles southeast of Logansport. His friends and associates have known him from boyhood, and in this one community he has led a life of quiet prosperity and substantial wealth, entitled to the high esteem of all who know him.

Mr Minnick married Miss Effie Wingrave on February 28, 1894, a daughter of Frederick and Mary (Staggs) Wingrave. They are the parents of two children. Lyle Edward and Maude Merrill. The former is a member of the high school class of 1914 and the latter, who was graduated with the class of 1913, has taken up the advanced study of music. Mrs Minnick was born in Cass county on October 30, 1873, and there was educated, fitting herself for the vocation of a school teacher and winning her teacher's certificate, although she never applied herself to the work. The family attend the Methodist church.

MARCUS M MORROW. Among the farmers of Cass county whose intelligent treatment of the soil has added materially to the agricultural prestige of this section stands M M Morrow, the owner of an eighty-acre farm in Adams township. Belonging to the new school of farming men, who have proven that modern methods and machinery and scientific measures obtain far better results than the old hit-or-miss style, he is gaining a full measure of success from his labors, and as a citizen he is known as one who has the welfare of his community closely at heart. Mr Morrow is a native son of Cass county, and was born on a farm in Bethlehem township, on January 18, 1874, a son of Abner and Marguerite (Teel) Morrow.

Abner Morrow was likewise born in Indiana, and during the Civil war he enlisted in an Indiana regiment of volunteers, fighting bravely through the war in the defense of the Union. At the close of the war he again took up his vocation of agriculturist, and he was so engaged during the remainder of his active career. He was one of the highly respected citizens of his community, and one who took an abiding interest in the success and activities of the Republican party all his days. He was a faithful member and a liberal supporter of the Baptist church. His wife passed away in 1904.

M M Morrow received his education in the public schools of Bethlehem township, and was reared to agricultural pursuits and taught in his home the benefits to be derived from a life of industry and integrity. On attaining his majority, he secured eighty acres of land from his father in Adams township, purchasing a part of the tract and this he has continued to cultivate up to the present time, his success being in every way commensurate with the extent of his labors. He has placed thereon all of its many improvements with the exception of the residence, and he has a comfortable home, fitted with modern conveniences, and located on Hoover rural free delivery route No 20. Mr. Morrow has never entered the political arena as an aspirant for public office, but displayed his public spirit on various occasions when he has stanchly supported movements for the advancement of good government in his community He was affiliated with the Republican party until the campaign of 1912 when he cast his lot in with the newly organized Progressive party. He is a consistent member of the Baptist church, where both he and his wife have numerous friends

On November 4, 1894, Mr. Morrow was married to Miss Jennie Fisher, and they have since made their home on the pretty homestead place which is theirs, and which as familiarly known as 'Old Reliable Stock Farm''

WILLIAM HENRY HARRISON TUCKER This venerable man, now in the seventy-eighth year of his age, who with firm step and unclouded mind still walks the streets and attends to his daily routine of affairs, has, during his long and useful life in Cass county, witnessed almost its entire development and borne a share in the starting course of its progress Although he is now retired from active business, and lives quietly on his neatly-cultivated tract of twenty-one acres, located just off the Logansport and Marion pike, about four miles southeast of Logansport, he still manifests a keen and intelligent interest in all that affects the welfare of his native county, and is widely and favorably known as a man of progress and public spirit William Henry Harrison Tucker was born November 9, 1835, in Clay township Cass county, Indiana, and is a son of James and Charlotte (Pursell) Tucker. His father, a native of Virginia, moved to Ohio in young manhood, and from that state came to Cass county in 1829, here spending the remainder of his life in agricultural pursuits He and his wife had seven children, namely John P, Harvey, Eleanor, Mary, Benjamin, Moses and William Henry Harrison The last named is the only member of this family now living

William H H Tucker passed his boyhood and youth as was customary with farmers' sons of his day and locality, dividing his time between attendance at the district schools in the short winter terms, while assisting his father in clearing, grubbing and general farm work in the summer months When he was but twenty-one years of age the management of the estate of his father devolved upon him, but so thorough had been his training and of such a high character was his ambition and ability that he was able to uninterruptedly continue the work that had been started by his father. As the years passed, he added to his acreage and made numerous improvements on the property, developing one of the handsome farms of his section, but when advancing years came on he was ready to turn over the heavy duties of management to younger hands and to retire to the peaceful quietude of his comfortable home. Mr Tucker was known as an excellent farmer and good judge of stock, and was uniformly successful in all of his ventures

On October 6, 1859, Mr Tucker was married to Mary E Grimes, who was born September 21, 1843, near Liberty, Union county, Indiana, daughter of George W. and Mary (Snyder) Grimes George W Grimes was born and educated in Tennessee, near Greenville, and shortly after his marriage came to Union county, Indiana. In 1856 he came to Cass county, and here spent the rest of his life in agricultural pursuits

Mr and Mrs Grimes were the parents of ten children: William and Sarah J, who are deceased, Nancy A, widow of Peter Bird, who has three children—Monroe, George A and Mary Ellmore, John W and Mrs Elizabeth Martin, both deceased, Mary E, who married Mr Tucker, George R, deceased. James P, a resident of Crawfordsville, Indiana, Mrs Eliza J Evans, of Linden, Indiana, and Thomas B., of LaFayette Indiana. Six children have been born to Mr. and Mrs. Tucker, as follows: Mary C, who married David Lichty, both being deceased, Nettie S, deceased, who was the wife of Joseph Whinnery, and had one child—Naomi S, now the wife of George Vanstenburg, Sherman L, who married Anna Fidler and has two children—LeRoy and Mabel, the Rev James G, a Methodist Episcopal minister, who married Ota Corlis, and has one child—John C, William Albert, who married Estella Bellman, and has two children—Verna Mae and Albert B, and Ernest, who married Amy Snell, who died without issue

Mr Tucker was for many years active in Republican politics and was frequently elected to public offices of trust and responsibility, large majorities giving evidence of his widespread popularity. In 1912 he cast his fortunes with the young Progressive party, the policies and candidates of which have since received his support. With his family, he attends the United Brethren church.

M H HUFFMAN As the efficient and successful manager of the Stutesman farm, one of the fine places of the county, lying in section 27 and section 28 of Tipton township, M H Huffman carries on the responsible duties of a farmer, and is one of the best known men thus occupied in Cass county. Like many another successful and prosperous man, he began his business career with a period of school teaching, but for the past fifteen years he has been identified with the rural industry and interests of Cass county, and while the county lost a capable and conscientious educator it gained one of its most able agricultural men instead. A man of the highest integrity his record in all departments of life has been an honorable one and in every way well up to standard. Men of his stamp have ever constituted much of the bone and sinew of the country, and wherever found will be accorded the esteem which they so well deserve.

M H Huffman was born on July 26, 1874, in Hamilton county, Indiana and is the son of A J and Martha (Boyer) Huffman. The father was formerly a resident of Madison county, Indiana, and his occupation during his active career was that of farming. He never resided in Cass county, but ended his days in Hamilton county. He was a Union soldier in the Civil war, seeing much service throughout, and making a valiant record first in the Indiana Infantry, the Thirty-ninth and later in the Eight Indiana Cavalry. His service continued throughout the war, and he arose to the rank of lieutenant in his cavalry troop, winning distinction for valor in the field on a number of occasions. The five children of the family who are now living are as follows: Linnie, Albert, John, M H, and Dollie

Mr Huffman attended the common schools of his native community, after which he took a preparatory course at Mount Morris, Illinois, becoming well equipped for the duties of a teacher in that place. His

career in the educational field continued for three years, one year of that time finding him employed in Cass county, but he abandoned the vocation wherein he had already made a successful record and turned his attention to farming

In 1897 he was united in marriage with Miss Carrie Stutesman, a daughter of Albertus and Mary Jane (Peterbaugh) Stutesman, and six children have been born of their union· Leland B , Esther J., Lawrence, Ralph, Russell and John Paul Mr Huffman and his family are communicants and supporters of the Church of the Brethren at Pipe Creek, and are prominent in other circles in their community.

GEORGE STRECKER, who died in Logansport, Indiana, on September 16, 1902, was a native of Wittenburg, Germany, born there on March 22, 1840 As a boy in Germany he attended the German Lutheran Parochial schools, and there also learned the trade of a baker He was sixteen years old when he emigrated to America even at that early age being impressed with the ideas that he would here find better opportunities for material advancement than would be his in the Fatherland He had an uncle living in Crawfordsville, Indiana, and that circumstance caused him to make Indiana his objective point when he arrived in New York For six years he made Crawfordsville his home, there working at his trade and becoming acquainted with business methods in America, and in 1862 he returned to Germany, returning to the United States at the end of a year This time he located in Jackson, Michigan, and for two years he worked at his trade in that city In 1865 he came to Logansport, Indiana working here for Mr Coulson for one year

During all these years of work he had saved carefully from his weekly stipend, and when he was about twenty-six or twenty-seven he concluded that he had saved sufficient to warrant him in establishing a home of his own In his boyhood home he had been reared in the neighborhood which also held the family of Wilhelm Schue, and in this family was a comely daughter, Rosina, who had been the sweetheart of the boy before he left home In 1866 she came to America and on October 16th of that year she met and married George Strecker at Buffalo, New York They came at once to Logansport, and in November 1866, they bought a bakery shop at No 324 Fourth street The building at that time was not more than a dilapidated old store building, and Mr. Strecker tore down the old structure, rearing a new one in its place, for doing which he received eight years' rent free from the owner of the property. Above the shop Mr and Mrs Strecker made their home In December, 1868, he sold out his interest and in the spring of 1869 bought a bakery at Fourth street and Broadway, and there they conducted a thriving business for two years He then sold again and bought the property at Fourth and Market streets, on which he erected a fine new building, which stands today as originally reared by him Here for a period of eight years Mr Strecker conducted a bakery, after which he sold the shop, but retained the ownership of the building, and with his wife and children returned to Germany, with the possible thought of making that their future home The call of America proved too strong for them however, and at the end of a year and a half the family returned to Logansport, and once more resumed the bakery business at the old place at Fourth and Market streets Later Mr Strecker built another store at Twelfth and Spear streets, where they conducted a splendid business for seventeen years, the family occupying an apartment over the shop

In 1895 Mr Strecker established his sons in business and retired from active participation in the work himself, but he continued, however to take a keen interest in business, and when he felt so inclined would enter into the work with all the vim and energy of his early days His residence in Logansport was continuous with the single exception of a three year period which the family spent in Andrews, Indiana, where they were engaged in the hotel business, this break occurring in the early part of their residence at Twelfth and Spear streets

The splendid success which Mr Strecker achieved in his business is especially worthy of commendation, and is a fit example for the youth of America, many of whom accomplish less with greater advantages and facilities at hand in early youth than Mr Strecker possessed A boy of sixteen in a strange land, unable to speak the language and without a penny at his command, he made rapid strides in the business field, and when he died at the age of sixty-two he was possessed of considerable wealth and a thriving business, which his sons are carrying on at the present time Energy, determination and a characteristic German thriftiness all entered into the making of his splendid prosperity, and he was known to be one of the shrewdest investors to be found in the community While he had the reputation of being what is called a "close figurer" in business dealings, yet he was known to be kind and charitable at heart, and no worthy cause ever lacked his support His chiefest characteristics were honesty, industry and unostentatious charity He was a German Lutheran in his religion and a Republican with regard to his political faith He died on September 16, 1902

Mr and Mrs Strecker had seven children, as follows Henry, who died in infancy, George, now in business in Logansport, Rose, now Mrs Edward Battenberg, of Bloomington Illinois; Charles, whose home is in Logansport Amelia, married to William Schroeder, and who died January 6, 1909; Kathrin and Daisy. Mrs Strecker, the widowed mother, still lives in Logansport, and enjoys the friendship of a large circle of the best people of the city She is a German Lutheran and a member of that church

GEORGE STRECKER, JR, was born in Logansport, Indiana, on November 12, 1868, and was here reared and educated in the public schools He is the son of George and Rosina (Schue) Strecker, both native born Germans, of whom more extended mention is made in another sketch dedicated to the late George Strecker, to be found in other pages of this historical and biographical work Further detail with regard to the parentage and ancestry of the subject are therefore not deemed requisite in this connection, and the account is carried forward with a direct relation of his life thus far in a brief and concise manner.

When he had completed the curriculum of the public schools of Logansport, George Strecker, Jr, attended Hall's Business College for a term He subsequently learned the baker's trade with his father, and when that worthy gentleman retired, the son succeeded him in the old established business. In the course of time Mr Strecker sold out and re-established himself in business on various occasions, until in the year 1894, when he permanently located in business at No. 8 Front street Here he opened a bake shop with one oven, and while the capacity of the shop was small, by judicious management of the shop, and carrying on both a wholesale and retail business, his trade reached a point in 1895 that made necessary the securing of more spacious quarters Then he located at No 508 Broadway, operating one oven to September, 1902, when he moved to No 520-22 Broadway, built by his father and there his retail establishment has since been located In order to successfully meet the constant increase in his trade, a large brick bakery was built at the corner of Canal and McKeen streets, 90x 165 feet This plant operates three ovens and has seven wagons in constant use, supplying not only Logansport, but the surrounding towns for miles around Twenty-five hands are required in the operation of the bakery in all its departments, and it is recognized as one of the stable industries of the city

Mr Strecker is a prominent member of various fraternal orders in Logansport, among them the Knights of Pythias and the Benevolent and Protective Order of Elks He is an adherent of the new Progressive, or Bull Moose faction, in politics, and takes an active part in the political activities of the city.

On November 26, 1896, Mr Strecker was united in marriage with Leona Hoffman, the daughter of George Hoffman, of Logansport, and three children have been born to them, Harry Strecker, deceased, Paul Strecker and George Strecker III

MERRITT W BURLEY Probably there is no better known family within the limits of Cass county than that of Burley, whose members have been identified with the agricultural interests of this section for more than eighty-five years, as well as with other matters which have added to the importance of the community A worthy representative of this name is found in Merritt W Burley, of section 27, Jefferson township, who has contributed his share to the material welfare of the county and is widely known as able farmer and stock raiser Mr. Burley was born December 8, 1860, in Burley's Hollow, Cass county, Indiana, and is a son of Joseph A and Hattie (Burkett) Burley

John Burley, the great-grandfather of Merritt W. Burley, was a resident of Virginia, where he followed the occupation of a boatman on the Ohio and Shenandoah rivers, near to Harpers Ferry, and while in pursuit of his vocation he met his death by accidental drowning near the Ferry. He married Margaret Harper, who was sole heir to Harper's Ferry, and they became the parents of three sons, one of them being Thornton Burley, the grandfather of Merritt W Burley Margaret (Harper) Burley was thrice married Her second husband was named Simes and her third husband was of the name of Downs.

Thornton Burley was very young when he was apprenticed or bound out to a harness maker in Ohio, and there he learned the harness making trade He was young when he married Polly Connors in that state, and in 1827 they came to Indiana, locating in what is known to this day as Burley's Hollow, where Mr Burley continued to reside until his death, which took place at the remarkable age of ninety-eight He was the father of seven children by his first marriage. Edgar, Thornton, Joseph A, William, Marshall, Mary and Jane A Burley His second wife was Nancy Rohen, and she bore him one child, Ella Burley.

Joesph A Burley was born in Ohio, and he was two years old when he was brought to Cass county by his family Here he grew to manhood, was twice married, and made his home for twenty-five or thirty years, when he moved to White county and lived there until the death of his second wife, at which time he returned to Cass county and here spent the remainder of his life. He was the father of one child by his first wife, who was Hattie Burkett, and that child was Merritt W Burley of this review. His second wife was Emma Swinehart and to them six children were born, as follows: Charles E, Harry, Joseph S., Harvey C, Jennie and Eben W. Burley

Merritt W. Burley was a small child when taken to Logansport and there he secured the advantages offered by the public and high schools Succeeding this, he took a course in Hull's Business College, from which he was graduated in bookkeeping and for some years thereafter was connected with various establishments in that capacity About twenty years ago, however, Mr Burley returned to the soil and has since met with marked success in his farming and stock raising operations

His well developed land, situated on section 27, has been made valuable by the introduction of numerous improvements, including a modern home, a substantial barn, and other attractive outbuildings Modern methods have always found favor in his eyes He employs the latest machinery and finds that his high-powered automobile is adapted not only to pleasure trips, but is also a great help in his business His fair and honorable dealings have won him many friendships, and the esteem and confidence in which he is held everywhere is ample evidence of his integrity

On March 21, 1892, Mr Burley was united in marriage with Miss Iva Binney, a daughter of Levi Binney, a well known citizen of Cass county. They have no children. Until the campaign of 1912 Mr Burley supported Republican candidates and principles, but at that time transferred his allegiance to the new Progressive party

GEORGE G HUBLER One of the old and honored families of Cass county is that of Hubler, which for many years has been identified with the agricultural interests of Deer Creek township. Among the representatives of the younger generation of this name, one who is worthily maintaining the family reputation for industry and progress is George G Hubler, who is managing his father's farm of 120 acres, located on the Pound stone road, not far from Young America Mr. Hubler's success as an agriculturist may be accredited to his energy and industrious habits, and to the fact that he is thoroughly conversant with conditions in this locality, having been a resident of the township all of his life He was born on this farm, June 19, 1880 and is a son of William and Nellie (Risher) Hubler His father, a native of Pennsylvania, left the Keystone State as a young man and migrated to Cass county, where he is now living a somewhat retired life. He has been successful in his business operations and is accounted one of the substantial men of his community Mr Hubler was married in Cass county to Nellie Risher, a native of Ohio, and they have been the parents of eight children. of whom four survive, namely Charles O , Mrs Cora Frier, George C and Mrs Ethel McClosky

George C Hubler began his training as an agriculturist as soon as he was able to do his share of the homestead chores, and was thoroughly acquainted with all the duties of the farmer by his father He continued to work during his school period, his education being secured in Young America, and when he had completed his studies gave all of his attention to the home place On attaining his majority, the management of the farm was turned over to him, and he has justified the confidence reposed in his ability by bringing the land to a high state of cultivation, making numerous improvements, and achieving a full measure of success along all lines of agricultural work He carries on general farming and stock raising, doing some dairying and raising diversified crops He brings to his work a thorough and practical knowledge of the needs of the soil, and relies upon modern scientific methods rather than upon the hit-or-miss style of former days Sober and industrious, he has gained a wide friendship among his fellow-citizens, and everywhere is known as one in whom the agricultural interests of the community have an excellent representative

On March 12, 1907, Mr Hubler was united in marriage with Miss Grace Ulerich, daughter of John B and Sarah (Keever) Ulerich, who came from Lancaster county, Ohio, to Cass county at an early day Mr and Mrs Ulerich had seven children, namely Joseph, George, Edward, Grace, Andrew, Mary and Amanda The union of Mr and Mrs Hubler has been blessed by the birth of three interesting children. William, Ruth and Edward Mr Hubler is a popular member of the Independent Order of Odd Fellows, of the Knights of Pythias and of the local lodge of the Masonic fraternity With his wife he attends the United Brethren church They have many friends in social circles of Young America, and their comfortable home is a center of refinement and hospitality

ARTHUR S BOYER The contracting and building business in Cass county has found in Arthur S Boyer one of its most successful adherents and operators, and for the past ten years he has been identified with that field of activity in a most striking manner His operations have long since extended beyond the confines of Cass county, and he employs an average force of twenty men in carrying forward the work of his contracts He is one of the substantial business men of Logansport and the county, and it is such as he who have been most effective in the development of this section of the state to its present splendid condition Born in the town of Walton, Cass county, Indiana, on March 19, 1875, Arthur S Boyer is one of the three children born to George W. and Mary E (Masters) Boyer.

Concerning the parentage of the subject, it may be said here that George W Boyer is one of the oldest native born citizens of Cass county, Indiana, his birth having occurred at Walton on January 12, 1848 He is the son of Peter Boyer, a native of the state of Virginia, who came to Cass county in 1840, and here followed farming for the remainder of his life. In 1847 that worthy gentleman married Mary Small, who was a native product of Ohio and came with her parents to this county in 1842 Four sons and three daughters were born to Peter and Mary Boyer, and of that number but three are living today George W Boyer was one of these, and he passed his youth and early manhood with his parents During those years he received the educational benefits conferred by the early schools of that time He learned the carpenter's trade, and has, for the most part, followed that work ever since To his marriage with Mary E Masters, daughter of James W and Martha J Masters, solemnized on March 20, 1873, three children have been born Arthur S, the subject of this brief review, born March 19, 1875; Annie R, now Mrs Shaver, of Walton, Indiana, born on December 6, 1879, and Lanford P, born July 12, 1882, a carpenter at Logansport

Mr Boyer is a Methodist in his religious belief, a Prohibitionist in politics, and socially is a member of the A F & A. M.

Arthur S Boyer was reared in Tipton township, and there received his early education in the district schools He began to learn the carpenter's trade when he was sixteen years old under the able instruction of his father, and continued with him for two years, when the family moved to Logansport There Mr Boyer finished learning his trade with the Thompson Lumber Company and in 1902 established himself in business as a carpenter contractor Mr Boyer has since continued successfully in the business, which he has conducted on an increasing scale, and today his operations extend far beyond the limitations of Cass county He employs a force of some twenty men and his annual business aggregates some $40,000

On March 20, 1895, Mr Boyer was united in marriage with Sarah E Congdon, of Logansport, and they have one son, Clarence A Boyer Mr and Mrs Boyer are members of the Wheatland Avenue Methodist Episcopal church, and he is fraternally affiliated with the Independent Order of Odd Fellows and the Masons He was twice senior warden, three times worthy master and seven years secretary of Tipton Lodge No 33, A F. & A. M, and has long enjoyed the confidence and esteem of a large circle of friends and acquaintances in and about Logansport, where he is known for one of the sound and reliable business men of the city and a citizen of distinctive order and merit

HON MARCUS W COLLETT who served four years as a distinguished member of the Indiana state senate, and is president of the Farmers and Merchants State Bank of Logansport, may justly be numbered with the representative men of Cass county For a number of years agricultural industries claimed a large part of his attention and business enterprises were financed and carried on through his well-applied energy, his whole life having been one of activity and of both public and private usefulness and accomplishment Largely it has been a peaceful one but his courage and patriotism were tested before his boyhood was over, and warfare and danger surrounded him during the closing years of the Civil war, in which he proudly wore a uniform of Union blue and did it credit. Mr Collett was born in Miami county, Indiana, February 6 1847, one of the four children (of whom three are still living) of William and Susanna (Color) Collett. The mother died in 1855, and the father afterwards married Mary Brower, by whom he became the parent of four children, all of whom are living. William Collett passed away in 1881, and was followed to the grave by his widow in 1912. He was a farmer by vocation, an occupation which he followed throughout life, was a Republican in his political views, and a German Baptist, or "Dunkard," by religion. He started life with no means, but by hard and industrious labor, constant thrift and well directed energy, accumulated a fair competency.

Marcus W Collett passed his youthful days on the home farm in Miami county, attending the district schools of that locality. He was but seventeen years of age when he enlisted, November 1, 1864, in the First Indiana Light Artillery, Capt Lawrence Jacoby commanding, his command being in the Sixteenth Army Corps. This organization participated in the bombardment of old Spanish Fort, in Mobile Bay, and was with General Banks on the Red river expedition. Mr Collett served bravely and faithfully, and after receiving his honorable discharge, at Indianapolis, August 22, 1865, returned to Miami county and at once began farming on his own account on his father's farm, receiving as his share one-third of all the produce he raised. He was thus engaged for three years, but on February 25, 1869, was married to Sarah A Stroud, and following this he began farming on eighty acres of land in Miami county. Two years later he moved to the town of Mexico, in Miami county, and embarked in the hardware business at which he continued about eight years, and in 1881 removed to Cass county, locating on 320 acres of land in Bethlehem township which he had purchased some time previously. Here, with the exception of the years 1895 and 1896, when he was living in Logansport, he farmed and raised stock until 1902, at which time he sold out and moved to Logansport, which city has since been his home. Mr Collett is a Republican in politics, and has always taken an active interest in the councils of his party. While living in Bethlehem township, he served four years as township trustee. In 1894 he was the nominee of his party for state senator, and was elected in the following fall. He served one full term of four years and introduced two bills which became laws. For many years he was identified as a stockholder in the Farmers and Marchants State Bank of Logansport. He early became a director in the same and in 1910 was elected its president, a position he has since occupied. He is also a stockholder in the banks at Twelve Mile, Walton, Royal Centre and Galveston, and in all of these institutions figured actively in their organization. Mr Collett is a director at the present time in the Twelve Mile bank. He has been a member of the state board of trustees of the Indiana State Soldiers Home at LaFayette for the past four years and was reappointed February 25th, 1913, by Governor Balston for four years more. His fraternal connections are with the Masons and the Elks, and he is also a valued comrade of the Grand Army of the Republic

DAVID FLORY, a native of Dayton, Ohio, came to Cass county, Indiana, in 1841, and for a time thereafter made his home with his brother, Emanuel Flory, who had preceded him hither and was then living in Clay township. He was born on November 23, 1820, and was thus twenty-one years old when he came to Cass county. It is assumed that the Flory family is one of French ancestry, their advent into this country having been in colonial days, and members of the family participated in the War of Independence. He received but a meager education in his youth, and the death of his parents when he was still young, caused him to be reared by relatives. In the year following his arrival in Cass county, on July 17, 1842, he married Hester Richason, and started work at the trade of a cooper soon after, at a place now known as Adamsboro. Hester Richason Flory bore him two children, William, who became a physician, and is now deceased, and Henry, a blacksmith now living retired at Minneapolis, Minnesota. The wife and mother died when her youngest born was five days old and on February 11, 1849, Mr Flory married Sarah Heffley. Soon after his second marriage he moved to a farm in Miami township, a place comprising one hundred and sixty-five acres of practically unimproved land. He built a double log cabin, which he later replaced with a more modern and commodious building, and there he made his home during the remainder of his life. He worked at his trade at intervals, and gave a portion of his time to the clearing and improving of his place, and eventually a fine farm resulted from his efforts.

Mr Flory was a member of the Dunkard church, now known as the Brethren, his membership covering a period of seventy years. Although he had but slight educational advantages in his youth, he was a great reader and in this way became unusually well informed for one of his time. During his later years he gave considerable attention to fruit growing, and he was the originator of the famous winter banana-apple. He and his second wife reared a family of six sons and three daughters, as follows: Francis, now living at Geneva, Nebraska; James, a resident of McPherson, Kansas; David M, of whom extended mention is made in an article following this; Charles A., Aaron Edward, both of Cass county; Mary, the wife of Dr J C Waite, is now deceased; Margaret, Isabelle, and Florence the two latter being now deceased. Mr Flory died on December 14 1910, and was preceded by his wife on October 5, 1909

DAVID M FLORY is a native son of Cass county, born on the home farm on November 10, 1861, and is the son of David and Sarah (Heffley) Flory. Of David Flory a detailed account will be found preceding this article, so that further mention of the family and ancestry of the subject is not called for at this point.

A common school education was all that David M Flory received, and he remained on the home farm until he was eighteen years old, when he started out on his own responsibility. He engaged in farming at first, but for the past twenty years the best part of his time has been

"THE MAPLES," RESIDENCE OF MR. AND MRS. WILLIAM MURDEN

devoted to horticulture For nearly fifteen years of that time he has also been engaged in handling fencing red cedar posts windmills and a patent heater of his own invention He is the owner of a farm of eighty-seven and a half acres in Cass county, but for the past two years he has made his home in Logansport

Mr Flory is a Democrat and a member of the Brethren church formerly known as the Dunkards, in which faith he was reared by his parents

On February 28, 1885, he married Margaret Kelly, daughter of Nelson Kelly, of Cass county, and to them have been born five children, as follows Schuyler M , Harry Byron, who died at the age of fifteen months, Jasper R , Orville M , and Ursula M

WILLIAM MURDEN The man who buys land today in Cass county has no conception of the obstacles which confronted the pioneers who began developing this property Now fertile fields yield banner crops the ground once covered with mighty forest trees smiles beneath modern cultivation, and where worthless swamps gathered green slime and sent forth pestilential fevers the rich soil eagerly responds to the hand of the farmer All this was not attained without endless hard work through all seasons When summer's crops did not require attention, fences were in need of building or repairing, new buildings were to be erected and numerous other improvements were constantly requiring the farmer's labors No man who has brought success out of his years of endeavor ever attained it unless he was ready and willing to make any kind of a sacrifice of inclination and strength to bring it about One of the men who has been the architect of his own fortunes and has brought his present handsome farm from a state of wilderness to one of high cultivation is William Murden, of Adams township, farmer, public-spirited citizen and veteran of the Civil war Mr Murden was born in Miami county, Indiana, May 25, 1841, and is a son of Imri and Rebecca (Woolpert) Murden, the former of whom died in 1900 and the latter in 1904

Mr Murden attended the schools of Miami county, and was reared on the farm of his father, whom he remembers telling of the Indians with whom he played in boyhood when the family first moved to that county. Reared to agricultural pursuits, Mr Murden was so engaged at the outbreak of the Civil war, and, with other youths of his vicinity, he hastened to offer his services to his country, enlisting in the One Hundred and Thirty-fourth Regiment, Indiana Volunteer Infantry With this organization he served his full term of four months, and would have re-enlisted but was compelled to remain at home on account of the ill health of his father at that time In 1871 Mr Murden first came to Cass county, settling in a log house near Hoover in Adams township, but subsequently removed to Miami for a short period, and then again came to Adams township and located on his present tract This farm was covered with heavy timber, and the only improvements which had been made were several small log buildings which were nearly worthless With determination and industry, Mr Murden at once set to work to clear his land, a task that took many years in the completing, but which he finally accomplished As the years passed, and his finances permitted, he erected modern buildings for the shelter of his stock and the housing of his grain and implements, and a comfortable residence was also built. The land is highly cultivated, and the farm now embraces 137 acres of some of the most valuable soil in Adams township. Mr. Murden is an able agriculturist, farming his land along scientific lines and taking advantage of all the aids which have been brought about by invention and discovery. He is a Republican in his political views, but has not aspired to public office, being content to devote himself to the cultivation of his land. With his family, he attends the Methodist church, and is known as a man of high business ideals and probity of character.

While still a resident of Miami county, Mr. Murden was married December 27, 1864, to Miss Sarah Jane Willson, daughter of Joseph R. Willson. Three sons have been born to this union: Mahlon, born June 13, 1866; Joseph R., born July 13, 1873, and Truman G., born November 10, 1879. Mahlon married Florence Sylvana Funk, daughter of Joseph G. Funk, and they have had four children. Harry F., born June 10, 1890. Iva Louise and Ida Grace, twins, born October 31, 1891, the latter of whom died in 1892; and Jennie E., born July 10, 1897. Joseph R. is a resident of Cass county. He wedded Myrtie Irene Woodhouse, and has four children—Marion M., Lyman R., Mabel Fern and Ralph Orion. Truman G. Murden married Edith Irene Barnhart, daughter of George Barnhart, and they have one son, Homer Clare, born October 19, 1903. Mrs. Murden is a native of Miami county, Indiana, born August 17, 1846, and reared and educated in her home county. Both her parents are deceased. The present estate of Mr. and Mrs. Murden is called "The Maples."

ALBERT H. DOUGLASS. It is in connection with the cause of education that Albert H. Douglass is entitled to a leading place among the men whose services have made them benefactors of Cass county. Entering upon his career as an educator when still a lad, in 1891 he was appointed superintendent of public schools of Logansport, and has continued to faithfully give his time, his thought and his work to the cause which enlisted the earliest sympathies of his boyhood and the matured interest of his later life. Few men have given better service to their city, none are more widely or favorably known. Mr. Douglass was born on the family farm in Clay township, Cass county, Indiana, April 23, 1858, the only child of Joseph and Harriet (Pugh) Douglass. His father, who was an agriculturist all of his life, died in 1891, having been twice married, his first wife being a Miss Keith by whom he had five children, of whom three are living. The second Mrs. Douglass survived her husband ten years.

Like many youths of his day and locality, Albert H. Douglass divided his boyhood between the farm and the school room, attending the district institutions during the winter terms and assisting his father to till the soil during the summer months. Of an ambitious and industrious nature, he applied himself closely to his studies, and at the age of seventeen years, in 1875, graduated from the Logansport high school. At this time he entered upon the career in which he has won such high honors. His first term as a school teacher was taught in

Rock county, Wisconsin, in a country school, and for the seven terms that followed he had charge of country schools in Cass county, Indiana Succeeding this, he was advanced to the principalship of the Walton (Indiana) schools, and then spent two years as principal of the McKinley school in Logansport and one year as principal of the Franklin school During the next three years he was principal of the Logansport high school, and in 1891 became superintendent of the schools of Logansport, a position he has dignified to the present time Mr. Douglass possesses in high degree that very desirable ability of being able to impart his own deep knowledge to others, without which no educator is ever really successful During his administration numerous innovations have been made that have considerably raised the standard of excellence in the Logansport institutions, and modern methods and ideas have served to place the system here on a high plane He has made himself a general favorite with pupils and teachers alike, who not only respect and esteem him for his many scholarly attainments, but have been drawn to him because of the manner in which he has been able to advise and assist them in various ways His career has been one worthy of emulation by those entering upon an educational life and illustrates forcibly the high honors to be gained through constant practice of industry and probity

Mr Douglass was married May 10, 1881, to Miss Elizabeth Barnett, and they have had three children, namely Bessie S , who is now deceased, Nina M , now Mrs C A Ballard, of Logansport, and Albert E

JAMES G GISH An excellent farm of 120 acres, in Deer Creek township pays tribute to the care and labor of James G. Gish, who has been one of his locality's leading representatives of agricultural interests for some years Numbered among those who have aided their community while aiding themselves, whatever success he has achieved is attributable entirely to his own efforts and his life of industry has been followed by a goodly share of prosperity Essentially a farmer he has not cared for other interests than those which center around his property and his home, content to gain a reputation in the peaceful pursuits of the soil, free from the strife of politics and the busy mart of trade and commerce Mr Gish is a native of the Hoosier State, and was born July 7, 1860, in Carroll county, a son of Henry and Elizabeth (Garst) Gish The family was founded in Cass county by Mr Gish's father, who had come from Virginia to Carroll county, with the grandfather of James G Gish, Abraham Gish and his wife Abraham Gish entered land from the United States government at an early day, and the remainder of his life was spent in Carroll county, where both he and his wife died Following in the footsteps of his parent, Henry Gish early became a tiller of the soil, and for years was prominent in agricultural circles of Carroll county, and there both parents died They had a family of five children, as follows Hester, who is now deceased, Catherine; Jeremiah, who is deceased; Mary, and James G

James G Gish received his early education in the old Blue schoolhouse in Carroll county, and after coming to Cass county continued to attend the district schools during the winter months, while helping his father in the summers He was reared to habits of industry and integrity and taught to work hard and realize the value of money, and by the time he had reached his majority he was thoroughly trained in all branches of farm work. He early learned to make a study of soil and climatic conditions, and a knowledge of crop rotation was also included in his curriculum. On coming to manhood, he began operations on his own account on 80 acres of land which he purchased, from which he cleared the incumbrance by faithful and persistent labor, well applied along well-defined lines. He has continued to add to the improvements and buildings on his property, and has met with a full measure of success both in general farming and stock raising being now accounted one of Deer Creek's substantial men. He has every modern improvement for the cultivation of the soil, his buildings are large and substantial, and everything about the property gives evidence of his skill and good management. Mr Gish has always labored faithfully in behalf of his community and its people, and holds a high place in the esteem of those with whom he has been brought into contact.

Mr Gish was married to Miss Emma Wills, and to them there have been born two children: Bruce, who married Maud Kay, and has four children—Ruth, Owen, Gertrude and Grace, and Grace, who became the wife of Harry Miller, and has one child, Wilbur. With his wife and children, Mr Gish attends the United Brethren church, of which he is a liberal supporter.

STEPHEN B BOYER A more notable illustration of the exercise of American energy, ability, integrity and superior skill would be hard to find than that exhibited by the firm of Obenchain & Boyer, which controls one of the leading enterprises of Logansport, and which has achieved a wide-spread reputation and by its able management, and steady development, has secured at Logansport the undoubted supremacy as regards the manufacture of a superior grade of chemical fire engines and automatic boiler cleaners One of the proprietors of this concern, Stephen B Boyer belongs to that class of men who have risen to prominence through the exercise of native ability, and not through outside assistance or influence. A veteran of the Civil war he came to Logansport, at the close of that struggle, poor in purse but rich in ambition and ideas and in the years that have followed has not only gained a position of signal prominence in the commercial world, but has contributed materially to the welfare of his adopted city, both as a manufacturer and as the incumbent of important office. Mr Boyer was born at New Bloomfield, Perry county, Pennsylvania, December 7, 1842, and is a son of William D and Mariah (Fritz) Boyer His parents, natives of Germany, and on the paternal side with an admixture of French, had nine children, of whom one son and one daughter still survive Stephen Boyer, the paternal grandfather, was a minister of the Presbyterian church at Little York, Pennsylvania William D. Boyer was a soldier, and fought through the Indian wars, in Florida

Before he had reached the age of twelve years, Stephen B Boyer had learned to set type in the office with his father, foreman of the *Perry County Freeman*, a Whig newspaper, and thus added to the few years of education he had secured in the New Bloomfield schools In 1854 the death of his father broke up the family and Stephen B Boyer went to his uncle's farm in the same county, and with the exception of one or two terms while here, this completed his scholastic training. When about fifteen years of age he began driving a mule team on the Pennsylvania Canal, after which he accepted a position as a clerk in a grocery store at Duncannon, on the Pennsylvania Railway, fifteen miles from Harrisburg He was thus employed at the outbreak of the Civil war, and, fired with the patriotism of youth and with the ideas that had been instilled in him while he was working in the office with his father, he enlisted, November 10, 1861, in the Ninth Pennsylvania Cavalry, Company A, which rendezvoused at Harrisburg This regiment was assigned to the Army of the Cumberland, and went into camp on the farm of Jesse D Bright, in Indiana, this gentleman having been previously expelled from the United States senate for treasonable utterances The command was ordered to Munfordville, Kentucky, on the Green river, and subsequently marched to Nashville, Tennessee, in the meantime being employed to a considerable extent in scouting After spending a short time in camp at Springfield, the regiment fell back at the invasion of Bragg, and was in camp at Crab Orchard when the battle of Richmond, Kentucky, was fought On that same day they were ordered to Richmond, but arrived after the retreat of the Federal forces, and became their rear guard as far as Louisville Upon the reorganization, in 1862, with Gen Buell in command, the army moved against Bragg and contested the battle of Perryville, the cavalry then following Bragg's retreat entirely out of Kentucky By a special request of the Kentucky Legislature, the Ninth Pennsylvania Cavalry was asked to remain in Kentucky and there they continued throughout the balance of the year, 1862, doing cavalry and scout work The battle of Stone river approaching, the Ninth Cavalry was consolidated with other commands and sent to destroy bridges on the railroad near Knoxville, to prevent reinforcements being thrown to Bragg's relief, and this mission was successfully completed, being known officially as Carter's Raid Returning, after twenty-seven days, to camp at Nicholasville, Kentucky, the regiment then went to Nashville, and on to Franklin, where they occupied the extreme right of Rosecrans' army, taking part in the campaigns of middle Tennessee, Chattanooga, the Giant campaigns around Chattanooga to Knoxville and with Sherman to Atlanta and to the sea and through the Carolinas to the end of the war

Returning to the occupations of peace, Mr Boyer taught school in Pennsylvania for a short time, and in the spring of 1865 entered a commercial school in Philadelphia, where he found himself at the close of the Civil war Believing that the west was the place for young men having nothing but the desire to do, Mr Boyer came in June, 1865, to Logansport, Indiana, and this city has been his home ever since He first took a position as bookkeeper with C B Knowlton and continued as bookkeeper and superintendent for Knowlton & Dykeman and Knowlton & Dolan up to 1882. In 1881, in connection with John S Obenchain, he erected the Logan Flouring Mills, which they operated some twenty years This mill was destroyed by fire in 1901 and the business was closed out About 1888 the firm of Obenchain & Boyer was organized, for the manufacture of an automatic boiler cleaner and in 1898 they commenced the manufacture of chemical fire engines this business and the mill being operated at the same time. In January, 1902, a new building was erected on the site of the burned mill, and the business was continued with the exception of the flouring mill. Since the death of Mr Obencham, in 1909, Mr. Boyer has continued the business as surviving partner This enterprise has a large trade all over Indiana and the surrounding states, and under Mr. Boyer's management is constantly adding to its prestige. Not only in business life has Mr Boyer left the impress of his influence upon that city, but also in public life, and during the sixteen years he served as a member of the city council and three years which he was police commissioner, he displayed the highest executive ability During his service in the common council many measures of a public interest were secured Among these was the building of the Electric Light Plant This plant was erected by a special committee of which Mr Boyer was chairman and the plant was enlarged and extended under his management as chairman of the electric light committee This plant is a financial success The Wabash and Erie Canal running through the city was purchased and Erie avenue built which is now one of the great thoroughfares of the city The natural gas situation was fought out and settled in favor of the city and the Interurban policy of the city was settled after passing through a situation bordering on civil war Mr Boyer has been a Republican in his political views but joined the progressive movement of 1912 He is a valued member of the Grand Army of the Republic, and with his wife attends the First Presbyterian church of which he has been elder for years

On September 12, 1872, Mr Boyer was married to Miss Josephine Goodwin, and they have three children Alexander B, Mary J, and Helen T

HOWARD H YORK, chief engineer of the Northern Indiana Hospital for the Insane, at Logansport, has been connected with this institution for many years, and during his long and honorable residence in the city has firmly established himself as one of its representative citizens. Mr York is a native of the Hoosier state, having been born in Hendricks county, June 11, 1849, a son of Aquilla and Rebecca M (Barker) York His father, a native of Alamance county, North Carolina, was born March 4, 1818, and came to Indiana in 1834, locating in Hendricks county, where he spent the remainder of his life in farming, and passed away in September, 1876 He was married in Hendricks county to Miss Rebecca M Barker, also a native of North Carolina, who died in 1866, and they became the parents of nine children, of whom six are now living John M, of Indianapolis, Indiana, Charles, a resident of California, Austin, living in Washington; Ellen, a resident of Indianapolis; Nettie, of Pekin, Illinois, and Howard H

Howard H York was educated in the public schools of Hendricks county, following which he entered Asbury University (now DePauw), receiving excellent advantages for his day and locality He secured a teacher's license, which, however, he never made use of, as his time was devoted to the work of the home farm until he reached the age of twenty-three years At that time he left the parental roof and came to Indianapolis, and during the next ten years acted in the capacity of fireman and assistant engineer in the Central Indiana Hospital for the Insane, then becoming chief engineer of the Northern Indiana Hospital for Insane. He has continued to be connected with this institution to the present time, during which he has been in the active discharge of his duties with the exception of ten months, when he was superintendent of the construction of the Hospital for the Insane at Evansville, Indiana He has made his home in Logansport since 1888, has made many friends, and is known as a man who regards the discharge of his duties as a sacred trust He and his wife are popular members of the Order of the Eastern Star, and Mr York is also well known in Masonry, having attained to the R and S M degree In political matters, his inclinations have led him to support the principles and candidates of the Democratic party, to which the members of both his and his wife s families have always given their aid These families have been well represented in military life, Mr York having seven uncles who served as soldiers during the Civil war, while Mrs York's stepfather and one brother also participated in that struggle

On November 8, 1882, Mr York was married to Miss Mary J Dent, who was born in Knightstown, Indiana, April 8, 1847, and educated in the common schools there To this union there has been born one son: George D, born August 27, 1886, in Indianapolis, Indiana. He was educated in the public schools of Logansport, and after his graduation from the high school became connected with the Northern Indiana Hospital for the Insane, where he is now acting in the capacity of assistant engineer

DeWitt Doran In the life of DeWitt Doran, of Adams township, there is presented a lesson for the youth of any land, something to be found in it of a nature encouraging to the young aspirant who, without friends or fortunes, is struggling to overcome obstacles in his efforts to acquire a comfortable competence, if not absolute wealth Some twenty-seven years ago, Mr Doran came to Adams township with a capital of fifty dollars in money, poor but ambitious, unknown but determined Today he is the proprietor of the noted Old Virginia Stock Farm, a tract of 300 acres, and is known throughout his part of Cass county Probably no better example of what may be accomplished through a life of industry, perseverance and strict integrity could be found, and a brief review of the height by which he has risen to his present position will no doubt prove interesting to those who are admirers of self-made manhood

Mr. Doran is a native of the Old Dominion state, and was born January 22, 1864, a son of Liza Ann Doran His parents were in humble circumstances and he was only able to attend school several months out of each year, as his services were needed in assisting in the support of the family, but he was an alert, intelligent and ambitious lad, and made good use of his opportunities, gaining thereby a good rudimentary education Moreover, he was reared to habits of industry, economy and thrift, and thoroughly trained in all the details of farm work When he first came to Cass county, in November, 1886, his cash capital was represented by the sum of fifty dollars but his stock of ambition, energy and determination was beyond estimation His limited pecuniary circumstances forced him to rent the poorest farm on the Taber Seven Sections, but his success on this property soon attracted the attention of Mr Taber, the owner, who subsequently rented him the best property he had, and there he continued to carry on operations for sixteen years. His success was commensurate with his faithful labor, and in 1902 he was able to purchase his present property, a finely-cultivated tract of 300 acres, which he named the Old Virginia Stock Farm, in honor of his birth state. He has cleared this land, has erected substantial buildings, and now devotes the greater part of his attention to the raising of thoroughbred stock, for which he finds a ready and lucrative market. From earliest boyhood, his life has been one of continuous and well-directed industry, and his success is all the more satisfactory in that it has been self-gained, without outside assistance. Mr Doran has been too busily occupied with his private affairs to engage in political matters and when he votes he recognizes no party lines, believing in voting for the man whom he deems best fitted for the office rather than the organization which he represents. With his family, he is a consistent member of Hoover Methodist Episcopal church.

In 1884, Mr Doran was united in marriage with Miss Frances Purdue, the estimable daughter of Daniel Purdue and they have had ten children, namely Mark, Ora, James, Myrtle, Bertha, Minnie Belle, Arlo Hugh, Katie and Wayne. The children have all been given good educational advantages and have been reared to fit any position in life which they may be called upon to occupy.

WILLIAM M SMITH has been a resident of Logansport for the past thirty years, and in that time has seen many changes in and about the city. He was born on August 23, 1849, in a log cabin near Kewanee, in Pulaski county, Indiana, and is the son of David and Elizabeth (Mitchell) Smith.

David Smith was a native of Southern Indiana, and a farmer and blacksmith by trade. When a young man in the early forties, he came to what is now Pulaski county, and there built a log cabin, after which he returned to his old home, married his youthful sweetheart, Elizabeth Mitchell, native of Kentucky and brought her with him to the cabin in Pulaski county. Here he worked with a will at his trade when he could spare the time from his regualr farm work and under the most adverse conditions succeeded in clearing up his farm. He and his wife passed through all the hardships and privations incident to pioneer life in those early days,—conditions which the present generation can have but the faintest conception of. They became the parents of seven children,—two only of the number now are living. The life of Mr Smith was a quiet and uneventful one, barring the happenings incident to the formative period of the county, and he died on April 18, 1880, his widow surviving him until 1896.

William M Smith was the oldest of his parents' children and much of the hard work in the carrying on of the regular farm work early fell upon his shoulders. He attended the country school in the winter seasons, and remained in the home until he had passed his twenty-first birthday. He rented land in Pulaski county which he farmed inde-

pendently until the fall of 1880 when he came to Logansport He secured work in a stave factory at which he continued for a time, but later went into the teaming business, still later engaging in the feed business Subsequent to his experience in that respect he once more took up teaming, and for a considerable time after that was in the employ of various grocery concerns in the city In August, 1902, he bought a lease and the building which stands on his present property, and at once opened up a general coal and fuel business In 1911 he built his present building, and it is needless to add he has prospered most agreeably in the business He has added cement to his stock, and cement blocks, in which he is now extensively and profitably engaged in manufacturing He handles more than one hundred and fifty car loads of coal annually and about four thousand barrels of cement, and the business is on the steady advance

Mr Smith is a Republican, a member of the Order of Ben Hur, and of the Methodist Episcopal church He was married on March 16, 1871, to Miss Margaret E Woods, of Cass county and they are the parents of three children Hugh, a druggist of Logansport, Jesse, who died in infancy, and Asa E, in the drug and jewelry business with his brother in Logansport

ZUINGLESS U LOOP, M D Industry and intellect have never been incompatible There is more wisdom, and will be more benefit, in combining them than scholars like to believe or than the ordinary people of the world imagine Life has time enough for both, and its happiness will be increased by the union To this combination add these other important qualities—enterprise and energy business tact and public-spirit—and the sum total is the make-up of that class of men in which Dr Zuingless Loop of Galveston, stands in prominent relief Dr Loop has long been a leading factor in the life of Galveston He is known as one of the prominent physicians of his part of the county, has wide and varied interests in the business world, is the owner of a valuable farming property, and in public and social affairs holds recognized prestige He was born July 9, 1851, in the village of Deer Creek, Carroll county Indiana, about twelve miles from Galveston, and is a son of James C and Sarah (Wertz) Loop His father, a native of Clearmont county Ohio, was educated in the common schools, read medicine and subsequently became a country physician, following his profession in conjunction with farming operations on his property in Deer Creek township, near the Abraham Smith farm He and his wife had five children namely William M, deceased, who married Laura Hyman, and had two children, Luna and Wade and Luna married Frank Brown, auditor of Carroll county, Zuingless, Kate Charles C; and Pearl The mother of these children still survives and although now in her eighty-fourth year, is hale and hearty and in full possession of her faculties

Zuingless Loop received his early education in the public schools of Jackson township, and was reared in Galveston where he worked until he was nineteen years of age He read medicine with his brother, Dr W M Loop, who was at that time practicing in Deer Creek, Carroll county, Indiana He entered a drug store in Galveston and by economy managed to save enough money to enter college. He entered Louisville (Ky.) Medical College, where he received his degree of Doctor of Medicine in 1882. He at once located at Galveston, where he has since been engaged in practice with the exception of the time he spent in taking post-graduate courses at Chicago and New York. In 1875 Dr. Loop entered the drug business and has been continuously engaged in the business up to April, 1912, and at the same time he was practicing medicine. He has built up a large and representative practice, which covers Galveston and the contiguous territory. is widely known in his profession as a man of the highest ability, and has the full confidence of his patients. He belongs to the Cass County and Indiana State Medical Societies and the American Medical Association, in the work of which he takes great interest, and keeps himself thoroughly abreast of the advances and discoveries of his profession by subscription to the leading medical periodicals of the day. His fraternal connections are with the Knights of Pythias, in which he has passed all the chairs, and the Independent Order of Odd Fellows. With his family, he attends the Methodist Episcopal church. Dr. Loop has various financial, business and realty interests, and is the owner of a valuable eighty-acre farm, located on the county line in Jackson township, to which he devotes a good deal of his attention. He is president of the First State Bank of Galveston organized June 7, 1913 and was a member of the county council of Cass county for three years.

In September, 1875, Dr. Loop was married first to Mary E. Atchley, who died a short time thereafter without issue. In 1882 he formed his second union with Miss Laura Darragh Wilson. She died in 1900, leaving three children. Clarence, who married Pearl Cook, Glen R., who is employed at Kokomo, Indiana, but makes his home with his parents, and Florence died in infancy. Dr. Loop married for his third wife Miss Ella Metcalf. He has been loyal and active in his support of all measures that have promised to benefit his community, and for a period served as town treasurer.

Dr. Milton B. Stewart has been a practicing physician at Logansport for the past sixteen years, and has taken front rank among the members of his profession in Cass county. He was born March 14, 1873, at Virgil, Kansas and his youth was passed in attending the schools where his father a pastor of the Methodist Episcopal church, happened to be stationed. When six years old the father was transferred to the North Indiana conference, and while living at Columbia City, he was graduated from the high school. In 1890 when but sixteen years old he began teaching in the public schools with the ultimate object of making that his permanent work in life. Through the influence of Dr. Barnhill, of South Whitely, he was induced to alter his plans and take up the study of medicine. He matriculated at the Cleveland Medical College, Cleveland, Ohio, from which he was graduated with the spring class of 1897. He at once located in Logansport which has ever since been his home, and where his skill as a practitioner is evidenced by a large and increasing patronage.

Dr. Stewart was married on April 24, 1901, to Miss Alice H. Larimer. He is a member of the Methodist church and one of the greatest pleasures he has is his association with this body, with which he became connected at the age of nine years, since when he has endeavored at all times to live the life of a Christian gentleman. His citizenship is of a high order, his unostentatious benefactions being freely bestowed where, in his judgment, the most good will follow. Dr. Stewart is a member of the Masonic order, the Knights of Pythias, the Independent Order of Odd Fellows, the Loyal Order of Moose, the I. O. R. M., and other fraternal and benevolent organizations of a similar nature.

JOHN E. SUTTON. In preparing such a historical and biographical work as this publication is intended to be, it is as essential that specific mention be made of those who have been identified with the best interests of a given community and have finished their earthly labors as of those who are yet active in their chosen spheres of labor. It is therefore consistent with the spirit of this work that somewhat extended place be given to the life of the late John E. Sutton who for eleven years gave the best that was in him to the publication of a wholesome, honest and capable newspaper in the city of Logansport. In his capacity as proprietor and business manager of the *Daily and Weekly Reporter*, one of the most efficient journals that Cass county has ever known, he made a lasting imprint upon the minds of his readers and upon the entire county in effect, and his influence is yet alive in the community which knows him no more. He was born on October 21, 1863, and died on the 6th of January, 1900.

John E. Sutton, who claimed Fulton county, Indiana, as his native place, was the son of Andrew J. and Barbara (Horn) Sutton. The father was born in Fayette county, Ohio, and the mother in Washington county, Pennsylvania. For some years they were residents of Logansport, but their residence in Cass county covered a much longer period. Andrew Sutton was a son of Ferdinand and Mary (Shellenberger) Sutton, natives of West Virginia and Pennsylvania and were of Scotch and German ancestry. Andrew Sutton was young in years when he accompanied his parents to Clark county, Ohio, and there he received his education which was complete enough to permit him to engage in teaching at the age of nineteen. His pedagogic work found him employed in the counties of Miami, Cass and Fulton, in Indiana, having taken up a residence in this state in 1844. For twenty winters he gave himself to educational work, and he was known to be one of the most successful teachers of his day, his services always being in demand from season to season.

In 1870 Mr. Sutton gave up his teaching activities and turned his attention to the business of merchandise in Logansport, to which he added operations in real estate. He was a man who gave considerable attention to the duties of public life, and served in varied capacities in the years of his residence here. In 1882 he was elected a member of the Board of Commissioners of Cass county serving a three year term in a most capable and efficient manner. In the latter nineties Mr. Sutton, then well advanced in years, retired from active business in a large measure. He was for many years an active member of the Methodist church, and he was a life-long Democrat. He married Barbara Horn in May, 1850, and five children came to them. It is to their son, John E., that this sketch is dedicated.

In Fulton county, Indiana, John E. Sutton was reared in the wise and loving care of his devoted parents. His father gave to the boy especial attention in an educational way, and he grew to manhood well fortified in his studies, which had, since he was six years old, been pursued in the city of Logansport. He was graduated from the high school of this city in 1882, and then gave some little attention to school-teaching in which work his father had for many years previous been occupied, but he soon changed his activities to other fields. Journalism attracted him strangely and he entered the office of the *Logansport Pharos* where he served for three years as city editor of that paper. He was ambitious, and, discontented with such experience as he might gain in that position, he gave up his work in Logansport and went west, finding employment readily with any of the metropolitan dailies he chanced upon from Indianapolis to San Francisco. In Los Angeles he became the publisher of the *Real Estate Reporter*, a paper, which though short lived, had a most prosperous career and a phenomenal circulation. The southern California *Bubble* of 1886 went the way of all such, and the *Reporter* shared in the general collapse of inflated values that had prevailed in that region. Two years of experience in independent journalism served to convince Mr. Sutton of his ability, and returning to Logansport, he founded the *Reporter*, although contrary to the advice of the wiseacres who predicted failure for any such project. Nothing daunted, however, Mr. Sutton went ahead with his plans and it is significant of his perspicacity and general good judgment that the paper proved a distinct success, from every possible view point. The first issue of the paper bore the date of October 1, 1889, and from then until the time of his passing, it maintained a high standard of excellence in the county owning a popularity second to none in the field. It is a fact worthy of record here that Mr. Sutton also founded and published papers in other parts of the state, among them the *Galveston Sun*, and another of his Logansport enterprises was the *Advance*, which also proved a successful venture. Mr. Sutton assumed an Independent attitude in politics, and his papers ever reflected that attitude, being conducted entirely upon neutral lines.

While Mr. Sutton was a resident of Los Angeles, he met and married Miss May Stanley, the ceremony being solemnized in that city in January, 1887. Two children, Psyche and Lindley, were born to them.

Mr. Sutton was a member of the Presbyterian church as is also his widow and children who survive him. They maintain a high place in the best circles in Logansport and enjoy the esteem and friendship of a select circle which widens with the passing years.

JOHN D. BEAL, now living retired in Logansport at the advanced age of eighty-six years was born on February 20, 1828, in Alsace-Loraine, then a part of France but now a province of Germany. In the old country the family name was De Biehl, but after the removal to America the name was simplified and Anglicized into its present form. John De Biehl was the name of the father of the subject of this review, and his career was a notable one. He was one of the famous soldiers who fought under Napoleon at the battle of Austerlitz, participated in the Russian campaign against Moscow and in its disastrous retreat, and was with Grouchy at the battle of Waterloo. He was born in 1787, married Elizabeth Coler who was born in 1801, and in the year 1830 emigrated to the United States. For the ensuing ten years he was employed in a distillery at New Lancaster, Ohio, and in the fall of 1840 he and his family came to Cass county, Indiana, making the journey in a wagon, drawn by a yoke of oxen. The first winter the family lived in a cabin on the present site of the Heppe Soap Factory, and the following spring he moved into a log house on a farm in Washington township, where he passed the remainder of his days. He died in 1879, and his wife having preceded him four years.

After coming to Cass county, Mr. Beal, as he came to be known in this country, made two trips back to his old home in Ohio to collect sale notes, both trips to and from being made on foot. He and his wife became the parents of five children, of which number John D. Beal, whose name heads this review, was the only son and is the sole survivor of the five. He was two years old when the family migrated to America, and twelve when they came to Cass county to live. His early years were passed in attending the neighboring schools in the intervals when his services were not in requisition in the work of the home farm, in which he early became proficient, his knowledge embracing all the various branches of agricultural life incidental to making a farm in a new country. He followed farming and farm life until 1896, when he moved to Logansport, where the evening of his life is now being passed in quiet and peace.

On October 29, 1859, John D. Beal married Katherene Long, whose people were also early settlers of Cass county and to them were born eight children. Three of that number died in infancy, the others being Joseph A., John H., Jeannette William, and J Adrian. The mother yet lives, at a ripe old age, and is a devout member of the English Lutheran church.

J. Adrian Beal, the youngest of the children of John D and Katherene (Long) Beal, was born on the home farm in Washington township, this county, on December 12, 1869, and was there reared to manhood. He was educated in the district schools and on attaining his majority worked two years at railroading, and the next two years at farming. He came to Logansport in 1896, and from then until 1900 was deputy county surveyor. He was then elected to the office of county surveyor, and was re-elected to this office two years later. The succeeding two years he was employed by the county at bridge building and road work, but the fall of 1906 he was again elected county surveyor.

On January 1, 1909, Mr. Beal formed a partnership with Harry M Bell, under the firm name of Beal and Bell and they have since been engaged in the work of engineering and contracting. Between the years of 1906 and 1912 he was also in partnership with his brother, William V., under the name of Beal Brothers Coal Company.

Mr. Beal is a Democrat. He is high in Masonic circles, being a member of its various bodies, including the Knights Templar, the Scottish

Rite and the Shrine, he is also a member of the Benevolent and Protective Order of Elks and the T P A

On September 28, 1905, Mr Beal was united in marriage with Miss Julia E Grover, daughter of General John B Grover, a veteran of both the Mexican and Civil wars Mrs Beal is also a granddaughter of the first mayor of Logansport

AUGUST GRUBE The A Grube Company, of which August Grube is the leading spirit was established in Logansport in 1910, its business being the handling of ladies' and childrens' ready-to-wear goods, exclusively The firm is located at No 427-29 Broadway Its manager, Mr Grube came to Logansport from Terre Haute, where he had been employed as the buyer and manager of the ready-to-wear department of a large establishment in that city, and he readily saw the splendid possibilities for such a concern in Logansport An exclusive garment shop catering solely to the wants of women and children, was a new departure for Logansport, and the success of Mr Grube's venture here has been most gratifying The corporation was here organized with a capital of $5,000, fully paid, in which Mr Grube is the half owner The first year the young concern did more than $60,000 in business, largely the result of a carefully planned advertising campaign Since that time the business has had a healthy increase annually, and the establishment is now regarded as one of the standard business houses of the city

August Grube was born in Danville, Illinois, on September 6, 1876, and is of German parentage. He was taken out of school when he was eleven years old and since that time has made his own way in the world, with a success which is well worthy of the name His entire life has been passed in mercantile lines, and he has learned the business from the ground up. He had charge of the silk department in which he was employed when he was twenty years of age, and is conceded to be one of the best versed men in his line of business to be found anywhere in the country Mr Grube maintains his home in Logansport, and his present expectation is that Logansport will be his home for many years to come

In 1896 he married Miss Alice Johnson, of Danville, Illinois, his native town as well, and nine children have been born to them of which number eight are now living

BERNARD A KROEGER, senior member of the undertaking firm of Kroeger & Winquist, in which business he has been long and successfully engaged in Logansport, was born at Cloppenburg, Germany, on May 30 1856, and is a son of Anthony and Elizabeth (Hochhertz) Kroeger He was reared to man's estate in his native country, and until he was seventeen years old attended the parochial schools In 1873 he entered the employ of the German government in the post office and telegraph department, and was thus engaged until he was twenty-two years of age In August, 1878, Mr Kroeger immigrated to the United States, and for one year succeeding his arrival he was a student at St Francis' Seminary, at Milwaukee, Wisconsin, where he bettered his already fair education and made rapid strides toward the mastery of the English language

When he had finished his schooling in Milwaukee, Mr Kroeger located in Logansport, Indiana, where he secured employment as bookkeeper for the firms of W T S Manley & Sons, undertakers, and Manly & Smith, furniture manufacturers He continued thus until 1882 when he associated himself with R W Weaver, who had succeeded Manly & Son, and the firm of Weaver & Kroeger was then established In 1884, Rodney Strain bought out the interest of Mr Weaver and the firm thereupon became Kroeger & Strain, until the death of Mr Strain in 1910 Subsequent to that event, the firm of Kroeger & Winquist came into existence, and the concern today occupies a leading place among the stable business institutions of Logansport The continued connection of Mr Kroeger with the firm during the past three decades, despite many changes, has won for it a reputation for integrity and fair dealing that has made it one of the respected business houses of the city

Although of foreign birth, Mr Kroeger is an American citizen in all that the term implies He is one of the progressive and enterprising men of this city and enjoys the confidence and esteem of all who come in contact with him in his business life

Mr Kroeger is a Roman Catholic in religion, as have been his ancestors for many generations He is a member of the Knights of Columbus, the Catholic Benevolent Legion, the Benevolent and Protective Order of Elks, and his politics are those of a Democrat To his marriage with Miss Veronica Hoffman, of Logansport, on October 25, 1887, six children have been born as follows Bernard A , Jr , Florence J , married Jos C Kienly of Logansport, Marie, Edith, George and Francis

JOSEPH MARTIN ELLIOTT, generally known in Logansport as Mark Elliott, was born on the old Elliott farm in Harrison township. on January 13, 1853 and is the son of Joseph and Martha (Lincoln) Elliott, who came to Cass county from Tippecanoe county, Indiana, at about 1850 The Elliott family is of Irish extraction, the father of the subject having been born in North Carolina in 1801 the son of an Irishman In an early day Joseph Elliott came to the north and settled in Drake county, Ohio, where occurred his marriage to Martha Lincoln, the mother of the subject The father died in Harrison township, Cass county, in 1855, his widow surviving him for some years A goodly family of twelve children were reared by them, and of this number Joseph Martin Elliott was the youngest Five of that number are living today After the death of her husband Mrs Elliott married one Alexander Elliott, a cousin of her first husband, and one child was born to them who is now dead

"Mark" Elliott was reared on the old home place in Harrison township, and such education as he acquired was gained through the medium of the district school of the neighborhood He began to shift for himself, as the old familiar saying goes when he was sixteen years old, working out as a farm hand, and when he was seventeen he set about learning the trade of a horseshoer For thirty-three years thereafter he followed that work in Logansport, and in 1904 he embarked in the livery business, in which he has since continued with pleasing success He was known for years as the leading blacksmith of the city, and had a reputation for honest work and dependability that has followed him in his newer venture

Mr Elliott is a Republican in politics, and in 1896 was the nominee of his party for the office of county sheriff At the previous election the Democratic state ticket had a majority of four hundred and fifty-nine votes, but in this election Mr Elliott met defeat by but seventy-eight votes He is a member of the Masonic order, the Knights of Pythias, in the Uniform Rank, and of the Benevolent and Protective Order of Elks and the Independent Order of Foresters

On March 14, 1877, Mr Elliott married Miss Priscilla Castel, and to them four children have been born, named as follows Blanche now the wife of Dr John Bradfield, Harry B, George M and Earl, who died in infancy

JOHN S SMITH, M D For thirty years Dr Smith has quietly performed his round of professional services and duties at Galveston and vicinity, and is not only one of the oldest, but one of the most highly esteemed practitioners in Cass county A physician cannot live and practice his calling for thirty years in one locality without possessing a faithful character and a certain high ability and skill in his profession which have contributed to make the splendid type of family physicians which is known both in literature and in actual life.

Dr John S Smith was born on a farm in Jefferson county Indiana, March 24, 1855 His parents were James and Catherine (Overturf) Smith. The mother was a daughter of Jacob Overturf, who was a farmer and a substantial citizen of his locality James Smith, the father, came from Woodford county Kentucky, to Indiana He was a man of versatile accomplishments and for twenty-five years during his residence in Jefferson county, Indiana, he was a farmer, school teacher and surveyor He was captain of Company A, Ninth Indiana Cavalry, and was the first man to chase John Morgan when he was on his raid through Indiana He and his wife were the parents of six children named as follows Elizabeth (Merrill) William, who married Olive O'Neil, and is now deceased, his four children being Nora Luther, Homer and James Sylvanis G , Mary E Hillis, Dr John, James H

Dr John S Smith attended the common schools of Jefferson county, Indiana, and during his early youth worked on the farm, and became thoroughly acquainted with the industrious life of the Indiana agriculturist He took up the reading of medicine under Dr S B Lewis, who had been an army surgeon and continued his education in the Ohio Medical College, where he was graduated in March, 1882 Since that time he has been engaged in practice at Galveston, and has built up a large patronage a great many people refusing to depend upon any other professional service in time of sickness than that of Dr Smith

On December 27, 1885 he married Miss Anna E Jump They are the parents of three children, now deceased, their names having been Chauncey, Lillian and Ernest Fraternally the doctor is a member of Masonic Order, both York and Scottish Rite degrees, of the Improved Order of Red Men, of the Eagles, and Sons of Veterans He has served on the pension board and as township supervisor, and in various ways

has given his services in public affairs as well as in the circle of people who are among his patients, and who esteem him for his professional ability and as a citizen and man.

JOHN W KISTLER has occupied a leading place in the business activities of Royal Center, Cass county, Indiana, for many years He is a native son of the county, born in Boone township, on October 3, 1862, and is a son of Amos and Anna E (Schlegelmilch) Kistler

Amos Kistler was born in Fairfield county, Ohio, and came to Indiana as a boy, while his wife was a native of Pennsylvania, and was of German ancestry, her father having been born in Germany, coming to the United States in his youth When Amos Kistler settled in Indiana his first position was with a corps of engineers who were engaged in the survey of the Pennsylvania Railroad through Royal Center In later years the young man located permanently in the village, which he continued to make his residence until death claimed him in 1909. He was a man of many excellent qualities, and an upright and honorable citizen of Cass county Ten children were born to Amos and Anna Kistler, of which number eight are now living They are Martha, who married D. B Artrum, George L, a resident of English Lake, Indiana, John W, the subject of this review; Lena C., the wife of J. M Verman, Cara D who married Thomas J Kistler Laura, the wife of M E Fisher, of Florida, August C., unmarried and a resident of Warsaw, Indiana, Mabel, the wife of John A Hardesty; Effie and Jennie are deceased

John W. Kistler was reared on the home farm west of Royal Center, and in the schools of the village received his early education He began farming early in life, at first on the home place and later on his own responsibility, his marriage in 1884 being the occasion for his launching out in independent agricultural activities His wife, who was Miss Sarah E Holmes, was born in Boone township on May 30, 1862, and there reared and educated She was the daughter of Jackson and Mary (Corbet) Holmes, old residents of Boone township The marriage of Mr and Mrs Kistler was celebrated on November 16, 1884, and one son has been born to them—Elden J, who was reared in his native community and finished his education in the Marion Normal School, and is now a member of the firm of John W Kistler & Son He married Catheryn Anderson and they are the parents of two children,—Eliza A, born in 1909 and May R, born in 1912

Mrs Kistler is a devout member of the Baptist church and a faithful worker in the various departments of its activities Mr Kistler is a member of the Knights of Pythias, the Independent Order of Odd Fellows and the Knights of the Maccabees, also F & A M He is a Republican and has held several township offices of more or less responsibility and is now a member of the village council He is a man of the highest integrity and honor and occupies a worthy place in the esteem and confidence of his fellow citizens in and about Royal Center

BRADEN F HARPER On the line of Cass and Carroll counties, in Clinton township is located the beautiful country home of Braden F

Harper a citizen whose activities have had a distinct bearing upon the development of his section. The work he has done and the success he has gained may be taken as examples of what has been accomplished by men of his character, the sturdy agricultural citizenship that Cass county owes its prestige to. Mr Harper is a native of the Old Dominion State, born in Loudoun county, Virginia, October 31, 1857, a son of Jonathan and Mary J (Woodard) Harper. On his paternal side he is descended from a native of Scotland, and on his maternal side from residents of England, although his parents were born, reared and married in Virginia. Jonathan and Mary J Harper came to Cass county, Indiana, in 1871, after a short stay in Fulton county, and here spent the remainder of their lives, honest, God-fearing people who well merited the high esteem in which they were universally held. They were the parents of eleven children of whom four are now living. James W, a farmer of Carroll county, Indiana, Nancy J, the widow of Benjamin Bear now living in Logansport, Robert R, who resides in Carroll county, and Braden F.

Braden F Harper was fourteen years of age when he came to Cass county, and here completed the education he had commenced in the schools of his native state. Like other farmers' sons of his day and locality, he divided his boyhood and youth between the district schools and the work of the home farm, and at the age of eighteen years had completed his education, and then turned his attention to agricultural pursuits. He continued to work for his father until he attained his majority, when he began working by the day, and when twenty-four years of age was married. He carried on farming operations for J. M. Justice for six years and for William Walker five years, and during this time, by careful management saved enough to invest in his present farm, a tract of eighty acres which was then covered with heavy timber. On this he built a hewed log house, 16x24 feet, in which the young couple settled down to housekeeping, while Mr Harper started to clear the land, a task that took years of steady, persistent labor. During the years that followed, Mr Harper encountered all the obstacles that are incident to the development of virgin soil, but his labors have borne fruit, and he may now point with a pardonable degree of pride to one of the finest farms of its size in Clinton township. The little log cabin home has been replaced by a modern residence, barns and outbuildings of appropriate size and substantial character have been erected, and the land is now worth $200 an acre. He is known as one of his township's substantial citizens, an excellent farmer, and an acknowledged judge of standard-bred stock and high-grade horses, his specialty being the draft.

On February 17. 1881, Mr Harper was united in marriage with Miss Melissa Dale, of Carroll county, Indiana, and they have had four children. June M., Estella· Clara B, who is now the wife of Ross Cree, and Julia F. The family is identified with the Methodist Episcopal church at Clymers, and Mr Harper's fraternal connection is with Burrows Lodge No 485, I. O. O F. With other men of advanced ideas, in 1912 he allied himself with the Progressive party, and its principles have since received his hearty support.

ALBERT R BECKLEY, president of the Citizens' State Savings Bank, farmer and stock buyer of Royal Center, is one of the more prosperous and widely known farming men of the township He is a native of Cass county, born in Boone township, on October 25, 1862, and is the son of George Ward and Margaret (Walters) Beckley.

George Beckley was also a native of Boone township, this county, and was one of the first children born in this section of the country He was the son of David and Lucinda (Wooley) Beckley, natives of Pennsylvania, who came from the old Keystone state to Ohio and settled at Caldonia There David Beckley was engaged in wagon making, which was the trade he had learned in his youth, but they only remained in Ohio a comparatively short time, coming on to Indiana, where the head of the family took up a claim, his land being that which is occupied by Royal Center today. At one time this pioneer settler owned about half a section of rich Indiana land Here George W Beckley was born and reared, and when he had reached young manhood he taught school for some time during the winter seasons, and farmed in summer It was while he was teaching school that he married Margaret Walters She was born in Virginia and came to Indiana with her parents, who were of German and Irish descent Eventually George Beckley bought a farm and settled upon it, there making his home until the end of his days, his death occurring in 1912 The wife and mother yet lives, and makes her home with her son, Albert R, in Royal Center To these parents were born five children, all of whom are yet living They are Albert R, the subject of this review, Ira B, also of Royal Center, Edward L, living in Boone township, Anna E, the wife of R C Roach, of Waterville, Ohio, George W, Jr, living in San Diego, California, where he has property interests

Up to the time of his marriage Albert R Beckley lived in his parents' home and shared in the work of the farm He received a common school education in the schools of his native community, but beyond that his educational privileges did not extend On November 23, 1888, he was united in marriage to Dollie Woods, the daughter of Thomas and Martha J. Woods, people of Indiana birth, and to them one child has been born Dottie L, now the wife of C G. Beach, of Fargo, North Dakota

Mr Beckley is busily occupied with the care of his fine farm of two hundred and forty acres and with his other interests in Royal Center His politics are those of the Prohibition party, and he is a member of various fraternal orders, among which are the A F. & A. M., Lodge No 585 at Royal Center, the Knights of Pythias, the order of the Eastern Star, and the Knights of the Maccabees He and his wife enjoy the good will and confidence of a large number of friends and acquaintances who have known them with more or less of intimacy for many years

WILLIAM C. THOMAS Practically the whole of the active business career of William C Thomas has been devoted to financial affairs, and no man in Cass county has been more prominently identified with the leading banking concerns of the county than has he Mr Thomas is a native of the state of Indiana, born at Royal Center on the 20th day of

February, 1863, and is one of the four children of his parents, James and Elizabeth (Little) Thomas.

Dr James Thomas was one of the pioneer physicians and surgeons of Cass county, and to this honored gentleman a sketch is dedicated on other pages of this work, so that further detail concerning him and his family history is not necessary at this juncture.

William C Thomas was reared to manhood in Royal Centre, and his preliminary educational training was secured in the public schools of that place In 1883 he entered Wabash College from which he was graduated in 1887 with the degree of B S , and following his graduation he was occupied for a year in the settling of his father's estate. In 1889, private matters having been disposed of, he found himself free to engage in business enterprise, and he helped to organize the Royal Center bank, of which the late D. P Baldwin was president and Mr Thomas was cashier In 1891 Ernest B Thomas a brother of William C , bought out the interest of Mr Baldwin, upon which he became cashier and Mr William Thomas was elevated to the position of president The bank continued as a private institution until 1902, when it was incorporated as the Royal Center State Bank, and Mr Thomas has continued in the presidency, with his brother Ernest as cashier up to the present time The Royal Center State Bank is today the second oldest bank in Cass county, and has a splendid reputation for stability and clean, wholesome methods of operation In August, 1907, Mr. Thomas organized the State Bank of Burnettsville, and he is and has been its only president thus far This bank also is one of the growing and solid fiscal institutions of the county, its management being on a par with that of the Royal Center State Bank

In 1893 Mr Thomas moved to Logansport and assisted in the organization of the Logansport State Bank of which he became the cashier, and in which capacity he served continuously for some fifteen years He resigned the position owing to a state of ill health, and for two years did practically no business, except that which absolute necessity forced him to attend to On February 23, 1911. Mr Thomas was appointed state bank examiner, his territory comprising fifteen counties in Northeast Indiana, and covering one hundred and thirty-nine banks and trust companies

Mr Thomas is a Democrat in his political faith, but has never been an aspirant for official preferment or favor. He is a member of the Sigma Chi college fraternity and the Indiana Democratic Club at Indianapolis

In 1889 Mr Thomas was united in marriage with Miss Nettie Minthorn of Royal Center, who died in 1901, leaving three children Walter, Paul and William In 1903 Mr Thomas married Miss Estelle Keiser, of Indianapolis She is a member of the Presbyterian church and enjoys the friendship of a wide circle of the best people of Logansport, as does also her husband

BEAUFORT BANTA is undeniably one of the most successful farming men in Jefferson township, where he has been engaged in agriculture and horticulture since 1892 but not continuously on present farm. He has a fine place of one hundred acres, and there engages in general farming and stock raising, giving a generous bit of time to fruit culture, his orchard of more than three hundred trees being one of the features of his well kept and productive farm.

Mr. Banta was born in Cass county in 1866, and is the son of John and Sarah Banta. In his childhood he suffered the loss of his hearing as the result of brain fever when he was but five years of age, and his wife, whom he married in 1891, suffered a like misfortune when eight years old, through an attack of measles to which she was subject at that age. She was Addie M. Hayden, a native of Elkhart county, Indiana, and her marriage with Mr. Banta has been blessed with four children, all of whom have perfect hearing. Neither Mr. nor Mrs. Banta experienced any detriment to their vocal organs in the illnesses which robbed them of their sense of hearing.

Since his marriage Mr. Banta has been devoted to farm life, and his success has been one that is well worthy of the name, and places him well up in the ranks of the prominent farming men of his township. Mr. Banta is a Republican, or has been all his life, until in the election of 1912 when he voted the Progressive ticket.

Mr. Banta and his wife were educated in the schools of Indianapolis, Mrs. Banta being a graduate. Mrs. Banta is a member of the Episcopal church and holds her membership in Indianapolis. As previously mentioned, they have four children, their names and the dates of their birth being as follows: Robert, born September 25, 1894; Lorena, born October 28, 1896; Bertha, born on July 27, 1903, and Thelma, whose natal day was September 16, 1906.

The farm home of the family is in Section 16, some ten miles distant from Logansport, and is one of the finest places in the township. Mr. Banta has some fine stock on his place, and gives careful attention to matters of breeding and selection, his success being of a most pleasing nature. His fruitful fields, his productive flocks and his fine orchard of more than three hundred bearing trees, all unite to further his prosperity and give him place among the leading agriculturists in the township, and the family is one which holds secure position in popular esteem.

WALTER ERVIN BALLARD. The advent of the automobile has created a profession altogether unknown only several decades ago. Its members have not learned their art in school or from books, but in the workshop, in daily contact with the work they have had to do. They have had no precedents to guide them, but have worked out the problem which their employment brought in the school of experience. In this school was educated Walter Ervin Ballard, of Walton, proprietor of the only automobile garage in Cass county outside of the city of Logansport. A machinist by trade, he early recognized the growing importance of the automobile, and had the courage to attach himself to this new vocation, and the ability to make a success of his operations. Although still a young man, he has attained a degree of success that places him with the substantial business men of his locality, where he has forced his abilities to be recognized. Mr. Ballard was born April 23, 1883, in Walton, Indiana, and is a son of N. A. and Luella (Noel) Ballard. His father, a farmer by occupation, was born in South Carolina, and came to Cass county when still a lad, his education being completed in the public schools of Walton He and his wife were the parents of three children, namely Walter Ervin; Leorus, and Hazel, who became the wife of Ernest Neblung, and has had one child—Noel.

Walter Ervin Ballard received his education in the common schools, and was brought up on the home farm, but early gave evidence of mechanical ability that presaged success in other fields than that of agriculture With commendable foresight he developed this inclination, accepting whatever honorable employment he could find in the machine shops of Kokomo until he was able to enter business on his own account, when he started to work as a machinist After about two years, however, he opened a garage, which, as before stated, is the only one in Cass county, outside of Logansport He has attended strictly to business, and the result has been the development of an excellent business and the gaining of a position of independence He is known to be thoroughly reliable, a master of his trade and conversant with all its details, and as a man who has won confidence and public esteem by the honorable manner in which he has conducted his operations He has been too busily engaged in his business to give much thought to public matters, but can be relied upon to assist in any way when progressive movements are inaugurated

On January 28, 1911, Mr Ballard was united in marriage with Miss Josephine Sullivan, of Keene, New Hampshire, and to this union there has been born one son and daughter, Nerious Daniel and Mary Alice Mr Ballard is a consistent member of the Universalist church Mrs Ballard is a Roman Catholic

WILLIAM C ROUTH was born in Logansport, Indiana, on March 31, 1854, and is one of a family of four children born to William Isaac and Emily (Cook) Routh Of these children two are living today The parents were natives of England, where the father was reared, and there he learned the trade of a tanner He came to America when a young man and in the thirties established a bakery on Fourth street in Logansport, Indiana, in conjunction with John Cook also a native of England, and who afterwards became his father-in-law The bakery thus established was one of the first, if not the first to be opened in Logansport, which was at that early date scarcely more than a trading post In time Mr Routh sold his interest in the shop and started up in tavern keeping about two squares east of the Sackett's bridge At that time the only possible means by which the point might be reached was by ferrying across the Wabash river Mr Routh finally gave up his inn-keeping venture and engaged in the buying and butchering of beef and in the sale of the product In 1853, or thereabouts, he moved to a farm which he had purchased, located some two miles east of the city, in Washington township, and there he made his home for about sixteen years His next move took him back to Logansport, and in the fall of 1871 he started a meat market on Twelfth street, near Spear street He continued to do business at that stand until his death, which occurred in 1877

Mr Routh was a man of conservative habits, inclined to be averse to branching out aggressively in business, but it was characteristic of the man that when he once embarked on a mission or venture, he clung tenaciously to the plans on which he had originally settled, admitting of no difficulties in the carrying out of his design The establishing of the meat market business on Twelfth street was the real beginning of what has become the pork packing industry of William C Routh & Company.

William C Routh has always made his home in Logansport He was educated in the public schools, and when old enough, began to assist his father in his various business undertakings after the death of whom the son continued the retail meat market business. In about 1879 Mr. Routh arranged for more suitable accommodations for the business at No 503-5 Twelfth street, and here, in connection with his retail business, he began the business of packing in a small way This little venture was the entering wedge of the real packing industry which has since been evolved from that modest beginning From the start, the industry grew apace, and while it was originally confined to winter packing, after five years, Mr. Routh built a refrigerating plant, which enabled him to continue the year around In 1889 his refrigerator plant and another of the principal buildings were destroyed by fire He immediately rebuilt on the south side of the city and continued there until 1898, when he erected the buildings at his present location, his actual outlay at that time amounting to approximately $30,000 Since that time Mr Routh has added other buildings and machinery to the extent of about $70,000 The present capacity of the plant is about two hundred and fifty to three hundred hogs per day, and the plant is run at its capacity The main building has a floor space of 13,225 square feet, and the entire basement and about one-half of the first floor space is used for refrigeration purposes The second floor is used for refrigeration and sausage room, and the firm gives employment to about eighty people The firm of William C Routh & Company was incorporated in January, 1905, with a capitalization of $110,000, and in December, 1908, the capital was increased to $200,000 The first officers of the firm were · William C Routh, president, Lillian W Chase, secretary, and W A Routh, treasurer The present officers are William C Routh, president, A C Routh, vice-president, Albert Cassube, secretary, and W A Routh, treasurer The aggregate business done by the firm in the year 1912 was about $1,000,000

Mr Routh is a Republican, and a member of the Presbyterian church Fraternally he is a member of the Independent Order of Odd Fellows

On October 24, 1877, Mr Routh was united in marriage to Miss Sarah Taylor, and to this union seven children have been born, as follows Edwin Wallace, Etta, now Mrs Charles S Tucker, Almon C.; William Arthur, Emily Cordelia, the wife of Guy Manaugh, John H. and Harry B Of the sons, Almon C, William Arthur and John H. are associated with their father in the business, and are accounted among the most progressive among the younger business men of the city.

WILLIAM H WALTER William H Walter is one of the well known builders and contractors of Cass county and is located in Royal Center, where he has carried on his work since 1880 Much of the principal building work of this place has passed through his hands, as well as that of other towns in the vicinity. He is a native of the county, born in

Harrison township, on the 17th of January, 1861 and is the son of Jesse and Margaret (Caloway) Walter The father was born in Ohio, while the mother was a native of the state of Delaware They met and married in Indiana both having located in Cass county, and there they passed the remainder of their days, the father having passed away in 1905 and the mother in 1877

William H Walter was the fifth born of the twelve children who came to his parents He was reared on the farm of his father and was educated primarily in the district schools, later attending the high school of Logansport, Indiana, and finishing the curriculum of that school Locating in Royal Center in 1888, since which time he has devoted himself to the contracting and building business

Since Mr Walter has been identified with the building activities of this community, he has reared many of the principal buildings that grace the town today, and he may be said to have experienced a most gratifying success in his work

On November 22, 1888, Mr Walter was united in marriage with Miss Cordelia A Kistler a daughter of Jonas and Amy Kistler, and a sister of Thomas J Kistler, Sr, the daughter of one of the finest and most highly esteemed old families in Cass county She was born and reared in Boone township and received her education in the public schools Five children have been born to them Durword G, who is married to Etha Chapman, Edna F, the wife of Bruce Chapman, J William, seven years of age Oliver E, four years old, and Ned R, now at the age of one year The family are members of the First Christian church at Royal Center, and Mr Walter is a member of Royal Center Lodge No 585, A F & A M and the Independent Order of Odd Fellows He is also a valued member of the Royal Center Commercial Club, in which he takes an active part He is Progressive in his politics, and bears his full share of the burden of civic responsibility as do all open-minded and generously disposed citizens

PETER MICHAEL One of the pioneers of Cass county, who did a worthy part in the development of the material resources of the county, and who established his family now well known in this and other sections of the middle west, was Peter Michael, who for nearly sixty years was a resident of Harrison township, and who during his life there witnessed practically every phase of development from the clearing of the original wilderness down to the time of railroads and electric facilities

Peter Michael who was of mingled German and Scotch ancestors, was born in Virginia but now West Virginia, January 15, 1811 His death occurred March 5, 1893 His father was a farmer in Morgan county, West Virginia, and the family belonged to that sterling class of Scotch-Irish people who gave character to the entire life of mountain district of Virginia, and other middle eastern states The other children in the family brothers and sisters of Peter were Samuel Andrew, and William, and Mrs Harriet Burk Mrs Martha Caw, and Mrs Nellie Bruner Peter Michael was reared in West Virginia, had the education of the old field schools was trained to habits of industry and to the strict religious life that prevailed in that section of the country during the early part of the nineteenth century In the fall of 1835 he accomplished the journey westward by river and canal and wagon road to Cass county, Indiana, settling in Harrison township on the farm, which continued to be his home until his death, nearly sixty years later. He was a farmer, was a man of thrift and good management, and provided well for his large family, and his later years were spent in comfortable circumstances He was a Democrat in politics until the Civil war, and after that a Republican He served as a trustee of his township, and was always held in the highest esteem in his community In religion he was non-sectarian with a preference for the Episcopal church

Peter Michael married Christina Frushour, daughter of Solomon Frushour, a farmer of West Virginia She was born in West Virginia, and their marriage occurred April 17, 1834 They were married fifty-nine years Mrs Peter Michael died December 22, 1907. The children of Peter Michael and wife with dates of birth, and present residence are as follows. William Uriah, born in Ohio, January 31, 1835, and now a resident of Harrison township, Susan Winn, born April 5, 1837, and died April 12, 1893, Albert P , born July 27, 1838, and a resident of Logansport, Harriet Beard, born December 25, 1839, living in Chillicothe, Missouri, Ellen McKee, born July 25, 1841, and living at Kahoka, Missouri; Mary Thomas, born March 18, 1843, living at LaFountaine, Indiana; George W , born March 14, 1845, living in Campbell, Missouri, Lydia J , born November 4, 1846, died June 11, 1855 , Celia E , born October 1, 1848, died October 8, 1848 , Samuel A , born December 25, 1849, a resident of Logansport, Martha Curl, born October 3, 1851, living at Bloomfield, Iowa, Margaret A , born June 1, 1853, died September 1, 1853 , Emily Puterbaugh, born October 5, 1855 All the children were born in Harrison township of Cass county, except the first

DR GEORGE M JEROLAMAN Among the doctors of the old time there were men of rare human greatness—strong but tender, brusque but true, with a devotion to duty that bestead them through all storms and stress The past generation knew such men in Cass county, and among them esteemed none more highly both for his professional and for his vigorous citizenship and personal character than Dr George M Jerolaman, who was not only one of the very first physicians in Northern Indiana, but also one of the pioneers of Logansport

George M Jerolaman was born in Bedminster township of New Jersey, May 10, 1811, and was a son of Nicholas and Elizabeth (Jessup) Jerolaman, the mother being a French girl The father spent practically all his career in New York City, and finally retired and died at Neshanic, New Jersey. Besides Doctor Jerolaman there were five sons and three daughters, none of whom ever came west to live

Dr George M Jerolaman was reared in the east, and is a student of Union College of Schenectady, New York While he was growing to manhood there were few regular medical schools in the country, and the majority of medical students pursued their studies under the direction of a preceptor Doctor Jerolaman studied medicine under a particularly fine authority. Doctor Schermerhorn of New York City In 1832 at the age of twenty-one Doctor Jerolaman went west, traversing the new and sparsely settled states of Ohio and Indiana, and from Fort Wayne came down the Wabash river in a row boat to Logansport In the boat he had a small stock of drugs, it being his intention to practice in Logansport. The boat capsized, and all his medicines were left in the bottom of the river. As there were no drug stores, in the modern sense of the term, it was a necessity that the doctor should combine the skill and ability of the pharmacist, and practically every pioneer physician compounded his own medicines, and in the saddle bags which he carried in his weary rounds of the country always had a liberal stock of medicines of all kinds and for all cases. Doctor Jerolaman, after coming to Cass county, practiced as a physician until his health failed, and he sought recuperation in New Orleans. When his health was restored he returned to Logansport, and formed a partnership with Doctor Lytle in the drug business. In 1838 Doctor Jerolaman was appointed attending physician to the Pottawatomie Indians, who were still dwelling on their reservations in Indiana, but who soon afterwards were compelled to leave their villages on Yellow river, Tippecanoe, and Eel rivers, and take their long journey to the west. For a number of years Doctor Jerolaman made his home on a farm three and a half miles west of Logansport on the Wabash river. In 1853 he moved back from the farm, building the brick house on the northeast corner of Market and Tenth streets, which has long stood as a land mark of the city. During the latter years of his life he gave practically all his attention to farming and to dealing in farms and livestock.

Doctor Jerolaman in politics supported the Democratic party. He was a member of the Presbyterian faith, and was affiliated with the Tipton lodge of Masons. In 1840 he married Margaret Weakley of Syracuse, New York. She died in 1845. In 1847 occurred his marriage with Mary Rush, a daughter of Judge James Rush of Ohio, who came to Cass county and settled on a farm two miles east of Adamsborough on the bank of Eel river. The five daughters of Doctor Jerolaman are mentioned as follows: Isabella married Egbert Phelps and lives in Joliet, Elizabeth became the wife of John W. Layne of Joplin, Missouri, Mary is the wife of Maj. W. H. Snider of Logansport, Martha married Thomas Forman, deceased, and Harriet died in childhood.

Dr. George M. Jerolaman died March 4, 1883, after a short illness and is buried in Mount Hope cemetery. During his long career in Cass county, his fellow citizens esteemed him as a man of energy and varied activity, his fine sense of humor and for his unselfish devotion to his community. He was a good friend and a frank enemy.

IRA A. SMITH. A representative of the progressive element among farmers in southern Cass county, Ira A. Smith is one of Deer Creek township's prospering farmers. He is the owner of sixty acres of land, and since making his home there has brought his estate into a high condition of productivity, and has made a comfortable home and one which reflects credit upon his own enterprise and upon the neighborhood of which he is a member.

Ira A. Smith was born on the Smith farm, just west of his present residence, on October 9, 1873. His parents were Artemus and Mary (Logan) Smith. He was reared on the old homestead and while attending the district schools of this neighborhood was also becoming versed in the varied duties and responsibilities of farm life. He belongs to the younger generation among Cass county farmers, and has succeeded to a gratifying degree. Mr Smith established his own home on the fifteenth of September, 1897, when he was married to Miss Mary Burious. They are the parents of two children, Edna Alice and Earl Van Buren. Mr. Smith has no fraternal affiliations but is an active member of the Church of the Brethren. In politics he is conservative

FREDERICK N. BOERGER is undeniably one of the most prominent men in Indianapolis, where he has for years occupied positions of trust in the administration of the affairs of the city, and where he is esteemed of all who know him for his many admirable traits of heart and mind

Born in Logansport, Indiana, on August 4, 1856, Frederick N. Boerger is the son of Frederick August and Margaret (Eberts), both native Germans. The father was born in Hanover, his birth occurring on November 4, 1854, and he came to America with his parents in 1852, making his way directly to Logansport, where his half-brother, Henry Miller, a tailor, had previously located. For a time after he came to Logansport, Frederick August Boerger worked on a farm, but later set about learning the trade of a wagon maker. He also found employment at the stone quarry at Kenneth,—the first quarry that produced stone that entered into the construction of the stone building which stands today directly north of the alley in the same block with the Masonic Temple. This building was occupied as a residence by Henry Miller, the half-brother of Mr Boerger, and the stone was conveyed to Indianapolis by canal boat. After completing the learning of his trade, Mr Boerger continued in wagon making until his death. He married Margaret Eberts in Logansport in 1855. Her parents had died in Germany, and she came to America in company with an uncle and aunt, and when she first arrived made her home at Roanoke, near Fort Wayne on the old canal. She was born on January 13, 1834, at Worms, province of Hesse, Germany. She remained but a short time at Roanoke before coming to Logansport and for sixty years this city has represented her home. Twelve children were born to Mr and Mrs Boerger, six of whom are yet living. Of this number Frederick N, Charles H, Minnie, William H, John and George W, all reside in Logansport. The father was a Democrat and served about five years in the City Council. He was a member of St. James Lutheran church. He was a man of excellent character and habits, highly industrious and a man who lived a clean, wholesome and straightforward life. He had a healthy dread of debt, and avoided undue liabilities at all costs. He died on January 16, 1896

Frederick N Boerger is the oldest of the twelve children of his parents. He was educated in the parochial and public schools of Logansport and at Hall's Business College, and when he finished school learned the wagon maker's trade with his father, and continued with him in the work until 1884. From then until 1892 he was in charge of the wood shops for Holbruner and Uhl, carriage makers, but in 1892, the failing health of his father induced him to give up his work in that connection and take charge of his father's shops, in which he continued until 1902. In that year he was elected city treasurer, and two years later was his own successor in the office. In the autumn of 1906 he became an assistant in the office of the county treasurer, and continued thus until January 1 1910, when he was appointed by the mayor as a member of the Board of Public Works, and as such is present street commissioner of the city. He has served faithfully and honorably in every office he has filled thus far, and is regarded as one of the ablest officials the city has known. Mr Boerger is a Democrat, and he is a member of the German Lutheran church, in which he was a deacon and trustee for twenty-one years

On October 22, 1885, Mr Boerger was united in marriage with Miss Minnie Hauenstien and three children have been born to them William, who died in 1902, aged twelve years, Emma who died in infancy, and Edward, who was born in 1900

ANDREW J ZANGER has been engaged in business in Logansport since 1897, and has enjoyed a pleasing prosperity in the passing year. He came from Kewanee to this city, although he was born in Fulton county Indiana on September 30, 1873 He is the son of Matthew Zanger, who was a native of Germany and there reared to maturity

Matthew Zanger married Lena Moser in his native land and came to America soon after He came to Indiana soon after his arrival upon American shores, and located in Fulton county, where he followed farming until death claimed him, in September, 1887, his faithful wife having preceded him in 1883 They were the parents of thirteen children, Andrew J of this review being the twelfth in order of birth

Andrew J Zanger was reared on the home farm in Fulton county and educated in the district schools of his home community He was nineteen years old when he came to Logansport and began learning the trade of a baker He worked at that business here and in Winamac, Indianapolis, Fort Wayne, Louisville, Kentucky, and numerous other places, but in March, 1897, he established himself in business at No 8 Front street, in Logansport, opening a modern bakery It was there that Mr Zanger got his start in business He remained there until in May, 1905, when he moved to his present quarters and built his present establishment He has prospered, but his success has not been the result of chance but rather through his hard work, economy, industry and excellent business judgment He employs from twelve to fourteen people constantly, and is constantly adding to and improving his place of business In the spring of 1912 he doubled his capacity The trade which Mr Zanger has established is not confined exclusively to Logansport but he supplies many of the surrounding towns as well, his products having a reputation for wholesomeness and general excellence that makes them particularly desirable

Mr Zanger is a Democrat, and in 1908 was elected a member of the City Council at large for a term of four years. He is a citizen of a high order, and one who has always consistently borne his full share of the civic burden in Logansport, where he enjoys the esteem and confidence of all who know him

On November 19 1901, Mr Zanger was united in marriage with Miss Lizzie Rech, of Washington township, Cass county, and they are the parents of four daughters Agnes E Mary M, Gertrude M and Dorothy C Mr and Mrs Zanger are members of the Roman Catholic church

SIDNEY A. VAUGHN whose name is so closely interwoven with the lumber industry of Cass county, was born in Niagara county, New York, on June 29, 1842, a son of Artemas and Eleanor (Hines) Vaughn. His early life was passed on his father's farm in Niagara county and in attending the district schools, and in 1861 he enlisted as a private in the Seventh New York Cavalry for three years. By an order of the War Department, in 1862, the cavalry arm of the service was reduced and the Seventh Cavalry, with others, was disbanded. Mr. Vaughn re-enlisted in the One Hundred and Twenty-ninth New York Volunteer Infantry, which in 1863, became the Eighth New York Heavy Artillery, which was recruited to its maximum of eighteen hundred men. While on the Peninsular Campaign, Mr. Vaughn applied to the War Department for permission to appear before the Carey Board and take the examination for a commission. This was granted, a creditable examination was passed, and he was commissioned a First Lieutenant by President Lincoln. He was then ordered to Kentucky to help recruit a command which became the Twelfth United States Heavy Artillery. With this he continued during the remainder of the war, and was honorably discharged at its close after having served a total of four years and four months. Succeeding this service, for a year he was in charge of the retail department of the packing house of A. E. Kent & Company, Chicago, and then came to Indiana, in search of a permanent location in a business way. With A. E. Richardson he bought a sawmill and a quantity of poplar logs located a short distance northeast of Lincoln, in Jackson township, Cass county, and after converting these logs into lumber, moved to Lincoln. In partnership with J. E. Parker, he then bought thirteen hundred acres of the best timber land in Jackson township one and a half miles north and west of Lincoln, and here they installed a saw mill and converted the timber into merchantable lumber. Mr. Vaughn was for many years one of the largest shippers of black walnut in this locality. The firm of Vaughn & Parker bought the old Johnson residence property on Fourth street, opposite the Fourth National Bank, in Logansport, which old building they razed and on the site they erected what is known as the Vaughn & Parker block. in this building was entered the first plate glass in Logansport. Mr. Vaughn has been an active figure in the commercial and political history of Cass county for nearly half a century, and has borne his full share of the civic burden and in the development and upbuilding of the city along the lines of its best good. He was a Republican in politics until 1896, when, owing to the financial plank in the platform of the party in that year, he went over to the Democratic faction, and has since affiliated with that party. He has served three terms in the city council of Logansport, one term as police commissioner, by appointment of Governor Matthews, and one term as mayor of the city, in all of which offices he acquitted himself with the utmost credit, his services resulting in much good to the common good of the city. He is a Mason of the Knight Templar degree, and is also a member of the Benevolent and Protective Order of Elks.

In 1880 Mr. Vaughn was married to Miss Lilla W. Rice, the daughter of W. H. Rice, of Indianapolis, the editor and proprietor of the Masonic Advocate. To their marriage three children have been born:

Lillian Ethel, now Mrs W H Mordhurst, of Fort Wayne, Indiana, Sidney R and Regina   Mrs Vaughn died July 14, 1911   Excellent educational advantages have been afforded the children of Mr Vaughn, for while he lacked similar privileges in his own youth, he has never been one to gainsay the benefits that accrue from such advantages, and he determined that his children should not be handicapped as he was in that respect   All three of his children have completed the curriculum of the Logansport schools, and Lillian is a graduate of the Chicago University, while Sidney has his degree from Purdue University

MRS. SARAH ELLEN TYSON   It has already been said that many a man who entered upon an unsettled, undeveloped section lived to be that section's most prominent man and largest capitalist, and this assertion found confirmation in the life of John Hoover, who was the father of Mrs Sarah Ellen Tyson, who is one of Cass county's best known and most esteemed residents   Ohio was the original home of the Hoovers and eighty-five years ago John Hoover and his father, Jacob Hoover, left Wayne county for what was then the border of civilization, the wilds of Indiana   Owing to their method of transportation their progress was slow, but after a journey of twenty-one days they reached their destination, Adams township Cass county   They had money with which to invest in land and the grandfather of Mrs Tyson, Jacob Hoover, secured six hundred acres, the purchase price being but a fraction of a dollar per acre   Concerning him, it should be said that he was born in Germany and that early in life he settled in Preble county, Ohio   His son, John Hoover, was born in Preble county, Ohio, on November 8 1808, and in his twentieth year he married Rachel Mandlin, who was born December 16 1811 and was a native of North Carolina, but who was residing with her parents in Wayne county at the time of her marriage March, 1829   Mr Hoover moved to Adams township, Cass county with his young wife, and there he purchased 300 acres of land, upon which he settled and lived for thirty-eight years   His father, Jacob Hoover, had already become the owner of a large estate in the county, and these men were pioneers in the truest sense of the word   Where they led, others soon followed, and as the value of this land became noised about travel in the county so increased that a railroad was projected   John Hoover owned so large a body of land that negotiations had to be opened up with him and a part of his property became railroad land about 1870, the new station that quickly developed being named Hoover in his honor. It may well be believed that Mr Hoover took a deep interest in the new town, and, eagerly watched the laying of the rails and the other construction work preparatory to the passing over of the first train of cars, which seemed to him the last advance of civilization   No doubt his life was somewhat prolonged by the hope of witnessing the arrival of the train that would assure the prosperous future of his namesake town but his ardent wish was not gratified, his death occurring November 28, 1872, only a few days before the road was in running order

John Hoover, became an extensive farmer, cleared his land and made it productive, and lived to see many changes take place   He related frequently to his children how small a village Logansport was when he first came to this section and the fact that he dug the first cellar in that place He was the father of the following children Martha Ann, who married Sebastian Moore, and both are deceased. 1866, Mary Jane, who married Augustus Moore, a brother of Sebastian, Noah B, who married Frances Obenchain both deceased, Sarah Ellen, who married Thornton Tyson, John M, who married Parthena Wilson and after her death married Nancy Boyai, nee Williams, Leah B, who became the wife of E B Forgy, Hannah Maria, who married William Dennison, Riley C, who married Irene Wilson, both deceased, George who died in infancy, and Emma Frances, who married William Fernald

Thornton Tyson was a son of Thorton F and Mary Ann (Teeter) Tyson, both of Virginia He served as a soldier in the Union army during the Civil war, after which he lived on the farm that Mrs Tyson now lives on, known as the Tyson homestead and devoted himself to agricultural pursuits until the time of his death, December 22, 1905 Mrs Tyson, as stated, is still living on the well cultivated tract of two hundred acres of land, not far distant from Hoover, in Adams township, the town named for her honored father Mrs Tyson is a consistent member of the Christian church, which she has liberally supported for many years, and she is widely known for her religious and charitable work She and her husband became the parents of the following children Morton V, born in 1865, who married Rebecca Moss, and has one son, Orvil and lives in North Dakota, Cora Jane, born in 1869, who became the wife of Simon Fisher and has four children, Florence, Fernald, Simon, and Earl, and lives in Rock Rapids, Iowa, Ora E, born 1867 married James H Fisher, and has one daughter, Ina C and lives in Peru, Indiana, John R, born 1872, is deceased, N Franklin, born 1874, now living at home, and married to Clara Hammon of Adams township, and the father of Martha Ellen, deceased Cecil, Byron, Harold, Clifford, Rachel and James

GEORGE AND WILLIAM CLYMER, pioneers of Clinton township, were natives of Ohio but came to this township when the Indian and wild beast held possession of the forests which then covered its present fertile fields This was in the years 1834-5 They were both active in the development of the township, and took a leading part in all its enterprises George Clymer built one of the first water power mills on Keeps creek, and later a steam sawmill at Clymers, and that town receives its name from him. This mill was later operated by his brother, William, and his son, David H Clymer The latter also became one of the leading spirits in Clinton township and was township trustee George Clymer bought the Biddle Island in Logansport and lived there for a time and in the latter 'sixties moved to Minnesota, where he died some years thereafter William Clymer was married to Martha McKaig She died at Clymers in 1873 and he died at the same place in 1881 One daughter, Ruth, became the wife of Robert R Reed, Sr, but is now dead Another daughter, Mary, married George Shideler, the first white child born in Clinton township Her husband is dead but she is now living in Logansport, over eighty years of age The son, David H Clymer, born in Ohio, 1828, married Margaret Conner, of Clinton township, 1850, and raised quite a family of children. He died in Logansport in 1901, and is buried in St. John's churchyard near the place of his activities and the home he loved so well.

JOHN R. CHILCOTT, a pioneer of Jefferson township, was born in Pennsylvania, 1788, came to Cass county in 1840, and settled on the northwest quarter of section 13, Jefferson township, where he continued to reside until his death in 1875, and sleeps his last sleep in the Fry cemetery. He was a soldier in a Pennsylvania regiment in the War of 1812 and for many years a justice of the peace and a prominent farmer of Jefferson township. He was united in marriage to Margaret Miller in Erie county, New York. She bore him six children: Mrs. Caroline Watts, now living on the home farm; John, who died in 1900; Benjamin died in 1908; Henry, now living in Harrison township; Columbus, dying in 1844, and Amos Chilcott. The four sons served their country honorably as Union soldiers during the Civil war.

AMOS CHILCOTT, now eighty-two years old, has a wonderful vivid memory and the writer is indebted to him for many historical facts contained herein. Mary Jane Banta, daughter of Beaufort Banta, became his wife in 1854, and they have seven children, 33 grandchildren living, 12 dead and 20 great grandchildren.

RICHARD PRYOR was born in Philadelphia in 1810, came to Logansport in 1835 and engaged in the manufacture of hats, appointed collector of revenue by the county commissioner in 1838, in 1840 was the nominee of the Whig party for county treasurer and soon after erected the first two-story stone building in Logansport. This was a landmark for many years and stood on the south side of the street at what is now known as No. 417 Market street. Here he engaged in the hardware business. He resided in Jefferson township, however, in section 14, on a farm now owned by his son Horace. Mr. Pryor was an earnest Presbyterian and was largely instrumental in organizing the congregation and erecting Pisgah church, in which he was an elder. He was thrice married and had several children. One son, Horace Pryor, now a respected citizen of Jefferson township, and D. E. Pryor, a brave soldier of the Seventy-third Indiana Regiment and for many years a prominent druggist at 516 Broadway, who died in 1900. Mrs. James W. Shim and Mrs. S. B. Pratt were daughters. Mr. Pryor died in Logansport in 1889, having been an active and influential member of society for over half a century.

JOHN COTNER, second son of Eli and Nackey (Mullennix) Cotner, was born in Ohio in 1818. He was one of a family of thirteen children. His grandparents, Daniel and Mary (Coble) Cotner, of German descent and natives of North Carolina came to Ohio in 1815. Eli Cotner, the father of our subject, came with his family to Cass county in 1831, where John aided his father to clear his farm in Noble township.

John Cotner was united in marriage to Eliza Walters, November 3, 1841, who was born in Michigan in 1822. To this union was born ten children, to-wit: Elmira, William, Eli, Easton, Sarah, Anna, Levi, Albert, James and an infant. The nine former grew to adult life

Mr Cotner settled in the northeast quarter of section 18, moving into a hewed.log house on Christmas Day, 1841 The house was afterwards covered with siding and otherwise modernized This house they occupied until their death, he dying in 1868 and the widow in 1908, sixty-seven years after she moved into it as a bride

Mr. Cotner was an industrious, hardworking farmer, and an admirer of fine horses, which he always drove. When this couple first moved into this cabin it was surrounded by dense forests Wild turkeys roosted in the boughs of the nearby trees and in the early mornings herds of deer could be seen browsing near their cabin door, and many a deer Mr Cotner has shot from a crack between the logs of his forest home

RICHARD FERGUSON A pioneer of Adams township was born in West Virginia, of Scotch-Irish parentage His education was limited to a few terms in the log schoolhouse of his native state where he was united in marriage to Phebe Payne and soon after embarked on a small flat boat, came down the Ohio river and up the Wabash to Logansport where, after many trials and hardships he landed in the summer of 1833 and erected a cabin near where St Joseph's hospital now stands About 1836 or 1837 he moved to Adams township, locating on the northwest quarter of section 32, where he purchased and improved one of the best farms in the township and for fifty years was regarded as the most respected and influential farmer of the township A short time before his death he moved to Miami township, south of New Waverly, where he died in 1884 after a long and useful life

The following children were born to Richard Ferguson and wife Mary, Sarah, Elizabeth Ann, Richard W., James P. and Sebastian C Ferguson and four children who died in infancy Of this number all are now dead except Sebastian C , who was born July 22, 1841, in Adams township, attended the log schoolhouse without windows and was raised a farmer's boy At the breaking out of the war in 1861 he enlisted in Company G, Fifty-first Indiana, and served nearly four years After the war he engaged in farming in Miami township until 1868 when he moved to Logansport and engaged in contract carpenter work and in 1906 retired and moved to Chicago. He was married in 1865 to Eliza Dillman of Adams township, a daughter of Daniel Dillman, and they have two sons and one daughter, all living

Richard Ferguson had a brother, John Ferguson, who was a pioneer settler in the northern part of Bethlehem township, where he resided, an honored citizen for many years, but about 1874 moved to Wisconsin, where he died.

John D Ferguson is a son of John Ferguson and was born in Bethlehem township about 1846, reared on the farm, educated in the district school and in the sixties moved to Logansport, engaged in the bakery business later in the clothing business, then real estate, and thus arose from an obscure country boy to be one of the leading business men and capitalists of our city

THOMAS SKINNER, SR a pioneer of Adams township and a most exemplary citizen, was born in North Carolina in 1795 Parmelia Cox, his wife, was born in Tennessee in 1800 They came to Cass county in 1837, locating in Adams township, where he became one of the most influential citizens of the county and was a leader in all things that had a tendency to a better and a higher life. He was not an office seeker and only filled minor township offices, but he held the highest official position in his church, the Twelve Mile Christian, which he was instrumental in establishing. He died in 1883, respected and mourned by all and lies at rest near the church he loved so well, his wife having preceded him seventeen years. They were blessed with five sons. John C., Daniel, Ira, Richard and Thomas H. Skinner. Ira served his country in the Twentieth Indiana Infantry, during the Civil war, John C., Richard and Daniel died in Cass county years ago leaving families and Thomas H. is at this writing, one of the oldest and most influential men in Adams township, and his large and respected family as well as all his neighbors can only speak words of praise for his beneficent acts.

HENRY LOGAN THOMAS was one of the earliest settlers of Adams township, locating on section 29 in the year 1831 or 1832. He was a sturdy character and one of the most influential and best known citizens of the township. He was a quiet, unostentatious man, a worker rather than an expounder of good deeds. He was a devout Christian and the first religious meeting in Adams township was held at his cabin, soon after it was erected in the midst of the forest. He was reliable, faithful and upright in all his dealings and his influence for all that is true and noble has left a lasting impression on the community where he spent the active years of his life. Mr. Thomas, son of George and Nancy (Logan) Thomas, who were natives of Ireland, was born in Virginia, 1805, moved with his parents to Ohio, where he married Nancy Williams and soon after moved to Cass county, where he raised an old time family of eleven children of whom Elizabeth, Esther, William, Nathaniel and Bruce are now living in Kansas and Edgar resides near the old home in Adams township. Henry Logan Thomas died on his original homestead in Adams township, February 14, 1873, beloved and respected by all.

BERRY FAMILY. While the early history of the Berry family is involved in some obscurity yet it is known to be of German origin and that its progenitor came from Heidelberg, Bavaria, about 1765 and settled in eastern Pennsylvania. This was Peter Berry, a man of influence in the community. He served as lieutenant in the Revolutionary war under Washington's immediate command and was promoted to the rank of captain. He died in Lebanon county, Pennsylvania, prior to 1796, leaving a wife, Margaret, six sons and four daughters, one son dying in youth. These children were all married and left progeny, some in Pennsylvania, others in the west. Among the latter was Peter Berry, the second son who was born in 1787, married Elizabeth Lutz, daughter of a German physician who was also a Revolutionary soldier. Peter Berry moved to Cincinnati about 1815 and opened a shop for the manufacture of edged tools. He made the boiler for the first steamboat that plied the waters of the Ohio river. He moved to Butler county, Ohio, for a time and came to Logansport in 1829, where he resided one year, then located on a farm in Miami township between Waverly and Hooverville, where he spent the remainder of his life, departing this life in 1872 or 1873.

HISTORY OF CASS COUNTY 1203

The following are the names of the children of Peter and Elizabeth Berry Henry, Catharine, who married David Miller, an early settler of Miami township, Peter C, Samuel, Elizabeth and John H

John H Berry, the second son of Peter and Elizabeth (Lutz) Berry, was born in Pennsylvania in 1812 and moved with his parents to Cass county in 1829 and spent the rest of his life on a farm in Miami township, where he died in 1872. In 1838 he was united in marriage to Harriet Reed, daughter of Abraham and Nancy (Cox) Reed, who were pioneers in Miami township Mrs Berry died in 1872 and some years thereafter Mr Berry contracted a marriage with Mrs. Ellen Conner (nee Sackett) who survived him and is now (1913) living in Richmond, Indiana. He died in Miami township in 1879 John H and Harriet Berry were the parents of thirteen children, namely Israel J, Peter A, Edwin R, James K P., Maria, Graham N, Wilson R., Eliza D., Elizabeth, John M, Harvey H, Harriet and Martha, six of whom are now living (1913).

Israel J., teacher, farmer and horticulturist, was born in Miami township in 1839 He taught school for a third of a century and is now retired and lives at Adamsboro, this county He married Miss Emmeline Spencer, 1866, daughter of John and Mary (Keeran) Spencer, a native of Ohio, born there in 1841 To this union were born four children, viz: John, now residing near Marion, Indiana; Clementine, now Mrs Howard Helm, Katharine, now Mrs Charles E Douglas, both living in Clay township, and Bertha, died in infancy Mr Berry is a devout Baptist and a Democrat in politics, although liberal in his views

Peter A Berry, teacher, lawyer and fruit grower, was born in 1842 and died in 1895 He was educated in Logansport's high school and Wabash College, studied law with the late Judge D. H Chase, and attended the law department of Michigan University. He practiced for a time, but the profession not being to his taste, he relinquished it and returned to teaching and educational work He served three terms as superintendent of the county schools

For some years prior to his demise he retired to his farm in Miami township and engaged chiefly in horticulture Mr Berry was married in 1868 to Miss Nancy Jane Crockett, she, dying in 1889, left four children, all of whom are dead except Emma, who is the wife of Lewis C. Brown

Edwin R Berry, born 1844, died 1865

James K P Berry, farmer and teacher, born 1846, married Miss Sarah Spencer, by whom he had four children He died in 1882 and his widow is now Mrs Nelson Scott, of Clay township

Graham Newell Berry, teacher and writer of local history and biography, was born in 1848, taught twenty-four years in the public schools, sixteen years of which was principal of the different schools of Logansport He has assisted in writing the history of scores of county and state histories and is a contributor to a number of magazines He was married June 20, 1876, to Miss Elvira, daughter of John S and Prudence (Harris) Winters, who was born at Wabash, Indiana, January 7, 1854. They have had six children, none of whom is living.

Wilson Reed Berry, artist and draftsman, born 1851 Has illustrated numerous books, magazines, etc, besides achieving more than a local reputation as a painter in oil and water colors. He was married

January 31, 1878 to Miss Emma Conner, daughter of Calvin and Ellen (Sackett) Conner, the union resulting in the following children Murillo, Percival (deceased), Virgil, Robin A and Inez Lillian

Mr Berry is now the owner and occupant of the old Biddle home on the island in Logansport and since the recent flood thinks we have a wet town

Eliza D Berry, born 1853, died 1895, unmarried

Elizabeth Berry born 1856, married Wm Obencham and has had seven children, only four of whom are living They reside in Logansport.

John Meek Berry, herdsman, was born 1858, is married and lives on a sheep ranch in Kansas

Harvey Heath Berry, born 1861, died in 1873

Harriet Berry, born 1863, died in 1880

Martha J. Berry, born 1868 married Joseph Stewart and is the mother of five children They now reside in Marion, Indiana

COL WM L BROWN, a veteran of two wars, was born in Ohio, November 19, 1817, and was killed at the battle of Bull Run, Virginia, in 1862 He came to Logansport in the early forties, was a brave soldier in the Mexican war, united in marriage to Elizabeth Purveyance in Logansport, June 27, 1849, from which union six children were born: Eleanor H., Frederick L, Daisy, James A, Charles H and William I, the latter still an honored resident of our city On the breaking out of the Civil war he raised a regiment, the Twentieth Indiana, and became its colonel, which he gallantly commanded and fell while bravely battling for his country. Colonel Brown was an energetic man and a leader in civil and business affairs of Logansport and was interested in banking and other business interests He bought and improved the old Fitch farm at Kenneth, west of town, where he lived for some time

He had three brothers, all Presbyterian ministers who occupied the pulpit of the First Presbyterian church of Logansport at different times during their ministerial labors They were the Revs James C Brown, Frederick T and Hugh A Brown

Colonel Brown's widow was postmaster at Logansport from 1866 to 1870

NOAH S LA ROSE, son of Philip J and Anna Maria (Sherer) La Rose, who were natives of North Carolina, was born in Ohio in 1817, came with his parents to Cass county in 1834, where his father lived until his death in 1871 Our subject had two brothers, John S. and Joshua S, and one sister, all of whom were honored residents of Cass county but are now dead Mr La Rose was educated in the public schools of the county and at Hanover College, from which he graduated in 1862 From 1834 to 1850 Mr La Rose made his home with his father on the farm In the latter year he came to Logansport, where he resided until his death in 1886 He is interred in the Bethel cemetery in Clay township He served as county clerk from 1856 to 1864, and again from 1872 to 1876 In 1868 he was the candidate of his party (Democratic) for clerk of the supreme court but was defeated with the entire ticket

Noah La Rose was a tall, slender man with a kind and gentle face, sociable in his manners, and made friends of everyone with whom he

HISTORY OF CASS COUNTY 1205

came in contact. He was never married and was not a member of any order, hence his energies were largely expended in the aid of others He affiliated with the Evangelical Reformed church, was charitably inclined, and materially assisted all enterprises for the betterment of the race. He was a public-spirited man and laid out several additions to the city of Logansport, and he was a familiar and well-known figure on the streets of Logansport for over a third of a century

ROBERT R. REED, SR , son of Robert and Mary (Megwood) Reed, was born in Fayette county, Indiana, November 7, 1824 His parents were born and married in Ireland and came to America with their four children, namely. James, William, Jane and Mary Ann in 1817 and settled in Fayette county, Indiana. His father was a weaver by trade and died in Fayette county August 7, 1824, and his son James died there in 1825. The widowed mother moved to Clinton township, Cass county, with her children, William, Thomas, Mary Ann and the subject of this sketch, October 13, 1834, and occupied a log cabin in the midst of the primeval forest which they helped to clear and develop the country where they all lived and died except Robert R He was educated in the old log schoolhouse on the Hewitt L Thomas farm, later he taught school and in 1850 moved to Logansport and engaged in the grain business with Pollard & Wilson Was appointed county treasurer November 30, 1879, in place of W T S Manly, deceased, ran for treasurer on Republican ticket but was beaten by Thos Pierce. Was united in marriage to Miss Ruth Clymer, daughter of David Clymer, of Clinton township on June 19, 1853. Mrs Reed died in 1893, leaving our aged yet honored subject alone in the world Mr Reed served several terms in the city council in the seventies and for a man of his age, being now past eighty-eight, has a remarkably vivid memory and the writer is indebted to him for much historical data found herein

HON. JOHN W. WRIGHT, son of Rev. John Wright, is a native of Lancaster, Ohio, where he was born October, 1811 He graduated from the Ohio University in 1832, read law for one year and in 1833 located in Logansport and began the practice of law In 1835 his brother, Williamson Wright, came west and entered into a partnership with him He was prosecuting attorney and in 1840 was elected president judge of the eighth judicial circuit and served for six years, when he retired to his farm, four miles north of Logansport on the Michigan road and was the chief actor in building the old plank road from Logansport to Fulton about 1853 He was instrumental in building the Wabash Railroad through Logansport and presided over the first meeting held in the courthouse, composed of men from Ft Wayne, Lafayette and New York, for the purpose of organization of the company About the same time his brother, Williamson Wright, was active in promoting the construction of the Pan Handle Railroad into Logansport and John W. Wright took the contract for the building of that road between Newcastle and Logansport and the first locomotive engine ever seen in Logansport was brought by him on the old canal, and hauled across the Wabash bridge onto the railroad During the run of the free banking system in the fifties he operated a bank in Logansport and one at Rochester, but the death of that system shut them up. In 1852 he was elected mayor of the city. In 1858 he was elected to congress but refused to take his seat, because of his interest in making Kansas a free state, whither he moved and was a member of the constitutional convention of that state and later a member of the legislature and became the speaker of the house About 1861-62 he returned to Logansport and built a residence on the east side of the First Presbyterian church, now occupied as a parsonage In the sixties he was appointed to an Indian agency in the West and later took up his residence in Washington, where he died, 1889, and on October 12 of that year, the bar of Logansport, at a meeting presided over by Judge D B McConnell, passed most complimentary resolutions on the distinguished services of Judge Wright and especially his work in the cause of freedom and opposition to slavery and the organization of the Free Soil party in Cass county.

COL JORDAN VIGUS was a native of Virginia, where he was born September 17, 1792 In 1810 he went to Lexington, Kentucky, and clerked in his brother's store He served with distinction in the First Kentucky Regiment during the War of 1812 In 1828 he located in Logansport and aided in the laying out and naming the town with General Tipton, Chauncey Carter, John B Durett and Gillis McBean. Was appointed by Governor Ray a commissioner of the Wabash and Erie canal in 1832-33 and went to Ft Wayne on February 22, 1832, to commemorate the commencement of construction of the canal and after delivering a brief address commenced the work by digging the first spadefull of earth amid great rejoicing Logansport was incorporated as a city by act of legislature, February 17, 1838, and the following May Colonel Vigus was elected its first mayor. He afterwards served two terms as postmaster, 1840, and, again, 1848 He was of medium height, stout build with dark hair and dark eyes He died September 20, 1860, leaving a wife and several children His remains are interred in the old cemetery on Ninth street.

DR JEHU Z POWELL, son of Jacob and Martha A (Troutman) Powell, was born in Bethlehem township, Cass county, Indiana, August 13, 1848 He was educated in the Logansport high school and Presbyterian Academy and graduated from the literary department of the University of Michigan in 1871 and from the medical department in 1874 In the same spring he took a post-graduate course at the Long Island Hospital Medical College. New York, and at once opened an office in Logansport, where he has been in active practice ever since. In 1892 and again in 1902 he took a practitioner's course in the Post-Graduate Medical School of Chicago.

The doctor has never sought office, being content to follow his chosen profession, but believes every citizen owes a duty to the public and was induced to serve as member of the city council for four years and was a presidential elector in 1896 and postmaster at Logansport from 1898 to 1902

In politics the doctor has always espoused the cause of the Republican party and has acted as the chairman of the Cass County Republican committee, 1892 to 1896

He has always been an earnest temperance advocate and has filled various offices in the local and grand lodge of the Independent Order of Good Templars, the only order to which he ever belonged, but is active in promoting temperance and moral reform.

The doctor is a close student and spends his leisure time in reading solid literature and writing along various temperance, moral and historical lines. He has been thrice married: First marriage to Mary J. Leffel, September 22, 1874, daughter of Arthur Leffel of Bethlehem township, by whom he had one son, Dwight C Powell, born in Logansport, March 28, 1876, was educated in the city high school and the University of Michigan and graduated from Bellevue Medical College in 1899, appointed surgeon in the United States army and served two years in the Philippine Islands; resigned from the service and not liking private practice, relinquished his profession and engaged in mercantile pursuits and is now located in Los Angeles, California. He was married June 25, 1908, to Miss Mildred Addlesberger, of Springfield, Illinois, and they have one daughter, Mary Louise, born September 9, 1909

Mrs. Powell died May 17, 1877, and on May 1, 1881, he was again united in marriage to Mrs. Louisa F. Ewing nee Harris, whose first husband died while serving as postmaster of this city and she succeeded him as postmistress in 1874. She died in 1899, death resulting from a fall through a cellar door He was again married to Miss Christine A. Markert of Logansport, May 1, 1901, and they are blessed with one son, Weldon, born January 4, 1903.

He is liberal in his religious views but was raised a Quaker and believes in plain, practical religion. He is a member of the Cass County Medical Society and was its secretary for nearly twenty-five years, also member of the Indiana State Medical Society and the American Medical Association

In 1903 he was a delegate to the International Medical Congress at Madrid, Spain, and visited the hospitals in all the European capitals in preparation for his duties as chief surgeon in charge of the hospital at the National Military Home at Johnson City, Tennessee, which position he filled. But tiring of the confinement and military discipline, he resigned after four months service in that capacity He then returned to Logansport to his old home, which he had never relinquished, nor lost his citizenship in the county that gave him birth, where he is still actively engaged in the practice of his chosen profession.